OFFICIALLY
WITHDRAWN

May 2018

SPEAKER JIM WRIGHT

Speaker
Jim Wright

POWER, SCANDAL, AND THE
BIRTH OF MODERN POLITICS

J. Brooks Flippen

UNIVERSITY OF TEXAS PRESS ⟨✦⟩ AUSTIN

Requests for permission to reproduce material
from this work should be sent to:
> Permissions
> University of Texas Press
> P.O. Box 7819
> Austin, TX 78713–7819
> utpress.utexas.edu/rp-form

The paper used in this book meets the minimum
requirements of ANSI/NISO Z39.48–1992 (R1997)
(Permanence of Paper). ∞

Book design by Lindsay Starr
Typesetting by Integrated Composition Systems

Library of Congress Cataloging-in-Publication Data

Names: Flippen, J. Brooks, 1959–, author.
Title: Speaker Jim Wright : power, scandal, and
the birth of modern politics / J. Brooks Flippen.
Description: First edition. | Austin : University
of Texas Press, 2018. | Includes bibliographical
references and index.
Identifiers: LCCN 2017037707
    ISBN 978-1-4773-1514-9 (cloth : alk. paper)
    ISBN 978-1-4773-1631-3 (library e-book)
    ISBN 978-1-4773-1632-0 (nonlibrary e-book)
Subjects: LCSH: Wright, Jim, 1922–2015. |
    Legislators--United States—Biography. | United
    States. Congress. House—Biography. | United
    States. Congress. House—Speakers—Biography.
Classification: LCC E840.8.W75 F55 2018 |
    DDC 328.73/092 [B] —dc23
LC record available at https://lccn.loc.gov
/2017037707

doi:10.7560/315149

Contents

PART III. Leadership in an Age of Dynamism

PART IV. Victory and Defeat in the Age of Reagan

The Long Shadow of Scandal

THE FORGOTTEN LEGACY

Sixty-six-year-old James Claude Wright Jr. was no stranger to the podium. Over his thirty-four-year career as a Texas Democratic congressman, Wright had been on the floor of the House of Representatives to make an impassioned speech so many times that his colleagues regarded him as one of the institution's great orators. According to one report, "When Jim Wright talks, people sit up and listen."[1] New York congressman Tom Downey was one. "Every time Wright spoke," Downey recalled, "I took the opportunity to listen, because he was the greatest orator I ever saw."[2] Confidently strolling to the microphone on May 31, 1989, Wright looked as dapper as ever. As he asked the presiding officer, Majority Leader Thomas Foley of Washington, for permission to address his colleagues on a personal matter, Wright's voice was strong as usual, his gaze shifting from side to side as it always did. Still, as everyone knew, this speech was different. For one, the chamber was full, with even the spectators' gallery packed. In that gallery was Wright's beloved wife, Betty, and a daughter from his first marriage. Friends were nearby. Sitting to Wright's side was Majority Whip Tony Coelho of California, who had just announced that he was leaving Congress rather than face possible punishment for an alleged ethics violation. Near Wright was another member of the Democratic leadership, William Gray of Pennsylvania, who, according to a report two days before, was the subject of a Justice Department investigation. Most notably, before Wright and sitting among the distinguished audience was Georgia Representative Newt Gingrich, a Republican who more than any other present had led Wright to the podium that day.

For weeks before the speech, speculation had been rampant that Speaker of the House Jim Wright, the fifty-sixth man to hold that powerful position, was going to resign from Congress. The scandal that had slowly enveloped him for more than a year had come to a head the previous month, with a critical report from the House Committee on Standards of Official Conduct, the "Ethics Committee," and an even harsher report from the special counsel that the committee had hired to investigate, the aggressive Chicago litigator Richard J. Phelan. The Ethics Committee report cited sixty-nine instances in which there was "reason to believe" that Speaker Wright had violated House rules. The official allegations were far broader than the initial complaints that Gingrich had filed 356 days earlier, and which the committee had dismissed.[3] The potential financial misdeeds had broadened as the investigation had unfolded, the politics as obvious as the sensationalized media coverage. Wright, the report alleged, had received improper gifts from Fort Worth developer George Mallick. With interest in legislation, Mallick had employed Betty in a do-nothing job and given the Wrights a car and a rent-free condominium. Moreover, Wright had surpassed the limits on honoraria for speeches with bulk sales of his book *Reflections of a Public Man*.[4] Other allegations, from unnecessary travel to legislation that benefited his own investments, had come and gone. As Wright approached the podium, the crowd at least expected him to refute the charges.

Wright had his defense, of course, noting that Betty did real work for Mallightco, the investment company he and Mallick had formed. The car and condominium were merely additional compensation. Mallick, a friend, had no legislative agenda. Moreover, Congress had explicitly exempted book royalties from outside income, and many congressmen had royalties far greater than his own. Noting Phelan's "mean and unsupported inferences," Wright's rebuttal resembled a legal brief.[5] It was dirty politics, Wright argued, a cynical attempt to remove from office a thorn in the side of Republican president Ronald Reagan. Gingrich, Wright added, had even hired a staffer to explore every nook and cranny in his past.[6]

The air was thick with anticipation as the networks covered the speech. Would Wright resign, or, like the boxer he had once been, dig in and launch his own offensive? Certainly, fighting back was uphill. With Watergate only fifteen years before, public approval of Congress, the institution Wright loved, was near all-time lows. Scandals had forced the Ethics Committee to strengthen its codes twice since the late 1960s. The first time, in 1967, had involved the flamboyant Harlem Democrat Adam Clayton Powell; the second followed the titillating sex and payroll escapades of Ohio Democrat Wayne Hays in 1976. Moreover, as Coelho and Gray certainly knew, Wright was hardly the only legislator under suspicion.[7]

In short, the committee report could not have come at a worse time for Wright. Weeks before, outrage over a proposed congressional pay raise had drained Wright's support. With the increase popular among members but unpopular outside the Washington Beltway, Wright had tried to broker a compromise only to have the growing medium of talk radio execrate him, including the newly syndicated show hosted by commentator Rush Limbaugh.[8] Republicans were already angry that questionable charges of womanizing and drunkenness had derailed President George Herbert Walker Bush's nominee for secretary of defense, former Texas senator John Tower. The rejection of a new president's cabinet appointee was unprecedented, and the obvious partisanship encouraged Republican retaliation.[9]

Throughout May, every development appeared to weaken Wright's position. When Wright hired a new team of attorneys, his defense appeared in disarray. As this team acquainted itself with his case, new charges arose, most of them frivolous, but still requiring immediate rebuttal. A false claim that the Internal Revenue Service planned to indict Wright took its toll, as did renewed reports that one of Wright's aides, John Mack, the brother of a former Wright son-in-law, had decades before brutally attacked a woman with a hammer. Although the Ethics Committee had dropped charges alleging that Wright had tried to block an investigation of a Texas savings and loan, new accounts surfaced claiming that Wright had intimidated a regulator by publicizing his homosexuality. The press even dredged up outlandish reports from the 1940s saying that Wright had been complicit in the murder of a former opponent. By mid-May, reporters were camping outside his house in a political deathwatch.[10]

No one appeared to hear Wright's side of the story. He insisted that Phelan was no impartial investigator but a politically ambitious prosecutor who wanted to reel in a big fish. Wright had testified earlier, but the Ethics Committee kept delaying his chance to address the new charges. Moreover, the committee had denied his defense team access to the depositions of more than seventy witnesses, 7,000 pages of documentation, and the advisory opinions that Phelan had employed in his ten-month, $2 million probe. "These past few months have been tough," Wright wrote a friend in the midst of the whirlwind. "But I am at peace with myself and I intend to work hard to merit the continued confidence of friends like you."[11]

Behind the scenes, Wright thrashed about, trying to save his reputation, if not his speakership. Wright later denied that he was aware of any negotiations for his resignation in exchange for the committee dropping the charges against Betty, but in the final days, the media correctly reported that Wright's representatives had met with committee members and even Phelan.[12] According to journalist John Barry's later account, Wright agreed to the demands only to have Phelan add that Wright would have to resign the next day and appoint a Speaker pro tem. No one, Wright insisted, would ever tell him how or when to resign. If he resigned, he would leave with dignity. Wright understood that when a Speaker, a constitutional officer, resigned, his appointment of a Speaker pro tem would also lapse, leaving no constitutional head of the legislative branch and a horrible precedent for America. Phelan, however, remained adamant; failure to resign would prompt further investigations into oil investments Wright held, and the committee would inevitably rule against him after months of further agony.[13]

Wright understood the politics. In mid-May, a group of Democrats discussed the possibility of Wright resigning. They included Wisconsin representative David Obey, the most outspoken congressman to argue that the committee had misread the ethics rules, no small claim, given that Obey had helped write the rules in the first place. The next day, the *New York Times* reported on the meeting, suggesting that Wright's days were numbered.[14] Many Democrats were skittish about Wright fighting the charges on the House floor, as the members of the Grand Old Party would surely couch their support as an endorsement of corruption. Already the pressure had swayed two Democrats on the Ethics Committee to abandon Wright. To many Democrats, the charges were unfair but the momentum too great; even Wright's grand rhetorical skills could not deflect the inevitable sanctions and the damage to their party. Others quietly recalled Wright's forceful leadership in advancing an ambitious agenda on which they did not always agree. And then there was the possibility of Wright's replacement, an attractive plum for the personally ambitious.[15]

Wright had no intention of damaging the party, but his mind was on more than petty self-interest. Scandal promised to grind Congress to a halt, and the continuation of a political brawl did not serve the common good. As Wright pondered the larger questions, Coelho, on May 26, set the stage for

Wright, announcing his own resignation. Like Wright, he had been charged with no crime but with financial improprieties. Two days later, Jim and Betty Wright slipped out of town for Memorial Day, switching cars at his office, and thus dodging the reporters who hounded him incessantly. As the two fled to a friend's house in the Shenandoah Valley for a chance to contemplate their future quietly, the press wondered why Wright had suddenly vanished. It was yet another good story.[16]

Returning to the Capitol on May 30, Wright remained noncommittal, but the tea leaves were obvious. The press had cast Coelho's departure as a selfless sacrifice for the common good, granting Coelho a degree of dignity that Wright wanted as much as assurances that he could keep his pension.[17] "I want to be fair to myself and my family and my reputation and I want to be fair to this institution that I have served for thirty-four years," Wright acknowledged.[18] The renowned Washington insider Clark Clifford advised Wright to continue fighting, and, in fact, a new poll suggested that Wright's constituents wanted him to remain in office. Others, however, cautioned that Phelan had the votes of a slight majority on the committee and that the end was a forgone conclusion, fair or not. Wright should fall on his sword.[19]

In later years, scholars would cite Wright's greatly anticipated speech as a rhetorical case study in seeking redemption.[20] Wright claimed that the speech was mostly extemporaneous, but his note cards suggested otherwise. Regardless, the emotions that bubbled up as he neared his conclusion were clearly genuine. Anger, sadness, righteous indignation, and resignation tore at him. For almost an hour Wright held his audience in rapt attention. He began by offering thanks, adding that he loved Congress and was proud of its accomplishments, implicit praise of his own leadership. "I want to assure each of you that under no circumstances . . . would I ever knowingly or intentionally do or say anything to violate [Congress's] rules or detract from its standards," he stated. After denying any criticism of the Ethics Committee, apparently forgetting his harsh private denunciations in the previous weeks, Wright offered a point-by-point rebuttal of the charges, the chance the committee had long denied him. As he spoke, wry, ironic smiles arose and he gestured with his hands. His inflection changed, his voice rising and falling for emphasis, the brief pregnant pauses a sure sign of a seasoned orator. Increasingly, he took off his glasses and wiped his brow. Critics stated that he was wiping away tears, but Wright maintained that it was perspiration from the heat of the chamber and its lights.[21]

It all memorably culminated with an ardent denunciation of the partisanship that consumed Congress. "When vilification becomes an accepted form of political debate, when negative campaigning becomes a full-time occupation, when members of both parties become self-appointed vigilantes carrying out personal vendettas against members of the other party, in God's name that is not what this institution is supposed to be about," Wright pleaded. It drowned out "the quiet logic of serious debate on important issues" and was "unworthy of the American political process." Wright's call to end such "mindless cannibalism," complete with a clasped fist and an angry edge to his voice, drew a prolonged standing ovation from the Democrats. The crescendo ended with his resignation, his eyes now obviously welling and his head drooping. "Let me give you back this job you gave me as propitiation for all this season of bad will that has grown up among us; give it back to you," he stated. "I will resign as Speaker of the House effective upon the election of my successor and I'll ask that we call a caucus on the Democratic side for next Tuesday to choose a successor." Neither side, he added, should try to avenge a perceived loss. "I do not want to be a party to tearing up the institution I love."[22]

To Texas Democrat Mike Andrews, it was a "sad day," the first time in history that a Speaker of the House had resigned in a scandal.[23] The Speakership was not new to accusation, of course, with no less a figure than Henry Clay having faced charges of impropriety. A half century later, James Blaine had survived more serious charges, and, at the beginning of the twentieth century, Joseph Conrad had refused to resign despite having lost his power over rules and appointments. Even Wright's own predecessors, Carl Albert and Thomas "Tip" O'Neill, had survived accusations, the former of intemperate drinking and the latter of influence-peddling.[24] Never before, however, had a formal inquiry brought down a man two heartbeats from the presidency.

Despite his eloquent speech, Wright was the first to face the ignominy of resignation. His troubles were "more serious," observed Ronald Peters of the Carl Albert Center for Congressional Studies.[25] No one had ever faced such a well-funded, lengthy, and broad-ranging formal investigation, one so closely aligned with media coverage. Wright claimed that he held "no rancor or bitterness," a contention that at least one acquaintance supported. "He may have had harsh comments about Gingrich," Texas Christian University's James Riddlesperger remarked, "but I wouldn't say he was completely bitter."[26] Wright's sister, Betty Lee Wright, recalled her brother as stoic, more angry at the Democrats who failed to rally to his defense than at the

Republicans. "He didn't want people to know how hurt he was," she concluded, recalling a conversation she'd had with Wright's wife, Betty, who undoubtedly harbored her own anger.[27] Certainly the letters Wright received comforted him. New Republican president George Bush released a gracious statement from London noting their long friendship and declaring Wright's tenure "one of effectiveness and dedication to the Congress."[28] From colleagues came anger and sympathy. "I have followed the 'witch-hunt' . . . with increasing ire," wrote one Democrat. "I have you and Betty in my prayers daily," said another.[29] Most of the letters came from Wright's district. "We want you to know how respected you are," penned a Fort Worth couple. "Your speech was extremely touching," noted Wright's former limousine driver. Many simply lashed out at their party colleagues on the committee. Democrats, complained one colorful constituent, "no longer have guts enough to whip a cowering stink bug."[30]

As Wright left the podium, Democrats crowded around him offering thanks while Republicans scattered. Reporters rushed down from the galleries but found the Capitol police blocking their access. "Hey, everyone says I don't have friends like Tip did," Wright exclaimed, shaking hands. "But I've got 'em. Look here." Back in his office, Wright spoke with the powerful chairman of the Ways and Means Committee, Dan Rostenkowski. Despite their frequent competition, no tension existed on this day. With his feet up on the desk, Wright declared himself liberated.[31] There would be no more concerns about the committee, no more Phelan. And there would be no more worry about the Republicans—at least for Jim Wright.

If the speech was historic, Wright's pleas for bipartisanship and collegiality appeared to ring hollow for most of his audience, standing ovations aside. The speech was just more "snake oil" to Virginia Republican William Whitehurst, another example of Wright's slick modus operandi, the very thing that made him so dangerous.[32] As Republicans such as Whitehurst reveled in Wright's fall, many Democrats openly pined for revenge. "What is this, 'Nail a Congressman Day'?" bemoaned New Mexico's Bill Richardson, adding that there was "no way" Democrats would forget. "I hope we can resolve all this but I just don't see how it stops here," New Yorker Gary Ackerman predicted.[33] Fellow New Yorker Charles Schumer was more ominous, saying, "When we get into [the continuing investigations of the savings and loan scandal], there is going to be plenty of blame to go around." Republicans knew what was coming. "Everyone is walking on eggshells," replied Californian Jerry Lewis, creating "a negative environment that is paralyzing the process." The politics of personal destruction were here to stay, *Time* magazine predicted, summarizing the obvious. "How many will fall?"[34]

If Jim Wright's resignation was not the turning point he had hoped for, it was important for more than its historical implications. It dominated the news and cast a long shadow over both Wright and the Congress. In many ways it defined Wright's legacy, with his supporters citing him as a political martyr, one who perhaps made mistakes but in the end selflessly sacrificed himself for the common good. He did not deserve his reputation for corruption and self-interest. For others he was the exemplar of just such corruption. His resignation was a tacit admission, his career deservedly tarnished, which no speech could erase.

The entire sordid affair of the resignation of Jim Wright was indeed a story of "ambition and power," as the journalist Barry termed it, with more than enough culpability to go around. Wright had mastered the art of pushing the rules to their limit, his actions at times audacious if not technically illegal. As Wright admitted, he had made too many mistakes to mention. If nothing else, he had left the door to accusation open. At the same time, Gingrich had been a driving force in Wright's downfall and had been more than willing to push open any additional doors that blocked his own rise to greater prominence, his motivations overtly partisan and his tactics Machiavellian, in some ways reminiscent of McCarthyism almost four decades before.[35] In the end, the story of Jim Wright is not simple, but neither is it complete. In fact, Jim Wright's long career in politics was historic in its own right. His influence was profound in his local community, his state, and the nation at large, separate from his infamous resignation. He played a major role in foreign policy, in the process becoming known worldwide. His accomplishments were manifold, if lost in the wake of scandal. Moreover, his career was a story of Congress, a dynamic institution that required constant revision and adaptation. At this Jim Wright was a master, calculating his every move and preparing for the future with one eye on the animated political culture that surrounded him. It worked—at least until the age of Gingrich. Jim Wright's success in mastering the machinations of Congress illustrates the evolution of politics and governance in post–World War II America. It made his many critical accomplishments possible. There is so much more to the story of James C. Wright Jr. than scandal.

In so many ways Wright represented what journalist Tom Brokaw later termed the "greatest generation."[36] Like the ancestors of millions of Americans, Wright's forefathers went west, living in an age not far removed from the frontier and instilling in their children an idealism and ambition uniquely American. Throughout Wright's life, his parents, especially his father, played outsized roles. Wright had his moments, but the youthful Jim was a pleaser, more than willing to absorb the message and model his parents imparted. Born in boom time but experiencing the Great Depression, Wright lived America's own evolution, his diverse experiences again molding the character that guided him in Congress. Out of the Depression came an appreciation for the New Deal. The poor needed assistance, and government could be a force for good. Wright learned the importance of water to the arid Southwest, and of Hispanic cultures just to the South. Like many in his generation, Wright dropped out of school to join the war against fascism, eventually becoming a decorated bombardier with a lifelong interest in aviation and foreign policy. Having participated in one of World War II's longest bombing missions, Wright knew firsthand the horrors of war. The experience had given him a tremendous, if idealistic, faith in diplomacy.

The end of the war brought Wright and many of his contemporaries wealth they had never expected. For Wright, at least, his employment at the National Federation of Small Business and at his father's company, the National Trade Day Association, was representative in another way, helping small-town America adjust to the more mobile, suburban economy that grew in the war's wake. Born to a generation of small-town values, Wright adapted well to the urban culture he encountered, which added another layer to his character in the making. Out of his youth continued to grow both ambition and idealism, two powerful forces not always in harmony or easily reconciled.

Money was not enough to fulfill Wright, whose impressive work ethic turned to public service. Elected one of the youngest members of the Texas Legislature, Wright failed miserably but, in the process, learned another valuable lesson. To pay for an aggressive populist agenda that included funds for roads and schools, he advocated for new revenue that angered the powerful oil interests. His stay in Austin was brief but instructive: swinging for the fences, his natural inclination, was not always the wisest path; success did not come quickly no matter one's good intentions. More to the point, Wright now better understood Texas politics, which were solidly Democratic but far from united. Southern conservatives carried on the tradition of states' rights, stressing the state's historical emphasis on individualism if not its racial animosity. Others promoted the activist federal policies of President Franklin D. Roosevelt and his successor, Harry S. Truman, who was then in office. The Democratic majority, as historian Karl Gerard

Brandt has noted, "was slim and vulnerable, as evidenced by the Dixiecrat movement and Eisenhower's success."[37] This conservative-liberal dichotomy in Wright's party was not new, but neither was it fading. In fact, the Roosevelt Democratic coalition became increasingly tenuous as Wright's career in politics progressed, always defining for Wright the realm of possibility.

Wright's defeat after only one term came after a sensational campaign of charges baptized him to the reality of hardball politics. It also launched the first of several periods of dismayed reflection that characterized the otherwise optimistic Wright. Given the confidence that he placed in his work ethic, Wright was prone to melancholy in defeat. He did not take losses well and occasionally struggled to contain a short temper. Once, writing in his diary, Wright spoke of the need "not to let myself grow too vulnerable to the deep personal disappointment."[38] In these moments of periodic reflection, he relied on his religion, which he took as seriously as the famous "Bible Belt" that surrounded him. Unlike many of his more fundamentalist neighbors, however, Wright had inherited a less doctrinaire and more tolerant faith. His attitudes on race, moreover, also distinguished him. His idealism taught equality, but his ambition required a pragmatism that was uncomfortable. Wright's stance on civil rights evolved, Wright as much a follower as a leader and always aware that a wrong step on such a violable issue could end a career. His failure to win reelection in an age when McCarthyism had just begun solidified in the young politician a commitment always to wage a positive campaign. It was another example of Wright's emergent idealism and, like other aspects, ultimately proved somewhat quixotic and difficult to maintain.

Desperately wanting to make a difference and seeking a stage on which to shine, Wright ran successfully for mayor of Weatherford, his family's hometown. It was a step back, but, unlike during his stint in the state legislature, in his term as mayor Wright had tremendous success—and gained additional experience. He was building his base, and learning, as Tip O'Neill famously stated, that all politics was local. Good governance won friends, and connections with friends made careers. These connections, collegiality, and keeping his constituents satisfied were cornerstones of Wright's long career. A city expansion, new water and sewage facilities, a renovated courthouse, and the occasional fight over rate increases, among other developments, made Wright, at the time, the youngest mayor in the state, one of the most popular. His efforts to pass a bond issue to pay for the improvements not only signaled his growing political skills but marked the beginning of his lifelong aversion to debt. The appropriate level of spending and taxes—the grist of government—was always controversial but forever a centerpiece of Wright's agenda. By the time he was elected president of the Texas Municipal League, Wright's growing list of powerful acquaintances ensured new opportunities—including, for example, the chance to witness a nuclear bomb test. That experience left an impression that strengthened his faith in internationalism and diplomacy.

His groundwork laid, Wright recognized another opportunity in Texas's 12th Congressional District, which included the urban center of Fort Worth. The famous Cow Town's growth had benefited Weatherford, but it had an established political order that now rejected the young upstart. Wright directly challenged the powerful newspaperman Amon Carter in Carter's own paper and, in defeating the Carter-backed incumbent, demonstrated not only gumption but also the power of the press. It was the beginning of the complicated relationship Wright would have with the media. He cultivated the media to his advantage when possible, but ultimately he grew distrustful of it, his scandal only the last example. Despite his lack of a college degree, Wright understood from history the power of what the British political philosopher Edmund Burke termed the "Fourth Estate." Well-read, Wright remained a lifelong student of the past and authored numerous books.

Wright was appointed to the Committee on Public Works, where he stayed for over three decades, helping to determine infrastructure spending that every congressman sought. The power was real as Wright mastered the art of the deal. To critics, it was "pork-barrel" politics, but it worked to Wright's advantage and to the advantage of the district he represented. Wright never forgot his district's constituents, winning for Fort Worth an array of projects that garnered government spending, including government agencies and defense contracts. The highways around the city, the development of the Trinity River through it, and the Fort Worth Stockyards, a famous tourist attraction that defines the city for millions, all carried Wright's stamp. Wright proved to be a force in the development of the Dallas–Fort Worth International Airport, not always to the applause of neighboring Dallas, but ultimately for the good of the sprawling "Metroplex" that the two cities eventually constituted.[39]

Flowing from Wright's idealistic notion of public service was his faith in bipartisanship and compromise. In this respect, Wright was fortunate. After McCarthyism faded, moderation grew. Dwight Eisenhower was no Robert Taft, Richard Nixon no Barry Goldwater. Although there were certainly exceptions, Congress largely maintained its clubby traditions: one took the word of a fellow member; one might tussle over legislation during the day but share drinks at night; success, all seemed to agree, required a bit of give-and-take. Wright's emphasis on collegiality and connections served him well in this environment, earning him respect across the aisle. The result was an impressive list of accomplishments. Wright played a major role in the development of America's interstate highway system and in the construction of its waste treatment plants. His economic initiatives were manifold and covered a broad range of topics, from monetary policy to energy independence. A major player in diplomacy to Latin America, he worked on the Inter-American Highway and encouraged bilateral relations with Mexico. His negotiations for peace in Central America were truly historic. Wright played a role in the Camp David Accords and became the first American politician to speak live on Soviet television. In the end, leaders worldwide knew him.

Wright played his political cards well, always positioning himself as the acceptable moderate between the Democratic Party's conservative and liberal wings, a bridge to help keep the party together. Having lost some of his early populism and aggressiveness, he always looked for a way to break an impasse, a true master at working his colleagues. Ratings agencies had difficulty classifying him. On issues such as the environment, organized labor, and energy production, Wright considered both sides, often countering a move one way with another in the opposite direction. Reconciliation always followed anger. It was no wonder that Wright began to rise in the party's leadership. It helped that Wright was from Texas. With the conservatives dominating the South, his liberal inclinations made him acceptable to the more progressive North. Wright's rise in the leadership embodied the "Austin-Boston connection" that had characterized the Democratic House leadership for almost half a century.[40]

This did not mean Wright's political ascension was easy. His driving ambition demanded forceful and immediate action, but the voice of experience often cautioned restraint. Wright made mistakes—for example, launching an ill-advised Senate campaign. He had always pined for higher office, and his rise from majority whip to majority leader and finally to Speaker seemed painfully slow. The House had rules, and its seniority system was a source of frustration early and always controversial. From early-morning office breakfasts to late-night fundraisers, Wright's preoccupation with politics carried a personal cost as well. He fathered five children, four of whom lived into adulthood, but the demands of Washington never allowed enough personal time to spend with them. Wright's first marriage failed, hardly an uncommon occurrence to the power brokers in the nation's capital.

Wright certainly enjoyed a front-row seat to history. He played a role in bringing John Kennedy to Dallas on November 22, 1963, and was with him on that fateful day. His bipartisanship obvious, Wright developed a close working relationship with Richard Nixon, though friendship was never easy for that complicated president. Despite all the evidence, Wright was reluctant to believe Nixon's complicity in Watergate. Close encounters with interesting and powerful people, from Egypt's Anwar el-Sadat to the Soviet Union's Mikhail Gorbachev, added color to Wright's life. He found mentors in the likes of Sam Rayburn and fellow Texan Lyndon Johnson, but he eventually developed his own following. He was also close to Jimmy Carter, a fellow southern moderate. Wright had, in short, close associates representing a virtual who's who of modern American political history.

As political history changed over his three decades of public life, Wright had to adapt. He found the New Left of the late 1960s frustrating, and he never embodied the shifting cultural norms of the times to the same degree as many of his Democratic colleagues. The youthful activism and disillusionment of the Vietnam War and Watergate eras brought a sudden influx of young, more liberal congressmen. With reform on the agenda, Wright struggled with how to recalibrate his balance. Central party leadership weakened in favor of democratization, and committee chairs became more independent. As the Democratic Party arguably moved leftward, the Republicans drifted in the opposite direction. Slowly, but in time irrevocably, conservatives began to abandon the Democratic Party for the GOP's southern outreach. Wright's efforts to bridge the growing party divide lifted his personal ship even as the seas grew increasingly stormy. The congressional traditions that Wright represented began to fade, with consensus politics giving way to harsher partisan discord, and compromise turning into personal invective. The many engines of this evolution spanned the realms of politics, culture, and the economy, but a new, more competitive media also played a role.

As the Texan Andrews recalled, the staff brought buckets of ice water to every congressional office, most of whom used refrigerators. When Andrews asked why the buckets remained, Wright replied, "Well, that's because they have always done it that way." Wright resisted efforts to remove the Capitol's elevator operator, despite the fact that the elevator was the "size of a phone booth" and the operator an elderly man who sat in a chair and used a cane. Wright loved it all and wanted it to stay the same.[41]

Wright remained a complex man, supporting campaign finance reform, another aspect of his idealism, even as he needed money to match his increasingly well-armed opponents. In time, ironically, he became a leading fundraiser, his well-regarded rhetorical skills a major draw for national audiences. Even as critics decried him as a "pork-barrel" spender, Wright remained a deficit hawk, arguing that his spending stimulated private growth and revenue and noting the larger cuts he advocated elsewhere. With truth on both sides, however, the reality of Washington remained: one congressman's stimulus was another's waste. Wright's idealism taught him that the nation needed to rally around the chief executive, the constitutionally ordained commander-in-chief, in times of war. At the same time, however, Wright became an ardent defender of congressional prerogative, noting Congress's constitutional role in declaring war, in oversight, and in appropriations. The distinction was not always clear. Wright brought from his war experiences the need for a robust military even as he championed diplomacy. A hawk on the Vietnam War in a party fast becoming dovish, he always had difficulty admitting that the war was a mistake. In short, Wright was as complicated as the political culture in which he operated.

The emergence of the charismatic Republican president Ronald Reagan, the embodiment of a "New Right" of fiscal and social conservatives, appeared to be the culmination of this dynamic political process. For Wright, it was the ultimate challenge. Despite Wright's robust leadership, the supply-side economic theories of "Reaganomics" found their way into law. Never before had Wright faced such a powerful and ideological opponent, one whom Wright believed failed to consider alternative arguments, never delving deeply into issues. Simplistic or not, Reagan understood his power and, at least in Wright's view, refused to compromise. Reagan was simply unlike his Republican predecessors, unlike Eisenhower or Nixon or the others who had served terms while Wright was in Washington.

Reagan's leverage ebbed and flowed, his failures as obvious as his successes, but following the 1986 congressional election Wright enjoyed a new momentum in the Democratic counterattack. In terms of legislation, the historic one hundredth Congress that met during Wright's tenure as Speaker of the House was one of the nation's most productive. It hardly solved the nation's problems, but it confirmed Wright's leadership abilities. Wright had the power he had sought for so many years, and he was not shy about using it, reaffirming the power of the position. Swinging for the fences at last, as he had always wanted to do, Wright was ready to emerge as one of history's most famous House Speakers. In foreign policy, he ended up confronting Reagan directly on the White House's Cold War policies in Central America. It was brazen and public. Jim Wright was a problem for Ronald Reagan and a thorn in the side of the Republicans. Fortunately for the GOP, and for all his enemies, Wright had also made mistakes. And despite it all, his tenure was brief. Only two years after taking office as Speaker of the House, Wright, a complex man whose life paralleled and influenced so much of modern American history, a man whose life was, according to his colleague Andrews, "amazing," stood at the podium giving the most painful speech of his career. He was in history as he had hoped, but not as he had intended—and, perhaps, not as he completely deserved.

PART I

The Rise of a Politician

CHAPTER I

The Foundations for Success

FAMILY AND CHILDHOOD (1922–1939)

Jim Wright's roots ran deep into the prairie soil of Texas, his ancestors part of those hardy migrants who ventured westward in the nineteenth century. He had English and Irish DNA—the latter evidenced, perhaps, by his red hair, and, as critics claimed, a quick temper—and descended mostly from men and women who arrived in America in the wake of the Civil War. At that time, Texas was just beginning the transition from the Old West to the New South—from cattle to cars, frontier to finance. It provided both challenges and opportunities, all of which helped to shape Jim Wright's large family, and ultimately, the foundations of his own life.[1]

Although it surely impressed few in Texas, Jim Wright's mother, Marie Louella Lyster, could trace her lineage back to the seventeenth-century English baron Sir Toby Caufield. She was also related to the famous Lee and Byrd families of Virginia.[2] Marie's mother, Lena Crowder, Jim Wright's maternal grandmother, was part of a large family that had settled in Weatherford, a town rising out of the prairie forty miles west of the booming cattle stockyards in Fort Worth and surrounded by peach orchards and melon fields. The extended family had no pretensions of wealth: Lena's father was the only teacher in a one-room schoolhouse in the Parker County community of Dicey. Nevertheless, Lena's family lived comfortably, displaying a degree of education and refinement uncommon in an area not long removed from the Wild West. In Weatherford Lena met and married Harry Lyster, Jim Wright's maternal grandfather. No common ranch hand himself, Harry had been born in Australia of English and Irish parents and had been educated as a civil engineer at the prestigious University of Heidelberg. He had come to Texas to join his uncle, who was a former surveyor general of Australia. The uncle's inventions had won him a considerable endowment from the crown, which had allowed him to buy a ranch in Parker County. Harry hoped to find work as an engineer on the railroads then crossing the West. It was a fateful decision; his uncle's ranch was immediately adjacent to the Crowder homestead.[3]

Finding employment with the Southern Pacific Railroad, Harry took his young bride to New Mexico Territory, where he began surveying a new rail route just above the Mexican border. Harry and Lena stayed in Eddy, now Carlsbad, for the duration of the project, and there, on September 11, 1894, Lena gave birth to Marie, Jim Wright's mother. Life was difficult without even Weatherford's basic amenities, and Harry suddenly died of a fever, leaving twenty-year-old Lena alone with an infant. Demonstrating a degree of self-reliance belied by her refinement but cultivated by her frontier experience, Lena employed her bilingual skills to land a job running the company store. Hawking necessaries to Hispanic laborers was arguably beneath her station, but the vicissitudes of life had already taught her important lessons. She valued education, hard work, persistence, and empathy for those less fortunate, all traits that eventually would manifest in her progeny.[4]

After carefully saving every cent, Lena was finally able to return to Weatherford. Disembarking from the train, she and Marie, still a toddler, appeared quite bedraggled. Fortunately they had a place to stay, as Lena's great aunt, Lenora Lisk Womak, and her husband, a former Confederate officer, owned the Victorian Terminal Hotel.[5] The railroad had arrived in 1880, and Weatherford had prospered. It now boasted an ornate 1884 French Second Empire–style courthouse. Covered wagons sold their wares on the grassy square while political events brought crowds from the surrounding communities. It was a good place to raise a daughter, even if vestiges of the frontier were still visible in the marketing of cattle and the occasional drunken brawl. It had, after all, been less than two decades since the city had proudly proclaimed freedom from "the incursions of hostile Indians."[6]

The bustling hotel, where Lena worked as a bookkeeper, was an exciting place for a child. Traveling salesmen known as "drummers" would come and go while the nearby Haynes Opera House ensured a constant influx of people from all walks of life. The transient actors, amused by the doting little girl with the big brown eyes, let Marie try on their costumes. Not surprisingly, Marie announced her intention to join the profession. In time, always good at mathematics, Marie expressed an interest in becoming an "Expert Accountant," and, later still, a pharmacist. Marie, it appeared, had quite the ambition.[7]

The Victorian-minded Lena, however, had other expectations. If women had to work as she did, they should seek employment in the "women's sphere," respectable female professions such as teaching. Marie, Lena insisted, would learn to be a proper lady. Accordingly, for two hours each day, Marie had to practice the piano and learn the feminine arts of poetry, literature, and painting. It was a cultured but strict environment.[8]

Lena, still relatively young, was an obvious object of attention for the city's male gentry. While she still treasured the broad-banded wedding ring that Harry had given her—Harry, her life's true love—society expected her to remarry. In 1902, Lena settled on William Dee Walker, a tall, dark-haired, and imposing man, the son of a land-wealthy Brazos River family who met her strict expectations. In true frontier fashion, the young Willie Dee, as he was known to friends, had been a hard-drinking gambler, reportedly lighting cigars with $5 bills.[9] In marrying Lena, however, he had sworn off such ungentlemanly ways. He would reinforce Lena's Victorian admonishments to Marie. "I really don't believe I have ever heard of a lady Expert Accountant," he told her.[10]

By the second decade of the twentieth century, Marie had grown into an attractive five-foot-six brunette absorbed in her mother's traits and training. As Jim Wright would later recall of his mother, her dignity was always paramount. She once refused to chase her large-brimmed hat blown off by the wind. Her sense of ambition was still intact, however, and she became a teacher—of drama, understandably, and "expression," as poetry was then known. She also enjoyed teaching English literature. One does not have to look far to see where Wright's famous ambition and oratory had its genesis. For a brief period Marie taught in Duncan, Oklahoma, a new state where additional relatives resided.[11]

At the Parker County Fair, Marie met James Claude Wright, a strapping, fair-skinned blond of just under six feet who was five years her senior. Jim Wright's father seemed energetic and gregarious but was an odd choice for the young teacher. While he, too, had English and Irish blood, and his family had also migrated to Texas from Virginia, albeit via Tennessee, he lacked refinement and education. The youngest of four siblings born to John Wright and Elizabeth Amanda Johnson, James Wright had suffered early like his wife-to-be. His father had died young, and polio, the most feared scourge of the day, had left his mother in a wheelchair. Without a broader clan to help raise him, James had quit school after the fourth grade and gone to work.[12]

As determined in spirit as his future mother-in-law, Lena, James took what opportunities were available for a poor, uneducated young man. After chopping cotton and laboring at a brick kiln, he became a boxer. It was the heyday of the black fighter Jack Johnson—the "Galveston Giant"—and the public searched for the next great "white hope."[13] Traveling to Detroit, New York, and Chicago, James learned the value of hard work and persistence, finding some success but quite literally taking his lumps. Never idle, he apprenticed as a tailor to learn a trade he could practice after his boxing days were over. On a trip home to Weatherford, James met Marie and was smitten immediately. After learning that she would not date a boxer, he opened a tailor and dry cleaning business in town and, surely to impress her, began to read more. In time, Jim Wright later recalled, his father became an "ecumenist," a Renaissance man interested in learning and challenging the status quo.[14]

James enlisted in the National Guard around 1910, and his Weatherford infantry company elected him a captain under an anachronistic policy that was soon ended. When Woodrow Wilson federalized the force in 1916 to combat Mexican revolutionaries such as Pancho Villa, James was sent south to the Rio Grande. Perhaps motivated by the separation, he and Marie married during James's deployment in the small Big Bend border town of Valentine, Texas. With the outbreak of World War I, James received a commission as a captain. After a period stationed in Spartanburg, South Carolina, in which his bride joined him, he won a decoration in the famous French Argonne Forest offensive, where shrapnel dimpled his face. Marie, meanwhile, stayed on New York's Long Island with the family of one of James's colleagues. It was an eye-opening experience. Her hosts were Catholic, and Marie, raised a Southern Baptist, had known only Hispanic Catholics.[15] "Mother," Jim Wright later recalled, "learned how hideously untrue the things said of the Catholic faith by rural fundamentalists with whom she had grown up."[16] In fact, with James a Methodist, the young couple developed rather tolerant religious views, eventually settling on Presbyterianism while later sending their daughters to Catholic schools. "The only prejudice we had was against Baptists who didn't drink, dance, smoke, or play cards," Jim Wright's sister, Mary Nelle, jokingly recalled. When the

Scopes Trial made national headlines just after Jim Wright's birth, James and Marie did not share their community's dominant condemnation of evolutionary theory.[17]

Sharing the trenches with men from across the globe solidified James's egalitarian spirit. All men, he later told his famous son, "wanted the same things, felt the same hurts, and bled the same color."[18] The nativism that flourished after the war repulsed him. From 1900 to 1930, over 600,000 Mexicans immigrated to the Southwest, many of whom, the University of Texas warned in 1920, were not assimilating. With Texas's own African American population growing by a quarter million over the same period, James fought a courageous battle against the Ku Klux Klan. When the Klan "branded" an African American bellhop with acid in Dallas, James signed letters to the *Weatherford Daily Herald* criticizing the organization.[19]

James and Marie were a bit iconoclastic, maintaining their Progressive sense of optimism despite the fact that Wilson's promise of a world safe for democracy had fallen flat. They supported the League of Nations, while many Texans questioned the Treaty of Versailles. They rejected their peers' isolationism, but were patriotic and had faith in government. When a friend remarked that she had not raised her son to become a soldier, Marie quipped, "Well, neither did I, but I will not raise him to be a slacker." Years later, despite his fifty-one years, James protested his rejection for service in World War II. "I've already been to war and I know how to fight," Jim's sister, Betty Lee, remembered her father complaining.[20] Unlike their fundamentalist neighbors, James and Marie resisted Prohibition, and, although Marie held no driver's license and was hardly a feminist, both supported women's suffrage. James once angered a school superintendent by arguing that girls should be allowed to wear blue jeans. While hardly quiet about their beliefs, neither were they quick to judge others publicly. The courage of their convictions was tempered by their innate tolerance. It was not always easy. James had a temper and a growing fondness for alcohol. Admired by his friends, if not by Marie, as a man who "could hold his liquor," James regularly had an African American employee drive him across county lines to purchase whiskey, though when they returned, he would drink by himself. James and Marie Wright were forceful characters hard to miss.[21]

Living with Lena and William Walker in Fort Worth, James and Marie gave birth to their first son, James Claude Wright Jr., on December 22, 1922. Given his strong work ethic, James had become the southwest regional sales manager for the US Chamber of Commerce, selling municipal memberships and the organization's journal *Nation's Business*. It was a great job, but the constant moving it required was hard on a young family. Before young Jim was even in school, the family had lived both in large cities, such as Lubbock and San Antonio, Texas, and in small towns, including some locations in Arkansas and Louisiana. This semi-transient lifestyle defined Jim Wright's boyhood well into his high school years. Although each successive year became more difficult for Jim, the constant moving developed skills that served him a lifetime. No natural extrovert, Jim learned to be flexible and gregarious, to feel comfortable in public and to read cues from his peers, and to ingratiate himself with new groups.

After Jim finished first grade in Houston in 1929, the family moved to Dallas. Like its sister city, Fort Worth, to which it was connected by a new interurban rail line, Dallas was in the midst of an oil boom. With a population exceeding 150,000, it was a center for the redistribution of eastern goods to southwestern markets. It boasted a major university, a federal reserve bank, an insurance center, a developed transportation network, a symphony orchestra, and over two dozen theaters.[22] Optimistic and prospering like the city itself, the Wright family rented a large two-room house in the Oak Cliff section of town. James traded his Dodge automobile for a Hudson, a status symbol. Of course, as Jim started second grade that fall, his parents—like everyone else—had no idea that the "New Economic Era" of the 1920s was about to end.[23]

The stock market crash of October 1929 changed everything. Slow to realize the magnitude of the emerging Great Depression, James quit his job to form a company that manufactured and sold signs that combined street names with advertisements. Despite their need, many small towns could no longer afford the signs after the crash, and many businesses had little to spend on advertising.[24] His father, Jim Wright later recalled, "had more ambition than prudence," a conclusion that others would later apply to Wright's own career.[25] As his father struggled, the family moved back to Weatherford, settling into a modest rental on Lee Street. Jim, a good student, skipped the third grade. But Weatherford gave him a front-row seat to the unfolding economic calamity.

At first Jim was still young enough to enjoy the simple—and free— pleasures of boyhood without much suffering. He and his friends still chased the horse-drawn ice wagon to see who could sit longest on the slab of ice. He never missed a meal, noticing only that his father no longer bought cigarettes but rolled his own. In time, however, hoboes began begging at his family's door. The hoboes traveled on the Texas and Pacific line that bordered the Wrights' property. Marie, who thought the term "tramps" derogatory, impressed Jim by offering food when she could. Asked in school to define the role of government, Jim, who had heard his parents complaining about Herbert Hoover, answered simply, "Depression."[26]

The family later spoke of 1931 as the year they "ate the piano." With James's company failing, the family sold Marie's cherished piano, despite the fact that the family had regularly gathered around it to sing. Years later, Jim still recalled the ragtime tunes and old Irish ballads that his mother had played. The loss was tough for Marie, who saw in the piano a symbol of the refinement she valued. Within the year, the Hudson was gone as well. It was six years before James Wright purchased another car, explaining nonchalantly to his son that it was easier to walk or take trains. Hearing of a mysterious "Hooverville" along the railroad tracks, Jim one night went to explore, and he found not the elaborate community he had expected but crude lean-tos and shabbily dressed men sitting before a fire, one of whom sang with a harmonica the plaintive lament of "Red River Valley." That night, Jim later remembered, he had never felt so "warmly snug."[27]

The fate of William Walker, Lena's husband and the only real grandfather Jim had known, left an even a greater impression. At age sixty-three, after twenty-three years of loyalty—and only two years before a promised pension—Walker lost his job selling equipment for lumberyards. The company explained that the dismissal was necessary to ensure the pensions of those who had served a quarter century, an explanation that undoubtedly stung. Now, James Wright explained to his son, his grandparents' house, which the young boy saw as a "sanctuary," a place to visit on Sundays for fried chicken dinners, might have to go. To prevent this, James broke his Weatherford lease and moved his family back into his in-laws' home, where they all shared a bathroom. Jim, who was only ten years old, noticed his grandfather quietly reading the job advertisements every morning. Walker would get dressed in his best outfits and leave the house hopeful only to return in the evenings despondent.[28]

The house was crowded. By this time Jim had two sisters, Mary Nelle and Betty Lee. Born in 1927, Mary Nelle had inherited her mother's artistic bent and her father's eclectic energy. Her interests were broader than her focus, however; she eventually attended five different colleges and never graduated. She was married three times and sired a child by each husband. A published poet and an accomplished painter, she also had a sense of humor and a zest for life. Betty Lee, born in 1929, inherited her mother's interest in education and her father's ambition, and in this way she was more akin to her older brother. Betty Lee became an Austin teacher and, later, a Southwest Texas State University professor. The children were always close, she recalled. They often played "dictionary," trying to stump each other by choosing difficult words for definition.[29] Both girls loved their brother as "Bubba," a nickname that thankfully did not progress into Jim's career.[30]

These were impressionable years for the growing Jim Wright. Once, when a horse threw him into a creek near Fort Worth's Sycamore Park, he refused to remount. Wet and crying, and still wearing the knickers of a younger child, he faced the taunting scorn of a visiting cousin. Not remounting, the older boy insisted, would "ruin" the horse. Later, at home, Jim asked his father if the admonishment was true. Yes, came the answer, and "the boy might be ruined as well."[31]

Sycamore Park, with its open spaces, pool, and tennis courts, was a special place to young Jim. Encouraged by his father to be competitive—a winner—Jim became a star halfback in the seventy-five-pound division of a youth football league sponsored in the park by a local newspaper. When the competition protested that he weighed too much, Jim confidently dismissed the charges and, demonstrating the moxie for which he was later famous, offered to weigh himself. The result, seventy-eight pounds, left him embarrassed and disgraced—and stark naked before a mocking crowd. While in later years Jim laughingly recalled that a female friend had told him, "Don't worry, no one saw it," it was clear that Jim Wright was developing a thin skin and hated to lose. As one newspaper put it decades later, "Jim Wright can be easily hurt by others' criticism."[32]

His father's approval mattered to him. As one of his grade school friends, James Bodiford, put it, "Jim was very fond of his daddy and his daddy was very fond of him."[33] While still in Dallas, James Wright had given seven-year-old Jim a book on the boxer Jack Dempsey, Nat Fleischer's *Jack Dempsey: Idol of Fistiana*. Promptly memorizing the text of what he called "his first real man book," Jim quietly hoped for his own boxing exploits—just like his father and Jack Dempsey.[34] By the time he lived in Fort Worth, Jim was subscribing to the magazine *The Ring*; when he was thirteen, he lied about his age to enter a boxing tournament. Throughout the years James kept his son interested in heroic stories, giving him biographies of such figures as Andrew Jackson and the football coach Knute Rockne. "I did what dad wanted me to do, whatever coach wanted me to do," Jim Wright recalled as an adult. "I wasn't a rebellious person. I wanted to be part of the team."[35] In one congressional-era interview, he acknowledged that a psychiatrist friend "had once told me I still was trying to please my father."[36]

Jim already knew that he had to be *somebody*. Even years later, his diary still spoke of the "insatiable thirst for approval that drives me."[37] From his elders came a constant reinforcement of ambition and ego. In one not-so-subtle example, his father introduced him at age five to Fort Worth congressman Fritz Lanham as "your successor."[38] Both their parents, Mary Nelle recalled, stressed that "we were something special." Anything was possible "if you want to do it strongly enough and are willing to pay the price."[39] This expectation of success created a lot of pressure. According to Mary Nelle, "I felt like I would be a failure if I didn't win the Nobel Prize."[40] When faced with evidence that he would not always get his way, Jim was not only thin-skinned but also quick to anger. As an excitable child, he threw quite the fit, and as an adolescent he had his share of fights. In one fourth-grade scuffle, Jim exploded when another boy called his book bag a "sissy-looking satchel."[41] "He was high tempered as hell," his friend Bodiford remembered, and "could throw out a lot of four letter words." As high-strung as Jim was, however, the tempest would invariably pass quickly, with few grudges remaining.[42]

Jim's gift for public speaking grew from his ambition and thirst for the limelight. While the family was still in Dallas, his mother entered him in a show to recite poetry at a local church. Practicing with him for days, she had him repeat the poem "until you can say it with feeling." His performance was a roaring success. Jim later recalled basking in the applause and seeking other opportunities for public acclaim, considering for the first time even a career in the pulpit. Preaching, after all, was an attractive option. Church was a staple of his life, and he saw preachers as respected leaders in the community. As a preacher he could do well and be good.[43]

If Jim Wright's ambition was obvious early, his growing idealism was less so. Once, fired up by riveting stories of cowboys and Indians and for the moment angry at his parents, Jim ran away to live with the Indians. "He took his Indian blanket and his good stuff," Mary Nelle laughingly recalled, but, after a rainstorm, "came home looking very bedraggled." As Wright remembered it, "I decided that the Indians had been given a raw deal. The white men had made promises and not kept them. I decided that I was on the side of the Indians."[44] He was also, he decided, on the side of the poor fellows arriving on their doorstep begging for work.

When Jim was about to enter the sixth grade—with his thoughts about the world and his future rattling about in his brain—his father decided to move again. As puberty neared, Jim would have to find his answers in yet another place.

In the depths of the Great Depression, James Wright got a break: his experience with small towns and marketing earned him the directorship of the Duncan Chamber of Commerce in Oklahoma. Ninety miles southwest of Oklahoma City, Duncan had prospered during the 1920s with the founding of the Halliburton Oil Company. Tudor Revival houses had sprung up, and the community of 8,300 had been optimistic for the future. Now, however, James's job was to stem the tide of the Depression in the town, a task made somewhat easier by the New Deal work programs that eventually brought Duncan a new library, high school, armory, and sidewalks. If James and Marie were not already committed Democrats, they were now.[45] "I remember that [the New Deal] had something to do with us," Jim recalled. The National Recovery Administration's symbol, a blue eagle, was in every storefront. Too young for the Civilian Conservation Corps, Jim nevertheless remembered Franklin Roosevelt's Inaugural Address. "The only thing we have to fear is fear itself," he joked, described his family's transient lifestyle.[46]

"If ever we were poor," Jim Wright recalled years later, "we never knew it." In fact, compared to the millions unemployed, they were not poor at all, their small town environment a bit of nostalgic Americana. The home, "ample in size for our family," he later said, allowed him his own room. Every night, the children would gather around the radio until their 8:30 bedtime, at which point, ensconced in their pajamas, they were permitted to select one story from *Book Trails* for their mother to read before prayers. Mary Nelle kept choosing the childish fantasy "Dolls Coming Alive," the volume's longest story and a blatant attempt to filibuster the inevitable. Life included football games, church revivals, band concerts, fireflies at twilight, and a county fair.[47] The family's backyard had a garden, a coop for bantam chickens, and, hanging from a tree, a punching bag made of two sewn pieces of canvas filled with cottonseed mill. With the home located just blocks from the town square and Jim's school, walking was the preferred option. Joining the family was a friendly pit bull that followed Jim home one day. They named him Caesar. On Saturdays, Jim sold advertising circulars to the farmers and ranchers who came into the square. He would spend a dime to attend the town's air-conditioned movie house and a nickel for a hamburger. With his remaining change he would purchase one of the big city newspapers that had just arrived, turning quickly to the sports section. Like many rural boys, Jim had a .22-caliber rifle for target shooting. Patriotism and religion were omnipresent, while urban crime seemed distant. The family was even able to send money back to Fort Worth to Jim's grandfather

William Walker, who lived on part-time employment and a small rental property he had constructed. Walker also had an extensive garden that helped him make ends meet.[48]

With their children growing older, the lessons still came from Jim's parents. After Jim used scissors to cut a girl's felt cap, which had been left unclaimed in study hall, to create a kind of skull cap popular with the boys, James and Marie played to Jim's conscience. Would not some little girl miss her hat? They should pray for God's forgiveness and the strength to return the stolen property, James suggested. The cap found its owner, of course, but more importantly, the point had been made. Jim's high energy and desire to be the center of attention always ensured that his parents would face challenges. After seeing a newsreel of Johnny Weissmuller—the famous swimmer and later star of the Tarzan movies—rubbing oil over his body to discourage shark attacks, Jim rubbed molten asphalt not only over himself but also on several girls. The result was an expulsion from the pool, and, undoubtedly, parental ire.[49] Punishment for such sins varied. "I could count on one hand the number of times my father took the switch to me," Jim later recalled. James was not above corporal punishment, but he preferred using transgressions as teaching opportunities. Like any boy, however, Jim feared his father's stern side. Emulating the comics he enjoyed in a sketchbook, Jim labeled one figure, obviously angry and wagging his finger, the "father."[50]

After hooking Jim on reading with Edgar Rice Burroughs's *Tarzan of the Apes* series, James gave him *The Complete Works of O'Henry*.[51] "Read these short stories with a pencil in your hand," James instructed. Every time Jim found a word he did not know, he should check a dictionary and then use the word in a sentence five times over the following week. "That way you will own them," his father said. Jim dutifully did as told, becoming a bibliophile like his parents, his arsenal an obvious tool to further his equally obvious ambition.[52] The lessons kept coming. "Imagine what it would be like if little red-haired boys could not use the water fountains," James commented one day in an obvious rebuttal to Jim Crow. "Imagine the world's religions the spokes of a tire with God at the center," he instructed on another occasion. If they were ants on different spokes, the further they were from God, the further they were from each other.[53] When Jim once called Pentecostals "crazy" for claiming they heard God talking to them, James asked, "What makes you so certain they do not?" He then switched on a radio with a man singing before turning it off. "Do you think he's quit singing?" The lesson was obvious; it was folly to criticize others who might simply be on different frequencies.[54] In Duncan, Jim and his father would visit a different congregation each week, "sermon sampling," as the writer C. S. Lewis would later decry it. The two would then discuss the sermons walking home, a lesson on tolerance.[55]

In later years, Jim recounted his father's lessons with fondness, repeating them in his writings. "I was convinced that geography was boring until Dad began telling me of things he'd seen in some of the countries," Jim recalled in one instance. James, still despising pretensions of class despite the bourgeois overtones of his wife's family, kept insisting that Jim never look down on anybody because of their circumstances. "There is no such thing as an upper class or lower class in America," he explained.[56] By this point Jim had clearly learned the art of a deal, no small skill for a future politician. After James promised to purchase a punching bag for Jim if he stopped teasing his sisters for six weeks, Jim approached Mary Nelle and Betty Lee with his own offer. If they would not complain for six weeks, he proposed, he would let them play with his new bag.[57]

Perhaps the most important lesson for Jim was the loving relationship James and Marie modeled. Although the two were quite different, they were open to communication and respected one another. In a book of poetry she gave James for one of his birthdays, Marie scribbled, "Wipe your eyes, dry your tears, it's you that counts, not the years." The inscription impressed Jim, who eventually gave the book to his own son as a family memento.[58] The pressure the Wright children felt came from high expectations and not from tension within the household. In later years, James's drinking undoubtedly strained relationships. James, the rugged mentor to an impressionable adolescent, became an inebriated old man sitting in a wheelbarrow in his garage scribbling poetry on the walls. Still, Mary Nelle recalled, James always remained a gentleman and provided for his family. "People who dwell on his alcoholism overlook his strengths," she said. "He had 'stickability,' a word he often used and pounded into all of us."[59]

There was, at least, a bright side to James's vice. The adult Jim Wright never drank to excess. According to family friends, he remembered the devolution of his old man.[60] In fact, as Jim prepared to leave home years later, James had a proposition. Explaining that he had missed out on "thousands of dollars of profitable deals by being too befuddled by drink," James offered to abstain if Jim would as well. Jim agreed—"a very small sacrifice for me"— and the two shook hands. Unfortunately, Jim later learned, his father's drinking had resumed. By the end of his life James had sought professional help numerous times, but in each instance surrendered to his demons.[61]

Jim, relentlessly pushed forward, was ahead of most of his Duncan peers academically. As fate would have it, Oklahoma had twelve years of common schooling and Texas only eleven. Duncan officials gave the Wrights the option of entering Jim into the sixth grade as scheduled or advancing him directly into the seventh. Jim insisted upon the latter, aware that in his old state the sixth grade was still in elementary school. In his own mind, he had no time to waste. The promotion, however, made Jim another year younger—another year smaller—than his contemporaries. For a competitive child always seeking to fit in, it proved to be a new challenge, further sharpening his ambition and will to win.[62]

In the end, Jim had relatively little time to bond with the town of Duncan. His family moved yet again. Jim started the eighth grade roughly eighty miles to the northeast, in Seminole, Oklahoma, where James had accepted a more lucrative job leading that town's chamber of commerce. While Seminole was slightly larger than Duncan, life was similar. Without a Presbyterian church, the family migrated to the Methodist congregation. Jim no longer had to take the mandated course in agriculture he had endured in Duncan, but he missed his chickens—his new backyard was too small for any coop. He became interested in the Boy Scouts, promising to be "as loyal as even a bulldog is to his master." As active as ever, he continued his drawing and exhibited a degree of real talent with faces and animals.[63]

It was in Seminole that Jim's father launched his "Appreciation Day" for local businesses. Most small towns competed to draw customers to their squares on Saturdays, which meant that the local merchants did not know where to focus their advertising and expansion. Moreover, many people drove to Oklahoma City to shop, convinced that the smaller towns charged more for goods. Believing that their chamber of commerce had done well with industry but not retail, which constituted 90 percent of its budget, Seminole merchants demanded action. After trying to discern Seminole's market from the subscription lists of local publications, James realized that he needed something original, something to define the town's market and not detract from business on Saturdays.[64]

The resulting plan was to advertise Seminole by getting customers to come on Wednesdays, "Appreciation Day." Each purchase earned a coupon of from 5 to 50 percent off, with the larger percentages reserved for the more expensive purchases, and each coupon recording the customer's name and address. The coupons were for a drawing on Wednesdays from the Community Treasure Chest, a fund composed of contributions from the local businesses. The winner of the Wednesday drawing received the stated percentage of the total till. The remaining funds were transferred to the next week's Community Treasure Chest, and thus the incentive grew weekly. To avoid violating state lottery laws, the program required winners to recite advertisements from the previous week's newspaper. Technically, therefore, it was a game of skill, not gambling.[65]

It was a huge success. Merchants knew where to focus their marketing, their sales increased, and other towns began to inquire how the program worked. James responded with Saturday "goodwill tours" to the nearby towns. On their squares, he organized exhibitions, including dancing, recitals, and singing. Young Jim even gave boxing exhibitions, undoubtedly loving having an audience while simultaneously pleasing his father. The goodwill tours proved popular on their own because without television, live entertainment was rare in such small communities.[66] Wisely seeking copyright protection for his ideas, James began to grow a business teaching other communities how to replicate "Appreciation Day." Of the first seven towns to adopt the program, four had a designated day every week. All reported increased sales.[67]

If this success ensured another move for the family, it was a turning point in more than one way. For the first time ever, the family had financial security to match its refinement and education. The growing wealth and prominence, moreover, brought opportunities and connections that, in time, opened doors for Jim Wright as he launched his political career. The constant traveling from community to community and his father's daily consultations with business leaders gave Jim as much as his father a connection to rural America. Jim knew from his boyhood what worried small-town America, and the aspirations of the common folk undoubtedly reinforced not only the egalitarianism and tolerance he had absorbed from his parents but also his budding idealism.

In the short term, James's success caught the eye of the owners of the Oklahoma City Chieftains, a minor league baseball team in the Texas League, who hired him to run their marketing. As he hawked the team, the elder Wright began to sell franchises for his "Appreciation Day" program under the banner of the National Trade Day Association. The franchisees purchased a region in which to practice the program with the local communities. By the end of the decade, James had state directors coordinating various regions. The NTDA's growth remained steady, the so-called Roosevelt Recession of 1937 only briefly tarnishing the company's profits and, in the Wright family's eyes, the towering stature of the New Deal. Indeed, years later, Jim Wright listed Franklin Roosevelt as his "teenage idol."[68]

Ninth grade in such a large city was a change for Jim. Oklahoma City was first settled in 1889, but by now it sported three high schools and six junior high schools serving a population approaching 200,000. The oil boom had hit the state capital as it had the smaller towns, and, in fact, only a few years before the Wrights' arrival, the May Sudik well in the city had gushed uncontrolled for eleven days, spraying 10,000 barrels of oil each day. The city that Jim Wright knew had an extensive trolley system, although, like everywhere else, it was just recovering from the Great Depression. The huge Hooverville on the south side of the North Canadian River had largely shrunk away by the time of the Wrights' arrival, a hopeful sign for the future. The Chieftains were popular with the locals, having won their only championship in 1935.[69]

Jim stayed busy, occasionally receiving permission to leave school early to collect money for the team coupons his father had sold. After supper, Jim took the trolley to the Chieftains' stadium, where he got in for free. The family now enjoyed at least a degree of air conditioning with an old water-driven window unit, which would soon go out of vogue. While Jim was still too young to partake of the drinking and smoking that some of his older peers indulged in—friends recounted him "turning green" on experimenting with cigarettes—he still did his best to fit in with his new crowd. "I didn't want my friends to know that I was younger," he recalled.[70] To keep his secret, he adopted the persona of the popular set. As it turned out, perhaps predictably, he need not have tried so hard. A new year brought a new change: his father's National Trade Day Association had grown to the point that James Wright felt it deserved his full attention. Resigning from the Chieftains, he packed up his family for Dallas. Here, at long last, Jim would find a degree of the continuity so critical for a boy quickly maturing into a young man.[71]

"I thought I'd died and gone to heaven," Jim Wright recalled of his high school years. It was the first time he had enjoyed the same friends and school and a real sense of home for more than a short time.[72] The family first moved into a large apartment on Marseilles Street back in the Oak Cliff section of town, near where they had lived years before. Marie needed surgery and feared the worst, so she enrolled the girls at Our Lady of Hope Catholic School to ensure they would receive proper moral guidance. Jim, she trusted, already had a strong foundation. After a brief rental of a small house just west of there, the family then found the perfect home, a big house with a sizable backyard in the Trinity Heights section of Oak Cliff. Although the smaller house had been in the district that served the new

Sunset High School, Jim stayed throughout his high school career at Adamson High, a large school of approximately 1,200 students. By the time he graduated three years later, he had taken every advantage of the opportunities the larger school had offered, and his extensive resume hinted at his ambition and ultimate career.[73]

Jim was still a decent student, but he devoted much of his time to extracurricular activities that established him as a leader among his peers. On any given day one might find him with friends at the Oak Cliff Public Library, a large building near the zoo and a popular hangout, or at the Oak Cliff YMCA, where he was captain of the club boxing team and a frequent participant in Amateur Athletic Union–sponsored tournaments. An aggressive fighter, Jim ended his senior year with ten victories and only one defeat, but his hatred for losing and well-practiced maneuvers had been more influential in his wins than any innate physical prowess. Reflecting his mother's influence, Jim also sang in the Oak Cliff Presbyterian Church youth choir and continued his interest in art, refining his drawing skills. Boxing matches, facial portraits, and animals were common subjects for his pen— perhaps appropriately, he drew an excellent bulldog. His reading favored the iconoclastic, including the writings of William Cooper Brann, a fiery and controversial Waco editor who had been assassinated in 1898.[74]

James Wright, still a bulldog of a man himself, continued relentlessly promoting his business as his son advanced. Never one to miss an opportunity, James created a promotion that gave away a flowing oil well to an out-of-state guest at the official Texas Centennial Exposition, a celebration that brought 100,000 people to Dallas's new Art Deco–themed Fair Park. By the time Jim graduated from high school, the NTDA had a national office that employed half a dozen people at its headquarters and forty-two field representatives. It had branch offices in Minneapolis, Louisville, and Oklahoma City and was the youngest organization ever to win the Certificate of Merit from the Trade Extension Bureau of America. Before its demise a generation later, the NTDA grew to serve more than 100,000 merchants in almost 3,000 different communities in 42 states.[75] The growth, however, came with a cost. At only forty-eight, James suffered a heart attack. Fearful that his end was near, he encouraged his son to develop marketable skills quickly. In response, Jim, hopeful of a career in cartooning, or, in a broader sense, journalism, enrolled in a class at Dallas Technical College taught by a professional newsman from the *Dallas Journal*. Journalism, like preaching, appeared to be a creative and public profession, and it sounded interesting to him.[76]

Also interesting to Jim was Latin America. In 1937, the year after the Texas centennial, Dallas's Fair Park hosted a Pan-American Exposition on the Southern Hemisphere. Jim had always been interested in Mexico because of the sympathetic stories his grandmother Lena had told him. "If you are honest with them," she had said of the Mexicans, "they'll be honest with you."[77] His father had added that President Woodrow Wilson's intervention in the Mexican Revolution had been a mistake, because it had stoked anti-Americanism and made Pancho Villa popular. Now, with the Pan-American Exposition, Jim discovered the elaborate history that lay behind such stories. He came to view men such as José de San Martín, Miguel Hidalgo, Benito Juárez, and his favorite, Simón Bolívar, in the same way that he viewed the American heroes he had learned about in school. It was the beginning of a lifelong love affair with Latin America, an interest that would eventually reach the floor of Congress.[78]

At the time, of course, Jim was still just a teenager trying to fit in, always subject to the peer pressure from his classmates two years older. He began to smoke, although he later claimed he did not do so "as a rule," and to drink. One evening, Jim and his friends got intoxicated at the Pig Stand, the local drive-in. When, walking home, the older boys mocked Jim for not being able to hit a store sign hanging above their heads, Jim eventually knocked the sign completely off. As the boys walked with their trophy, the police stopped them, charged them with vandalism, and took them to the Dallas jail. When the police called Jim's mother, it took three calls to convince her that it was not a joke. Meanwhile, in the background, one could hear Jim and his accomplices, still drunk in their cell, singing "When the Saints Go Marching In." In the end it all proved to be another opportunity for one of James's lessons. Jim had to face the store owner alone and offer to re-hang the sign or work to pay for it. Jim had always hated public embarrassment and disgrace, and although the owner kindly replied that the sign fell down all the time, the painful lesson lingered.[79]

In short order Jim had a wide swath of friends. Although he was hardly a ladies' man, he dated occasionally, always trying to hide his age. It was a simpler day, before the Beat Generation or the hippies transformed teenage America. While dating usually just meant a drive-in or a movie, it still taught its own lessons. In his senior year, for example, Jim developed a crush on his fellow door monitor Betty Jane Wagner, the girlfriend of his close acquaintance Louis McBride. Facing a moral dilemma, Jim, apparently deciding that all was fair in love and war, took Betty to dinner. In another instance, a female classmate signed Jim's yearbook asking, "When are you going to get rid of that Goddamn temper and be the man I know that you can be?" All Jim noticed was that it was signed "Love." It was the first time anyone had ever used the term toward him outside of his family. During the summer, Jim dated a girl visiting from Arkansas, a daughter of a friend of his mother's. In the words of one former date, Jim was "extremely outgoing" and obviously seeking to impress, taking her to the plush Golden Pheasant restaurant in Dallas. Despite all the dates, however, Jim never had a steady girlfriend, perhaps because he was too busy to spare the time.[80] Jim's ambitions were even evident in his romantic daydreams. When the aviator Amelia Earhart vanished trying to fly solo across the Pacific Ocean, Jim dreamed of being the one to find her, but in the dream, Earhart had "grown much prettier and become a sex goddess ruling a Polynesian tribe."[81]

One immediate ambition was football glory. Despite his 137-pound build as a tailback, Jim endeared himself to his coach by not being afraid of contact. The coach, Bob Harris, impressed Jim as "the most admired man in the community."[82] With high school football as big in Texas then as it is today, coaches commanded the type of respect ambitious boys admired. Like Coach Harris, Jim finally decided, he too would become a coach. Jim began diagraming new plays, anxious to prove himself to his beloved mentor. Then, however, everything changed. Early in the 1937 season, Jim suffered a chipped cartilage in his right knee. His leg was in a cast for six weeks, and Jim's season was over.[83]

It was another turning point in Jim's life. Recognizing the boy's despondency, Coach Harris suggested that Jim abandon football and take up debate. "What we really need, even more than a good halfback," Jim quoted his coach as saying, "is somebody to represent the school in debate. You're the best prospect we've got."[84] This, Jim Wright later claimed, was when he first thought seriously about using his superior speaking abilities. In time, he continued, it was this decision to enter competitive debate that sparked his interest in history and politics. Ultimately, it gave him a new career ambition. He would not be a cartoonist, after all, or a coach, but a politician. Still an adolescent, Jim Wright had set his sights on winning the presidency.

Although Jim Wright repeated this story for years to come, and it was a colorful anecdote, it smacks of embellishment. There is ample evidence that Jim had at least entertained the idea of debate and politics previously. He had taken debate classes in Seminole, and while there he had been impressed by a visiting senator who had painted a "rosy" vision of the nation's capital.[85]

At the very least, Jim already knew that he spoke well and enjoyed the public limelight. Politics and world events had spawned frequent discussions at his family's dinner table. "Daddy would have liked to have been a congressman himself," concluded Mary Nelle, suggesting the possibility that from a quite early age Jim had absorbed his father's own subliminal political aspirations.[86] Politics indeed seemed a natural fit; in the words of one former classmate, Joe Bailey Irwin, everyone already recognized Jim as a "natural born politician." In one later interview, Jim Wright himself acknowledged that he had harbored presidential ambitions since his childhood.[87]

Moreover, from a contrary perspective, one might question whether Jim was as certain in his new aspiration as his later story indicated. Evidence suggests that preaching and journalism still held their allure. Within a few short years after high school, Jim began serving as a lay pastor at the Presbyterian church in Granbury, Texas. "He could preach a sermon," his friend Bodiford remembered. "He could get that Bible and open it up, and he didn't have to go referring to a lot of stuff." Several years later, his sister Betty Lee still assumed that her brother would become a preacher. Jim told her, "The world has enough good ministers, but there are not enough good congressmen."[88] When it came time to state his future plans for his high school yearbook, Jim listed not politics but journalism and law. In any event, regardless of any possible embellishment, there is little doubt that Bob Harris wielded true influence in Jim's life. Most people can name that special someone who inspired and mentored them, and often that person is a teacher. So it was with Jim Wright and his coach.[89]

Coach Harris, like many other high school coaches, also taught an academic class, history. Jim, still trying to impress him, jumped into his studies for the class, raising his hand at every opportunity. Soon he was "hooked," reading on his own at the library and earning his highest marks.[90] "There came to me at that time a very strong conviction that this is what a man ought to do with his life," Jim Wright later recalled. "The battles are not out there on the gridiron, or even in the field of war, but in the halls of Congress."[91] Undoubtedly influenced by his parents' dinnertime conversations, Jim began to reflect more on the Senate's postwar rejection of the Treaty of Versailles and America's failure to join the League of Nations. It was a terrible mistake, he began to argue, and might contribute to the breakout of another war. It was, of course, the late 1930s. Adolf Hitler had not yet invaded Poland, but even a teenager could see the ominous headlines. Calmer heads needed to prevail. "Armies cannot kill an idea," his father had always told him. "Only a better idea can do that." Honest discussions were more powerful than fists or guns. If only the country had listened to Woodrow Wilson.[92]

With the hindsight of history, such sentiments may appear a bit naïve today, smacking of appeasement in the face of determined ideological aggression, a war that no diplomacy would have prevented. Nevertheless, Jim's arguments did reflect his growing idealism, if not the Progressive optimism that he had inherited. Reading a volume of Wilson's speeches, Jim organized with his friend Joe Irwin a Progressive Club in his school. Its humorously audacious goal was "Peace, Progress, and Prosperity." The club was, his senior yearbook reported, "the only one of its kind in any of the Dallas high schools . . . a figment of Jim's versatile mind." It was a "political body, taking part in school elections and other activities and having discussions on national and international subjects."[93]

Not surprisingly, Jim was known by his senior year as "the senator." Not only was he president of his Progressive Club, but also of the National Thespians and the Debate Club. Jim represented the school in extemporaneous speaking and won seventeen of nineteen debates. He then immersed himself in student politics, formed the Future Democrats Club, and won election to the school's student council. During his senior year, he served as a delegate to the annual convention of the Southern Association of Student Governments. There, his fellow delegates nominated him for president of the organization. Although Jim campaigned hard, he lost the election. It must have hurt, but the defeat was solid training for a newly aspiring politician.[94] His father, meanwhile, continued to encourage his son, in one instance presenting him with a copy of Dale Carnegie's newly published book *How to Win Friends and Influence People*. He asked Jim if he thought it would be appropriate to give copies of the book to his employees, but the real reason he gave it to him, of course, was that he wanted Jim to read it.[95]

Jim did not limit his political oratory to school events. He joined the Oak Hill Speakers Club, a group of men who met periodically to debate assigned topics. In one instance, Jim spoke on world peace to the Young Democrats of Dallas, a group of attorneys who met at the Adolphus Hotel. Developing a reputation as a teenage prodigy and undoubtedly helped by his father's growing prominence, Jim began giving speeches for his father's friend Ernest O. Thompson. Thompson was one of thirteen candidates for the 1938 Democratic nomination for governor. He won the primary, and many people thought he was sure to win the general election, given the party's dominance. Throughout the summer of 1938, Jim gave brief remarks supporting Thompson to small crowds throughout Dallas County. As Jim later recalled, "Whenever they needed a speaker, they would send me. And by gosh they got to sending me, instead of lawyers and people like that because I got them fired up." When the candidate himself came to a rally in Oak Cliff's Kiest Park, Thompson suddenly asked Jim to come onto the stage and talk. It was the ultimate extemporaneous speech, to a crowd of over one thousand, but Jim performed brilliantly and basked in the applause. "He turned me loose for ten minutes. It was heady wine to make them whoop and holler and respond." It was, once again, a siren call for a career in politics.[96] As the end of his senior year approached, the oracle for the school yearbook made predictions for May 1955 with uncanny accuracy. "Congressman Jim Wright delivered yesterday what is said to be the most erudite speech heard in the Congressional Hall," it proclaimed, unaware that its fictional reporting had selected the very year Jim would begin his long congressional career.[97]

As student body president, Jim gave a four-minute address to his graduating class in June 1939, giving thanks and calling his audience to action. "Well, here we are," he told his classmates, "on the threshold of the time when we shall leave the school and prepare to cast our lots on the seas of time and fate, to weave our lives into the empyrean tapestry of a complex twentieth-century world." It was classic Jim Wright, the type of speech full of soaring oratory that would characterize hundreds of congressional speeches to come. It demonstrated just how well prepared his parents, his school, and his own efforts had made him.[98]

James and Marie were undoubtedly quite proud as they sat in the audience watching their son. "The whole idea of posterity is for one generation to improve upon its predecessors," James had always told his son.[99] Now, having worked hard to instill the foundation for success, they hoped, indeed expected, such success to follow. Most likely, however, they had no idea just how high their first-born child would fly and the impact his long career would have. Sadly, they never knew. Marie died in 1959 in a tragic car wreck, and James passed away three years later of throat cancer, just as their son was beginning his career in Congress. Jim Wright always remembered his youth, his mentors, and, most importantly, his parents. Their pictures figured prominently in every office he ever held, and he repeated their stories constantly in his writings. Jim Wright always knew that his past molded his future.[100] Just before the graduation ceremony, James had solemnly summoned his son to his downtown Dallas office on Elm Street. There Jim received a gift box bearing the name of a jeweler. Jim had not expected a graduation gift, much less the expensive $50 watch that lay inside. His father, however, made the present on a condition. "I want you to promise that each time you look at the face of this watch you'll think of the words inside the back cover." Turning the watch over, Jim found a verse from the Lord's Prayer: "Lead us not into temptation, but deliver us from evil."[101] It was one last lesson for Jim as he embarked on a new stage in his life. Jim Wright carried the watch with him as his career took off, only years later gifting it to his own son with a similar admonition. It was a constant reminder that time was passing, that work was to be done, and that high expectations surrounded him.

CHAPTER 2

The Lessons of Life

COLLEGE AND WAR (1939–1944)

As Jim Wright looked to the future following his 1939 high school gradua-tion, his father, James, sought to return to his past. In a "family meeting," James announced that because his National Trade Day Association served smaller towns, the family should return to Weatherford. James and Marie had obviously waited in order not to disrupt Jim's education. Although Jim had clearly bonded with Dallas, the sixteen-year-old did not protest. He had graduated; Dallas was his past and a new challenge awaited.[1]

The return proved fateful. Weatherford gave Jim a sense of belonging that not even his three years at Adamson could match. Over his long life Jim Wright lived longer in Washington and Fort Worth, but he forever iden-tified Weatherford as his home. "I learned the arts of compromise and of understanding, the art of getting along with people and making things work harmoniously," Wright recalled. "God bless the Weatherfords of this world for there is the only permanence."[2] In the end the town reciprocated. In April 1986, forty-seven years after Jim Wright's arrival and only a year before his election as Speaker of the House, Parker County citizens planted a tree in Wright's honor and presented him with a gavel made of Parker County wood. A visibly emotional Wright responded by quoting a former

Speaker of the House. "Sam Rayburn used to love to go home to Bonham [Texas] because it's a place where people know when you are sick, and they care when you die," Wright said. "That's a good description of community."[3] Weatherford was Jim Wright's community.

James and Marie quickly purchased a large, two-story house on a corner lot and began to put down new roots. They lived there for the rest of their lives.[4] Built in 1910, the Victorian had all the amenities: high ceilings, hardwood floors, a partial wrap-around porch, and bathrooms on both floors. A wrought-iron fence surrounded the yard, which included a fish pond and pecan trees. Making it their own, Jim and his father planted rose bushes, while Marie, who had adopted a new hobby, photography, put in a dark room. The family hired a cook, Martha Thomas, who worked for them for years. Her specialty was a breakfast of fried chicken and biscuits. It was all, Jim Wright later wrote, an "earthy outpost of heaven."[5]

The outpost was perfectly situated: it was two blocks from the city square, two blocks from the First Presbyterian Church, and two blocks from Weatherford College, the latter Jim's first stop after high school on his long career. In a way, Weatherford College was an odd choice. A two-year Methodist school of only 300 students, it was no longer a baccalaureate-granting institution. It resembled the community colleges of today except that it had not embraced the vocational curriculum of the Progressive-era reformers. While providing, in Jim Wright's description, a "classical" education, it was hardly the prestigious 13,000-student University of Texas campus in Austin, which Jim had identified as his preferred destination.[6]

The reason he went there, Jim Wright later claimed, was simple. At $150 per semester, Weatherford was cheaper than a four-year college, and a transfer to Austin for his bachelor's degree was still possible. While that was undoubtedly true, other factors surely contributed.[7] Given the fact that James's success could certainly have covered the larger tuition, Jim's relative age, still two years younger than most freshmen, must have been a consideration. Keeping Jim at home until he was the normal age to leave for college allowed him additional time to mature. One might think that such an ambitious young man as Jim would have chafed at such restrictions, especially since, in his words, Weatherford's culture was "sedate, religious, and conformist."[8] If he had cause for complaint, however, Jim never did. Whether recognizing the finances or simply wanting to please, he took to Weatherford College as he had to every school he had ever attended—he was determined to adapt and make the most of his opportunities.

In the end, Weatherford College proved a wise choice. Jim fit in easily and emerged a leader, thriving in a way that perhaps would not have been possible for him at a larger institution. He gained confidence, and his sense of ambition grew. With its "Old Main," a large brick and sandstone building with a prominent bell tower, Weatherford College was an attractive place. Most professors were young, and classes were small. Jim was not afraid to speak up and challenge the information presented. This often earned him a wry smile and a polite "that's an interesting idea" from his theology professors.[9]

Not surprisingly, debate and chorus occupied a great deal of Jim's energy. With the former including competition against prestigious universities, Jim struggled with his tendency to wax lyrical. "Jim, the purpose of words is to reveal thought, not conceal thought," one of Jim's teachers admonished.[10] If Republicans in later years claimed Jim's florid rhetoric amounted to intentional obfuscation, never, from Weatherford to Congress, was he at a loss for words—he only seemed to lack the time and place to say them all. He never mastered the thirty-second sound bite, and his often theatrical comments could appear less than genuine without full context.[11] Whatever the effectiveness of his rhetoric, Wright's continuing interest in competitive debating reinforced the necessity of proper preparation. A misplaced word or incorrect fact, he learned, could undermine a debate score as thoroughly as a congressional vote.

Jim's participation in chorus pleased his mother and provided another stage on which to shine. The stage was, occasionally, impressive. The huge sanctuary at Fort Worth's First Methodist Church, Wright recalled, "awed" him. Augmenting the limelight, Jim and three friends formed their own singing group, the Tramps Quartet, a play on a popular local group, the Stamps Quartet. The foursome had more gumption than talent, singing of drinking beer outside the girl's dormitory.[12]

Drinking remained a way to fit in, although, unlike in high school, in college thankfully there were no legal repercussions. In one instance, when his parents were away from home, Jim had to borrow $40 to restock his father's bar, which he and his buddies had drained in a poker game. Although he did not join a fraternity, Jim hardly avoided social events. He and his friends camped annually under Parker County's rural Tin Top Bridge—there, his friend Don Kennard recalled, they barbecued a pig, drank whiskey, and sang songs until the early morning.[13] During Jim's college years, his parents hosted numerous reunions in which distant family members descended upon Weatherford. "I reveled in those," Jim recalled. The summer the family moved to Weatherford, his uncle William took Jim to numerous sporting events, "reinforcing the lessons I had learned from my father." On some holidays the family drove to visit cousins in Bakersfield, California, which was always an adventure before interstate highways. In later years Jim denied that his family dispensed advice as he maneuvered in Congress, a claim reinforced by Betty Lee, and most likely true, despite the closeness of the clan. His father, however, was the probable exception. The elder Wright was so prominent in Jim's life that it is hard to imagine him completely removed from his son's policy positions. Before his death, James regularly asked his son questions and pointed out concerns, but they always avoided arguments. Jim's mother, meanwhile, simply worried about the stresses her son faced.[14]

Given that Nazi Germany invaded Poland just one month after he matriculated, Jim joined the International Relations Club (IRC) and was active in the student government. The IRC was sponsored by the Carnegie Foundation and held weekly debates on such topics as the Spanish Civil War or the fate of Chiang Kai-shek's nationalist China. In Jim's freshman year, the members chipped in for gas to attend the national conference at the University of Arkansas. Although the Weatherford club was one of the smallest, a friend circulated a petition to elect Jim the national club president. Ultimately, Jim won the vice presidency instead, which meant he would be coordinating and chairing the following year's convention, to be held at Louisiana State University.[15]

Jim was anxious to become head of the student government and, like any good politician, cultivated influential friends who might help him achieve that goal. Having contributed stories for the college newspaper, the *Coyote*, he befriended its editor and won the paper's endorsement. The competition, however, was fierce. Jim's loss to the ministry student Erving Gathings stung, but it came with a consolation prize. Jim was elected editor of the *Coyote* for his sophomore year. If he did not recognize the power of the press before, his new position would make him keenly aware of it for the rest of his career.[16]

"I learned a lot more as editor of the paper than I ever would have as student body president," Jim Wright later recalled. The job required extensive organizational skills. The paper put out biweekly editions costing sixty dollars to publish, and the editor held responsibility for generating the stories, running the copy on a linotype machine, submitting the copy to the downtown printing shop, and distributing the resulting paper, usually six to eight pages long. Equally important was selling advertisements to cover the cost. Enlisting the help of energetic freshman Harold Owen—hardly the last time his career benefited from a strong staff—Jim had an ambitious and revolutionary plan. By releasing a new pre-enrollment edition and publishing an additional one thousand copies of each paper for free distribution, he could argue to downtown businesses that the wider circulation required higher advertising rates.[17] The plan proved ingenious, and the new charge of sixty cents per column inch raised more revenue than the additional publication costs required. The paper increased its coverage of community events, and Jim and Harold were regularly able to pay themselves ten to fifteen dollars apiece.[18]

It was not always easy. Local businesses sometimes complained that the college sought to drain them, and the student writers, who were not always as committed as Jim, often failed to meet their deadlines. Sometimes there simply was not enough news. In one instance, with the number of columns set in linotype, Jim's newfound sense of entrepreneurship again came to the rescue. At the time, Generalissimo Francisco Franco was promising in his Spanish revolution a new wave of support from a secret "Fifth Column." Setting the headline type to run vertically in their one unfilled column, the fifth column, Jim wrote, "Let there be no Fifth Column here!" It appeared a patriotic appeal, but with readers none the wiser, it solved the problem.[19]

Occasionally the problems were more serious and the lessons more profound. Ambitious to make a name for himself, Jim ran an editorial complaining that the newly implemented peacetime draft was a product of a "militarist state" and insulted "the patriotism of American youth."[20] Many readers viewed the comments as unpatriotic and complained. Another editorial criticized the lack of school-sponsored dances. The conservative church-led administration viewed dances as part of a larger moral breakdown, reflecting the antagonism many rural Texans felt for the libertine "flapper" culture of the 1920s. The college, Jim recalled, was "flooded by letters." Challenged to their core, the administration pressed the paper's faculty adviser to relieve Jim of his duties. The adviser, Sam Householder, agreed with Jim that freedom of the press was paramount, but he was worried about his job. Only after Householder pleaded did Jim agree to submit future editorials for review. "It must have been embarrassing for [Householder] to have to confide his own sense of economic insecurity to a student," Jim later wrote.[21] The larger lessons—of ambition, censorship, unintended consequences, and, of course, the importance of the press from every perspective—were part of an education Jim Wright needed way beyond the classroom.

Jim had plenty of collegiate interests, but Mary Ethelyn Lemons, or Mab, drew his attention the most. The attractive Mab was an effervescent brunette with big blues eyes, a drama major known as the campus's best actress. Jim won the role opposite Mab in a two-person play about a World War I British officer and a German prostitute, and from that point on, he was smitten. Although he had little time for new activities, Jim was soon volunteering for every play that included Mab. The romance blossomed as the couple starred in the play *Blue Beards*, advancing to the state finals for junior college drama. "I wasn't really a very competent actor," a self-effacing Jim Wright later wrote, although one suspects that, given his theatrical flair and love of the limelight, he excelled.[22] "I thought that he had a future and I wanted to be part of that future," Mab recalled.[23] Indeed, in time she would be.

As Mab knew, there was never a dull moment with Jim Wright. Once, after borrowing $300 to speculate on Karakul lambs, Jim used his $150 profit to help purchase, with his friend Harold Owen, a 1931 Ford Model A Coupe. The two didn't care that the ten-year-old car's horn did not work, or that starting the engine required one of them to crank it manually while the other pumped the gas. It did not even matter that the car burned a ridiculous amount of oil; Harold worked part-time at a Gulf gas station and reused the best oil from the fancy cars that had come in for an oil change.[24] Automobiles were ubiquitous by 1940, but, in Jim's world, even a clunking 1931 Ford was a status symbol. Jim enjoyed squiring Mab about town and learned how to make the car backfire at just the right moment. When the wealthy local Ford dealer purchased a British-made Austin for his daughter, threatening to upstage Jim and his friends, they found that the sportster was so light they could move it around campus as a joke. In the end, all the status and fun proved another entrepreneurial venture. Jim sold the car for a profit of five dollars.[25]

Sometimes opportunities just presented themselves. After the *Dallas Herald* solicited writers to cover high school sports, Jim traveled to Dallas on Friday nights for football games, rushing to the local Western Union office afterward to file his story. With writers paid by the line, Jim's natural verbosity finally worked in his favor. His writing was impressive, and soon his reports appeared in the *Fort Worth Star-Telegram*. The money he earned, ten to fifteen dollars every three weeks, was enough to keep his Ford running and Mab sufficiently impressed.[26]

As his June 1941 graduation from Weatherford College approached, Jim had the opportunity of a lifetime. His friend and partner in sheep speculation, Bob Lott, earned a pilot's license and thrilled Jim with a flight in a small

Piper Cub. Bob climbed into a steep ascent before feigning a loss of control, suddenly swooping down just above the trees. For most of the public, flight was still something novel; commercial airfare had advanced but was still less than two decades old. Fort Worth's airport, Meacham Field, was only fourteen years old, and it had been less than four years since Amelia Earhart had disappeared. Most people, Jim Wright included, had never flown. The result, for Jim Wright, was a lifelong interest in flying that later guided his war experiences and made him a congressional champion of aviation.[27]

With his associate's degree in hand, eighteen-year-old Jim Wright departed for the University of Texas in August 1941. In Austin he campaigned for Attorney General Gerald C. Mann, a New Dealer trying to win the Democratic nomination to fill a US Senate vacancy.[28] The experience was "wonderful," Wright later recalled, and included his first exposure to Lyndon Baines Johnson. The future president and Wright ally was then a thirty-two-year-old seeking the same nomination as Mann. With the public debating possible American intervention into World War II, which at the time was going badly for the Allies, Johnson declared in an Austin speech that if it ever came to casting the deciding vote to go to war, he would resign his congressional seat and go himself. This impressed Wright, who was unaware that behind the scenes Johnson had undercut Mann's candidacy with the White House and potential donors. Perhaps sensing a winner, Wright began to follow Johnson's career, the start of what Wright later termed "a strong sense of devotion to LBJ."[29]

Meanwhile, in a real coup for Wright, Mann rewarded his eager young supporter with a part-time job in his Austin office. Mann, who was known for his loyalty, appealed to Wright's idealism. A plaque in his office declared, "I sacrificed no principle to gain this office and I shall sacrifice no principle to keep it."[30] Essentially a political internship, the job was great for Wright's resume and promised powerful connections. Predictably, Wright thrived, designing a new filing system for court cases. The job also paid $30 monthly. Wright often cashed his checks at Charlie's Liquor Store, and unfortunately for Wright, the bank mistakenly forwarded the canceled checks to his father, who also had an account. James, who obviously knew of the dangers of drink and assumed the checks were for alcohol, admonished his son. How, he wondered, could one attend classes, given the quantity of liquor obviously being consumed?[31]

Whether he recognized it or not, Jim Wright was swimming in a larger pond. The University of Texas was in turmoil. New conservative members of its board of regents were pressuring university president Homer P. Rainey to weed out perceived radicalism on campus. When Rainey, citing tenure and academic freedom, resisted efforts to censure "communist" books and fire offending faculty, the young activist in Wright had to participate. Although he was only in his first year, he began giving speeches against the governor and the regents, in short, cultivating his radical and activist image in a new venue. He did not conceive of the notion that he might make enemies or color his own political ambitions, an oversight he would later regret.[32]

The intellectual life at the University of Texas suited Jim Wright. With his coursework heavy in political science and economics, he was never shy about arguing his position. The academic rigors did not, however, stifle his feelings for Mab, who had transferred to Texas Woman's University in Denton, over 250 miles away. Telephone calls and long-distance commutes were now the order of the day. Mab was a "nice girl," Wright recalled, not someone "to play around with." While her serious nature appeared formidable to many men, to Wright she had substance. She was "someone to settle down with."[33] Continuing competitive debate, he traveled to Baylor University in November 1941 to argue the affirmative on the question of whether America should proactively declare war. Citing the growing antagonism, Wright argued that an attack was eminent. It was not a hard case to make. The United States had begun preparing for war, and many idealistic young men—including several of Wright's Weatherford friends—had already traveled to Canada to join the Royal Air Force and fight. Wright later wistfully noted that he encountered some of these men during the war and that they outranked him, implying that, in retrospect, he should have joined them, a rare instance in which he had missed an opportunity for advancement.[34]

Wright remembered that his position in the debate was hypothetical; the reality of such a war was hard to fathom. Unfortunately, of course, Wright proved prescient. Japan attacked Pearl Harbor less than two weeks later. Like many Americans, Wright heard the horrifying news on the radio, and like many young men, he left school to volunteer. Hitching a ride to Fort Worth with three friends, he hoped to join the Army Air Corps. As he recalled, "I wanted to be part of it."[35] Today, in a more complex world, it is difficult to imagine the anger, nationalism, and unity the surprise attack evoked. The members of Wright's generation had suffered through the Great Depression, and their patriotism was paramount. Wright was, in the end, one of the lucky ones, later recounting the names of over half a dozen close friends who made the ultimate sacrifice. Included was Harold Owen, Wright's old newspaper colleague and car co-owner, who was killed in 1944 flying a P-38 combat mission.[36]

Of course, in all probability, more than American honor entered into Wright's decision. To miss a war on which so much rested, a war that drew so heavily from everything and everyone he knew, was to miss history. Wright later wrote, "It became second nature to recite name, rank and serial number for a whole generation of men."[37] This meant, of course, that military service was essential for any future political resume. Indeed, every president from Dwight Eisenhower to George H. W. Bush was a veteran of the war. Moreover, there was the matter of the draft. If he did not act first, he might have to go anyway. Enlisting meant more choices. Wright never mentioned whether he discussed his options with Mab, but it would have made no difference. On December 30, three weeks after the declaration of the war and a week past his nineteenth birthday, Jim Wright enlisted. Wright and the friends who went with him to enlist were given a small cash stipend and ordered to report the following morning. Later, they went to the movie *Sergeant York*, each undoubtedly envisioning himself in the role of its World War I hero. They were in many respects still boys. Although they peer-pressured themselves into visiting a brothel that night, only two of them stayed. Wright and the majority of his friends awkwardly slinked away.[38]

The next day they took their oaths, received their uniforms, and were given a one-day reprieve—the New Year's holiday. Wright had previously planned to attend the Cotton Bowl, a family tradition. There, he said goodbye to his proud father and mother, his father cracking jokes to break the tension and his mother fighting back tears. That evening, Private Wright reported for duty and boarded a bus for Camp Wolters in Mineral Wells, Texas. His destination was only fifteen miles away from Weatherford, but the journey represented no small milestone in Jim Wright's life.[39]

As Wright underwent his physical checkup and indoctrination at Wolters, the magnitude of his decision hit him. Lying in his bunk one night, he later recalled, "I buried my face in the pillow and wept silently."[40] He had applied to flight school and a commission, but the only thing certain was that he would miss his family. As he waited for word on his application, he joined his fellow enlistees as they were bused to Sheppard Field, a new Army Air Corps training facility outside Wichita Falls, Texas. There, at boot camp, the memory of Pearl Harbor cast a long shadow. Just before Wright's arrival, spooked officials had woken up sleeping enlistees shouting that Japanese planes were attacking.[41]

Following graduation three weeks later, Wright took a troop train to Riverside, California, the home of Marsh Field and the 14th Fighter Group. There he saw the comedian Bob Hope conducting one of his famous United Service Organizations tours. It was then off to Hamilton Field, north of San Francisco, where a routine finally emerged. Paid $21 monthly, Wright landed at G-2, the group headquarters' intelligence office. "Oh, my God, another ubiquitous, loquacious Texan!" his colleagues exclaimed. "Every time somebody discovers there's another Texan in the crowd, you all holler and start singing that lousy 'Eyes of Texas' song."[42] Nevertheless, it was a heterogeneous group, and being part of it reinforced the message of equality that Wright's father had learned from his own military service. Writing Mann back in Texas, Wright proudly reported that the skills he had learned in the attorney general's office still served him well. Wright recognized that maintaining connections was as important as making them in the first place.[43]

Despite the fact that his work involved classified information, it was still just routine office work and not what the ambitious Wright had in mind. He had beefed up—added sixteen pounds of muscle—but it had been months and he was impatient to hear of his application for flight training. Faking the clipped accent of a supposed group commander, Wright called to inquire.[44] Four days later, he received orders to report to flight school at Santa Ana Army Air Base south of Los Angeles. In retrospect, the incident not only spoke to Wright's ambition but also his risk-taking nature. Although his call was impulsive, impersonating an officer was a serious violation of the Articles of War, which promised harsh penalties.[45] A court-martial would have ended his nascent political aspirations before his career even got started. Wright may have known his actions were impetuous and a bit Machiavellian. Despite speaking of the incident in later years, he did not include the phone call in his 2005 wartime memoirs, *The Flying Circus*. "I fumed," he wrote of the wait, conveniently skimming over the full story.[46]

According to the soldiers, Santa Ana was a "hellhole of the Earth," a "1,300 acre torture chamber." In reality, it was a well-run machine, producing in three hectic months aviators ready for advanced training to become pilots, bombardiers, and navigators. Its demanding schedule, Wright noted approvingly, taught him more than an entire year in college. No longer was he just pushing office papers. Wright completed his preparation at Santa Ana in early fall 1942 and departed for Arizona's Williams Field and specific training as a bombardier. When people asked him why he did not become a pilot, Wright had a ready answer: the bombardier was the cutting edge of the sword, the one who inflicted the punishment and enacted the retribution.[47]

Wright's days were now spent flying and dropping bombs on targets constructed in the desert. He was soon recording direct hits—"shacks," in the parlance of the flyboys—in one-third of his attempts, an impressive record. It was, Wright recalled tellingly, a great way to "satisfy one's expectations." The danger did not bother him. The Army Air Forces, which just after Wright's arrival incorporated the Army Air Corps, suffered over 50,000 accidents stateside, costing almost 15,000 lives. Whether it was his religion, his innate optimism, or his supreme confidence in his skills, Wright later said, he always "had an overwhelming faith that I would return."[48]

Mab was never so confident. The two kept in contact with letters and, less frequently, the telephone. His father wrote often, typing out his letters on a portable typewriter to tell Wright about local politics and people, but Mab's letters were the highlight of "Mail Call." Their correspondence was touching. "My sweet honey darling," Wright penned. "I shall always love you more than life's other gifts. You are the fairies' magic wand. You are the alchemy which makes everything else golden. And without you, all else would be a tarnished corroded brass." It was classic Jim Wright, and it made Mab's head swirl.[49] Considering themselves "alternatively engaged or engaged to be engaged," the couple had even spoken of marriage—eventually. Wright, predictably, had always thought of marriage in the context of his career. "In ten years I am going to run for Congress," he promised, "and I want you to marry me at that time." But if death came, she pleaded, "then we'd never be together."[50]

After having dinner with a fellow officer and his wife—an endearing, cozy scene—Wright began to reconsider. After all, his parents had married in wartime. On December 12, 1942, Wright graduated and received his gold second lieutenant bars. His mind, however, was elsewhere. Driving to the Davis-Monthan Air Force Base near Tucson, to report for duty with the 380th Bombardment Group, Wright stopped and telegrammed Mab. He now had, he declared, bars on his shoulders, wings on his chest, and a ring in his pocket. Would Mab come to Tucson and marry him?[51]

Mab was on her way in less than three weeks, arriving by train on Christmas Eve. The next day, Christmas 1942, a local Methodist preacher married them. The brief, small ceremony was hardly unusual. Wartime couples across the land were saying their vows in haste. Although it was only three days past his twentieth birthday, Wright listed his age as twenty-two. "He lied about it," Mab later remembered. "He was embarrassed I was two years older." It mattered little, of course, except that in retrospect, perhaps it again underscored Wright's concern for image and his willingness to do what he thought necessary.[52]

His second lieutenant rank bumped his salary up to $225 per month. Wright and his bride lived frugally, however. They moved into a one and a half room apartment in the motor court Sage and Sand. Their meager possessions included an alarm clock, a toaster, and a coffee pot, the latter doubling as a pot in which to boil eggs. Although busing to the base required a transfer downtown, Mab occasionally met Wright for a movie.[53] Despite it all, the newlyweds lived happily.

The 380th Bombardment Group consisted of B-24 Liberators, a huge plane with four engines that allowed it to cover over 2,000 miles at 200 miles per hour. Clumsy and difficult to handle, it was to the pilots "like sitting on the front porch and flying the house." The plane carried up to ten crewmen and was known for its mechanical failures—many called it a "death trap" or "flying coffin." While most men preferred the newer, sleeker B-17 Flying Fortress, Jim Wright's optimism allowed him to see the glass half full rather than half empty. The plane, after all, was heavily fortified, with a top turret gunner, a nose gunner, a belly gunner, and a tail gunner. The bombardier—Wright's assignment—was in the lower nose of the plane, in a small compartment below the nose gunner and the pilot.[54]

For the first phase of Wright's training with the B-24 he remained in Arizona. In January 1943, he was transferred to Biggs Field in El Paso, Texas, where the men learned to fly as a unit. The following month, it was off to Lowry Field in Denver, Colorado. The group became quite cohesive, Wright recalled, even bailing out a jailed and drunken colleague in Mexico. Their departure for the war was imminent—and the men obviously knew it. Mab patiently followed Wright, her burden lightened by her camaraderie with the other military wives. It was in Denver where Wright's outfit earned its name. General George Kenney, who two years later would award Wright medals, scoffed at the rough landing of one of the B-24s. The 380th, he quipped, was a "flying circus." Wright and the others embraced the moniker and carried it with them for the remainder of the war.[55]

The 380th, which included four squadrons of nine planes, finally received its orders in late March. Australia, threatened by a possible Japanese invasion, needed the long-range bomber for the Pacific's vast expanses. Wright was ready. The one short year of training since his time at the University of Texas had transformed him. No longer was he crying in his bunk. He was still only twenty years old, but he was now a true man—more physically developed, more worldly, and, with the support of a loving family, ready for the hardships and responsibilities of war and an uncertain future rife with danger. He also felt as though he had a new family—the once disparate but now cohesive group of aviators whose survival depended upon each other. Seventy years later, he could still recall their faces and intimate details, and he wrote about them frequently. Wright and his colleagues were about to make their own contribution to the Greatest Generation.[56]

First Wright had to say the painful goodbyes, and he had been granted a three-day pass before reporting for overseas duty for this purpose. Wright returned to Weatherford while Mab stayed behind, suggesting that the price of her ticket might cover a bassinet. It was a not-so-subtle hint that she hoped for a child, as well as a display of supportive optimism. Weatherford was hard. The clan sang at their new piano just like the old days, and Wright told his father how much he valued all the lessons over the years. The graduation watch was going abroad as well, Wright added.[57]

The home front was never easy during the war. Shortages, rationing, and the constant worry that a telegram would arrive with horrific news colored every day. The National Trade Day Association lost business, but James Wright always remained upbeat in the letters he wrote his son. The elder Wrights planted a "Victory Garden," a volunteer effort to save food, a program that extended back to World War I. Mab returned to Weatherford to move in with James and Marie, living in Jim's old bedroom. While Mab did not become one of the famous "Rosie the Riveters" working in the defense industry, she was one of the millions of women returning to the workforce. In fact, Fort Worth was a major employer of female industrial workers during the war. One aviation plant transported women to work from neighboring towns in converted cattle trucks. Mab, however, decided to help neighbors run a clothing store. Marie, meanwhile, simply wore her son's jacket, a way to make herself feel closer to Jim. It all made sense to Lieutenant Wright, confident that Mab was busy and safe.[58]

On April 24, 1943, the Flying Circus left San Francisco for a semicircular trip of almost 9,000 miles. The planes, flown by skeleton crews in sequential order, made stops in Hawaii, Christmas Island, Fiji, New Caledonia, and, finally, Brisbane, Australia. The trip took eight days because they had to fly around Japanese-controlled areas. During every stage, danger lurked, if for no other reason than the relatively primitive navigation. With no radar, the navigators had to rely on maps, compasses, and the night skies. Frequently out of radio contact, they could easily miscalculate and run out of fuel. In fact, in the next two years, 400 Army Air Force planes vanished on their way overseas. The Polynesian cultures at each brief stop entranced Wright even if the stories of the veterans alarmed him. One returning bombardier explained the necessity of low-level bombing, a skill for which Wright's crew had not been adequately prepared.[59]

The bombardier was perhaps the most important job outside of the pilot. Sitting in the nose of the plane, his vision covering the vast expanse, the bombardier employed the cutting-edge Norden sighting system, essentially an $8,000 analog computer. After locating the target, he would calculate air speed, altitude, wind, and other factors and feed the data into the system, which would then automatically fly the plane, calculate the angle, and name the precise time to release the bombs. This procedure was ineffectual at low-level skip bombing but proved quite accurate otherwise. Still working well as a team, Wright's crew named their plane *Gus's Bus* for their commander, Gus Connery. [60]

Arriving in Australia, the 380th learned that the Pacific had claimed one of its own. The commander of that plane, like Wright, had just married before deployment. Assigned to the Fifth Air Force, the group reported to Townsend, one of General Douglas MacArthur's headquarters, and then received orders to proceed south 100 miles into the northern outback. There, at Fenton Airfield, still under construction, the 380th worked with the Royal Australian Air Force. Fenton was connected to the distant city of Darwin only by a hard clay rutted road. It consisted of a runway with thirty-five paved abutments for the planes, each protected by earthen mounds. Nearby were buildings for the group headquarters, the mess hall, and the necessary storage and maintenance. There were also tanks for fuel and water. Wright's 530th Squadron was to stay just under a mile away, where a headquarters shack, a small kitchen, and several bathrooms were located. The crews, assigned four to a tent, had to construct their own dwellings from the trees and materials at hand. If Wright thought the accommodations rough, life was relatively comfortable for a combat zone. Unlike for the infantry in the tropical jungles to the north, dengue fever and filariasis, a common lymphatic infection, posed no risk for the men, and malaria was less common. [61]

It all struck Wright as being a bit like Texas. The land was sparsely populated and dry, the people fiercely independent but hospitable. They were proud, but capable of rowdiness. The only local community, a tiny poor settlement along the Adelaide River, "looked like a remnant of the old American West." In fact, there had been unsuccessful attempts at ranching and gold mining. The Aussies thought the Yanks overpaid, but the two got along well. "I liked the Aussies," Wright later wrote. [62]

As Wright settled into his new life, General Kenney, who coordinated air strategy, decided to deemphasize high-level bombings of ships at sea by planes such as the B-24. Instead, Kenney sought additional lower-level sweeps by lighter and more agile medium bombers armed with fragmentation bombs. The veterans who had warned Wright that lower-level bombings were more accurate had been correct. Because the smaller bombers had less range to find the targets, however, the larger bombers were still necessary. Accordingly, while Wright's crew still spent considerable time hunting targets of opportunity, most of their missions were to bomb larger, fixed infrastructures, such as port facilities and airports, many located at great distances.[63]

Wright's first taste of combat, on June 11, 1943, was such a mission. The 380th had been ordered to bomb a Japanese airport at Koepang on Timor Island, a five-hundred-mile flight each way, or, as Wright calculated, roughly the same distance as Santa Fe from Fort Worth. It was payback time, as Japanese bombers, probably from Koepang, had struck Fenton a few nights before. The American attack went well, but six Japanese "Zeros" retaliated, attacking from the rear. Wright got off a few rounds, but, as he was in the plane's nose, probably contributed little to its defense. *Gus's Bus* arrived home intact, but Wright witnessed another B-24 spiral into the ocean below. Pleased to see life rafts, he then watched with trembling hands as the Zeros strafed the defenseless men. There was nothing romantic about this fight.[64]

The Japanese prided themselves on their ethnic purity, the "Yamato Race," and saw the Americans as a contemptuous polyglot. Their "Code of Bushido" demanded loyalty, austerity, and indifference to pain. Wright knew after his first taste of combat that capture was unthinkable, and that decent treatment for those who were captured impossible. In reality, while Wright never embraced such brutality, racial stereotypes were common on both sides of the Pacific war, which became particularly horrific. His trembling aside, Wright adapted to it all amazingly well. He focused on pursuing retaliation for an affront he had personally witnessed, simply assuming in general terms that the Japanese were evil. It was not the time for complexity, he convinced himself; once again, the ends justified the means. For Jim Wright, there was never any moral ambiguity or emotional trauma to blight his future.[65]

By the summer of 1943, the Japanese had constructed a defensive shell that extended 3,000 miles above the Australian coast from the Solomon Islands to Malaya. Connecting their island defenses were ports, communication facilities, airports, and army bases, many only within reach of the B-24. After the military transferred a number of B-24s to the European theater in the spring of 1943, *Gus's Bus* had its dance card full. If one could call combat missions routine, so it became for Wright.[66] Most attacks were at squadron strength, although, on occasion, a smaller number of planes still randomly hunted for ships at sea. Wright's crew began to mark with pins on a map where they had bombed. Fortunately, they suffered only one broken jaw from enemy fire.[67]

Between missions, Wright passed the time the best he could. After receiving permission to dig irrigation ditches, he planted a garden, providing the crew with tomatoes, which they loved. He led efforts to build an outdoor theater with plank seats. Weekly films were a pleasant diversion, as were the dogs the men adopted. Wright, in true Texan fashion, purchased a horse, only to regret that he had neither the time nor the money to care for it.[68] He also hung a lightweight speed punching bag from a tree and, after locating two old boxing gloves, tried to find sparring partners. In time Wright was the official "athletic officer," which proved to entail more than just organizing intramural competitions. After the medical officer reported that too many men were sick, the commanding officer ordered Wright to increase squadron fitness. The result was calisthenics every morning at eight o'clock. When the local population complained that soldiers were causing trouble swimming in a nearby lagoon, Wright banned guns and cigarettes and ordered commissioned officers to accompany them as escorts.[69]

Wright's performance as athletic officer reflected his emerging leadership style. He was not afraid of taking charge, but he also wanted a degree of camaraderie. He explained himself to subordinates when it was unnecessary and even injected humor into his orders. His calisthenics command was a "pill," Wright later acknowledged, but it would prove effective against the men's "ever expanding middle." If calisthenics were earlier, he quipped, it would interfere with breakfast and the shower water would be too cold. Any later would prove "too darn hot for man or beast." Thanking the men for their compliance with his swimming order, Wright declared, "The athletic officer is grateful . . . for this splendid cooperation."[70] Later, in Congress, Wright worked in a similar fashion, always personal and collegial, always trying to build consensus, but never afraid to enforce a firm position. According to Mab, Wright could get angry, but at his core he always wanted admiration and respect. Perhaps it was a vestige of the transient lifestyle of his family during his youth and his need for friends. "I think he wants to become the person who[ever] he's with thinks he is," Mab concluded. "He's a very kind man."[71]

Wright was still Wright, of course, and so with an eye to history he wrote a dramatic article titled "Appointment with War." Hoping to impress Mab, he dedicated it to "the sweetest girl who ever kept a home fire burning." The article recounted developments in the war and listed actions the home front could take. "The dye [sic] is cast; the wheels are turning; History is waiting," he wrote as encouragement.[72] Never losing his eye on politics, Wright wrote Minnesota senator Joseph Ball in March 1943 on the need to create a United Nations. After Ball introduced a resolution, Wright thanked him. "We feel very strongly that now is the time to get the United States foreign policy clarified and out of partisan politics," Ball replied. It was heady stuff for a young second lieutenant on the other side of the globe, but it was characteristic of the outspoken, confident Jim Wright. He had applauded Woodrow Wilson's internationalism while he was still in school, and he was going to encourage those who held power now. In fact, his call was prescient; just over nine months later, the major powers agreed in Tehran to create some form of international body.[73]

Ever the politician, the popular Wright became the official greeter of new crews. Still, however, his temper remained his Achilles' heel. Once, after a fellow soldier's accidental bump caused hot coffee to spill, Wright, uttering an expletive, whirled around and decked the offender. "I didn't think I'd shoved him," Wright later claimed, although it was obvious that he had initiated the fight. Embarrassed, and with all eyes on him, Wright regained his composure and apologized. The men, after all, had to stay united.[74]

In another instance, trying to prove his leadership, Wright took his confidence and outspokenness too far. After a major had ordered disciplinary actions against several tardy men, Wright complained to the major's superior that "the offense was certainly not one to warrant humiliation." The major's "ill-considered" order, Wright wrote, "bespeaks of bad manners, short sighted policy and poor leadership." Wright argued that the men were unaware of the original time constraints. But the result of Wright's protest was predictable. "Basic communication not favorably considered," came the curt reply. "It is noted with interest that such protest comes only from an officer recently commissioned." Such communications "will not be tolerated in the future," and the incident had been noted in Wright's permanent record.[75] Wright, it appeared, needed to keep his certitude and self-righteousness in check, even if they were born of his idealism. Aiming too high, after all, carried its own costs.

Wright's most important mission—and his claim to wartime history—was the August 13, 1943, bombing of Balikpapan, Borneo. With a massive air field and seaport, the site was a linchpin of the Japanese perimeter and

provided more than half the fuel the Japanese needed in the war. Balikpapan was 2,700 miles away, however, and no bombing mission had ever gone
so far. It would be the "longest bombing mission on record," Colonel F. W.
Miller explained, but afterward, the Japanese would be "running out of
gas."[76] The danger was real; between Australia and Balikpapan were a number of Japanese airports. Intelligence was minimal, and the weather always
dynamic. Each of the eleven B-24s assigned to the mission would carry an
overload of 3,500 gallons of fuel—but only six 500-pound bombs. Departing from Darwin to get as close as possible, Gus's Bus was one of the first
planes to take off, in late afternoon, and, twenty minutes past midnight,
one of the first to reach the site. The timing, it turned out, was fortunate.
Assuming the facility beyond the reach of attack, the Japanese had all the
lights ablaze. Without flak, Wright hit his mark; two separate storage tanks
burned in a towering inferno.[77]

The Japanese, however, were now awake. Not only did the subsequent
B-24s face intensive ground fire, but Zeros swarmed around all the planes.
For more than an hour Gus's Bus fought off the attackers, its diversionary
flying risking depletion of its fuel. Seventeen hours after leaving, Wright's
plane barely made it back. Soon, however, they were aloft again, searching
for another plane that had lost fuel in evasive action over Timor and ditched
into the Australian outback. Gus's Bus located the downed crew because
they had used parachutes to spell out "H20" in the red clay sand. Flying low
and dropping canisters of food and water within fifty yards of the stranded,
Wright's crew steered rescue operations to the site.[78]

The Balikpapan mission helped Jim Wright earn the prestigious Distinguished Flying Cross, the kind of heroism all too common during wartime
but essential to victory. More importantly, the mission helped set the stage
for increased American "island-hopping" in the coming months. The Americans coordinated attacks at key locations but avoided the most heavily fortified island outposts, cutting them off and starving them.[79] Missions such
as Balikpapan helped weaken the enemy's communication and supply lines
and were critical to the strategy. One can forgive Wright, therefore, a little
hyperbole. The Balikpapan mission, he wrote in Flying Circus, "was the
decisive defining moment of change in the Pacific War's momentum." Later,
in a reflective article, he called it "a turning point."[80] In fact, while important, the Balikpapan mission was not as decisive as events that had taken
place the preceding year. In May 1942, the Battle of Coral Sea had stunted
the initial tide of Japanese success, helping the Allies retake the critical city
of Port Moresby. The following month, the Americans had won at the Battle

of Midway, ending forever Japanese hopes in the Central Pacific. Then, between August 1942 and February 1943, the Americans had taken Guadalcanal in an offensive that lives on in military lore. During all of this, Wright was in training.[81]

In an even broader context, the American war machine had finally reached optimum production by the summer of 1943, producing almost 40 percent of the world's arms. American personnel were flooding into the Pacific theater. American intelligence had largely cracked Japanese codes. New fighters, such as the twin-engine P-38 Lightning, could now outmaneuver the Zeros. The United States was finishing production of the B-29 Superfortress, a bomber that surpassed the B-24. Finally, four months before Balikpapan, in an event that was perhaps symbolic of coming victory, an American fighter had shot down Japanese admiral Isoroku Yamamoto, the architect of the Pearl Harbor attack. The Balikpapan attack was important and historic in its own way, and Wright's medals were well deserved. It was hardly, however, the seminal event he had suggested.[82]

The following months brought more of the same, including a second raid on Balikpapan that sank 30,000 tons of shipping. The title of *Gus's Bus* was superimposed on a green Shamrock leaf on the side of the plane, which seemed appropriate. With continued attacks on targets as far away as Java, Wright's crew obviously had the luck of the Irish. The Flying Circus received the Presidential Citation Medal, itself well deserved, with the 380th having suffered over a 45 percent casualty rate in the preceding six months. Wright, now promoted to first lieutenant, received the honorary title of "squadron bombardier," recognition of his own professionalism. By October he had finished his twentieth bombing mission and received a well-deserved week of rest. A C-47 transport flew Wright and his colleagues to the southern Australian coastal city of Adelaide. There, Wright, too relaxed away from combat, swam too far from the shore and almost drowned; a death on break would have been deeply ironic.[83]

By the end of 1943, preparing to launch a large-scale invasion of New Guinea and New Britain, the Allies integrated the Flying Circus into a massive strike force. Now more than ever Wright flew with British and Australian accompaniment, often with fighter escort, their goal to soften defensive fortifications in preparation for the invasion. Wright, transferred temporarily to an airfield on Dubodura, New Guinea, just outside of Japanese control, found the "miserable rain-drenched base" smelling of mildew, swarmed by mosquitoes, and subject to sniper fire. It was a taste of what the ground combat troops had experienced for almost two years. The December invasion proved a tremendous success, offering Lieutenant Wright, as it turned out, his last combat missions.[84]

As 1944 dawned, Jim Wright had flown thirty combat missions and logged over three hundred combat flying hours. The crew of *Gus's Bus* was free to leave as soon as they could pack up from Fenton. Wright could have volunteered for another tour of combat duty. Gus Connery, *Gus's Bus* namesake, did just that. He was rewarded with a promotion to major and became a group commander. The rest of the crew, however, had had enough. Whether it was exhaustion, a sense that he had done his duty and had a record he could run on, or simply that he missed Mab, Wright opted to leave. He even acknowledged that perhaps his unfailing optimism had begun to ebb. How many more close encounters with the Grim Reaper could he survive?[85]

The Flying Circus was over. The military bestowed upon *Gus's Bus* a new crew but, perhaps appropriately, the old warhorse finally fell apart only two weeks after Wright's departure. Wright and his colleagues proceeded to Townsville, where General Kenney held an awards ceremony. There, Wright received the Legion of Merit as well as his Distinguished Flying Cross. The former, an award only established a year before, recognized "exceptionally meritorious conduct in the performance of outstanding services and achievements." The latter, dating back to 1926, was a bit more prestigious, having been awarded to such noted aviators as Charles Lindbergh and Robert Byrd. It recognized "heroism or extraordinary achievement in participating in aerial flight." From Townsville it was on to Brisbane, to board a Liberty Ship with other happy combatants. One of the 2,700 famous cargo vessels mass-produced during the war, the Liberty Ship had become a symbol of the miracle of American production. With soldiers stacked in bunks, however, it was uncomfortable and offered no privacy. Wright could not have cared less. The Liberty Ship was taking him home at last.[86]

CHAPTER 3

Ambition and Frustration

STATE LEGISLATURE (1944–1948)

On St. Patrick's Day, 1944, seventeen days after departing from Brisbane, Wright's Liberty Ship reached San Francisco. The ship passed under the Golden Gate Bridge, which was then only eight years old and seemed like a monument to America's greatness. A marching band awaited the men with cheering crowds nearby. It all made an impression on Wright. "Everyone felt like we were really something," Wright recounted years later. "There was a kind of national mood, and in those days our guys wore white hats and the media didn't think it was their responsibility to paint us as villains." If only, Wright concluded, the men returning from Vietnam had received the same welcome.[1]

Another impressive crowd greeted Wright when his train pulled into Weatherford a few days later. On the platform were Mab, his parents, his sisters, and even his minister. For six weeks Wright enjoyed the leave he had dreamed of for months, three weeks at home and an additional three weeks in Miami with Mab, the honeymoon the newlyweds had never taken. Even there, however, politics was never far behind. Mab, at Wright's insistence, had to endure a speech by Miami's longtime congressman Claude Pepper.[2]

The war continued, of course, and Wright was still in the military. When his leave ended, he received orders to train airmen at Nebraska's Lincoln Army Air Base. The base contained hundreds of wood buildings, because the war consumed so much steel and concrete. It was, Wright learned, always hot in the summer and cold in the winter. Nevertheless, the accommodations seemed luxurious compared to what he had experienced in Australia. There was a commissary, a library, a hospital, an officers' club, and, at the insistence of First Lady Eleanor Roosevelt, a chapel. Wright, predictably, remained as busy as ever. Instruction went around the clock, seven days a week.[3]

Later acknowledging himself an "eager beaver," Wright continued to submit articles of his experiences to various publications.[4] Some were works of advocacy, while others were little more than travelogues. Air Force Academy cadets, Wright wrote of one visit to Colorado Springs, were "young men in whose hands will rest the safety of tomorrow." The Strategic Air Command, he recalled of a trip to Bolling Air Force Base, was the "nerve center" of American defense. He had "sat today behind the big control room console," he added. In another post, Wright argued that America's massive war effort was money well spent.[5] In one perceptive piece, he countered the economists who were predicting a return to depression after the war. Large personal savings, Wright suggested, would create a "huge post-war demand for almost every kind of commodity." The Serviceman's Readjustment Act of 1944, moreover, was "too good to be true." Because the legislation provided veterans a weekly pension of $20 for a year, Wright joked, a "52/20" Club had formed in Weatherford.[6]

In letters to newspaper editors around Fort Worth, Wright always cited his home as Weatherford and not Nebraska, a clear sign that he was trying to make a name for himself before his return. In one such letter from October 1944, Wright applauded the efforts of the Dumbarton Oaks Conference in Washington, DC, to create a United Nations. The League of Nations had failed to prevent World War II, he argued, and thus a "united nations police" was essential. "The time to stop aggressors is before they start."[7]

The most impressive effort Wright made to establish himself, however, was a program he tried to market to smaller towns in the Fort Worth area. Entitled "Jobs and Small City," Wright's program called for a series of committees—perfect for the "town's civic spirited women"—to predict post-war surpluses, shortages, and revenues. A "Veteran's Contact Committee" would determine the number of men who planned to return, while a "Business Employment Committee" would coordinate local businesses. If the town's elders thought such a plan worthwhile, Wright concluded, "please let me know if there is any service I can render you."[8] It was entrepreneurship worthy of his father, but, unfortunately, no offers of employment resulted. Many towns had already begun planning. As Wright well knew, however, he had established connections, adding to the foundation for his future.[9]

Although Wright was anxious to start this future, his self-promotion continued to carry the risk of overstepping his bounds. Just prior to the 1944 election, Wright protested that the Nebraska State Fair had invited a Republican congressman to speak on behalf of the GOP's presidential nominee Thomas Dewey, but no Democrat to support President Roosevelt. "I think you owe it to us who believe in Mr. Roosevelt," Wright complained to the fair's manager, offering to fill the role himself. The result was, in hindsight, predictable. The base's commanding officer, Wright recalled, "skewered me like a hot dog on a stick." The military, he stated, "does not mess in politics." Wright tried to argue, suggesting that "free speech is one of those things we are fighting for." The commander, however, would have none of it. "I don't think you understand me, Lieutenant," he stated before designating Wright the official Officer of the Day, requiring Wright to remain deskbound for twenty-four hours.[10] The episode, like the military reprimand the year before, spoke to Wright's self-confidence and willingness to take risks. When he felt he was on the side of justice, Wright did not accept defeat easily. Of course, his position was untenable. Although the military won the right to vote in presidential elections in 1944, a partisan military would have certainly weakened public support and undermined the command structure.

It was clear that Wright's heart was not in the military, especially when Mab got pregnant. As the due date approached, he sent Mab to his parents' home in Weatherford while he stayed in the Lincoln apartment they had rented. "I felt strongly about it," he later explained. His parents lived near a medical clinic and welcomed the chance to help, and he could remain focused on his career. On January 31, 1945—one day past FDR's sixty-third birthday—Mab gave birth to James Claude Wright III. Wright was a proud father, as one might expect, but, if anything, it only increased the pressure he felt to succeed. Looking back years later, Wright's friends noted that the child-rearing duties fell largely to Mab. "It was obvious he was more interested in politics than he was in his family," said one longtime friend. "We didn't have a married life like a lot of couples," Mab recalled. "He was always working toward his career."[11]

Years later, his children agreed. Wright was a loving father who helped with homework and listened to their problems—when he was at home. His son, dubbed Jimmy, recalled that "weekends were about all we had." Wright's daughter Ginger, born four years later, recalled that Wright "tried to be a pal." He was easy to approach and genuinely cared, but work often distracted him. "Often he would carry home the tensions of his office and those were unapproachable times." All of Wright's children agreed that their father sensed what he had sacrificed for his career and never encouraged them to go into politics. He tried to impart his idealism and the importance of fairness, but the family never had the piano sing-alongs or the close bond that Wright had enjoyed with his own parents. Late in his career, with the wisdom of old age, he even admitted to pangs of guilt over not spending more time with his children.[12]

In 1944, however, Wright was chomping at the bit to get his political career under way. He read *Southwest Reporter*, a digest of Texas Supreme Court cases, and bristled at the internment of Japanese on the West Coast. Always a joiner, he found the Masons particularly attractive. His father and a banker friend agreed to sign for Wright so that he could join the fraternal organization. In Lincoln, Wright was just an apprentice, but everyone recognized the young lieutenant as an up-and-comer. Wright's gregariousness and drive won him a number of Cornhusker friends who wanted him to stay. Bypassing many of the usual requirements, they bestowed upon Wright the rank of Master Mason. By the end of 1944, Wright had received several post-military offers of employment from his new friends, one of them a fellow Mason, and another from a local insurance company. Wright, of course, was not about to take the offers. He realized that his future in politics was better served by returning to his own hometown.[13]

By the spring of 1945, the time had finally come. Wright applied and received an early release, one of the first soldiers to take advantage of the military's new "point system" that considered factors such as time overseas, time in combat, and personal issues, such as parenthood. Despite the friction his outspokenness had incurred, the military still recognized Wright's potential, and he was offered an appointment to the Fort Leavenworth Command and General Staff School in Kansas. If he stayed in the army, Wright would receive a promotion to major. For Wright, the decision was a no-brainer. He agreed with the sarcastic comments of a colleague: "The only thing I ever really wanted from the army was out." In May 1945, just days after V-E Day, Wright traveled by Greyhound bus to San Antonio's Fort Sam Houston. There, at the mustering-out center, Wright and thirty-five other happy soldiers received their honorable discharge papers. Jim Wright was now a civilian again, free to return home and launch his career in earnest.[14]

Wright took an early morning train from Fort Sam Houston to Weatherford, proudly attired in his new $27 "civvies" purchased from San Antonio's Joske's Department Store. Once back in Weatherford, he, Mab, and five-month-old Jimmy moved out of Wright's parents' house and into a monthly $45 two-bedroom rental. Wright's father knew the head of the National Federation of Small Business and convinced his friend to hire Wright as a salesman, the pay solely commission. The fledgling NFSB, headquartered in San Marcos, California, was an organization formed to rival the official US Chamber of Commerce, which operated on behalf of the large, more urban businesses that dominated it. The NFSB planned to focus on the small rural operations that were often neglected. It was perfect for Wright. His job was to travel a circuit selling memberships. For a while, he traveled by bus and train to save money, but eventually he purchased a used eight-year-old Dodge.[15] The appeal of the job was not just the money but also the exposure. "I traveled throughout the 12th Congressional District meeting small businessmen," Wright recalled, a telling description, given that his region did not depend upon political districts. Wright talked politics, listening as the men explained their concerns. He was building on the familiarity with small-town America that he had inherited from his father and solidifying critical friendships.[16] The businessmen's concerns were real. With improved transportation, growing suburbanization was costing small-town commerce and transforming American life.[17]

Wright's correspondence from this period reflected the political overtones. "I hope you will be the representative from Parker in the next legislature," wrote one new acquaintance. "I appreciate your letter concerning the possibility of a Congressional campaign, but I am not in a position to offer a commitment," wrote another. Wright's sales job, meanwhile, still included constant travel and the occasional complaint. One city manager, for example, wrote of his "dissatisfaction with your program" and requested a refund. Wright was on each incident quickly, the consummate salesman. Still, it was obvious that he was selling more than just the NFSB.[18]

When one of Wright's friends, Bernard Rapoport, approached him about the Young Democrats of Texas (YDT), Wright quickly recognized an opportunity. Rapoport was working with Jack Carter, a Fort Worth attorney and the county Democratic chairman, and Carter's wife, Margaret, a well-known liberal, to revive the defunct organization. With its membership overseas and with partisanship muted, the YDT had dwindled during the war. Working with this energetic trio, Wright began calling former classmates and businessmen he had met on his sales circuit. Together they organized a convention to be held at Fort Worth's Hotel Texas in December 1945. "We got people from all over the state," Wright proudly recalled.[19]

The convention, however, was not something all the Democratic elders applauded. The Democratic Party was prominent throughout the South, and the key elections were often the primaries, not the fall general elections. "All local and statewide offices were held by Democrats. That's just the way it was," Wright recalled.[20] The party, however, like small-town America, was beginning a period of tremendous transformation. Many southern Democrats still embraced economic populism and admired FDR's New Deal, which had profoundly impacted impoverished Texans. Others, nevertheless, had become more reactionary in matters of foreign policy, race, and a litany of social concerns. While not exhibiting the same degree of ideological conservatism that is prominent today, they had parted company with their more liberal colleagues, certainly with many northern Democrats. This split had been evident in the candidacy of New York's Catholic governor Al Smith in the 1920s and in the matter of Prohibition, but, in Texas at least, the split had grown quite acrimonious. In fact, the Texas Democratic State Convention of 1944 had, in the words of historian Robert Dallek, resulted in "an all-out fight" with personal insults. Roosevelt reportedly had been livid at Texas's conservative Democrats, and leading Texas Democrats such as Sam Rayburn and Lyndon Johnson had to walk a fine line to keep the split from widening into a third party.[21]

Wright's convention placed the Young Democrats of Texas firmly in the liberal camp. It advocated a degree of desegregation in education, abolition of the poll tax, a voting age of eighteen, and the inclusion of women on juries. This platform, together with the group's apparent tendency to favor taxation and heavier regulation than many conservative Democrats thought prudent, made the Young Democrats worrisome to many of the older, more staid members of the Democratic elite. Wright and his colleagues, whether they recognized it or not, were in the vanguard of a new Democratic Party that within decades would come to alienate much of the party's traditional southern base. Like young people throughout time, they were more open to change than their elders and impatient to implement their ideas. Jim Wright quickly emerged as their leader, and he was elected to represent the state chapter at the Young Democrats' national convention.[22]

Meanwhile, back in Austin, the drama at the University of Texas finally concluded with President Homer Rainey's resignation. Wright, who as a student had defended Rainey against charges of radicalism, now attacked Rainey's critics on the Rotary Club circuit. No longer just a student, however,

Wright enraged many conservatives and earned him his first serious political criticism. Watching it all was Wright's father, James, who became
increasingly worried that politics would not offer his son a stable or lucrative
career. Arguing that financial security was paramount, James finally convinced him to buy a quarter share in the National Trade Day Association.
While the elder Wright certainly wanted the business that he had launched
to survive into the next generation, he told his son that part ownership
would provide a salary and not just a commission while still allowing time
for politics. Still trying to teach a lesson, he told Wright it was best to borrow the necessary funds and not just inherit the shares. It would be good
for Wright's self-respect and political career. Wright agreed, and taking out
a GI Bill of Rights loan, he joined his proud father.

Jim Wright, finally ready for political office, announced his intention to
run for the Texas Legislature from Parker County, the 103rd Legislative
District. Employing every connection he had made, and with his father's
help, Wright campaigned with a stamina that would come to characterize
all of his campaigns. He returned favors as well, campaigning for his old
high school friend Joe Irwin, his fellow founder of the Future Democrats of
Texas club, who was running from the Dallas area against the future
Speaker of the Texas House, William Otey Reed. Moreover, when the disgruntled Rainey decided to seek election as governor, an obvious rebuttal to
his dismissal from the University of Texas, Wright campaigned hard in
support. Wright's willingness to work endlessly for others was another trait
that would come to characterize his politics. He was a friend in need, and,
when in need himself, he had friends.[23]

The campaign was lively. At the Weatherford Veterans of Foreign Wars
Hall, an intoxicated legionnaire called Wright a "commiesonofabitch" and
threw a punch. In true Golden Gloves fashion, Wright ducked and returned
a left jab. Six blows later, Wright recalled, his assailant lay on the floor
"crumpled like a sack of wet laundry." The veterans loved it. Once his Democratic challengers were defeated, the general election was predictably anticlimactic. Years later, Wright could not even recall if he had a Republican
opponent.[24] Asked to speak before the Texas Democratic Party's Executive
Committee, Wright sought to bridge the party's differences with humor. The
famous Democrat William Jennings Bryan, Wright explained, was once
asked the difference between a Democrat and a Republican. When a
Republican saw an afflicted beggar surviving by "eating the crumbs which
fell from the lavishly loaded table" of an affluent family, he concluded that
it was a blessing that the table was so well stocked that the beggar got

substance. When a Democrat saw the same thing, he wondered why the beggar was not invited to join the dining.[25]

"I made a lot of mistakes," Wright laughingly recalled of his first real election. "I publicly supported the losing candidate for governor, managed to alienate the speaker-to-be of the House in which I sought membership, spoke out needlessly on the most controversial issues, accosted the state's dominant economic interest and opposed the governor-elect at the state Democratic convention."[26] Jim Wright was not quite twenty-four years old, barely past the minimum age required for election, and entered the House against headwinds. Even if his election promised a rough start, however, the year 1946 was a milestone, and not only for Wright but also for other World War II veterans who were launching long and ultimately influential political careers. Joining Congress were John F. Kennedy from Massachusetts and Richard M. Nixon from California. In time, they all would know each other well.

The Texas Legislature met for only 120 days every two years, though its biennial schedule was becoming increasingly rare across the country. Adjourning for the weekend at noon on Thursdays, members earned only ten dollars daily and, if additional time was needed beyond four months, only five dollars. It all meant that sessions were hectic and long, and that some outside income was essential. The NTDA allowed Wright to bring Mab and Jimmy, who was now a toddler, to an apartment only a few blocks from the state capitol and to support the legislature's unsuccessful efforts to extend the workweek without additional pay. Although he later argued for a pay increase "to enable [legislators] to give all their time" to their work and as a tool against corruption, he initially insisted that legislators "knew what they would get from the state when they offered themselves for the offices." Jim Wright, it appeared, was bringing both his idealism and his work ethic with him to Austin.[27]

Of course, he also brought ambition. "For some time I have thought that it would be good for those of us who are counted in the liberal column to meet," Wright, obviously trying to assume leadership, wrote early in the session.[28] "I am taking you up on your kind offer . . . to introduce me to the Parker County citizens," replied one legislator to a separate Wright offer.[29] Everyone, it appeared, knew Wright had bigger ambitions. "I am a stranger here," one freshman wrote, "but by the time you get ready for Congress (now don't be modest about it), I'll be entrenched here and can help you."[30] James

Wright certainly recognized his son's ambition. "If one aspires to a political career," he advised, "his needs must look out for the taxpayer's dollar."[31]

Wright's continued interest in foreign policy gave away his broader horizons. In a speech to the Lions Club, Wright, still sharpening his political tongue, supported the famed Marshall Plan.[32] While remaining active in the Veterans of Foreign Wars and the American Legion, he proved receptive to a new, more liberal organization known as the American Veterans Committee (AVC). The AVC supported the desegregation of the military and a more internationalist stance. Unlike the other veterans groups, it welcomed membership from other countries' veterans. This latter position, Wright claimed hyperbolically, constituted "one of the most significant developments for peace in this time." Wright agreed to help form a Weatherford chapter but noted that the *Fort Worth Star-Telegram* had editorialized against the organization. Many readers, he said, believed erroneously that the paper "made up its collective mind independently on public matters."[33]

More often, of course, Wright worked to please his constituents, shrewdly casting himself as a prairie populist. He recognized that a feeling of "separateness" permeated much of Texas, a belief arising from the Depression that large old-money interests exploited the common Texan. In fact, eastern manufacturers had earlier enjoyed cheaper shipping rates than their Texas competitors. This, Wright noted, gave an "impetus to people who beat their breasts and said that they would not be dominated by Tammany Hall and Wall Street." It was "no longer necessary to appeal to people's regional prejudice," he later recalled, "but there are some vestigial remnants of that old brooding resentment in Texas culture."[34] In fact, Wright was not above a little mild breast-beating himself. After stopping at a vegetable stand and hearing complaints, he charged that the large dairy companies were operating as an illegal cartel. Falsely claiming a surplus of milk, they were paying the local farmers less. Taking up the farmers' cause, Wright wrote a letter to the state attorney general, building momentum for a lawsuit and an eventual ruling that there was, in fact, a restraint of trade.[35]

Wright also reflected the populist sentiment that powerful economic consolidation undermined democracy, a vestige of what Mark Twain had termed the "Gilded Age." Large corporations, many believed, controlled the state legislature through financial contributions. Undetected, the money undermined the average voter, created conflicts of interest, and encouraged corruption. In fact, as Wright entered the Texas Legislature, the US Congress had just passed the Federal Registration Lobbying Act of 1946.

The law required those who made sizable contributions to register their personal information.[36] Joining his fellow Texan populists, Wright sought to do the same thing at the state level. This effort, of course, was doomed. The bill challenged both potent financial interests and the power of incumbency. Others raised First Amendment questions. In any case, the bill never emerged from committee. Wright's support for it was the first evidence of his career-long interest in ensuring political integrity. As he stated in one 1966 speech, politics "doesn't have to be filthy and corrupted." Morals mattered. "Each of us to whom has been given the mantle of public trust," he later wrote, "is the recipient of a gift more sublime than title of royalty."[37] Born of his youthful idealism and populism, this theme resonated throughout Wright's long career, sometimes, as in his ultimate political demise, ironically.

The best example of Wright's populism, however, was the manner in which he dealt with the politically influential oil interests. A ten-dollar donation from a Weatherford gas station owner, Wright proudly proclaimed, was the largest he received from the industry.[38] In fact, in Austin at least, almost all of Wright's legislative agenda rested on taxing big oil, natural gas, and sulfur. Wright's acquaintance Bob Eckhardt, later a liberal congressman from Houston, worked with Wright to draw up a heavily progressive tax on the largest producers. They argued that the larger corporations let the smaller independent drillers spend time and money locating new wells only to buy them afterward, saving the large oilmen money but raising the price of energy for everyone else. Accordingly, Wright's plan spared the smaller independents and focused on the wealthy. "There is the explorer and the exploiter, and my sympathy is with the explorer," Wright remarked. Wright's rhetoric sometimes approached the breast-beating he attributed to others. "The major sulfur producers," he once declared, "are dominant members of a world-wide cartel which has realized enormous profits from its monopoly maintained prices." Cartel, monopoly—the famed agrarian rebel Tom Watson could not have described such populist sentiment better. Wright even hired graduate students to ascertain the revenue his tax would raise. The proposed tax was so high, the students determined, that it raised three times the funds necessary to accomplish their goals.[39]

In no way, however, did this suggest that Wright's legislative goals in Austin were timid. Far from it, Wright had hardly forgotten his swing-for-the fence style of play. He had grand plans to spend the money that his tax would raise. First was education, an obvious reflection of his past. "I intend to introduce bills designed at appreciably raising our per capita student apportionments and substantially increasing minimum allowable teacher salaries," Wright stated soon after his election. True to his word, he introduced, with five others, the Teacher Pay Increase Support Bill of 1947, raising average per student appropriations $20, to $55. Texas ranked thirty-eighth in teacher pay but first in oil revenue, he noted. Because the state was losing teachers, Wright proposed that teacher pay should be raised $2,000, for a total of $26 million in additional funding, a considerable sum in 1947.[40] He also sought to spend more money on Prairie View Normal School, a college for African Americans, so that it could reach "the standing of a first-rate university." Wright sought to diminish political interference into the work of the Text Book Board and to give teachers a "place on the policy making agencies of education."[41] He worked tirelessly for his bill, writing the Oklahoma Board of Education to inquire about its recent efforts to raise teacher pay.[42] Arguing that education was key to future economic growth, Wright received numerous invitations to speak to teachers. The cost of his bill was going to make it difficult to pass, he warned the Classroom Teachers Association of Fort Worth. Some legislators were sure to "follow the path of least resistance" and argue that the surplus in the state's rainy day fund—"pitifully inadequate" and temporary—would suffice.[43] This was folly, Wright insisted.

Other priorities included more money for a "thorough network of hard-surface, year-around rural roads." The improvements were essential, Wright argued, because inclement weather made dirt roads impassable for many farmers. He also promised to "oppose efforts aimed at stifling R.E.A. cooperatives." Cutting funds for the Rural Electrification Administration was folly, Wright claimed. The Depression may have ended, and much of rural America may have been electrified, but many farmers remained in need. In defense of another New Deal–era program, he argued that continued soil conservation efforts were necessary to prevent a recurrence of the infamous Dust Bowl. Although Wright was unable to attend all the meetings of the soil conservation districts, he distributed literature that documented his strong advocacy.[44] "The farmers are powerless and voiceless," Wright concluded, like a true populist. He did not always take the lead with every liberal bill—his efforts mostly focused on his tax and education proposals—but by the end of the legislative cycle he had a record that could prove both a sword and a shield.[45]

Of all the issues that challenged Wright personally, matters of race stood out. He brought with him the egalitarian lessons of his parents and of his own experiences abroad, but at the same time he realized that demonstrating too much advocacy on behalf of African Americans risked conservative wrath that could undermine his entire agenda. In this he was similar to many other liberal Democrats of the era. FDR had sought to assist African Americans, too, but, fearful of alienating southern conservative Democrats, he had not proposed any significant civil rights legislation.[46] Two key ingredients in Wright's political DNA, idealism and ambition, appeared to be at odds. Years later, Wright still recalled his surprise upon finding blacks at an early political meeting in the home of liberals Jack and Margaret Carter. "While intellectually accepting the doctrine of equality," Wright reflected, "some of us felt nevertheless a trifle awkward talking politics in a racially mixed gathering."[47]

The solution, he determined, was not to repudiate his beliefs but to downplay his positions. He quietly supported efforts to assist African Americans, but he never sought leadership in this area. In early meetings of the Young Democrats of Texas, for example, he did not invite "my Negro friends," but he did welcome them when they came. "It never occurred to me to invite Charlie," Wright remarked of his family's black employee Charlie Bailey Smith. While rejecting the poll tax, Wright recalled, he only "played around with it."[48] He supported admitting African Americans to the University of Texas School of Law—particularly when it came to a case then under litigation involving the law school that foreshadowed the more famous *Brown v. Board of Education of Topeka, Kansas*—but he rarely mentioned his stance in his own speeches.[49] In fact, when he did so, his conflicted feelings were evident. "In general," he wrote *The Emancipator*, "I am inclined to defend segregation while wholeheartedly opposing discrimination." Wright probably knew that segregation without discrimination was inherently impossible, just as the *Brown* case would soon rule, but for the present the stance sufficed.[50]

Wright never had a moment to spare. There had been no official orientation for new members, but Wright had wisely sought the counsel of more experienced legislators. His extensive networking gave him a foundation for the personal dynamics at play, not just the official protocol but also the rivalries, pet peeves, and individual personalities. With no office or staff, and no formal mentor, Wright worked directly from his desk on the floor of the legislature. Although he was anxious to advance his own agenda, the routine was usually mundane. Requests arrived almost daily. One alumnus of Weatherford College wanted Wright to help get football at their alma mater. Now that the war was over, the Veterans of Foreign Wars wanted help acquiring buildings at Camp Wolters.[51] One publication asked Wright to list his chief likes and dislikes. The former, Wright replied, included "people, autumn, and food," while the latter included "small talk and gossip." He might have added wasted time. In scribbled handwriting, an elderly man asked that Wright, as a Christian and World War II veteran, fight the "money-changers and the big corporations in Austin." On this, at least, he needed not worry.[52]

Joe Kilgore, elected to the Texas House the same year as Wright, recalled his colleague as more liberal than most members but not caustic. "We didn't vote alike but I had a lot of respect for him," Kilgore said. "He was easy to work with, quick and understanding. You didn't get anger or frustration from him, but you did get vigorous opposition if you disagreed with him."[53] Wright successfully kept his temper in check while in Austin, but it was often challenging for him to do so. "I'd like to cultivate a more equitable disposition," Wright wrote years later in his diary, "one able to remain unruffled in the face of unexpected and unreasonable demands."[54] In Austin, Wright worked to find consensus, later stating that his experiences solidified a valuable political lesson: "One's success in the legislature depended less upon his ideology than on his acceptance as a person."[55]

Whatever Wright's efforts, of course, many conservatives did not share Kilgore's begrudging respect and felt that Wright's liberalism was just too difficult to overcome. "To the well-established power structure in Texas," Wright recalled, "I was as abrasive as sandpaper." In fact, some hardline conservatives even sarcastically called Wright and his allies the "Russian Embassy."[56] Politics in Texas had never been for the faint of heart, and the national political scene did not help. For the first time in years, the GOP had won back the House of Representatives in 1946, which facilitated its campaign to paint Democrats as weak on communism. Throughout 1947, the Republican-dominated House Un-American Activities Committee played prominently in the news, especially in the conservative South.[57] After a group known as The Christian America leveled charges of communism against a number of liberal Texas legislators and groups, including the YDT, the Texas attorney general authorized an investigation that ultimately exonerated them. "No member of the honorable body of legislators of Texas is or ever has been a Communist," his report declared, "and furthermore, no official of the Young Democrats of Texas, past or present, is or ever has been a Communist."[58]

None of this boded well for Wright's ambitious agenda. The one key ingredient, the tax proposal, died a slow, agonizing legislative death. "I had no concept of the power of [the oil] lobby," Wright later admitted. When Wright's bill finally won a hearing, the lobbyists ensured that it came before the Committee on Revenue and Taxation, to which they had given sizable contributions. A motion to assign Wright's bill to a "s-l-o-w subcommittee to study this bill very, very carefully" brought laughs from the conservatives, who knew that the bill would never emerge. Meanwhile, the other portions of Wright's agenda fared no better, most never making it to a floor vote. In Wright's words, they "never got to first base." Wright at least had a chance with his education bill, but he refused to compromise. In what amounted to an honor for a first-term representative, the governor called Wright and asked if he would support an average pay increase of $2,000 in place of a uniform increase of at least the same amount. Wright, perhaps foolishly, refused, and the bill died.[59]

Like most representatives from rural areas, Wright did support successful efforts to fund soil conservation districts, promoting a bill to provide matching funds for local efforts to acquire equipment and to assist with terracing and cover cropping. He had seen a bit of the Dust Bowl as a boy in Oklahoma and, while a teenager in Parker County, had befriended the county agricultural agent. By the time he reached Austin, Wright was an acquaintance of a prominent district soil conservation supervisor. In short, he knew from firsthand experience the importance of water. Indeed, matters of water and environment would play prominently throughout his career.[60]

In most substantive ways, Wright's first session in the Texas House was a complete failure. Nevertheless, for good or bad, he had made a name for himself and won his share of headlines. More politically astute, his list of friends had already become quite long. Already aware of the importance of personal relationships, he now understood the need for patience, the need to lay better groundwork, and, when necessary, the need to accomplish goals piecemeal. Wright's well-developed sense of ambition and confidence always motivated him to think big. Sometimes, he now understood, it was better to think strategically. "I learned not to bite off more than I could chew," Wright concluded. Also, he had learned not to "mingle in too many fights," which risked facilitating opposition coalitions. In general, he learned not to just "assume that you know everything."[61] It was wisdom born of experience, but, for Jim Wright, it remained a constant struggle.

Given it all, perhaps the fireworks that Wright's 1948 reelection effort produced were inevitable. Wright faced two challengers in the Democratic primary. Floyd Bradshaw, a thin, bald, thirty-nine-year-old graduate of East Texas State and, like Wright, a war veteran, was a Weatherford teacher who sought to capture the district's sizable conservative constituency. More outspoken than Wright in support of segregation, Bradshaw struggled to overcome his relative obscurity, running what Wright recalled as a "colorless and inoffensive campaign." Eugene Miller, meanwhile, had a stronger pedigree—Southern Methodist University and the University of Texas School of Law—but a tarnished reputation. Not surprisingly, it was Miller, not Bradshaw, who brought the proverbial fireworks.

A bit younger than Wright's father, Miller had served two terms in the Texas House and one in the Senate. Ever since a defeat in his early thirties, however, his career had taken a frustrating nosedive. He had run unsuccessfully for office so many times that rumors swirled that he ran not to win but to defeat others by drawing votes away. Some suggested that various lobbies supported Miller in this effort, while others claimed that he was a gambler in debt. He reportedly lived in an Austin hotel, but he claimed Parker County as his residency. One thing was for sure: Miller's campaigns were quick to level personal insults and unsupported accusations. In fact, in 1946, the same year Wright had won his seat, Miller had challenged the integrity of his State Senate opponent Ben Hagman, a friend of Wright's and the father of actor Larry Hagman, who was later known for the television drama *Dallas*. Miller's unsubstantiated claims that Hagman had cheated his clients brought a liability lawsuit that solidified Miller's reputation as, at best, a right-wing Huey Long–like character, and, at worst, a paid political assassin.[62]

At the outset Wright promised to run a positive campaign, another lifelong commitment that challenged him throughout his career. "My whole idea," he later recalled, "was that if I had to get elected saying what a sorry fellow my opponent was, then that did not say much for me." Although Wright was able to withstand Miller's verbal blows, three weeks before the primary election the unbelievable happened. On July 7, 1948, three men drove a red Chevrolet to a Parker farmhouse where Miller was staying and shot him twice with a .45-caliber Army-issue revolver. One bullet hit just below the heart and the other in the right leg.[63] An ambulance rushed Miller to the hospital, and one of its drivers later recalled that Miller, still conscious, told him "left-wingers" had probably shot him because "I am hot on their trail."[64]

Wright was at a church prayer meeting when he got the news. He had given blood before, and the hospital called him. In an ironic twist, Wright had the same blood type as Miller and the hospital wanted Wright to come quickly. Wright donated the blood, but no one recognized how dire the situation was, certainly not Miller. "This is going to get me elected," county attorney J. B. Hand recalled Miller stating in the hospital. What Miller actually said is unclear, but according to most accounts, he stated that communists had hired "henchmen" to "liquidate" him. Miller ended up dying nine hours later. There was no direct accusation against Wright, but throughout the campaign Miller had argued that Wright was a communist sympathizer. Wright's colleague Bob Eckhardt was livid. Only hours before his death, Miller had "rebaited" Wright. "It was probably the dirtiest piece of political work I've ever seen an older man pull on a younger challenger," Eckhardt said, especially given the fact that Wright was a "young, fresh, completely guileless person."[65] Eckhardt's description of Wright was charitable but shared by the county attorney. "Jim Wright was a comer," concluded Hand. "Eugene Miller was a has-been. Jim Wright didn't need him out of the way. He would have won that thing hands down had it not been for the murder."[66]

The whispers started almost immediately. Witnesses said they had seen Wright in the area with a gun. One farmer said he had seen Wright taking target practice. Wright replied that several days before the shooting he had been in the area tacking up campaign posters with a hammer, but he had never had a gun. Others spoke of how Wright's Irish temper matched his red hair and recalled his fight during his previous campaign. Wright, they concluded knowingly, would react violently when called a communist.[67] Authorities said there never was credible evidence to connect Wright to the murder and, although many of the files were lost, the case technically remains open. The Texas Ranger who led the investigation, George Roach, stated that he believed Miller's gambling debts were involved.[68] Miller had a "multitude of enemies," Roach concluded. One informant claimed that Houston gamblers had demanded money. Roach's investigation uncovered ten possible suspects as far away as Louisiana and New Mexico, but no solid evidence.[69]

It made little difference. As Wright decried the "slander," there was clearly more at play than public titillation. Someone asked Charlie Bailey Smith, the Wright family employee, to retrieve Wright's father James's pistol. James, like many other World War I veterans, had kept his side arms. Smith did not know the man who had asked, but it was obvious that he wanted to check it for evidence. Jim Wright decided to turn the gun over to the police, countering James, who worried that it would fuel more speculation and a mistaken analysis might result. In the end, the gun was ruled out, but the speculation continued.[70]

Wright was worried—and with good cause. In a desperate election-eve appeal, he purchased an ad in the local paper. "I despise communism," it stated. "I believe in States Rights. . . . I believe in the Southern tradition of segregation and have strongly resisted any and all efforts to destroy it. . . . I believe [labor leader] John L. Lewis one of the most dangerous men in America today." Wright, it appeared, was frantically trying to regain conservative votes. It was a difficult moment for Wright. Facing the possibility of defeat, his idealism pulled him in one direction and his ambition and pragmatism in the opposite direction. Wright, in fact, did not personally embrace segregation, but he knew that many voters did. He did not think of himself as an enemy of organized labor, but many voters in his district thought unions were the vanguard of communism. His choice was stark and, in the end, disconcerting. It was, arguably, not his finest hour—and it ultimately paid little dividends.[71]

Wright was starting to gain ground when the clock ran out. He recalled giving a speech at the Weatherford Court House just before the election. Three hundred supporters cheered wildly, but others, either swayed by the anticommunist zealotry of the day or simply caught up in a good conspiracy theory, refused to give him any benefit of the doubt. Most agreed that Wright probably was not personally involved in the murder but insisted that his "radical" friends might truly be to blame. Had there been more time, Wright probably would have won. As it turned out, however, he lost by a mere thirty-nine votes.[72]

The defeat hit the entire Wright family hard. Mab later recalled that the months in Austin had been for her the "happiest of our marriage."[73] Despite his lack of legislative success, Wright had never seemed so content. "I always thought that he wanted to be president of the United States, and I always thought that he could make it," Mab remembered of those days. "But you know we never once discussed it. It's a matter of knowing something without being told." Now, however, her husband's limitless potential seemed suddenly and unfairly quashed. He was depressed, and his future was uncertain. Bradshaw, meanwhile, went on to a thirteen-year career in the Texas Legislature. Wright, a good loser, called to congratulate him. "We never became friends," Wright recalled, "but we were always polite."[74]

The loss was so disillusioning and difficult to process that it left, in Wright's words, "lasting psychic scars." Like Mab, Wright had never been more confident or sure of his destiny. He may not have accomplished much legislatively, but he had loved every minute of being in the legislature. He had tasted the career and now wanted it more than ever. Moreover, the horror he had seen overseas during the war had only amplified his idealism. In politics, he could prevent another such calamity. No other career promised such an impact. "I was certain in my vision of the road to world peace and of what I considered my mission in life," Wright later recalled. "I had sort of a messiah complex." Now, however, it all suddenly appeared to be over, and Wright would have to recalculate everything.[75]

If Wright ever had been the "young, fresh, completely guileless person" that his colleague Eckhardt described, he was no longer. The defeat made him "overly cautious politically," Eckhardt now concluded. "I think he began to understand the truth did not necessarily pay."[76] More cautious, more cynical—it was, perhaps, yet another lesson in the political evolution of Jim Wright. It may have been a valuable education but, at the time, Wright surely wondered if he ever would have a chance to apply the lessons learned. He appeared to be a political failure, his life ambitions crushed by an unfair and inexplicable twist of fate. Perhaps he never again would be able to serve in public office. At the ripe old age of twenty-six, Jim Wright was in a life crisis.

CHAPTER 4

Preparation and Payoff

BUSINESSMAN, MAYOR, AND ELECTION TO CONGRESS
(1948–1954)

The Wrights' return to Weatherford was painful. With the rumors of Jim
Wright's involvement in the Miller murder persisting, Mab suggested the
family move. "If we leave now, people will assume that everything that's
been said was correct," Wright answered. Wright appeared to have become
more cynical and cautious in a political sense. He also had become more
reserved personally. He remained congenial and still cultivated a wide network of acquaintances, but he relied more now on a small circle of family
and friends. He socialized less and became, in the words of one of his top
congressional staffers, Craig Raupe, "a very private man."[1]

His future still uncertain, Wright threw himself into his work at the
National Trade Day Association. His success was astounding. Within three
years he was earning $50,000 annually, almost thirteen times the median
family income at the time.[2] Every year, Wright and his father hosted a
national conference for their legions of salesmen. The business allowed
Wright to purchase his first home. Even in this Wright employed his connections. His friends Fred and Bob Ray were homebuilders, and Wright
enlisted them to construct a large home for him and his young family in a

new northwestern Weatherford development. Built on three lots and finished in shingles, the house boasted three bedrooms and a spacious living
room with a built-in fireplace. Wright even had room to build a rental property. A small hut housed a Shetland pony that Wright bought for Jimmy. In
time, in true Texan form, all the Wright children developed a love of horses.
The youngest, Alicia, who was not yet born in 1949, especially loved horses
and worked with them throughout much of her life. The home was a wise
purchase. Soon after Wright's bitter defeat, Mab gave birth to Ginger, their
first daughter. Wright was overjoyed. The two young children were undoubtedly a salve for the lingering pain from the election.[3]

Wright's expansive list of activities now included both efforts to advance
his business and efforts to maintain possible political connections. He taught
Sunday School in Weatherford's First Presbyterian Church, where he solidified a friendship with Conrad Russell, who had worked for the NTDA.
Russell had been Weatherford's mayor and led the Texas Municipal League.
Almost two decades older than Wright, he was, Wright recalled, "my mentor
in many ways." Although Wright later claimed that he had "given up 100
percent on a political career," Russell's encouragement and Wright's extensive civic involvement spoke to the embers of political ambition.[4]

Wright became a beloved scoutmaster for Boy Scout Troop 76, where
Russell's son Bill was a member. In later years, the troop and their parents
volunteered for Wright's campaigns—in Wright's words, they did "all the
mundane things."[5] Remaining active in the veterans' organizations, Wright
served on the American Legion's Americanism Committee, which was dedicated to fighting communism, and became chief of staff for the Department of Texas in the Veterans of Foreign Wars. He was active in the Jaycees,
served as chairman of the Parker County Cancer Fund Drive, and became
a member of the Council of Social Agencies. Most notably, he began coach-
ing Golden Gloves boxing. His athletes included the actor Larry Hagman,
who was still a boy. "I'm the man who taught J. R. [the character J. R. Ewing
in TV's Dallas] to be mean," Wright later quipped. "He taught J. R. how to
finesse," Hagman laughingly added.[6]

"In a town like Weatherford, they give you all these free jobs," Wright
later joked.[7] Wright clearly grew to enjoy this interregnum in his political
life. He had time with his young children, was surrounded by friends, and
had more wealth than he had ever imagined. Later, he even purchased a
four-hundred-acre Kerr County ranch southwest of Fort Worth, where he
raised turkeys and pheasants. Wright enjoyed the ranch for almost a decade
before selling it to pay for campaign debts, a decision he later regretted.[8]

The life of a wealthy and beloved businessman certainly had its attractions. But somehow, for Jim Wright, something was still missing.

As if by fate, in late 1949 Weatherford's mayor, William Sadler, resigned, and a special election was scheduled for January 1950. Wright, hesitant at first to run, announced publicly that he would not enter the campaign. His father believed being mayor would be a waste of Wright's time, abilities, and money. The town was small, with only 8,500 people, and the position was part time and paid only $75 per month. Though it might satisfy his itch for public service, it seemed to be a step down from the Texas Legislature. The people who knew him best, however, were particularly insistent that he give it a go; the city would benefit from his obvious energy and abilities. Even people who had voted against Wright's reelection urged him to run. A Veterans Committee for Jim Wright formed and, while Wright was at the annual NTDA conference, lobbied by telephone. Russell called as well. Finally, still in Chicago, Wright called Russell back to give him the news. He had decided that a "public career was what I always wanted." Signing an affidavit from Chicago making Russell his power of attorney, Wright asked the former mayor to file for him.[9]

After Russell advertised Wright's candidacy in the *Weatherford Daily News*, Wright's primary opponent, E. B. Buffington, the owner of Weatherford's two movie theaters, pounced. The veterans had promised to support his campaign, Buffington claimed. They might now deny it, but "it is true nevertheless." Moreover, Russell wanted to serve as the power behind the curtain. "Do you want a proxy mayor, or do you want one with no strings attached who will be under obligation only to the people?" Wright, Buffington continued, was young and inexperienced and had an extensive legislative record of radicalism.[10]

Wright, who knew how rough politics could get, laughed at the contradiction. It was "Buff's idea of a big expose" and "not worthy of a response."[11] Wright knew that Buffington was "not a popular person" and that old charges of radicalism would not fly in a local election where everyone knew everyone else. The results, accordingly, were predictable. In what the *Daily Herald* termed a "surprisingly heavy" turnout, Wright won by a vote of 490 to 175. A crowd on the square swarmed Wright. Thanking the public and praising the heavy vote, Wright asked for "the continued goodwill, prayers, advice and active cooperation of every citizen." The following day he purchased an ad in the paper repeating the sentiments.[12]

Wright, at twenty-six the youngest mayor in the state at that time, was not shy about his inexperience. First, he stated, he needed a "detailed study of the city charter to find out . . . the mayor's prerogatives." He needed to visit with all city departments and the leaders of nearby towns. Only after becoming "thoroughly indoctrinated," Wright stated, could he "dispense intelligent service." If Wright's comments spoke to his experiences in the state legislature, the *Daily Herald* editorialized, they promised "a wise sound beginning." Wright was "young in years but very mature in the realms of government."[13] Wright's plan was to devote his mornings to the NTDA and his afternoons to City Hall across the square. He would cover his absence at the NTDA with a new employee. Wright enjoyed no real assistance in his public duties, however. Serving with just two City Commission members and one secretary, he was responsible for almost forty municipal employees divided among police, sanitation, fire, revenue, and public works.[14]

Wright's entire family joined a crowd of sixty admirers for his swearing-in at City Hall. Wright promised that the city's books would be open for inspection and invited the public to news conferences every Wednesday afternoon, in time for the next day's paper. "There has been an inherent suspicion in the media," Wright explained. In fact, there had never been press conferences in town before and the media only consisted of reporters for the *Daily Herald* and the weekly local newspaper. In time, a radio reporter from nearby Mineral Wells attended as well. The conferences, Wright later claimed, proved "quite beneficial." They represented an early expression of Wright's career-long interest in open government and demonstrated, if nothing else, that he was anxious for accomplishments.[15]

One characteristic defined Weatherford during Jim Wright's tenure as mayor—growth, part of what Harvard economist John Kenneth Galbraith termed America's "affluent society" in the 1950s. Unlike some small rural towns that continued to decline as citizens migrated to the new suburbs, Weatherford was close enough to Fort Worth to benefit from that city's expansion. Just before Wright's election, US Highway 180 was improved through Weatherford, later assisted by the expansion of US Highway 80. The new highway barreled through downtown, eliminating a portion of the square and changing the character of the business community forever. Nevertheless, it placed Weatherford on a growth corridor while other small towns remained isolated. In time, Weatherford would be adjacent to the Dallas–Fort Worth "Metroplex," a massive sprawl of postwar growth unmatched almost anywhere in America.[16]

This growth proved both a blessing and, if not a curse, at least a challenge for the new mayor. With greater population came more employment.

After only a month on the job, Wright announced that annual tax collections were up almost 20 percent.[17] At the same time, however, growth mandated more services. The arrivals strained the municipal power plant's ability to meet electrical demand, and the city's network of wells struggled to provide sufficient water. Private services such as telephone and gas needed to adapt as well, often presenting local lawmakers with additional problems. In fact, the city was operating with an uncomfortable level of debt in spite of the new revenues, and the financial records were in arrears.[18]

This reality was evident in Wright's first City Commission meetings. Wright appointed a committee to plan a new park, including a baseball diamond and a bandstand. He led efforts to make parks of the city's three school playgrounds, which required new lighting and equipment. He even promised to write welcome letters to each arrival.[19] The city also announced plans to design unique new street signs and new plaques on the downtown square.[20] At the same time, however, the City Commission rejected a new housing project, lacking the funds necessary for the water and sewage lines. The original sewage system, Wright explained, "was written up in technical magazines as an outstanding job." Nevertheless, it was now "serving three times as many people."[21] When an argument broke out over public utilities in a Jaycees meeting, Wright declared that the city was "not big enough for factionalism" and promised to purchase water from nearby areas. "Everyone in the city should unite to see that [municipal plant expansion] succeeds," he added.[22] Once again, a congenial Wright worked to build consensus.

Wright hardly shied away from the harder issues. Although he had sought to abolish poll taxes in Austin, he now deputized Chamber of Commerce members as tax collectors. Better enforcement meant more revenue. He supported parking meters on the square and a slight tax increase for additional street improvements.[23] As he wrestled with water and electricity, he launched a major initiative against the deficit. Authorizing a citizens' advisory body, he invited public comment. A recent study, he noted, indicated that Weatherford had $13 million more in real property values than sixteen nearby cities of comparable size, and yet the lowest assessments. While tax rates should be kept low, Wright insisted, the city needed a fair evaluation and better enforcement of delinquency. Accordingly, Wright authorized the city attorney to begin the "unpleasant undertaking" of initiating lawsuits.[24]

Wright's efforts proved popular. When the time came for the regularly scheduled mayoral election in April, he faced no challengers. In local politics, at least, politicians could speak of taxes without being branded communist, perhaps because the revenues were tied so specifically to a town's needs. The people applauded Wright's stance on eliminating the city's deficit financing, even with a pay increase for city employees.[25] Wright's open government stance was also popular. "You should not resign yourself to the fate that nothing can be done in the community," Wright told a group of students, with the caveat that it was not wise to "tackle something too ambitious." A "well-rounded program involving a few immediate objectives" was essential.[26] Wright, it appeared, was still willing to take risks and wanted to accomplish great things, but he had learned from painful experience the wisdom in his own words.

The public welcomed his sense of calming reassurance. The Cold War was raging, and when Texas governor Allan Shivers asked all the state's municipalities to develop emergency plans for nuclear disaster, Wright appointed a permanent emergency panel to coordinate the Red Cross, the National Guard, medical officials, the police and fire departments, and private volunteers. He emphasized, however, that the system was "probably unnecessary," and applicable for natural disasters as well. Wright had experienced red-baiting firsthand and had no intention of emulating Senator Joseph McCarthy, who was then near his peak of popularity.[27]

For the most part, however, it was the mundane issues of water and electricity that drove Wright's popularity. Under Wright's leadership, the city agreed to share the cost of extending water mains with developers. The charges would be determined by the length and location of the pipes. Renegotiating with the Rural Electrification Administration, Wright won reduced electricity rates while converting the municipal power plant to natural gas. Although the initial cost was greater, Wright argued, the conversion made long-term savings "absolutely certain."[28]

Extending the water pipes helped, Wright told the Lions Club in June 1950, but a new "permanent water supply" was essential to sustain city growth. Eventually, he predicted, water would be more valuable than "oil, gold, or uranium." The problem was money. Piping water from "every possible lake site within a practical radius" would cost at least $2 million. Similarly, the town's sewage pipes were inadequate and the processing plant was old. Money from past sewage bonds would not cover the costs.[29] Without new revenue, city expansion would have to wait.

The city had other needs, Wright told the club. The city dump was inadequate and a new location was mandatory. Until new funds were identified, Wright promised, the city would do "everything within our power to keep the present grounds as clean as is humanly possible." In fact, as Wright spoke, the city was spraying the chemical DDT. No one, Wright included, knew of its environmental hazards.[30]

Wright had dealt with taxes and spending in Austin, but now he had more power—and more of a dilemma. He had already raised taxes and promised to end deficit financing. How could he meet spending needs? To complicate matters, a fire destroyed Weatherford's warehouse just before Wright spoke to the Lions Club, claiming $23,000 in municipal property. Of the city's paltry $17,000 in insurance, $10,000 was reserved for a possible boiler explosion. The city had only $7,000 to cover its losses.[31]

Of course, the little demands strained Wright as well. Requests for appearances were as constant as complaints and personnel decisions. The "Polar Bear Club" wanted to swim at the city pool. The American Legion needed help with school safety patrols.[32] It was always something. Wright even considered hiring a city manager—"at least one full-time paid man at the executive level"—but did not want to surrender power.[33] And then, of course, there was the NTDA. The daily grind was enough to exhaust another man, but not Jim Wright. His idealism intact, Wright still, somehow, wanted to accomplish more. The life of a wealthy businessman had not completely satisfied him, and now service as mayor did not satisfy him either. Certainly his family had benefited from his dedication. With his son Jimmy reveling in a new battery-powered toy car, and his daughter, the baby Ginger, growing rapidly, Mab gave birth to the couple's third child, daughter Patricia Kay. On the surface, everything seemed fine. Nevertheless, quietly, out of the public eye, Wright remained unsettled, his life-crisis lingering.[34]

Wright turned to his faith. As he pondered the larger questions of life, he began taking theology classes at night and serving as a lay preacher at the Granbury Presbyterian Church. With only forty members, the church lacked the funds for a full-time minister and relied on Wright and a Texas Christian University theology student. Wright had pondered the ministry as a child, but now, having tasted private and public life, he began to question his career ambitions again. Pastors were respected and influential and left a legacy of helping others, the type of thing that appealed to Wright. He already knew that he was a good speaker, and so it was worth exploring again.[35]

The day after Christmas in 1950, Wright applied to Iowa's University of Dubuque, planning to finish his degree and enter the school's seminary. "Since early adolescence and until very recently I have consistently believed that I could render the greatest possible service to God and man in the field of public service or politics," Wright's application stated. "Business holds no fascination for me," he wrote, and there was "inadequacy to do good" in politics. The application was classic Jim Wright, with all the rhetorical flourishes. He noted that going back to school was a risky decision for him—he would have to sell his property in order to pay the tuition. Mab was "a wife of vast integrity and understanding," and they had "been blessed with fine, healthy children." The application even reflected Wright's sense of humor. Asked to list relatives' occupations, Wright added six-year-old Jimmy as a "cowboy."[36]

The university accepted Wright and promised to help the young family find an apartment.[37] Before Wright committed, however, a turn of events gave him a different perspective. With the winter of 1950–1951 one of the coldest on record, the Upham Gas Company found that its smaller pipes were freezing. Noting that it already possessed larger pipes, Wright extracted a company promise to divert gas from industrial uses and employ more valves until the larger replacements were installed. As Weatherford College closed its classes and Wright opened City Hall as an emergency shelter, Upham, however, reneged. Wright had had enough. "We are not going to have citizens of Weatherford freezing to death," Wright wrote, threatening to cancel the city's contract. The threat worked, and Upham had the new pipes installed in a matter of days. If Wright needed a reminder that his job was, in fact, quite meaningful, he had it.[38]

Meanwhile, Weatherford's one milk bottler, Thomas Dairy, complained to Wright that Fort Worth would not allow the company to sell its milk, claiming that it was too expensive for its health officials to inspect farm and pasteurizing businesses outside of city limits. This was unfair and a possible restriction of trade, Wright quickly protested. Weatherford's health officials had inspected Thomas Dairy but had not inspected Fort Worth's bottlers, which, in fact, sold their products in Weatherford. Testifying before the Fort Worth City Council, Wright noted that legal precedent favored Weatherford and that he was willing to file suit. Citizens were "ready to put up money in a kitty if necessary to supply funds for a legal test."[39] Moreover, Weatherford would boycott Fort Worth products and, without approval from its own health department, no longer sell Fort Worth's milk. The nearby community of Mineral Wells agreed publicly with Wright, promising Fort Worth a problem that might metastasize. Wright was playing hard ball—and it worked. Fort Worth caved, dispatching inspectors to Thomas Dairy. Once again Wright had proved to himself the value of his efforts.[40]

As the anniversary of his election passed, Wright had one additional reminder of his influence. Southwestern Bell Telephone Company announced that it would seek substantial rate hikes with the City Commission. Unlike the situation in Fort Worth, Southwestern Bell had a strong case, as its rates had held steady for thirty years. On the other hand, it sought a 125 percent increase in business one-party service and a 10 percent increase in multi-party residential lines, which would lead to rates beyond what Wright thought most citizens could afford. When Wright asked the company to provide rate surveys of other towns—a useful tactic he had employed before—company officials only showed their losses for Weatherford. Refusing to negotiate, the officials brought in attorneys, and the situation appeared deadlocked. Keeping his temper intact, Wright continued to press for common ground. By the middle of 1951, he had won considerable concessions. Residential rates would remain the same, while business rates would rise to a lower rate than initially solicited. The company also agreed to upgrade its equipment. It would replace its antiquated central operation system and provide for more direct calls. The work was completed by the time Wright left office two years later.[41] It was, Wright wrote in his scrapbook, "what can be done . . . when one really tries to see both sides fairly and impartially and keep the public interest paramount."[42]

It was becoming more obvious that Wright's work did matter in tangible and profound ways—and not just to Wright. In July 1951, Wright led a committee of Weatherford and Mineral Wells citizens to meet with Texas senators John Connally and Lyndon Johnson. It was Wright's first official visit to the nation's capital. He also met with Weatherford's congressman, Wingate Lucas, a man who would soon hear from Wright again. Arguing that Wolters Air Force Base created a severe housing shortage, the committee won a new designation for their cities as a "critical defense area for housing." This designation relaxed credit controls and contributed to the construction of one hundred new houses. While rubbing shoulders with the most powerful Texans in Washington helped put Wright on the map, his election as vice-president of the Texas Municipal League was a more tangible accolade. The League represented over five hundred cities, making Wright known statewide. Conrad Russell had served as president of the League and was now operating Weatherford's municipal power plant, having arranged the original city purchase of the facility years before. Russell was another example of Wright's extensive connections, and the support of such a prominent man undoubtedly helped Wright's candidacy for League vice-president. Wright's political career, it suddenly appeared, did have a future. Whatever his reasoning, Wright's flirtations with the ministry fell once again to his political aspirations. When he came up for reelection as mayor, there was no opposition.[43]

Wright's momentum continued for the next two years. With the winter freeze giving way to a devastating drought in 1951, Wright implemented a water rationing program that was acknowledged as fair. The location of residents' homes determined the days that they could water. As the drought worsened, Wright allowed watering of shrubs and other larger plants but not lawns. "A toast-brown lawn," Wright lobbied, "was a badge of good citizenship."[44] More significantly, Wright helped purchase Sunshine Lake from the Texas and Pacific Railroad. It was an outstanding solution to the problem he had warned of earlier. The property had 61 of 145 acres covered by water and extensive filtration and pumping facilities. Realizing that diesel engines diminished the railroad's water needs, Wright won the property for only 10 percent of its $200,000 appraisal. The railroad maintained mineral and fishing rights for twenty years, but Weatherford had what it needed. Wright quickly helped win approval of $25,000 to raise the levee two feet, thereby increasing the lake's capacity from 170,000 to 300,000 gallons, and to connect the facility's pipes to the city's operations.[45]

While the lake deal spoke to Wright's business savvy, his efforts to pass a bond issue to improve the city's sewage system—another concern noted early—spoke to his growing political skills. With many Weatherford citizens hesitant to incur more debt, Wright first made allies of the state's health officials and then won over the Weatherford Chamber of Commerce, the Lions Club, and the Rotary Club. Only then did he lobby the public. It was a choice, he stated, not a mandate. The city might patch up its existing pipes and plant, which would not cost much but would last only five or six years, or, alternatively, spend more money for a system that allowed for future expansion. The existing plant, he noted, had been built in 1907 to serve 3,000 inhabitants, just over a third of the existing population. Moreover, Odessa had suffered a polio outbreak, partly as a result of insufficient sanitation. Finally, he added, the tax rate would increase only 25 cents for every $100 in property value, so taxes would still be lower than in most cities.[46] Supporting Wright, a number of organizations passed out fliers declaring that the bond issue would "make Weatherford the kind of clean, attractive city which will encourage people to come here."[47]

It was a persuasive campaign. On February 12, 1952, voters passed a $440,000 bond issue in a landslide of 768–85. As he had done after his own election, Wright thanked supporters and deflected personal credit. Now Weatherford was "in a position to welcome industry and housing with open arms." In only a hint at his own leadership, Wright added, "We are ahead of the growth for the first time in many years."[48] In fact, the plant was operational by the time Wright left office. Weatherford had extended its boundaries twice, and its population exceeded 10,000 people. The city was also out of debt, meaning that another one of Wright's initial goals had been met. Still, however, Wright did not rest. He pressed the Brazos River Authority for more water and discussed options with state officials, a process that ultimately led to the acquisition of another large lake, named Lake Weatherford.[49]

Not surprisingly, the accolades continued to accumulate. By late 1952, Wright was president of the Texas Municipal League and lobbying for additional aid to urban communities, a call that his fellow Texan Lyndon Johnson later repeated. Wright invited Johnson to speak to the League's conference. Senate Democrats had just elected Johnson as majority leader, and his acceptance of the invitation confirmed Wright's bright future. Working with Johnson's staff, Wright befriended Austin's liberal congressman Jake Pickle, another valuable connection. As Wright led the Municipal League, he also served as vice-president of the Texas Construction Council, a group of city administrators and industry professionals. He even offered to mediate a statewide telephone strike. At the end of 1953, the Texas Jaycees voted Wright one of five "outstanding young Texans of the year." A Wright friend summed up public sentiment succinctly: "Jim Wright was not long for Weatherford."[50]

"I've never had such a sense of raw power," Wright later joked about his days as Weatherford mayor. While glossing over his life crisis, Wright's recollections suggested that he had finally accepted his place, that he now understood that politics could fulfill both his idealism and his ambitions. Once, Wright recalled, a woman on the south side of town called early one morning to complain about boys shooting songbirds in her yard. "As I was leisurely wiping the sleep out of my eyes and wondering what I might do the telephone rang again," Wright laughed. "And, so help me, it was a lady on the north side complaining about all the sparrows roosting in the eave of her house." Did not the city have some ordinance? "I sent for the boys. I said, 'Hey, you want to shoot some birds? Let me show you where there are some birds.'"[51]

Wright certainly handled the issue of race adroitly. It was the most obvious issue where his idealism and his ambitions clashed. Weatherford's one school for African American children stopped at the eighth grade. For high school, the children had to travel thirty miles to Fort Worth's black school, I. M. Terrill. There was no bus service, and few students had cars. This was unacceptable to Wright, who recognized a tricky remedy. "We've got trouble, fellas," Wright told the City Commission late in 1952. The NAACP was planning to file a lawsuit and the evidence was compelling. Weatherford should "strike first," Wright suggested, and provide bus service to Terrill. It was a bluff, of course, but it worked. The threat of a lawsuit, Wright recalled, "struck terror" in the commission. Wright had achieved his objective without incurring conservative blowback. The incident once again spoke to the risk-taker and Machiavellian in Wright, but it also proved that he had matured as a politician.[52]

Wright now knew when to choose his battles. During the long hot drought, he watched uneasily as segregated black children peered enviously through the fence of the municipal pool while their white friends swam. When Craig Raupe, the pool manager and Wright's future congressional aide, suggested that he would admit the black children if they asked, Wright once again had a dilemma. "OK, I'll back you," Wright replied. "But let's hope they don't ask." Both men "knew what was right," Raupe recalled, "but it was political suicide."[53] The wise politician, Wright knew, moved cautiously on racial matters.

As Wright's father James had advised him, Jim Wright never held grudges and always sought to turn events to his advantage. It proved to be good advice. Three prominent Weatherford citizens—the owners of a peanut-shelling plant, a tool manufacturing company, and a funeral home—all continued to oppose Wright's career. "Well, now, that's a rare opportunity," James again mentored his son, recounting how Abraham Lincoln had suggested that the only way to destroy an enemy was to make him a friend. "Why not make friends of them?" James asked. "Show them you're a better man than they supposed." Taking his father's advice, Wright deliberately cultivated the three, eventually winning their support.[54]

If he were to advance in the Cold War era, Wright recognized, he needed foreign policy experience. Fortunately for him, an invitation arrived to discuss the 1952 presidential campaign on air with College Station congressman Olin Teague and Killeen businessman Bill Elkins. Both of these men, like Wright, were combat veterans who supported Democratic candidate Adlai Stevenson. Citing the "failed" presidencies of William Henry Harrison, Zachary Taylor, and Ulysses S. Grant—and conveniently omitting George Washington and Andrew Jackson—the three agreed that a "military man," such as Republican Dwight Eisenhower, was ill-suited for the civilian position of president. Soldiers, Wright claimed, were trained "to play under a completely different set of rules." Eisenhower would listen to the failed advice of "isolationists" in the ongoing Korean War, he argued, a prediction that belied Eisenhower's record and spoke to the broadcast's partisanship. While the program apparently swayed few Texans, and the state ultimately broke from the Deep South to support Eisenhower, it put Wright on record concerning a national issue.[55]

Another opportunity arose in March 1952, when the Atomic Energy Commission and the Federal Civil Defense Administration authorized Texas governor Allan Shivers to invite ten Texans to witness an atomic bomb explosion at Nevada's Yucca Flat Proving Ground. Wright was invited because of his position with the Municipal League and joined five hundred observers from around the country in the dawn chill outside Las Vegas for the test. All were provided with safety goggles. The papers reported on Wright's attendance, and the *Fort Worth Star-Telegram* asked him to write of his experience. "You gasp involuntarily and then gape in awed silence," Wright reported. "You watch the angry ball of flame churn in the sky for maybe seven seconds, then disappear in a boiling purple cloud that seems to foam and spill out over its own top."[56] These were not the normal experiences of a small-town mayor, readers must have known, but rather part of a portfolio of a man with greater responsibilities to come.

Everything spoke to a new chapter in Wright's life. Weatherford celebrated a renovated city hall, the *Weatherford Democrat* said, opining that the city was like a teenager "in that you can almost see it grow." Delegations from other towns arrived hoping to learn from the city's success.[57] In demand as a speaker, Wright was no longer a failed, one-term state legislator. He had an outstanding record as mayor. Experience had taught him the virtues of patience, hard work, collegiality, and consensus. One did not act emotionally or precipitously, but calculated every move and relied upon connections. Politics could be a brutal profession, but still could be quite rewarding. Wright was wiser—and believed himself ready. Texas's 12th Congressional District beckoned.

The district consisted of five counties, including Wright's Parker County. Given his background, Wright felt that he could compete in the four predominantly rural counties, but despite his birth in Fort Worth, the urban Tarrant County appeared problematic. The "Seventh Street Establishment," a group of powerful bankers, utility executives, and corporate titans, dominated as Fort Worth's version of a big city political machine. Its money and command of the media made its support crucial. At its head was the mag-nate Amon Carter, who had founded Texas's first radio station, WBAP, and owned both the state's first television channel, Channel 5, and the *Fort Worth Star-Telegram*. The latter was not the only newspaper in town, but its rival, the *Fort Worth Press*, had a much smaller circulation. Carter was a political kingmaker—and he appeared to have already settled on his king, the incumbent, four-term Democrat Wingate Lucas. Defeating Lucas, Wright knew, was no small order.[58]

Wright, however, was characteristically confident. Lucas "wasn't inartic-ulate," Wright recalled, "but I thought I was a better speaker."[59] Moreover, Lucas had bucked Democratic president Harry Truman, which irked many loyal Democrats. Lucas's stance was indicative of the conservative nature of the Texas electorate and the split in the Democratic Party, but Wright rec-ognized that Lucas had especially antagonized organized labor. He had supported the Taft-Hartley Act, which unions called the "slave labor bill," and had fought wartime wage controls.[60] In fact, years before, Willard Barr, the publisher of the periodical the *Labor News*, had tried to win Carter's support for the candidacy of M. M. McKnight, a union printer in Carter's paper and a member of the Central Labor Council. The two had worked well negotiating company contracts. With McKnight thinking of running, Barr had gone to Carter's office to ask for his support. "I couldn't do any-thing like that," Carter had stated, adding awkwardly, "I ask nothing of [Lucas]." In the end, McKnight decided not to run, but Wright knew that labor still sought a champion.[61]

As the 1954 election approached, Jim Greer began to press Wright to run. Greer had a background in public relations and was a member of the liberal Tarrant County Social and Legislative Conference. He had free-lanced for Barr at the *Labor News* and was exasperated with conservative Democrats. He had first met Wright at a labor-organized charity and had quickly recognized his positive attributes.[62] Greer and his wife began visit-ing with Wright on Sunday afternoons Around the same time, a group of liberals, including Barr and Jack and Margaret Carter, met with Wright for lunch in Weatherford. Wright, Barr recalled, "was a little hesitant about tackling the establishment," and worried about integration in the wake of the Supreme Court decision in *Brown v. Board of Education of Topeka, Kansas*. Although African Americans would surely oppose Lucas because of his conservative "Dixiecrat" connections, Wright understood that cham-pioning civil rights too prominently risked alienating the district's many conservatives. "I might be on the losing side," Wright stated. He left the luncheon with a promise to mull over a candidacy, but called several days later to announce that his hat was in the ring.[63] In the interim, he had won the approval of Mab, who was aware of what it meant to him, and of his father, who had been reluctant about politics. "Maybe in his heart of hearts, Dad might have secretly hoped that I wouldn't win so that I'd come back and devote my energies more wholly to the business," Wright recalled, "but I doubt it." The constant encouragement from Weatherford's citizens was undoubtedly the most influential factor. With such support, Jim Wright was ready at last to fulfill his "ultimate ambition."[64]

The first step was a meeting of forty local ranchers and businessmen in a small room above Weatherford's chamber of commerce, a fundraiser that collected a "nest egg of twenty-six or twenty-seven thousand dollars." Wright announced that he would accept no contribution of more than $100, a pledge that took some fortitude, since the labor unions offered a huge $5,000 donation. He was beholden to no one, Wright told voters.[65]

He certainly was not beholden to Amon Carter. Citing a hectic schedule, Carter declined in a telephone call to meet with Wright. Wright, however, recounted that years before, Carter had gone to the home of a man who had refused to do business, waiting on his doorstep until he had relented. "Now, would you want me to do that?" Wright half-jokingly asked. Carter chuckled and the conversation ended amicably—but without Carter's support.[66]

When a supporter donated office space in Fort Worth's "Insurance Building," Wright had his headquarters. Although Wright officially had no campaign manager, Jim Greer agreed to serve as the campaign's only paid employee. Wright made virtually every major decision, although he was rarely in the office. The campaign employed a small travel trailer with a microphone and speaker, occasionally adorned with balloons. Wright campaigned ferociously, often working sixteen- to eighteen-hour days. Although this was again classic Jim Wright, the campaign was obviously dependent upon volunteers. Here Wright's collegiality and networking paid dividends. The lengthy list, enumerated in an office card filing system, included everyone from Weatherford schoolchildren to elite Fort Worth families.[67]

In addition to Barr, Greer, and Jack and Margaret Carter, prominent contributors included Fort Worth attorney Clyde Thomas, who focused solely on Tarrant County. In Parker County there was James and Jimi Bodiford, lifelong friends, while in Johnson and Somervell counties Louis Armstrong assisted. Among the massive Weatherford contingent were Jack Knox and George and Louise McCall. George Karaboom, a recent journalism graduate, helped with marketing, although Wright insisted on composing his own speeches. Bill Wills, a General Dynamics attorney and a would-be politician, submitted sixteen pages of suggestions. General Dynamics had just purchased the airplane manufacturer Convair, Wills noted, and Convair's Fort Worth employees were willing to help. Wright, he argued, should reach out to other large urban businesses as well. Behind it all remained Conrad Russell, who was still operating as Wright's political mentor. The campaign tried to organize female volunteers as "Women for Wright," but the effort floundered, lacking solid leadership.[68]

The advertising executive Julian Read was particularly helpful. With Wright adopting the slogan "A Congressman for All the People," Read helped cast the campaign as an epic battle between David and Goliath, the average working man against the wealthy Seventh Street establishment. Although it was a clear return to the populist playbook, the strategy also reflected Wright's persistent idealism. Even if he was hardly a naïve "Mr. Smith Goes to Washington" character, Wright did have a record of advocacy for open governance, campaign restrictions, and public morality. He did care about the common man. Read advised Wright that a tall, skinny newspaper advertisement was better than a short, fat one. Fridays were best, he explained, as the papers were thinner and people had more leisure time to read them. Clearly ahead of his time, Read recognized the depth of political marketing. Certain words turned off farmers, he explained, while others appealed to women. He guarded against any gaffe that might capture headlines. Wright was fortunate to have him.[69]

To officially launch his campaign, Wright optimistically scheduled a large fundraiser for the Fort Worth Coliseum. Used for rodeo and cattle shows, the facility was less regal than its name implied but could still host thousands of people. Fort Worth restaurateur Walter Aetpon agreed to cook barbeque for only a $1.25 per plate, "a silent campaign contribution," Greer later joked. In the end, over 1,200 people turned out, raising over $4,000. Although newspapers and television ignored it all, a radio station broadcast Wright's speech—one of his best—live.[70]

With this additional cash, Wright wisely turned to television, still a relatively new medium for politics. "I traveled around the area and found that about three out of five homes had TV antennas," Wright recalled. With only two stations for the district, a TV advertisement thus held tremendous potential. Rates remained remarkably cheap; a thirty-minute advertisement still cost only $520. Looking straight into the camera, a flag behind him, Wright spoke as though his audience were directly before him. To modern audiences, Wright's spots would appear more infomercial than political ad, more a discussion than a quick sound bite. But the script was largely his own. Wright had an announcer introduce him and ended with "God bless America."[71]

Looking back, Wright recalled, "TV was the key." Suddenly he had more volunteers and cash. People would remark with astonishment that he was the fellow on television. At the time, his opponents were slow to recognize Wright's momentum. Wright had aired most of his programs on Channel 5, the station owned by Amon Carter. Carter and Lucas simply thought Wright a long-shot and gave him little thought. Lucas did not want to give Wright additional publicity by addressing him directly. In a throwback to the nineteenth century, politicians still scheduled competing speeches together at venues throughout their jurisdiction. With television, Greer later noted, "they don't do that sort of thing anymore." Confident incumbents sometimes sent surrogates to speak, an obvious slight to their challengers. So it was with Lucas.[72]

All of this played to Wright's advantage. Not only was Wright invariably the better speaker than Lucas's surrogates, but he appeared to be unafraid of pressing the flesh with the common folk. He seemed, as one supporter put it, like "one of us." After each encounter, Wright would confer with his inner circle on possible revisions, a sort of "political war room." Wright's quick wit served him well. His message was always fresh, and he adapted it for each individual town.[73] Although he occasionally spoke about labor or water problems, more often it was about American pride and old-fashioned values.[74] "Why are we so rich?" he asked. "Isn't it because of the atmosphere of freedom?" America, Wright claimed, "was commissioned by destiny."[75] Wright's lifelong interest in foreign affairs and his fear of isolationism were evident, as was the larger Cold War zeitgeist. The 12th District's top priority, Wright informed one reporter, was "the same as every other district in America . . . to avoid an atomic war by winning the worldwide competition between Democracy and Communism."[76]

As the months passed, Lucas began to recognize that this small-town mayor was actually a real threat, which forced him to appear at the traveling debates himself. Soon the campaign was a "rough-and-tumble affair," in the words of one later account.[77] Lucas, reflecting a common Republican tactic, called Wright a tool of "corrupt labor bosses." He was part of a "left-wing conspiracy," an attack reminiscent of Eugene Miller and the ugly McCarthyism that had just begun to ebb with the Army-McCarthy hearings then unfolding nationally.[78] Wright had promised to run a positive campaign, but it was hard not to respond in kind. Wright had his temper and his goal appeared so near. Lucas, the Wright campaign replied—if not Wright himself—was an "ineffective" leader, a tool of a political machine who cared little for the common man. Downplaying Lucas's experience, Wright said that "Congress wasn't meant to be a lifetime job," an ironic statement in retrospect, given Wright's long tenure. Wright knew that politics was brutal, and he was going to do what it took.[79]

Still, however, Wright's charges paled in comparison to those of the Lucas campaign. Lucas drove the negativity, not Wright's responses. In one of the milder assaults, Lucas suggested that Wright had thought of the ministry only for political advantage.[80] In one of the more troubling instances, a member of the Fort Worth Chamber of Commerce threatened the husband of the chairman of "Women for Wright." The husband was a member of the chamber as well, Greer recalled, and the threat was blunt: "You know she really shouldn't be doing things like that. I am sure that you would like to keep your job here." The threat was also effective; the chairman promptly resigned.[81]

With the election only weeks away, Wright faced his most troublesome attack. The United States Postal Service suddenly charged that the National Trade Day Association was operating an illegal lottery through the mail. In fact, seven years before federal officials had dropped a similar complaint. Wright and his father had even signed an affidavit promising no violations. Now, however, despite the earlier vindication, Wright faced the same charge. It was a last-minute bombshell, an eerie replay of Wright's 1948 campaign for reelection to the state legislature. To a livid Wright, it all appeared to be too strange a coincidence. With all his dreams riding on the following two weeks, he worried that once again his campaign had been dealt an unfair but deadly blow.[82]

Wright had little time but fought back ferociously. If the NTDA were a lottery, Wright stated on television, why had it been operating so openly for so long? Why had the charges just appeared only days before an election that was increasingly close? The purpose of his business, Wright continued, was to "help small towns stay on the map." Keeping his own suspicions under wrap, Wright added that Lucas had "assured me personally that he knew nothing of these charges."[83] It was, in the end, another brilliant Wright performance. The televised reply tied the NTDA into his key small-town constituency. Noting Lucas's denial made Wright appear gracious while still implying a political motivation. It was brilliant politics, turning the charge to Wright's own advantage. In time, Wright's supporters concluded that Assistant Postmaster General Ben Will, a former Texas congressman and friend of Lucas, had instigated the charges while other congressmen tied to Lucas had called the attention of the press to them.[84]

Letters began to pour into Wright's campaign. "Of course this move was politically inspired," wrote one supporter. The charge was "sinful," said another.[85] People wrote that they knew Jim Wright, a fact that Lucas's campaign had not fully considered. Wright's efforts, after all, had made him a familiar character, and he was now difficult to paint as a crook or a radical. For the first time Wright appeared to have the momentum. In one of the dueling speeches that immediately followed the charge's publication, Lucas claimed that congressmen "should be beyond reproach," a comment that infuriated Wright's brother-in-law. "Jim," he whispered, "I wish you had slammed that suspicion down his throat." The following night, when Lucas repeated the comments, Wright did exactly that. "I agree with the distinguished gentleman that a congressman should be above reproach," Wright replied to sustained applause. "But I also believe that a congressman should be above casting suspicion upon his fellow man."[86]

The Wright campaign played its hand beautifully as the election approached. The owner of the Fort Worth Cats, a minor league baseball team, sought to attract people by inviting candidates to give speeches before the beginning of a game. The various campaigns were allotted seats that their supporters could purchase. One candidate running a long-shot campaign against Lyndon Johnson, Dudley Dougherty, found that he could not sell all his tickets. Moving smartly, Julian Read struck a deal. If Dougherty would let Wright dispense his excess tickets, Wright would help Dougherty get additional time. Dougherty agreed, and Read packed the crowd with Wright supporters. The deal helped Wright speak earlier, when people were ready to listen, and required Dougherty to speak last. By the time Dougherty spoke, the crowd was tired of the politicians and chanting for the game to begin.[87]

The Lucas campaign, meanwhile, continued to struggle. After Wright had repeated that he had turned down a large contribution, Lucas appeared on TV. "I demand to know who it was that came and offered Jim Wright that money to run against me," Lucas stated. "Was it the labor goons and racketeers, my fellow Texans? Was it the Communists?" Again the unsubstantiated charges did not play well. One of the last competitive speeches was in

Weatherford, Wright's base of support. Here, of all places, Lucas noted the Miller assassination from Wright's 1948 campaign. "I'll come to Weatherford but I am going to ask the sheriff to meet me at the county line," Lucas remarked, implying that Wright was a physical threat and complicit in Miller's death. The crowd promptly booed, a first for Lucas. Pressing his advantage, Wright then rose to defend his opponent. "We're a hospitable people here," Wright told the hecklers. "This is the congressman and we're going to show him the courtesy that we'd want to be shown if we were in his hometown."[88]

With Wright's momentum building, Amon Carter moved to save Lucas. For the longest time, Carter had largely ignored Wright, believing that anything that he or his newspaper might say would just give Wright publicity. Suddenly, however, three days before the election, the paper ran a front-page editorial criticizing Wright. Wright stood for nothing and voters had no idea what he would do, it said. "So far Mr. Wright has skirted the questions, or answered only in the vaguest of generalities," the editorial claimed. "Sure, he is for avoiding atomic war and winning the allegiance of the world's people for democracy. Who isn't? But does Mr. Wright have any formula, any well-defined ideas for bringing this about?"[89]

Wright was in Julian Read's Fort Worth advertising agency when he received word of the editorial, a fortunate location to respond quickly. Dispatching Read to the Star-Telegram's office to reserve space for his reply in the next day's edition, Wright sat down at a typewriter and began channeling his anger. The rebuttal, Wright recalled, "just spilled out of my brain."[90] Wright did not know if Carter would publish the rebuttal, and, sensitive from the constant personal attacks, clearly had to struggle to control his temper. Wright began by noting that he was paying for the response with $947.40 from his own pocket. "For you have at least met a man, Mr. Carter, who is not afraid of you . . . who will not bow his knee to you and come running like a simpering pup at your beck and call," he wrote. He continued by saying that he had thought Carter a "bigger man" than to engage in such "misrepresentation." After noting what he specifically advocated, Wright claimed to respect Carter and appreciate "the wonderful things you have done for Fort Worth." Nevertheless, it was "unhealthy for anyone to become too powerful." It was not good for democracy. "I will be your congressman just as I will be everyone's congressman," Wright concluded, but not "your personal private congressman." He would be "a congressman for all the people." Ending with his campaign slogan was a nice touch. Satisfied, Wright sent the draft with Read for delivery.[91]

The *Star-Telegram*'s advertising manager forwarded Wright's letter to its lawyer, Abe Herman, who, according to Wright, called the publisher at home. "Do you think his check is good?" Carter simply asked. Told that it was, Carter was brief: "Well, run with it then."[92] "People loved Amon," recalled one copy editor, but they also "loved the underdog." Carter's decision impressed his employees. "Amon didn't have to do that," one concluded.[93] Even Wright agreed. Publishing the letter, which took up three-quarters of a page, was "to Carter's everlasting credit." Wright's own staff thought that Carter would not do so, but "he was a bigger man than that."[94]

Writing the letter was the type of big, risky move that attracted Wright. Perhaps it was his temper, but for the moment he seemed to forget his campaign's cautious, calculated approach. It was three days before the election. With his momentum, Wright might have been able to ignore the editorial and still win. Now, however, the letter was a wildcard. Would Wright come off as too thin skinned and angry? "Just the effrontery of anybody to stand up against Mr. Carter, that just wasn't done," recalled Luther Adkins, a vice-president at the *Star-Telegram*. Don Kennard, a future state senator who was with Wright at the time, agreed. "We thought it was well-written," Kennard recalled, but "it was like throwing the dice."[95]

It did not take long to learn the results. Two days later, Wright beat Lucas by approximately 14,000 votes, winning well over 50 percent. "I don't think there is any question that [the Carter letter] was a very important element," concluded Julian Read. Wright thought otherwise. Lucas had won election eight years before campaigning as "just a country boy," Wright concluded. He had simply stolen that mantle from him. With his late personal attacks, Lucas had seemed like just another Washington politician. Wright had strong support from labor, farmers, African Americans, and his own townspeople. Teachers came out for him strongly, aware of his record in the state legislature and the fact that Lucas had opposed federal aid to education. Organized as Public School Teachers for Jim Wright, the group declared Wright's record on education "perfect."[96] Whether the last-minute letter was determinative or not, Wright was thrilled. The campaign had cost him $32,000, half of it from his own pocket. Wright heard about the returns coming in on the radio at the home of Conrad Russell, appropriately enough, who was hosting a victory party. Wright's family and friends were there, as was his minister. After the "momentary exaltation" when the race was called, the press began phoning. Still a bit afraid to admit to himself that he had won, Wright drove with Mab to Fort Worth, where his campaign had a party set up in the Hotel Texas. Perhaps afraid of jinxing himself, Wright had not prepared comments. For once in his life he was brief, simply thanking his supporters over and over as the crowd cheered. The media all wanted interviews, and, for a bonus, the *Star-Telegram* took his picture for the front page of the next day's edition.[97]

Letters of congratulation poured in. "I just wanted to say thanks for liberating us from the Republicans disguised under Democratic rule," wrote one man from Mineral Wells. It was good that the "turncoat Democrat" was out, added a woman from Weatherford.[98] All the letters from his hometown were special for Wright, most notably the many from city employees who had worked under him. In a bit of enjoyable irony, members of the Fort Worth Chamber of Commerce who had known Wright and his father wrote of their support, clearly not sharing the sentiment of the organization's leaders.[99] With no credible Republican to run in the general election, Wright was going to Congress. At the ripe old age of thirty-one, he had taken an important step toward reaching his ultimate goal, the Oval Office.

Within a few days of Wright's victory, Amon Carter's *Star-Telegram* wrote a new editorial offering to bury the hatchet and urging the new congressman to "hop at it in full force and good humor."[100] It was an amicable send-off and it dissolved any lingering animosity. True to the advice of his father, Wright cultivated a friendship with Carter and other Fort Worth power brokers, turning enemies into friends. After Carter died the following year, his son Amon Carter Jr. became a close personal friend of Wright's, even serving as chairman of the Wright Congressional Club until his death in 1982. As it turned out, Carter Sr. and Wright had a lot in common. Not only were they both charismatic, ambitious men, but they both left an indelible mark on Fort Worth and its surrounding counties. For almost half a century, Carter had dominated; now it was Wright's turn. The election was in many ways a symbol of the old order giving way to the new. It was a new chapter for Fort Worth and Texas's 12th Congressional District—and it was a new chapter for Jim Wright. Wright had prepared almost his entire life for this position. He was anxious to get started, and he had no intention of failing.[101]

PART II

Congress in an Age of Tradition

_____

CHAPTER 5

Learning the Ropes

THE NEW CONGRESSMAN (1954–1956)

Wright's family arrived in the nation's capital several weeks before the 84th Congress was scheduled to convene on January 5, 1955, but the task of settling into their new home was more than enough to keep them busy. Wright rented an apartment in a four-story townhouse near the National Cathedral, only two blocks from Massachusetts Avenue's stately Embassy Row—and a long way from Weatherford. A mosque was under construction nearby, and the diversity and density of people required some adjustment. As Wright prepared for his new job, his two oldest children, nine-year-old Jimmy and five-year-old Ginger, prepared for school. Even this was not easy. Only three months previously, the District of Columbia schools had become one of the first systems nationally to desegregate, and there had been instances of racial confrontation. The Wrights' decision to enroll the children in public schools, therefore, spoke well of their true attitudes on race. Wright later recounted dropping the children off on their first day and warning them that there might be African Americans in their class, a fact that mattered little to either child.[1]

Jim Wright's adjustment was arguably less problematic than the children's. Not only had the Democrats won back control of Congress in 1954, but seventy-two-year-old Sam Rayburn was set to return as Speaker of the House. The indomitable Rayburn, an institutional patriarch and one of the most effective Speakers in history, hailed from Bonham, Texas, just north of Dallas. Rayburn took special pride in his state and quickly took an interest in the young Fort Worth congressman, becoming, in Wright's words, a "conscious mentor."[2] Wright, moreover, had already cultivated his relationship with Lyndon Johnson, who was set to become Senate majority leader, and he knew other powerful congressmen as well. Among them were Texans Frank Ikard, who served on the powerful House Ways and Means Committee, and Jack Brooks, who was just beginning a four-decade congressional career.

The Democratic leadership certainly welcomed Wright. Wright, after all, had defeated Wingate Lucas, a prominent Boll Weevil. Named for a beetle that infested cotton crops, the original Boll Weevils were southern conservative Democrats who had resisted Franklin Roosevelt. By 1954, FDR was long gone, but the Boll Weevils were still known for breaking with their party leadership. In Wright, Rayburn now assumed, he had an acolyte and counterbalance. "It will be a pleasure to serve in Congress with you," Rayburn telegrammed the freshman, a thrill for Wright—just as Rayburn expected.[3]

Wright was fortunate in other regards. President Dwight Eisenhower was a Republican, but no ideologue. A moderate pragmatist who claimed to be liberal regarding people and conservative regarding finances, Eisenhower had no intention of dismantling the New Deal. "Should any political party attempt to abolish Social Security, unemployment insurance, and eliminate labor laws and farm programs," Eisenhower concluded, "you would not hear of that party again."[4] Willing to work across party lines, Eisenhower believed it was "impossible to do anything just by asking for the loyalty of your party."[5] Eisenhower's legislative liaison, Bryce Harlow, kept in close contact with both Rayburn and Johnson, and their discussions were often unknown to other party elders, part of what historian Fred Greenstein termed a "hidden-hand presidency."[6]

Wright later recalled that Rayburn insisted upon members of Congress accepting that their colleagues were always honest. Members might disagree, but they did not have to be disagreeable. Rayburn regularly invited Republican leaders such as Minority Leader Joe Martin to his golf outings. In fact, with a Republican House for two brief periods, 1947 to 1949 and 1953 to 1955, Martin and Rayburn had been switching offices as Speaker. Returning as Speaker in 1955, Rayburn let Martin remain in the larger office, a gesture Martin never forgot.[7]

In short, partisanship had hardly died, but with McCarthyism just beginning to ebb and the nation well into a period of prosperity, all the ingredients were present for a productive legislative session. Wright did not enter a gridlocked Congress. Although the party leadership could exert tremendous pressure, a rigid system of seniority still determined committee chairmanships. The rules invested tremendous authority in these chairs, who had little incentive to toe the party line and could carve their own legislative niches. Moreover, in the words of political scientist Norman Ornstein, the two parties "didn't have as strong fundamental principles as they do today."[8] "Every legislator faced two distinct seasons," one former congressman remarked, "a campaigning one and a governing one." Pollsters were not as omnipresent once governing began. Once elected, another former congressman recalled, "I had crossed a line from candidate and partisan to legislator."[9] The media was not as omnipresent as well, with much negotiation remaining behind closed doors. Wright had advocated open governance as mayor, but the lack of transparency allowed legislators to make agreements that blurred party allegiances. It put a premium on knowledge of parliamentary procedure, deal-making, and personal relationships. This all suited Wright, whose experiences had taught him the value of networking and consensus building.

Because of his long interest in internationalism, Wright pressed for an assignment on the House Committee on Foreign Affairs, and his preference was reported in the Texas media. Rayburn, however, advised otherwise. The House committee had less constitutional power than its Senate counterpart, he noted. With the important taxing and appropriations committees unlikely for a freshman, the best choice was the House Committee on Public Works. It had authority over highways, bridges, public buildings, and all forms of water reclamation. In short, the committee determined where federal money was spent and the jobs that resulted. This was true power, Rayburn explained, constituting negotiating leverage on virtually every issue.[10]

While there was some truth to critics' claims that the Committee on Public Works represented "pork-barrel" politics adding to the national debt, many projects were in fact desperately needed. Whether others derided the process or not, constituents lauded their own representatives for advancing their own interests. It was only pork barrel when the money went elsewhere, and bringing home the bacon promised reelection. Wright knew this. His efforts to improve Weatherford's infrastructure without incurring debt had made him a popular mayor. The same thing, he assumed, was possible at the national level. After all, if the money did not come to his district, it would go elsewhere. Wright claimed that he was "dumbfounded" when he first heard the term "pork barrel" applied to his committee. "Pork, hell," he replied. "That's bread and butter."[11]

Rayburn was correct, Wright concluded. The committee assignment did not have to be permanent, and Lyndon Johnson agreed. When Wright had remarked that a possible diplomatic appointment might offer a new career path, Johnson had rebuked him. It was better to make policy than carry it out. The seniority system required new members to be deferential and patient, and Wright did not want to repeat the same mistakes he had made in the Texas Legislature. Wright, therefore, set out to learn the protocol for long-term gain. He would work within the system. Ultimately, he commanded Congress by becoming a creature of it. This meant that early in his congressional years Wright was "not one for tilting at windmills," recalled Frank Ikard. Wright never went "way out front on anything."[12]

Wright put his leadership ambitions on the back burner and told the *Weatherford Daily Herald* that he was "very happy about . . . serving on the Public Works Committee." Watershed development and conservation was "vital in our state," he added. A quick study, Wright also noted that Arlington in his district needed a new post office. "I intend to do what I can for them."[13] Wright, with his desire for higher office paramount, did not know it, but he was embarking on a twenty-two-year tenure on the committee that made him one of the most prodigious providers of federal aid ever. By the mid-1980s, a Michigan State University study had ranked his district first among 435 in federal spending. By then Wright had the power Rayburn had predicted he would gain. He had greater exposure than most to the economic conditions and political attitudes throughout the country, and numerous state and federal officials approached him on a wide variety of issues. "I came in contact with others in a way that I wouldn't have otherwise," Wright later recalled, reflecting on how the committee had given him an entrée to national stature. "There's a lot of luck in politics," he said.[14]

This, of course, was all in the future as Wright waited for the congressional session to begin. With his office on the sixth floor of the Longworth House Office Building not yet ready, he worked out of temporary space that Ikard provided. A White House reception for new members was particularly memorable. "What a ridiculous costume," Wright, trying to hide his excitement, complained to Mab about the formal attire. President Eisenhower, Wright remembered, reminded him of his father. Born in Texas only six days apart, they shared "physical similarities, similarities in mannerisms, and were similar in the way they responded to questions." Wright was already inclined to work with the opposition, but the reception encouraged him. The similarities, Wright reflected, "were bound to have influenced my attitudes toward his policies."[15] Finally, five days into the new year, Wright stood in the well of the House with his family in the visitor gallery. Along with his new colleagues, he raised his hand and recited the oath of office. At the ripe old age of thirty-one, Jim Wright was, at last, a congressman.[16]

Wright's commitment to his constituents was apparent from the start. Given his district's going drought, Wright clamored for the Department of Agriculture to raise the production quota for cotton and the allotted acreage for peanuts. Claiming that quotas favored western ranchers, he lobbied for the appointment of a central Texas cotton farmer to the Agriculture Stabilization Committee. All such production limits grew from the New Deal, but when it came to his district, Wright was more prudent than ideological.[17] Making his first move for district funding, he requested expanded postal facilities for the city of Arlington.[18] When he was allowed a floor speech only weeks into his first term, Wright challenged the recommendations of the Truman-appointed Commission on Organization of the Executive Branch of the Government. The so-called Hoover Commission wanted to turn federal soil conservation programs over to the states. While expressing "sympathy" for conservatives—a conciliatory move—Wright argued that the transfer would prove "disastrous." He did not, however, mention that many farmers in his district feared cuts with state control.[19]

Given his position on the Public Works Committee, it was no surprise that so much of Wright's early work in Congress revolved around water and soil. Appearing before the House Appropriations Committee, Wright helped win an additional $5 million for the 1956 flood control budget.[20] He lobbied for dams on the Brazos River and for the development of the Trinity River watershed, which flowed through Fort Worth. The New Deal–era Trinity Development Plan, Wright told conservatives, was "unmatched" because it combined local, state, and federal jurisdiction. Working with the US Army Corps of Engineers to complete the mandated studies, he had begun a fight that would continue for years.[21]

Part of the resistance Wright faced emanated from Eisenhower, who sought to reverse the trend toward federal funding of reclamation projects with a "partnership" of government and private industry.[22] With the secretary of the interior, Douglas McKay—"Give Away McKay" to liberals—implementing the plan haphazardly, and with the overall budget cut, hopes for funding rested on the merit of individual projects and the abilities of their congressional backers. To this extent Wright's position on the Public Works Committee was key, even if he still faced strong headwinds. Wright admired Eisenhower and sought consensus, but the winds still promised a storm.[23]

The winds were at his back regarding tariffs. Not only did Wright and most other Democrats favor free trade, but Eisenhower did as well, bucking the protectionist Republican Old Guard. Arguing that lower tariffs encouraged peace, Wright supported the White House's efforts to renew the Reciprocal Trade Act of 1934, which gave the executive branch greater control. Wright, predictably, worked for consensus, appealing to conservatives by suggesting that lower tariffs meant less need for foreign aid, and trying to be conciliatory by acknowledging merit in their position. The tactics worked. Congress passed a compromise one-year extension.[24] When this extension came up for renewal, Wright tacked for his own political cover. To assuage the complaints of labor, he proposed higher wages for workers in exchange for free trade. Although it was an imaginative, if unrealistic, proposal even as the new extension passed, it demonstrated that Wright was learning the ropes.[25]

Wright took the low-hanging political fruit, proposing legislation that weakened reporting requirements for churches to maintain their cheaper postage. Wright argued that there was "no real logical reason for denying the churches the same privilege" afforded other nonprofits. His bill appealed to the conservative religious element in his district while proving difficult for most congressmen to oppose. When the bill passed, Wright had a legislative accomplishment for his first session of Congress that had cost little and won goodwill among many.[26]

Wright's chance to impact foreign policy came early when a dispute arose between Chairman Mao Zedong's People's Republic of China (PRC) and Chiang Kai-shek's Nationalist Chinese government, which had recently been forced onto Formosa, now Taiwan. Both claimed the islands of Quemoy and Matsu. The United States had a treaty with the Nationalists, but the question of congressional support for a possible Eisenhower military intervention remained open. Eisenhower argued for a show of support as a deterrent to the PRC, and Rayburn promised a majority for a legislative blank check. "I am with the President," Wright declared, believing a show of American unity important.[27] He was not alone; the Formosa Resolution passed the House 410–3. It was an easy victory, and perhaps not surprising, given the prominence of the Cold War, but it set a precedent and foreshadowed the Vietnam War's Gulf of Tonkin Resolution a decade later. It was also an issue that would bedevil Wright later in his career when the relative roles of the legislative and executive branches in foreign policy became more convoluted.[28]

Wright's stance on the Formosa Resolution was instructive. Having seen war firsthand, Wright believed that his foremost objective was the maintenance of peace, underscoring his long-held faith in internationalism and diplomacy. At the same time, however, Wright, like many of his generation, took from his experiences the necessity of standing up to aggression. As a result he was an ardent Cold Warrior and an advocate for military preparedness. An outspoken critic of communism, he shared a relatively uncritical view of America's historical role globally. In one early speech, for example, he praised Cuba's "irresistible urge for self-government and national self-expression" in the Spanish-American War, forgetting the powerful American economic self-interests that had also been at play.[29] Wright supported a rigid form of containment, but agreed with the initial architect of containment policy, George Kennan, that economic development was as critical as military might. Wright, for one, supported the famous Marshall Plan. He sought military power but publicly refuted bipartisan calls for preemptive strikes as a means of defense.[30] In short, Wright truly believed in accord through reasoned dialogue, but, as his approval of the Formosa Resolution indicated, a more complex amalgam of reason and emotion frequently informed his specific positions.

In his first few months Wright set the mold for his early career. He catered to his constituents. He had clear liberal leanings and a faith in the federal establishment, but he also recognized the potency of the conservative critique, which tilted him toward moderation. Favoring bipartisanship, he sought consensus in domestic affairs. In foreign affairs, he had faith in Eisenhower's executive leadership and shared the dominant ethic of the day.

As the 84th Congress progressed, Wright's position on the Public Works Committee placed him at the center of some of the decade's most important developments. With the problem of water pollution only beginning to become apparent in the 1950s, the matter fell to the existing committee structure in Congress.[31] Because of its role in water development, the Public Works Committee took the lead. Policymakers, as historian Paul Milazzo has noted, interpreted pollution as "a national water resource problem." It exacerbated already limited supplies and threatened economic growth.[32] Not only did committee members relate water quality to quantity, but a broader jurisdiction promised the autonomous committee chairs more power. The elderly Charles Buckley of New York was not such a strong chair, leading the Committee on Public Works, but Minnesota Democrat John Blatnik more than filled the void. Blatnik, Milazzo concluded, worked to "recast the issue in the more familiar New Deal mold of government-promoted resource development," and thus to combat Republican efforts to devolve regulation to the states.[33] Wright certainly welcomed the augmented power, but he knew from his experiences in Texas the importance of clean water. Water pollution, he argued, was an issue of "over-riding national importance." Effective sewage control was an "urgent necessity."[34]

Accordingly, Wright supported legislation to expand federal authority originally granted in 1948. The proposal offered states additional grants for the construction of waste treatment centers and provided for federal enforcement of industrial polluters in interstate waters. Water pollution, Wright explained, was a "national disgrace."[35] To calm conservative worries, he noted that federal funds required a state match, and state health officials had to approve all projects.[36] Such arguments carried the day, and when Congress passed the Water Pollution Control Act Amendment, Wright fairly took some credit. Wright's advocacy gave him an early claim for environmental stewardship.[37]

The issue of water quality was actually more complex than the 1956 legislation suggested, however. In fact, water resource development did not always equate with environmental quality, as reclamation projects frequently altered fragile ecosystems. When preservationists complained that a proposed dam at Echo Park on the Upper Colorado River would flood the scenic Dinosaur National Monument, Wright found himself in an uncomfortable position. Opponents sent him a picture book of the park's beauty, while proponents appealed to partisan loyalty. Defeat of the dam proposal, they wrote, would have a "great bearing on the future of the Democratic Party here in Utah."[38] Weighing his options, and undoubtedly glad that the debate was centered more in the House Committee on Interior and Insular Affairs than in the Committee on Public Works, Wright still left no doubt where he stood. Describing objections as "propaganda," he noted that California had piped Colorado River water for years. He mocked Californian Craig Hosmer, who had sent each congressman Echo Park clay and argued that since water dissolved it, the water was undrinkable.[39] In this instance, Wright's arguments did not carry the day. It was a statement on the growing influence of environmentalism, a statement that Wright surely noticed.[40]

If the water-quality debate spoke to the future, so did a proposal for a system of federal interstate highways. Despite the idea's Democratic origins in the New Deal, Eisenhower was an early convert, appointing General Lucius Clay to lead an investigatory panel.[41] The Clay report reached Congress just as Wright took his oath of office. The report called for a ten-year construction program financed with $24 billion in bonds, which would be retired in part by a federal fund drawn from gasoline and tire taxes. Resisting bonds, Democrats advocated greater taxes on the trucking industry, among other users. When the Clay proposal came before his committee, Wright protested that Clay's taxes did not cover all the costs and would increase the national debt, a complaint popular back in Texas.[42] "People have howled for years about the Roosevelt spending program," Wright wrote home.[43] When Tennessee senator Albert Gore and Maryland representative George Fallon introduced an equally massive Democratic alternative without the bonds, Wright offered his own bill for $750 million annually, a level Wright said the nation could afford.[44]

The debate continued into 1956. Still arguing that the other Democratic alternatives were "excessive," Wright insisted that the government was overpaying for a mile of road construction. Interstate highways were desperately needed, he said, but the government still needed to be a good steward of the people's money.[45] Lobbyists were "like a swarm of bees around an overripe melon." It was the first time Wright had felt such pressure, and it was exhausting. "We've heard from everybody but one fellow," Wright stated, "the average fellow who actually does most of the driving and will pay the great bulk of the costs."[46] Wright was empathetic but less than persuasive. After the Committee on Public Works requested an audit of the proposal's cost, the Federal Bureau of Roads supported the larger $25 billion estimate.[47]

If Wright had little luck reducing the scope and costs of the proposal, he did help to persuade Eisenhower to abandon a bond issue, which was something most Republicans still supported. Wright and Iowa representative Fred Schwengel complained to Rayburn about the bond, who agreed. "In time of war or depression, we have to go into debt," Rayburn told the two, "but not now."[48] When Rayburn arranged for Wright and his allies to meet with Eisenhower, Wright was as nervous as "a hotdog on a bun." If user taxes were expansive enough, Wright told Eisenhower, a highway trust fund could pay not for bonds but for construction as it proceeded—a "pay as you go" trust fund. "Gentlemen, if you think that you can sell that to the American people," Eisenhower responded, "you have my blessing."[49] Eisenhower realized that the Clay proposal would never pass with Democratic objections, and he wanted a bill before the coming election. After the meeting, he instructed his party colleagues to "yield to Democratic insistence on financing." The GOP should not oppose a popular highway system in an election year.[50]

The pressure worked. The Federal-Aid Highway Act of 1956, "the greatest road building program in history," according to historian Piers Brendon, provided for $25 billion in construction funded entirely through Wright's pay-as-you-go trust fund.[51] Gasoline and user taxes went up, but the massive project ultimately employed thousands and proved an economic incentive. It literally changed the way Americans lived. Wright still thought the cost excessive, but by the end of the decade he had come to recognize that even the sums allocated were insufficient. The cost of materials had risen more than expected, and the task of building urban roads had become more complex than imagined. While the slowing construction worried Wright, he successfully defended the program's self-funding system. The entire episode was a huge success and one of his greatest contributions early in his career. Wright took pride in his accomplishment and became prickly when others glossed over it. "It is somewhat surprising to me that you were not already aware of the efforts I extended in this direction," Wright replied to one constituent. "I suppose it just goes to show that the old axiom is correct which says that it doesn't make any difference how hard a congressman works on legislation, he must keep reminding the public of it."[52]

As the 1956 election approached, Wright did not always agree with the most strident liberals, but he remained a team player. He lobbied to raise the minimum wage and supported public power for New York's Niagara Falls, a position that one critic called "creeping socialism."[53] Wright introduced a bill to place postmasters in the competitive civil service to remove patronage. "The average American," he explained, "has nothing but contempt for the spoils system."[54] Liberals welcomed the proposal, because civil servants had greater protections, making it more difficult for conservatives to diminish the federal bureaucracy. Eisenhower certainly did not like it. The way to get rid of a Democrat, he joked, was to "transfer him around until he's sick of it."[55]

Wright was certainly a team player in regard to taxes. The year he entered Congress, the nation still had high marginal income tax rates to reduce the wartime debt. Conservatives had pressed for reductions, but Eisenhower, worried about the debt, cautioned moderation. Spending cuts had to match revenue reductions. Few suggested, as became common during the 1980s, that tax cuts produced sufficient revenue increases to pay for themselves.

The debate centered more on the size of possible cuts and who would receive them. In 1954, Republicans had enacted tax reductions, but liberals protested that the cuts were too large and favored the wealthy. With each side accusing the other of fiscal irresponsibility, Wright joined with his Democratic allies to propose a flat $20 per dependent income tax reduction, a plan they argued was manageable given the debt and helped the average American. The Republicans, he stated, had "rammed through billions in tax reductions for their special friends" and still sought massive decreases in corporate taxes.[56] With an election-year stalemate looming, Wright told one group that it was better not to reduce rates than to adopt the Republican alternative. "Eighty-four percent of the budget goes to the task of paying off past wars," he noted.[57]

As the election approached, Wright remained popular in his district. Whenever tilting to the political left, he protected his right flank. When he joined liberals demanding increases in federal aid for education, he sought guarantees "that not even a modicum of federal control will accompany federal aid."[58] When he stressed the virtues of individual initiative, he also praised the value of collective action.[59] While he largely sided with the liberals on spending and taxes, he regularly touted states' rights. It would "only be a matter of time," he stated, "until state governments will be deprived of practically all legislative initiatives." Wright supported a proposal by Virginian Howard Smith to declare the rights of states to enact laws similar to those of the federal government so long as Congress had not specifically established federal preeminence in the field. Implicit was the chance that such state laws might run counter to the federal ones. "It is not a reactionary doctrine," Wright insisted.[60]

Many of Wright's proposals transcended partisan lines. The Electoral College, for example, had been "outgrown by the American people," Wright argued, failing to mention that its elimination might favor larger states like Texas.[61] Continuing his populism, Wright advocated campaign reform to diminish the role of large corporations. He supported limits to campaign donations but also tax deductions for modest contributions by the average citizen.[62] Wright, moreover, asked the Justice Department to investigate the US Trust and Guaranty Company for possible mail fraud. The company, he complained, had lost the savings of thousands of Texans by, in part, misrepresenting its investments.[63] As Wright surely knew, it was tough to be against someone who advocated for good governance.

Wright genuinely believed in cooperation, but he also assumed that bipartisanship helped inoculate him against conservative attacks. He publicly praised Eisenhower, Rayburn, and Johnson as being responsible for the "national harmony," a tactic that also endeared him to each man. He lauded lawmakers of all stripes who were willing to work together "for the welfare of the nation."[64] The country was in great hands, he told constituents, fully aware that prosperity benefited incumbents.[65] Following his father's old advice, Wright worked to win over past enemies. When his old nemesis Amon Carter died, Wright eulogized him on the House floor, adding that his heir, Amon Carter Jr., shared his father's "unfeigned modesty."[66]

Wright crafted his appeal masterfully. He contributed a regular column to several newspapers, ostensibly to bring his constituents up to date on Congress, but also, of course, to explain his own positions. Likewise, he began a weekly radio address every Sunday afternoon at one o'clock. During the three-month congressional recess between the two sessions of the 84th Congress, Wright returned to Texas and gave an astounding 104 speeches.[67] When Parker County reached its centennial in 1956, he published a letter of congratulations in the *Weatherford Democrat*.[68] His name appeared in the newspapers constantly. When one constituent contracted polio while on active military duty, Wright joined with Lyndon Johnson to press the case as service-related, thus covering all medical expenses.[69] When a hungry Weatherford runaway turned himself in to Virginia police, Wright supervised the boy's return.[70] The newspapers had a camera ready when Wright visited a soup kitchen, and again when his secretaries began decorating his congressional office with native Texan plants. When constituents showed up at the Capitol, Wright often greeted them personally, releasing a picture for the hometown press.[71]

Wright knew how to win friends as well as headlines. Once, when Congress was debating a huge defense bill, Wright showed up in a full tuxedo. "I think we owe it to the taxpayer to dress for the occasion," Wright stated to bipartisan laughter.[72] When a colleague stated that a Soviet satellite country had no more right to be in the United Nations than the state of Texas, Wright joked that Texas had a better chance; it had the Texas Rangers to put down international aggression.[73] When word got out that Wright's office was distributing free maps of the United States, Wright laughed off the resulting flood of requests. "I hate to be a cheapskate," he joked, "but four dollars a throw can get kinda tiresome after a hundred times or so."[74]

Wright's now obvious skill in protecting his district's interests impressed his constituents the most. When budget cuts threatened his old military base, Fort Wolters, Wright lobbied successfully to keep it open.[75] When there was a ground-breaking ceremony for new construction, Wright was there—a boat factory in Weatherford, an electronics plant in Mansfield, the Brazos Power Plant outside Weatherford, a portion of the Trinity River Flood-way near Fort Worth, and, dating back to his days as mayor, the new Lake Weatherford.[76] When Dallas won funds for a new federal building, Wright received assurances that Fort Worth civil servants would remain employed. He also fought hard to keep a regional postal transportation facility from moving.[77] The Fort Worth Chamber of Commerce felt comfortable enough with Wright to make specific requests for him to "contact the proper offi-cials in Washington" when specific needs arose.[78] When it came to his district, Wright never missed the smallest detail, regularly responding to constituent letters requesting assistance. In several instances he helped constituents gain federal employment.[79]

Everyone soon recognized Jim Wright as an up-and-comer. When citi-zens of Weatherford nominated him for their Outstanding Citizen Award, Wright smartly declined in favor of someone "at the forefront of every worth-while civic effort." Modesty, Wright understood, was an attractive quality.[80] More substantively, the twenty-four-man Texas congressional delegation elected Wright its official secretary, a reflection of both his popularity and his legislative skill. Rayburn agreed, asking Wright to preside ceremoniously over the House in one of his brief absences. It was symbolic, of course, but symbolism in politics was powerful.[81]

It all paid dividends in the 1956 election. Announcing his intention to seek reelection, Wright noted that he had missed only two roll-call votes out of 192. The announcement won immediate endorsement from several local newspapers, an obvious disincentive to any potential challengers.[82] Wright also benefited in an unexpected way from the early announcement. When the Texas Democrats decided to charge a high filing fee of $4,500, Wright had the advantage of an incumbent. "I called a few friends of mine in the business community," Wright recalled, and the result was astounding, a total 27 percent more than what was required. Taking pen and paper in hand, Wright then calculated 27 percent from the sum that each contribu-tor had submitted and reimbursed them. "People laughed that it was the first time a politician had given anything back," Wright recalled, acknowl-edging that the reimbursements "helped establish my honesty." Not sur-prisingly, therefore, when the Democratic primary arrived in July, the only opposition Wright faced was a write-in campaign by an ardent segregation-ist, Bob Stuart, who had suggested that Texas should secede from the Union. "The people of Texas are in favor of segregation and I don't think Jim

Wright is," Stuart declared. Even if the racist Stuart was correct about Wright's true beliefs, Wright's public positions protected him, and not many voters shared Stuart's extremism. Stuart received only two hundred votes.[83] The primary was nevertheless memorable for Wright. Mab gave birth on Election Day to a second son, Parker Steven Wright. As the press noted that the boy's name "doesn't hold any political meaning," Wright beamed, a proud father of four facing no threat in the November general election.[84]

Characteristically, neither the birth of his new son nor his own secure position kept Wright from active campaigning in the 1956 election. In a testament to his popularity, speculation even grew that Wright might enter the race for the US Senate if the incumbent, Price Daniel, decided to run for Texas governor. While Daniel in the end did so, Wright's pragmatism overcame his ambition. The race "would take a lot of money," Wright noted, wisely deciding that such a run would be premature.[85] Wright jumped instead headfirst into the ongoing battle within the Texas Democratic Party. The governor, Allan Shivers, controlled the party apparatus, but he was so staunchly conservative that he had been listed on the 1952 ballot for governor as both a Democrat and a Republican, a practice that has since been abolished. With Shivers supporting Eisenhower over the Democrat Adlai Stevenson, Wright joined other Democrats in pressing for Lyndon Johnson to head the Texas delegation to the National Democratic Convention, in essence seizing control of the state's party. Praising his mentor in the *Congressional Record* and campaigning with him, Wright termed Johnson a "middle of the road Democrat" who could unite the party.[86] Wright later recalled that just prior to the Texas State Democratic Convention, Shivers had claimed that Johnson was a tool of the NAACP. Johnson's failure to reply had impressed Wright. "I am not going to die with that on my conscience," Johnson explained.[87]

Johnson's victory over Shivers and his subsequent domination of the state convention confirmed Johnson as a national contender. Still, the state convention broke down in fighting when Johnson threw his support for control of the state's executive committee not to the liberal Ralph Yarborough but to the moderate Daniel. When Johnson moved to unseat several liberal delegates, Wright fell in line, even supporting Johnson as a potential vice-presidential candidate. As the Texas Democrats battled, the vice-presidential nomination went to Estes Kefauver. Wright, like Johnson, was hardly despondent. Both men thought their positions wise; they were comfortably in the middle of a divided party.[88]

In retrospect, the "war among Texas Democrats," as one national magazine termed it, spoke to the future. With forced integration of public facilities just beginning to unfold, the issue of race promised to reshuffle the political deck.[89] Shivers's flirtation with the GOP was an early indication that many southern conservatives might take their allegiance elsewhere if, indeed, the Democratic Party moved leftward. In fact, Eisenhower had carried Texas in 1952, the first time the state had gone Republican in twenty-four years. Moreover, the Republican Bruce Alger had won the Dallas congressional district that year, becoming the state's only Republican representative. Wright recalled that every Wednesday, Speaker Rayburn met with the Texas delegation and, as a display of collegiality, invited Alger. When Alger broke the rule of confidentiality, however, Rayburn was outraged. With Alger "attributing bad motives," Wright recalled, "we banned Alger." Asked what he thought of his new Republican colleague, Rayburn was blunt. "I don't think about Alger," Rayburn snapped back. "He's a shitass."[90]

If the Alger incident was any indication, Rayburn's stated ideal of trusting every congressman and valuing compromise for the good of the nation was at risk. For his part, Wright's criticism of Eisenhower grew harsher as the November election approached. Never, however, did Wright get personal. His comments were never slanderous. Eisenhower, he suggested, had ignored the ongoing Texas drought. He had twisted Stevenson's positions.[91] Republicans were "servants of the privileged few." While claiming not to "cast aspersions on people's motives," Wright nevertheless came close. Eisenhower, Wright suggested, "wanted to repeal federal programs" because he appointed hostile administrators. "We have not had a nonpartisan government this term," he added. Wright knew that Eisenhower remained popular and tried to tie him to less popular Republicans. A vote for Eisenhower was "also a vote for the whole party."[92] Heading a campaign bus touring small towns in his district, Wright attended one fundraiser after another—but he never lost his sense of humor, which was good for donations. Asked if he thought the state should have voting machines, Wright quipped, "Definitely not. I think people ought to vote for themselves."[93]

In only one instance did Wright arguably go too far. He took the lead in publicizing the claim that Republicans were using the Internal Revenue Service to harass Democratic politicians. While Wright acknowledged that it was "congressional cloak room rumors," there was no evidence for the charge, and subsequent investigations found nothing untoward. Although there had been credible evidence of such foul play in the past, Wright should have remained quiet until he had proof. It was a small instance, but nevertheless cast the shadow of the type of politics Wright abhorred.[94]

Casting a long shadow over the end of the campaign was a crisis in Egypt over control of the Suez Canal. In what was later dubbed the Suez Crisis, the Egyptians seized control of the canal from the British and the French, who responded with an invasion that the United States thought unnecessarily provocative. Standing against traditional allies was uncomfortable for Eisenhower and held the potential for great criticism just as the campaign was reaching its culmination. Wright, however, had long valued the role of the chief executive in foreign policy and realized that in times of international turmoil Americans had always rallied around their commander-in-chief. Like most Democrats, therefore, Wright avoided criticizing the president.[95]

The election, on November 6, 1956, was, for Wright, a disappointment. Eisenhower won in a landslide, doubling his margin from 1952 and carrying more than 56 percent of voters. Wright remained sanguine, however, convinced that he had done all he could to support Adlai Stevenson's effort. He had faced no opposition in his own campaign, and he had done yeoman's work for Johnson and the national ticket. Both surely would prove useful for the future. Best for Wright, however, was the fact that Democrats had carried both houses of Congress. Now, he assumed, the period of partisanship would end, and Eisenhower would return to his moderate policies. Wright reflected little on the election. Before the year ended, he was telling the Texas media his plans for the 85th Congress. First on his list was a water transportation authority that would aid arid cities such as Fort Worth by supplying long-range water pipelines. Wright was back in form. Having only completed one term in Congress, he was looking toward the future with grand plans.[96]

———

CHAPTER 6

Building a Record

THE EISENHOWER YEARS (1956–1960)

Wright, it turned out, had reason for optimism. Just after the 85th Congress convened in January 1957, Eisenhower promised a bipartisan group of legislators that partisanship "will not move me one inch."[1] As Eisenhower promised cooperation, Illinois senator Paul Douglas told national reporters that Wright was a young congressman to watch. The magazine *Esquire*, meanwhile, included Wright on its list of America's notable "bright young men," and Democrats selected him cochairman of the Democratic National Committee Speakers Bureau. In the words of one Washington observer, Wright had already earned a reputation as "one of the more eloquent men on Capitol Hill." Wright's task was to line up speakers to support candidates, the perfect job for someone who wanted to expand his network of connections. By the end of the Eisenhower administration, one reporter neatly summarized the first six years of Jim Wright's congressional career: "Jim Wright," he wrote, "has arrived."[2]

At the center remained Wright's carefully crafted political persona as a man who was able to bridge divides, especially among the warring tribes of Democrats. While the Americans for Democratic Action, a left-leaning political lobby, listed Wright as one of the most liberal members of the

Texas delegation, with a "liberal quotient" of 75, the *Houston Chronicle* described him as "a middle-of-the roader."[3] Indeed, extolling the virtues of government even as he warned of it becoming "overly protective," Wright continued to campaign for both liberal and conservative Democrats.[4] He also continued to maintain friendships with Republicans, telling one group that "there's never been a time in history when we have so desperately needed unity."[5] Put simply, Wright's persona and modus operandi remained perfectly suited to the day.

Certainly the early months of 1957 made Wright's pleas for greater water resource management seem prescient. Still suffering from alternating extremes of severe drought and sudden floods, Wright's constituents never let their congressman forget that water was one of their foremost demands. The year began with a drought, for which Wright and the other Texans in Congress proposed a significant relief program for farmers and stockmen.[6] Wright fulfilled his promise to propose a water transportation authority and also proposed a program to help states finance long-distance water pipelines. The federal government would buy a portion of the bonds, while the Army Corps of Engineers would approve each project. Water, Wright exclaimed, was one of the nation's "most urgent domestic problems."[7] The debt financing proposal for pipelines, one newspaper reported, got an "enthusiastic response" and even attracted Lyndon Johnson, who introduced a similar bill in the Senate.[8] In the end, however, both of Wright's proposals faced stringent opposition and failed to pass. Expanded aid for farmers angered Secretary of Agriculture Ezra Benson, who questioned "the wisdom of a far-off political bureaucracy."[9] A modest package of drought aid passed Congress in 1957, but the following year, when Midwestern Republicans joined with a majority of Democrats to pass additional aid to farmers, Eisenhower sided with Benson and vetoed the measure.[10] As for the debt financing proposal, it smacked of California's Central Valley Project, which had not been able to sell all of its bonds. Many conservatives balked even as Wright's support among the Texans never wavered.[11]

As if to mock the continuing overall drought, a brief period of torrential rain in May 1957 brought severe flooding to parts of Texas. Appointed the head of a subcommittee to investigate, Wright and his colleagues took boats and helicopters to inspect the damage. With his blue suit soaked and photographers nearby, Wright wasted little time in using the disaster to back his call for more public works funding. "Without these flood control dams . . . almost all of Fort Worth would be under water," he claimed.[12] The subcommittee held a meeting in Fort Worth's federal courthouse and over one hundred citizens testified.[13] After returning to Washington, Wright received a handful of new hats from constituents who had seen pictures of a waterlogged Wright holding his own ruined hat. Wright quickly succeeded in winning funding to study the need for additional works along Fort Worth's Trinity River watershed.[14] When Congress turned to the larger fiscal budget, Wright supported much of the Hoover Commission's recommendations on trimming expenditures—except for those involving water and soil conservation. While denouncing the debt and wasteful spending, Wright declared that the conservation effort was "an investment."[15] Other congressmen whose districts had projects Wright opposed thought his position hypocritical, but Wright's own voters did not care. After praising Wright for his flood control efforts, one columnist wrote approvingly of his other cost-cutting proposals. To help Wright be more effective, he said, "let's demand that the budget be cut sharply."[16]

Wright remained relentless in his advocacy for his district. When, early in 1957, the United States Postal Service announced plans to move a regional transportation division from Fort Worth to Dallas, a "very upset" Wright led a protest rally in his city.[17] With partisan patronage hanging in the balance, he prevailed in this matter over the Republican representing Dallas in Congress, Bruce Alger. Not only did the regional office remain in Wright's district, but the postal facilities in nearby Arlington grew as well.[18]

Wright continued to help bring a flow of Washington money to the district, spearheading a new armory in Weatherford, a school in Burleson, additional flood control improvements on the Trinity and Brazos Rivers, and a number of other items, all in the first months of 1957.[19] He also won a new federal judgeship for the Northern District of Texas.[20] With the planning for the interstate system unfolding, Wright pressed for a highway to connect Fort Worth and Dallas, objecting, like Alger, to the possibility of tolls. "For once," Wright said, "Dallas and Fort Worth are united." Growth in the Dallas–Fort Worth metropolitan area, he correctly predicted, would far exceed the national average.[21] This growth, he also said, would continue to pour pollutants into his district's rivers. Accordingly, he proposed an additional $45 million for water pollution control. "Already," Wright stated, "streams which ran pure and fresh and clear have been reduced to corrupted cesspools." When Wright made these comments, it was still more than half a decade before Rachel Carson's bestseller *Silent Spring* would awaken the public to the problem of water pollution. And his comments on Dallas–Fort Worth growth were just as prescient as his comments on rivers. Wright was ahead of the national curve, and certainly ahead of the

Eisenhower administration. Pollution control, Eisenhower answered, was "strictly local in character."[22]

Returning to his legislative roots, Wright pressed for increased federal aid to education. He supported a school construction bill, a tax credit for teachers who continued their education, and greater emphasis on technology. Educators, Wright claimed, had not fully utilized television, "the greatest medium ever discovered." Columbia University professor Charles van Doren, Wright even suggested, should lead a federal program of instruction. Only later did Wright learn that van Doren, who had won fame by winning over $100,000 on the television quiz program *Twenty One*, had received help from producers.[23] When a Purdue University study noted a lack of civic knowledge among American youth, Wright publicized the results to make his case. "We'd all better get back on the track," he declared.[24]

The federal budget, the money necessary for all such activities, was, of course, one of the major issues that faced the 85th Congress upon its return. With the national deficit approaching $12 billion, Wright joined congressmen from both sides of the aisle in protest. "Everyone seems to agree," Wright noted.[25] In fact, it was a complicated issue. As Wright continued to insist that his proposals would grow the economy and were acceptable with cuts elsewhere, the White House's moderation drew the ire of fiscal hawks within his own party. Even Treasury Secretary George Humphrey predicted that a failure to make additional cuts would produce "a depression that will curl your hair."[26] Eisenhower clearly hoped that moderate Democrats, such as Wright, would rally around his budget, but Wright's own position remained controversial. As his constituents continued to praise him for his aid to their district, others claimed that he was hypocritical. "Unnecessary government spending is one of the major threats to our prosperity," wrote a bank president. "Has Uncle Sam become a confirmed spend-happy nation?" asked another writer.[27] Joining a group of bipartisan conservatives, and with the approval of the Hoover Commission on government reorganization, Wright supported annual accrued expenditure budgeting mandating that unused funds from previous appropriations lapse unless specifically authorized. This position burnished Wright's credentials as a budget hawk even as he continued to be relatively successful in winning his own allocations.[28]

To curb the national debt, Wright said, the military needed a central supply services administration. Eliminating duplication would save up to $1.2 billion per year without hampering military preparedness, he argued,

reminding critics that he had always defended robust military appropriations. Reform, he added, would prove difficult, however, "because of the
absolutely chauvinistic attitude so many of the career officers hold concerning the merits of their own particular service."[29] In the end it was indeed
challenging to sell the idea, but Wright was successful. The debate spurred
the Department of Defense to create the Defense Supply Agency, embodying in concept much of what he had proposed. For his efforts at cost cutting,
Wright even received an award from the Citizens Committee for the Hoover
Commission.[30]

Of course a growing economy was the best way to attack the national
debt, Wright argued. Noting that the Federal Reserve had raised interest
rates six times since he entered Congress, he suggested that the higher rates
increased the cost of living and thus stifled economic growth. Most economists and the Fed, however, believed that a liberalized monetary policy
would exacerbate inflation. More money in the system might prove an economic stimulus, but the even higher cost of living would destroy whatever
economic progress took place.[31] Wright did not specify how he might lower
inflation. "Hard money policy, initiated to halt inflation, has not done so,"
Wright stated simply. "Instead of deferring their spending, people have gone
right ahead and borrowed."[32]

In retrospect, Wright had a solid argument against the administration's
hard money policies even if his singular focus on borrowing appeared to
others to be too simplistic. The higher rates, combined with budget cuts, led
not to inflation but to growing unemployment. The higher cost of borrowing was hardly the sole cause of the economic slowdown that began early in
1957, as the natural economic cycle and the liquidation of inventories were
undoubtedly influential, but it did contribute. By early 1958, unemployment
reached 7 percent in what critics termed an "Eisenhower Recession."[33]
Democrats pounced, pressing for tax cuts and increased spending. Wright,
predictably, focused on public works, and the slowdown served as merely
additional ammunition. In this, at least, he appeared at first glance to be a
model Keynesian. In fact, however, he always denied that the term applied to
him. As his warnings about the 1957 deficit, his stance on interstate funding, and his earlier calls for budget cuts all suggested, Wright was too uncomfortable with the use of debt as an economic tool to be a true Keynesian.
He wanted to spend to aid a recovery, but he remained ill at ease with the
debt that such spending implied.[34]

The new Congress brought frustrations that went beyond the deteriorating economy and the growing debt. Developments in civil rights throughout

1957 kept Wright in the uncomfortable position of having to choose between personal belief and political pragmatism. He was willing to praise working women, unlike many conservatives, who were blaming working mothers for a degeneration in youth culture, but he continued to struggle with the rights of African Americans.[35] Wright had been fortunate to avoid much of the acrimony in his first term, although once, in 1956, he had faced a meeting of parents where one complained of "niggers in our schools." Caught off guard, Wright had replied with his true sentiments, speaking of Christian love, and noting the responsibility of citizens to obey the law. "The [Supreme] court has ruled," Wright stated, referring to the *Brown v. Board of Education* case. An awkward period of silence resulted before another questioner saved the day by asking Wright who would win the Southwest Conference football championship. "TCU," Wright quickly declared, aware that Texas Christian University was the crowd's favorite.[36]

Wright urged a "cooling off period" on integration, but other conservative Democrats pressed a "Southern Manifesto" denouncing the *Brown* decision as an "encroachment on rights reserved to the States." Wright at first showed the courage of his convictions, joining only nine other southerners who refused to sign the measure.[37] In time, however, the pressure built and Wright retreated. "I personally believe the Supreme Court erred in judgment when it said discrimination is inherent in segregation," he stated.[38] When New York's African American representative Adam Clayton Powell proposed denying funds to school districts that did not desegregate, Wright voted against the amendment. "You have to remember that there wasn't nearly as much federal money for education in those days," Wright later rationalized.[39] As Congress debated the school construction bill, Wright proposed an amendment declaring that it was not the "intent of Congress" that federal officials control local school districts. The amendment did not explicitly mention segregation, but with the civil rights controversy unfolding, southern conservatives supported Wright's efforts.[40]

Events had a momentum of their own. In Little Rock, Arkansas, Governor Orval Faubus openly refused to desegregate Central High School, claiming that it would ignite violence. Wright supported Eisenhower's subsequent decision to enforce the court order with troops, but he thought their number excessive, risking additional violence. "The President would have been better advised just to send in one marshal to escort the children," Wright later explained. Wright simply wanted to avoid the cutting edge of the sword. He denounced violence while declining invitations to lead rallies against the federal efforts. At the same time, however, he concluded, "I would have been a damn fool to push civil rights."[41]

Lyndon Johnson, now Senate majority leader, recognized trouble as well but was willing to take the lead. If southern conservatives continued to filibuster civil rights legislation, Johnson worried, African Americans would turn increasingly to the Republicans. Johnson, moreover, assumed that a legislative compromise would improve his shot at the presidency.[42] When the Eisenhower administration introduced a bill that provided for the Justice Department to prosecute in federal court people who denied the voting rights of African Americans, Johnson recognized an opening. Many southern conservatives demanded assurances that any legislation would deal solely with voting rights and not education, and that any prosecutions would take place only before juries. If Congress adopted these provisions, Johnson calculated, a civil rights bill might just pass. For his part, Wright joined with the conservatives in denouncing the absence of jury trials, insisting that a trial before one's peers was fundamental. "In states like Texas," Wright remarked, "this fundamental right has been accepted in practice as well as history." What Wright did not state, but his constituents undoubtedly knew, was that African Americans were frequently denied service on juries. In the end Wright assumed that his position advanced civil rights while still muting conservative criticism.[43]

It was still not easy. As the diehard segregationists in his district lobbied him, his mentors, who had done so much for him, wanted him to vote for the compromise. It was the give-and-take of politics, and it was Wright's turn to give. Rayburn was certainly persuasive. After sending a page to summon Wright, Rayburn told him, "Jim, I think you want to vote for this bill." Wright should ignore the angry chorus and "in the future years you will be proud that you did."[44]

Wright did vote for the Civil Rights Act of 1957, the first civil rights legislation since Reconstruction, later concluding, "I am proud of having done so."[45] Although the final bill was a shadow of its original, a "sham" to some liberals, a fact Wright conveniently left out of later recollections, it was still symbolically important. It set a precedent for the preeminence of the federal judiciary in civil rights. While the law created a Commission on Civil Rights with little enforcement power, it could still document data concerning illegality. Although the law allowed juries in criminal cases, it did prohibit them in some civil matters. The Justice Department's small civil rights section grew. Overall, Wright did have some cause for pride. Civil rights had advanced, and he had further endeared himself to the powers-that-be. He had also, however, once again protected his right flank.[46]

As Wright weathered Washington's political storms, changes took place back in Texas. The Texas Legislature passed a redistricting bill that gave Fort Worth its own congressman, effectively splitting Wright's district. With his Parker County home now in the 17th District, Wright announced that he would move to Fort Worth. The move would allow him to retain his seat and avoid a contest with another incumbent. This meant, of course, that he had to sell his beloved Weatherford home, not an easy task with Wright tethered to Washington. Mab took the lead, and Wright insisted only that any new house be on high ground, because of the chance of the Trinity River flooding again. The result was a new home in Arlington Heights, a nice section of town near the upscale River Crest community. "I loved the new home," Wright recalled. He promised not to forget Weatherford, which "would now have two congressmen."[47] The reality remained, however, that the Wrights were effectively citizens of both Washington and Fort Worth, and the commute between them was becoming increasingly frustrating. When Congress was in session, the Wrights lived in Washington; otherwise they lived in Texas. In Washington they had moved from their initial rented apartment near the National Cathedral to a suburban house in Arlington, Virginia, which they leased from an Italian air force colonel. Wright recognized the status quo as untenable. Uprooting their children was growing more difficult each year, and home ownership in the DC area made more sense than renting. Satisfied that he had positioned himself well politically, in 1957 Wright purchased a new home in Arlington County, Virginia. There they would live year round, and the Fort Worth home would become a necessary but secondary abode. The house had two stories, cost $25,000, and came complete with a basement, an amenity that the Texan Wrights found unique.[48]

Amid all the changes, Wright was fortunate to have a dependable staff. His Washington office had approximately eight employees, and his Fort Worth office had several more. Leading the lot was Wright's chief of staff, Craig Raupe, a former Weatherford College history professor. "We worked virtually twenty hours a day," Raupe recalled, "and it was hell on family life." Wright expected from his staff the same dedication he himself displayed, but Raupe recalled that "Jim never asked us to do anything he did not do." Wright's temper could explode, but he always appreciated his staff—in one instance he devoted almost an entire newsletter to their "skill and dedication." In the days before computers, Raupe maintained a card filing system of Wright's connections—never an easy task—and did all the hiring. His most notable assistant, Kathy Mitchell, stayed with Wright his entire career.[49]

As Wright jumped from one issue to another, and from one home to another, he lost ten pounds, but not his sense of humor. When his son Jimmy asked what "checks and balances" meant, Wright quipped, "Write too many checks and you haven't got any balances." Jimmy was a handful—at one point, he announced he was a Republican.[50] If Wright was hoping for more time between congressional sessions to spend with his family—to turn Jimmy around or otherwise—he was hoping in vain. In late 1957 he received orders to report for three weeks to the Middle East. Still an Air Force Reserve captain, Wright did not complain about missing his family, however, but instead spoke of a "splendid opportunity" to "make me a better congressman."[51] Wright undoubtedly understood that the trip would burnish his foreign policy credentials and allow him to write of his experiences in the *Fort Worth Star-Telegram*. Turkey reminded him of West Texas, he wrote. Morocco was important strategically, and the Italians were firm American allies.[52]

In retrospect, Wright might have wished for additional time at home. Only weeks after he came back, tragedy struck. Days before Christmas in 1957, his seventeen-month-old son, Parker Steven, who suffered from Down syndrome, began to have respiratory difficulties. At the time, Mab was in Washington's Providence Hospital for another matter, and it was left to Wright to get help. With his other children in tow, he drove to the same hospital where Mab was. Sadly, Stevie died only hours later. Wright had to tell the other children, and the family knelt to pray in the hospital parking lot. Stevie was buried in Washington, and more than a dozen of Wright's colleagues attended the ceremony. Mab was "disconsolate," Wright recalled. The death was "the hardest blow I've ever had," he said.[53] For Wright, the best consolation was work. The new session of Congress beckoned.

The new year brought much to distract Wright from his grief. In October 1957, the Soviets had launched Sputnik 1, the first manmade satellite, shocking Americans and suggesting a national deficiency in science. According to the *Washington Star*, the "atmosphere was urgent" as the new congressional session convened.[54] Despite the loss of his son, Wright moved quickly to take the lead, proposing legislation to spend $75 million annually on a program to stimulate secondary school science. Taking a cue from the Future

Farmers of America, Wright termed his proposal the "Future Scientists of America." It was "a red hot idea," in the words of one commentator, a view shared by many.[55] Wright's office reported "scores of letters" that approved. With bipartisan support, the only resistance Wright received was from a minority of voters who still feared a federal takeover of education. When one high school student admonished Wright in this vein, Wright instructed the boy to "be a little kinder in your appraisal of others." Cooperation and collegiality were important in politics, Wright reminded him.[56]

By April, the bill had received approval from the House Committee on Education and Labor, where Wright testified that without improvements, "complete scientific mastery could lie in the hands of a godless colossus."[57] Although he was being a bit hyperbolic, Wright's comments adequately reflected public sentiment. By August, the House had passed Wright's proposal and Lyndon Johnson had agreed to press the matter in the Senate.[58] When Eisenhower signed the resulting legislation in September, Wright had only one regret. His proposal had been incorporated into a broader bill termed the National Defense Education Act, denying Wright full authorship. His time would come, Wright assumed; seniority had its perks.[59]

Wright took every opportunity to indulge his interest in foreign affairs, consistently encouraging diplomacy. His idealism was intact, even if his commitment to anticommunism and a strong military never wavered. "Be ye therefore wise as serpents and harmless as doves," Wright said, quoting the Bible, although without explaining how his militarism related to the passage.[60] The United Nations, he suggested, should become more involved in the Middle East. Lebanon was a "possible springboard for aggression." Wright still had little patience for isolationists. "If we are to win in the long run," Wright explained, referring to Palestinian nationalists, "we must show them that we sympathize with their desire for dignity and economic betterment."[61] In budget negotiations, Wright sought more money for "mutual security," wisely avoiding the more controversial phrase "foreign aid," and applauded Eisenhower's role in the creation of the Southeast Asia Treaty Organization and the Central Treaty Organization.[62]

Wright still believed that the president, the designated commander-in-chief, deserved considerable leeway in international relations. "When he speaks to the world for America," Wright concluded, "he speaks for me."[63] Congress had a role to play in oversight and funding, but a united front internationally was vital. Such views were easy for Wright to maintain—at least in the 1950s. He respected Eisenhower's experience and stated policies. When the administration dispatched Richard Nixon to South America

only to meet viole·
vice-president ⊦
crats, but al·
met with
nucle·
far

Wright was at the airport to welcome the
.ad used the term "traitor" to define Demo-
ented the country. A few months later, Wright
Worth. Wright supported Eisenhower's buildup of
.e so-called New Look policy—even though he was no
State John Foster Dulles, its primary architect. "Mutu-
struction," Wright later recalled, "probably helped somewhat
e détente." Eisenhower, at least, "was no warmonger." Wright
ned with the administration on defense budgets but still insisted
isenhower deserved the right to appoint his own foreign policy advis-
. "I thought he certainly must be better informed than I," Wright recalled.
While others criticized Eisenhower's ill-fated "Open Skies" proposal with
the Soviet Union, Wright supported it. Mutual surveillance of nuclear facilities suited Wright's idealism and, once again, he trusted Eisenhower.[64]

The leeway Wright granted the executive in foreign affairs increasingly
contrasted with his defense of Congress in matters of overall authority. In
fact, more secure in his seat, Wright was quicker to defend the legislative
branch when he thought the judicial or executive branches had encroached
on it. While Congress "was closer to the people," Wright argued, its powers
had been in a "state of gradual decline." Wright's mentor, Rayburn, had
claimed that he served "with" presidents not "under" them, and Wright
thought the same way. In time, Wright would find his ideas about the balance of powers between the branches of government troublesome—even in
matters of foreign affairs. He would serve for decades after Eisenhower had
departed, after all, and Wright's own long-standing interest in world affairs
would not always easily mesh with the ideas of Eisenhower's successors.[65]

Wright's position on the Public Works Committee afforded him a strong
say on a project that both asserted congressional rights and jibed with the
Eisenhower administration—the Inter-American Highway, a joint project
with several countries to build a road 3,351 miles from Texas to Colombia,
South America. Construction had begun in 1941, but Wright quickly became
the strongest advocate for continued funding. It would improve the economy to the south and help contain communism, Wright argued. The project
combined his interest in the Southern Hemisphere with his defense of congressional prerogative, his idealism, and his stout anticommunism.[66] "The
highway comes as near as any other [public works project] in combining our
economic and foreign policy interests," Wright insisted.[67] In the fall of 1958,
Wright flew to Central America to inspect the progress, meeting with leaders and reporting none of the anti-Americanism Nixon had encountered.[68]

Wright had brushed up on his Spanish—later laughing that he "didn't have over a hundred words in my vocabulary"—and was scheduled to give a speech to the Costa Rican Congress; the speech, however, was canceled after the unexpected death of a prominent Costa Rican politician.[69]

His idealism aside, Wright understood that many Americans were ambivalent about their southern neighbors. The Eisenhower administration, for example, supported the Inter-American Highway but also implemented an overtly unfair immigration policy. "Operation Wetback"—a telling name— clamped down on immigration in a way that broke apart families, even deporting legal residents. Wright never commented on the program, either deferring to the administration or simply unaware of the program's impact. He applauded passage of funding for the Inter-American Highway but otherwise kept his comments general. The Southern Hemisphere and immigration were both vital for America's future, he noted. If the Mexicans should learn English, Wright once stated, "we are going to have to do the same thing and learn Spanish."[70]

Both Wright's idealism and his views on racism were evident when, in 1958, the territories of Alaska and Hawaii applied for statehood. As Wright well knew, the issue was complicated. Many Republicans feared Alaska would vote Democratic, or, like Eisenhower, worried that it would prove a financial burden. Many conservative southern Democrats, meanwhile, thought it unwise to approve statehood for either territory. Alaska would probably prove pro–civil rights, while Hawaii would become the first state with a nonwhite majority. When legislation arose to admit both territories simultaneously, Wright supported the measure even as the Democratic leaders Rayburn and Johnson did not, fearful of dividing their party. When this bill failed, Alaska moved to force Congress's hand, declaring itself a state and holding elections, a gambit that Tennessee had pulled off successfully at the end of the eighteenth century.[71] As the Democratic leadership began to sway in favor of statehood, sensing two new Democratic states, Wright argued that Alaskans did not enjoy self-determination, and that they had to pay taxes and could be drafted but did not have voting rights or representation. "It should be a matter of great pride," he said, that people wanted to join the union. In his newsletter, Wright asked bluntly, "Do we as a nation really believe what we professed as a nation 182 years ago?"[72] Such comments impressed the territorial governor of Alaska, Ernest Gruening, who declared Wright's speech "the best and most persuasive address ever heard in support of statehood."[73] At least one of Wright's constituents agreed, writing, "We have been far too slow in keeping our promises."[74]

Suddenly, Wright had a pivotal role to play. Late one night, Hawaii's nonvoting congressional representative, John Burns, called Wright at home and stated that he had heard that Johnson planned a floor speech the following day supporting the Alaska bill. Would Wright, Burns asked, contact Johnson and get him to insert into his speech a promise to pass a Hawaiian statehood act the following year? It would win Hawaiian support for Alaska's admittance. Wright agreed. He told the majority leader that it was both the right thing to do and advantageous politically. Johnson had already warmed to the idea of admitting Hawaii and now viewed admission as a rebuttal to Soviet claims of American racism. Wright helped convince him that Burns's concession was important. The result was passage of both the Alaska Statehood Act, and, early in 1959, the Hawaiian Admission Act. In the latter, Wright broke from his more conservative Texas colleagues to vote for the measure.[75]

It was no coincidence that Burns and Gruening had noticed Wright. Wright had powerful friends, and he was an eloquent speaker and an astute political craftsman. He was also increasingly in the news. In July 1958, Wright witnessed two rockets being launched at Cape Canaveral, the Thor missile and the Explorer IV, America's fourth and largest satellite. The Thor missile failed at liftoff, but the Explorer was successful. Wright maximized his chance to be in the national spotlight by reporting on the experience for several newspapers. The "little cigar shaped moon," he wrote eloquently, would determine if "man can penetrate this menacing formation [of space]."[76] Several months later, just before Christmas, Wright received considerable press once again, when his newsletter included a letter to a hypothetical Soviet. Perhaps, Wright suggested, if average Americans wrote letters to the "plain, afraid, average men who live in Russia," such intimate communications might encourage mutual bonds and peace.[77]

"I've been thinking about you," Wright's "Letter to Ivan" began, acknowledging mutual fear. "This military business can get out of hand." Perhaps, the letter proposed, each side could agree to a "binding contract" to cut military spending by 10 percent for five years. This would save billions of dollars for more productive purposes, such as eradicating diseases, improving education, and eliminating poverty. If both sides "would only play square and fair," it did not have to be a "wonderful dream." People would no longer have to be afraid, and that would be the "greatest Christmas present since the first Christmas."[78] Whether it was a naïve reflection of his idealism or a crafty political stunt, the timely letter hit a nerve with the public. The Associated Press picked up the story, and a number of newspapers ran editorials praising it. In a nod to his disciple, no doubt, Johnson inserted a copy of the letter into the *Congressional Record*. Wright, it appeared, kept catching the eye of Washington's politicos.[79]

Eisenhower noticed Wright for another reason. The recession that had begun the previous year slowly ebbed throughout 1958 as legislators debated the appropriate response. The Democrats, Wright later wrote, offered a "well-timed package of anti-recession measures." The centerpiece for Wright was the omnibus rivers and harbors bill, a massive $1.5 billion public works program to fund over 130 reclamation measures, including the Trinity River Floodway. In response, Eisenhower suggested a $2 billion post office building program that in Wright's view "hardly amounted to a comprehensive anti-recession program."[80] The lines were drawn for a struggle as Wright dismissed Eisenhower's claim that the Democrats' program would explode the debt. The answer, Wright countered, was to be "ruthless ruling out wastes" while funding "ways that will actually grow the capital wealth." When the Citizens Committee for the Hoover Commission, the same anti-debt group that had earlier given Wright an award, suggested cuts beyond $4 billion, Rayburn and many other Democrats exploded. Playing the conciliator, Wright noted some merits among the cuts but reiterated the importance of public works. Such projects would help fight communism and, if delayed, would grow in costs. When rumors grew that Eisenhower might veto the omnibus rivers and harbors bill, Wright feigned disbelief. It was "wholly inconsistent" with Eisenhower's support for the economy.[81]

In reality, Wright had no reason to be surprised; Eisenhower had made his objections clear. Moreover, in a move that spoke to Wright's confidence but appeared presumptuous, Wright stated that the Public Works Committee had information the president needed to consider and asked Jack Anderson, Eisenhower's congressional liaison, to deliver a one-page summary to the White House. Wright expected a reply, but it never came. The silence was undoubtedly a blow to his ego but also another indication of Eisenhower's true intentions.[82]

When Congress passed the bill in early April 1958, Eisenhower vetoed it as a "waste of public funds."[83] Wright was furious, and his temper gained the upper hand. The president, Wright told the media, should spend less time on the golf course and more time with ordinary people. "Those who object have never seen a flood and the human wreckage it leaves," Wright stated about a man who clearly had seen his share of human wreckage. Wright even implied that if the president did not approve water projects at home, perhaps Congress might not approve water projects abroad. It was a not-so-subtle reference to Eisenhower's request for foreign aid; the statement was also ironic, given Wright's own support for mutual security.[84] Such political red meat was unlike Wright and it caught the eye of the media. "I don't know who the Congressman is," Eisenhower answered the press, "but I have probably visited many more small towns than he has."[85] It was a blunt rebuke but it helped Wright recognize that he had overreacted. True to form, Wright apologized, stating that he meant "nothing personally offensive."[86] If Eisenhower genuinely did not remember Wright from his White House meeting on interstate funding two years before, he definitely knew Wright now.

In retrospect, Eisenhower's veto comments—seemingly dismissing public works projects as a waste of public funds, in essence dismissing what had been at the center of Wright's career—was sure to raise Wright's quick temper. Still, for a thirty-five-year-old second-term congressman to imply that a worldly sixty-six-year-old president was inexperienced was audacious, more so given that Eisenhower had signed a $1 billion reclamation bill just before Wright had entered Congress.[87] In any event, Wright had the last laugh, as Congress overrode the veto. The White House, an obviously pleased Wright later wrote, "bowed to the righteous wrath of a scorned Congress."[88]

Although the public works battle was Wright's most notable domestic accomplishment in the 85th Congress, no issue appeared to escape Wright's notice. Wright led unsuccessful efforts to outlaw subliminal advertising, a precursor to a Federal Communications Commission rule prohibiting the practice two decades later, and suggested that the surgeon general was "outdated" in listing all mentally handicapped children—"retarded" in the parlance of the day—as custodial cases. In a bit of populism reflective of his past, Wright complained that the lack of stronger oil import quotas helped the large oil producers at the expense of the smaller ones.[89] Foretelling a battle that would grow in the future and define Wright for many of his constituents, he complained that the Civil Aeronautics Board, soon to be replaced by the Federal Aviation Administration, restricted all flights westward just to the Dallas airport. Fort Worth residents were "forced to go to another city."[90]

The end of the 85th Congress brought the 1958 congressional elections. Wright, again running unopposed despite his civil rights vote, jumped into the fray, struggling to remain true to his principles. When Democrats attacked Eisenhower's chief of staff, Sherman Adams, as corrupt, Wright declared Adams "essentially an honest man."[91] When a group of architects renovating the US Capitol criticized Rayburn in hyperbolic terms, Wright rushed to his mentor's defense. The remarks "might be more fitting for

Attila the Hun," Wright stated equally hyperbolically.[92] As head of the Democratic Speakers Bureau, Wright arranged dozens of speakers, many of them more caustic than himself, and remained constantly on the road. Given his position, Wright declared, it was "good policy" for him not to campaign actively for any one Democrat. In fact, however, he could not avoid making specific speeches on behalf of congressmen he admired.[93] After all, favors begat favors in politics.

On November 4, 1958, Republicans suffered their worst defeat since the advent of the Depression. With Democrats in the new 86th Congress outnumbering Republicans by nearly two to one, with the economy improving, and with developments in civil rights temporarily calm, Wright predicted less friction. Democrats who advocated "open hostilities upon an aging lame-duck President are quite likely to be disappointed," Wright claimed, calling for bipartisanship.[94] Eisenhower, Wright understood, wanted to leave office with a balanced budget. Wright agreed this goal was both appropriate and achievable.

"We've got to convince Americans that thrift is not a bad word," Eisenhower told congressional leaders early in January.[95] Wright concurred, but he sought the initiative, introducing within days a concurrent resolution for a "definite plan for systemic debt retirement." Congress should commit to "pay on the principal [of the national debt] an amount equal to not less than one percent of the present indebtedness," Wright proposed. Simply put, future Congresses should "pay an amount not less than $2.8 billion annually to . . . the eventual retirement of this burdensome obligation." Although it would cost more upfront and take almost a century, Wright added, it was "cheaper to pay than to owe."[96] Two weeks later, Wright spoke of the "extremely heartening public response" he had received. "The American people," he insisted, "do not have to be pandered to and spoon fed."[97]

Wright was correct about the positive press. A *Washington Star* columnist spoke of the "beauty of Wright's plan." The *Dallas Morning News* concluded that "it makes sense." In the weeks that followed, the resolution gained eighteen bipartisan cosponsors.[98] In the end, however, the plan's demise was predictable. It never dealt with the core issues; in the words of Illinois congressman Leo Allen, "Where would Wright get the money?"[99] Where exactly would Wright raise taxes or cut spending? The proposal, Wright's nemesis Bruce Alger said facetiously, "took a firm stand for motherhood and against sin."[100] When the administration's budget office warned that deficit spending was essential in emergencies, Wright began to retreat.

His plan was politically impractical, and he began to acknowledge that. It was "quixotic," he admitted.[101]

Wright, of course, still had his own ideas on the appropriate level of taxes and spending cuts. Claiming that Americans "will respond adequately if they are treated honestly and straightforwardly," he supported reform of wartime excise taxes but not massive cuts. Moreover, he saw waste in spending, if just not in public works. When he learned that public housing units had gone unused, he agreed to reduce allocations.[102] With Wright's pay-as-you-go highway trust fund already overdrawn and facing accusations of corruption, Wright welcomed an appointment to a House select committee to investigate.[103] It was important to ensure that his legacy was intact. "The investigation," Wright promised, "will be neither a 'witch hunt' nor a 'whitewash.'"[104] Indeed, the committee ultimately determined that inflation in the costs of materials, bureaucratic delays, unexpected construction expenses in urban areas, and litigation over eminent domain were as much a problem as waste and corruption. After discovering that funds diverted from other appropriations had failed to cover the entire shortage, Wright's committee faced three unpleasant options: abandon the pay-as-you-go mandate and adopt deficit financing; increase the gasoline tax; or slow construction to fit the existing revenue. The first, the core of his legacy, was untenable for Wright, and the second was not much better. "Texans have been very vigorous in their opposition to this idea," Wright noted, fearing that any temporary tax would become permanent.[105] With no good options, Wright and his colleagues had to acquiesce to a construction slowdown in the end, which, of course, brought its own headaches.[106]

As he warned of the evils of debt, Wright remained sensitive to criticism that his continued advocacy for his district and public works constituted "pork barrel." "Your criticism of public works troubles me greatly," Wright told one commentator. Public works, investments that stimulated economic growth, "paid for themselves." Wright wrote that Congress had already cut from Eisenhower's 1960 budget over $1.5 billion, and thus the projects his committee advocated were affordable.[107] Eisenhower thought otherwise, following his veto in 1958 with another in 1959. Wright was more restrained in his reaction this time, but the new veto still hardly cowered him.[108] Without missing a beat, he began pushing for new funding for an array of projects, including a new Fort Worth federal building and improvements to the city's airport.[109] Wright's continued advocacy of additional water pollution funds earned him a "thanks for your timely and effective work" from the National Wildlife Federation.[110] His efforts on the debt notwithstanding,

Wright advocated increased Social Security payments and a higher minimum wage. The former covered almost 60 million Americans by 1960. In the end, the growing economy, rebounding rapidly by the end of the Eisenhower administration from its brief recession, made all of Wright's priorities, from spending to deficit reduction, easier to afford, and politicians on both sides of the aisle claimed credit. The nation began the 1960s with a budget surplus, and the country appeared to be going in the right direction.[111]

Throughout the 86th Congress, Wright, undoubtedly moved by the evidence of fraud in the highway program, returned to another of his pet issues, openness and integrity in government. Other nations, he noted in his newsletter, looked to America for "spiritual leadership and moral example."[112] Standing against corruption paid political dividends, of course, but for Wright the issue became increasingly complex. The press had begun to level corruption charges against organized labor—which Wright usually supported—and Republicans sought to press their advantage in order to diminish labor's power at the behest of business. It was tough to be a crusader for integrity and still support unions, Wright recognized. "If you can't stand the heat, get out of the kitchen," he mused.[113] In fact, the debate divided Senators John F. Kennedy and Lyndon Johnson, who both had an eye on the upcoming 1960 Democratic presidential nomination. To make matters even more complex, Rayburn supported Kennedy over Johnson. With his mentors at odds, Wright was in an awkward position. In a tough call, Wright voted against the Kennedy anticorruption bill that most unions favored and for the so-called Landrum-Griffin Labor Bill, which also curbed picketing rights and secondary boycotts, provisions cheered by big business. Rayburn was furious, convinced that Johnson had pressed the Texas delegation to vote for a bill that hurt labor but strengthened his own presidential chances. Caught in the middle, Wright immediately began to hedge his positon, reminding unions that he had always been "more sympathetic to their cause than anybody else," and promising to seek revisions to the new law.[114] As with civil rights, with labor issues Wright knew that he had to tread carefully.

In fact, with presidential politics once again at the fore, the labor reform efforts coincided with renewed efforts to strengthen civil rights protections. When the Republicans introduced a relatively broad bill of protections, hoping to split the Democrats, Democratic leaders worked to narrow the focus in a way that would satisfy both their northern liberal and southern conservative wings. Johnson, seeking political advantage, took the lead, pressing for "responsible moderation." The result, the Civil Rights Act of 1960, allowed for court referees to investigate inequities in voting registration and strengthened some of the federal penalties established in the 1957 act, but did not include the stricter sanctions that civil rights advocates thought necessary. Given all the considerations—the pressure from Johnson, and the fact that his support for the 1957 bill had cost him little—Wright voted for the compromise. As many liberals complained, Wright was more worried about the conservative criticism in his district than about pressure from the left. "It does not have one cotton-picking thing to do with integration," Wright reminded one worried conservative. "All it has to do with is voting rights." In any event, the impending election quickly swept the new law from the headlines, and Wright, most assuredly, was not going to raise it himself.[115]

At the end of the decade, Wright certainly had much to contemplate. In May 1959, Mab gave birth to the Wrights' last child, Alicia Marie, named in part for Wright's mother. After the death of Stevie, Mab had been desperate for another child. Wright had not felt ready, but he hoped that an addition to the family would alleviate her continued grief. The baby did not come easily. A delayed pregnancy raised the possibility of adoption, and the delivery required emergency surgery and blood transfusions. "The baby is destined, no doubt, for operatic fame," a relieved Wright wrote once the drama had passed. Although they had purchased their Arlington County home not long before, Mab began to press for a more spacious home to accommodate the larger family. Wright, meanwhile, remained active in Washington's historic New York Avenue Presbyterian Church, his deep faith an obvious source of strength through it all. Wright taught a couple's class there, and the church members elected him to the Permanent Judicial Committee of the General Assembly, the faith's ruling court on ecclesiastical law, in 1960. As a reward for his continued support of defense appropriations, the military also granted Wright a demonstration flight on the Texas-built B-58 bomber, making him the first legislator to fly at twice the speed of sound. To Wright it no doubt seemed appropriate, with his own life seeming to travel at equally fast speeds.[116]

And then there was the matter of foreign policy, with the end of the decade bringing some momentous developments that overshadowed domestic issues and also occupied Wright's time. Soviet leader Nikita Khrushchev was angry over West Germany's new membership in the North Atlantic Treaty Organization (NATO), and to calm the growing tensions, Eisenhower invited him to visit the United States. Before Eisenhower could accept a reciprocal invitation to visit Moscow, however, the budding détente abruptly ended. On May 1, 1960—May Day—the Soviets shot down an American U-2 spy plane flying over the Soviet Union. Wright publicly downplayed the new crisis as a "disappointment," but he recognized that the troublesome developments posed a challenge for his idealism. The U-2 flights violated international law and contradicted American claims. At the same time, however, they made sense in practical terms. Wright later concluded they were "appropriate given the failure of Eisenhower's Open Skies proposal."[117] Conflicted, Wright fell back on his default position, respect for the executive in a time of crisis. He praised the Democrats for not leveling partisan criticism, "tempting though it undoubtedly was," but in the process ignored many of his colleagues who did exactly that. In hindsight, one can only wonder what Wright would have thought had he known of the Central Intelligence Agency's covert actions throughout the 1950s to rig elections and overthrow popular regimes. From Mohammed Mossadegh in Turkey to leftist regimes in Latin America, the CIA's version of practicality appeared Machiavellian, and they were a far cry from Wright's noble principles of international relations.[118]

If these developments were not enough, Fidel Castro seized power in early 1959 from Cuba's pro-Western dictator Fulgencio Batista. As Cuba's relations with the United States deteriorated, the anticommunist in Wright overcame his more nuanced knowledge and interest in Latin America. The revolution was a communist-inspired plot to gain a foothold in the Western Hemisphere, Wright agreed with Eisenhower, in no way a nationalist movement for independence.[119] Once again Wright rallied to the executive in crisis. In fact, despite the pending 1960 elections, Wright agreed to help the White House bring the headquarters of the Pan-American Health Organization to Washington, DC. It appeared, after all, a great way to win friends and prevent another Cuba. Assistant Secretary of State Roy Rubottom phoned Wright to explain that Eisenhower had promised the organization's members that the United States would host the headquarters, but that many Democrats were resisting the funding, hoping to embarrass the administration. Would Wright, Rubottom asked, serve as floor leader for the fight? Appreciating that Eisenhower appeared to hold no grudges from their public works spat, Wright agreed. Wright spent hours on the phone, and his impassioned floor speech soon thereafter was telling. "Although I did not personally vote for this president, I want everyone in this House to know that he is my President," Wright stated. "If he is embarrassed in the eyes of the world, then I am embarrassed because my country is embarrassed." It was a classic Wright speech, and it carried the vote by a margin of six to one. Not only was the White House relieved, but Rayburn invited Wright into his small hideaway office, his inner sanctum, for a bourbon and branch water. It was an unstated honor to be invited to what Rayburn called the "Board of Education." Wright had truly arrived; he was on the inside now both literally and figuratively.[120]

Not surprisingly, therefore, Wright anticipated playing a major role in the 1960 elections. Everyone sensed that with the Eisenhower years finally coming to a close, and America's paterfamilias retiring to his farm in Gettysburg, Pennsylvania, the country was on the cusp of a new period in its history. Speaking to a Dallas audience in June 1960, Wright summed up this sentiment. "Once to each civilization comes an opportunity for enduring greatness," Wright stated with his usual rhetorical flourish, "and we in America are upon the threshold of that opportunity."[121] Wright spoke of the nation, but he might as well have been speaking of himself. Like the nation, he was ready for the next step. The 1960 election, Wright believed, promised a new chapter in his own life and in the life of his country.

CHAPTER 7

Challenges

THE KENNEDY YEARS (1960–1963)

Wright was not coy about who should lead America into the new decade. As early as February 1959—when Rayburn declared it to be "too early" for predictions—Wright joined fourteen members of the Texas delegation in supporting Lyndon Johnson. Johnson, the only southerner capable of winning the Democratic presidential nomination, would heal the intraparty rift, Wright suggested, without mentioning the advantage Johnson's candidacy promised his own career.[1] While everyone knew of Johnson's ambition, Wright recalled, the candidate himself thought it best "not to go out and hustle for votes." But feigning disinterest was antiquated, Wright argued. Voters "didn't pay attention to that."[2] In fact, according to historian Doris Kearns Goodwin, Johnson's political instincts failed him at a much deeper level. Mistakenly assuming that senators had power over Democratic delegates, he bargained behind the scenes while his competition frenetically campaigned across the country raising money, doing what Wright, as a surrogate, could never do. By 1960—the "first postbroker convention," in Goodwin's words—a wave of populism had weakened traditional Democratic powerbrokers. Johnson did not recognize the new reality.[3]

Johnson certainly had stiff competition. While Vice President Richard Nixon stood as the favorite to carry the banner for the GOP, the Democrats, true to their nature, had an open field. Of the lot, Hubert Humphrey of Minnesota and John F. Kennedy of Massachusetts appeared to have the best chance, and the latter was buoyed by a youthful charisma. Several years before, hosting a Fort Worth television program, Wright had interviewed the young dynamo about his new Pulitzer Prize-winning book *Profiles in Courage*. The book's tale of courageous politicians suited Wright's idealism and, in Wright's words, "really rang my bell." Kennedy was nice and agreed to sign copies of the book for the winners of a high school essay competition Wright had organized. Surprisingly, Wright didn't think Kennedy was "particularly magnetic."[4] Wright had no inkling that he had just met a seminal individual in postwar American history or that the books he awarded would become collector's items.[5]

As Wright did yeoman's work for his mentor Johnson, he had no idea of Kennedy's potential, even suggesting that Kennedy might make a good vice-presidential running mate. The "Kennedy mystique" began to dawn on Wright at Washington's annual Gridiron Dinner in early 1960. Just before Kennedy spoke, a comedian portraying him threw out money to the crowd, an obvious nudge at the Kennedy family's wealth. "I felt sorry for him," Wright recalled. At the podium, however, Kennedy announced that he had a telegram from his father. "Don't buy a vote more than necessary," he said it read. "I'll be damned if I am going to pay for a landslide." While the audience exploded in laughter, Wright thought to himself, "This guy's smart."[6]

After several primary victories, it was obvious that Kennedy was a serious contender. In a poor part of West Virginia, Wright watched Kennedy explain that his wealth did not keep him from caring about those who faced challenges he could only imagine. "He showed his humanity," Wright later said admiringly. Afterward, a coal miner quipped to Kennedy, "I've been poor all my life and you ain't missed noth'in."[7] At the Kansas State Democratic Convention in March, Wright watched the proceedings. Kennedy, who seemed to recognize that the crowd was growing restless after a long speech by Humphrey, cut his speech to only eight minutes. Wright recalled that Kennedy had the audience "in the palm of his hand."[8] As Kennedy continued to gather delegates into the summer of 1960, Wright took the only tack left to a Johnson surrogate. Only Johnson, Wright told the Texas State Democratic Convention, could "weld together divergent factions into one united and fairly harmonious whole." The implication was clear: a Massachusetts liberal would alienate southern conservatives and cost the party.[9]

By the time the Democratic National Convention convened in Los Angeles in July, Wright believed that Kennedy's lead was unsurpassable, but he said nothing. In a last-minute ploy, Johnson invited Kennedy to debate at the Biltmore Hotel's amphitheater, packing it with his own partisans. Far from intimidated, Kennedy deflected the crowd with compliments and humor, even bringing Wright to laughter. When the first ballot concluded, Kennedy, to no one's surprise, had the nomination.

Many observers believed—correctly, as it turned out—that Kennedy had been soft on Johnson because he wanted the Texan, who would be the perfect bridge to southern conservatives, as his running mate. This arrangement, however, worried Rayburn, who knew how important Johnson was in the Senate. In the words of historian Herbert Parmet, Johnson's "own brand of dependents" were "primarily interested in how much more he could do for them if he remained as majority leader."[10] To his credit, perhaps, or simply out of loyalty to whatever Johnson chose, Wright did not share Rayburn's concerns. The party, Wright calculated, needed the unity that only Johnson could bring to the ticket. Moreover, Johnson had served as the de facto party leader with Eisenhower in the White House. With Kennedy there, however, Johnson's role in the Senate would be nothing more than "a glorified errand boy." On the one hand, if Johnson refused the VP nomination and the Democrats lost, Johnson would take a lot of the blame and might even lose his leadership position. On the other hand, if Johnson accepted and the Democrats lost, Johnson could still serve as majority leader. "There seems scant likelihood of the Senate going Republican," Wright concluded. Johnson would surely "more than hold his own" in the White House.[11] It was a perceptive political analysis, demonstrating all that Wright had learned. Johnson, in any case, accepted Kennedy's offer.

With the Democratic ticket set, Wright campaigned actively in his district and throughout West Texas.[12] Like many in his generation, he could relate to Kennedy. He, too, was a young veteran with a wife and small children. Wright thought Kennedy's wife, Jacqueline, a political asset but difficult to know. "I never really felt as though I was connecting with her," Wright remembered. Wright certainly had reason to be jealous of Kennedy, who, after all, was born to wealth and was higher on the political ladder that Wright had devoted his life to climbing. Not once, however, did Wright express envy. Once Johnson joined the ticket, Wright was a Kennedy man just as ardently as he had been a Johnson man previously.[13]

What particularly annoyed Wright was the question of Kennedy's Catholicism. Many fundamentalist Protestants remained wary of the Catholic faith, and the nation had never elected a Catholic president.[14] Nixon had denounced attacks on Kennedy's Catholicism as a "malignant ugliness," but to Wright his words were "not quite true."[15] In fact, Nixon knew of bigotry from his Quaker upbringing but could have done more to distance himself from the more overt criticism. At the same time, Wright's district had its share of fundamentalists. When complaints arose, Wright professed his own "misgivings about the Catholic Church per se," but added that religion was "irrelevant to the question of a man's fitness for office."[16] It was Wright's modus operandi. In a heated campaign, he might become sharper than the bipartisan persona he cultivated, but in personal communications he employed friendly persuasion. In fact Wright had no reservations about Catholics, because the ecumenical lessons of his youth were so ingrained.

In any event, Wright felt fortunate to witness history when Kennedy, in a speech in Houston, assured Protestant ministers that he would follow the Constitution. As president, he would not enforce the edicts of the pope on any American, for to do so would be to deny the religious liberty of all Americans. The famous speech, author Garry Wills noted, made Kennedy a "symbol of American pluralism."[17] Impressed by the speech, Wright compared Kennedy to the biblical Daniel in the lion's den. The comment, Wright laughingly recalled, led to complaints that Wright had compared Protestant men of God to lions.[18]

The campaign had its rough moments, and the level of acrimony still made Wright uncomfortable. When Johnson came to Dallas's Baker Hotel, a "cacophony of epithets" greeted him and the crowd drowned out his speech. The Republican Bruce Alger, it turned out, had arranged for several hundred women to come and stage a "tag day." On such days, activists would hand out fliers, or "tags," but, as Alger undoubtedly intended, Johnson's presence ensured a raucous protest for the cameras. When Johnson subsequently refused a police escort as he walked to the nearby Adolphus Hotel, the taunts were equally vicious. Wright confronted Alger, but the Dallas congressman replied that it was fine to "tell a socialist and a traitor what you think of him."[19]

Many pundits later attributed Kennedy's narrow victory to the first nationally televised presidential debates. Kennedy was more telegenic than Nixon, which Wright appreciated. Wright always considered himself to be innovative in using television, but had failed to realize that his own lyrical style came across as theatrical. Kennedy's style was a pithy, to-the-point brevity. "The tube is Wright's Achilles' Heel," one report read. Throughout the 1960s, aides had to resist Wright's efforts to purchase larger blocks of time for televised advertisements.[20] Wright was always confident, certainly no more so than after the 1960 election. He arranged—without approval—for a group of Texas mounted police to ride in Kennedy's inaugural parade. When the Inaugural Committee later agreed, it appeared that Wright's influence now extended all the way down Pennsylvania Avenue.[21]

With the wind at his back, Wright assumed that it was time for him to swing for the fences again. Kennedy's victory left Johnson's Senate seat open. The upper house beckoned. It was a chance for Wright to win his first statewide election. Governor Price Daniel appointed William Blakley, a conservative Democrat who had voted for Eisenhower, to fill the seat until a special election could be held in April 1961. Liberals, Wright recognized, sought an alternative. On November 18, Wright announced his candidacy, downplaying his burning ambition. "Since no other member of the Texas delegation has demonstrated any great desire to make the race," Wright stated, "I respectfully offer my services." Wright, in reality, had rushed his announcement, making it less than two weeks after the presidential election. Assuming that his growing stature would be intimidating, he wanted to discourage potential rivals. Denouncing "extremism . . . of the right or the left," Wright followed Johnson's lead, promising to keep the fractured Democrats together. Wright also stressed his connections—as he put it, his "friendly working relationship with the executive and legislative leadership of our country."[22]

Wright's efforts to scare off opponents failed miserably. Almost seventy candidates filed, including liberals Henry B. Gonzalez, a popular San Antonio state senator, and former congressman Maury Maverick, whose grandfather had originally given the term "maverick" its meaning. The broad field, the League of Women Voters concluded, made it "impractical to publish a Voter's Guide." On the Republican side, college professor John Tower had gained considerable publicity in his ill-fated run against Johnson only weeks before. He sought to consolidate conservatives who had been angered by Kennedy's election. "Double your pleasure, double your fun," he campaigned. "Vote against Johnson two times and not one."[23]

Wright, hardly a lightweight himself, adopted his old populist campaign theme. In slick fliers, he was now a "senator for all the people," not merely a "congressman for all the people."[24] Wright's district—both in its original configuration and in its later Fort Worth incarnation—came out strong for his candidacy. When over four hundred supporters rallied in Fort Worth, the campaign touted that both Republicans and Democrats attended. It was important to unite Texans, Wright stated. Both the *Fort Worth Star-Telegram* and the *Weatherford Democrat* endorsed Wright, that latter noting without any apparent sense of contradiction that "the young red-haired man" had accomplished wonderful things for Texas and had helped cut the debt.[25]

Lacking a strong presence outside his district, Wright established chairmen in all state counties. "Project Motorcade," meanwhile, stopped in town squares to distribute fliers and solicit volunteers. The campaign kept lists of "block workers" and their "captains," and, quietly, "negro pastors" who might assist.[26] Reminding small towns that he had been Weatherford's mayor as well as Fort Worth's congressman, Wright claimed to understand both urban and rural issues. In time, over twenty-nine newspapers endorsed his candidacy.[27]

Wright had some help. Because of Wright's role in the presidential campaign, Kennedy had appointed him to a natural resources advisory committee, which, just before Kennedy's inauguration, issued its report. The appointment allowed Wright to remind voters that he had experience with the water shortages much of the state faced. The key, Wright explained, was better coordination with the federal government, a subtle hint of his connections.[28] After Johnson lent one of his staff members to Wright to help with the campaign, Wright challenged all the leading candidates, including the Republican Tower, to individual debates in their hometowns, even offering to pay the costs.[29]

Despite all his efforts, the polls did not look good as the election approached. Wright was still relatively unknown throughout much of the state, and he had raised only $260,000, which was insufficient to match the media onslaught of his many opponents. Moreover, Julian Read, Wright's campaign manager, suddenly resigned on account of the demands of his family's brick business. Worse still, the Texas Democratic Party, which usually did not make endorsements, did so for Gonzalez. Wright still had the support of Fort Worth's General Dynamics workers, but many unions followed the party's endorsement.[30]

The results of the early April election were a blow to Wright. Tower received the most votes. Wright came in at third place, just behind Blakley. Although he performed well in Fort Worth and in some southern and panhandle counties, he lagged in Houston, San Antonio, and along the Rio Grande.[31] State law required a runoff between Tower and Blakely, and this created a problem for the Democrats. Many liberals decided to protest

Blakley by voting for Tower. If Tower won, they reasoned, he would surely lose to a "real Democrat" in the next election cycle, given the Democratic majority. A Blakely victory, however, would entrench a conservative in the seat. Wright found such a plan destructive and supported Blakley, hoping that the Senate would mute his conservatism. When his own supporters suggested a write-in campaign in the runoff, Wright dismissed the idea as "not the responsible thing for me to do."[32] When his longtime supporter Margaret Carter announced that she would vote for Tower, Wright minced no words. Tower was "a vicious, and opportunistic, and dangerous nincompoop who has such a closed mind that he thinks that he and [arch-conservative Arizona senator] Barry Goldwater are conducting a Holy Crusade."[33]

Wright, it turned out, had reason to fear Tower. Defeating Blakley by more than 10,000 votes, Tower became the first Texas Republican to be elected to the Senate since 1870. Liberal Democrats, *Texas Monthly* declared, "had fouled their own nest and then fouled the conservative Democrats."[34] Looking back, Wright thought Blakley had run a poor campaign— he had even denounced crop price supports to farmers. "Blakley was a natural for saying the wrong thing to the wrong people," Wright laughed. Although no one could have known it at the time, Tower's election on the heels of Alger's new presence in the House signaled the beginning of a worrisome trend for Wright and his allies. Tower would remain in the Senate for over two decades, and his victory was evidence of a slowly rejuvenating Texas Republican Party. A tectonic shift in Texas politics, fueled in part by the perceived liberalism of the Kennedy administration and the ongoing civil rights struggle, and aided by the Democrats' bitter divisions, had begun. Several weeks after the runoff, Jim Bertron, Tower's campaign chairman, confidently predicted that the Texas GOP would defeat five incumbents in 1962, including Wright. Two years later, the prediction proved untrue, but the Republicans did win the governorship and two of the five seats. It was only the beginning of a new reality that would challenge Wright for the rest of his career.[35]

"Right now I am uncertain what my future may hold," Wright acknowledged just after his defeat.[36] In fact, he took the loss hard, and it precipitated another crisis in his life. He had not lost an election since the state legislature, when he had made obvious mistakes. Now, however, he had applied the lessons learned and still lost. He had even passed up a lucrative job offer from a large transportation company. His ambition thwarted, suddenly everything seemed in doubt. If he could not advance his congressional career, what should he do? His supporters also worried. "We need to think in terms of what we can now do to promote this outstanding young man," wrote one contributor.[37]

As Wright pondered the big picture, a more pressing problem emerged. Campaign volunteers in Houston and San Antonio had charged approximately $90,000 to the campaign for which there was no money. Wright had been blissfully unaware of the charges, but he now realized that leaving vendors in the lurch might jeopardize his future. Unaware that many candidates in similar situations negotiated reduced payments, Wright believed it was his moral duty to repay his debts in full. The first priority, he believed, was the smaller businesses that had provided supplies and services. After a fundraising dinner raised less than $5,000, a new controversy blossomed, the last thing Wright needed.[38] The *Fort Worth Press* reported that employees at Convair, a business that had benefited from Wright's advocacy, were being forced to contribute funds. When Wright heard of the matter, he wrote the newspaper that he welcomed voluntary donations "even though it might appear a bit embarrassing," but never condoned forced contributions. Quietly, Wright complained that the report "left so much to the imagination," and he had no idea of who was "master-minding this effort."[39] Wright asked Convair's management to find out who was responsible and inform whoever it was "that I don't want a single penny from anybody who is giving it grudgingly."[40]

In the end, Wright sold his Kerr County ranch to cover part of the bills. Nevertheless, he later wrote, the campaign debt "would hound me for the next sixteen years." The entire episode signaled the beginning of a period of financial troubles for Wright; it also begged the question of how someone so controlling in other aspects of his career could be so casual about the money he needed. Critics would later claim that Wright was not ignorant but manipulative, and indeed, the story of forced contributions was hardly the last charge of financial corruption. A fairer interpretation, however, was simply that Wright, at this point in his career at least, was so focused on the larger picture that he had little time for details, and money not his raison d'être. "If he had spent as much time in business as he did in politics," one friend explained, "he'd be chairman of some large corporation."[41] Wright relied on subordinates who in this instance failed him. If anyone besides Wright held blame, it was campaign manager Read. Wright, however, refused to criticize his aide, remaining generous to his supporters. Indeed, in the midst of his troubles, Wright contributed a portion of the ranch sale to Weatherford's Presbyterian Church.[42]

The media did not help. Seeking to earn extra money, Mab agreed to help a friend, Borden Seaberry, form a building company, WSB Corporation. While Mab's relationship with WSB was brief, her name remained on the incorporation papers. "It was just like Lady Bird's name got on everything," Mab later recalled, referring to the future First Lady. The oversight probably would not have mattered except that in 1963 the Federal Housing Administration began to investigate allegations of illicit loans at the company. Once again Wright had to defend himself from charges of cronyism, explaining that Mab had left the business "many months" before.[43]

Mab and the children were clearly growing restless. Mab was well liked in Washington's social scene but the hectic pace of life and her husband's long hours were beginning to wear thin. In addition, Jimmy, their oldest child, was doing poorly at Arlington's Washington and Lee High School. "None of us liked it," Jimmy later recalled.[44] Just after Wright's Senate defeat, Mab announced that she planned to move to their Fort Worth house with their daughters. Jimmy would attend a military school in Texas, and at the end of the year they could purchase a house in a different school district in the DC area. Wright did not protest, as critics had claimed the empty house was merely a tool to feign residency.[45] In addition, the move allowed Wright to sell his Virginia home and use the proceeds to help retire his debt. The move made sense, but Wright could not avoid its implications: he and Mab were growing apart, and their separation was more than just physical distance.

Without his family, Wright moved temporarily into Washington's Coronet Hotel. "God it was lonely," he recalled. On the advice of Weatherford's Presbyterian minister, the family enrolled Jimmy in the Schreiner Institute, a Kerrville, Texas, military academy. If they hoped the discipline would help their son, they were disappointed. Jimmy, always mischievous, broke into the school's broadcast booth one night and blasted a recording of reveille, sending sleepy cadets into formation and earning himself an expulsion. The Wrights then prevailed upon Weatherford friends to board Jimmy, allowing him to attend the small town's school.[46] To save on airfare, the Wrights purchased a station wagon. Fortunately, the commuting did not last long. At the end of the year, Mab was indeed back in Washington. With new money from renting their Fort Worth home, the Wrights then purchased a house in North Arlington. It was not far from their earlier home, but in the Yorktown School District. On a corner lot with almost two dozen dogwood trees, it had once been the home of singer Kate Smith. It was not elaborate, befitting Wright's troubled finances, but he loved it and the family stayed there for almost eight years.[47]

The challenges the family faced and the direction of his career continued to weigh heavily on Wright. He was "a fretter and a brooder," according to one former staffer.[48] Just after his Senate loss, Wright surmised that his troubles had been exacerbated by the disorganization of the Democratic Party. "The party must rebuild from the ground up," he insisted. It must "never be the captive of any one group."[49] Years later, Wright appeared to understand just how systemic the problems were and how difficult, if not impossible, it was to achieve party unity. He appeared to place more of the blame on his own overconfidence and outspokenness. "I felt invincible," he recalled. "I had made the mistake of thinking I could get way out ahead of the public."[50]

At the time, however, Wright had no shortage of supporters whispering in his ear to think big again. The loss was not Wright's fault, avid supporter Silas Grant wrote a colleague. "I think Jim is the man we need for Governor of Texas and our job is to give the people an opportunity to know him better." Grant thought Wright should seek the governorship in 1962 as a platform for the Senate in 1966. Tower, Grant argued, was "not going to be easily defeated," but four years as governor would make Wright "visualized on a state-wide basis."[51] Another close Wright confident disagreed. Reagan Legg advised Wright to "stay in the middle as a Congressman" and avoid getting "caught in a squeeze on labels in another race." As "a middle-of-the-roader," Legg argued, "one side or the other is going to have to come to you."[52]

Wright, accordingly, wrestled with his ambition, acknowledging his frustration at waiting for a committee chairmanship and, after authoring legislation, watching others get credit.[53] When the media began to speculate on him running for governor, Wright hardly tamped down the possibility. If he were to run, Wright remarked, it would not be to lay the groundwork for the Senate, but to unite the fractious Democrats.[54] In another instance, Wright remarked that it was "really no secret" that he wanted Tower's Senate seat.[55] While Wright stated publicly that it was "too early" for "definite conclusions," quietly he enumerated his assets: an organization still mobilized from his Senate race; a "public office from which newsworthy pronouncements can be made"; a reputation as a unifying moderate; and, finally, "enough physical energy." His liabilities included his campaign debt; his continued lack of name recognition in parts of the state; and a problem with fundraising due to the fact that many donors thought him insufficiently conservative. Accordingly, Wright concluded, he should "proceed as though I had made up my mind definitely to run for governor," but delay any official announcement.[56]

Soon Wright's "itinerary for the fall" included fundraising, organizational meetings, and events for publicity. With Grant influential in the nascent campaign, newspapers began speculating on a gubernatorial run.[57] By midsummer, polls had Wright performing well in hypothetical matchups, but still trailing the incumbent, Daniel.[58] In September Wright proposed that the state revise its constitution "from the horse and buggy era," something a gubernatorial candidate would say, not a congressman.[59]

Just as Wright appeared to be picking up steam, the race shifted. John Connally, a close associate of Johnson, announced his intention to run for governor. As the press speculated on whether Johnson might endorse Wright or Connally, Connally stated that he did not anticipate the vice-president intervening but that Wright had just assured him that he was not running. When reporters tracked down Wright on a Washington street, Wright did not deny the comments. He would, Wright answered, have an announcement in the next two days. Wright's supporters were less restrained. "John Connally must be stopped," the liberal Margaret Carter stated in an open letter.[60]

Wright could read the tea leaves. Not only had Connally entered the fray, but Daniel had announced that he would seek reelection, and new polls had Wright fading in the larger field.[61] Not surprisingly, therefore, Wright announced on December 15, as promised, that he would not be a candidate for governor. Although Wright stated that it was a matter of where he "could do the most good," other factors were clearly influential. Wright longed for a rebound from the worst defeat of his career, and the governorship would have given him excellent executive experience for a national candidacy. Now, however, his decision made, he had to return quietly to the fold, still brooding about his future. [62]

As Wright campaigned, the new president was anxious for legislative action but faced his own frustrations. The coalition of conservative southern Democrats and Republicans remained, most notably in the House Rules Committee. There, Virginia's Howard Smith and Mississippi's William Colmer often sided with the four Republicans to block bills from reaching the floor. For remedy, Kennedy tuned to Speaker Rayburn, and Rayburn threatened to remove Colmer from the committee. Moderates, however, complained that any removal undermined the seniority system, which benefited southerners of all stripes. Rayburn then turned to an alternative that particularly annoyed conservatives, the temporary addition of three new committee members, two Democrats and one Republican. This, he knew, ensured an

8–7 majority for allowing floor votes on Kennedy's proposals. To mollify conservatives, Kennedy publicly stated his intention to balance the budget. Rayburn, suffering now from pancreatic cancer, placed his reputation on the line to lobby for the plan. Wright was in a difficult position.[63] His district's conservatives were unhappy, but Wright had high hopes for Kennedy and could not break from Rayburn in his time of need. Wright, accordingly, voted for the temporary Rayburn additions, and two years later he voted to make them permanent. He was simply defending democracy, Wright told his conservative critics. An "arbitrary" minority had "handcuffed" the will of the people.[64]

Kennedy, Wright later remarked, undoubtedly reflecting on his own tempered ambitions, "opted for boldness over timidity."[65] When the White House proposals came, Wright, predictably, largely fell in line. When Kennedy proposed raising the minimum wage to $1.25 per hour, Wright's support brought out his conservative critics. Fort Worth business owners complained that the higher wage threatened "the survival of many of us."[66] Wright not only had his populist leanings, however, but understood that his support for the Landrum-Griffin Bill during the Eisenhower administration had cost him valuable union support. Wright wanted to vote affirmatively, but he also welcomed exemptions to protect his right flank. "If you will read the law," he told one conservative, "it only applies to firms engaged in interstate commerce and then only if they do $250,000 in interstate business and a minimum of $1,000,000 in all."[67]

Increased Social Security benefits, additional highway construction, and the Manpower Redevelopment and Training Act all won Wright's support. Wright welcomed Kennedy's famous challenge to get a man to the moon, and he also voted for the funding. More money for science, he noted, promised "technological mastery as well as potential military mastery."[68] In the future, Wright predicted excitedly, the morning mail could be "delivered anywhere in the civilized world before nightfall." "Electronic signals" could carry the letters through satellites.[69] Wright welcomed increased spending on veterans and civil servants, making him a "friend of postal employees," as one grateful recipient put it.[70] When Kennedy, worried about inflation, confronted the steel industry over price increases, Wright publicly praised the forceful response.[71]

Wright's fight for additional water development as a member of the Public Works Committee continued, as did the conservative criticism. "I may get my neck chopped off by voting to restore the funds," Wright joked to one supporter.[72] Wright was slow to recognize the impact that Rachel Carson's seminal bestseller *Silent Spring* was having on environmentalism, but he continued to perceive himself as one of Congress's foremost pollution fighters. Wright read the book, he later noted, but "not as carefully as I should have."[73] In fact, while Wright's concern for pollution was genuine—he supported the Clean Air Act of 1963, which set standards for stationary sources of pollution and created a research program for monitoring emissions—water quality remained a complex issue. The budding environmentalists did not always welcome the reclamation Wright advocated, while the pesticides that Carson bemoaned were important to the farmers, whom Wright still supported. When Carson testified before Congress, Wright advised caution.[74]

While Mab was in Texas, Wright spent time socializing with some of the younger members of Kennedy's staff, solidifying his connections to the administration. His "favorites," Wright recalled, were Kenney O'Donnell, Henry Hall Wilson, and Larry O'Brien. O'Brien later became chair of the Democratic National Committee during the Watergate scandal. Wilson and Wright became particularly close, Wright later writing that he helped Wilson "promote support among southern members."[75] Wright's position as a rare southern ally won him invitations to Robert Kennedy's home, although the attorney general remained suspicious of Wright's connections to Johnson. "I was never pushed in the pool as [the Kennedys] did with their close inner circle," Wright later laughed. The younger Kennedy, the true liberal ideologue, questioned Wright's commitment to civil rights even as he recognized the alliance as important.[76]

Bobby Kennedy had been appointed to his position, of course, and could safely ignore politics; Wright could not. The conservative criticism Wright received grew. "Our president," one constituent wrote, "is issuing orders so rapidly that it is impossible for an average citizen to keep up." Another warned that Kennedy would confiscate America's guns.[77] Wright continued to assure critics that he was no minion of the administration, and when he broke from the White House, he made sure they knew it. Wright supported the Public Housing Act of 1961, but he voted against the creation of a Department of Urban Affairs. Supporting government action was one thing, Wright's votes implied, but adding to the bureaucracy was quite another.[78]

Kennedy's proposal for health insurance for the elderly, dubbed Medicare, and his call for dramatic increases in aid to education proved particularly troublesome. The former promised an increased bureaucracy, while the latter appeared to infringe on states' rights. With the House deferring on Medicare and the Senate narrowly defeating it, Wright never had to cast a final vote. The education bill, meanwhile, appeared to many southern conservatives to be unconstitutional, and to the Catholic hierarchy it seemed unfair in its exclusion of religious schools. Wright wanted to support education, but he hedged his bets. At least one constituent noticed, complaining that Wright had not voted "one way or the other." Wright replied that he had an excellent voting record—without, again, stating his specific position.[79]

The debate over trade was also a challenge. The growth of the European Common Market, Kennedy believed, mandated reciprocal tariff reductions. Early in 1962, therefore, the administration proposed a bill authorizing the executive to reduce tariffs.[80] Wright applauded the initiative and agreed with Kennedy that economic unity defended against communism, but he knew that many in his district, including key unions, were opposed. In the end Wright voted for the Economic Expansion Act of 1962 but hedged by complaining that it hurt unemployment compensation and the oil industry. Noting that he had "actively opposed executive encroachment on legislative prerogatives," Wright insisted that the bill was not "ideal," but had been necessary.[81]

Wright's most notable departure from the administration was, predictably, over debt. Wright strongly supported administration requests to fund projects that he thought were essential, including public works and the military. "It is time for some very plain talk," Wright told the American Legion, supporting Kennedy's call for upgraded missile systems.[82] At the same time, however, Wright resisted projects that he thought unnecessary. In 1962, Wright ignored a personal call from Kennedy and opposed an increase in the national debt ceiling. Kennedy's Keynesian advisers, Wright thought, should "rethink their economics." Tax cuts, properly placed, were possible, but they never paid for themselves through economic growth. Wright applauded when Kennedy proposed to raise revenue by eliminating corporate deductions, but he insisted that his proposal to cut income tax rates for the wealthy was unfair to the poor and increased debt.[83]

Of course not every congressman shared Wright's view that spending on his district was essential. For years Fort Worth's General Dynamics plant had employed approximately 18,000 people, producing a succession of big bombers, such as the B-52. With the subsonic B-52 fleet aging, however, the military was considering upgrading to the supersonic B-58. The plane was state-of-the art but more expensive. Viewing the additional costs as unnecessary when missiles promised similar but cheaper lethality, Congress removed budgeting for the newer plane, forcing Wright to become, in his own words, a "self-appointed one-man sales force."[84]

It proved a hard sell. After Wright won $525 million for the B-58, Air Force Chief of Staff Curtis LeMay decided that the new funds were better suited for the B-52s that Boeing Corporation still built in Seattle. Lyndon Johnson warned Wright that LeMay was blunt. When Wright suggested diplomatically that surely LeMay had not made up his mind, LeMay retorted that, yes, he had.[85] With the cuts beginning at Fort Worth's largest employer, Wright learned that Defense Secretary Robert McNamara was pushing development of an experimental tri-service airplane, the TFX, a supersonic fighter-bomber hybrid. Pressing his case, Wright met with McNamara and employed his connections to meet with Kennedy. There Wright appealed to Kennedy's love for sports, suggesting that General Dynamics was like a winning football team. They had sufficient training, practice, and coordination. Wright's rehearsed eight-minute presentation appeared to have been effective; Kennedy implied that he agreed.[86]

Several months passed before Wright, in Texas, received a phone call from Johnson. "You'd better get up here," the vice-president exclaimed. McNamara, Wright learned after taking the first plane available, had recommended Boeing for the TFX only to have the White House request a second opinion. Rushing to the White House, Wright explained to congressional liaison Kenney O'Donnell that Kennedy preferred General Dynamics. O'Donnell called McNamara and explained that a second opinion meant a different recommendation. A few weeks later, Wright learned the good news. Calling the company to let them know of the contract, Wright heard screams of joy. Kennedy's decision was surely due to a number of factors—his dislike for LeMay and the need to cultivate support in Texas among them—but to Fort Worth it was simple. Wright was the hero of the day.[87]

Hardly resting on his laurels, Wright pressed again for his district, insisting that Fort Worth needed equity with Dallas in aviation. This, too, proved a long struggle. In 1940, the Civil Aeronautics Board (CAB) had agreed to study the possibility of a regional airport to serve the two cities, which had resulted in the construction in Arlington of Midway Airport, a dozen miles west of Dallas's Love Field. Competition between the cities and Fort Worth's continued reliance on its old Meacham Airport, however, had doomed Midway, and it had closed. A decade passed before Fort Worth reopened the airport as Amon Carter Field, transferring all its commercial flights from Meacham. Still, however, the airport suffered. Since Amon Carter was close to Dallas, the CAB had restricted all flights westward just to Love Field. In 1960, moving to stimulate the airport once again, the city of Fort Worth had purchased Amon Carter, infusing it with cash and renaming it the Greater Southwest Airport. Even this, however, had little impact. By the time of the Kennedy administration, it was apparent that Greater Southwest Airport had the better site but suffered from its restrictions.[88]

Wright jumped into action, first arguing to the Federal Aviation Administration (FAA), which had replaced the CAB, that Greater Southwest's flights were "inferior," creating a "tale of two cities." Twenty-three times, Wright complained, he had been forced to drive thirty miles east just to fly west. It was an insult to Fort Worth. Wright's pressure won for Greater Southwest a new aviation tower and better flights from American Airlines and Braniff International, but the central problem remained.[89] The only solution, Wright believed, was one large international airport for both cities. Although the effort had failed earlier, Wright won concessions. The FAA agreed to conduct another study on the feasibility of a large, joint endeavor.[90] It was only a beginning, but a beginning that Wright's constituents applauded. No one had any idea just how far the roots he planted would grow.

Forever in tune with his district, Wright continued to tack on each issue. In June 1962, he broke with the White House when the Supreme Court ruled in *Engel v. Vitale* that voluntary, nondenominational public school prayer violated the Constitution's Establishment Clause. "The country," one angry southern fundamentalist declared, "had turned its back on God."[91] Kennedy stated that he supported the decision and tried to move on, but Wright recognized the repercussions the decision would have back in Texas.[92] "The First Amendment did not mean that there is to be no religion . . . in public places," Wright stated, playing to his home crowd. He supported a constitutional amendment to correct the matter.[93]

Kennedy did not always make Wright's job easier. A year later, Kennedy reversed what Martin Luther King Jr. had termed a "cautious and defensive" position on African American civil rights—in order not to offend southern conservatives—and proposed legislation to encourage equal employment and outlaw discrimination in all private facilities that served the public.[94] It was the Holy Grail for the civil rights movement but an ugly bombshell for conservatives in Wright's district. "This is a country of the White Man," wrote one constituent. "The greatest book of them all," another obviously struggled to write, was clear about the "Ethiopkian the Negro the Ruler of Sodom Gomrrah [sic]." More thoughtful letters insisted that racism was an issue of morality that government could not legislate, that the proposal violated private property rights, or that the matter was best left to the states.[95]

Wright was in a bind. While Johnson urged support for the proposals, Wright sensed that this time he could not vote his conscience or hedge his bet. On the House floor Wright spoke about the "insanity of racial hatred," reflecting the believe in equality that he had learned from his parents.[96] When it came time to vote, however, Wright sided with the conservatives, breaking from Kennedy, Johnson, and, in a way, his own conscience. Idealism be damned; it was a matter of staying in office. Denouncing the "hotheads on both extremes" and noting that he had supported civil rights bills earlier, Wright couched his opposition as a defense of property rights. In time, he would regret his decision, but, as 1963 concluded, at least the debate had turned to the Senate.[97]

Kennedy's foreign policies presented Wright with no such challenges. Kennedy was a consummate Cold Warrior but also idealistic, and his policies reflected his own internationalist assumptions. In Wright's words, they were "consistent with our history and national character."[98] The demands for both national security and international freedom at times presented unavoidable conflicts for both men, but throughout it all, Wright remained firmly in the Kennedy camp.

The Bay of Pigs fiasco had unfolded three months after Kennedy's inauguration, but Wright never criticized the ill-fated plan to assist Cuban exiles in overthrowing dictator Fidel Castro. Stressing that the plan had originated during the Eisenhower administration, Wright commented admiringly of the way Kennedy "did not attempt to avoid responsibility."[99] Wright later proposed a resolution authorizing Kennedy "to take such action as may be necessary" to prevent foreign militarization of Latin America. The proposal spoke to Wright's long interest in the region and his respect for presidential authority in foreign policy; ironically, given Wright's idealism, it also smacked of the Roosevelt Corollary to the Monroe Doctrine, an old rationale for American imperialism.[100]

When the Cuban Missile Crisis developed just over a year after the Bay of Pigs, Wright thought Kennedy's military mobilization and boycott appropriate. When Kennedy sought to inform Congress, congressmen were home on recess for the 1962 elections, and Wright helped organize a private, televised address in Fort Worth for congressmen from nearby states. Again Wright spoke admirably of Kennedy. Soviet leader Nikita Khrushchev, Wright stated, "underestimated John F. Kennedy."[101] The same was true when Khrushchev began to threaten West Berlin, ultimately building the

Berlin Wall. "Let us get behind Kennedy's admonition," Wright advised. "We are the night watchmen of freedom."[102]

Nothing spoke to Wright's idealism more than Kennedy's creation of the Peace Corps and the Alliance for Progress. As the Republican John Tower bashed the Peace Corps as a "bunch of starry-eyed liberals," Wright "worked the floor" for funding, becoming a key administration liaison with hesitant southern conservatives. After Congress approved the Peace Corps Act, Wright received an invitation to speak with the first volunteers. Reciprocating, he then invited the new Peace Corps director, Sargent Shriver, the president's brother-in-law, to speak in Fort Worth.[103] The Alliance for Progress, meanwhile, promised $100 billion in economic development for Latin America and thus spoke even more directly to Wright's idealism. Latin America, Wright explained, was "the most important area to the United States." Like the Inter-American Highway, which he had long advocated, the Alliance for Progress "raised hopes throughout the whole hemisphere."[104]

Wright's long-standing interest in Latin America was becoming obvious to all. Accordingly, congressional leaders appointed him to a new bipartisan delegation to meet annually with the Mexican Congress. Ultimately, he would serve in the delegation for almost two decades. At the time, he began taking lessons in Spanish at the State Department's Foreign Service Institute. Moreover, the Panamanian government turned to Wright when it feared that Kennedy might replace the American ambassador it favored, Joseph Farland. Employing his connections, Wright interceded and got Farland retained.[105]

Wright still had little time for neo-isolationists, and he struggled to understand why so many conservatives still questioned the United Nations. "Russian leaders are ready for the UN to die," Wright argued, appealing to the hearts of skeptics and arguing for the purchase of UN bonds. Noting that he had received letters "filled with slogans, inspired by misinformation . . . dripping with hate, and condemning the bonds as worthless," he noted that his own poll indicated support "by almost three to one." The United Nations was "not perfect," Wright acknowledged, employing his usual rhetorical nod to opponents as a way to gain their trust, but it was no one-world government.[106]

Wright, not surprisingly, also strongly supported the White House's efforts to increase foreign aid and create the United States Agency for International Development (USAID). After Congress approved the Foreign Assistance Act of 1961, which for the first time separated military and domestic aid, Wright still argued that the money did not "filter down to the average people." The solution was to harken back to the New Deal and have locals form cooperatives to which America might guarantee loans. It was "a sensible aid program," in the words of one columnist.[107] "You are one of the real bulwarks of strength during House debate on many of the most difficult issues of foreign policy," Secretary of State Dean Rusk told Wright. Kennedy was "most appreciative."[108]

Foreign aid hit home for Wright in more than one way. Craig Raupe, a vital cog in Wright's office, announced that he was joining USAID. It was a smart move; Raupe ended up coordinating all of the agency's programs for the Pacific Islands. It marked a turning point for his career; later he became a vice-president for Eastern Airlines. When Wright became majority leader years later, Raupe returned, but, at the time, Wright acknowledged that he had grown "dependent" on his young assistant. Wright temporarily hired Don Kennard, a friend and state senator who worked between legislative sessions, and, upon Kennard's departure, Larry L. King, who would later pen the musical *The Best Little Whorehouse in Texas*. With all these changes, Wright faced a period of difficult adjustment.[109]

Perhaps, Wright began to wonder, he, too, should join the administration. His frustration from his Senate defeat remained, and the death of Sam Rayburn left a great void. Rayburn had represented the Old School, the civility that Wright valued. Now, however, things seemed different. Wright's emotions were obvious in his eulogy on the House floor. Wright voted for the new Speaker, John McCormack, but he was just not Rayburn.[110] Moreover, just as Wright was beginning to reconcile himself to a career entirely in the House, media reports on elaborate overseas congressional trips threatened to diminish the institution.[111]

Serving in Congress certainly was not getting any easier. The magazine *Texas Observer* complained that Wright had won liberal votes in spite of his conservative record, citing his stance on debt and civil rights. The implication was that liberals needed a replacement. Wright was "having his cake and eating it too," one friend joked.[112] A year later, the media reported that conservatives, not liberals, were considering a primary challenge. In the end no Democrats ran, but Wright did face his first Republican challenger, the archconservative Del Barron, an insurance broker who embraced the John Birch Society.[113] Barron ran a vicious campaign in the 1962 general election, describing Wright as a "pious fraud." Wright's friends wanted him to reciprocate, but Wright declined, assuring them that he would not "take any chances on overconfidence."[114] Indeed, the mudslinging was "extremely difficult," and Wright's victory disconcerting. The fact that an individual so far right on the political spectrum received almost 40 percent of the vote was, perhaps, a reflection of troublesome political dynamics in Wright's district.[115]

Disgruntled and employing his connections again, Wright asked Vice President Johnson about an executive appointment. "Do you think I'm not frustrated?" Johnson replied. The real policy power was in Congress. Johnson concluded that he could probably get Wright "a spot in the cabinet or certainly the sub-cabinet," but recommended against it.[116] Several months later, another connection, deLesseps Morrison, offered to recommend Wright to replace him as the American ambassador to the Organization of American States. It was another tempting offer, but Johnson's advice was still ringing in Wright's ears.[117]

If he was going to remain in Congress—at least for the time being—Wright felt he would need to defend it against the growing charges of corruption. Writing an editorial in the periodical *Roll Call*, he argued that sensationalism overshadowed the dedication that congressmen performed daily.[118] He proposed better oversight of travel, a requirement that members disclose their transactions with private entities that had business before Congress, and a prohibition of congressmen conducting their own business with the public sector.[119] Wright's proposals were ironic in light of the charges that a quarter century later led to his political demise, but they added to the momentum for reform. Four years later—in 1967—and with Wright's support, Congress created the House Committee on Standards of Official Conduct, the first watchdog on congressional behavior and a forerunner of the House Ethics Committee. For his part, Wright began to contemplate a book along the same themes as his article. The result, *You and Your Congressman* in 1965, was, as Carl Albert termed it, a "primer on government."[120] Clearly the article, the proposal, and the book were outlets for Wright's frustrations.

Nothing, of course, compared to the shock of November 22, 1963. With the 1964 presidential election approaching, Johnson pressed Kennedy to make a campaign-style two-day visit to Texas. Kennedy agreed, according to his adviser Ted Sorensen, "to harmonize the warring factions of Texas Democrats."[121] Johnson envisioned Kennedy speaking in Houston and San Antonio on the first day and Fort Worth and Dallas on the second, culminating with a dinner in Austin. Predictably, Wright called Texas governor John Connally about his own district. Connally was interested in fundraising, while Wright wanted to appear in public on a dais with the world's most powerful man. Wright agreed to help raise $100,000 if Connally would support efforts to have Kennedy speak to a pre-breakfast crowd outside Fort Worth's Hotel Texas, where the presidential party was staying. Connally agreed, and Wright, with the help of unions, began organizing a fund-raiser with $100 tickets. The result was $78,000 in sales, more than Wright expected, and suggesting a fundraising prowess that his ill-fated Senate campaign had not fully utilized.[122]

Wright was at Carswell Air Force Base to welcome Kennedy to his city. Despite the late hour, a crowd of supporters cheered. "Take me over to the fence, Jim, and introduce me to some of these good people," Kennedy remarked.[123] Wright had little sleep that night, aware that forecasters had called for rain. Fortunately for Wright, the weather cleared quickly on Friday, November 22. Wright went up to the presidential suite and escorted the president down to the street, where a flatbed truck was parked as a stage. An enthusiastic crowd, still damp from the rain, waited there for the president's speech. Kennedy performed magnificently, Wright by his side. "Where's Jackie?" a supporter shouted. "It takes Jackie a little longer to get herself together," Kennedy responded. "But then she's prettier than we are. After all, nobody ever asks what Lyndon and I were wearing." For Wright the best was still to come. At the formal breakfast speech to the Fort Worth Chamber of Commerce, Kennedy praised Wright, catching the congress-man off guard. "I'm glad to be here in Jim Wright's city," Kennedy stated. "He speaks for Fort Worth, and he speaks for his country, and I don't know of any city that is better represented in the Congress."[124] The crowd exploded in cheers, a moment that Wright would cherish for the rest of his life.

Of course, the day was not over. Wright enjoyed a flight on Air Force One from Carswell to Love Field, talking with Kennedy and Connally about Dallas's reputation as a right-wing bastion. A full-page advertisement against Kennedy's visit had appeared that morning in the *Dallas Morning News*. Wright suggested the right-wing media as an explanation for the city's brand of conservatism. Connally countered that, unlike Fort Worth, which was known for its union workers, Dallas was known for its wealth built on the white-collar banking and insurance industries, which favored less regula-tion. After arriving at Love Field, Wright joined Kennedy's motorcade driv-ing through downtown Dallas, trailing a few cars back and traveling with fellow area congressmen Jack Brooks and Earl Cabell. Wright recalled that the crowd was larger and more enthusiastic than he had expected. As Ken-nedy's convertible limousine rounded the corner just in front of the Texas

Book Depository, and Wright's car was approaching the building, Wright heard three shots—"of that I am absolutely clear," he later recalled. At first he thought someone was giving a twenty-one-gun salute. This impression did not last long. Wright unfortunately had a front-row seat to the horrible drama that then unfolded—Jackie attempting to crawl out of the vehicle, the limousine speeding up out of Dealey Plaza, and the bewildered and silent crowd passing by Wright as his own car followed the now speeding motorcade to the hospital.[125]

Wright arrived in time to see the medical personnel removing Kennedy's limp body, the bloody vehicle that remained, and the chaos that ensued. As reporters gathered, desperate for news, Wright heard that Kennedy and Connally, who had also been hit, were still alive. When Wright reported the rumor, newsman Walter Cronkite repeated it on national television, quoting Wright by name.[126] Sadly, of course, in reality only Connally lived. After confirmation of Kennedy's demise, Wright was also present when Johnson learned of his promotion. Johnson, Wright recalled, was stunned, only recovering when Congressman Brooks suggested that tighter security was necessary in case of a broader plot. To swear in the new president, Brooks contacted a Dallas federal judge, who agreed to meet Johnson back at Air Force One. Johnson invited Wright to return to Washington on Air Force One with him, but Wright declined. There were reports of another shooting in Fort Worth, and it was best, Wright figured, to remain if the hunt for the assassin turned to his city.[127]

"For several days most of us moved around in a cloud," Wright later wrote. So much seemed surreal. The highs and lows, the peaks and valleys of his life, just somehow seemed starker. If Wright's career had seemed uncertain and frustrating before, now everything seemed even more in doubt. Wright's close acquaintance, one of his mentors, was now in the ultimate position of power, with implications for Wright's own career. Wright, however, was too disjointed, too much in disbelief, to think of matters like that. It was all so tough to process.[128]

CHAPTER 8

Access to Power

JOHNSON TAKES CONTROL (1963–1965)

Lyndon Johnson had grand ambitions, Wright later wrote, but "knew the dangers of being too progressive, too outspoken, too far ahead of the pack."[1] After the horror in Dallas, Johnson set about "subordinating his own agenda to that of the fallen president." In reality, of course, it was much more than that. The calculating Johnson recognized that associating himself with the martyred executive offered him a chance for his own great accomplishments. It allowed an activism he could never have advocated before. "Anybody that ever smelled of the Kennedys," Johnson remarked a month after the assassination, was welcome to join him.[2] As he claimed to be the "dutiful executor" of his predecessor's will, Johnson in fact unleashed a torrent of government—the "Great Society"—that far outstripped anything envisioned in Kennedy's Camelot.[3]

Wright had much in common with his old mentor, and the liberal in him reveled. Eradicating poverty, Wright gushed, "fulfilled my concept of what government was all about."[4] Although he had not read Michael Harrington's 1962 bestseller *The Other America: Poverty in the United States*, which influenced the Great Society, Wright accepted the assumption that properly placed government might break poverty's cycle of economic deprivation.[5] "Once a family moves into the ghetto," Wright wrote, "it begins a cycle of no job, illegitimate children, and all over again."[6] The key, for Wright, was to utilize government wisely, not simply to throw money at the problem. In the years that followed, Wright proved a reliable foot soldier in the Great Society, though he did not always see eye-to-eye with the new president on exactly what constituted wise spending. If he was quietly concerned about the debt, he certainly remained conscious of the conservative nature of many of his district's voters. Wright recognized that he did not share the now-liberated Johnson's national constituency. He agreed with Johnson's overall ideology and wanted to support his mentor, but, as always, Jim Wright would make his own political calculations. Republicans later decried Congress's rapid approval of the Great Society by labeling it "Johnson's hip-pocket Congress." Wright supported the Great Society, but he was in no one's hip pocket.[7]

This was evident only weeks after Kennedy's assassination. Because Wright would "vote right," Johnson urged him to make another run for the Senate in 1964. "There's a lot that I can do for you," Johnson stated. If Wright were to lose, a federal appointment could follow. The White House could get Texas governor Connally, "his arm in a sling" from his bullet wounds, to appear with Wright and allow him access to his "rich, fat-cat money." Playing off the frustrations he knew Wright was still experiencing, Johnson remarked that Wright could "just come back to the House" or "shoot the works." Wright, however, stood firm. "Damn, I appreciate that Lyndon," he answered. The offer was "tempting," but another run was just too risky. Although his own future remained in doubt, Wright simply thought it too soon to shoot for the moon again.[8]

Johnson was applying pressure on multiple fronts. Wright was at the White House when Johnson phoned a reluctant Supreme Court chief justice, Earl Warren, to convince him to accept the chairmanship of a bipartisan commission to investigate Kennedy's assassination. "This is your president," Johnson stated, "and I'm asking you to do this as a service to your country." Wright supported the resulting Warren Commission, assuming, like Johnson, that Castro or other communists were involved. While later acknowledging that its report was flawed, Wright, like Johnson, accepted its conclusion that the assassin Lee Harvey Oswald had acted alone.[9] Oswald was from Fort Worth, and thus Wright's staff scoured their records for helpful information. As it turned out, Oswald's mother had contacted Wright's office seeking help for finding her son, who was then in the Soviet Union. Wright had passed the request on to the State Department, which then had contacted the US Embassy in Moscow, but to no avail. Later, when political opponents speculated that Wright had assisted Oswald with his return, Wright got the Warren Commission's general counsel to write "unequivocally" that Wright had played no role.[10]

Unfortunately for Wright, the first legislative order of business for Johnson was passage of Kennedy's civil rights bill. "No memorial or oration or eulogy could more eloquently honor President Kennedy's memory," Johnson declared.[11] Once again Wright was in an uncomfortable position, with a new wave of opposition letters arriving daily. The bill, wrote one constituent, was "10% civil rights and 90% extension of federal executive power." Another wondered about "laws to give the white man an equal opportunity."[12] Once again, Wright decried the evils of racism on the House floor while denouncing the legislation as government overreach. "We can do it through the voluntary method . . . providing incentives rather than penalties," Wright suggested.[13] Wright's predicament was evident in April when Republicans claimed that he had criticized the proposal but had also apologized to the African American community. In fact, days after complaining that the bill had "leap frogged" the state courts, Wright had appeared before the Tarrant County Precinct Workers, a group with a strong African American presence, and cast the legislation in a more positive light. In the end the passage of the monumental Civil Rights Act of 1964 was, if anything, a relief to Wright. It removed a burr in his political saddle and ended an episode that he later concluded was one of his greatest regrets.[14]

When Johnson pushed the tax cuts Kennedy had proposed, Wright suggested that the nation—"never more dynamic and healthy than it is today"— could afford it. If the cuts were a bit of Keynesian economics, designed to stimulate the economy—a method that normally Wright opposed—he rationalized that its impact on the debt would be minimal. Johnson, moreover, coupled the tax cuts with targeted spending cuts, which allowed Wright to title one of his newsletters "Chronicle of a Budget Cutter."[15] Wright understood that the cuts, which were popular with conservatives, shielded him from criticism when he supported Johnson's liberalism in other realms. Indeed, over the next several years Wright reported progress for the "beleaguered taxpayer." Even as Wright supported the unfolding Great Society, he touted "economy as the new official watchword."[16] To Wright, the promise of a Great Society was not a promise of overwhelming debt.

The first proposal that portended the Great Society, the Economic Opportunity Act of 1964, provided almost $1 billion in government activism, including Job Corps, a vocational training program; a domestic group resembling the Peace Corps known as Volunteers in Service to America; and an early childhood education program called Head Start. The bill provided for a Community Action Program to organize local citizens and the Office of Economic Opportunity to oversee it all. Wright was among the strong Democratic majority voting for the bill. The proposal obviously reflected his old Populist sentiments and interest in education.[17]

Wright was surprised that almost three-fourths of conservative Democrats also supported the bill. It proved, Wright claimed, that attacking poverty "was generally more popular than some had originally thought." The easy passage made support for Johnson's other initiatives easier, and Wright always reminded conservatives that defense spending still dwarfed domestic allocations.[18] In reality, of course, any conservative support for Johnson quickly ebbed as the Great Society unfolded. Wright plowed ahead regardless of the coming 1964 elections, voting in favor of almost every new initiative while promising that he would not "hesitate to oppose President Johnson when he is wrong."[19] Among the new initiatives was a permanent food stamp program, which Wright reminded critics was not mandatory and shared expenses among jurisdictions.[20]

Given his own personal interests, Wright's support for the National Arts and Cultural Development Act of 1964, which created the National Council on the Arts and foretold the following year the creation of national endowments for the arts and humanities, was hardly surprising.[21] The same was true for Wright's support for the Wilderness Act of 1964, which removed pristine natural areas from development. After all, Wright's district included no such designated areas.[22] Wright, of course, supported expanded funding for public works, but protected his right flank by breaking from the White House in its promotion of mass transit. Fort Worth, Wright understood, did not have the same level of congestion as many older eastern cities. Still touting himself as an anti-debt crusader, he could still say he was fighting "wasteful spending" even as the term remained as nebulous as ever.[23]

Wright's support for the president's foreign policy never wavered, certainly not in Johnson's first year, which, in retrospect, was a seminal year for what would become known as the Vietnam War. By this point the story of American involvement was already more than a decade old, marked by incremental increases in support for the capitalist South Vietnam against the communist North.[24] Kennedy had even secretly approved of a coup against South Vietnam's unpopular president, Ngo Dinh Diem, a plot that had done little to stabilize the war-torn country. Wright had watched these developments, though he was unaware of Kennedy's role in the Diem coup; like most of America, however, he had given it little attention.[25]

In retrospect, the arrival of the Johnson administration might have been a propitious time for the United States to depart from Vietnam. In later years historians would suggest that the conflict involved elements of nationalism and anticolonialism and should not have been interpreted solely through a bipolar Cold War lens.[26] At the time, however, few thought in such terms, certainly not Johnson, Wright, or the majority of Wright's Capitol Hill colleagues. America had already invested considerable funds and manpower in Vietnam, which a withdrawal would waste. "The whole business of Vietnam should be put into the context of the times," Wright later said, beginning to explain his consistent support for America's longest war and its most notable defeat.[27] Not only did Wright accept the famous "domino theory" and America's containment policy, but he continued to believe that the president deserved leeway to guide foreign policy. The Constitution gave the chief executive the power to wage war, and dissention emboldened America's opponents. This view had held firm throughout Wright's career, and with his mentor Johnson in the Oval Office, he was not likely to change now.[28]

So it was in August 1964 when the destroyer USS *Maddox* came under attack by North Vietnamese gunboats. Seeking authority to retaliate for an obvious act of war, Johnson sought approval from Congress with a resolution similar to the one Congress had passed during the Eisenhower years regarding Formosa. "We must make it clear to all that the United States is united," Johnson stated.[29] In reaction, Congress moved swiftly—and, as some historians have suggested, with too little debate. Only two days later, the Senate passed the Gulf of Tonkin Resolution 88–2, and the House followed unanimously. Satisfied with Johnson's assurances of "no rashness and no wider war," Congress granted Johnson a blank check for further military action.[30] Wright strongly approved. Johnson's call for unity reflected his own desires in the matter. In fact, Wright's newsletter took a triumphant tone. "North Vietnamese military leaders must be suffering serious doubts about the wisdom of their precipitate attacks," he wrote.[31]

Lost in the rush, perhaps, was a chance to debate the larger issues at hand. Perhaps afraid of being cast as weak on communism, or recognizing that an authorization short of a war declaration left room to avoid blame if matters went bad, many congressmen did not delve deeper. How far was America willing to go? What exactly constituted victory? Were there limits to the regional conflicts that promised to characterize containment? In this sense, at least, it was not Congress's finest hour.[32] Faced with this argument years later, Wright defended the institution. "I don't agree with that," he explained. "It may not have been Congress's finest hour but neither was it Congress's weakest hour," he stated. Wright believed that Congress needed to react quickly and forcibly, and that Johnson's efforts to enlist Republicans were admirable. Years later Wright still could not bring himself to declare the conflict a mistake, although he acknowledged that as the war dragged on he had harbored growing reservations about the strategies employed. He could understand that the enemy might have been more nationalist than communist, or that the South Vietnamese government might have been fundamentally flawed. He had grown to understand the arguments of those who had objected, and accepted the reality that the growing lack of public support had made victory difficult. It just remained too painful to think that it all might have been for naught.[33]

Indeed, as Congress debated the Gulf of Tonkin Resolution, Wright's stake in Vietnam grew exponentially. Wright's son Jimmy, now a strapping nineteen-year-old, announced that he wanted to join the army. The year before, Wright had discouraged Jimmy from joining the Peace Corps, but now Jimmy had the stronger hand. Wright, after all, had left the University of Texas to fight in World War II. As Jimmy argued that draft deferments were unfair, Wright simply had to acquiesce with mixed emotions. He was undoubtedly proud of his son, but, perhaps not even consciously, sensed that the matter might not turn out well.[34]

In any event, the resolution in hand, Johnson did not want to be seen as a warmonger with his 1964 presidential campaign in full swing. In the words of historian Stanley Karnow, Johnson "exercised caution immediately after the Gulf of Tonkin affair."[35] The first step was simply to get through the elections.

Jim Wright had his own election to get through. For the first time, he faced a significant challenge in the Democratic primary: the popular Fort Worth city councilman Tommy Thompson. Noting that Wright had cited Congress's "unfinished business" as a reason for his reelection, Thompson claimed that Wright had been ineffective. Thompson even cited the uncompleted Trinity River project, a task for which no man could have done more than Wright. When this line of attack failed, Thompson began describing Wright as a "career politician."[36] This was a more realistic attack, but the economy was growing and, unlike in later years, in 1964 the public still held their legislators in relatively high esteem. Wright had positioned himself well in the divided party, leaning leftward but with a defense against the right. Some, at least, complained. "Jim Wright is so anxious to get the support of divergent groups that he does a little bit for each and does not take a stand on an issue," wrote one liberal. Most of Wright's constituents, however, appreciated his bipartisan pragmatism. Moreover, in his moderation he tended to avoid the political wrath that extremism could have engendered. Indeed, when the primary arrived, Wright overwhelmingly won the nomination.[37]

Another credible opponent, Fred Dielman, faced Wright in the general election—another sign, perhaps, that the Texas GOP was growing. Polls showed that both Johnson, who was still carrying the Kennedy baton, and Wright were still popular, but the Texas Republicans planned to use their new "EDP machines." These electronic data machines instantly processed voters' names, addresses, telephone numbers, and the "hardness" of their partisan attachments.[38] They spoke to the future, but, as it turned out, did little to influence the present. Wright still had the power of incumbency. When a Texas cowboy rode his Brahman bull "Bobo" through Washington on his way to the World's Fair, Wright was photographed atop the animal, his own cowboy hat in hand. To offset Wright's continuing financial constraints, his supporters held a "Jim Wright Appreciation Dinner" at Fort Worth's Will Rogers Memorial Center. The dinner was laughingly cast as a "non-partisan" rally, and it helped Wright boost his moderate, trans-party image.[39] Avoiding the issue of race, Wright cultivated conservatives by noting his anti-debt credentials while boasting, ironically or not, of his district's appropriations.[40] The media helped. Wright, the *Fort Worth Press* declared, was "fighting for the local cause." When the November tally came, voters agreed. Wright garnered almost two-thirds of the electorate.[41]

In the midst of it all, Wright found time to campaign for Johnson against the Republican nominee, Arizona senator Barry Goldwater. Wright knew Goldwater, who commanded the Capitol Hill reserve air force unit in which Wright served. Goldwater was a "fine commander," Wright recalled, but politically was "not amenable to discussions." He was so ideological it made the consensus and compromise Wright valued difficult. During the campaign, Wright traveled the Southwest, but mostly in West Texas. "I did everything I was asked to do," Wright remembered.[42] Following the campaign script to make Goldwater appear extreme, Wright spoke favorably of "responsible conservatives." Goldwater, however, was part of a "bitter, fanatical fringe group."[43] Goldwater, who recommended eliminating Social Security and suggested military control of nuclear weapons, certainly made

Wright's task easier. "Extremism in the defense of liberty is no vice, and moderation in the pursuit of justice is no virtue," Goldwater declared.[44]

The campaign quickly became bitter. As the Johnson campaign aired the infamous "Daisy Girl" television commercial implying that Goldwater would lead to nuclear Armageddon, Wright saw no irony in arguing that Republicans ran their campaign "on a level much below that to which the American public is entitled." Years later, Wright still thought the "Daisy Girl" commercial was "quite effective." It depicted Goldwater "as a quick-tempered guy, which was what he was."[45] Wright, it appeared, prided himself on running clean campaigns but was not above bare-knuckled politics.

Befitting his growing stature, Wright even took time to campaign for congressional candidates in six different states, and his ability as a speaker became quite the draw. Occasionally joining him was the actor Dan Blocker, the character Hoss Cartwright on the popular television western *Bonanza*. With each appearance, Wright expanded his connections. A favor done was a favor owed. On November 3, 1964, all the work paid off. Johnson won the largest popular vote ever up to that time, thumping Goldwater in the Electoral College 486–32. Equally important, from Wright's perspective, was that the Democrats gained 38 House seats. In the Senate Democrats held more than the critical two-thirds majority. To top it off, Texas's two Republican congressmen lost, including Wright's old nemesis Bruce Alger.[46]

On the surface, at least, the overwhelming victory laid bare the Republican claims of rejuvenation, their EDP system notwithstanding. At closer inspection, however, the situation for the GOP was not quite as dire as it seemed. Undoubtedly Kennedy's aura swayed some voters, and Goldwater was arguably a poor candidate, so the landslide was somewhat of an anomaly. More significantly for the long term, Goldwater won a swath of the Old Confederacy from Louisiana eastward to South Carolina. Today it is clear that this Republican strength in the South was a precursor of a tectonic shift in politics. The full impact of the turbulent 1960s had yet to unfold, but the 1964 results spoke to a growing conservative reaction deep in the heart of Dixie. In 1964, Texas went solidly Democratic, with one of its own at the top of the ticket. But the state was a part of the South and had more than its share of conservatism. It was a reality that Jim Wright already knew and one that would continue to challenge him.

As 1965 began, however, Democrats claimed a public mandate. It was almost enough to make Wright forget—at least temporarily—his recent frustrations. Once again supporters pressed Wright to run against the Republican

John Tower in the Senate. "Everyone is itching for 1966 and the timely burial of John Tower," one loyalist wrote just after the election.[47] To celebrate the triumph, Wright hosted a buffet for the Texas delegation on the eve of Johnson's inauguration. Wright had arranged for one bus to bring guests early in the evening and another later. The first crowd, however, was so celebratory that they remained, and the Wright house became packed with over one hundred guests, all anxious for the new session to begin.[48]

"The broad outlines of the Great Society began to take form as Congress reorganized last week," Wright wrote his constituents at the beginning of the 89th Congress in January 1965. Months later, as the first session wound down, Wright quoted one of his colleagues. "I can't believe that we will have anything left to work on next year," the congressman had joked.[49] In fact, the 89th Congress was historic in the volume of major legislation it passed, rivaling the Roosevelt Congress at the beginning of the New Deal. Much to his frustration, Wright was still not a senator or even a committee chair. None of the momentous bills officially carried his name. Nevertheless, just as the new Congress convened, Wright was enough of a presence to earn a spot on the bipartisan delegation to the funeral of former British prime minister Winston Churchill, one of the largest state funerals in history. The trip also included a week conferring with British legislators at a historical country estate. Clearly, although Wright held no leadership post, he was not a backbencher.[50]

Public Works Committee chairman George Fallon, for one, asked Wright to serve as floor leader for legislation to address the blight along America's highways, a pet cause of the First Lady. After the White House hosted a conference on the issue in May 1965 and the Senate passed a bill, the House appeared to present a problem. Many conservatives feared infringements on private property. The bill restricted billboards, required junkyards to be screened, and funded landscaping. With Wright working for a compromise, White House aides reported that "House leaders were counting noses and twisting arms."[51] The final compromise ensured "just compensation" for seized property and allowed localities additional say in implementing restrictions. "I knew that a Texan could do it," Vice President Humphrey congratulated Wright.[52]

Another appointment came when the Appalachian Regional Development Commission, which Kennedy had created to explore ways to stimulate the economy in that region, issued its report.[53] Named to a committee tasked with turning the recommendations into a specific bill, Wright helped craft a package of just over $1 billion in subsidies for infrastructure, vocational training, and crop conservation. With the bill's provisions set, Wright then served as chairman of a Democratic task force to ensure passage, a difficult task, given that Republicans boycotted the Public Works Committee to deny it a quorum. Only when Speaker John McCormack threatened to keep Congress in session until it had dealt with all poverty programs did the Republicans relent. When Congress passed the Appalachian Regional Development Act in March 1965, Wright sought to reassure conservatives by distinguishing the law from welfare. It makes "productive taxpayers from tax liabilities," he explained. It was "not a hand-out but a hand-up," an argument Wright would come to use frequently in advancing Johnson's agenda.[54]

Wright's support for Johnson's 1965 education initiatives, the Elementary and Secondary Education Act and the Higher Education Act, was hardly surprising, given his record. Wright had increasingly lamented an educational "achievement gap," and the former provided funds to improve schools serving low-income children. With his own children nearing college age, Wright applauded the latter, which provided aid to universities, authorized low-interest student loans, and created a National Teacher Corps. Once again Wright worked to find consensus. He assured conservatives that both bills required reauthorization and prohibited any federal curriculum. Wright surely understood, however, that both were revolutionary in their extension of federal authority.[55] It was not an issue of states' rights, Wright argued, but rather one of "national values."[56]

The historic passage of the Medicare and Medicaid health reforms as part of the Social Security Act Amendments of 1965 was more problematic for Wright. The United States remained the only industrial democracy without some form of national health insurance, but for almost two decades the American Medical Association (AMA) had joined with many conservatives to defeat comprehensive reform. The AMA worried about physician compensation, and conservatives warned of "socialized medicine." Recognizing such conservative sentiment in his own district, Wright stated that he feared "the insidious dangers of socialized medicine" and would always protect the "sanctity of the doctor-patient relation." Hoping to avoid either extreme, he suggested giving the "Kerr-Mills Bill a chance to work." That 1960 legislation had allowed matching funds for states that set up programs for their elderly and poor.[57]

With the new Congress, however, came new efforts for comprehensive insurance. The Democratic Study Group, a group to develop party policy, reported "a particularly heavy mail barrage" pressing for reform.[58] Caught in the middle, Wright was vague, telling one liberal that he did not "remember having expressed my definite opposition" to national coverage.[59] More often, Wright simply responded that he had "not had a chance to study the various proposals."[60] Into this uncomfortable void came Wilbur Mills and Robert Kerr, the authors of the original 1960 legislation, who proposed a compromise that did not include universal coverage but expanded their earlier program to the national level. The Democratic leadership urged support and Wright fell in line. To mute conservative criticism, Wright noted that the program utilized private companies, ensured individual choice of doctors, and was paid through expanding Social Security rather than through new taxes.[61] In the end, therefore, Wright supported passage of Medicare and Medicaid, two cornerstones of the Great Society, and later took considerable pride in his stance.[62]

Wright knew how to mute conservative criticism. He agreed with a report from the Truman-era Commission on Immigration and Naturalization that America's system of national quotas for immigration perpetuated racial inequities.[63] Nevertheless, when southern conservatives pressed him to resist reform, Wright mollified them without giving them what they wanted. "I shared your concern before I had the opportunity of becoming familiar with the proposal," he replied. The bill "would make no abrupt changes . . . with plans to phase out the national origins formula over a five year period." Limits to immigration still existed, he added, with the total number "not substantially changed." By focusing on individual circumstances, the United States could more easily contain radicals. When Wright voted for the Immigration and Naturalization Act of 1965, another cornerstone of the Great Society, his arguments swayed many of his colleagues. The bill passed with considerable majorities.[64]

The issue of "home rule" for the District of Columbia was particularly contentious. In a debate that reflected both racial and partisan overtones, many Democrats complained that residents had no vote. For Wright, it was an affront to his idealism. "If it was unfair in 1776 to impose levies on people without giving them the right to express themselves in the councils of government," Wright argued, "it is doubly wrong today."[65] Characteristically, however, he proposed a compromise. Congress should retain control over a smaller federal area within the District of Columbia, allowing residents elsewhere suffrage. Wright's proposal was still too much for many conservatives, however, who envisioned a new wave of liberals and blocked any reform until 1973. Even then, residents of the District of Columbia won no voting privileges on the floor of Congress.[66]

The bills kept coming, and Wright dutifully obliged. He voted for the Housing and Urban Development Act of 1965, which expanded funds for public housing, and for the creation of the Department of Housing and Urban Development.[67] More to Wright's heart, however, was his support for the Clean Water Act of 1965, which provided for stronger federal oversight and required states to develop water quality standards for all navigable interstate waters. By this point Wright had a considerable record supporting clean water, even as he still did not fully appreciate reclamation as a potential environmental threat.[68] When he was appointed the chairman of a subcommittee on watershed development, Wright's emphasis remained more on ensuring clean water for consumption than on maintaining natural water ecologies. This emphasis was evident in Wright's second book, which came out in the midst of Johnson's legislative wave. In *The Coming Water Famine*, Wright argued that both stopping pollutants and expanding development projects would ensure adequate supply. Water development, Wright added for good measure, was not "pork barrel." The book, he later joked, did not sell well. Just as it was released, a severe drought broke in New York City, forcing local officials to consider flood relief.[69]

To be fair, few Americans yet thought in ecological terms by the mid-1960s. The environmental movement was still in its infancy. In time, Wright's words began to reflect the evolving consensus as he acknowledged the "cry for pure air, pure water, noise abatement, open spaces and scenic preservation."[70] He later cited "the abatement of water pollution" as "one of the things I am most proud of."[71] Nevertheless, at the time, Wright envisioned a massive grant program to states for dams and desalinization. Moreover, despite his later endorsements of preservation, Wright also never lost his fondness for large reclamation projects. Wright, as he was so often, was still the moderate. He never could be easily categorized.[72]

Johnson's 1965 call for new voting rights legislation was, predictably, a challenge for Wright. Wright quickly remembered how difficult moderation and consensus had been in the civil rights debate the year before. On matters of race, critics were never easily assuaged. Johnson's proposal required federal approval for states with a history of denying suffrage rights to change their voting regulations. It applied to all jurisdictions that had used a "device" to disenfranchise voters and those in which less than 50 percent of the population had been registered to vote in 1964.[73] In short, it applied to Texas, where many in Wright's district were sure to object strenuously. Wright, however, had felt the pangs of not voting his conscience the year before and, in any event, saw voting rights as separate from private accommodations. Suffrage was the key to democracy, the idealist in Wright believed, the reason he had voted in favor of voting rights legislation in 1957 and 1960 despite the conservative criticism.

Wright did not initially take the lead in pushing for Johnson's bill. "You have my word that I will study closely all committee actions on this bill," Wright promised one critic of the enforcement provisions. "Should it reach the floor with any provisions I consider dangerous, I will speak out against them."[74] In fact, when the proposal reached the full House, Wright knew exactly what he wanted to say. "Coming from a state of the Old Confederacy and steeped in the traditions and customs of the changing Southland, I believe we are ready to let all the people vote," Wright confidently declared for the record. "I have no fear of the result."[75] Whether Wright was fearful or not, letters of protest flooded his office. Once again, Wright did his best to mollify his conservative critics, reminding them that he had resisted the Civil Rights Act of 1964. In short, it appeared, his pragmatism the previous year had made it easier for him to follow his idealism in the new year.[76] Wright's strong support was no doubt influential among his colleagues. They recognized that he was subjecting his own constituency to a higher standard. When the vote finally came, more than fifty southern conservatives voted against it. Some, however, sided with Wright and the president. Passing the House by a vote of 333-85, the Voting Rights Act of 1965 won 78 percent of Democrats.[77]

When Johnson signed the Voting Rights Act, Martin Luther King Jr. applauded its passage. After all, the Voting Rights Act and the Civil Rights Act the year before stood as the hallmarks of the nonviolent civil rights movement. Johnson, however, still foresaw trouble. The Democratic embrace of African Americans threatened to cleave their coalition further apart, sending southern conservatives into the hands of the GOP. "I think we just delivered the South to the Republican Party for the next generation," Johnson reportedly told journalist Bill Moyers after the 1964 legislation passed.[78] Accurate or not, Johnson was even blunter speaking to Texas governor Connally after the 1965 legislation passed. "Now my judgment is we're going to lose every Southern state. . . . I just don't think they can take this nigga stuff," Johnson remarked. Southerners were going to "pour it on."[79] Perhaps Johnson envisioned something like Richard Nixon's famous "Southern Strategy" three years later or Ronald Reagan's wholesale Republican takeover of Dixie in 1980. If Wright thought likewise, he at least assumed that he personally remained on solid electoral grounds despite his vote for the 1965 legislation. After all, just as the letters of complaint arrived, developments offered Wright another chance to win the hearts of all of his constituents, conservative and liberal alike.

The debate over Fort Worth's beloved Trinity River development came to a head, casting Wright in the role of hometown hero. For years Wright had pushed the project, winning funding for various portions and for a comprehensive Corps of Engineers feasibility study. In the middle of 1965 the Corps issued its long-awaited report, which noted not only the high price tag but also the economic advantages of having barge traffic reach upstream to Fort Worth. Pressing the report's conclusions with Charles Schultze, director of Johnson's Bureau of the Budget (BOB), Wright found the report did little to sway Schultze's fear that the additional spending would prove inflationary. Wright, however, knew that Johnson had just thanked him for his support of home rule in the District of Columbia and thought that he might press his advantage with Schultze's boss.[80]

Meeting the president in a small room on the ground floor of the White House, Wright first recounted how bureaucrats had frustrated Johnson's efforts for reclamation projects on the Colorado River. It was the same now, Wright stated. Johnson replied that Governor Connally had made a similar plea but that the BOB's concerns were real. Annoyed, Wright thought to himself that Johnson was simply protecting his own political backside. If he were to approve the project, opponents would argue that he was favoring his own state, that he was encouraging inflation, and that he was for free spending, with the costs for the Great Society and Vietnam War continuing to grow.[81]

Unwilling to cave, Wright suggested that legislation authorizing the project did not need BOB approval. Trying to push a bill without BOB approval, Johnson quipped, would get Wright "laughed off the floor of Congress." Wright replied that he did not care. "I can pass the bill with them laughing," he boasted.[82] His challenge before him, Wright started lobbying his colleagues, employing every means available, including calling in his own chips. He reminded colleagues from the upper South that he had supported the Appalachian Regional Development Act. "I paraded representatives of some seventy Texas cities before the [Rivers and Harbors] subcommittee," Wright later wrote.[83] Wright fought off efforts to remove the navigation provisions, leaving only flood control. When the House passed an omnibus rivers and harbors bill that included funding for the Trinity, Wright worked with Texas senator Ralph Yarborough to ensure that it remained in the Senate version. When the House-Senate Conference Committee subsequently reported a final bill that included the Trinity but eliminated many other projects, Wright then had to deal with his colleagues who had lost, members who obviously did not enjoy Wright's clout. "Compromise is the name of the game in conference," Wright explained. "If each side didn't give in, there'd be no purpose to having a conference and subsequently no legislation." It was Wright at his congressional best, proving that he had political skills to rival Johnson. Indeed, Wright had compromised. The omnibus bill of 1965 did not fund the entire Trinity. It still required Texans to raise additional funds for the project's completion, a task Wright was confident they could achieve.[84]

In the end, perhaps Wright was overconfident. In the years that followed, Texas politics continued to evolve. Environmentalists, who had backed Wright on so much, sued to stop the project even as conservatives increasingly found the required $150 million bond issue too costly to swallow. When the measure came to the ballot eight years later, a growing hesitancy to take on more taxing and spending helped doom it—and, ultimately, Wright's grand vision. "It was a big miscalculation on my part," Wright later acknowledged.[85] At the time, however, the future for the Trinity appeared bright, and Wright was its heroic champion, feted by Fort Worth's civic leaders and wealthy power-brokers. Wright constantly reminded voters that he was "proud to say that I have been its leading champion."[86] With his support for the city's airport and General Dynamics to boot, Wright figured that he could afford the occasional vote against his district's conservatives. With his support for so much of the Great Society, he could even afford the occasional break from his president and mentor. Wright, as always, made his own calculations and demonstrated that he well understood how to bridge the divisions that surrounded him.

Johnson understood Wright, any differences in their political calculations aside. He respected Wright's obvious political skill and knew that Wright had supported so much of his agenda. Their rifts were relatively minor, and Wright was, overall, an invaluable ally to cultivate. Johnson began to push him to challenge Senator Tower in the coming 1966 elections. Wright could be the perfect candidate to pull enough conservative voters from the Republicans to deny Tower reelection. He could claim moderation and help maintain the struggling Democratic New Deal coalition. Wright thought so too. His supporters explained that the liberals who had turned on the conservative Democrat Blakley in 1961 and helped elect Tower now realized their mistake. Wright's ambition quietly burned. He wanted to run; he even needed to run. At the same time, however, beyond the obvious concern over additional debt, he feared that a loss would define him as too personally ambitious. "Doggone it," Wright complained to one reporter who had speculated that he might run. "What you wrote . . . portrayed me as an opportunist."[87] Certainly any campaign promised formidable opposition. The Texas attorney general, Waggoner Carr, had already declared, and the media reported that he had over $1 million on hand.

Wright had first seriously thought of running in 1964. "Let me ask you one candid question," Wright then asked a financial contributor. "Do you feel if I run against Tower in 1966 that the great bulk of the good Democrats would rally to my support regardless of whoever else might enter that race?"[88] By early 1965 Wright was clearly leaning toward taking the plunge. "[Tower] notes that he expects 'formidable opposition' next year," Wright wrote another supporter in February. "I hope that I can see to it that he is not disappointed."[89] By the summer, Wright had decided to run if it appeared he could raise sufficient funds and attract support from all over the state. He encouraged supporters to use his book signings to garner publicity and to put up fliers in areas where he was not well known. He began working with an Austin marketing firm, Clyde Johnson and Associates, on "advertising layouts, suggested letters, and various mailing list compilations." Writing the firm's namesake, Wright explained that "the problem is a familiar one." He wanted money to ensure a valid campaign before he announced his candidacy, but only an announcement would raise sufficient funds.[90]

By the fall of 1965, it was becoming difficult for Wright to feign disinterest publicly. "It probably comes as no surprise to you that I would like to be in the Senate," Wright stated directly in a fundraising form letter.[91] When some supporters suggested a run for governor, Wright stated that he only wanted to be a senator. "As a matter of fact, I have never desired to be Governor of Texas," Wright responded, conveniently forgetting his earlier flirtation with the governorship.[92] Supporters began to organize on their own. "I believe that his candidacy is a strong probability at this time," one Fort Worth attorney wrote his legal colleagues.[93] Even the Democratic National Committee was starting to notice. "The library here at the DNC has a thick file on John Tower," wrote one Washington staffer to Wright. "This sounds like a real gold mine," Wright replied, whatever his hesitancy to attack opponents personally. "Material such as I suspect you have will not only be helpful but essential in giving Texans a true picture of the Junior Senator's Birch-like philosophy and utter ineffectiveness." Wright was ready to run, it appeared, and anticipated a rough campaign.[94]

Then Wright hit upon a plan. He would purchase television time and ask voters if he should run. He would explain the high cost of campaigning and solicit donations, noting that unlike other candidates with deep-pocket contributors, he needed wide support from the working people. It would play off his populist appeal. If he could get 25,000 Texans to contribute $10 each, he would run. It was a bold move but not unprecedented. In 1938, W. Lee O'Daniel had asked voters if he should run for governor and had subsequently won. In 1956, Price Daniel had asked voters if he should resign his Senate seat and run for governor, and had also won. While Wright, unlike Daniel, was not planning to risk his existing position, a public plea had nevertheless worked before. Spending $10,000, therefore, Wright purchased thirty minutes on seventeen Texas stations for the evening of December 16, 1965. As the night approached, he also bought newspaper advertisements. "Hear Congressman Jim Wright in one of the most frank, candid and revealing statements in Texas political annals," the ads declared.[95]

The response was discouraging, in part because the ads had had to compete against a popular western starring Jimmy Stewart. After two weeks, Wright had received only 7,000 replies, garnering just under $49,000. The responses came from 167 separate counties, but almost 100 counties had contributed nothing. In fact, almost 50 percent of the total came from his own district. Accordingly, on January 8, 1966, Wright announced that he would not be a candidate. If he were to run, Wright explained, he would have to be a constant "beggar," or, alternatively, get the assistance of wealthy groups who were "more interested in what I can do for them." He refused to do either. "I am not temperamentally suited for the former nor conscientiously fitted for the latter." Wright promised to return the contributions, but his disappointment was obvious. "It is sobering to realize how little known are the works of any member of the US House of Representatives beyond the area of his constituency," he lamented.[96]

The press did a brief postmortem, some suggesting that Wright had been disingenuous in claiming that the Senate would not benefit him personally. While it was true that the salaries were similar, the Senate had more prestige, a larger staff, and additional power. Others suggested that the age of thirty-minute political advertisements had passed. A more skeptical public simply changed the channel. Wright had his own conclusions: too many people thought the advertisement was just a political stunt. "Apparently they thought I would pretend to have heard from 25,000 people even if such was not the truth," Wright remarked, hardly hiding his frustration over what might have been.[97]

The letters of support comforted Wright, as did an editorial in the *Fort Worth Star-Telegram* declaring that he had made the "right decision."[98] Any way he cast the result, however, the reality remained—he was in the same position he had held for over a decade. Even the chairmanship of the Public Works Committee seemed distant with fifty-four-year-old John Blatnik next in line. While Speaker John McCormack was seventy-four, he had waited for years during Rayburn's long reign and appeared unlikely to surrender the position now. Even if he did, fifty-seven-year-old majority leader Carl Albert was poised to assume the title. Below him were a bevy of other powerful— and more senior—committee chairmen. Wright, after all, was not alone in his ambition.[99]

Wright was concluding one of the most productive years in congressional history. By the end of 1965, Johnson had been in the White House for two years and his Great Society was a reality. So much of what Wright believed in was going so well. Wright was proud of his role in the wave of momentous legislation, but he still hoped for something more. It appeared Wright had no choice. He had just turned forty-three. He would have to bide his time and just hope for the best.

CHAPTER 9

———

The Rough Path Forward

YEARS OF CHANGE (1965–1968)

The new Congress quickly tempered Wright's hopes and optimism. Wright supported successful efforts to raise the minimum wage, improve automobile safety standards, create public broadcasting, and expand funding for a number of federal programs. Nevertheless, as 1966 progressed, it became obvious that the Great Society's momentum had stalled.[1] Its cracks had begun to show, and the inevitable conservative backlash had begun. The country, Wright increasingly found himself saying, was not "going to hell in a hand basket."[2]

It was not just conservatives who worried about the country's direction. Wright had earlier described Vietnam as "that nasty little war." By 1966, however, he spoke the obvious in concluding that nothing could be "appraised apart" from it.[3] His continued support for the war angered the growing number of protesters. Years later, after the Pentagon Papers disclosed that Johnson and the military had not been forthright with the facts, Wright acknowledged that he had not been "sufficiently attuned" and that he had incorrectly assumed "that the South Vietnamese elections were fair."[4]

"Wars are for winning," Wright assumed at the time, adding that he had given "100% support to our fighting forces."[5] The escalation, of course, cost money, but Wright still saw no threat to the Great Society or the national debt. Supporting early in 1966 a supplemental appropriation and "the taxes to pay for it," Wright hoped to send the enemy a message.[6] Failing to support the appropriation, Wright warned, would give "a false impression of indecision," prolonging the war.[7] Adding that taxes remained lower than at any time since the Korean War, Wright declared that the nation was "far better prepared to sustain a prolonged effort." In fact, he hoped, the booming economy would still shrink the debt despite the escalation. Through the end of 1966, at least, it did.[8]

Wright, of course, was hardly immune to the reality of war with his son "in country." Wright understood the soldiers' sacrifices and supported expanded veterans benefits.[9] What Wright could not understand were the growing protests, which he believed encouraged the enemy. It perplexed Wright but did little to challenge his assumptions. By 1966, Wright was quietly acknowledging at least "some reservations," but he believed that "no simple solution" existed for an administration that had little choice.[10] The war "must indeed be stopped before it consumes us all," he told college students. "But the only way . . . is for the aggressors to be forced to stop their aggression."[11]

Despite the fact that Wright was beginning to think that there was "no simple solution," ironically he proposed just such a solution in February 1966. The proposal spoke both to his idealism and to his presumptuousness. Holding no significant foreign policy post or secret intelligence, Wright suggested to Johnson a diplomatic offensive. Stating that "no truly free election" comforted communists, Wright proposed two elections supervised by the United Nations. First, after a six-week truce, the South Vietnamese would vote on their form of government. Two years later, an election, North and South, would determine the leaders for one national government. The United States might even promise economic assistance. "We could probably help electrify every village, pave every major road in South Viet-Nam, build a water purification and sewage disposal plant in every town of 10,000 or more, and indemnify the government for its promised land reform programs," Wright suggested. It was as if Wright had no knowledge of the failed Geneva Accord elections or of the millions of dollars already plowed into the country, or that he little appreciated the nationalistic popularity of North Vietnamese leader Ho Chi Minh. While Wright had a point when he said that the plan might "put Hanoi on the psychological defensive," his suggestion to use the elections to highlight "that America has never sought territorial aggrandizement" whitewashed America's own history.[12]

The plan's simplicity might suggest that Wright had his own public relations agenda, but in fact, he did not go to the press but lobbied privately,
which suggests that he truly believed it was a viable plan.[13] The responses
he received predictably—but politely—tamped down his optimism. Senate
Armed Services Committee chairman William Fulbright noted that
Wright's "objective" was "similar to mine," but that the White House would
think the plan impractical.[14] UN Ambassador Arthur Goldberg noted that
North Vietnam believed the United Nations to be a tool of the West, and
that the losing side would declare the results invalid.[15] Assistant Secretary
of State Douglas MacArthur II, the nephew of the famed general, added
that elections had already been scuttled.[16] "What makes sense to us doesn't
make sense to them," Johnson simply replied. If Wright wanted to pursue
the matter, he could take his suggestions to Walt Rostow, an adviser who
was pursuing diplomatic alternatives. Wright did so only to be shuttled
to Abe Fortas, a Johnson confidant newly on the Supreme Court. "The only
thing we can do is to make the war cost them more than they're willing to
pay," Fortas stated, putting the matter to rest.[17]

To make matters worse, the problems abroad had begun to metastasize at
home. By the end of 1966, the combination of increased consumer demand
from the tax cuts, increased domestic spending, and the new massive outlays for the war had finally begun to cause troublesome inflation.[18] When
Johnson began to press for a tax increase to soak up spending power, Wright
protested that it would raise the cost of living. Congress would never support taxes as "an anti-inflationary device." The answer was to increase
production with a tax credit for business investment and, as he had suggested before, to loosen the money supply.[19] Johnson, like Wright, worried
about higher borrowing costs, but the tight-fisted Fed chairman, William
McChesney Martin, disagreed. Accordingly, the discount rates remained
the highest in over thirty years.[20]

Soon the rising war costs began to cannibalize the Great Society. A
military appropriations bill in 1967 that Wright noted surpassed any in
World War II coincided with targeted domestic cuts.[21] Angry liberals
reacted by encouraging wage and price controls, but Johnson resisted.
Wright, for his part, then declared consumer debt "the culprit" and proposed requiring large down payments on significant credit purchases.[22]
Acknowledging it "a matter of great concern to Texas," he demurred on
any proposals to limit oil prices, which certainly would have impacted

higher costs. He would give the issue his "close attention," Wright stalled, a "great deal of watching and evaluation."[23]

As Wright watched and waited, deficits began to rise in spite of domestic cuts that soon surpassed $8 billion. It was too much for Wright, who had been both a Great Society supporter and a longtime foe of national debt. Reversing his stance and suggesting the need for new "balance" in economic policies, he now pronounced a tax increase necessary.[24] In the end, Wright voted to adjust taxes. A temporary surcharge would be added for individuals and corporations, but additional domestic spending would be cut.[25] Wright defended his change by explaining that the nation had never fought a war without raising taxes, conveniently omitting that the military spending benefited Fort Worth. America had to support its troops—"fighting in a coin far more precious than dollars"—and a greater national debt was intolerable.[26]

As inflation and Vietnam ate away at its effectiveness, the Great Society faced other challenges. Reports grew that communities were misappropriating federal dollars. When charges arose in Houston, Wright suggested that it was a "simple and innocent" mistake.[27] When he learned that federal officials had misapplied some of the highway beautification funds that he had worked so hard to achieve, Wright explained that the standards were complex and that there had been no intent to hurt local advertising firms. He was angrier, however, when he found out that certain construction grants had not been awarded in compliance with his own committee's rules—they had gone not to a Texas company operating in an area of poverty, but to an Oklahoma company where sufficient services existed.[28]

The more Wright looked, the harder it became for him to defend the Great Society. Rent subsidies had gone to families that earned too much. The comptroller of the currency had manipulated policy outside of congressional intent. The IRS had ignored congressional prohibitions on wiretapping. In short, Wright wrote in his newsletter, Johnson needed to "tighten the screws" on the officials running the Great Society. "Congress makes the laws," Wright sarcastically commented. Wright made sure the White House knew of his newsletter and, according to Wright, Johnson waved it around at his next cabinet meeting, demanding improvement.[29]

The 1966 congressional elections were, perhaps, predictable. Although the Democrats maintained solid majorities, the GOP picked up seats in both houses. The victors, much to Wright's dismay, included John Tower. Emboldened, many Republicans began to call for truly dramatic cuts. Such calls certainly resonated among conservatives in Wright's district, one of whom complained that Wright had failed to grasp the "growing antagonism" against "money wasted on every 'do-gooder' idea."[30] When in late 1967 Republicans proposed that additional billions be cut from the Economic Opportunity Act, Wright recognized a dagger at the heart of Johnson's "War on Poverty." Wright's impassioned plea helped defeat the proposal, but three Texas Democrats voted for it. Wright could not avoid the fact that Texas was slowly changing.[31]

The problems the Great Society faced did little to help Johnson's relations with Congress. Johnson's strength was in legislating and not implementing law, Wright believed, and Johnson did not always appreciate his new role. When Wright's committee had first considered highway beautification, for example, White House aide Larry O'Brien had frequently interrupted the deliberations. He was demanding things that were "not contemplated in the act," Wright had explained.[32] Only Congress could make the laws, and Johnson was no longer a member. Now, with much of the legislative agenda in place, Johnson needed to refocus his attention on implementing congressional intent.

"The real problem is with the Congress, not the bureaucracy," one Johnson aide countered. Congress made constant demands, "insisting that we handle the most people with the least cost." If the White House admitted "difficulties with our programs," Congress would then slash funds. "Better to send the reports in as they are, even knowing that the situation is more complicated than it appears, and then work from within to make things better."[33] Had Wright been cognizant of such attitudes, he would have been irate. Frustrated on multiple levels, and consigned to Congress for the foreseeable future, he was increasingly sensitive to slights against the institution— from whomever.

Wright, accordingly, had little patience for Adam Clayton Powell, a Harlem congressman who faced growing accusations of corruption. Powell, moreover, tended to make inflammatory statements that brought ridicule upon Congress. When Powell resisted paying a court-ordered judgment for slander, Wright joined Democrat Morris Udall in an effort to divest Powell of his committee chairmanship. Congress, however, went further. With only a majority vote, it excluded Powell from taking his seat. Hardly a fan of Powell, Wright nevertheless thought his colleagues had gone too far. The Constitution allowed Congress only to expel a representative, and then only by a two-thirds majority. If Congress did not follow the rules, Wright argued, how could it be worthy of any public respect? It was a principled position but an unpopular one, and it cast Wright in the role of defending corruption. "I happen to believe that the Constitution means exactly what it says," Wright responded defensively. The entire affair did neither Wright nor Congress any favors, and the case lingered until Powell sued and ultimately won his seat back.[34]

With characteristic vigor and once again reflecting his idealism, Wright began a campaign to improve Congress's image. The first steps were restrictions on large campaign contributions and public financing of campaigns. He knew firsthand, Wright said, that the "skyrocketing cost of politics" meant that men of modest means required big donors. This arrangement imperiled "the integrity of our political institutions."[35] Politics was a noble profession. To love democracy but disdain politics was "to pretend to honor the product while despising the process that creates it."[36] Wright also called for a financial disclosure act to reassure the public and encourage lawmakers to "hew hard to the straight path."[37] Accordingly, he reported on his income back to 1952. Going back to his most successful days at the National Trade Day Association allowed him to demonstrate how congressional service had reduced his income by $74,000. His income was only $35,000, including what he earned from investments and books.[38] Not all congressmen were getting rich on the public dime, Wright's comments implied, Powell notwithstanding. A trip to a home district, Wright argued, "could hardly be classified as a pleasure trip." In fact, he added, he had often funded his own trips to Fort Worth. "If it had been my purpose . . . to build a huge estate," Wright continued, "I assuredly would have not sought to serve in Congress."[39]

To improve its image, Wright concluded, Congress needed to realize that compromise was necessary. With closed minds too many legislators increasingly demonized their opposition. Realizing that no one was infallible was "the beginning of political wisdom," Wright argued, reflecting what he had been taught by his parents and his religious training. It was not a betrayal of one's beliefs to give ground for the common good. Moreover, constant bickering and personal attacks made Congress appear petty.[40]

As for congressional seniority, Wright had become more ambivalent about reform. Seniority had kept him from a committee chairmanship, and yet he now approached fourteen years of service and had learned the system well. His success legislatively spoke volumes. Seniority "has worked fairly well over the years," Wright wrote in 1967, even if reform "does merit further study." Further study, Congress decided, was the watchword for all of Wright's reform proposals. At least the Department of the Interior noticed

Wright's advocacy, selecting him to explain the role of the legislature in a movie shown to tourists. Wright was in heady company; Vice President Hubert Humphrey spoke for the executive branch, and Justice William O. Douglas for the judiciary.[41]

In some respects, Wright's life was a bit like a personal purgatory. He liked serving in Congress and thought highly of his accomplishments, but he still harbored hopes of personal advancement. A statewide office seemed beyond his grasp—he rejected out of hand any suggestion that he run for the governorship in 1968—and his ardent defense of Congress spoke to a realization that he did not want to return to the private sector, whatever wealth it might afford.[42] To recover from his debts, Wright invested in a Leesburg, Virginia, Pontiac dealership, but, absorbed in the Great Society, showed little interest in its management. When the dealership lost money, Wright surrendered his share. Wright, it appeared, remained a poor steward of his finances almost a decade after he had paid so dearly in his Senate race. Appearances still mattered to Wright. When the NTDA asked him to intervene with the Federal Communications Commission to assure local stations that its advertisements did not promote an illegal lottery, Wright refused, not wanting to appear to favor family and friends.[43]

If this were not enough, the tight finances and long hours continued to strain his marriage. In late 1966, a Fort Worth newsman shadowed Wright on his daily rounds, publishing a story headlined, "If He's Jim Wright, He Stays Busy." Homework often followed twelve-hour workdays, and lunch was often just orange juice at his desk. Speeches, meetings, and dinners often occupied his weekends. His dog, Sir Winston Muggs, barely knew him. One could forgive Mab if she felt a bit neglected.[44] Moreover, the recent deaths of his parents "remained very painful and hurt for years," he later said. A car wreck south of Weatherford had claimed his mother; his father had succumbed to throat cancer, his drinking no doubt influential. Wright was executor of their estates and buried them in a family plot in Weatherford. Meanwhile, his children were growing older, and their interests were naturally being drawn elsewhere. Jimmy's return from Vietnam hardly ended Wright's worries about his son, as Jimmy's future appeared as uncertain as his father's. "For a while there, Dad and I didn't get along too well," Jimmy later recalled. "I got radical for a while."[45]

At the office, nothing was the same. Wright's new assistant, Marshall Lynam, a Fort Worth reporter who had helped in Wright's first congressional campaign, added a new dimension, as did updated accommodations in the new Rayburn Building, which was appropriately named, Wright believed. A Xerox Model 650 copy machine forever changed the nature of the daily grind, as did a device by Chapman Telephonics that allowed his office to make three recorded telephone calls a minute, each at only six cents. Wright immediately recognized the potential of the "robo calls," but insisted that the device only operate during the day. In short, Wright's life, like that of so many other Americans in the late 1960s, was in flux. And like so many others, Wright struggled to find his bearings.[46]

The birth of what pundits termed the "New Left" posed challenges to Jim Wright. It was more than the fact that by 1968 Wright was approaching fifty. He had faith in government born of the New Deal and World War II. Wright's sideburns grew and his tie widened, but "sex, drugs, and rock 'n' roll" were hardly his "bag." Wright certainly shared many of the New Left's concerns, but he struggled to relate even as the movement captivated some in his own party, suggesting further cleavage. Wright, for example, supported equal pay for women even as he still thought of the Women's Army Corps in World War II as "men's work." He recognized feminists as potential allies, but never read Betty Friedan's seminal 1966 bestseller *The Feminine Mystique*. Wright was once again in the middle, his efforts to hold his political coalition together in such a dynamic period even more difficult than before.[47]

Wright could dismiss as naïve the Port Huron Statement of the Students for a Democratic Society (SDS), which proclaimed a new humanistic age of love. He understood—at least in general terms—the ideals of the so-called Free Speech Movement. When, however, criticism turned personal and ugly, or, worse, violent, Wright's patience ran thin. "The House Internal Security Committee has already made plans to conduct an investigation into the SDS," Wright wrote approvingly in 1967.[48] The horrible events of early 1968 only hardened Wright's reactionary tendencies. To many protesters, police were "pigs," executives were the "the man," and soldiers returning from Vietnam were "baby killers." From the massacre of the Vietnamese village of My Lai in March 1968 to the assassination of the civil rights icon King the following month, there appeared to be no shortage of outrage—or riots. Clouds of smoke literally covered the Capitol building. "The so-called New Left," Wright noted sarcastically, "ridicules [Johnson] for preserving and honoring the very institutions and processes of our constitutional system which he is sworn to defend."[49]

Still hoping to bridge his party's great divide, Wright highlighted those times he had agreed with liberals even as his revulsion at the disorder brought out his own conservatism. "If a person is old enough to fight, he is old enough to vote," Wright stated, promoting a voting age of eighteen.[50] When Wright spoke of the poor, many in the New Left applauded. When he fought to repeal a portion of the Taft-Hartley Act, which prohibited "secondary strikes," unions praised him. Shutting down operations at businesses whose subcontractors were problematic was unfair, many conservatives argued. At first Wright vaguely agreed; shuttering "an entire building project" because of a "grievance with some extraneous supplier" was unwise. Upon reflection, however, he sided with the AFL-CIO, which was still annoyed by his support of the Landrum-Griffin Bill eight years before.[51] Wright, one conservative complained, had been "masquerading as a middle-of-the-roader" but really stood "with the far-left."[52]

In fact, the "far-left" was equally angry at Wright, who repeatedly reaffirmed his support for Johnson's war effort. "It was hard for any middle-aged member of the so-called establishment to comprehend [the youthful protesters'] exact message," Wright stated.[53] On a trip to Hawaii with Massachusetts Democrat Tip O'Neill, who had just announced his own opposition to the war, Wright met several Asian students through his daughter Kay. "It is wrong to come and bring more war to us," the students argued, adding that Indochina had known only foreign domination. When Wright responded that America was different, it was clear that the group only saw Americans as "light-skinned people with uniforms and weapons." The conversation gave Wright pause and, years later, his memoirs implied that he understood. "Self-congratulatory paternalism can be culturally blind and blind to its own blindness," Wright wrote.[54]

If the exchange challenged Wright's assumptions, it did not change his public stance at the time. "We are winning," Wright proclaimed.[55] On the House floor just days before Martin Luther King Jr.'s death, Wright praised Johnson for his "courageous determination" and argued that history would prove him right.[56] While acknowledging that the draft was "unfair in certain cases," Wright resisted the "drastic changes" that the protesters demanded. No system was "absolutely fair to everyone in every single case."[57] Arguing that the media was biased against the war, Wright suggested that the North Vietnamese Tet Offensive had become a loss only when public opinion had shifted. The enemy "staged the attack for just that purpose." The My Lai tragedy was a horrible anomaly played for effect.[58]

Wright thought that those advocating nuclear weapons were dangerous, but his rather hawkish stance alienated him from the younger generation, including his own children. It was not just Kay. Like many veterans, Jimmy returned from Vietnam against the war, publicly quiet out of respect for his father but vocal at home. A friend of Ginger's, meanwhile, launched into an angry tirade as Wright held his tongue. Even Wright's sister Mary Nelle was so critical, Wright recalled, it was "no longer pleasant for me to be in her company." Everywhere he turned, "I would get bombarded with anti-Vietnam talk."[59] What bothered Wright more—but again failed to shift his stance— were Johnson's own reservations. "In fact," Wright recalled, "one of the first expressions [of antiwar sentiments] I heard was from Lyndon Johnson himself." Johnson, Wright recalled, complained that the percentage of African American deaths in the war was double their percentage in the general population. The objections of religious leaders also worried Wright, challenging his assumptions that the protesters were misinformed.[60]

Such disagreements made Wright introspective, and yet the riots that took place aroused his more reactionary tendencies. "The right of peaceful protest has become something else indeed when a group of people wave the flags of the enemy, shout obscene imprecations against the leaders of our country and try, however futilely and absurdly, to storm the Pentagon," Wright stated. "If this is not treason, it is so close to it as to be almost indistinguishable."[61] It was the "politics of disruption," and police "must not stand by and countenance it."[62] Wright accepted Johnson's creation of the National Advisory Commission on Civil Disorders, charged with finding a resolution to the turmoil, but he harbored doubts about any economic solution. "Conditions comparatively are so much better than they have been," Wright explained. While Wright listed nine separate options to address protesters' grievances, he insisted that such remedies were "not the most important thing." A firm crackdown was.[63] Perpetrators were "idiots," and their prosecution was "gratifying," Wright stated, adding that he wanted to make flag burning a crime.[64] He also sought to make crossing state lines to promote a riot illegal and proposed larger federal grants for state law enforcement. "It was greatly encouraging," one conservative attorney general wrote, that Wright's proposal "has the benefit of the State's discretion."[65]

Wright had some success. For months, southern conservatives had blocked fair housing legislation that the liberals advocated. In the wake of the King assassination, however, Congress passed the Civil Rights Act of 1968, also known as the Fair Housing Act, hoping to cool tensions. As a salve to conservatives, Wright's anti-riot provisions were added as amendments. Wright acknowledged that the bill "will not solve all of our problems" and sought to soothe critics on both his left and right. "I agonized over this vote," he stated, "knowing that some of my cherished friends will feel that I have done wrong."[66] Wright continued to encourage compromise as Congress reacted. He supported the Omnibus Crime Control and Safe Street Act of 1968 which, while adding $50 million for law enforcement and clarifying wiretapping and confession rules in a way that conservatives advocated, also strengthened gun control as the liberals demanded. Wright reiterated his unwavering support for the Second Amendment but added that compromise was necessary if Congress was to combat rampant lawlessness.[67]

If Wright sensed that society was coming unhinged, his continuing interest in foreign policy did not help. "A decade of hemispheric idealism began to fade," Wright later recalled of Latin America during the late 1960s.[68] The Kennedy-era aid programs had, it appeared, done little to diminish domestic turmoil as the idealist in Wright had hoped. When violence broke out in the Dominican Republic, Johnson, fearing communism, deployed 20,000 American troops and asked Wright to travel to the beleaguered nation and mediate. It was, Wright recalled, a "witch's brew of smoldering resentments."[69] For a solution, Wright turned to one of his friends, Waco businessman Bernard Rapoport, who proposed to attract American investors in new corporations jointly owned with employees. After the military reestablished control and the immediate crisis faded, however, the five large investors that Wright had solicited lost interest. The nation was again calm, but the episode suggested that military force, not economic aid, would increasingly define Latin America.[70]

Although Wright supported the continuing American boycott of Castro's Cuba, he found the growing cuts to Latin American foreign assistance frustrating. "Military hardware plays only the defensive role of a holding tactic," Wright argued.[71] In his usual way of acknowledging his opposition's point to drive home his own, Wright agreed that waste was rampant. The solution, however, was more efficiency and oversight, not cuts. When, for example, problems emerged with loan guarantees for El Salvador, Wright suggested that a "private initiative" could augment public funds.[72] He strongly supported the Voice of America, celebrating its twenty-fifth anniversary, and a Puerto Rican plebiscite on statehood.[73]

Wright was still a member of the Mexico–United States Interparliamentary Conference, where he had served since 1963, and chaired the American delegation hosting the 1968 meeting in Honolulu. Returning to his idealism, he spoke of the "bridges of understanding" between the two nations and bemoaned that the North Vietnamese would not "sit together and talk" like the Mexicans and Americans.[74] In reality, immigration and illegal drugs were divisive issues and conciliation required work. The problem of drugs, Wright acknowledged, lay with American demand as much as with Mexican production. The Mexicans had a point, he added, that the water they got from the Colorado River was polluted. He promised to seek redress in Washington.[75]

Dialogue, not just strength, remained key to Wright's foreign policy. Wright found French leader Charles de Gaulle's nationalism annoying and labeled the House's negation of an agreement to buy British minesweepers "irrational." When Congress threatened to cut aid to Spain because the Spanish traded with Cuba, Wright reminded his colleagues that American military bases in Spain were critical. Answers, Wright reminded his colleagues, "are not always simple."[76]

China certainly was not simple. Trying to understand the People's Republic of China, Wright wrote, was like "trying to guess what a mentally unbalanced person will do."[77] In fact, Chairman Mao Zedong knew exactly what he was doing. Worried about the growing American presence in Southeast Asia, Mao was not only solidifying his control with the infamous Cultural Revolution, but urging a "people's war" against "U.S. imperialism and its lackeys." Mao dramatically increased the Chinese military and tested his nation's first nuclear bomb.[78] China, Wright understood, was no ordinary belligerent but a dangerous behemoth. The United States needed to project strength but should proceed with caution. When North Korea attacked the American vessel USS *Pueblo* in 1968, taking hostages, congressional war hawks, including many southern conservatives, recommended an ultimatum under the threat of a nuclear attack. Such recklessness, Wright countered, might spiral out of control. The situation, rather, "called for cool heads, clear eyes and strong hearts." In the end, such caution proved wise, as negotiations led to a release of the crew with no loss of life.[79]

The "harder task," in Wright's words, was the amalgam of religion, culture, and politics that constituted the Middle East. After the Six Day War in 1967 ended with an Israeli occupation of the Gaza Strip, the Golan Heights, and the Sinai, the United States had an international dilemma whose complexity befuddled world leaders like no other. Wright, ambitious to the point of presumption, offered a solution. His plan basically embodied the "two-state solution" for the Israelis and Palestinians that leaders would debate for decades—without much success.[80] Energetic and idealistic, Wright had solutions, but the problems, both at home and abroad, just kept coming.

As the 1968 elections approached, Wright was definitely in a get-tough mood, accentuated perhaps by meeting one of his childhood heroes, Jack Dempsey. Wright had met the famous boxing champion over thirty years before in Oklahoma, when Dempsey had autographed Wright's chewing gum wrapper and impressed the lad with his aggressive style. With Dempsey in Washington, Wright now won a photograph and a conversation. Certainly the "Manassa Mauler" would not let radicals push him around.[81] Wright faced no credible challenger in the election, as redistricting in the wake of the Voting Rights Act, controlled by the Democrats, had moved much of southern Tarrant County into the more rural 6th Congressional District. The more Democratic and labor-friendly Fort Worth and Arlington remained for Wright. Accordingly, Wright's plans for an aggressive campaign centered on his fellow Democrats, which, of course, promised Wright its own rewards.[82]

Initially, at least, most political pundits expected Johnson to win the Democratic nomination easily despite the party's obvious rift. Liberal senator Eugene McCarthy launched a campaign as a New Left peace candidate, but Wright was not worried for Johnson. Southern voters, Wright reported, "greatly prefer Johnson to McCarthy."[83] More troublesome was the entrance of Senator Robert Kennedy, the late president's brother with all the advantages that offered. Wright began to wonder if the primary season might not be as easy as he had hoped.[84]

Then the first bombshell dropped. In late March, Lyndon Johnson announced that he would not seek reelection. Although Wright understood the toll the complex challenges had taken on Johnson, the announcement "more than surprised" him. At first Wright still hoped that fellow Democrats might persuade Johnson "that his decision to withdraw is not irrevocable," but then Wright "saw relief in [Johnson's] face, in his demeanor, and in his manners."[85] Moreover, media speculation that "the Texas leadership mantle had been passed to Wright" certainly took some of the sting out of Johnson's announcement. Regardless, Wright wasted little time defending Johnson's legacy. History, he claimed, would record Johnson's "personal sacrifice in the cause of peace."[86]

Thanking Wright for his long support, Johnson stated that he hoped to accomplish something Wright wanted in his remaining months. Never one to miss an opportunity for networking, Wright immediately asked if Johnson would address graduation at Fort Worth's Texas Christian University (TCU). The phone conversation lasted two hours; during part of that time, Johnson was getting his hair cut as the two talked. Johnson's promise to speak at TCU demonstrated, the press reported, "Wright's closeness to LBJ." When the graduation arrived in May, Wright had a reception and press conference ready. Johnson even made news by endorsing the eighteen-year-old vote.

"We rank it as a triumph!" the obviously ecstatic TCU chancellor wrote Wright. Wright deserved "a great deal of the credit."[87]

With Johnson out of the race, his vice-president, Hubert Humphrey, took his spot, continuing to envision the war as leverage for a negotiated peace and retaining the support of much of the Democratic establishment. As Kennedy attracted the ethnic and poor while McCarthy the intellectuals and most of the New Left, former Alabama governor George Wallace ran as the southern conservative option, a neo-Dixiecrat. Much to Wright's chagrin, it was hardly the unity the party needed.

Wright's allegiance to Humphrey surprised no one. Not only were the Democratic elders—whom Wright had so cultivated—supporting Humphrey, but he admired the vice-president's "candor, his spirit, his genuine friendliness." Humphrey was also loyal, a commodity Wright understood from personal experience. In the words of one supporter, Wright quickly offered to organize a "flying around squad" of congressmen.[88] Predictably, no one was going to outwork Wright, and his rhetorical flashes were always a welcome attraction. "Kennedy could not carry a single state in the South," Wright argued. McCarthy would repel every conservative. Polls indicated that Humphrey, not the others, was "the strongest candidate against Richard Nixon."[89] Working to dispel attacks by those who said Humphrey was the pro-war candidate, Wright claimed that the candidate had "not just talked about peace" but "worked for peace."[90]

As Wright campaigned, a second bombshell fell. After nipping McCarthy to win the California primary, Kennedy fell to an assassin's bullet in Los Angeles. While the nation reeled in horror, the murder solidified the antiwar vote behind McCarthy and refocused Wright's attention. Referring to McCarthy as a "man of decent purpose and good intentions"—classic Wright style—Wright crafted an "open letter" to the senator. If America deescalated, Wright asked, what assured that North Vietnam would follow? How would the coalition government that McCarthy advocated be determined? How would other allies feel if communists subsequently threatened them? Wright's questions were not personal, but they were harsh nevertheless. They suggested that McCarthy was undercutting the ongoing peace negotiations.[91]

In August, the battle culminated in Chicago with the Democratic National Convention, a disaster that proved to be the election's final bombshell. Humphrey selected Wright and Michigan congressman Jim O'Hara to represent his interests on the Rules and Credentials Committee. The sudden departures of Johnson and Kennedy complicated the selection of delegates, and McCarthy supporters quickly complained that Wright and his allies were manipulating the rules to Humphrey's advantage, a charge Wright denied. Wright ended up supporting a rules change for the 1972 convention but not for the Chicago convention at hand. Starting in 1972, a "freedom of conscience" provision would give delegates more leeway, but for the moment the "unit rules" remained. These rules required delegates to follow the lead of their state conventions, a requirement that to Wright was "the only way to ascertain that the wishes of the majority would be carried out." What Wright did not mention was that party elders favoring Humphrey dominated the state conventions; keeping the unit rules helped his candidate.[92]

Humphrey also asked Wright to testify against an antiwar resolution that McCarthy supporters were pressing in the Resolutions Committee. Wright did so, hitting all his familiar themes. He suggested first and foremost that the resolution would undercut negotiations and make peace less likely. Wright had his rhetorical skills but still faced stiff opposition. Appearing on behalf of the resolution and drawing significant coverage were the actors Paul Newman and Shirley MacLaine.[93]

If the bitterness inside the convention did not attract enough negative coverage, outside brewed events that would enter political infamy. Thousands of angry antiwar demonstrators convened. When Chicago Mayor Richard Daley, who had wanted to use the convention as a shining star for his city, cracked down, a riot resulted. Tear gas floated into the convention hall and mace hit innocent bystanders. Rocks and clubs flew as the multitude of media captured it all. In the end, the nomination of Humphrey and the defeat of the antiwar resolution may have divided Democrats further in a way that benefited no one, but the mayhem outside ultimately defined the party. The Republicans, meanwhile, nominated the veteran Richard Nixon in Miami. Their convention was quiet and orderly, quite the contrast to Wright's party.[94]

Wright recognized the damage immediately and vented his frustrations by complaining about the media's coverage to the FCC.[95] A Humphrey campaign statement acknowledged Wright's critical role in the convention, suggesting that Wright "did as much as any other in the country to assure Humphrey's nomination." Not only had he served on key committees, but he had traveled "from New Jersey to Utah, from Michigan to Alabama." The statement concluded with Humphrey's hopes that Wright would "accept a prominent role in the [general] campaign and play a prominent role in the Humphrey Administration."[96]

Wright was already at work. Assigned, along with Dallas attorney Bob Strauss, as a co-coordinator of the Democratic efforts in Texas, Wright opened a headquarters at Austin's Commodore Perry Hotel. That fall Wright was in Texas more than Washington. With many liberals disengaged and the party's divisions raw, Wright arranged for the liberal Edmund Muskie to make a speaking tour of the state. The following week, Humphrey embarked on his own three-day, six-city blitz, including an appearance with Johnson at the Houston Astrodome. While fearing that appearing with Johnson would further alienate liberals, Wright still admired Humphrey's loyalty, a trait Wright continued to value.[97]

There were "slip ups," Wright recalled, and the media was always frustrating. Rather than highlighting Humphrey's speeches, the press stressed that Texas governor John Connally had not met the Democratic candidate at the airport. Several outlets reported that Wright had been a McCarthy man before the convention, an error that Wright tried to turn to his advantage. It was, he said, an "understandable" mistake, as he had worked closely with McCarthy delegates for consensus.[98] Wright struggled to get the liberals coalescing around Senator Ralph Yarborough and the conservatives around Connally to coordinate with each other. In fact, ill will remained between the two groups from a fight over the state convention chairmanship. Wright was able to get both state leaders to a Fort Worth luncheon, which Strauss suggested showed a lot of "brass." Wright, Strauss joked to Humphrey, "has all the pride and reticence of a whore." It was a compliment, Wright laughingly replied.[99]

Nixon was a formidable opponent. He vaguely promised to end the war with honor, draping it around the Democrats' neck, and stressed "law and order," obviously tapping into resentment against the riots. It was, historians would later conclude, a deliberate effort to win disaffected southern conservatives who were angry over civil rights. Nixon's famous "Southern Strategy" held profound implications for Wright's efforts to hold his party's coalition together, which Wright quickly recognized.[100] No novice himself, Wright raised enough money to purchase a twenty-eight-minute statewide television broadcast only days before the election. In what he later recalled as one of the "most frantic twenty-four hours of my life," Wright wrote the script, hired the crew, edited the footage, and narrated the show, which was the only statewide Humphrey broadcast. Although Wright's aides still favored shorter, more targeted commercials, Wright's efforts helped Humphrey narrowly carry Texas even as Nixon became the nation's thirty-seventh chief executive by an equally narrow margin. "The success you realized in Texas was nothing short of a miracle," Larry O'Brien, Humphrey's campaign manager, wrote Wright. Humphrey agreed. Wright "made a big difference."[101]

The results on November 5 put Nixon into the Oval Office but gave neither party a mandate. While the Democrats lost seats in both houses of Congress, they retained control. Although one can debate whether Wallace's five southern states denied Humphrey a victory, the election indeed suggested that the Democratic consensus had fractured. Nixon's popular vote in the eleven former Confederate states exceeded those of both his opponents. Wright, of course, was crushed. Not only had he invested so much time and energy, but a Humphrey victory would have surely opened new avenues for his own future. Wright still considered his career stuck in neutral. He was beginning to reconcile himself to an entire career in Congress, but he certainly remained open to new options for advancement. The day after the election, Wright issued a statement that could not hide his disappointment but did stress a central theme of his own career. "The most essential business of this country today is to recapture our spirit of national unity," Wright stated. Richard Nixon was everyone's president, and "I will trust him."[102] For Wright, the country had come far in the eight years since the optimism of John F. Kennedy's inaugural. Wright had held such hope, for the country and for himself. Now, as the end of the decade approached and a Republican was about to take the helm, the Democrats in disarray, Wright's feelings were more ambivalent. The Kennedy and Johnson presidencies had witnessed manifold and historic legislation that embodied much of what Wright believed. At the same time, however, nothing was where Wright had hoped, not his private life nor the life of his country. It was a bit ironic, almost too difficult to understand, and too challenging to predict what would come next. Only time would tell.

PART III

Leadership in an Age of Dynamism

_____

CHAPTER 10

Old School

A MODERATE IN THE NIXON YEARS (1968–1972)

At first glance the new president, Richard Nixon, and Jim Wright made an odd pair. No one could have foreseen their friendship. Nixon, after all, a Republican, had a solid resume as a rabid anticommunist partisan, while Wright, a veteran Democrat and no red-baiter, openly avowed compromise and collegiality. In fact, strong forces drew the two politicians together. It began with Nixon's inaugural. As Wright sat on the Capitol's East Front listening, Nixon spoke eloquently of peace and unity. If the skillful oratory smacked of Wright's ability to turn a phrase, Nixon's sentiments reflected the Texan's exactly. Wright applauded heartily.[1]

A foundation for the two to connect existed on multiple levels. Not only had both experienced the Great Depression and served in World War II, but they shared a distaste for the recent national turmoil. Nixon's campaign included an appeal for law and order, and Wright's disgust at the riots drove him in the same direction. Nixon was no fan of the New Left, and neither was Wright. Wright remained angry at the media, believing it biased against the war, while Nixon was famously estranged from the press. Moreover, Nixon's call for a peace with honor in Vietnam appeared to be more akin to Johnson and Humphrey than McCarthy or Kennedy.

Nixon did not promise to withdraw precipitously but to force a negotiated settlement through "Vietnamization" of the war. Given Wright's belief in executive leadership in foreign policy and the need for a united front, more ingredients were in place for consensus than conflict. In domestic affairs, Nixon appeared to be moderate, hoping for electoral success more than any ideological agenda. Like Eisenhower, he did not perceive all government as evil, and he appeared to pose little threat to the recent Democratic accomplishments. Wright was hopeful, declaring that he had "found a lot of [Nixon's] publicly stated positions, particularly in the international arena, with which I agreed."[2]

Nixon had little time to rest. Just after his inaugural, the North Vietnamese launched a massive assault; angered, Nixon ordered a new round of saturation bombing even as he began, as promised, withdrawing troops. Meanwhile, the antiwar movement's "Moratorium to End the War," a series of large rallies, frustrated Wright. The protests, he complained, were "giving a superficial impression of a nation almost fatally crippled by internal division."[3] To counter such perceptions, Wright proposed a congressional resolution of support for Nixon's efforts and for an open election in South Vietnam supervised by an impartial international body. Later Wright offered conflicting explanations for how he got the idea: a *Fort Worth Star-Telegram* editorial; a letter from a J. C. Penney store manager; or discussions with Democrat Wayne Hays and Republican Ross Adair.[4] Later still, Wright stated that he was not even aware of the Moratorium at the time of his first draft, a claim hard to believe, given that the protests were front-page news two weeks before the first reports of Wright's resolution appeared.[5] Whatever the case, Wright circulated his draft to Speaker McCormack, Minority Leader Gerald Ford, and House Foreign Relations Committee chairman Tom Morgan. When Ford promised to forward the draft to Nixon, Wright promised any changes necessary. "It's fine just like it is," Nixon said in a telephone call the next day. Finding cosponsors proved easy. When Nixon had spoken of a "silent majority" of Americans, his approval ratings had risen. The White House had received thousands of telegrams of support for his Vietnam policies. Clearly, signing onto Wright's resolution required no profile in courage.[6]

With over one hundred cosponsors, Wright introduced his resolution on November 4, 1969. "Under our Constitution the President is charged with the responsibility to speak for the nation in its critical relations abroad," Wright stated, later adding that Democrats should "subordinate . . . party pride" to a "higher responsibility."[7] Happily for Wright, outside of the *New*

York Times and the *Washington Post*, the press was positive. Wright attributed the *Times* and *Post* critiques to bias. His staff distributed talking points differentiating the proposal from the Gulf of Tonkin Resolution and stating that any amendment urging troop withdrawals would "seriously dilute the message." The president had to act on a "day-to-day basis," which the Congress could not do.[8]

By November 12, three days before the Moratorium's culminating march, Wright had three hundred congressional supporters, including almost half the Democrats. The ambassador to South Vietnam, Henry Cabot Lodge, also offered support, which "elated" Wright. Anxious to augment publicity for the plan before the throngs descended on the Capitol, Nixon called Wright and asked him to assemble a bipartisan delegation to the White House. In the press conference that followed, reporters were skeptical. "I'm not here today in the interest of being a Democrat," Wright shot back, prompting Nixon to advise that Wright should ignore the media.[9] In fact, Wright sarcastically recalled, the following day the "anticipation of a colorful protest rally" still dominated the news. Frustrated, Wright's "hopes soared" when Nixon then scheduled a congressional address to push the resolution, only to find that once again the Moratorium simply overshadowed what they were trying to accomplish.[10]

Two weeks after the march, Wright was ready when the resolution reached the floor of Congress. Antiwar Democrats argued that Wright's proposal was a "blank check" and that debating it under closed rules stifled public objections. Wright countered that he was not aware of the closed rule but that similar conditions had guided earlier foreign policy debates. Besides, the opposition had enjoyed "ample time . . . to muster its forces."[11] Wright was collegial—acknowledging that the resolution was not "beyond the possibility at least of improvement"—but also plaintive, appealing to the liberals' commitment to free speech.[12] When the resolution finally passed 333–55, eighty-two liberals signed a letter reiterating that they had not surrendered any rights of future action. The internal Democratic squabble concerned Speaker McCormack, who, while acknowledging that he supported Wright, would not agree with Minority Leader Ford that the resolution had settled the matter.[13]

It may have been a "whole lot of nothing," as many liberal Democrats claimed, but Wright still welcomed the praise of his would-be Senate opponent John Tower and the continued thanks from Nixon, who claimed himself "deeply appreciative." To acknowledge the *Fort Worth Star-Telegram*'s positive editorials, Wright arranged a luncheon to thank its staff.[14] The resolution's real impact was more difficult to discern. Nixon was just getting ready to dispatch National Security Adviser Henry Kissinger for a new round of Paris peace talks, but the negotiations continued for another three years. Certainly the resolution solidified the odd relationship that Nixon and Wright enjoyed. Within days of the resolution, Wright and famed Oklahoma football coach Bud Wilkinson were Nixon's guests on Air Force One, flying to Little Rock for the Texas-Arkansas football game. Nixon, like Wright, calculated his every move. Few associates ever saw him relaxed or knew him intimately. To some extent, at least, Wright had crossed that line. In the coming years Nixon invited Wright, and even Wright's children, to the White House for social occasions.[15]

As the 91st Congress progressed, few issues threatened the connection that Nixon and Wright were establishing, partly, perhaps, because Nixon devoted little time to domestic policy.[16] One domestic issue that did win considerable attention was the environment, and even this largely strengthened the bond. "I always welcomed someone in the White House who supported the same train I was on," Wright recalled.[17] Like the Democrats, Nixon recognized that the nation had a new voting constituency, and the competition for political credit soon proved fruitful when the new Congress passed historic environmental legislation.[18] Competition even existed over committee jurisdiction. When Democrats created the Joint Committee on Environment and Technology, Wright lobbied for a position. "I have been co-sponsor of numerous environmental bills," Wright wrote, adding his long interest in water conservation.[19]

As Nixon dispatched subordinates on the nation's first Earth Day on April 22, 1970, Wright stressed environmental bipartisanship at the University of Texas at Arlington, specifically tipping his hat to Nixon's proposed "national growth policy."[20] In private, Wright acknowledged that Nixon was "trying very hard to grab the title of 'Mr. Clean' on environmental problems," and that he had no intention of surrendering the political advantage.[21] In the weeks before and after Earth Day, Wright gave more environmental speeches than all the White House surrogates combined.[22]

Wright and Nixon had their differences early over specific federal spending, but, in the big picture at least, they shared similar views on the national debt and the Federal Reserve. At the outset, Nixon resisted the liberalized monetary policy that Wright advocated and remained preoccupied with Vietnam. Privately, Wright welcomed White House inaction, suggesting to fellow Democrats that it was "the very best issue we have." Democrats should seize the initiative with new anti-inflationary methods.[23] Soon, however, Nixon began to feel the pressure, growing more concerned with unemployment than inflation and urging the Fed to lower discount rates. Wright applauded the decision, suggesting that the Democrats issue a "strong statement in support."[24]

In the aggregate, both Wright and Nixon were willing to accept a combination of budget cuts and tax reform even as they differed over their application. Wright thought the Republican cuts draconian and counterproductive and advocated instead targeted cuts in less effective programs and tax reform. This included middle-class rate reductions and higher individual exemptions, balanced with a greater burden on "those with multimillion dollar incomes who get rich with paying little or no tax." Such rhetoric gave Wright momentum, and, with news reports of tax inequities abounding, Nixon—reluctantly—signed legislation creating an "alternative minimum tax" on the wealthy and raising corporate taxes. It all did little to combat the debt, with its tax reductions elsewhere, but it did shift priorities to Wright's liking.[25]

Given the necessary but spiraling cost of national defense, Wright believed Nixon was wise in 1969 to embark upon arms control talks with the Soviets in Helsinki, Finland. Dubbed the Strategic Arms Limitation Talks (SALT), the negotiations represented the diplomacy that Wright had long advocated, more so because Wright increasingly believed that the Cold War threatened bankruptcy for both nations. At the same time that Wright supported "all hopeful measures designed to reduce tensions," however, he remained clear that he continued to support a robust military, any contradictions aside. After all, in his view, Fort Worth's defense contractors remained an absolute necessity.[26]

Nixon's decision to invade Cambodia in early 1970 posed a dilemma for Wright. Wright recognized the need to stem the flow of weapons along the infamous Ho Chi Minh Trail, but the explosion of negative coverage and the shootings of four protesters at Kent State University had undermined the war effort and could potentially hinder negotiations. The Gulf of Tonkin Resolution had only authorized action in Vietnam, and thus in pursuing the invasion Nixon had ignored Congress. That was a growing sore point for Wright.[27] Conflicted, he resisted liberal efforts to defund the invasion but also cosponsored a bill defining "the limits of Presidential power in any troop commitments."[28]

So it went, Nixon and Wright occasionally at odds but always recognizing some commonality. When Nixon proposed welfare reform that would entail providing a minimum income but also mandating work, Wright joined conservatives in complaining that "no reliable estimate of the cost" existed.[29] When the National Commission on Obscenity and Pornography concluded that pornography did not contribute to crime or sexual deviation, Wright joined Nixon in complaining that the courts "have let the barriers down." People "who actually wish to receive this kind of thing" had privacy rights, Wright declared, but no right to send "smut" through the mail. The prohibition Wright proposed won hearty White House support.[30]

Partisanship, of course, remained. While Wright periodically but inevitably charged that Nixon was "playing politics on the economy," frequently he defended the White House from the press.[31] "It offends me as an American for someone to misrepresent or characterize the President unfairly," Wright stated in one instance.[32] When author Joe McGinnis criticized Nixon, Wright declared that McGinnis had been "too hard" on the president.[33] Criticizing Nixon for defending the legitimacy of South Vietnam's government was "fashionable" but unfair, Wright concluded. The government had won "a better percentage [of the vote] than we get in Texas."[34]

Just before Christmas 1969, Nixon once again invited Wright to the White House. Opening his desk drawer, he pulled out a sapphire and pearl pendant. "Pat [Nixon's wife] and I would like for Mrs. Wright to have this little holiday remembrance," Nixon stated. Later, when Nixon hosted the comedian Bob Hope, Wright received an invitation. Nixon also invited Wright to religious ceremonies in the East Room, which Wright believed to be constitutional. Wright was no close friend of Nixon, who had few such intimates—another trait they had in common—but their relationship was more than political expediency. The two had a connection, odd as though it appeared.[35]

In the wake of its Chicago debacle, the Democratic National Committee formed a commission to review convention rules. DNC Chairman Fred Harris appointed three Texans, but not the biggest backers of Humphrey—Wright and San Antonio's Henry B. Gonzalez. Smelling a conspiracy to stack the 1972 convention, Wright predicted "no good coming from it." More impoliticly, he added that Humphrey "had lost control of the party" to the liberals. The comments from such a "dear friend," an obviously wounded Humphrey replied, were "just so sad."[36] After the Committee on Party Structure and Delegate Selection held hearings in seventeen cities, Wright, in a more politic mood, judged their proposals "in general quite good." Nevertheless, unit rules were still necessary for "the wishes of the majority."[37]

A battle was brewing. The elderly John McCormack remained as Speaker, although many younger Democrats thought the teetotaling New Dealer was insufficiently liberal, a member of the staid Old Guard. In fact, the powerful committee chairs, and, in a sense, the seniority system, benefited from McCormack's more lenient leadership. After a failure to oust the septuagenarian, the liberals succeeded in having the Democratic caucus declare a lack of confidence in McCormack's leadership. Reading the writing on the wall but not wishing to become a lame duck, McCormack decided to retire, but to delay his announcement until May 1970. Wright thought the younger liberals were being impatient, but he saw opportunity in the shifting tides. Representative Jack Brooks had asked Wright to replace him as a zone whip, charged with gaining votes for the leadership. It was the lowest position on the leadership ladder, but it offered a new avenue for advancement. Wright's zone consisted of the Texas delegation, which was large enough to form its own zone. Perhaps most importantly for Wright, Majority Leader Carl Albert stood ready to assume the Speakership. The 5'4" "Little Giant" shared Wright's political outlook and recognized the Texan as helpful in uniting the party factions. Twice he had asked Wright to mediate disputes between turf-conscious members of different committees, and he knew that members admired Wright for his collegial nature. Albert's ascension would clearly expand Wright's clout and horizons.[38]

Wright, taking every opportunity to act like the leader he so desperately wanted to become, proposed a new plan to "broaden participation" and raise party revenue. The plan called for "sustaining members" of the Democratic Party, each contributing $5 annually. Each county would have a quota, Wright explained, not so subtly adding that he was "willing to dedicate a great deal of time" to the project.[39] In another instance, he presented a group of Democratic leaders meeting in "Senator Muskie's hideaway" a packet of new initiatives. "I am cribbing from you already," former presidential candidate Adlai Stevenson replied.[40]

Wright was certainly adept at keeping his name in the news. When Representative Martin McKneally proposed a sparring match in Washington between boxers Joe Frazier and Jimmy Ellis, a prelude to their championship fight, Wright took the bait. "Please count me in," he wrote McKneally, adding that he would like to propose for himself a short, one-round spar with either contestant. "I would give my eye teeth to be able to say to my grandchildren that I once sparred with the champion of the world."[41] The media reported the offer without commentary, but Wright's colleagues were not so restrained. "What makes you think you can get by with just your eye teeth?" asked one. Noting that Wright was a fellow Texan, Ralph Yarborough joked, "I have no doubt that [Wright] will triumph." One liberal added, "You were always excellent in moving to your right, but why don't we mix it up and move to your left?" The Washington sparring match never took place in any configuration, but Wright had nevertheless made his point.[42]

As Wright lobbied and McCormack waited, Majority Leader Albert moved to calm the younger members by calling for monthly meetings of the Democratic caucus, an effort at democratization. McCormack had held only one meeting every session, which limited the agenda to leadership elections and a few critical issues. Albert's initial meetings were contentious but provided him time and goodwill to solidify his leadership.

Albert needed it. Many of the younger, more liberal members wanted more reform. To appease them, Albert appointed the Committee on Organization, Study, and Review, chaired by Washington's Julia Butler Hansen. The result, in time, was the Legislative Reorganization Act of 1970. The reforms eliminated the "Teller Rule" allowing frequent unrecorded votes, somewhat limited the power of committee chairs, strengthened minority rights, and allowed for computers in the House chamber, a farsighted advance that was not widely implemented for some time. While expanding the membership of the Steering and Policy Committee, which made Democratic committee assignments, Albert also required the committee to have two females and one member representing a minority group. Wright, happy with Albert's new position, accepted the reforms and laughed at the way Albert dealt with the new quota by filling two spots with Houston's Barbara Jordan, an African American woman.[43]

Still, however, the most ardent reformers remained unsatisfied and demanded a complete overhaul of committee structure. When the House created the Select Committee on Committees to explore this option, Albert appointed Missouri's Richard Bolling as its chair. Albert had defeated Bolling for the Speakership, and the appointment smoothed ruffled feathers. It also, however, assured controversy. When Bolling, a liberal reformer, led his committee to propose realigned jurisdictions, protests grew. Fortunately for Albert, the Democratic caucus referred Bolling's proposal to a reconstituted Hansen Committee, whose more conservative membership assured moderation. In fact, over the next several years, as the Hansen Committee studied additional reforms, the Democratic caucus moved on its own and expanded the size and number of subcommittees, thereby further weakening committee chairs.

Even this worked to Wright's advantage. The Committee on Public Works became the Committee on Public Works and Transportation with broader jurisdiction and more power. Wright's subcommittee, the Highway Investigating Subcommittee, became the Public Works Subcommittee on Investigation and Review. It was assigned to monitor almost every construction and stimulus program. It was perfect for Wright because he was always anxious to weed out waste.

Quick with a suggestion, Wright remained busy as the ground shifted below him. As the summer of 1970 ended, he joined fellow congressmen traveling to the South Pacific, once again writing of his experiences to keep his name in the papers.[44] If all the reforms were not enough, he continued to argue that the Electoral College was antiquated. "The system makes voters unequal," Wright concluded, without mentioning that it arguably diminished the power of large states like Texas.[45]

The changes—unfortunately—were also at home. Frustrated by Wright's never-ending work and unhappy with her hectic public life, Mab asked for a divorce. The financial strains, now magnified with two children in college, did not help. Wright did not resist, and the couple embarked on the two-year separation that Virginia law required. In 1971, their relatively amicable, no-fault divorce was final. Perhaps relieved by the end of the tensions or feeling a bit guilty, Wright gave little attention to the money, taking only books and clothes with him. For a brief time he moved into an apartment near the Supreme Court, sharing the building with other congressmen who were in Washington without wives. After a year he moved into a basement apartment with a small rear yard near the Library of Congress. For two summers during this period, Bill Lamb, his oldest sister's son, stayed with him working as a congressional intern. After Lamb left, Wright sent him a souvenir, a ticket stub from the last Washington Senators home baseball game.[46]

The divorce hit Wright's children hard, particularly the youngest, Alicia. Known as Lisa, she moved back to Texas to live with a former classmate of both Wrights at Weatherford College. Thankfully, by this point, the older siblings were largely independent. Jimmy worked for a Houston transportation firm, while Ginger, returning from Hawaii, lived nearby with her husband Rich Brown. The couple had given birth to "the smartest child to come down the pike," in Wright's words, and surely this was a salve to the proud grandfather.[47] When Brown expressed an interest in working for the

Selective Service, Wright made use of his connections and helped his son-in-law land a job.[48] Daughter Kay, meanwhile, had dropped out of Ferrum College after an automobile wreck that required plastic surgery, but was working for a bank. At least in Texas, Wright mused, Lisa had her beloved horses.[49]

Wishing that he had been more involved in their lives when they were younger, Wright kept up a stream of letters. When the NCAA basketball championship took place in Maryland, Wright gave tickets to Ginger and Rich, and when the couple had problems with their Pontiac, he pleaded their case with General Motors' Government Relations Division. He even helped Jimmy with some research by getting the Library of Congress to assist.[50] When his son caused a car wreck, however, he promised "full and adequate recompense." Wright's letters to Lisa exhibited a certain melancholy. "The pumpkin vines you planted are growing faster than you would guess," Wright wrote. "I sure am missing you."[51]

Wright maintained cordial relations with Mab, helping her get a job as a Capitol tour guide. After their house sold, Mab moved to McLean, Virginia, and, in time, to Maine. The separation divided loyalties among many of Wright's friends, as Mab was admired in her husband's circles.[52] Wasting no time in dating—characteristically in a rush—Wright asked out Betty Jean Hay in the middle of his separation. The dating was not easy for Betty, given, in the words of one friend, the "impression that she stole him from Mab." Even Wright's former assistant Craig Raupe remained aloof for a time toward Betty. "Everybody loved Mab," Raupe remembered. "I was friendly on the surface but it just took me longer to accept [Betty]. Here she was this knockout."[53]

Wright, in reality, did already know Betty well. Betty had grown up in St. Louis, the only child of an ill mother and a father who abandoned the family. To help pay the bills, Betty had worked as a tap dancer in nightclub chorus lines. "It's made me more independent," she recalled. Marrying a pilot and moving to Fort Worth, she got a job in the hotel business and, ultimately, as an assistant to the mayor. It was at the Texas Hotel when she first met the young congressman. After several years and a divorce, Betty, "seeking to make more money," applied through the Texas Employment Commission for a secretarial job in Wright's Washington office. Her spelling impressed Marshall Lynam, Wright remembered, and "Marshall was a stickler for spelling." Soon Betty became the principal aide in the front office, and, impressing Wright's colleagues, moved on to lead Humphrey's 1968 campaign advance team. In 1971, just as the two had begun dating, Wright had hired her to lead his powerful subcommittee's staff. If anyone knew of their relationship, it remained quiet. As his marriage became strained, Wright needed someone to accompany him to constituent functions. Betty complied. "It just kind of grew from there," Wright recalled.[54]

"It went slow," Betty insisted. "This one night he asked me to go out for dinner . . . but he was dating." With Wright "playing the field," Betty played hard to get, declining one of his invitations by claiming another date. As she stayed home, the phone started ringing. "He must have called up until midnight," Betty laughed. "The next day he said to me, 'Oh, you must have had a good time last night.' I said, 'I sure did . . . listening to that telephone ring!'" After that, Betty concluded, "things started to change."[55]

Unlike Mab, Betty loved Washington's bustle. They were, Betty later joked, "the only couple in Washington who sat down to dinner and discussed the interstate highway program."[56] Betty, Wright agreed, identified "with my exhilaration over minor victories and my despondency over petty failures." More importantly, her personality complemented Wright's—she could calm his temper and help him maintain perspective. "Jim," Betty told an exasperated Wright, "what do you think they elected you to be, the leader or a dictator?" When, in another instance, Wright flung the contents of a freezer across the room because he couldn't get the door shut, a composed Betty knew to remain quiet.[57] Noting the pressure Wright faced daily, she hoped to create a rejuvenating "oasis" for him.

Wright was falling in love but hesitated to propose. Still frustrated with his debt, and, amazingly, still battling a sense of failure, Wright did not want his workaholic ways to destroy another marriage. With Wright doubting that he was "a very good catch," Betty recalled, "I finally had to go and talk to him."[58] The talk made a difference, but even the nuptials proved complicated. As the wedding approached, Betty became ill and had to spend two weeks in a Waco, Texas, hospital. Once Betty recovered, the two married at the Calvary Methodist Church in Arlington, Virginia. It was November 12, 1972, approximately one year after Wright's divorce had been made final. It was "a kind of old-fashioned wedding," Wright recalled. "Betty wrote the script and I wore a Rhett Butler kind of tux." It was also, predictably, a bit of Washington high society. Anxious no doubt to project a powerful image, Wright asked Speaker Albert to secure the Cannon House Office Caucus Room for the reception. There were strawberries and champagne, and the guest list was unusually long for a second marriage of a couple in their forties. It was also quite impressive. Befitting Wright's bipartisanship, it included a number of Republicans.[59]

After a nice but hardly elaborate honeymoon in a Pennsylvania resort that included the opportunity to hear one of their favorite musical groups, the do-wop sound Ink Spots, the newlyweds stopped at a campaign event for one of Wright's colleagues. Betty, it appeared, surely knew what she was getting into. Back in Washington, the two rented a South Arlington house that Betty had found; after a year, they purchased it. Ever trying to be collegial, Wright thanked his "excellent landlord" with a gift of his autographed book. In Arlington, the couple settled into their new routine, Betty joking that being both aide and wife went "together like bacon and eggs." After Wright's aide Lynam gave the couple bikes, Wright no longer devoted his limited free time to painting but rather to riding with his beloved along the Potomac River Canal towpath.[60] If his professional life still appeared unsettled, Wright had at last found happiness on the home front.

Wright, it turned out, needed his domestic bliss. When the new 92nd Congress convened in January 1971, Nixon shifted his more centrist domestic agenda rightward. The 1970 congressional elections—in which Wright had faced no opponent—had cost the Republicans twelve House seats and numerous governorships. With polls showing his favorable ratings underwater, Nixon concluded that it was time for something new. As Wright sat in the audience, Nixon proposed a new concept in his 1971 State of the Union Address: "Revenue Sharing," returning to the states billions from existing federal programs.[61]

It was an outrage to Wright, a clear blow to his quasi-alliance with the White House. Many states would not use the funding on behalf of the poor, Wright protested, his old populist feathers ruffled. Left unstated was the reality that the proposal diminished Congress and, implicitly, Wright's own power base—his ability to distribute funds. Wright went on the attack, arguing that federal revenue was meant for the national interest. It was a solid argument, but in the end it did not carry the day. The legislation that resulted did not give Nixon all he wanted, but, despite Wright's impassioned pleas, revenue sharing made its way into law.[62]

Wright reeled—but Nixon moved again, proposing to reorganize and deregulate government. Wright, of course, applauded the effort to root out waste, but the new proposals appeared to be ideological and extreme. Once again, one man's waste was another's necessity, and the fight played out in the details. In reality, the situation was complex, with self-interest on all sides. No one had a monopoly on the truth.[63] Postal reorganization was a case in point. With inefficiency a real problem, Nixon supported efforts to create a new governing panel and to remove Congress's ability to make appointments and set rates. The proposal was balanced, ensuring postal workers collective bargaining rights and a pay raise. Wright immediately protested the infringement on congressional prerogative, which he had used so adroitly to win postal services for his own district.[64] He also predicted higher postal rates and service cuts beyond those necessary. In fact, Nixon's postmaster general, Winton Blount, soon used the position to solidify his conservative bona fides in planning a campaign for the Senate. Wright argued for Congress to "restore our proper jurisdiction," but for once his efforts to stem the new drift rightward proved inadequate.[65]

Nixon found his veto pen increasingly attractive, often to establish his own conservative bona fides. When Congress passed legislation increasing funds for day-care facilities for single working mothers, Nixon slapped the legislation down, bemoaning "communal approaches to child rearing over the family centered approach."[66] Wright replied that day care was voluntary and that Nixon had previously advocated mandatory ones for welfare mothers. Nixon, Wright added, perpetuated "a great deal of misrepresentation." Again, it was a solid argument, but it proved unwise. Conservatives in his district flooded his office with objections and Wright began to retreat. The bill was "not perfect," he now acknowledged, "a little too loosely drawn."[67]

When Nixon began to impound congressionally appropriated funds, suggesting that the amounts specified were only the top limits of what the president could spend, Wright had more success. Despite precedents back to Thomas Jefferson, Nixon's impoundment far outstripped that of his predecessors and clearly was intended to emasculate federal programs. Predictably rushing to Congress's defense, Wright declared Nixon's actions an "infringement of constitutional powers."[68] Matters came to a head when Congress passed new water pollution legislation that included billions for waste treatment facilities, which Wright called "one of my favorite programs." A Nixon veto, a congressional override, White House impoundment, and litigation all followed in due order.[69] Finally, in 1974, Congress settled the matter with the Congressional Budget and Impoundment Control Act so important to Wright in later years. It required congressional approval of all future excisions within forty-five days, which, to Wright's great satisfaction, almost never occurred.[70]

The struggle over the balance of powers continued with legislation to contain campaign spending. Wright knew the ramifications of unregulated cash from his own campaign debt. "I simply don't have that kind of money," he had frequently told supporters.[71] When Democrats passed legislation to restrict money for television, Nixon vetoed the measure as unfair to the broadcasting industry. He was, however, obviously aware of the traditional Republican advantage in fundraising.[72] The Democrats used the debate to cast Republicans as champions of the wealthy, an argument that won a few GOP defectors and allowed Wright to promote a new, broader bill as "bipartisan" and more "meaningful." Soon Wright was part of a "bipartisan steering group" to lobby the holdouts.[73] He accepted a formula based on an individual district's population and media costs, but resisted using thirty-second commercials to gauge the standards. A congressman was not a "carnival pitchman." Limits on individual donations, Wright countered, were better.[74] In the end, legislation included public financing through tax form check-offs, limits on what congressmen could spend on themselves, and, most significantly, public disclosure of all large contributions. Nixon finally agreed once he was assured that the law would not apply to his reelection. Wright welcomed Nixon's surrender but was now painfully aware that his odd alliance with the president would never be the same.[75]

Nixon's emerging conservatism was in some respects a shot across the bow of the Democrats. The only Republican presidents Wright had dealt with before were the centrist Eisenhower and the rather domestically nonchalant first-term Nixon. Now, however, Nixon seemed to exhibit a growing disdain for government that spoke as much to the likes of Barry Goldwater as to the more moderate Eisenhower. Though the years that followed brought Nixon's infamous demise and, apparently, a liberal revival, in fact the reaction to Great Society activism continued apace. By the end of the decade, Wright and his colleagues would face a Republican president that challenged Wright's central political assumptions far more than Nixon ever did. For the time being, however, the political pendulum had only begun to turn, and both Nixon and Wright remained committed to working together whenever possible. Although it became strained, their connection remained. Wright was no left-wing liberal, after all, just as Nixon was no Ronald Reagan.

This fact was evident in the direction Wright took his new, more powerful subcommittee. His first action was to call hearings on unnecessary public works bureaucracy. Fighting red tape, Wright explained, was like "cutting a path through the Amazon." Wright hoped to augment faith in government, attack the debt, and counter charges that the Democrats were prolific spenders, and Republicans believed that any focus on government inefficiency worked to their advantage. Republicans, and even nervous private contractors, wrote Wright to compliment the "splendid job" he was doing, adding that they were "anxious to cooperate in every possible manner."[76] When, in an acknowledgment of his reputation for cooperation and collegiality, Wright was named chairman of a bipartisan commission assigned to investigate waste in the Johnson-era highway beautification program, he played to both sides. His efforts would serve the common good, he stated, not just the "environmentalists and the outdoor advertising men."[77] Like the liberals, Wright thought the regulations worthwhile; like the Republicans, however, he had concerns about federalism and property rights.

Wright's reference to environmentalists was instructive. By the end of the 92nd Congress Wright was beginning to find the environmentalists frustrating, his strong advocacy for water pollution legislation notwithstanding. Emboldened by its successes, the environmental movement had matured, and it was now less likely to compromise and demanding ever more. At the same time, however, a conservative backlash had started to spring from this success. Clearly the bipartisan coalition on the issue was fracturing, with Nixon moving into line with his new conservatism and Wright and many moderates feeling pressure to adapt.[78]

Once again, Wright proved that he and Nixon could still find common ground. Explaining that congressmen did not have the luxury of being single-issue advocates and needed to "reach independent conclusions," Wright joined Nixon in supporting funds for the Supersonic Transport, or SST. Environmentalists objected, noting the plane's noise and impact on wildlife, but Wright's own aeronautical interests drove him into Nixon's corner.[79] Rather than dismissing the environmental concerns, as the White House did, Wright argued that the plane "could easily be limited to transoceanic flights."[80]

When it came to water reclamation projects, Wright became more ardent. A moratorium on stream channelization represented "a desire to lock up our rivers," he said. Suggestions that dams hurt stream ecology represented a "scapegoat syndrome."[81] Wright supported the Cross-Florida Barge Canal and the Tennessee-Tombigbee Waterway, two large canal projects with environmental implications, and complained that Supreme Court Justice William O. Douglas was "sloppy and careless" in his criticism of Texas dams. When columnist Jack Anderson wrote that Wright had remarked "to hell with the fish," Wright acknowledged it. "If I had known there was a transcript, I would have said, 'To heck with the fish.'" Never before had Wright's wise-use conservation diverged more from his environmentalism.

Wright's position, consumer advocate Ralph Nader said, revealed "the conflict between what is good for his district and what is environmentally good."[82]

Like Nixon, Wright increasingly believed that environmentalists were abusing the National Environmental Policy Act's impact statement requirement. The "unfortunate process," Wright recalled, "stopped projects that were good for the country." Wright laughingly remembered a lawsuit to stop a Fort Worth highway because of possible threats to an obscure species of endangered wildlife. The suit failed, but it reinforced a growing impression on the city's congressman that at least some environmentalists were anti-growth zealots.[83]

In later years Wright proudly described himself as an environmentalist, and indeed, there is much to support such a claim. Nevertheless, in context, it is fair to describe Wright as a moderate, a man whose attitudes and policies evolved—just as Nixon's did. In the end, Wright's record, like Nixon's, was complex. Although he strongly supported federal aid for waste treatment, he voted against requiring the best available technology and mandating increased oversight by the Environmental Protection Agency (EPA). He supported ending underground nuclear testing in Alaska, fearing radioactivity, but resisted comprehensive land use legislation, envisioning a violation of property rights. While he supported strict logging limits, he did not believe the EPA should ban nonessential pesticides. In 1972, based on his solid record on environmental issues, the League of Conservation Voters gave Wright a grade of 71, a score higher than Nixon's but lower than that of many liberals. Whether this record warranted the title of environmentalist was always a matter of opinion.

Wright and Nixon continued to share their disdain for New Left radicalism. When Wright's son Jimmy noted that many of the continuing protests were nonviolent, Wright replied that they were "clearly directed by anarchists." Like Nixon, Wright supported full funding for the Committee on Internal Security, formerly the controversial House Un-American Activities Committee.[84] When civil libertarians complained that his rhetoric mirrored that of Attorney General John Mitchell, Wright brushed off the comments.[85] Like Nixon, Wright was no fan of modern art, complaining that a mural selected for a federal building was worse than what his preteen daughter could have produced. Still dabbling in painting himself, Wright preferred more conservative and traditional art.[86]

Wright's continuing criticism of the media's "slanted coverage" still sounded eerily like Nixon's. "I don't want to sound like Spiro Agnew," Wright stated, referring to the vice-president's well-publicized complaints. In fact, Wright congratulated the *Fort Worth Star-Telegram* for its law-and-order editorials and its support of Nixon in Vietnam.[87] When Nixon called for a "war on cancer," Wright quickly enlisted, cosponsoring legislation that emerged as the National Cancer Act of 1971.[88] Although later questioning harsh prosecution of marijuana, Wright shared Nixon's perception of drugs as more of a criminal than a health issue; he believed that the government needed to crack down on this "monstrous evil."[89]

When Nixon, in an attempt to control inflation, instituted wage and price controls and took the dollar off the gold standard, Wright applauded the move. He had also approved of Nixon's belated embrace of a more liberalized monetary policy, but it had not solved the problem of spiraling costs as Wright had predicted. Inflation, along with the nation's growing deficit in its balance of payments, made for a complex set of issues, but both Nixon and Wright realized that the American voter demanded action. The wage and price controls were certainly ironic, given Nixon's growing conservatism in so many other ways, but Wright refused the opportunity to criticize the president. The controls were temporary, with a Cost of Living Council to determine their future, and Wright appreciated that Nixon had appointed his Texas acquaintance John Connally as treasury secretary. Nixon's initiatives, Wright later reflected, "may have averted a crisis." In fact, had there been a run on gold, one certainly would have developed. In any event, while the economic data improved slightly, the controls ultimately proved unequal to the task of inflation. The floating currency promoted growth but also risked financial bubbles.[90]

The Supreme Court, meanwhile, continued to set the context for Nixon and Wright. When the Court ruled in 1971 that busing to achieve desegregation was constitutional, Nixon calculated that southern conservative anger would further split the Democratic Party, facilitating his "Southern Strategy." Indeed, defiant letters flooded Wright's office.[91] Once again Wright had to face his civil rights dilemma. He did not agree with the racist sentiments expressed by many protesters, and he recognized the problem of inequality in the schools, but the social engineering busing implied rubbed him the wrong way. The politics were obvious. Accordingly—and at least somewhat uncomfortably—Wright joined Nixon in criticism of the Court's decision. The decision, Wright said, in comments that others later used against affirmative action, promoted "a color conscious society," not a "colorblind society."[92] It was an "arbitrary" decision by "activist judges."[93] When southern

Democrats began to push for a constitutional amendment overturning the decision, both Nixon and Wright supported the effort.[94]

When the Supreme Court essentially confirmed its 1962 ruling that prohibited voluntary school prayer as unconstitutional, Wright's reaction was in many ways more ardent than Nixon's.[95] Nixon understood that the decision once again angered many southern conservatives, but he also recognized that at least some Protestants, such as the Baptist General Convention of Texas, still feared a government-led prayer contrary to their own beliefs.[96] Qualifying his criticism, therefore, Nixon denounced the decision but opposed a constitutional amendment overturning it. Wright, meanwhile, criticized the decision and still supported the proposed amendment. School prayer was an "enriching experience," Wright stated, to the chagrin of civil libertarians, adding that no one would be forced to pray.[97]

In foreign policy, the end of Nixon's first term only solidified Wright's support for the White House. Nixon's realpolitik overture to the People's Republic of China, including his historic 1972 visit to Beijing, and his subsequent agreement with the Soviets in the SALT talks made sense to Wright on multiple levels. Diplomacy appealed both to his pragmatism and to his idealism. When Nixon, in Beijing, spoke of a "peaceful new world," Wright later wrote, "Nixon spoke for me." That moment, Wright concluded, was the "high point of his presidency."[98]

Wright had growing concerns about Vietnam, of course, but in his view Nixon still seemed headed in the right direction. The liberals in his own caucus threatening to deny military appropriations worried him more. When the liberals passed a resolution denouncing heavy bombing to press negotiations, Wright lashed out. "I disassociate myself entirely from that expression," Wright stated. It was senseless "unless one desires a victory for the North."[99] If the resolution's proponents thought such comments unnecessarily caustic, the White House also noticed. Vice President Spiro Agnew thanked Wright, and National Security Adviser Henry Kissinger acknowledged "how difficult this can be for a member of the opposition." Wright was "putting country above party," Nixon declared, "and events will prove the wisdom of your courageous act."[100]

When CBS televised a "special report" suggesting that the Pentagon had sought to sway public opinion in favor of the war, Wright protested the award-winning telecast even as many Democrats claimed that the military had misused public funds. When conservatives demanded the show's records and CBS refused, citing freedom of the press, Wright supported a resolution of contempt. Moreover, when the infamous Pentagon Papers became public, Wright's anger was aimed as much at the leaker, Daniel Ellsberg, as at government malfeasance—just as Nixon's was.[101]

Nixon and Wright were willing to give each other the benefit of the doubt. Their connection was not what it was in the previous Congress, but neither were they bitter enemies. As part of the Mexico–United States Interparliamentary Conference, Wright had promised to press Mexican concerns that American runoff was polluting the Colorado River. When Wright, true to his word, raised the issue with the White House, Nixon agreed to support the legislation Wright proposed. Thus assured, Wright played an integral role in what finally emerged as a new agreement between the two neighbors. The agreement, which included an American-built desalinization plant near the border, gave Wright "enormous satisfaction."[102] When reports arose that the CIA had covertly undermined the left-leaning but democratically elected government of Salvador Allende in Chile, Wright worried about an affront to American ideals. The State Department and Kissinger, however, personally assured Wright that America had played no role. Wright accepted the denials. In the end, such trust proved misplaced. Several years later, after the right-wing dictator Augusto Pinochet seized power and suspended constitutional government, Nixon's successor, Gerald Ford, acknowledged CIA involvement. Wright was aghast, and his perception of Nixon was shattered.[103]

In 1972, Chile was not the only reality about Nixon that Wright failed to grasp. It was an election year, and Wright refused to believe that a reported break-in at the Democratic National Committee headquarters in Washington's Watergate complex had anything to do with the White House. Nixon had just given him one of the first Eisenhower silver dollars minted, undoubtedly a token to soothe recent ruffled feathers, and Wright once again gave the president the benefit of the doubt. To Wright, he and Nixon remained partisans on opposite sides, but they were both Americans sharing the same basic morals and ideals. Their policies might increasingly differ, but they still recognized some commonality between them. As events unfolded, of course, Wright would have to revisit this assumption. The 1972 election changed everything—for Nixon, for Wright, and for the country at large.[104]

_____

CHAPTER 11

Bombshell

THE WATERGATE CRISIS (1972–1974)

Eight months before the 1972 election, the *Haltom City (TX) News-Tribune* declared the "long shot of '54" Jim Wright as the "strongest man in politics today."[1] If a bit of hyperbole, there was some truth in the claim. With Wright straddling the divide in the Democratic Party, potential presidential candidates solicited his support almost a year and a half before the election. First was the apparent front-runner, Maine senator Edmund Muskie, whom Wright liked for his collegiality, moderation, and defense of clean water. Although Wright let Muskie know that it was too early for any endorsement, but that he welcomed Muskie's candidacy, Muskie still replied that it was "very gratifying, indeed, to know of your support at this time."[2] Hubert Humphrey, the defeated 1968 nominee whom Wright had supported, followed. "I simply can't make a move without getting your advice and hopefully your support," Humphrey wrote.[3] Joining these two Democratic stalwarts were South Dakota senator George McGovern and Alabama governor George Wallace. Sharing a flyboy past, Wright was friends with the former, although McGovern had led the resistance to Nixon's Vietnam policies and courted the New Left. His efforts to democratize the party, Wright feared, risked weakening party unity. As for Wallace, Wright feared he would be a troublesome wildcard just as he had been four years before. Adding to the uncertainty were two long shots: Senator Henry Jackson from Washington State, and Representative Shirley Chisholm of New York, the first African American to run for president and the first woman to seek the Democratic nomination.

Wright had positioned himself well for what Muskie described as the "long and vigorous campaign ahead." After all, Wright still faced no challengers for his own office. Despite his growing role in national politics, he had hardly forgotten his own constituents or lost his ability to bring home the bacon. Once the Vietnam War had begun, for example, Wright had won lucrative helicopter contracts for Fort Worth's Bell Helicopters. The experimental TFX plane that Wright had won for General Dynamics had evolved into the F-111, a plane worth millions. Referring to that company's aerospace division, some described Wright as the "Congressman from Convair."[4] Wright had fought once again to keep Fort Wolters Air Force Base open and worked to diversify the city's economy. Voters applauded his efforts to promote private employment and win a broader range of government expenditures. In short, Wright's popularity dissuaded potential challengers. Once again he was free to focus on the national campaign.

Always networking, Wright was among Lyndon Johnson's "host of friends" in Austin to celebrate the opening of the former president's library.[5] Always a draw as a great speaker, he was constantly campaigning for his colleagues around the country.[6] Increasingly, it appeared, Wright favored Muskie for the Democratic nomination, even submitting "a little speech I scrawled out on the plane" for Muskie's review.[7] The speech, effusive in praise, listed Muskie's admirable qualities, which, Wright concluded, "add up to a somewhat old fashioned trait that we call integrity."[8]

Muskie, it turned out, may have had integrity, but he did not have a thick skin. After several early victories, an exhausted Muskie attempted to address charges that he had made racist remarks about French Canadians and that his wife drank excessively. The charge that he was racist had been made in the so-called "Canuck Letter," a letter to the editor that had been published by a New Hampshire newspaper shortly before the state primary. The letter later proved to be a hoax. Standing on a flatbed truck in New Hampshire as the snow began to fall, Muskie appeared to become emotional. Critics soon claimed that he had cried, although Muskie insisted the "tears" were only melted snow. Of course, it did not matter; the damage had been done. As his support plummeted, it was effectively the end of any real chance Muskie had at the nomination—and the beginning of Wright's support for

Humphrey. Wright, "trying to be honest," publicly urged Muskie to withdraw. Muskie tried to fight on, but, perhaps proving the integrity of which Wright had spoken, held no grudges. He later thanked Wright for his "help and support."[9]

Three "realistic alternatives" remained, Wright explained, but only Humphrey had the "experience necessary." Wallace, Wright charged, would "divide the country dangerously," and McGovern had endorsed "legalization of marijuana, unqualified amnesty for draft evaders, and indiscriminate cuts in national defense." Wright's criticism of McGovern predicted the harsh Republican attacks to come and reflected Wright's disdain for the New Left.[10]

Wright pressed for Humphrey in the Texas state primary and precinct conventions, but the Fort Worth senatorial convention exposed the party's deep divisions. Liberals and conservatives openly battled, and Wright tried to play the conciliator in his keynote address. "Out of our disorganization, our diversity, and even our disagreements," Wright stated, "comes our strength."[11] Wright's efforts to spin the convention were not completely successful. One delegate complained that the convention was "frustrating" because the leaders could not maintain order. Wright only replied that he had "refrained from taking any personal role at all in the floor tactics."[12]

It was a momentous spring and early summer. In May, a gunman shot Wallace at a Maryland shopping center. One of the bullets injured his spinal cord, paralyzing him from the waist down. Although Wallace, like Muskie, remained in the race, the bullet effectively ended the Alabaman's campaign. Then, in mid-June, the media reported that five burglars had been caught inside the headquarters of the Democratic National Committee, located in Washington, DC's, Watergate complex. Speculation immediately arose of White House involvement and the investigations began, but Nixon said he knew nothing of the matter, and Wright took him at his word. Wright could not fathom such presidential corruption and, in any event, the battle for the Democratic nomination demanded all of his time.[13]

The July Democratic National Convention in Miami was all Wright had feared it would be. With Humphrey's chances hinging on a desperate challenge to McGovern delegates, the party's revised rules for delegate selection proved pivotal. The more diverse participation magnified the contention and, while thankfully lacking the violence of Chicago four years earlier, the protracted debate arguably weakened the ultimate victor, McGovern.[14] The champion of those who were young, who were members of minority groups, or who held antiwar sentiments, McGovern was too liberal for many southern conservatives, who promised to vote Republican. Among them were Wright's patron Amon Carter Jr., John Connally, and much of the Texas oil money. While Wright was too loyal a Democrat for something so drastic, McGovern's nomination arguably accelerated the Republican ascent in the Lone Star State. Perhaps anticipating the result, Wright skipped the party's convention for the first time since he had held national office. Humphrey, like Muskie earlier, graciously thanked Wright for his "strong friendship and support," and Wright promised to "support the nominee."[15]

Wright was loyal but not optimistic. "You and I seem to be suffering the same trauma as [a] result of the Democratic nomination," Wright wrote one friend. "It is a new day and a new ball game." There were too many "freshmen on the field."[16] While Wright knew that McGovern was no rookie, events suggested otherwise. After reports emerged confirming that vice-presidential nominee Thomas Eagleton, a senator from Missouri, had sought psychiatric help, McGovern first vowed his support only to later ask his running mate to step aside. Wright admired Eagleton as a "thoroughly decent man" and complained openly that he had been "thrown overboard." Increasingly, Wright later acknowledged, he "entertained no illusion about [McGovern's] electability."[17]

Wright clearly did not have as much enthusiasm for the general campaign as he had had in the past. When he agreed to introduce Eagleton's replacement, J. Sargent Shriver, at a Texas campaign stop, Shriver sounded almost surprised. "I was genuinely happy to see you at the rally," Shriver later wrote before asking Wright to help "rally" local Democrats. It was, of course, telling that Wright, campaigner extraordinaire, needed any such prompting.[18] If McGovern had any hope of winning, it ended when Henry Kissinger announced in late October that an agreement had been reached with North Vietnam. With the bombing halted, the promise of an armistice appeared to validate the administration's policies, political gold only days before the vote.

The 1972 election, accordingly, proved to be one of the most lopsided victories in American history, with McGovern carrying only Massachusetts and the District of Columbia. Even Texas, which outside of the Eisenhower administration had voted Republican only once since Reconstruction, went for the GOP. Much to his dismay, Wright's district followed suit. The Texas congressional delegation now included four Republicans, and Senator John Tower won reelection. In total, Democrats still held the congressional majority but now appeared to be on the defensive. Most voters shared Wright's view that the lingering Watergate investigation had nothing to do with Nixon personally.[19]

Wright's lack of enthusiasm for the national campaign was understandable in more than one way. Not only did the campaign pit a Republican with growing conservative tendencies against a true liberal opponent of the Vietnam War, leaving Wright without an ideal horse in the race, but Wright had more than enough on his own plate. For one thing, the redistricting that followed the 1970 census was troublesome. This was unexpected. All redistricting plans, State Representative Joe Christie announced during initial negotiations, "appear absolutely safe for Jim Wright of Fort Worth." Wright's overpopulated district would have to shrink, but he would not suffer a greater Republican presence. "He can't be hurt at all by any plan," said Christie.[20] In time, however, a Voting Rights Act revision mandated by the courts dismantled the district of one of Wright's colleagues, Olin Teague, leaving Teague the option of running in one of three new districts. When the press then reported that Teague, a popular Democrat, was considering moving to Fort Worth and challenging Wright, Wright had to acknowledge that his plans had been "thrown into a cocked hat." In the end, thankfully for Wright, Teague chose to run in another district, reminding Wright that he could take nothing for granted.[21]

The shocking plane crash death of House Majority Leader Hale Boggs really brought the message home. Wright and Boggs were friends. When Wright's mother had died, his father had traveled to New Orleans, Boggs's district, to get away from all the memories. Boggs had promised Wright to use his connections to keep a protective eye on the old man. "I had been friendly with Lindy [Boggs's wife and congressional successor] and knew their children," Wright recalled. At the time of his death, Boggs had been flying to a campaign event for Alaska congressman Nick Begich. Begich had, in fact, asked Wright to come if Boggs was unable to make it, and had also died in the crash. "I later learned," Wright recalled, "that Speaker [Carl] Albert had called a delay in a conference committee that [Boggs] was to attend so that he could make the trip."[22]

As fate would have it, however, the tragedy had a silver lining for Wright. The position of majority leader was open. With the moderate Oklahoman Albert as the Speaker of the House, Majority Whip Tip O'Neill, a Massachusetts liberal, was the logical choice for the caucus, promising the leadership a degree of regional and ideological balance. Set to challenge O'Neill were Floridian Sam Gibbons, who hoped to marshal southern resentment against northern liberals, and Californian Phil Burton, who hoped to win support with his advocacy of making the whip an elected, not appointed, position.[23] Wright voted for O'Neill not only because of party balance but because O'Neill still championed an appointed whip system. Wright had won his zone whip position through appointment. He was still hoping for a promotion, and the process played to his strengths. Accordingly, after precedent held firm and O'Neill emerged as majority leader, he appointed Californian John McFall as his replacement for majority whip. McFall, in turn, appointed Wright as one of the four deputy whips, a step up that made Wright responsible for the votes of the Democrats from one-fourth of the country.[24]

The Texas delegation, led by Jake Pickle and Eligio "Kika" de la Garza, lobbied Albert and O'Neill on Wright's behalf. Although Albert was from Oklahoma, they argued, many southerners still felt slighted. Former speaker John McCormack telephoned O'Neill to reinforce the importance of the southern-northern balance. Noting that he had served with Rayburn, and Johnson with Kennedy, McCormack asked O'Neill to "tell Carl Albert that I would appreciate it if he would keep the Boston-Austin axis going."[25] When he was later asked about these events, Wright sought to diminish the role of his personal ambition. "I don't think there was any contest," he recalled of O'Neill's election, brushing off the reality that Gibbons and Burton had dropped out only after considerable negotiation. His own appointment as deputy whip, Wright continued, was a "pleasant surprise." In fact, to conclude that the possibility had not occurred to him defies not only his career frustrations and his inherent ambition but also his actions beforehand.

Regardless of what role his ambition played, Wright took to his new role with the energy he had left out of the presidential campaign. When a bill arose, he instructed his zone whips to canvas their members and then coordinated an appropriate lobbying strategy. Employing his full arsenal of rhetoric, collegiality, and connections, Wright was good at his job, and rarely did a vote not go as planned.[26] Wright was, according to O'Neill, critical "in making the whip organization work."[27]

Wright still loved the limelight, even appearing as an "extra" in the television movie *Scorpio*, which was filmed in Washington. When he dressed for his role as a priest, Wright laughingly recalled, the film's crew picked him as the real cleric from a group of Georgetown priests who were also present. Wright donated his $25 payment to charity, but he kept a picture of him meeting the movie's star, Burt Lancaster.[28] Meanwhile, Wright agreed to a large exhibit of his paintings at the Jack Bryant Gallery in Azle, Texas, appearing for the opening with Betty. The reviews of Wright's paintings, most in watercolor and oil, were largely positive.[29]

More significantly, Wright joined a bipartisan delegation on a three-week trip to Europe and the Soviet Union to study how other countries dealt with public transportation and—though it was unstated—to advance détente. Predictably, Wright, writing of his experiences for the Fort Worth press, said he found the Soviet Union "most interesting."[30] He reported on the short daylight hours, the emerging yet clandestine free markets, and the remarkable history of the country. The friendly nature of the people, however, surprised him. Years before, Wright had written his "Letter to Ivan," addressing the common Soviet citizen, and now he found his sentiments reciprocated. A local merchant, for example, refused a payment upon learning that Wright was American. It all reinforced Wright's long-held idealism. Officially, Wright reported back that the European subway systems were inexpensive and efficient. A "coordinated approach" of automobiles and mass transit was best for America, he concluded, adding that a tax on parking had served a number of European cities well.[31]

Although Wright welcomed the press coverage of the trip, he might have considered that his narratives could leave the wrong impression. When a constituent complained of the cost, Wright found himself defending congressional travel, as he had in the past. "Firsthand observation" was essential, Wright insisted, and the "free circus atmosphere" of earlier trips had ended.[32] In fact, it was the first trip Wright had taken since marrying Betty, and it caused him to miss Christmas with his children. The fact that he went at all was testament to the importance he assigned to his career. To be fair, Wright later shared many Christmases with his children—and even Mab. Once, after his daughter Ginger asked Betty if her mother could attend a holiday fundraiser, Betty even insisted that Wright introduce Mab as "the mother of my children." Mab was gracious; the press reported that there wasn't a dry eye in the house.[33] Wright's preoccupation with his career was all right with Betty, and it appeared that Mab had found peace as well.

"The great tragedy of Watergate," Wright wrote late in 1973, was the way the scandal had "dominated the attention of so many Americans."[34] Few appreciated the momentous developments that otherwise characterized the 93rd Congress. Although Wright had no idea of the historical nature of the investigations then under way, their result unknown, there was some truth to his claim.

The Vietnam War, for example, did not end easily. After the announcement of peace just prior to the US elections, the accord broke down and fighting resumed. When Nixon launched saturation bombing during the holidays—the infamous "Christmas Bombing"—the peace movement erupted. Wright approved of the attacks as leverage for the resumption of negotiations, but he thought that Nixon should have consulted Congress first. When, in late January 1973, the accord was reaffirmed, Wright claimed a degree of vindication. "The Christmas bombing spree, while unauthorized, apparently achieved its purpose," Wright stated. The accord was not perfect, he believed, but Nixon's strategy had ended the war honorably. In fact, of course, Wright said nothing of the reality that North Vietnamese troops were allowed to remain in the South with vague promises of future reconciliation. The communists, many predicted, would simply resume their assault once the Americans had departed, a reality that subsequently unfolded in 1975. At this point, the new president, Gerald Ford, understandably refused to return, with the result that America experienced its first significant defeat.[35]

Although Wright clearly struggled with these events as they unfolded, his support for the war never wavered. Just after the final accords were signed, Nixon offered Wright congratulations and termed the war a "stern test nobly met." Wright, however, largely limited his comments to doubts that North Vietnam had returned all the prisoners and documented all of those reported missing in action.[36] When colleagues resisted reclassifying undocumented MIAs as "killed in action" until North Vietnam had completely complied, Wright supported the measure.[37] When others suggested the possibility of the United States providing humanitarian aid with "specific safeguards," Wright thought the idea might help America "retain some influence." When the end finally arrived and Ford refused re-intervention, Wright simply pointed out that Congress had not promised aid. "The treaty was negotiated by Mr. Kissinger without approval by Congress," Wright said.[38]

In his memoirs, Wright simply brushes past the war's tragic denouement with one cryptic sentence: "The Vietnam war, finally ended, brought a sense of relief but left little room for national pride."[39] In later years Wright recounted his concerns, but his actions at the time never really indicated he had such doubts. Like many Americans, Wright continued to wrestle with the war's implications, perhaps privately questioning whether he had been on the wrong side of history. At the time, for a congressman of his stature, such opinions were difficult to state publicly. When he later was asked about his impressions of the Vietnam War Memorial, for example, he was dismissive. "I was not fixated on the status of memorials," he curtly replied.[40]

Wright's support of the War Powers Act of 1973 suggested that even at the time he may have recognized the historical error of the war. There had not been an official declaration of war, and the growing opposition had sought to use the congressional power of the purse to defund the military operations. Early in the 93rd Congress, legislators had begun to recognize this situation as untenable for the future. Accordingly, the War Powers Act provided for the president to order troops into combat zones without prior congressional approval—but only for a designated period of time. At that point Congress had to declare war to ensure funding or the president had to withdraw the troops. The question struck at the heart of two competing beliefs that Wright had always held: his belief that a wartime commander-in-chief deserved a united nation, and his belief that Congress needed to reassert itself against the increasing consolidation of executive power. Although, in one sense, his support for Nixon's war policies spoke to the former, his support for the War Powers Act suggested the growing prominence of the latter. In another sense, more subtle perhaps, his support for the legislation implied that if the rules had been clearer, things might have turned out differently. The War Powers Act, after all, reinforced for many the impression that the conflict had been one colossal debacle.[41]

In any event, if Wright ever hoped that a greater degree of unity might emerge from the war's passing, the issue of abortion quickly extinguished the idea. Early in 1973 the Supreme Court ruled in *Roe v. Wade* that a right to privacy under the due process clause of the Fourteenth Amendment extended to a woman's decision to undergo the procedure.[42] The decision shocked the Roman Catholic Church, which argued that life existed from conception, and increasingly alienated many conservative Protestants who viewed the decision as part of a larger decay of American culture. Legalized abortion, homosexuality, new restrictions on school prayer, and, in the largest sense, the libertine sexual mores attendant to the 1960s, they argued, demanded a "fight to save the family."[43]

Recognizing the long history of religious conservatism in Texas, Wright saw trouble. Polls suggested that opposition to abortion was growing fastest in the South, and Wright feared the issue might tear the tenuous Democratic coalition apart. Many feminists, a key constituency, supported abortion rights, whereas Nixon denounced the decision, additional evidence of his evolving conservatism. Republicans, Wright worried, might use the issue as a political wedge.[44] Wright still believed that victory demanded winning the moderate middle, but abortion evoked so much emotion that compromise appeared impossible.[45] Wright, who knew that McGovern had angered both sides during his presidential run, saw no advantage in raising the matter. The smart move was to downplay it whenever possible.[46]

Much to Wright's dismay, by the end of the 93rd Congress more than fifty proposals for constitutional amendments on abortion existed, and the debate appeared to have begun to unfold just as Wright had feared it would. Some Democrats were attacking each other. There were bills restricting federal funding for abortion research, bills restricting foreign aid for abortion, and a slew of other proposals.[47] By the end of Jimmy Carter's administration seven years later, the debates had only hardened, and a clearer partisan allegiance had emerged. It had for Wright become a nightmare.[48] For the moment, however, whenever he was forced to address the matter, Wright declared his personal opposition to abortion but suggested that the matter was best left to the states. Opposing both *Roe* and constitutional prohibitions was the closest that he could get to a compromise. With no partisan allegiances yet demanded, Wright quietly supported both financial restrictions on fetal research and the "right of conscience" for health-care providers opposed to abortion. "We just didn't talk about such things," Wright later said, adding that he tried to quickly dismiss anyone who raised the matter. For the most part, he was fortunate, and the glare was focused on the ardent warriors on each side. Watching it all, he undoubtedly sensed that his juggling act would not always be so successful.[49]

While avoiding the spotlight on abortion, Wright kept his focus on the newly expanded Public Works Committee. The committee work and his growing status as a party leader ensured him a critical role in the passage of the Federal-Aid Highway Act of 1973. Soon after learning that Speaker O'Neill had appointed him as floor manager for the bill, Wright found that the Senate version divided his colleagues. Although the bill provided billions of dollars more for the maintenance that the highway system desperately needed, it also allowed states to divert almost $1 billion from the Highway Trust Fund for urban mass transit. This pleased liberal urban Democrats but worried southern conservatives, especially those from rural areas, who feared a loss of their road money. Wright agreed with the southerners, not out of any disdain for mass transit or a repudiation of his recent reports from Europe, but out of a desire to protect his own legacy. The trust fund had been his idea, and it had worked well. Diverting the funds, he exclaimed, would "bust the trust."[50] Moving to calm tensions, Wright pressed for the open hearing the young liberals demanded, quietly assuming that such hearings might make additional floor amendments more difficult. Next he proposed a compromise. In lieu of diverting fund money, cities could return their allotments to the trust fund and then seek an equal sum from the Treasury Department. States could also return money for projects they considered noncritical and seek the same amount from general federal revenues. With Wright at the helm, the House moved swiftly. Not only did it provide billions of dollars more than its Senate counterpart and expand safety programs, but it included Wright's compromise as well.[51]

Next came a conference committee to iron out the differences between the two chambers' bills. Wright advocated restricting the total cost, which brought the bill closer in line with the Senate version, pleasing the White House, and worked to ease the bill's environmental restrictions, demanded by many of his House colleagues. The issue of mass transit, however, drew out negotiations for over two months, requiring almost thirty meetings and necessitating a temporary continuing resolution. By this point, energy shortages had added momentum to mass transit funding. Working with Texas senator Lloyd Bentsen, Wright once again forged an acceptable compromise. The final legislation allowed cities in 1974 to divert trust fund money and receive an equal allotment from general revenues. In 1975, they could divert millions for urban buses, and in 1976, almost $1 billion for light rail, provided that the states also paid a portion of the total cost. The final bill included the House's safety programs, as well as money for bike trails, but not the proposed state diversion of trust fund money. In the end, the entire debate demonstrated again Wright's modus operandi and his mastery of the system. If Wright was a more muted congressman when it came to abortion, and a more chastened one when it came to the Vietnam War, his role in getting the most influential highway bill since the Eisenhower years passed confirmed his continued political ascent.[52]

A crisis in the Middle East soon shifted the debate once again. In fact, developments in the Middle East would play an outsized role in most of the economic and environmental issues the United States was to face for years to come. The Yom Kippur War of 1973 and the subsequent embargo of oil sales to America by the Organization of Petroleum Exporting Countries (OPEC) signaled the beginning of the infamous energy crisis of the 1970s. With gas shortages and inflation threatening to escalate, the Nixon administration wrestled with price controls and rationing as the public grew more frustrated and impatient.[53] By the time the Nixon administration had launched its "Project Independence" to make the United States self-sufficient in its energy needs by 1980, Wright had taken steps to make sure the public's ire would not metastasize to him. The shortages could have been avoided, Wright argued, if the government, "several years ago," had only adopted the alternative energy sources he had long advocated. Now, unfortunately, a "crash effort" was necessary. Wright supported many of the administration's proposals, and even demanded that they be imposed on a larger scale. Like Nixon, Wright supported the Trans-Alaska Pipeline System and the easing of environmental restrictions to promote domestic oil production. He agreed with Nixon's calls for conservation and alternative fuels, but thought them insufficient. Nixon's approach, he said, was a "cop out."[54]

Perhaps befitting his renewed political momentum, Wright unveiled his somewhat grandiosely termed "National Energy Plan of Action," calling for billions of dollars in an Energy Conservation and Development Trust Fund—an obvious reflection of his Highway Trust Fund. Wright envisioned not only expanded domestic oil production, additional oil shale recovery, and new waves to employ coal, but also expanded financial incentives for conservation and a massive research agenda in solar, nuclear, and geothermal power. Wright's call for inter-city commute systems was obviously intended for the Dallas–Fort Worth metropolitan area. To pay for the spending, the new fund would draw from additional taxes on oil, natural gas, gas-guzzling automobiles, large parking lots, and the biggest corporate users of electricity, among others. For workers adversely affected by the shifting energy priorities, Wright proposed compensation and retraining.[55]

It was indeed a grand scheme, although, as such, it faced stiff resistance. The Democratic leadership remarked that Wright was "on the right track" and thought the idea of a trust fund worth exploring, and many urban lawmakers liked Wright's focus on coordinated commuting systems. The problem, of course, was the taxes. Wright tried to compromise in order to give the new trust fund a better chance of passing, suggesting early on that his proposal would "need refining," but with so many oxen gored, the debate devolved into the minutiae before fading away in the shadow of Watergate.[56] In the end, Congress passed smaller, more focused initiatives that forced Wright to prioritize and trade off his specific reforms. Wright had advocated for expanded nuclear power, for example, but he resisted additional funds for such because the bill included only a "pittance" for solar energy.[57] He favored additional gas taxes, but he thought the ten-cent per gallon tax that emerged in debate was too high. Such a tax, he concluded, would "hurt those who can afford it the least." Moreover, he favored taxing oil production, but he argued that the result unfairly affected the small independent drillers, something that had been a concern for Wright since his earliest days. His relationship with the oil industry was complicated, if not ambivalent, and Wright insisted that the government focus the taxation proposals on the many "integrated, internationally operating companies who have racked up awfully high profits."[58]

With the problem persisting, the 93rd Congress ended with 32 committees having held over 650 days of hearings on more than 1,000 energy-related bills.[59] The results included the Emergency Petroleum Allocation Act of 1973 and the Energy Supply and Environmental Coordination Act of 1974, which together provided for expanded federal power to encourage conservation—including a national 55-mile-per-hour speed limit—but clearly favored expansion of fossil fuels at the expense of environmental safeguards. Recognizing that the large oil companies found much to like in the legislation, Wright supported a windfall profit tax that passed Congress but ultimately fell to a Nixon veto.[60]

Not only did the legislation not meet Wright's hopes, but it left him vulnerable to criticism from both the Left and the Right. "Attacking the oil industry per se," Wright wrote one liberal, who was outraged that the oil industry would benefit, would in a sense kill "the goose that laid the golden egg."[61] When Wright spoke of the "importance of completing the Trans-Alaskan Pipeline," environmentalists protested him as just another Texan tool of big oil. At the same time, however, Wright's National Energy Plan of Action naturally repelled many conservatives. It showed, they believed, his true colors—he was a big tax-and-spend liberal who wanted government in the free market. The reality was that Wright was in the middle. Open to negotiation, he was more pragmatic than ideological.[62]

Then again, few noticed. In fact, while the gas lines and the rationing were hard to miss, Wright was on the mark when he complained that the Watergate scandal stole the national spotlight. Vietnam and abortion received wide publicity, and Wright might have garnered a headline or two with his highway and energy proposals, but Wright, like the rest of Congress, increasingly labored in the shadow of Nixon's scandal. When Wright's Public Works Subcommittee on Investigation and Review, for example, documented the many ways in which bureaucratic red tape hampered production, barely anyone noticed. Rhyming on such phrases as "governmentese," Wright crafted a sarcastic poem to garner what publicity he could. "You might think there's no man alive who understands Circular A-95," he artfully penned.[63] Despite such efforts, no one cared when Wright proposed a bipartisan Commission on Federal Paper Work. Not even the conservatives mocked the obvious irony that such a commission would, in fact, produce its own new paperwork.[64] Wright quietly resisted higher postal rates and continued to insist that lower interest rates combated inflation. As a symbolic gesture to mark his hatred for debt, he voted against raising the national debt ceiling, confident that it would in fact rise. Out of the headlines, he served on the National Water Policy Commission, developing a relationship with New York governor Nelson Rockefeller that would soon serve him well, given Rockefeller's own ascent.[65] It may not have mattered to those outside the Washington Beltway, but Wright helped form the Coalition for a Democratic Majority, which was dedicated, Wright believed, to promoting "harmony and unity within the Democratic Party." In reality, Wright later learned, many in the group thought its goal was to "reduce the influence of the McGovernites."[66] "The proposed list of directors doesn't appear to represent a sufficiently broad base," Wright soon lobbied his colleagues.[67]

A celebratory roast organized by Amon Carter Jr. to mark Wright's twentieth anniversary in office received local press but little attention outside of the Lone Star State. This was despite almost 3,000 people attending. "Connally Republicans and Ted Kennedy Democrats" both attended, noted one observer. "If you looked hard enough, you'd even find a survivor of the Goldwater tragedy." Befitting Wright's career, a number of Republicans did in fact attend. Rockefeller presented Wright with a crystal fish symbolizing clean water, while John Anderson of Illinois told the crowd, "If you have to send us Democrats, please send us more Democrats like Jim Wright." Dignitaries throughout government wrote letters of praise, including Senator Muskie, who noted Wright's "ability to bridge the gap between conflicting points of view." Thanking the crowd, Wright bemoaned "public cynicism of the political process" and insisted that government was still capable of great accomplishments.[68]

Wright's defense of the political process appeared, by 1974, to be tilting at windmills. The 93rd Congress had by this time witnessed Watergate grow, step by miserable step, into what White House counsel John Dean famously described as a "cancer on the presidency." As the investigations, now including the Senate Watergate Committee, began to uncover additional evidence of administration culpability, Wright wrestled with each new revelation. "I felt a surge of anger," Wright later wrote, "still wanting to believe the president." When it became known that the White House maintained an "enemies list" of administration opponents subject to unethical abuses, Wright still kept his criticism vague. "Politicians who keep enemies' lists . . . are not worthy of having any position of power," he declared. After a Gallup poll showed that the public thought such Machiavellian politics were widespread, Wright countered that it was "most emphatically not commonplace."[69] Throughout the summer of 1973, as the televised Senate hearings captivated the public, culminating in the revelations of an Oval Office taping system, Wright watched it all with "a sick feeling in the pit of my stomach."[70]

The fall of 1973 was no easier. On October 10, Vice President Spiro Agnew resigned, facing corruption and tax charges. Speaker Albert informed the leadership that he had agreed with Nixon that since Agnew was still criminally liable, impeachment would serve no purpose. On October 11, Nixon called Wright to ask him whether he favored Minority Leader Gerald Ford or Wright's old colleague John Connally for Agnew's replacement. Answering the call in a private booth off the House floor, Wright replied that either would do well. When Nixon pressed, Wright suggested that the media "tend to like Connally," while Ford "has more friends on the Hill.[71] Nixon's confidence may have surprised Wright, but it made sense. Not only did their connection—while strained in the 93rd Congress—remain, but Nixon recognized that southern Democrats might prove key to his own survival.[72]

Wright approved of the Ford nomination. Four years earlier, Wright's daughter Kay had landed a part-time job working in Ford's office without letting anyone there know that her father was a powerful Democratic congressman. Upon learning of her job and recognizing that public disclosure of their relationship might raise uncomfortable questions, Wright had informed Ford on the House floor. "I've got to meet that girl!" Ford had replied. "I know that no daughter of yours would think of being anything but trustworthy and loyal to whomever she worked for."[73] This response had impressed Wright and, accordingly, Wright urged Judiciary Committee chairman Peter Rodino to confirm Ford quickly. Ford had the "quality of trust" and was "steeped in the tradition of civility," he told Rodino. Although some commentators claimed that Ford was "pedestrian and undistinguished," they were wrong about him. "Honor is more important than humor and character more essential than charisma," Wright concluded to the powerful chairman.[74] Ford appreciated Wright's efforts. "The tried-and-true phrase 'thank you' seems a bit inadequate to fully express my gratitude," Ford replied.[75] While Wright undoubtedly thought Ford's confirmation a good thing for the nation, he also clearly recognized the smart political path.

As the nation digested these developments, the "Saturday Night Massacre" exploded into the headlines. The quick resignations of two attorneys general, the product of Nixon's efforts to keep the White House tapes from the special prosecutor, confirmed for many Americans Nixon's guilt. In Fort Worth for a speech before the North Texas Homebuilders Association, Wright was called from the dais to take a phone call. His aide, Marshall Lynam, wanted Wright to know what was happening before he was asked by the press for a comment. With "my head reeling," Wright remembered, "my first reaction was disbelief."[76]

At the end of a leadership meeting the following Monday, Speaker Albert announced that the House Judiciary Committee would begin an initial impeachment inquiry. After researching "an ancient set of books my mother had given me," Wright recalled, he concluded that the nation's only other impeachment—the 1868 trial of President Andrew Johnson—had been politically motivated.[77] While he worried about Nixon's consolidation of executive power and, in a larger sense, about the reputation of government, Wright concluded that any appearance of a politically motivated prosecution would harm not only the Democrats but the entire nation. Wright had already warned Albert of the zealous partisanship of many in his own party, and Wright now urged the entire leadership to proceed with caution. Still apparently giving Nixon the benefit of any remaining doubt, Wright found the criticism he received from his district's Republicans annoying. "I don't believe that anyone would contend that I have tried to exploit the so-called Watergate disclosures to the President's detriment," he replied to one writer.[78]

Letters, both for and against impeachment, began flooding into Wright's office. "There is a growing feeling here that the attacks on President Nixon are and have been politically inspired by the majority of Democrats in Congress," wrote one constituent, expressing a sentiment that Wright believed remained strong in his district.[79] Although many of his colleagues were demanding Nixon's head, Wright had no intention of leading the charge, and he continued to insist on caution and moderation. Wright also had, it turned out, something else to divert his attention.

Surprisingly, in the middle of this growing constitutional crisis, and with all the political energy it absorbed, Congress moved in another way into the thorny issue of the balance of powers. The Budget and Impoundment Control Act of 1974, a long-brewing reaction to Nixon's impoundment of congressionally appropriated funds, was one of the most significant laws the 93rd Congress passed even as it remained in Watergate's shadow. The bill had profound implications for the future of American government—and, as it turned out, for Wright's own career. In addition to requiring, within forty-five days, congressional approval of impounded funds, the law further facilitated congressional control of the budget process. Rather than simply reacting to a presidential proposal, both houses of Congress now had new budget committees to propose their own budgets. Subsequent passage of a concurrent budget resolution would establish parameters for the regular work of the normal appropriating committees. To ensure that Congress had more to rely on than just the economic analysis of executive departments, the law also created the Congressional Budget Office. Nixon had fought the legislation, of course, but it was now 1974 and Watergate colored his every move. Needing all the friends he could get, Nixon acquiesced.[80]

As members clamored for appointment to the new, powerful committees, Speaker Albert came under pressure. The process called for the Speaker to name two members to the new House Budget Committee and for both the Democratic and Republican caucuses to elect the others proportionate to their percentage in Congress. Wright later denied any campaigning for a nomination and claimed that he had no idea who put his name forth. Certainly, however, he was an obvious choice. The year before, he had written letters to the leadership urging a "coordinated effort to reclaim Congressional powers and prerogatives." The letters had even suggested that Wright was becoming less willing to allow the executive leeway in foreign policy. Congressional influence internationally, the letters had stated, had sunk to a "pitifully low point."[81] Now, with Wright a well-known critic of debt, a party conciliator, and a defender of Congress, it was hardly surprising that he was the only member elected to the new committee on the first ballot. The "overwhelming vote," Albert remarked, demonstrated the "high esteem" Wright had earned in Congress.[82]

Wright had tried for years to advance his career without much success, blocked by the seniority system and his own electoral oversteps. Now, however, in a period of a few short years, things had suddenly begun to break his way. His divorce was in the past, and his personal life was more stable. Although he did not hold a higher office per se, he was now an important member of the Democratic leadership. He served on two key committees and held real power. Wright was more optimistic than in prior years, thinking of swinging for the fences just as he had at the outset of his career. He was, perhaps, too optimistic. A man in his early fifties, Wright agreed to spar with young boxers at a boys' club in Southeast Washington. Leaders, he wanted to teach, never surrendered. The result was, of course, a black eye and sunglasses for Wright. "Where are those bushy eyebrows that so easily identify him?" the press joked. "I decided to show the young man some moves," Wright answered. "And I hit his fist with my eye."[83]

Wright was quickly voted chairman of a task force to work out the internal rules of the new committee. It was like a cherry on his sundae. No one, one fellow committee member noted, "commands more respect." As he began to work through the weeds of procedure, Wright told the media that the new budget structure was critical to redeeming government from the stench of Watergate. Using what little spotlight was left over from the scandal, Wright reinforced his desire "to balance the budget and begin to make some modest payments on the public debt." He promised his opponents fairness and respect but a strong fight for what he believed. No one had reason to doubt him.[84]

Years later, Wright noted that his selection to the House Budget Committee was the first time anyone publicly suggested him as a possibility for the Speakership. In fact, columnist Charles Bartlett wrote that a Democratic insurgency against Speaker Albert considered Wright the best alternative. Undoubtedly flattered, Wright was still smart enough to recognize that such speculation would annoy Albert and work against him in the leadership. Accordingly, Wright claimed that any palace intrigue "shocked" him. He was a friend and admirer of Albert's. Wright did, however, add one caveat: "Should Albert resign then that would be a different situation and I might be interested in making the race."[85] Whether such speculation hurt or helped Wright, in the end it mattered little. Every day, after all, brought new developments in the drama unfolding at the other end of Pennsylvania Avenue.

By the summer of 1974, events were spiraling out of Nixon's control. As the fight over access to the White House tapes progressed, Nixon released edited transcripts that lacked any evidence of criminal complicity but still cast him in an unfavorable light. Demands for his impeachment grew. Wright, however, remained noncommittal, casting himself as an impartial juror. "I think it best to say no more at this particular time," he stated.[86] What Wright did not acknowledge, however, was that a vote for impeachment was not a final resolution of guilt but rather a statement that the evidence was sufficient to go to a Senate trial. Wright, it appeared, was still giving Nixon every benefit of the doubt. Not surprisingly, therefore, Nixon invited Wright and a group of southern conservatives to dinner in early July. The president, Wright recalled, looked tired and nursed a glass of scotch. It was a "soft sell," with Nixon apparently pained even at the mention of Watergate. Wright felt "deep sorrow for him" but did his best to remain noncommittal. While he still refused to support impeachment, neither did he promise to support Nixon if impeachment took place. Louisianan Joe Waggoner was working with Nixon to round up conservative support, but Wright kept his distance. "I don't think Joe Waggoner was someone I was trying to contact at that time," Wright later laughed.[87]

Finally, in late July, the Supreme Court ruled in *United States v. Richard Nixon* that executive privilege did not cover the tapes and that Nixon had to release them. Wright praised the decision, which, after all, confirmed the rights of congressional review. The Court, Wright stated, "used a scalpel rather than a meat ax in delineating the precise line between the demands of process on the one hand and the realistic requirements of Presidential confidentiality on the other." The decision "showed commendable restraint and I trust that the President will abide by it."[88]

The die was cast. As the Judiciary Committee voted to level three articles of impeachment, Nixon promised to abide by the Court ruling. Privately, however, he spent the night before the release attempting to erase all incriminating evidence. In the end, in early August, the tapes revealed a conversation that Nixon had missed—the "Smoking Gun Tape." In June 1973, it turned out, Nixon had ordered the FBI off the case, an obvious obstruction of justice. Nixon knew that he had played his last card. On August 9, he resigned, becoming the first president in history to do so. Gerald Ford, who had spent only a month as vice-president, became the thirty-eighth president of the United States on the same day. It was a day of "great sadness," Wright declared, "both for the President and the country." Now it was time to "lay completely aside every vestige of recrimination and division, to come together in thought and purpose, and to approach the future in a spirit of unity."[89]

In retrospect, Wright, through it all, remained remarkably loyal to Nixon. Even years later, with all the illegalities well documented, and with Nixon's personal professions of innocence to Wright now clearly lies, Wright still refused to state whether he would have voted for impeachment. "I never had to reach that judgment," he replied. "I would have listened to both sides." In his memoirs, Wright suggested that had Nixon immediately revealed administration complicity in the initial Watergate break-in, the public would have forgiven him. Nixon, Wright even concluded, acted as much out of a misguided sense of right and wrong as out of any true malice. He simply conflated what was best for his administration with what was best for the country.[90] Perhaps, but such conclusions nevertheless diminish all the illegalities that were subsequently revealed, the litany of dirty tricks and corruption that went beyond the burglary and the cover-up, and that ran counter to the good governance that Wright valued.

If the lack of anger in Wright, a man with an admitted temper, is difficult to understand, his sadness is less so. Watergate added greatly to growing public cynicism about government, a problem with which Wright had wrestled for some time and that he would face again in the future. Partisanship was rampant, and the nation was angry and demoralized. Wright, however, wanted to look forward, not backward. He had seen his own career suddenly rebound, and his ambitions were rekindled. It all was, in the broader context, a bit ironic.

———

CHAPTER 12

The Ripples of Watergate

A NEW CONGRESS AND NEW OPPORTUNITY (1972–1976)

If Wright was optimistic for his own career, and, perhaps, hopeful for a massive, post-scandal repudiation of the GOP, he knew not to get too ahead of himself. After all, Wright faced his first credible general election challenge in over a decade in the candidacy of James Garvey, a Fort Worth businessman who owned a large chain of grain elevators. Although Garvey was a novice candidate, he had made significant contributions to other Republicans and was willing to spend considerable cash for his own race, another indication of Republican hopes for the South.

Garvey clearly understood the GOP game plan. Wright was just another budget-busting big spender, he said, a bureaucrat who raised taxes and meddled in civil rights. Loose with facts, Garvey claimed that Wright had only supported cutting spending once, then later claimed there were "only two cases in the past six years."[1] Conflating procedural votes and the give-and-take of the legislative process to paint Wright as unconcerned about the national debt or bureaucratic overreach was a bit ironic given Wright's record. As Garvey understood, however, the same tactic had worked for other southern Republicans. Anticipating that Wright would cite his service on the congressional committee to reduce wasteful paperwork, Garvey mocked the committee's recommendations as "typical" for Democrats. Wright, he claimed, wanted to "set up another commission, spend some more money, and do a lot more paperwork."[2]

Wright, meanwhile, savvy enough to realize that stressing taxes to the corporate boardrooms and states' rights to the masses might indeed seed a Republican rebirth, replied forcefully. His long record, he argued, exposed "the utter falsehood and total fraudulency of the extravagant, florid claims" Garvey had leveled.[3] Mobilizing in a way that it had not done in years, the Wright campaign announced the creation of a "Committee of 500," a group of local leaders who endorsed Wright. "Originally we set out to form a committee of 100," campaign manager Joe Shosid said, "but we kept running into additional people." Wright's "effective community leadership," the committee claimed, was the reason that its diverse membership could "harmoniously unite."[4] Wright was no liberal ideologue.

Requesting support in "small contributions, volunteer help or simply the word of mouth," Wright's campaign unveiled a fundraising machine to match Garvey's wealth.[5] It organized 6,500 block captains. To win Hispanics, it stressed Wright's work in Latin America. Whether noting his views on busing or the war, the campaign highlighted Wright's differences with liberals, muting Garvey's strategy. At the same time, however, it lined up an impressive list of endorsements, many of them from liberal groups: teachers associations, unions, and even firefighter and police groups. To attract these endorsements, the campaign cited Wright's efforts to protect civil servants in the recent riots.[6] Casting Garvey as a tool of big, moneyed interests, Wright publicized the fact that 94 percent of the contributions to his own campaign were in amounts of less than $100. Wright was the populist once again. "The Republicans have the money but the Democrats have the people," Wright declared, conveniently ignoring his own large haul of cash.[7]

One instance particularly inflamed Wright. After a White House reception for all the Republican congressional candidates, Garvey claimed that Ford was endorsing him because Wright was a "notorious voter for spending bills" and "one of the major causes of inflation." Outraged and taking advantage of his connections, Wright called Ford, who denied the statement and agreed to let Wright publicize his denial.[8] In his subsequent comments, Wright was blunt. He expected the "titular head of the Republican Party," Wright stated, to "issue a routine blanket endorsement of all the Republican candidates." It was normal politics and it did not "diminish my regard for [Ford] in the slightest." Still, however, for Garvey to put words into Ford's mouth that were known to be "altogether untrue" was an insult to the presidency. If anyone doubted Ford's denial, Wright added, for good measure, that several presidential aides were "familiar with the conversations I have just recited."[9]

Wright had always taken great pride in running clean campaigns and staying above the malicious mudslinging and patent untruths. Such campaigns violated his sense of government as a noble calling. At the same time, however, there was frequently a fine line between a tough but fair campaign and a malicious, personal one. Although in later years Wright stated that he held no grudges against Garvey and assumed that the false Ford quotes had simply emanated from an inexperienced staff, at the time he wasted no time in implying—if not directly stating—that his opponent was a liar. Wright's campaign arranged for several prominent Fort Worth citizens to denounce Garvey's "spurious charges."[10] His staff, meanwhile, researched Garvey for weaknesses. Aide Marshall Lynam wrote campaign manager Shosid saying he had evidence that Garvey, who regularly denounced government, had received more than $25 million from the US Department of Agriculture in regard to land Garvey owned in Kansas. The campaign, Lynam suggested, should clandestinely arrange for a supporter to write the Kansas government for more damaging evidence. "This information needs to be guarded very closely," Lynam concluded, adding that all evidence uncovered should be kept "in Jim's safe room at the office."[11]

Working to tie Garvey to the stain of Watergate, Wright stated that people were "sick and tired of . . . the 'dirty tricks' of smear and fear and exaggeration." Even Ford, "unworthy of his better instincts," had stated a "ludicrous falsehood" in describing Democrats as spendthrifts. "I blush for my friend Gerald Ford," Wright remarked. Politics, it seemed, was indeed a dirty business—for all concerned.[12]

When the election finally came, it was clear that Wright's ability to bring home the bacon while appearing a pragmatic moderate carried the day. With 78 percent of the vote, Wright won virtually all of the district's 153 precincts. As a bonus, Democrats gained 49 seats in the House for more than a two-thirds majority. With 4 new seats in the Senate, the party claimed a filibuster-proof 60-vote margin.[13] Clearly, while voters approved of Wright, the Watergate scandal had become an albatross for the GOP.

New, younger Democrats—the "Watergate Babies"—poured into Congress, anxious for quick action. Not only did they bring new energy for institutional reform, but they also promised a level of liberalism that conflicted with much of the Washington establishment and, therefore, did not bode well for the harmonious government that Wright hoped to see emerge.

Despite the many Republican obituaries, Washington's political culture remained complex. The 1974 results notwithstanding, the perception of Democrats as budget-busting big spenders who undermined cultural traditions continued apace, especially in the South. In his memoirs, Wright concluded that the Voting Rights Act of 1965 and the Supreme Court's "one man–one vote alignment" of congressional districts had increased African American urban political power at the expense of rural, whiter regions. Whites fled to the suburbs, forming enclaves for a new Republicanism to flourish. Compounding the South's demographic changes, Wright continues, were longer sessions of Congress. With less time to meet with constituents, congressmen increasingly had to raise exorbitant sums of money for mass media, arguably augmenting negative attacks. With energy shortages and inflation still rampant, harmonious government was, perhaps, a bridge too far, even if newly emboldened Democrats were anxious to get started.[14]

The ground certainly remained fertile for continued congressional reform. Just before the election, the Democrat's Committee on Organization, Study, and Review, known as the Hansen Committee and the principal architect of the earlier Reorganization Act of 1970, moved again to encourage reform. Speaker of the House Carl Albert helped to reconstitute the committee, in part to consider a proposal that many younger members favored to completely realign House committee jurisdictions, a proposal originally put forth by Richard Bolling's House Select Committee on Committees. The Hansen Committee now proposed additional democratization, but it avoided the complete overhaul the Bolling Committee had recommended. The result was the final blow to the seniority system in selecting committee chairmen, who now faced a secret ballot of the caucus. In addition, the new subcommittees already created by the caucus received augmented powers, sometimes known as the "subcommittee bill of rights." Granting additional autonomy from the committee chairs, these rights included control of the subcommittee calendar. If the younger reformers gained ground, so did the party leaders. The Speaker gained the ability to appoint the Rules Committee and set legislative deadlines, in essence keeping committee chairmen from blocking the Speaker's will. Finally, the Democratic Steering and Policy Committee gained the ability to appoint committee members, a power previously held by the Ways and Means Committee. The Speaker, all recognized, had much greater control of the former than the latter.

Having so recently gained power with his expanded subcommittee and his appointment on the Budget Committee, Wright, not surprisingly, lobbied the Hansen Committee to reject Bolling's more radical jurisdictional reforms. A complete overhaul, Wright argued, would create "a nightmare of unraveling."[15] While resisting allowing the Speaker alone to name committee chairmen, noting that earlier leaders had "badly abused the power," Wright largely welcomed the stronger party leadership. He was, after all, a rising star on the leadership ladder.[16] For some reform but against revolutionary change, Wright wanted to remain the bridge between the Democrats' warring factions.

Also jockeying for political advantage in the shifting sands was California liberal Phillip Burton. Befriending Wayne Hays, chairman of the Democratic Congressional Campaign Committee and a powerful distributor of cash, Burton let the new Watergate Babies know that they needed his help. Cultivating his own liberal constituency, Burton won election as caucus chairman. Though the position had traditionally been somewhat ceremonial, Burton immediately demanded personal interviews with any potential committee chair. By organizing the Watergate Babies, he clearly hoped to move the party leftward in a way that had not been possible before.

Wright was friendly with Burton, but he thought his obvious competitor was "too personally ambitious" and his methods "distasteful." In one instance, Wright recalled, a Texas colleague complained that Burton was promising choice committee assignments for support and punishment for opposition.[17] In fact, Wright was not above strong-armed politics himself, though he was smoother in his interpersonal dealings. It was no wonder that the two men rubbed each other the wrong way.

Wright watched in dismay as Burton lobbied to oust W. R. Poage as chairman of the Committee on Agriculture. Poage was a fellow Texan, and Wright respected him, but Poage was also a seventy-five-year-old southern conservative and an obvious target. So was Louisianan Edward Hebert, chairman of the Armed Services Committee, who had referred to the new members as "boys and girls." When Burton turned his attention to another Texan, Wright could hold his tongue no longer. Wright Patman, chairman of the Committee on Banking, Currency, and Housing, was a crusty eighty-one-year-old with enemies, but, to Wright, another ardent foe of higher interest rates. As the caucus balloting began, Wright noted that Patman had opposed the Ku Klux Klan years before and had been an early critic of Watergate, implying the octogenarian was a reformer at heart. Patman was also a prolific fundraiser, Wright added, a fact Wright figured would resonate. In his classic style, Wright praised the man the young reformers touted as Patman's replacement, Wisconsin's Henry Reuss. The reformers had under-standable motivation, Wright insisted, but age and seniority alone should not damn anyone.[18]

Wright knew how to read the tea leaves. His unsuccessful defense of Patman, and, in a broader sense, his own experience, appealed to the old establishment. At the same time, Wright recognized that he was roughly the same age as many of the reformers, his two decades of seniority notwith-standing, and that it was wise to keep his dislike of Burton quiet. Wright wanted all of his lines of communication open. Recognizing Wright's trans-generational appeal, Albert asked Wright to help mitigate some of the younger members' complaints. Wright handled the situation with aplomb. When the reformers argued for both party unity and even more democ-ratization, Wright defused the tension. "I'll tell Carl Albert he's got to become . . . either a timid dictator or a tyrannical wimp," Wright replied to broad laughter.[19]

Wright's endorsement of new campaign finance restrictions endeared him to the reformers. He had long argued against the influence of money and supported new amendments to the Federal Election Campaign Act of 1972. Wright "enthusiastically" advocated not only limits on individual donations but also tax credits for the smallest donations.[20] The resulting law limited donations from individuals to $1,000 and from Political Action Committees (PACs) to $5,000. It also created the Federal Election Com-mission to police the process.[21] In later years, Wright became somewhat defensive about the legislative result—and with good reason. The PAC pro-visions proved inadequate to their objectives. Money flowed into hundreds of PACs, the lines between candidates and causes were murky, and "lead-ership PACs" proved a major loophole. Party leaders were able to solicit funds for independent issue-oriented bodies in their name. "I was not aware of the PAC provisions until later on," Wright later recalled, "and, regardless, I always responded to the law."[22]

Perhaps Wright was removed from close control of his campaign expenses, as he had always claimed; his reduced but still continuing personal debt arguably suggested a laissez-faire attitude. And yet the harsh reality of big money's continued influence demanded that he play the game for survival. The lessons of Garvey's challenge were obvious. Indeed, within a few short years, Wright was operating well in the reformed, post-Watergate political culture. As Wright's career advanced, so did his fundraising prowess. The Wright Congressional Club, initially a group of Fort Worth acquaintances helping Wright fly back to his district, grew into a huge operation, the Wright Appreciation Club, which required annual $200 dues and included multimillionaires such as Fort Worth philanthropists Sid and Lee Bass. In time, Wright had his own leadership PAC, the Jim Wright Majority Committee. It made sense, because better name recognition meant more cash. By the end of Wright's career, the committee enjoyed national donors and was distributing hundreds of thousands of dollars—and, with it, influence. In the mid-1970s, however, it must have been frustrating for Wright. He was, after all, a prolific fundraiser, but in personal debt.

As Wright pondered this irony, the younger liberals began to advocate limits on outside income. Wright understood the potential for abuse and wanted to curry favor with the new reformers. He also recognized that such limits would improve Congress's image. At the same time, however, Wright worried that restrictions might discourage candidates of lesser means. And, of course, his own financial insecurity weighed heavily. Approaching his mid-fifties, Wright still had not retired his debt fully and had a net worth of $70,000, less than when he had entered Congress. All around him he saw colleagues benefiting from their own amalgam of business and politics. Wright recognized the impropriety of congressmen holding stock in businesses with interests before Congress, but, at the same time, why should he continue to suffer personal debt when few others did? He had his idealism, and yet, in practical terms, he needed to augment his estate.[23]

As Wright wrestled with his conscience, news reports broke that a former Miss Virginia, Elizabeth Ray, was on the payroll of the House Administration Committee only to perform sexual favors for Congressman Wayne Hays, a Democrat. Ray's subsequent book suggested that her situation was not unique.[24] As debate over continued reform unfolded, Wright found himself again defending Congress. "No," Wright replied to one critic, "Congress is not extravagant."[25] Wright, like many politicians, had both used the media and complained about it, and perhaps in the moment he forgot about the complicity of congressmen like Hays. Watergate, he worried, had eroded what respect the public and the press had still had for government in the years preceding the scandal. "There is a sickness in American journalism," Wright wrote in his diary. "Now it's professionally unfashionable for a newsman to write anything complimentary."[26] Congress was right to reform its own house, Wright assumed, but the muckrakers who had helped speed the process should turn a mirror on themselves.

In any event, Wright's carefully crafted position at the vortex of his party remained as Congress evolved in the wake of Watergate. Wright could afford to rise in defense of the old guard, including the octogenarian Patman, for most reformers did not see Wright as an enemy. Wright supported strengthening the Freedom of Information Act and joined the liberals in overriding Ford's veto of the Privacy Act Amendments of 1974.[27] When proposals arose to televise congressional debates live—to encourage open government—Wright, to the delight of the reformers, supported the measure.[28] It was clear that Wright was willing to work with rookies and veterans alike, reformers and traditionalists, always aware of his own position, and his eyes always on the prize.

Wright also still hoped to work closely with Ford, writing the president a number of times early in his administration with various congratulations, statements of admiration, and even a request for an autographed photograph.[29] When Ford issued an unconditional pardon for Nixon, Wright once again found himself in the troublesome middle. He agreed with Ford that it was best to leave Watergate behind, and he found conspiracy theories of a quid pro quo—a vice-presidential nomination in exchange for a subsequent pardon—nonsense. He knew Ford's honesty and, regardless, Ford's nomination had come while Nixon still hoped to survive the scandal. The liberals Wright hoped to cultivate, however, demanded criminal prosecution. Trying to maintain balance, Wright noted that additional prosecution was a "moot question," given the executive's complete pardoning power. Nixon's pension was also unassailable, set by law. At the same time, Wright let the liberals know that he had advised Ford that a mass pardon of Watergate offenders would be a "very serious mistake."[30] He had also voted to reduce funds for the disgraced president's transition to private life. When Ford nominated New York governor Nelson Rockefeller as the new vice-president, Wright rejected the calls of some liberals to block confirmation. Rockefeller, Wright argued, was "a decent and intelligent man." In the end, the pardon remained, Rockefeller was confirmed, Wright avoided harsh criticism from any side, and Congress set about its agenda with harmony in short supply.[31]

First on the agenda, of course, was the stagnant economy and inflation. Unveiling a catchy slogan—Whip Inflation Now, with the nice acronym WIN—Ford endorsed higher interest rates and curtailed spending.[32] Carl Albert, recognizing the need for a united Democratic alternative, appointed Wright chairman of the ad-hoc Task Force on the Economy, which was charged with outlining a consensus that the individual committees might turn into specific bills. Wright, who, like Albert, was still sensitive to his colleagues' demands for democratization, wrote his caucus suggesting that together the Democrats could craft an alternative and not just react to presidential initiatives. "Something quite different is happening this year," Wright promised, recognizing another chance to make his mark.[33]

The result was what Americans would later call a stimulus package of spending—emergency housing and health initiatives, more aid to farmers, and, not surprisingly, given Wright's prominent role, expanded public works and a looser monetary system. Wright had helped persuade Nixon to push for lower interest rates, but now, Wright insisted, the rates were still too high. Contradicting Ford, Wright continued to insist that higher rates had not stifled borrowing but had added additional financial burdens and exacerbated the debt.[34]

Sitting in the new Budget Committee and still considering himself a deficit hawk—still refusing to fully embrace Keynesian economics—Wright argued that spending cuts remained possible in areas less critical to the economy and individual well-being, such as national defense. The real solution to the national debt, however, was to grow the economy—and growing the economy demanded government action.[35] The appropriate combination of targeted tax and spending reductions, along with a "stimulative budget," would grow the economy and "get the debt back under control."[36]

What followed was far from harmony: a series of presidential vetoes. The Democratic-controlled committees hashed out the specifics of Wright's task force plan in quick order, in some cases in a matter of weeks. In a national address that appeared timed to drown out the unveiling of Wright's task force plan, however, Ford demanded austerity. He sought to raise the tariff on oil and add taxes on other fossil fuels to discourage consumption even as many other Republicans argued for deregulation of gas and oil, sure to raise prices but helpful in weaning the nation off foreign imports.

Wright saw himself as an expert on the subject. He was from an oil state, and, although he had long been concerned about the dominance of Big Oil, he had frequently encouraged the oil industry. He had also advocated synthetic fuels before the Arab oil embargo. The grand energy agenda he had unveiled during the Nixon administration had gone nowhere, but it had demonstrated his expertise. Once again, therefore, Wright found himself appointed to a new ad hoc body, the Task Force on Energy. Once again, he was charged with proposing an expansive energy agenda.

Little, however, had changed. Democratic divisions alone assured no grand scheme. Welcoming conservation, many liberals protested increased production, viewing oil-state legislators such as Wright with cynicism. When Wright, pressing for a balanced "fair energy plan," called for more fuel-efficient automobiles and a long-range plan for alternative fuels, environmentalists heard only his simultaneous call for an increase in coal and nuclear energy. When he floated the idea of a petroleum allocation program to guard against future shortages, southern conservatives heard only big government.[37] With committees locked in debate, Wright proclaimed that legislators of all stripes lacked the "necessary sense of urgency." Ford's politically advantageous criticism of the Democratic-controlled Congress's inaction only added to Wright's exasperation.[38]

Soon Wright's early optimism faded to resignation. Announcing himself "disappointed," he predicted the result would be "weak and wishy-washy."[39] Fulfilling Wright's expectations, the Energy Policy and Conservation Act of 1975 included only modest efforts to increase domestic production and restrict consumption, including new automobile emission standards. Although it extended price controls and created the Strategic Petroleum Reserve—which was critical for the future—it did little to address the broad systemic causes of the shortages, or, for that matter, to mitigate the high prices.[40]

At every turn, it appeared, Wright ran into his party's divisions. When he supported expanded funds for waste treatment plants, hoping to reestablish his environmental credentials after they were tarnished by the energy debate, liberals complained that his incorporation of bureaucratic streamlining provisions weakened antipollution and financing guidelines. "We have to have a program that will work and not keep bogging down in red tape," Wright insisted. The bickering became so intense that it came down to "arguing about the shape of the table," in the words of one participant, paraphrasing an issue that had hampered the Paris peace talks.[41]

When the congressional Democrats could agree, Wright found more frustration with Ford. Ford wielded his veto pen more than sixty times.[42] When Wright prevailed upon southern conservatives to support over $6 billion for public works, Ford dismissed the bill as "election year pork barrel." Answering the objections, Wright then convinced northern liberals to compromise with $2 billion less. Still, however, Ford issued a veto. Not one to surrender, Wright then prevailed upon enough Republicans to override the veto.[43] On the Budget Committee, Wright had ample time to battle Ford, still insisting that Ford's cuts hurt the deficit. Money spent to put people back to work, Wright said, would shrink the debt.[44] Wading into bureaucratic accounting minutiae—on such issues as veterans' benefits, forest fire prevention, commodity credit costs, and, in an area he felt that he knew something about, postal expenditures—was taxing in its own right. The inevitable confrontation just made it worse, at times testing Wright's patience. Ford was not being "honest," Wright stated, without directly calling Ford a liar. Such deliberate distortion was "unworthy" of the White House.[45]

The battles even drained into foreign policy, proving a new challenge to Wright on several fronts. Wright applauded negotiations on the status of the Panama Canal, which suited his idealism. The Panamanians, he argued, had legitimate complaints on the canal's operation. Arguing that America had not lived up to its ideals was powerful, but, in the end, insufficient to meet the jingoism of an election year. To Wright's dismay, his colleagues passed a resolution prohibiting the talks from continuing.[46]

Wright still harbored romantic notions of America's role in the world, his perceptions relatively untarnished from Vietnam. While many of his colleagues, citing high unemployment, resisted additional immigration, Wright was passionate for the acceptance of Vietnamese refugees. To block them was to put "a moratorium on that noble message inscribed on the base of the Statue of Liberty."[47] To Wright, the United States remained a great force for good in the world, and it should not shrink from upholding its principles. When the communist Khmer Rouge ruling Cambodia seized the American merchant ship the *Mayaguez*, Wright favored "giving the Cambodians 48 hours to return the ship and its crew unharmed." If there were no action, the United States should then act with overwhelming military force. America should not tolerate "every little tin pot dictator who wants to show his disdain."[48] When Turkey, an American ally, launched an invasion of Cyprus in a dispute with Greece, another ally, Wright's reaction was as idealistic as it was pragmatic. While many of his colleagues argued restraint, fearful of jeopardizing the many critical American bases in Turkey, Wright sought to cut off military supplies. The United States had sold Turkey weapons for its defense only, he argued, and should never countenance aggression when diplomacy could resolve the matter. Although Wright's arguments carried the day, he later found a new, more moderate Turkish government worthy of the support, provided that no weapons made their way to the disputed island. This time, however, Wright failed to convince his colleagues and the sanctions remained in place. It was unfair, Wright argued, but politicians wanted to win the Greek-American vote. "The temptation to use foreign policy votes to curry favor back home is a recurring phenomenon," Wright later mused.[49]

Wright was not completely above the partisan sniping on foreign policy, his idealism notwithstanding. For years he had argued that foreign aid provided essential food and medicine while augmenting America's reputation. When Ford proposed an expansive package exceeding $6 billion, however, Wright surprised many with his opposition, in the process demonstrating that despite the calluses he had gained from years in Congress, his thin skin still remained. Only weeks from his battle with Ford over public works, a vindictive Wright could not resist striking back. "The President says we cannot afford to spend more for streets, for sewer lines, for waterworks, for libraries and schools and parks in American communities because they were nothing more than pork barrel," Wright sarcastically remarked. "Is it pork barrel to build such projects in the US but statesmanship to build such projects abroad?"[50]

The difficulties Wright faced in foreign policy ran deeper than disputes over individual pieces of legislation. He still wrestled with the tenuous balance of powers, weighing his traditional belief that the commander-in-chief deserved leeway and national unity with his increasing concern that the executive branch was encroaching upon congressional prerogatives. Just after Ford's ascension, Wright nicely summarized his evolving view in a lengthy address. Beginning with a history of the constitutional parameters, Wright left little doubt the direction he was heading. The president could command the military forces, Wright noted, but the Congress reserved "the power to declare war, to determine the size and shape of the armed forces, and to provide for, maintain, and govern those forces." Over the years, Wright continued, maintaining these distinct roles had been a constant struggle, but such balance was necessary if the nation was to avoid dictatorship. Whenever one branch had left a vacuum, it had been "quickly filled by the other," he said. Now, however, two developments required Congress to assert itself. First, international relations had changed. Because nuclear weapons had "made general warfare too dangerous," aggressors had turned to "political and economic warfare." This development naturally empowered the legislative branch. Moreover, in recent years, Congress, facing the "enormous escalation of the functions of the federal government," had abdicated its responsibilities. Wright did not mention Nixon by name— or his relatively unwavering support for Nixonian diplomacy—but his broader point was obvious.[51]

Whether as a product of the changing circumstances, or, perhaps, of his own rising power in Congress, Wright supported the National Emergencies Act of 1976. Motivated by Nixon's use of emergency powers to maintain troops in Cambodia without congressional approval, Congress formed a committee to investigate the statutory basis for such declarations. Hundreds of emergency powers, the committee found, often declared in brief crises over the years, remained on the books, and they would be loopholes for future presidents. The new law, therefore, required annual congressional renewals of emergency declarations and provided Congress with the power of revocation.[52] For Wright, it was just what the doctor ordered.

As 1975 came to a close, the *Sherman Democrat* of Sherman, Texas, ran an article titled "House Rise for Wright Predicted." Speaker Albert was "expected to bow out of next year's race," the newspaper reported, and Wright was "definitely the Texan to watch." Sources quoted Majority Leader Tip O'Neill suggesting that if he became Speaker himself, Wright was a strong candidate for "either the second or third spot." The paper said Wright was remaining coy: "He does not even want to discuss the question, saying it is up to other people to say who would make the best choice."[53]

The rumors of Albert's retirement appeared well-founded. During Ford's 1975 State of the Union Address, a camera caught the Speaker apparently dozing. Albert also admitted hitting a parked car and leaving the scene before returning, negotiating a cash settlement, and letting his wife drive him home. Soon charges of drinking, womanizing, and erratic behavior grew. Most damaging, however, was the charge that Albert had received gifts from a Korean businessman, Tongsun Park, who later turned out to be a government operative. The "Koreagate Scandal" persisted for months, with Albert acknowledging the donations but denying knowledge of anything unethical. In the end, Albert decided to retire at the end of the 94th Congress. All of these problems probably contributed to Albert's decision to retire, but, regardless, many believed that O'Neill had earned his chance at the top spot.[54]

Despite what he told the press, Wright understood that his own actions as much as those of others determined his future. When New York City mayor Abe Beame informed Washington in 1975 that the Big Apple could no longer meet its financial obligations and needed federal assistance, Wright recognized opportunity. Many southern conservatives saw New York as a bastion of elitism and an example of the failure of liberalism.[55] "If I tried to tell my poor constituents in South Texas that New York City needed their help," one of Wright's colleagues remarked, "they'd think I'd lost my mind."[56] Wright, however, knew Mayor Beame, who had come to Washington to meet with him personally. The two shared an interest in boxing and had first met at the second Muhammad Ali–Joe Frazier fight. When Ford announced his opposition to aid—a decision that caused the *New York Daily News* to blast the headline "Ford to NY: Drop Dead"— Wright decided to tack the opposite direction. Supporting aid would burnish his image with the new liberals and endear him to urban colleagues who might help in any subsequent leadership race.[57]

Wright crafted his support of the Big Apple carefully, appealing to his many dubious constituents with both idealism and pragmatism. Texas had benefited from the success of other parts of the country, he declared, and Americans should support one another. Moreover, he said, a loan guarantee was no "blank check or a handout."[58] If New York City defaulted, the nation's bond market would suffer. Rising rates "would mean higher local taxes to pay for necessary improvements in our own state and elsewhere."[59] When Beame began canceling construction projects, Wright stressed that the city had shown its good intent. Pressing for additional austerity, Wright eventually helped convince his colleagues, and, surprisingly, Ford, to authorize a loan of $2.3 billion a year for three years, one percentage point above the going rate.[60] Had New York not complied, Wright would have been on record supporting a failure. As it happened, however, the city did rebound, paying off its loans in full and on time. In later years, Wright took to the floor of Congress to publicize the initiative's success and his own role in it.[61]

Of course, Wright covered his bases. He still opposed federal funds for abortion and busing for school integration. Arguing that forced integration had hurt student learning, Wright even supported a constitutional amendment prohibiting busing. He publicized his support for the stiffer punishments of criminals and for "the constitutional rights of law-abiding citizens to keep and bear arms."[62] Whether it was his disdain for drugs or his support of the police, Wright maintained his conservative image even as he reached out to the new liberals.

He also always kept the home fires burning. Over a decade before, Wright had sought to end a long-fought competition between the airports of Dallas and Fort Worth—which Wright believed worked to his own city's disadvantage—by lobbying the new Federal Aviation Administration to study the feasibility of having one united operation. The study, it turned out, fulfilled Wright's hopes. Federally mandated mediation began and, in 1974, the Dallas–Fort Worth Regional Airport opened. Virtually every carrier but the fledgling Southwest Airlines, which served only the local region, left Dallas's Love Field. As Wright's constituency applauded, the new airport quickly grew into the Dallas–Fort Worth International Airport, a boon to Fort Worth. American Airlines alone brought hundreds of employees from New York City to Wright's district. "I still don't understand how [Wright] accomplished all he did," the airline's chairman remarked.[63]

For the rest of his career Wright continued to lobby for both the airline industry and Fort Worth's stake in it. When high energy prices hit the industry hard in the mid-1970s, he suggested "something like the old Reconstruction Finance Corporation to help them work their way out of their economic dilemma."[64] When people referred to the "Dallas Airport," Wright noted its official designation. "If that is too big a mouthful," Wright suggested, "they might use DFW." Wright even complained to Braniff Airlines' chairman that his employees cited only Dallas. The onetime flyboy had become, in the words of one aviation journal, "aviation's ranking man in the House."[65]

If Wright's stamp was increasingly in the skies over Fort Worth, his imprint on the ground continued to grow. He was an early supporter of turning the old cattle stockyards on the town's north side into a historic district, which he hoped might encourage tourism. With Wright's help, Fort Worth received a US Department of Commerce Economic Development Administration grant in 1974. By the end of the Ford administration, the Fort Worth Stockyards Historic District promised to become another economic engine.[66] Moreover, with Wright's help, the US Department of Housing and Urban Development moved several hundred jobs to Fort Worth in the mid-1970s, rejuvenating the dilapidated but historically designated Texas and Pacific Railroad Building.[67] Because of his support for the "820 Loop" around Fort Worth, a portion of the highway became the "Jim Wright Freeway." Wright's picture appeared often in the Fort Worth press in stories large and small—once for something as minor as greeting a local spelling champion in Washington.[68]

Encouraging her husband in his ambitions for the party's second position, Betty worked to soften his image, to change the style of his glasses, and to get him to quit smoking. She asked his colleagues what they thought of his speeches "in substance and style."[69] At Betty's urging, the couple purchased a larger house—on, appropriately enough, Weatherford Court in McLean, Virginia. There the Wrights remained until their days in Washington were over. Both loved the property, which abutted woods where Wright would later tell his grandchildren that Tarzan of the Apes lived. For Betty the home was perfect, given Wright's increasing absences. "A political wife has to be independent," she noted. She tried to reserve every third weekend and one week annually for a vacation, but she accepted that Wright's leadership aspirations meant that her private hopes were unlikely. Wright had clearly positioned himself well for a possible run—in all respects.[70]

It was also clear early in 1976 that the race for majority leader would be unusual. Majority Whip John McFall had the benefit of tradition, as his ascension from the number three position on the leadership ladder would follow normal protocol, and his low-key nature suited many members. McFall hailed from California, but he was still conservative enough for many southern Democrats. At the same time, however, others questioned whether he had a forceful enough personality to marshal the rambunctious younger liberals. More troublesome were news reports tying McFall to the Koreagate Scandal. Like Albert, McFall denied knowledge of illegality but also found himself on the defensive.

Campaigning early as the champion of the Watergate Babies was the liberal Phillip Burton. Burton had already cultivated supporters with his fundraising prowess, but, abrasive and ambitious, had obvious disdain for the southern conservatives. Told that Wright supported the farm bill, Burton exploded. "Fuck Jim Wright, fuck the farm bill," he said. "I will single-handedly sink all this redneck Texas special interest shit." Consensus was not Burton's goal; he preferred pressure and deal-making. "I don't want Jim Wright to have a meeting with a favored constituent without feeling me breathing down his neck," Burton later explained.[71] Also in the running was Richard Bolling, the liberal who served on the powerful Rules Committee. A decade older than Burton and with a much longer list of valuable contacts and a more respectable legislative dossier, Bolling despised the young upstart as competition for the same constituency. Less abrasive than Burton, but regarded by some as intellectually snobby, Bolling was a onetime history professor who shared Wright's interest in preserving congressional prerogatives, but not his admiration of Lyndon Johnson.[72]

Understandably hesitant, Wright initially focused on ensuring Majority Leader O'Neill's election as Speaker. The big Irishman, Wright proudly reported, could count on every Texan. With O'Neill facing no serious challenger and the majority leader's ascension the normal protocol, Wright also made an early endorsement in the coming presidential race. Conservative Texas senator Lloyd Bentsen, Wright declared, was in "the mainstream of American thought." Universally respected, Bentsen sought "solutions rather than scapegoats."[73] At the start of the campaign, Wright paid former

Georgia governor Jimmy Carter little attention, and was somewhat annoyed by his tendency to talk down Washington. Betty, however, saw potential. "I just have a good feeling about him," she told her husband. As Carter began to gain steam, Wright recognized that they had much in common, particularly since Carter, a Washington outsider, was somewhat of a southern moderate. When Carter won the Texas primary, where Wright had been a Bentsen delegate, Wright knew that Bentsen was doomed. Wright met Carter and found his sincerity appealing, although he viewed the candidate's promise not to lie a sad sign of the times. Increasingly convinced that a southern moderate might just prevent the South from going to the GOP, Wright predicted that Carter would do well in Texas in November if he won the nomination. If Carter won, Wright promised, he would support the ticket "without reservations."[74]

While keeping his focus publicly on O'Neill and the presidential election, Wright quietly weighed his chances for majority leader. Well-liked, he appeared to be a good compromise to hold the party together. As McFall faltered, conservatives worried about the abrasive Burton and the haughty Bolling. Not only did Wright get along well with O'Neill, but he provided the perfect geographic and ideological balance, the old Austin-Boston connection. And there was, of course, the yeoman's work he had done for others—the bridges, dams, and roads in his colleagues' districts, the years of campaigning and money raised. He had chits on which to call. On just such a campaign trip to West Virginia, Wright first raised the possibility of throwing his hat into the ring. Riding with his key aide, Craig Raupe, who had returned as a staffer, Wright talked through all the possibilities. A loss, Raupe noted, would make his life miserable. One should not think of failure, Wright answered. His intention to enter the race was obvious.[75]

Wright began polling his allies and found only two members of the Texas delegation, Jack Brooks and Bob Eckhardt, opposed to his election. With strong support from the Public Works Committee, Wright began to acknowledge his interest publicly, provided that "my colleagues wanted me to have it." When reporters began to suggest Wright as a compromise candidate, Wright hardly stifled the speculation. The declared candidates deserved "the first chance at winning the support of their colleagues," Wright told the press, but he would not object to "an effort by my colleagues to put my name forth should a deadlock occur."[76] With Wright's encouragement, his Texas allies kept floating the possibility of Wright's entrance, making it appear a groundswell of support. "I hope that he can find that he can make the race," Bob Kreuger told the media in June. By this point,

Wright, unable to deny his behind-the-scenes maneuvering, acknowledged that he was "definitely interested." His aide Marshall Lynam confirmed the internal polling. "Of the list of sixty-eight members we contacted," Lynam stated, "thirty-two said that they would be for him." Wright's announcement of an exploratory committee was therefore hardly surprising.[77]

Encouraging Wright was Dan Rostenkowski of Illinois, a representative who ultimately proved critical to the election. A bear of a man whose large stature matched his powerful persona, Rostenkowski remembered how the Texas delegation had not supported him earlier in the 1970s—before Burton's rise—when he had run for caucus chairman. Nevertheless, he despised both Burton and Bolling, who had cast stones against the Chicago-style machine politics from which he arose. Wright had helped Chicago win government money from the Public Works Committee, and Rostenkowski needed a new champion for his own advancement. He had earlier supported Hale Boggs as the majority leader in the hope that Boggs would appoint him majority whip. Boggs had won, but had selected O'Neill, initiating the beginning of O'Neill's meteoric rise. Now Rostenkowski needed a new political horse to ride, and Wright appeared just the man.[78]

Spurring Rostenkowski into action was Leo Diehl, O'Neill's chief aide. Diehl quietly notified Rostenkowski that the presumptive Speaker of the House welcomed the possibility of Wright as majority leader, as the thought of working with the ambitious Burton or the arrogant Bolling was unattractive. Rostenkowski knew what this meant—the chance to curry favor and put himself on the leadership ladder. Inviting Wright to a breakfast meeting in a downtown Chicago hotel with the powerful Chicago mayor Richard Daley, Rostenkowski promised the endorsement of big-city mayors across the country. Not surprisingly, New York's Beame was first aboard. When others joined, Wright had some momentum, thanks in no small part to Rostenkowski.[79]

While O'Neill had to remain officially neutral so that he could work with whomever won, his clandestine support did not surprise Wright. Several months before, O'Neill had inquired if Wright was interested in the position. When Wright had voiced concerns over the time commitment required and his hopes for the chairmanship of the Public Works Committee, O'Neill had tried to reassure him that the number two position "wouldn't take any more time than Public Works." O'Neill's support may not have surprised Wright, but it likely surprised Bolling. Bolling had won the support of O'Neill's good friend Edward Boland, which had led him to believe that the Speaker-to-be was in his camp.[80]

Wright's success in fundraising for his own November reelection despite the lack of any serious challenger spoke to his leadership potential. A successful fundraising dinner at Washington's Channel Inn Motel in late June attracted an array of PACs and raised more than $80,000, a large sum at the time. The fundraiser, it turned out, was another turning point for Wright. A lobbyist and former staffer of Oklahoman Robert Kerr, J. D. Williams, convinced Wright that he should use some of the proceeds to retire his long-standing personal debt. A loophole in the campaign financing law made transferring campaign funds to personal use legal, Williams correctly pointed out. As Wright surely recognized, such transfers were unseemly and held potential for abuse. In fact, Congress later outlawed them. At the time, however, the reality remained: Wright was tired of watching others manipulate the system while he remained idealistic and in debt. When he had first started out, Wright told a reporter shortly before the fundraiser, he had been a "purist" that "took no contribution of more than $100 and nothing from people affected by legislation." With experience, however, one recognized that "everyone is affected one way or another." Politicians had to do what it took. "My position now is if the law says it's all right, I'll take the money. I've complied with the law."[81]

If a bit of Machiavellianism now tinged Wright's idealism, he was, technically, still operating within the system. The press hardly noticed. When Joe Shosid of the Wright Appreciation Committee acknowledged that the fundraiser would help pay off Wright's debts, reporters asked only if the cash was for a possible race for majority leader. "I'm not giving you a run-around," Shosid replied, deflecting the question. "I just can't recall."[82] Shosid sought to assure both ample cash and legal compliance—he even provided potential donors with "the stationary and the stamps you need to handle your mailing." Donors might miss such costs and the committee might misreport its final figures, Shosid wrote. It was important to "comply with both the letter and spirit of the federal election law."[83]

Wright arrived two days early for the mid-July Democratic National Convention in New York City, reserving a hospitality room at the Essex House to meet with an exhaustive list of congressional candidates. With each of his thirty-minute-long meetings, Wright provided fruit, cheese, and coffee, and he ensured that Betty was on hand in case the candidate brought his own wife. No Burton, Wright was gracious as ever, never demanding a commitment but just consideration. The new majority leader would win election through a series of secret ballots, each eliminating the last place finisher. Wright knew that if he survived the first ballot, he might pick up those committed delegates who had lost their first choice. Quietly encouraging Wright was fellow Texan and friend Bob Strauss, chairman of the Democratic Party.[84]

Despite his own aspirations, Wright did his due diligence for the convention's choice, Jimmy Carter. At September's Texas state convention, Wright praised Carter's ability to unite Americans—and, implicitly, Democrats—with his "common sense approach."[85] When Carter faced blistering criticism following an interview he granted *Playboy* magazine, Wright called to commiserate, aware that Carter had been trying to express his Christian values. When Wright welcomed Carter to Fort Worth in late October, the nominee impressed Wright by attending church services before his scheduled speech. After the speech, Wright arranged a "family-style meeting" for citizens interested in meeting the candidate, once again praising Carter's "genuineness."[86] Whenever criticism arose about Carter from his own constituents, Wright set them straight. Carter, he wrote to one critic, had made Georgia's government "streamlined and efficient."[87] Throughout the fall, Wright was a team player even as his focus remained on leading the team himself.

In the years that followed, Wright insisted that the late announcement of his candidacy for the position of majority leader—two weeks after the national convention—was his greatest disadvantage. Although an earlier entrance might have kept some colleagues from endorsing others, in fact Wright had already done his homework. He had written hundreds of letters, each seemingly with a personal touch. "I felt I owed you the courtesy of letting you know directly from me," the letters began.[88] Wright aides Raupe and Lynam had spent weeks in Texas with potential donors, often couching their efforts as party teamwork. "We'd like you to raise money for these candidates, not Jim," they stated, adding when necessary that the money would not go to extreme liberals.[89] Wright supporter Bernard Rapoport submitted ten blank $1,000 checks. Such large contributions, Wright told another wealthy contributor, were important for "the continued development and well-being of the Southwest."[90] While Burton and Bolling undoubtedly raised more than the $50,000 Wright's efforts garnered, Wright was the one who had personally handed out checks to the rookie candidates seeking election. For the incumbents, it was Wright, not Burton, Bolling, or McFall, who had done the laborious day-to-day speeches in individual districts across the nation. It was Wright who had promised to hold Public Works Committee meetings on topics critical to them. Almost every evening, Wright met with his aides to review the latest intelligence. Wright's surrogates hounded those who were undecided, even following them into restaurants. The *Fort Worth Star-Telegram* did its share, declaring, "Wright's Right for Majority Leader."[91]

McFall was often on the defensive, and Burton attacked his opponents as champions of entrenched privilege unwilling to make the necessary reforms. Bolling, meanwhile, focused mostly on Burton, his intense dislike obvious. Support for Wright, he warned, would lead to a Burton victory. When Bolling did attack Wright, he implied nepotism. Wright's committee employed Wright's wife, he pointed out, while ignoring the fact that Wright had little connection to the employment and that Betty had a full Washington resume.[92]

Ultimately, however, Wright had an ace in the hole against Bolling's charges. Nick Masters, a Budget Committee aide, was friendly with Bolling but quietly preferred Wright. When Masters learned that Bolling planned to charge that Wright was too soft on African American rights and too cozy with oil interests, he informed Lynam at a secret breakfast meeting in the Rayburn House Office Building cafeteria. This valuable political intelligence allowed Wright to respond preemptively. The campaign began to stress that Wright had refused to sign the "Southern Manifesto" against school desegregation or to support efforts to oust the African American congressman Adam Clayton Powell. Wright's campaign, meanwhile, asked the oil industry lobbyists to back off, while stressing that Wright had favored the small producers, not the large behemoths.[93]

Two weeks before the scheduled election for majority leader, Rostenkowski and seven other Democrats endorsed Wright in a letter that was sent to the entire caucus. Wright was in the "mainstream of the party," the letter read, and would provide the "balance" the party desperately needed. He would work well with O'Neill and "never embarrass the House." Members would be "proud to present him to any group in your home district." He was, after all, "one of the most persuasive speakers" in Congress.[94] Days later, all four candidates appeared on the popular television program *Meet the Press*. Asked by the moderator how he would discipline Florida congressman Bob Sikes, who was under investigation for financial improprieties, Wright was indignant. "That's none of your business," he shot back. The decision rested with Congress and was not for public debate. The answer, one reporter suggested, spoke to all congressmen fearful of being embroiled in public charges, truthful or not. It endeared him to the constituency he needed at that moment.[95]

Wright had little time to celebrate Carter's victory in the presidential election. On November 2, 1976, Carter defeated Gerald Ford in a relatively narrow 297–240 Electoral College victory. Carter, the first man to win the presidency from the Deep South in over a century, carried Dixie completely. This included, much to Wright's satisfaction, his own district and state. If Wright celebrated, he undoubtedly sensed at the same time no new dawn for his party or the economy. Democrats picked up only one House seat, while the Senate essentially remained unchanged. Behind the results was the reality that many southern conservative Democrats remained disenchanted with the growing liberalism within their party. In a way, their votes for a fellow southerner at the top of the ticket masked their underlying sentiments.[96]

Wright moved quickly after the national election, inviting the forty-eight newly elected Democrats to a lunch that turned out to be the only time they had together before the vote for new leadership. Wright also invited the other candidates to speak and graciously introduced them. The comments did not go well for Burton. After he stood and stressed his support from the "Class of 1974," one member from that group, Kentucky's Carroll Hubbard, proclaimed his support for Wright "one hundred percent." Wright then stood and stressed unity and collegiality. After the caucus election approached, Raupe, his aide, prevailed upon a former staff colleague, Larry King, who had become a writer, to craft a pro-Wright piece. The article implied that though Carter could not make an endorsement, he favored a fellow southerner and pragmatic moderate. To maximize publicity, the Wright campaign distributed over three hundred copies of the article to House Democrats on the morning of the caucus vote.[97]

The vote, at noon on Monday, December 6, less than a month before the new 95th Congress convened, included official nominations. Wright selected a fellow Texan, Charlie Wilson, to do the honors. Wilson then struck the need for unity, while adding that Wright had supported the Voting Rights Act of 1965, which, Wilson claimed, "was about as popular in Fort Worth as terminal cancer."[98] The comments implied that Wright was a man who could get things done while insulating him from charges that he was too weak on African American rights. When the first ballots were tallied, counted from boxes, the order was not surprising even if the tally was. Burton led with 106, followed by Bolling with 81, Wright with 77, and McFall with 31. With McFall out, Rostenkowski came to Wright's aid again, making a secret deal with Burton. Burton considered Bolling his greatest challenger and ceded to Rostenkowski's plan to encourage some of his own supporters to vote for Wright on the next ballot. This would help make Bolling the new last place finisher and thus eliminate him from the third ballot. Burton, as cocky as ever, assumed that he could easily defeat Wright. Rostenkowski and Wright, meanwhile, calculated that with Bolling out of the race, Wright would gain more votes than Burton. In reality, of course, no one truly knew what would actually happen. "The second ballot's the key," one Rostenkowski aide leaked to the press.[99]

It was a risky plan, but it worked—just barely. Burton won with 107 votes and Wright came in second with 95. Two votes behind Wright was Bolling, now out of the race. As the third ballot approached, Rostenkowski lobbied his colleagues on Wright's behalf, winning for Wright the last-minute vote of Ohio's Thomas Ashley. Ashley's switch proved crucial. When the results came in, Wright had 148 and Burton had 147.[100] Wright had won—by one vote. Wright saw his fellow Texan Ray Roberts leap for joy and then heard Arkansas's Bill Alexander shout, "You won." Wright stood briefly in stunned disbelief before letting out a happy yelp. Betty, watching from the gallery, rushed down with a congratulatory kiss. Members swarmed around the obviously gleeful Wright, while O'Neill, the new Speaker, pushed through to offer his own congratulations. "Let's have a drink," he said.[101]

Jim Wright's parents, Marie Louella Lyster and James Claude Wright, circa 1915, just before their marriage during World War I. The unrefined Wright appeared to be an odd choice for the proper Lyster, but they shared both a driving ambition and an idealism that they passed on to their son.

Marie Lyster just before Jim Wright's birth in 1922. Marie instilled in her son a love of public speaking and a thirst for the limelight. In the end Wright proved to be one of Congress's greatest orators.

Toddler Jim Wright with his father, circa 1924. For the boy, his father's approval always mattered. The elder Wright grew a business into considerable wealth but struggled with alcohol. Through his father's business, Wright witnessed firsthand the Great Depression and the struggles of a small-town America that had begun to fade.

Wright with his girlfriend, Geraldine Brazeale, in 1935. The Wright family moved frequently when the boy was young, and he was advanced two grades beyond his age. Wright became a master at adaptation, always winning friends and trying to fit in.

Teenager Wright in the late 1930s. Wright was a decent student and took an early interest in history and current events, but it was his constant efforts to make a name for himself in extracurricular activities that dominated his time. Wright developed an interest in the theater, the school newspaper, the football team, and the debate club. From these experiences grew his decision to enter politics.

Lieutenant Jim Wright returning from combat duty in the Pacific, 1944. Greeting Wright is his old college friend Joe Sutton, who was serving at Carswell Air Force Base in Fort Worth. Wright served on a B-24 Liberator and flew one of the longest combat bombing missions of the war. Wright's worldview, like that of many other members of the "Greatest Generation," was shaped largely by his war experiences.

JIM **WRIGHT**

STATE
REPRESENTATIVE
[SEEKING SECOND TERM]

Left: A poster from Wright's failed reelection campaign for the Texas Legislature in 1948. The loss hit Wright hard. Throughout his life the driven Wright suffered from periods of melancholy and doubt.

Below: Mayor Jim Wright on horseback parading in Weatherford, Texas, 1952. Serving as a small-town mayor after being in the Texas Legislature appeared to be a step backward, but it allowed Wright to form connections and develop managerial skills. It laid the foundation for Wright's congressional run two years later.

GRAND JURY INDICTS NOTED 'WIREPULLER'

WASHINGTON, July 22 (AP).— Henry W. (The Dutchman) Grunewald, noted Washington wirepuller, was indicted Thursday on 10 charges of perjury.

The indictment charges he lied four times in the grand jury and six times before a House subcommittee and means subcommittee about ...

Count No. 1 charged Grunewald falsely testified to the House subcommittee in April 1953 that he had never discussed tax cases with Daniel A. Bolich once the nation's No. 3 tax collector. Bolich himself is now under indictment on charges of evading his own income taxes.

The subcommittee record showed Grunewald was asked the before "saying this time that Mr. Bolich was strong in your circle at the Washington hotel, did he ever discuss tax cases with you?"

Grunewald's reply was rounded. "At no time did Mr. Bolich discuss any tax cases with me in any way, shape or form, in my recollection."

Bolich was one of several officials at the Internal Revenue Bureau during the Truman administration with whom Grunewald was on friendly terms.

Previous court and congressional proceedings have shown "the Dutchman" also had contacts with Republicans in Washington and one court witness once described him as a "man who could walk into senators' offices with his hat on."

The jury said he lied when he swore he knew nothing of any tax fraud investigation involving Patullo Modes, Inc., a New York clothing firm. It said he eventually consulted the internal Revenue Bureau about it.

It also said he lied about an investigation of Gerard E. Catherwood, a union leader at Pine Bluff, Ark. The jury said Grunewald obtained confidential income tax returns of Catherwood "in an improper and unauthorized manner."

Joint Funeral Planned for 2 Killed in Crash

JACKSBORO, July 22 (Staff).— Joint funeral services will be conducted at First Baptist Church here at 10 a.m. Friday for Carl Howard Pippin, 23, and Enoch B. Rover, 32, who died Wednesday night after their car crashed into a bridge abutment six miles northeast of Breckenridge on U. S. Highway 183.

Pippin, a resident of Postoak, seven miles west of Jacksboro, was paralyzed from the neck down. He was fatally injured in an auto accident near here several years ago at a Breckenridge hospital.

Rover will be buried in Oakwood Cemetery here, Pippin in Wesley Chapel Cemetery, west of Jacksboro.

Pippin is survived by his wife of Postoak, his father, Edgar B. Pippin, who resides west of Jacksboro; three brothers, Mrs. Maudie Massingale and Mrs. Ruby Brison; four brothers, J. L. Lewis and Henry Pippin, all of Jacksboro, and his grandmother, Mrs. Ida Graham of Duncan, Okla.

Rover is survived by his mother, Mrs. Bessie L. Rover of Jacksboro, three sisters, Mrs. Bessie Ruth Barnett of Mineral Wells and Misses Susie and Dora Nadine Rover of Jacksboro; three brothers, William Rover of Mineral Wells and Thomas and Robert Rover of Jacksboro, and his grandmother, Chauf Dodd of Mineral Wells.

Funeral services will be conducted at 4 p.m. Friday in the Lawson Methodist Church, Bartlett will be in Lawson Cemetery.

Silas Y. Hamilton, 84, Of Colorado City Dies

COLORADO CITY, July 22 (Spl).—Silas Y. Hamilton, 84, died Thursday afternoon at his home in Loraine.

He was born in Mississippi and had lived in Mitchell County since 1918. He was a member of the First Methodist Church here. He was a retired farmer.

Surviving are two sons, Charlie Hamilton of Loraine and J. W. Hamilton of Pecos; three daughters, Mrs. U. W. Wilkerson and Mrs. C. W. Groom of Abilene and Mrs. Helen Allen of Fort Worth; a brother, W. L. Hamilton of Langtry, 17 grandchildren and 28 great-grandchildren.

Austin Boy Drowns While Wading in Creek

AUSTIN, July 22 (AP).—A 16-year-old boy who couldn't swim drowned in Barton Creek Thursday while wading with two companions.

Dead is Arnold Smith Jr., 16, the only son of Mr. and Mrs. Arnold Smith. He wandered into deep water in the area infested creek, went under and became entangled in the moss.

Ten thousand (a fifty thousand?) hysteria plated side by would measure on inch.

Synthetic resin coated on heavy paper makes a light, unbreakable phonograph record.

> *"If you can walk with crowds and keep your virtue, Or talk with kings, nor lose the 'common touch' ... If ALL men count with you, but NONE too much"*   —Kipling

AN OPEN LETTER TO MR. AMON G. CARTER
AND THE FORT WORTH STAR-TELEGRAM . . .

Dear Mr. Carter:

This is hurriedly written to meet your deadline which comes right on the heels of the appearance of your yesterday afternoon paper and its front page editorial.

Therefore, it won't be well written . . . but the facts will be here!

The $974.40 for this ad is coming out of my own pocket and it's going to be worth it to me . . . even if it overdraws my savings account.

For you have at last met a man, Mr. Carter, who is not afraid of you . . . who will not bow his knee to you . . . and come running like a simpering pup at your beck and call.

I expected you to editorialize against me, Mr. Carter . . . in spite of my many good friends and supporters among the working and writing staff of your paper.

But I didn't expect you to engage in misrepresentation. I thought you were a bigger man than that! I still think you are, and that you will retract it.

You say in your editorial that I have given no formula, no "well-defined ideas" for bringing about the things I've discussed as the goals of this nation . . . such as winning the cold war for the minds of men and women, preserving our freedoms, and avoiding atomic warfare.

You say that I have not commented on the farm program, taxation, federal spending, etc.

But I have, Mr. Carter . . . and your editorial writers KNOW that I have. In my very first announcement speech over your TV station . . . in subsequent speeches . . . and notably on May 14th at the barbecue dinner attended by more than 1000 people . . . I went in considerably greater detail on my stand on these issues than your private errand boy Congressman have ever done.

You say that I have kept my feelings on these things "well concealed." Let's tell the truth, Mr. Carter. YOU and your personal newspaper have kept them well concealed!

You had reporters at the May 14th barbecue . . . two of them. They wrote good stories . . . the type the huge attendance and the positions I took would have justified. And then somebody in your organization KILLED the most important

facts in those stories. The biggest political dinner in the recent history of Fort Worth and you gave it less space than an obituary of some Chinese laundryman in Seattle who once passed through Fort Worth!

Yes, I have commented publicly on the issues, Mr. Carter. I have spoken out against socialized medicine . . . on how to reduce foreign aid by increasing trade through Reciprocal Trade Agreements and the lowering of tariffs . . . against the proposed sales tax . . . against the "hard money" policy . . . I have gone into detail in my speeches on the farm program and the changes I would recommend . . . and I have devoted an entire TV program to how best we can clean up "the mess" in Washington and restore dignity to the sacred calling of free government . . . I devoted half a TV speech last Monday noon to how to solve the critical water supply problem for our area.

None of these things has been quoted in your paper. Am I to blame for that? In most cases . . . in fact, every case, I believe . . . I went to some pains to see that your paper had a copy.

Is this how you have controlled Fort Worth so long? By printing only that which you WANTED the people to read? By refusing to quote a man in your paper when he does take a stand and then running a front-page editorial saying he has not taken any stand?

The people know only what they read in the papers. For that reason, a newspaper has a sacred obligation.

"Ye shall know the truth and the truth shall make you free" is a holy promise. But how are we going to know the truth when it is suppressed by the papers?

Your personal ownership of the TV station, too, has been a part of this campaign. In late March, your TV lawyers first approved my original announcement script, then called it back after conferences to delete my request that the public share in the costs of the campaign. "Against FCC rules," they said. I didn't complain. But less than two weeks later, a Congressional candidate made the same identical request unchallenged over the Dallas station which is required to abide by the same FCC requirements.

And Governor Shivers was permitted to make such a request over YOUR station.

You have permitted ads intended to cast aspersions upon my business, Mr. Carter . . . in which the opposition has purported to print an affidavit bearing my signature. But they left out the one significant part of the affidavit . . . the part where it says it is not to be construed as indication that any statute or regulation had been violated.

I respect you, Mr. Carter . . . and I think, if the truth were only known, you respect me much more than you do the people who are always cowtowing and catering to you.

I admire the many wonderful things you have done for Fort Worth and our area. It is because of the inspiration of such "doers" as yourself and others that I have aspired, too, to try to do things for our area and our people.

But it is unhealthy for ANYONE to become TOO powerful . . . TOO influential . . . too dominating. It is not good for Democracy. The people are tired of "One-Man Rule".

This is a new day. New blood and new minds and new thoughts, fresh from the people themselves, are needed.

On Saturday, Mr. Carter, the PEOPLE are going to vote for me . . . in great numbers, unless I am terribly mistaken. And I mean people of all sorts. And let's not bring in that old "labor leaders" bugaboo that has been used against everyone who has run against the "rubber stamp" boys.

The labor leaders know, just as you know, that they don't control me. I have talked to them just exactly as I am talking to you now.

And if I am your Congressman, as I think I am going to be . . . I want you to know I will be delighted to work WITH you . . . not FOR you . . . in building a greater America, a greater Southwest, and a greater Fort Worth area.

I will be YOUR Congressman, just as I will be EVERYONE'S Congressman . . . not your personal, private Congressman . . . but a Congressman for ALL the people!

Very Sincerely yours,

Jim Wright

—Paid Political Adv.

Four Generals Topped For Additional Stars

WASHINGTON, July 22.— President Eisenhower Thursday named a member of the Army's elite Joint Chiefs of Staff and three others to four-star general rank as he is in his present command as chief of the Army field forces. Dahlquist has held that assignment since August.

Eisenhower also named three major generals to the rank of lieutenant general while assigned to corps commanders. These three are:

Maj. Gen. Henry I. Hodes, who commands the 7th Corps in Europe; Maj. Gen. John H. Collier, commander of the 1st Corps in the Far East, and Maj. Gen. Charles E. Hart, head of the 5th Corps in Europe.

During Wright's underdog 1954 congressional run, he faced the opposition of publisher Amon Carter. In a risky gambit, Wright took out an advertisement in Carter's own paper, a "Letter to Amon Carter," criticizing the Fort Worth power broker. Wright credited it with his surprise victory. Wright felt firsthand the rough nature of Texas politics and the sting of McCarthyism.

The Wright family just after his election to Congress in the mid-1950s. Pictured are his first wife, Mab; his son, Jimmy; and his daughters, Ginger and Kay. Wright's career took a toll on his family life.

Top: New Congressman Wright, always busy, on the phone in his office, circa 1956. Wright learned early the ways of Washington. A position on the Public Works Committee proved a real advantage. The committee oversaw publicly funded projects and thus gave Wright leverage early.

Bottom: In 1956 Wright helped host a dinner in Fort Worth honoring the powerful Speaker of the House, Sam Rayburn. Rayburn was in many ways a mentor and model during the early part of Wright's career. Seniority ruled in the House of Representatives, and while Wright had to cultivate connections and wait his turn, he also went about mastering the institution's rules and procedures.

Wright in front of the US Capitol in the late 1950s. Wright grew to love Congress, which at the time was more collegial and bipartisan than it is today. Wright developed a reputation as a moderate who was able to work across the aisle and get things done, but could also keep the fractured Democratic Party together.

When a special election was held in Texas in 1961 to fill Lyndon Johnson's Senate seat, which had become vacant when Johnson won the vice presidency, Wright threw his hat into the ring for the Democratic nomination. The Democratic Party was changing, torn between its liberal and conservative elements. Wright would have to straddle this line for the rest of his career, but, unfortunately for Wright, his 1961 run was unsuccessful, launching yet another period of reflection and frustration.

Wright played an important role in bringing President John F. Kennedy to Texas on November 22, 1963. Wright arranged for Kennedy to speak in front of Fort Worth's Hotel Texas the morning of that fateful day. In the background, from left: Wright, Fort Worth Chamber of Commerce president Raymond Buck, state committee woman Marjorie Belew, Senator Ralph Yarborough, Governor John Connally, and Vice President Lyndon Johnson. Wright, who flew with Kennedy to Dallas's Love Field and participated in the presidential motorcade, had a front-row seat to one of the nation's most tragic events.

Wright with Lyndon Johnson on a presidential visit to Fort Worth in 1968. Wright, like Johnson, became a legislative master. He worked to find consensus, advocating compromise, and the result was a flood of legislation. Wright played a key role in the Great Society and his legacy includes an array of laws that still stand today.

Wright worked closely with Johnson, who was yet another key Wright mentor. The emergence of the New Left and the turmoil of the Johnson years frustrated and confused Wright, making his task of appealing to the growing number of liberal Democrats difficult. Wright, after all, represented a southern district that was growing increasingly conservative.

Perhaps the most prominent of all the matters that alienated Wright from Democratic liberals was his support for the Vietnam War. Wright authored a congressional resolution that explicitly supported the efforts of Richard Nixon, shown here in December 1969 holding a copy of the resolution with Wright next to him. Wright had an oddly close relationship with the Republican Nixon and refused for a long time to believe the Watergate allegations.

Top: Wright always maintained a keen interest in Latin America, a product of his youth. Here he is shown with the American ambassador to Panama, Robert M. Sayer, on a 1971 trip to El Real, Colombia, to inspect the Inter-American Highway.

Bottom: Here Wright speaks at the dedication of the Dallas–Fort Worth International Airport in 1973. Wright was influential in getting the airport approved and constructed, and today the airport remains an engine of economic growth for the Dallas–Fort Worth "Metroplex."

Top: With his position on the Public Works Committee, Wright had a leading role in the construction of the Interstate Highway System. He never lost sight of his home district and became a master of "pork barrel." Here, in July 1976, Wright celebrates the opening of the "820 Loop," a highway around Fort Worth named in his honor.

Bottom: Wright helped spark negotiations that led to the famous Camp David Accords. Here he is shown with Israeli prime minister Menachem Begin in 1978.

Top: Wright with Egyptian president Muhammad Anwar el-Sadat in 1978. Wright got to know a number of world leaders personally and made numerous diplomatic trips abroad. After Sadat was assassinated in 1981, Wright attended his funeral, traveling on Air Force One.

Bottom: Wright with Carter on Air Force One in 1979. Wright admired Carter's moderation and faith but thought his reaction to the energy crisis weak.

Wright with his second wife, Betty, circa 1980s. Betty shared Wright's interest in politics and became his foremost confidante and supporter.

Wright with Ronald Reagan before Reagan's State of the Union Address, January 26, 1981. Wright struggled to answer the rise of the New Right and found Reagan a formidable opponent. The two clashed on numerous occasions.

From left: Vice President George Bush, Speaker Jim Wright, Senate Minority Leader Bob Dole, and President Ronald Reagan, negotiating the budget on a White House patio, summer 1985. Wright became a leader of the Democratic opposition to Reaganomics, the battles rocking the political world.

Finally elected Speaker of the House, Wright ensured that he had an office worthy of the position, shown here in 1987.

Wright, shown here with Vice President George Bush listening to Ronald Reagan's State of the Union Address on January 27, 1987, proved to be a powerful Speaker of the House. The 100th Congress was one of the most productive, but Wright's domineering style and the ever-present competition between rivals made him enemies.

President Reagan and congressional leaders announce the "Reagan-Wright Peace Plan" for Central America, August 5, 1987, at the White House. From left: Bob Michel, Tom Foley, Bob Dole, Ronald Reagan, Robert Byrd, and Jim Wright. In time, divisions over Central America would embroil Wright in controversy and contribute to his political demise.

Wright, joking while tending to his roses, 1987. Wright had little time for recreation during the years that his life was defined by his work in Congress.

Wright giving his emotional resignation speech before Congress on May 31, 1989. He holds the book whose publication contributed to the scandal that ended his career. Wright had made enemies, and the political culture of Congress had changed, leaving him, with his carelessness and excesses, an easy target for charges of corruption. The club-like bipartisanship and collegiality of Congress had become things of the past.

In his retirement Wright returned to Fort Worth. He awarded his papers, shown here, to Texas Christian University, which offered him an office and archives in his honor. Wright taught classes, wrote articles, and remained active politically.

The Lion in Winter, 2012. Wright suffered health issues, including cancer of the mouth, before his death in May 2015. The city mourned a true Texas giant, whose long life told so much about how Congress had evolved and reflected so much of how America had lived.

CHAPTER 13

The New Majority Leader

CRITICAL DECISIONS IN AN AGE OF PARTISANSHIP
(1976–1978)

The initial reviews of Wright's election were largely positive, touting him as the perfect choice for a productive Congress. Conservative pundits thrilled in the defeat of the liberal Phil Burton. Noting approvingly that the progressive Americans for Democratic Action had rated Wright "correct" on only 32 percent of his votes, syndicated columnists Rowland Evans and Robert Novak wrote that the victory constituted a "counter-revolutionary reaction following turbulent radical reform."[1] Acknowledging Wright's reputation for compromise, the more liberal *Washington Post* concluded that O'Neill and Wright promised "a strong, persuasive team." Common Cause, which billed itself as a nonpartisan lobby for good government, praised Wright's advocacy of campaign reform.[2] Many media reports enjoyed leading their stories with a play on Wright's name. "He's Wright on the job," declared the *Dallas Morning News*. Constituents, meanwhile, flooded Wright's office with letters of congratulations.[3]

The honeymoon, however, proved brief. "Wright Has Kin on Hill Staff," blasted headlines only weeks later. His wife, Betty, the press announced, earned $25,000 annually working for the Public Works Committee; one of his daughters, Ginger, had earned $13,000 working for the House Banking

Committee; and John Mack, the brother of Wright's son-in-law, worked directly in Wright's congressional office. While noting that Betty's employment predated her marriage and violated no nepotism laws, the implication of malfeasance was obvious.[4] Soon the press rediscovered Wright's transfer of campaign debts. Wright's "casual approach to bookkeeping," the *Washington Star* stated, had "the characteristics of a personal charitable operation." Reports then claimed that Wright had mentioned publicly that he had already retired his debt. By early summer, more damaging reports had emerged, claiming that Philip Lacovara, counsel for the House Ethics Committee, had confirmed that O'Neill and Wright had been under investigation as part of the Koreagate Scandal.[5]

It all seemed to confirm Wright's suspicions that the media were obsessed with scandal. Moving quickly to limit the damage, he acknowledged that Wisconsin's Henry Reuss had first suggested Ginger's employment. It was, however, a Banking Committee staffer who had made the hire and his own office had played no role. Mack, Wright added, was a "young man of enormous potential" who only helped with the office mail. In any event, the employment of both was completely legal.[6] As for Betty, Wright convinced his reluctant spouse to resign her position. Betty enjoyed the bustle of Capitol Hill politics, and one of Wright's aides, Marshall Lynam, insisted that the negative stories would pass. Wright, however, convinced Betty to declare that it was a "mutual decision" for her to be "just Jim's wife." Betty's frustration subtly showed. "Up until a few months ago," Betty reminded one audience weeks later, "I had a job too."[7]

To answer the renewed questions about his transfer of campaign funds, Wright volunteered to pay the IRS an additional $49,250 to cover taxes on all personal gain. "Fundraising is to me the crabgrass in the lawn of political life," Wright stated truthfully, belying his expanded operations.[8] The Koreagate story, however, was the one that was the most difficult to defend. Writing Lacovara directly, Wright stated that the press must have "misconstrued" what Lacovara had said. "I am anxious to get this entire matter cleared up today," Wright pled. Replying in a telegram that any reports that Wright had received a bribe were indeed "inaccurate," Lacovara released a statement apologizing.[9]

Between politics and the media, however, the story had a life of its own. With the majority of congressmen now implicated Democrats, many Republicans demanded a special prosecutor to supplement the House Ethics Committee. Carter refused to make any appointments, and Wright was left to angrily deny the continuing suggestions that he had received bribes. "I categorically, emphatically and unequivocally state that is a lie," Wright snapped, his temper showing.[10] Believing that the matter would never resolve otherwise, Wright decided to press for the appointment of former Watergate investigator Leon Jaworski. After Congress appointed Jaworski, new reports emerged that Jaworski had first agreed to limit his investigation. Noting Wright by name, Jaworski denied the charges and stated that if anyone had ever suggested limitations he would have resigned. In time the scandal passed, with the central figure, Tongsun Park, fleeing, and with Wright fully exonerated but frustrated by the entire affair.[11]

Frustrated or not, Wright arguably failed to glean from all the negative reports a central lesson—the power he had always sought brought scrutiny he had never before faced. Rather than guarding against any chance that events could be twisted against him, Wright continued to make questionable moves that if ever exposed publicly would surely invite criticism. For example, he apparently assumed that criticism of John Mack's employment had passed with the fading charges of nepotism. Left unreported—at least at the outset—was Mack's horrific background. When he was nineteen, Mack had brutally assaulted a woman with a hammer and a knife. After dumping her into a car, he had casually gone to a movie. During the trial, Wright had requested leniency, promising employment at the conclusion of Mack's sentence. True to his word, the new majority leader had hired him. It was, Wright claimed, Christian forgiveness for a changed man who had paid his dues. That may have been true, and the answer may have sufficed—at least for the moment. In the end, however, Wright would learn a painful lesson. Given the scrutiny he faced as majority leader, he should have seen it all coming.[12]

And then there was the matter of his finances. The loss of Betty's income, twice the national average, hit hard. Wright knew his estate was woefully inadequate.[13] It was this growing sentiment that helped solidify his relationship with Fort Worth businessman George Mallick, a friendship that left ample opportunity for attack and, like the Mack affair, would in the end come back to haunt Wright. Once again, facing the unprecedented scrutiny, Wright should have seen it all coming.

A large man of Lebanese descent, Mallick had first met Wright in 1963. By 1967, Mallick was a wealthy developer who shared Wright's ambition, penchant for hard work, and up-from-the-bootstraps background. The two became close. When many of Wright's acquaintances were initially cold to

Betty, Mallick welcomed her, endearing himself to the rising politician. Mallick, according to author John Barry, enjoyed the close connection to power but had no grand political agenda. He simply enjoyed the status, never directly asking Wright for favors. Neither Wright nor Mallick ever intended to break the law, and Mallick even tried to confirm compliance with regulations. Nevertheless, Mallick, like Wright, was willing to do all that he legally could to push the rules as far as possible.[14] In retrospect, the two were a natural pair; indeed, just as Wright began serving as majority leader, Mallick was becoming an increasingly important business adviser.

Wright assumed his relationship with Mallick to be personal, and no one's business but his own; he certainly would have ended the friendship if Mallick had sought to sway his policy positions to his own advantage. After all, just after Wright's election as majority leader, Eddie Chiles did just that. Chiles, the wealthy owner of an oil services company, approached Wright's campaign adviser, Joe Shosid, who recognized a potential donor. Soon Wright and Chiles were close, even visiting each other's homes, and their wives became friendly as well. Chiles, however, began to demand to see Wright every time Wright returned to his district, and with his relationship established, began to press for deregulation of the oil industry. When Wright refused and supported a "windfall profits" tax on large oil companies, the relationship ended. The friend became an enemy. In sum, Wright knew Mallick was no Chiles, but he failed to realize the shadow that others might cast on the relationship. It was a mistake much greater than his flirtation with Chiles and an oversight he would later regret.[15]

As the 95th Congress was set to convene in January 1977, Wright had more than enough on his plate. Meeting with the president-elect and the other Democratic leaders in Plains, Georgia, Wright could tell that Carter might have trouble with Congress. According to historian Kenneth Morris, Carter's troubles arose from two sources: the Democrats' "intraparty rivalry," and Carter's tendency to be the "moralist" outsider who dictated to the established Washington order. Carter later acknowledged as much. Congressional Democrats, he wrote in his memoirs, were "not about to embrace me as a long-awaited ally."[16] When Carter explained that as governor he had gone around the legislature and appealed to the people, O'Neill sensed a threat. Later, when he and his wife were assigned poor seats at Carter's inaugural gala, he saw a slight. Soon, at Carter's weekly Tuesday morning breakfast meetings, O'Neill was complaining about the menu and even the blessings offered. "Hell," he groused, "Nixon treated us better than this."

According to one assistant, O'Neill later recalled the Carter presidency as a "bad dream."[17]

Wright saw things differently. Carter, it appeared, a fellow southerner with strong connections to the conservatives, shared his concern for the debt, his idealism, and his emphasis on honesty. In the future, Wright would have his disagreements with the White House, but, as he later concluded, Carter became a friend on "a deeper, personal level."[18] Wright remembered the Plains meeting in a positive light. When Carter asked Wright to intercede with his fellow Texan Jack Brooks, who had the power as a committee chair to block Carter's proposal for a "sunset law," Wright explained that most programs already required reauthorization and that the request would challenge the prideful Brooks's jurisdiction. Carter, Wright remembered, was not condescending, but he agreed that it was best not to make an unnecessary enemy.[19] Perhaps sensing Wright's sentiments, Carter invited Wright for individual luncheon meetings, occasionally held in a shady alcove outside the White House. Wright had been to the White House a number of times, but never had he held such routine one-on-one access to the world's most powerful man. Of course, his opinion of the new president soared.[20]

Most congressmen, of course, relied on Carter's congressional liaison, Frank Moore. Moore, unfortunately, struck many of Wright's colleagues as uncommunicative. Moreover, Carter had brought his Georgia team with him, and none of them held much experience in the nation's capital. When they appeared dismissive of experienced congressional staff, resentment grew. Even Wright's aide Raupe agreed. "I gave Carter credit for being new, and for the people being new," Raupe remarked a year after Carter assumed office. "Now I just think they're just fuck-ups."[21]

None of this made Wright's new job easier. The majority leader's task was to work with the Speaker to define a legislative agenda capable of passing Congress and being signed by the president. This meant, Wright later explained, that he had to work with "diverse constituencies" both to form and enforce policy. He had to master legislative rules. Although he was loyal to the Speaker, he still had to be "a mediator and a peacemaker." He could not, he knew, "afford the luxury of vendettas or internecine feuds."[22]

But the feuds were particularly difficult to avoid. Wright had largely learned to contain his quick temper. It had been so obvious when he was younger, but it could still explode with higher stakes and greater pressure. "I've seen him [angry] more at the office," Betty told a reporter in 1986, "so by the time he gets home he's usually in a pretty good humor." His aide

Marshall Lynam concurred. "I've seen him angry and fifteen minutes later he literally cannot remember it," Lynam explained." Wright's trigger points were "carelessness, incompetence, or giving a job less than your best."[23] Another aide, Larry L. King, recalled that Wright occasionally cussed him out and once threw a book across the room. Within minutes, however, Wright apologized. Wright would quietly "fret until a molehill became a mountain," and then he would briefly erupt and the pressure would dissipate.[24]

Showing such temper on the floor of Congress was rare for Wright, but it occurred. Once after the liberal Californian Pete Stark called Wright a "cocksucker," colleagues had to constrain both men. Wright, the old Golden Gloves boxer, invited Stark outside. "I remember thinking I'm about to be hit in the face and I think it's going to hurt a lot," Stark later recalled. On another occasion, Wright, angry but grinning, threatened to punch a junior Republican who had accused him of being unfair. "I'm smiling because if I wasn't I'd punch you in the nose," Wright stated. The obvious intensity— the kettle threatening to boil—undoubtedly helped Wright to a degree in maintaining party discipline, although it hardly matched Wright's perception of his job. "You get the sense you wouldn't want to cross him," Ford's former chief of staff Dick Cheney observed.[25]

If the job of Majority Leader meant that Wright needed to control his temper and avoid feuds, he was not above the hard-boiled politics of which both were a part. His first order of business as majority leader was the selection of the whips. Asked who he thought might serve as chief deputy whip, Wright did not commit, but verbally he slapped his former caucus opponent Phillip Burton. The job, Wright stated, should go to someone "who will work in tandem with the speaker and the majority leader." Asked if that meant he had eliminated Burton, Wright simply smiled.[26] The resentful Burton, Wright understood, was already plotting his revenge.[27] Wright's ultimate choice for the job, Dan Rostenkowski, made sense. It was a reward for his assistance and an assurance of future loyalty. For the next in line, the majority whip, Wright agreed with O'Neill that the job should go to Indiana's John Brademas, a liberal who might placate the supporters of Burton and Bolling.[28]

The tenuous relationships within the Democratic leadership, and between Capitol Hill and Carter, played out in the early weeks of 1977. Invited to speak to the annual Washington Prayer Breakfast, Wright translated a passage from the Apostle Paul's Letter to the Philippians with the term "y'all." Paul, Wright joked, turning to Carter, "apparently came from our part of the country." Carter laughed. "May we resolve that we shall learn together," Wright continued. Afterward, Carter approached him. "Jim,"

Making the pill a bit easier to swallow for Wright was Carter's first specific proposal, a cabinet-level Department of Energy. With the Democratic leadership in agreement, Congress passed the Department of Energy Organization Act of 1977 relatively quickly.[51] The unanimity was, however, just an illusion. Carter's other reorganization plans promised a complete reshuffling of committee jurisdictions—and, in many cases, would diminish congressional power. When Carter began to propose a Department of Education, Wright understood that the reorganization proposals would linger legislatively for some time.[52]

Wright had proved himself a reliable White House ally, however, and he anticipated that Carter's broader economic agenda would match his own. Carter also worried about the federal deficit, and Wright assumed he recognized that stimulating the economy and attacking unemployment was the best strategy. Wright believed that both the massive spending and tax cuts that some Republicans suggested and the equally massive federal assistance that some liberals advocated would invariably add to the debt. Carter and Wright appeared to be on the same page, and, as Wright wrote one constituent, "I am anxious to cooperate with him."[53]

Of course, the devil was in the details. The key was finding the right balance of spending and taxes, never an easy task. One man's stimulus, of course, was another's pork barrel. At the outset, Carter proposed small tax reductions, a jobs program, increased spending for public works, and a one-time fifty-dollar tax rebate. While Wright publicly applauded the package, he once again had to lobby his flock diligently. In the end, Congress agreed, although it forced Carter to drop the rebate and crafted a compromise on an increase in the minimum wage. There was a "serious debate over budget priorities," Wright said in an understatement, once again lauding the compromise that made the bill possible.[54]

Surprisingly, Carter did not appear to appreciate the helpful role Wright had played. The Democratic leadership, Carter recalled of one early economic meeting, had "stricken expressions" when he proposed balancing the budget—"even Jim Wright." It was "anathema to them to be talking about balancing the budget."[55] Carter's recollections were understandable, if a bit unfair to Wright. During the debate, Wright had supported many of the cuts Carter had proposed, but he had also—predictably—protected his own interests. When his constituents pressed him for additional Department of Agriculture funds, Wright won the allocations.[56] As deficit hawks began to question defense spending, including spending for the B-1 bomber, Wright insisted that a better alternative was another experimental aircraft under development in Fort Worth, the FB-111.[57]

Most notably, Wright believed that Carter's proposal to increase public works was insufficient to stimulate the economy.[58] Employing his newfound power once again—this time against the White House—Wright helped Congress pass additional appropriations. When Carter spoke of the additions as classic congressional pork barrel, he struck at both Wright's own career and Congress's image. Wright was furious. As Carter's liaison, Frank Moore, wrote, "Wright takes this confrontation very personally and can get emotional." Wright believed that the White House "was getting some very bad advice from some young kids who are no growth environmentalists."[59] In fact, Wright admired what Carter was doing in the aggregate, just not in the specifics. When Carter vetoed the bill, Wright lobbied for an override, just as he had done with Eisenhower and Ford. "I come to this moment sadly," Wright stated.[60] It was, according to columnist Carl Rowan, "a costly fuss for Carter."[61] It also did Wright little favor, solidifying his reputation among conservatives as a captain of pork barrel even as it strained his relationship with a president he still admired.[62]

Both men wanted to quickly put the episode behind them, and Wright returned to his father's advice to let bygones be bygones. Quoting from the play *Camelot* and writing in longhand, Wright told Carter, "At least we are dealing in water and money and not in blood." Implying that he, too, was concerned about the debt, Wright professed to "understand the necessity which requires you to take the position that you do." Carter replied in kind and also in longhand, citing scripture. "To my friend," Carter wrote, "at least we understand one another."[63]

Nothing indicated that such disputes would pass as much as Wright's unbridled support for Carter's foreign policy. Here as nowhere else the two leaders shared the same outlook. If Carter was the "moralist," as historian Kenneth Morris believed, his moralism was embedded in an idealism that matched Wright's own. Nowhere was this more apparent than in Latin America, a special area of interest for Wright. When Carter reinvigorated efforts to negotiate the future of the Panama Canal, dispatching two emissaries, Ellsworth Bunker and Sol Linowitz, Wright understood the courage of conviction it took.[64]

Ruling Panama was General Omar Torrijos, who had seized power in a coup and installed Demetrio "Jimmy" Lakas as president. Torrijos had promised to have free elections once a new treaty was in force, but he remained an easy target for conservatives, who feared looking weak, and Republicans, who sought to paint Carter as exactly that. In the words of one columnist, Torrijos was a "morally decrepit leader."[65] Wright had known Torrijos for two decades working on the Inter-American Highway and believed him to be a nationalist with his country's best interest in mind. In fact, while Torrijos was no radical demagogue and assumed a good relationship with the United States to be essential, neither was he any true democrat. He enjoyed holding power, occasionally abused it, and arguably suffered from alcoholism.[66] Championing the treaty was risky, for both Carter and Wright. Polls showed that the majority of the members of Congress objected, and letters flooded into Wright's office. "There is no logic in surrendering our possessions to the enemy," wrote one constituent, promising to campaign against Wright's reelection.[67] Reflecting on the entire debate years later, Wright agreed that Carter's stance had contributed both to his loss in 1980 and to the growth of conservatism throughout the South. It was, however, still the right thing to do.[68] For his part, Carter appreciated Wright's help, thanking him "for your efforts to increase public awareness about the Panama Canal Treaty."[69]

Throughout 1977 Wright kept in close contact with Bunker and Linowitz, as well as with Torrijos. When Venezuela's president, Carlos Andrés Pérez, visited Washington, Wright stressed that Latin Americans viewed the Panama Canal Zone as "a colonial enclave."[70] When the Joint Chiefs of Staff essentially agreed, Wright circulated their conclusions. "If you have sincere reservations, please keep an open mind," Wright advised his fellow legislators.[71] When the iconic actor John Wayne declared negotiations in the "legitimate fundamental interests of our country," Wright knew that his support would help win over conservatives.[72]

The final treaty that Carter signed in the fall of 1977 provided for joint operation of the canal until the end of the millennium, when Panama would assume control. Guaranteeing free passage to all nations' ships, it provided for American intervention to protect such passage. As debate over ratification began, however, Torrijos implied that angry Panamanians might destroy the canal if ratification failed. Wright dashed off a letter to President Lakas asking for clarification, and, after speaking with Torrijos, concluded that the comments were an ill-advised effort to exert Panama's own pressure.[73] As Wright continued to lobby, an apologetic Torrijos praised the "coordination that we have begun to establish" and described Wright as a "good friend."[74]

Finally, in the spring of 1978, the Senate ratified the treaty. The following year, both chambers debated the specifics of the transfer, technically a last-ditch chance for opponents to stop the treaty. After Wright spoke eloquently for passage, Michigan's Carl Levin declared the bill's final success "a tribute to [Wright's] leadership."[75] Secretary of State Zbigniew Brzezinski agreed, calling Wright's statement "superb."[76] Wright had done a "masterful" job, according to David Jones, chairman of the Joint Chiefs.[77] Back home, of course, not everyone agreed. The Texas Republican Party even called for repeal. "I'm considering shifting to the GOP," complained one Fort Worth conservative.[78] Wright had real reason for pride, although Carter inexplicably failed to acknowledge Wright's key role in his own memoirs. Wright had acted in this instance on his idealism, not on political calculation. In the end, Torrijos did indeed liberalize his policies, and, until his death in 1981, he always insisted that he would, as promised, step down in 1984. Torrijos may not have been the man Wright believed him to be, but for years Panama remained an ally with the canal open and secure.[79]

If Wright took pride in the Panama Canal Treaty, he played a greater role in the famous Camp David Accords. He understood that peace between Israel and Egypt would not come easily. When, in early 1977, he described Israel as "an oasis of reason surrounded by a desert of hostility," the Syrian ambassador complained. Trying to walk back his comments, Wright remarked that perhaps his speech "painted a somewhat starker picture that I would have liked."[80] Wright applauded Carter's promises of human rights and equity in international relationships, but obviously understood that diplomacy was never easy.

For several years, the Speaker had allowed the majority leader to select a delegation to travel abroad to areas of international concern. Wright immediately scheduled a bipartisan trip of fifteen members of Congress, together with their wives, to Israel and Egypt. As Wright and his staff began making preparations, their hopes for the trip skyrocketed when Egypt's Muhammad Anwar el-Sadat stated that he was willing to go to the ends of the earth, "even to Jerusalem," if it might accomplish a lasting peace. The idea of an Arab leader going to the capital of a nation he did not recognize—a disputed city in itself—seemed farfetched even as it heightened interest in Wright's delegation.[81]

Just after the 95th Congress adjourned for Christmas, Wright and his colleagues departed on an air force plane for Cairo. On November 15, Sadat greeted the group at the Barrages, his presidential retreat several miles up the Nile River. When Sadat described Carter as a "man of the book," Wright recognized that Carter's oft-spoken professions of faith were critical. At the press conference that followed, Wright, having made sure in advance that his question was acceptable, inquired about Sadat's desire to go to Israel.[82] Sadat replied that he was willing to go "without any precon-ditions" and would like to address Israel's parliament, the Knesset. Asked about Palestinian land claims, Sadat suggested a "Palestinian settlement in confederation with Jordan," a position at odds with the views of many Arab leaders but not automatically rejected by Israel. "But I am an Arab," Sadat continued. "It is we who are threatened." Wright immediately inter-jected, suggesting that it was "time to sit down calmly together and try to understand, and thus assuage, one another's apprehensions." Sadat agreed, adding that he never worried about his own security, a profound claim, given his assassination several years later. For his part, Wright saw a man whose fearlessness grew from his own deep personal faith. In that way, Sadat was much like Carter. Wright recognized that it would be difficult for Israel to object.[83]

What happened next, Wright recalled, took place "with lightning-like swiftness." By the time Wright's delegation landed in Tel Aviv two days later as planned, Israel had made its invitation, and its leader, Menachem Begin, had announced that Sadat would arrive the following day. With his delega-tion staying at the King David Hotel, the same hotel as Sadat, Wright tele-phoned Begin to let him know that the Americans would depart in time for Sadat's arrival. "I want you present in the Knesset," Begin objected, surpris-ing Wright. The presence of the international community would make it difficult for hardliners on both sides to block an accord. Wright then knew that Begin, like Sadat, hoped for true peace.[84]

"Jerusalem was alive with anticipation," Wright recalled. "I saw Israeli soldiers hugging Arab girls." Security was tight at the flag-draped hotel. A full honor guard greeted the Egyptian leader and even Begin got caught up in the events, suggesting that he would like to "see the Pyramids" in a recip-rocal trip to Egypt. "After all, we helped build them." When the time for Sadat's speech arrived, Wright had his front-row seat to history, earbuds in place for the English translation. Sadat made an appeal for the "legitimate rights of the Palestinian people" but spoke of getting past the "prejudices of the Crusades." Both sides should respect the "spirit of tolerance."[85]

Upon returning to Washington, Wright debriefed Carter, helping to launch more intensive diplomacy that continued into 1978. In one Israeli visit to Washington, Carter called on Wright for a toast. "To Ishmael and Isaac, who were brothers, and to their children's children, may they have peace," Wright stated, his glass aloft. Welcoming an Egyptian delegation, Wright spoke of a "country whose civilization has lasted ten times as long as the recorded history of the American continent." As he took part in the negotiations, he clearly knew how to put his well-honed congressional col-legiality to good use.[86]

"Israel has substantial military investments in the Sinai" that would prove expensive to remove, Carter informed Wright and his colleagues. Moreover, Egypt was pressing for American grants and loans. Given all the issues, including mutual security, settlement, and access to the Suez Canal, Congress should be ready to appropriate over $1 billion. Wright, it appeared, had a new cause for lobbying.[87]

The press noted Wright's role, which resonated back in Texas. Although one Fort Worth man wrote that American interests "require leaning on Israel," Wright knew that many southern conservatives worried that the United States was abandoning its traditional support for the Jewish state.[88] In May, when it became public that Carter was considering selling arms to Saudi Arabia, a group of conservatives released a statement implying that the Democratic leadership thought the sale "an act of retreat."[89] It was left to Wright to deny the statement and ensure the impartiality Carter needed to succeed.

"The talks have become virtually stalemated," Wright reported in late summer, when Carter announced that both Begin and Sadat would meet with him in his presidential retreat at Camp David, Maryland. The announce-ment, Wright declared, renewed "the hopes of the civilized world."[90] Carter, Wright insisted, deserved considerable praise. A week before Sadat and Begin arrived, Wright released "An Open Letter to Friends" in his regular newsletter. Addressing both Begin and Sadat as though the letter were to them, Wright recounted the remaining obstacles and urged compromise, ending with his old Ishmael and Isaac toast.[91]

When the Camp David negotiations commenced on September 5, Wright waited like the rest of America. Appearing on the television news show *Face the Nation*, he remarked that the United States should play no enforcement role and denied that more pressure was being put on Israel than Egypt. "I think there's leaning on both sides," he answered diplomati-cally. The results, less than two weeks later, could not have pleased Wright more. Technically there were two agreements. The first called for a tempo-rary, semiautonomous authority in the occupied West Bank and Gaza Strip that would lead within five years to Palestinian self-governance. The second called for the return of the Sinai to Egypt in exchange for the Arab state's recognition of Israel.[92] After the official treaty confirming this second agree-ment was signed in March of the following year, Wright once again had reason for pride. Carter, Wright correctly noted, "deserved all the credit he could get." At the same time, however, Wright, too, had been part of a major historic event, an event that once again confirmed his idealism and faith in diplomacy.[93]

Jim Wright, in fact, was quite proud of the entire 95th Congress, his first as majority leader. As early as May 1977, he had praised his colleagues for their "congressional productivity." At the end of the first session in late 1978, Wright described the record as "a long one" worthy of "justifiable pride." O'Neill agreed, telling Wright that he was "impressed with our achievements." In some ways, such self-laudatory comments were understandable, if for no other reason than to build political momentum. When, however, Wright spoke of the 95th Congress as "paralleled only by the first year of Franklin D. Roosevelt's Administration," he had clearly crossed into hyperbole.[94] In most respects the historic events were in foreign policy, where legislators shared credit with the president, at best. There were still unresolved problems brewing: the economy, for one, still struggled. It was, no doubt, a productive Congress, just not the historic one Wright portrayed.

Wright, of course, had his hand in everything. From January 1977 until October 1978, he spoke on the floor of Congress 198 times, solidifying his reputation as a rhetorical master.[95] "We desperately need Jim Wright," Vice President Walter Mondale wrote Carter in 1977.[96] Wright, for example, played a key role in the passage of the Foreign Intelligence Surveillance Act of 1978, which is hardly surprising, given that it strengthened congressional oversight of data collection and created the House Permanent Select Committee on Intelligence. As Wright lobbied, Carter heard the pleas. "Congress can and should share oversight," he conceded.[97] "Without your help," Attorney General Griffin Bell wrote Wright, "we could not have been assured that this landmark piece of legislation would have become a reality."[98] Only later did the public learn that the secret Foreign Intelligence Surveillance Court, created by the bill to approve warrants, had failed to protect civil liberties. With virtually every government request approved, the court may have protected against terrorism, its critics claimed, but it was also a rubber stamp for abuses.[99]

The Surface Mining Control and Reclamation Act of 1977 was exactly the type of compromise Wright welcomed, although to many environmentalists it fell short of what was necessary. Carter appeared to be open-minded about the issue, asking his adviser Stuart Eizenstat to "explain to me the surface mining criticism," and Wright wanted to avoid the vetoes that had followed similar bills during the Nixon and Ford years.[100] The final result granted the Department of the Interior regulatory authority but still allowed the coal industry considerable influence in drafting the specific requirements. By the end of 1979, the secretary of the interior, Cecil Andrus, was writing to Wright requesting help in maintaining stringent rules. Wright worked for compromise, but Carter's Republican successor, Ronald Reagan, emasculated the program.[101]

The surface mining bill did little to help Wright's reputation with environmentalists. When the Environmental Protection Agency released its new air quality standards, Wright thought them excessive and spoke of their "serious scientific flaws." Under pressure from the Texas Utilities Commission, he argued that environmentalists were abusing the impact statement requirement of the National Environmental Policy Act.[102] He supported the Clean Water Act Amendments of 1977, which encouraged "best management practices" and stronger wetlands protection, but then introduced exemptions for farming and complained that the permitting process jeopardized the rights of states. When a Carter aide stressed environmentalism, Wright complained to Carter that the comments were "ill-advised" and "typifies the problems we face."[103] Environmentalists had won major advances over the previous decade and perhaps failed to appreciate the inevitable backlash fueled by the energy crisis. Wright recognized that the political culture had changed and, true to form, sought compromise. He still thought of himself as an environmentalist, and it was frustrating to him when critics called him "deeply biased" or grumbled that he had not joined the Environmental Study Conference.[104]

Laud the successes of the 95th Congress as he might, Wright could not ignore that beneath his strong record, the power of conservatives lay ready to explode. The Carter era, historian Melvyn Dubofsky concluded, was a "parenthetical" period, a "pregnant pause between the halcyon years of postwar productivity and the Reagan-Bush years of supply-side economics, neoliberal politics, and unregulated markets."[105] As Wright touted his successes, the labor law reform the unions demanded died on the vine. Sensing that growing numbers of Texans saw union leaders as "racketeers and muscle men," as one constituent put it, Wright was left to downplay his support for the bill, suggesting that it would "not make any significant difference." Still the conservatives attacked him. Wright should be "ashamed," one critic wrote.[106] Moreover, when New York City needed additional loan guarantees, Wright found the struggle to obtain them surprisingly difficult despite the success of the earlier loan. In the summer of 1977, the news highlighted the massive electricity blackout in New York City and the infamous "Son of

Sam" serial murders, but New York was also an easy target for critics of government spending. The city had "tightened its belt," Wright insisted, and made "impressive" cuts in spending. While Wright's plea once again helped carry the day, the angry reaction from home surpassed that which had taken place three years before. If Wright continued to take such stances, one Texan penned, it was time "to switch to the Republican Party."[107]

When Republicans helped pass the Airline Deregulation Act of 1978, Wright had a particular problem. He was not against deregulation per se, was still anxious to eliminate government inefficiencies, and in general welcomed loosened restrictions on fares, routes, and market entry for new competitors. The problem, however, was Southwest Airlines, which still operated from Dallas's Love Field. When Southwest gave notice that it planned broader interstate routes, the DFW Airport and the Fort Worth government recognized a threat and appealed to Wright. Wright, always the champion of his hometown, noted that the legislation stressed deregulation "where consistent with the regional airport plans of regional and local authorities." Southwest's application, he argued, violated an understanding between the two competitive cities.[108] Employing his full arsenal of persuasion yet again, Wright pressed the issue into the next Congress, ultimately getting new legislation passed that carried his name. The "Wright Amendment" stipulated that all large and midsized passenger service from Love Field could only fly to states contiguous to Texas. It was a blatant demonstration of congressional power, but it had its effect. Southwest proved no competition to the growing dominance of DFW even as, in the long run, conservatives began to cite the entire episode as an example of bureaucratic cronyism. Eventually, as the South turned ever more conservative, Republicans took up the cause as a threat to free markets. Almost thirty years later, in 2014, an agreement finally settled the matter by repealing the Wright Amendment.[109]

Wright recognized the conservatives' growing power but knew his constant defense of his district provided him strong immunity. He met, for example, with Fort Worth citizens to discuss the expansion of Interstate 30 through the city. "Fort Worth would be a great choice for a location," he told potential employers, often citing the city's proximity to DFW and thus hitting two birds with one stone.[110] Along with the growing conservative criticism continued to come the praise. "Even when Jim's vote rankles," one observer wrote, "Texas gains."[111]

Wright lobbied successfully to have Carter visit Fort Worth, telling the president that the newspapers had given "positive assurances . . . for total cooperation."[112] With 5,000 people greeting the president at the Tarrant

County Convention Center, Wright once again noted Carter's "courage" in pressing what mattered and not what was politically expedient. Carter reciprocated, describing Wright as a "man of judgment and sensitivity who has a knowledge of our country that above all represents the epitome of what is the spirit of Texas."[113] After the visit, Wright's reviews were positive.[114] Carter's, however, were not. Carter, implied the chairman of the Texas State Democratic Party, Calvin Guest, was only "fence-mending" with conservatives. Nationally, Guest predicted, Republicans looked strong. The coming November congressional elections might not prove a Democratic year.[115]

With the elections looming, Wright and many of his colleagues on both sides of the aisle supported the Full Employment and Balanced Growth Act of 1978. As much politics as policy, the legislation set targets for employment and called on the president to expand the public sector if the targets were not met. At the same time, however, the bill endorsed a balanced budget and called on the Federal Reserve to guard against inflation. Other than requiring the president to issue economic goals and to report periodically on the progress, and also for the Federal Reserve to make similar reports, the vagueness and apparent contradictions in the bill ensured that its only immediate impact was in protecting incumbents from charges of economic impotence. In the words of one economist, it was the "triumph of heart over mind."[116] Wright told the media that the bill would please the "most conservative constituency in this country." In fact, with something for everybody, the bill arguably did little.[117]

Wright and his fellow Democrats felt uneasy. The Republicans were campaigning hard and the Conservative Coalition, an alliance of Republicans and southern conservative Democrats, reported an increase in voting strength.[118] Wright faced no real opposition to his congressional seat, so he could freely tout the productivity of the 95th Congress. He could praise the presidential incumbent. Privately, he indeed had reason for pride in his own accomplishments. The success of his first term as minority leader was impressive, if not as historic as he sometimes claimed. Still, however, the economy remained stagnant, and the public was becoming restless and discontented, a "malaise," as Carter would term it the following year. Wright could fairly tout the past, but he knew that he had to keep his eye on the future—like any good leader. The past, after all, was only prelude.

———

CHAPTER 14

The Struggle for Unity

THE CARTER YEARS (1978–1980)

No one prepared harder for the 1978 congressional elections than Jim Wright. As the year began, the press suggested that Phillip Burton, still seething from his loss to Wright, might try to unseat the majority leader. "The return of Phil Burton?" asked one columnist. Burton was coy. Asked if he planned another challenge, Burton replied that he was "headed in that direction."[1] Soon Wright allies reported that Burton emissaries were canvassing members. Wright, of course, was having none of it and launched an aggressive campaign of fundraising and favors.[2]

Wright's fundraising, reported the *Dallas Morning News* early in the year, appeared to be more "formal and ambitious" than in his previous campaigns.[3] First was a $1,000 per plate fundraiser at Washington's Madison Hotel that promised $300,000 for the Wright Majority Congress Committee. Wright would spread the money around, the *Houston Post* added, which "won't hurt his own effort to get himself reelected majority leader" when the Democratic caucus met in December.[4]

When the day arrived, the glare was bright. Wright arrived "with a retinue of people who always seem to follow people in power," read one report. He appeared "a little embarrassed to find his fans lined up at the stairs."

Wright was the star, the "fund-raising dean," with his dinner the "Super Bowl of fund-raising."[5] In a more critical assessment, the dinner was a "lobbyist delight." To Common Cause Wright was hypocritical, raising unprecedented cash even as he denounced its influence. There was no choice, a prickly Wright replied. "There is nothing either new or cynical in this activity," he said, citing the Republicans, and he had nothing "for which to apologize."[6]

The dinner was only the beginning. Wright organized campaign seminars for colleagues, invited pollsters to speak with the Democratic caucus, and warned constantly of a rightward shift. When pollster Louis Harris noted that organized labor was in "the public's dog house" and that cynicism about government was rampant, Wright claimed that Harris had "put his finger on the problem."[7] Wright frequently dispensed advice, suggesting the party create block captains and "town hall style" meetings. Candidates should be collegial, Wright said, but the foreboding outlook demanded "low-cost, hard-hitting campaign radio spots."[8]

Given all this, perhaps Burton's ultimate decision not to challenge Wright was smart politically. As Burton faded, however, Bedford engineer Claude Brown announced for the Republican nomination in Wright's district. Wright, Brown declared, was a "big spender" who had forgotten about people back home.[9] The latter charge, of course, was ludicrous to Fort Worth's voters, and Wright recognized that Brown was no James Garvey, whom he had vanquished four years before. A group of farmers organized as the American Agriculture Movement promised to "take a hit at Jim Wright," because they were frustrated by Wright's efforts to find a compromise on a farm bill that Carter would not veto as inflationary.[10] Most farmers, however, understood that Wright had gotten them as much aid as possible. In the words of one Wright supporter, such opposition "would never be able to make a very big dent in the tremendous vote Jim always racks up."[11]

Not greatly concerned about his own reelection, Wright made over one hundred appearances for fellow Democrats. From Florida to California, he was always an attraction.[12] As thanks poured in, Wright took a special interest in candidate Martin Frost, a Dallas attorney and family friend. Frost was "bright, articulate and personable," Wright explained to one supporter while promising Frost to keep "in touch" and mentor the young man.[13] When Frost won, beginning a congressional career that lasted a quarter of a century, Wright had the loyal acolyte he obviously had wanted. Wright arranged for him to serve on the powerful Rules Committee, providing a tutorial for Frost in the way Congress actually worked.[14]

Wright needed lieutenants like Frost. Texas Democrats voted along party lines only 51 percent of the time. Recognizing the dissatisfaction of southern conservatives, Republican Jesse Helms, running for the Senate in North Carolina, proposed an alliance with southern conservative Democrats. "Isn't this incredible?" laughed one Wright aide.[15] It was no joke to Carter, who worried about the Democratic coalition fracturing, or, at the very least, failing to turn out in November. "I am deeply concerned," he wrote congressional leaders.[16]

Perhaps it was in light of this common wisdom that, on the surface at least, the actual results in November 1978 did not seem that bad to most Democrats. The Republicans gained only fifteen seats in the House and three in the Senate. When they viewed the situation more closely, however, Democrats recognized worrisome trends. Key Republican gains were in the South. One of the two new Texas Republicans was Ron Paul, who later became a presidential candidate. Other victors included future vice-president Dick Cheney from Wyoming and, from Georgia, a former college professor who would prove a thorn in Wright's side, Newt Gingrich.[17] Noting that regardless of party affiliation the number of self-described conservatives had grown by more than seventy-five, one periodical was blunt: "Congress Turns Rightward."[18] Outside of Congress, Republicans gained six governorships and picked up seats in state legislatures from New England to the Mountain West. Texans elected their first Republican governor since Reconstruction, William Clements. Clements immediately began working with Senator John Tower, who had easily won reelection, to build a new Republican state machinery.[19] National polls suggested that a massive tax-cut plan advocated by New York Republican Jack Kemp was popular; meanwhile, California had just enacted Proposition 13, slicing property taxes. Many Americans sensed that a tax revolt was imminent.[20]

Wright put the best spin on the election. He had almost tripled Brown's vote, and he easily maintained his leadership position. "I've tried it with opposition and without, and I prefer it without," Wright joked.[21] When the Texas press predicted that Wright would follow the well-worn path from majority leader to Speaker—becoming the "next Sam Rayburn"—Wright dismissed the speculation even as he obviously enjoyed it. In fact, just after the election, Wright visited Bonham, Texas, the late Speaker's hometown, hardly the move of a man trying to dismiss such talk.[22] In his acceptance speech as majority leader, Wright reiterated the successes of the 95th Congress and alluded to conservative dissatisfaction. The caucus, he acknowledged, faced steep "challenges."[23] In more reflective moments he bemoaned the "vulcanization" of America, the loss of common purpose. He would do his best, he promised, to address this fundamental flaw.[24]

First, however, there was the matter of Michigan's Charles Diggs—just what the Congress did not need. An early African American civil rights activist convicted of mail and tax fraud, Diggs had won reelection while awaiting sentencing. Diggs was appealing the case, and much of the public was clamoring for his expulsion. Wright agreed with O'Neill that the Democratic caucus would discuss the matter in a closed session where members would be "free to speak with utter candor."[25] Emerging from the meeting, Wright told the press that expelling Diggs before the final legal resolution would be to deny his constituents their own choice for representation. "Membership is not ours to bestow," Wright stated, a conclusion that conservative columnist George Will mocked as the "Wright Doctrine."[26] "I expect I'll face criticism in my district," Wright correctly predicted.[27] Indeed, the letters were personal and harsh, reflecting the growth of partisanship in Congress. "I remember in about 1970 you being on TV and picking your nose," one Texan wrote Wright. "President Nixon was a saint compared to you and 99% of the democrates [sic]."[28]

As Wright stuck to the letter of the rules, the newly elected Gingrich jumped at the chance to denounce the twelve-term Diggs as the exemplar of entrenched Democratic corruption. To Wright, televised congressional sessions were good open government; to Gingrich, they were opportunities for publicity. Cable television's C-SPAN began its operations in March 1979, and Gingrich quickly appreciated the significance of the new cameras. "My hat is off to the courageous congressman from Georgia," wrote one Diggs critic, suggesting that he had seen Gingrich on television and was switching from the Democratic Party to the Republican.[29]

"How could Gingrich simply call for Diggs's removal without formal consideration?" Wright mused in his diary. "Perhaps there is forgivable innocence in a first-term member's simplistic view."[30] In time Wright would learn that it was not Gingrich's perceptions that were simplistic but his own. Gingrich, Wright soon concluded, had an ambition to match his but fewer political scruples. According to Wright, Gingrich crowed to him on the House floor, "One day I'm going to be as good as you are."[31] True or not, the Democratic leadership maintained their judicious approach while Gingrich increasingly provided the media with the sensationalist quotes they sought. In the end, Diggs resigned and Gingrich appeared the champion of good government, not Wright.[32]

"The [*Washington*] *Post*," Wright seethed in his diary, was "loath to tell anything ever that Congress does constructively." The headlines were "always the usual petty, frothy and inconsequential drivel."[33] Presenting Congress as an "antagonistic and partisan competition," Wright lamented publicly, fed "the very forces which would destroy us both." President Carter agreed, adding, "God Bless You!"[34] For his colleagues Wright advised accountability. They should simply work hard and ignore the press's sensationalized accusations and headlines.[35]

As if to mock Wright's advice, the FBI had just begun a sting operation to uncover political corruption, the infamous "Abscam Scandal" that by 1980 would result in the conviction of one senator and six congressmen—all Democrats. The Department of Justice, moreover, refused to cooperate with the House Ethics Committee out of fear of compromising the agency's operations. Always sensitive to slights against the institution he loved, Wright felt like Congress was under assault.[36]

Suddenly, just weeks after the 1978 elections, the "Jonestown" tragedy put it all—his new position, the partisan politics, and the muckraking media—into perspective. Investigating reports of abuses at a separatist religious compound in Guyana led by former Californian Jim Jones, Congressman Leo Ryan led a group to South America. There Jones's followers killed Ryan and his entourage before committing mass suicide. The "Jonestown" tragedy dominated the news for several weeks and hit Wright hard. Wright had just campaigned for Ryan's reelection. Wright praised Ryan, stating that even as Americans were "impatient" with their government's "obvious imperfections," they should remember that government service was noble—and even dangerous.[37] At Ryan's San Francisco funeral, Wright eulogized his friend as a compassionate man who had made sacrifices for the important work of Congress.[38]

The tragic events reminded him once again of his own mortality. While the position of majority leader increased his salary by $12,000, to just over $52,000, and allowed an office budget of almost $300,000 and an expanded staff of fifteen, Wright remained a man of almost sixty with little financial security.[39] If he should die like Ryan, his family would suffer. Fortunately, Wright assumed, his friend George Mallick had a viable solution, hiring Betty with a salary of $18,000. Betty's job was to assist Mallick in his many real estate investments, none of which apparently involved Congress. Mallick had no political axe to grind and just enjoyed the association with power and the prestige it brought. Wright saw no legislative conflict of interest, just a friend who had never asked for any favor. Moreover, when Mallick offered Betty a free apartment as part of her employment, Wright again saw no cause for concern. Mallick supplied all his employees free housing, which provided him tax advantages explicitly approved by the IRS. Wright had no need for the Fort Worth abode and, in the end, stayed there only a few days per month.[40]

Failing to see the arrangement as a potential violation of congressional ethics, or, at least, a potential club that political opponents might use—an oversight Wright would come to regret—Wright and Mallick formed their own investment company, Mallightco. While Wright's contribution from stock represented a considerable portion of his estate, Mallick's share was nominal to his own estate—the investment was valuable simply through the association it created with Wright. In fact, the company prospered, quickly doubling its assets and providing Wright with the security he desperately needed. Surprisingly, he continued to overlook the potential for ethical charges in the new world of sensationalized partisanship.[41]

Better still—or worse still, from a different perspective—was Wright's decision to invest in several wells owned by the legendary Fort Worth oil-man W. A. "Monty" Moncrief. Unlike Mallick, the multimillionaire had a vested interest in federal policy and a willingness to make his views known. His other investors included prominent friends such as Bob Hope and Bing Crosby. Moncrief had never met Wright and made Mallick appear small time. He did not need Wright's money but clearly wanted his ear. Confident that he would never be swayed to act against his better judgment, and aware of many similar arrangements among his colleagues, Wright borrowed $50,000 for the purchase. It proved another wise investment, in strictly financial terms. Within five years the wells had returned between $70,000 and $222,500, according to Wright's own reports.[42] Wright now had the wealth that he thought Betty and the children deserved.

Of course, the payback did not take long to rear its head. Moncrief had helped Israel drill its first commercial oil well off the Sinai coast only to have the Camp David Accords promise the land back to Egypt. With his $100 million Sinai investment in doubt, Moncrief turned to Wright. Recognizing no harm to the United States, and, in his view, simply helping a constituent, Wright wrote Secretary of State Cyrus Vance warning of a "financial injustice . . . upon two U.S. firms which discovered the Alma Field in the Suez Gulf."[43] When Vance refused to move, Wright turned to Carter, but still he gained little traction. At last, with Sadat in Washington, Wright pressed into the Egyptian leader's hand a letter pleading Moncrief's case. "Egypt could benefit greatly over the next three years," Wright's letter read, "if your government will encourage your oil concessionaire . . . to cooperate with [Moncrief's company], which has discovered and developed the Alma Field."[44] Sadat proved no more open to Wright's pleas than Vance or Carter, thus costing Moncrief his investment.[45] It was, arguably, not Wright's best moment.

It was also not unique. Six months after pressing Moncrief's case directly with Sadat, Wright lobbied the secretary of the interior, Cecil Andrus, on behalf of the Texas Oil and Gas Corporation, a separate company, unrelated to Moncrief, fighting for leases on federal property. Wright wrote to "acquaint" Andrus with the firm and make the case against a competing company. Stating that it was important to "set forth the facts," Wright conspicuously left out one such fact: five months earlier, he had purchased over $15,000 of the company's stock. Once again Wright saw his efforts as benefiting the nation by expanding production and combating the ongoing energy crisis. In fact, Texas senator Lloyd Bentsen and Wright's own political acolyte, Martin Frost, had also lobbied Andrus. Wright rationalized his actions regarding both Moncrief and the Texas Oil and Gas Corporation as simply representing supporters, just as he had since his earliest days on the Public Works Committee. His own investments were immaterial if it was the right thing to do.[46] Wright was confident—but he should not have been. He was now walking a fine line that his critics would cast in a different light.

Certainly Wright welcomed the sudden wealth. Betty joined the governing boards of both the National Theatre and Ford's Theatre while Wright picked up his golf game. Tip O'Neill loved golf, Wright knew, and hitting the links was clearly was an avenue for expanding connections. Wright began inviting many Republicans to play with him and, later in his career, helped organize a formal congressional golf retreat. But Wright was still swimming against the tides of partisanship and rancor, the very seas in which his own actions would, in the end, drown him.[47]

Across a different sea, isolated protests against the government of the Iranian shah, Mohammad Reza Pahlavi, had grown into a full-scale revolution, just as the Organization of the Petroleum Exporting Countries (OPEC) announced a massive price increase. As the new Congress convened in January 1979, Wright found Carter's lack of action frustrating. "The issue turns men to cowards," Wright told the press.[48] In his diary Wright was more explicit: "I am reluctantly concluding that, conscientious though

Jimmy Carter is, he simply lacks the force of character to do what is necessary on energy."[49] Wright was, perhaps, a bit harsh. Carter had convened a new task force to make recommendations and the stakes were indeed high. Not only had Congress shredded his earlier initiatives, but new efforts to decrease foreign oil or to encourage alternatives and conservation would mean higher prices, exacerbating inflation. At the same time, a weak response ensured continued shortages and perhaps even worse inflation. It was easy for Wright, who was secure in his congressional seat, to demand hard choices. For Carter, not so much.[50]

When Carter called for the "moral equivalent of war" in response to the energy crisis, Wright, growing increasingly frustrated, gently mocked him, saying the White House's response so far represented the "Maginot Line."[51] When Carter proposed emergency gas rationing—an example, perhaps, of the sacrifice Wright advocated—Wright still complained that Carter had avoided the problem's systemic causes. In early March, when Carter told the Democrats that his new plan would "cut down on the consumption of oil," Wright replied that without corresponding production increases such conservation "would shrink the economy." Wright even floated a deal: the authority to ration for augmented production. The oil industry and many conservative Democrats applauded, as Wright well knew they would.[52]

One month later, in April, Carter unveiled his new agenda. Included was the deregulation that the oil industry sought and the corporate "windfall profits" tax that the liberals demanded, with the proceeds to help consumers and promote alternative energy. Although Carter insisted that existing legislation had empowered him to remove controls unilaterally, Wright recognized the compromise and thought the suggestions were a good start. Much to his dismay, however, Carter's proposals further cleaved Democrats. Northern liberals complained of the higher prices, while southern conservatives resisted any new tax whatsoever. As Wright frantically worked to break the resulting deadlock, the lines at gas stations grew longer and the public's patience shorter.[53]

Frustrated by it all, Carter returned to the airwaves several weeks later and spoke of a "malaise" that had overcome the nation. He also added two new proposals: a government corporation to develop synthetic fuels and a new emergency board to speed construction of pipelines and refineries, both paid from company profits. Wright once again fell in line and supported the proposals, but he still believed Carter lacked a sufficiently forceful agenda.[54] When, in a meeting with Carter advisers, Carter's aide, Stuart Eizenstat, appeared dismissive of his concerns, Wright's old temper returned. In World

War II, Wright snapped, "FDR didn't wonder philosophically what might be a realistic expectation but rather saw the need and resolved to meet it."[55]

In the end, of course, the energy crisis did ebb, as much a product of changing global dynamics as domestic legislation. Congress eventually passed a synthetic fuels bill and a new solar energy program funded by a windfall profits tax. Gas prices rose, consumption gave way to conservation, and increased production resulted even as the political fight exacerbated internal Democratic tensions and did little to help inflation. While the long battle had done Carter no favors, Carter still graciously wrote Wright to say he was "grateful" for Wright's leadership.[56] Even the stalwart conservative Barry Goldwater thought Wright's leadership effective, though he added cryptically that "some private group" should have taken the lead.[57]

While Wright undoubtedly appreciated the thanks, Carter's subsequent appointment of the economist Paul Volcker as the new Federal Reserve chairman confounded him. With Wright's approval, Carter had initially embraced government stimulus to combat unemployment, leaving conservatives to claim that federal spending, like energy, drove the higher prices and debt. Volcker, however, appeared to advocate another strategy against the stubborn inflation. He immediately began to tighten controls over private bank reserves and raise interest rates to constrict the money supply. This was too much for Wright, who had long argued that lower rates stimulated the economy and reduced the debt, and thus the cost of living. Higher rates, Wright protested, were "clearly price inflationary" and would drive the economy into a tailspin.[58] In fact, ultimately, Wright was both right and wrong. The constricted money supply contributed to a recession that hurt Carter's reelection and bottomed out in the early years of his successor, Ronald Reagan. By the end of the recession, however, inflation had fallen to 3 percent and continued to fall. While an improving energy climate—in part because of Carter's and Wright's efforts—surely played a role, the tighter monetary policy undoubtedly did as well. The initial recession was a bitter but necessary medicine.[59]

Blind to this future, of course, Wright found Carter's claim to be powerless even more frustrating. "If you say those who are elected don't have any control," Wright grumbled, "you've just enthroned [the Federal Reserve]." President Truman had browbeaten the Fed into lower rates, and Carter should as well. If Carter did not move forcibly, Wright concluded, the voters in the 1980 election would.[60]

Suddenly, in the middle of this debate, Chrysler Corporation demanded its own forceful action. The iconic automobile company had failed to adapt adequately to the dynamism of energy supply and technological change and desperately needed loan guarantees. A Chrysler bankruptcy would prove a "calamity to the nation," Wright argued, "creating a chain reactive fear" that would reverberate throughout the economy.[61] Once again, as in the threatened bankruptcy of New York City, Wright found himself trying to convince hesitant southern conservative Democrats that the issue was critical to organized labor and the industrial states on which their party counted. Such arguments, it turned out, carried the day. The guarantees passed, the company rebounded and paid back the loans, and the government netted $350 million.[62]

Oddly, to Wright, much of the public just did not seem to care. Wright saw another example of good governance, but all cynical voters seemed to see was a tax-supported bailout. When Congress passed Carter's Department of Education bill, Wright was pleased that Congress had affirmed America's young people as a priority. Now there would be adequate funding and coordination for education, a cause for national celebration.[63] Voters, however, seemed to see nothing more than another bureaucracy sucking up wasteful spending. Many southerners, Texas governor William Clements tried to explain to Wright, saw it as a states' rights issue.[64] Wright replied that people just blamed the government for everything—the nation's economic and energy woes and, now apparently, even the problems of education. Wright did not understand such cynicism about Washington, but by the late 1970s he could not avoid it.

Wright's fits of melancholy returned, and he poured out his frustrations in his diary. "I go around tired and dissatisfied, determined to correct the misperceptions," he penned. Congress—and his own role—never received "what I regard as credit due."[65] Wright had suffered lows before—after his reelection loss as a state legislator, after his failed Senate bid, after his divorce, and over other events before his path to the leadership had broken open. This time, however, he was stymied. He was enjoying so much success, and yet things still looked so bleak. People held the institution to which he had devoted his life in such poor esteem. The battles more caustic, the problems more complex and intractable, Wright began once again to flirt with the idea of chucking it all. His ambition demanded recognition, and his idealism demanded accomplishments. In a way, the notion of walking away from it all in protest seemed, somehow, romantic. "So should I quit?" Wright scribbled. "Perhaps." In the end such sentiments were, of course, more the product of Wright's emotions than reason. In reality, he had no intention of quitting, which would have gone against his workman-like, never-say-die nature. Indeed, by the end of the year, Wright's mood had lifted even as the situation had not. "It is my 57th birthday," Wright noted in his diary on December 22. "I've been in many ways the most fortunate of people."[66]

Of the recent accomplishments that Wright cherished, by far the most notable were in foreign policy. As the decade wound down, Wright returned with a congressional delegation from Mexico, having concluded productive negotiations over immigration and trade. Crowds had greeted the delegation warmly, and he had toasted the Mexican president. The press, however, "always seeing the negative," had noticed none of it. Diplomacy took time and patience, he insisted, and the public deserved to know when it was succeeding.[67] Not surprisingly, therefore, when Wright helped negotiate an agreement on natural gas with Mexico two months later, he went on radio to offer his own praise.[68]

In July 1979, Wright departed with a congressional delegation to Europe. Spouses came along "for protocol purposes," Wright emphasized, "not at government air travel expense."[69] Praising the Europeans for their synthetic fuels—a subtle suggestion that America needed to do more— and stressing the importance of NATO, Wright's comments reflected both his pragmatism and his idealism. Europe needed a strong military, he argued, but diplomacy was always the key.[70] When Carter formalized relations with the People's Republic of China, Wright applauded the move while reiterating America's commitment to Taiwan. When Carter concluded a new round of the Strategic Arms Limitation Talks—the so-called SALT II agreement that restricted the development of new strategic missile systems—Wright was enthusiastic while insisting that a strong arsenal remained essential.[71]

Also in July, Wright took a "quick trip" to speak at Puerto Rico's annual "Constitution Day." Ever the diplomat, Wright had stated that he would support whatever Puerto Ricans decided in regard to possible statehood. Not surprisingly, the crowds greeted him warmly, acting as the "perfect sounding board for an orator," as he put it in his diary.[72] Six months later, concluding a year of impressive travel, Wright was off again with another delegation to the Middle East and Africa, meeting among others with King Khalid of Saudi Arabia, the president of Nigeria, and the British governor of Zimbabwe Rhodesia.[73] Wright kept Carter informed, suggesting, for example, that starvation in Uganda demanded aid. Interestingly, Wright wrote highly of South Africa, citing its potential for energy but ignoring its racial apartheid.[74]

Wright impressed his hosts. He was, Saudi Crown Prince Fahd stated, "articulate, informed and sensitive." Others predicted that Wright's importance "would extend far beyond the next presidential elections."[75]

At home, the reviews were not so positive. When criticism grew that Wright's delegation was just enjoying a vacation at taxpayers' expense, Wright requested and received a letter of support from Secretary of State Cyrus Vance. "Working trips," Vance wrote, were the "duty of the Majority Leader," and Wright had conducted himself in "an exemplary fashion." Vance left out that Wright had traveled more than almost all previous majority leaders or that spouses frequently attended.[76]

Latin America remained Wright's primary interest, and, in many respects, his greatest challenge. Here balancing his idealistic hopes for peace through justice and economic development with his pragmatic desire to remain vigilant militarily against communism had never been easy. Recalling the frustrations of the Dominican Republic during the Johnson years, or the more recent right-leaning junta of Chile's Augusto Pinochet, Wright did not let his globe-trotting elsewhere blind him to developments in Nicaragua. Watching with apprehension, Wright hoped for the best even as he had little idea just how significant a challenge Nicaragua would ultimately pose. In time, that small Central American nation would come to define much of his remaining time in Congress.

When Carter began his presidency, the right-leaning Anastasio Somoza ruled—corrupt and no friend to civil rights, but, with aid, an American ally in the Cold War. After it became clear that Somoza had embezzled funds intended for earthquake victims, Wright broke with Carter over the proper reaction. Carter canceled aid that Wright thought essential to defeat the growing left-leaning opposition, the Sandinistas. Wright tried to argue that continuing aid would win civil rights concessions and that Cuba supported the Sandinistas, but liberal Democrats reacted with fury. Wright's "type of anti-communism," wrote one, was a "great destructive force." After all, "the object of the whole nation's hatred was put into power by the Americans." Another was more personal: "I do not admire persons who relish . . . dictatorial regimes rather than democracies."[77]

Such criticism hurt. Wright's goal was democracy, even if Somoza had not yet come around. In fact, Somoza never did, and, in 1979, the Sandinistas, led by the brothers Humberto and Daniel Ortega, forced Somoza from office—and forced Wright to tack. Wright had supported aid for the Somoza regime, but now he argued the case for the country's new rulers. If this stance made sense in ensuring continued American influence, it was in another sense jarring and difficult to explain. Writing of the episode years later, Wright did not mention his earlier support for Somoza, disdainfully noting that the regime had departed with "much of [Nicaragua's] remaining wealth."[78] This reality, Wright now argued, called out for aid not only to moderate any drift toward communism but also to avoid a humanitarian crisis. Carter agreed and proposed a $75 million aid package while asking Wright to lead a delegation to Managua to investigate. The package was "imperative," Wright told Carter, and had "enormous symbolic importance."[79]

Now, however, it was the conservatives—with whom Wright had earlier agreed—who viciously attacked him. Preparing to depart on his mission in the summer of 1980, Wright took the new criticism in stride and led efforts to pass a compromise that reduced the aid and called on Carter to report to Congress every three months on the new rulers' observance of democratic rights. It was "the widest margin of any vote on aid to a Central American country during the entire decade of the 1980s," an obviously proud Wright wrote. The "right-wingers" had now learned a lesson.[80]

His mission, Wright noted privately, was to "move things an inch or two in our direction." The aid and his trip were "rolling the dice," and his critics were sure to pounce if it backfired.[81] Wright was unable to secure complete Republican participation. The notice was too short, he explained publicly, even as he privately knew otherwise. It was an election year, and for the Republicans, couching the Ortega brothers as committed communists promised votes.[82]

Arriving in Nicaragua on a military aircraft, Wright's delegation met with a number of public and private officials.[83] Daniel Ortega, now recognized as the nation's leader, assured Wright that the new government would respect civil rights and private property, excepting only banks and utilities. Elections would be held as soon as there was "enough tranquility," but establishing security was paramount.[84] Ortega appeared to be earnest, and Wright left pleased but wary. While acknowledging in his diary the "Marxist influence," Wright still hoped that Ortega was more nationalist than communist, a man America could deal with.[85]

The events that followed, however, made such sentiments seem naïve. Cuba's Fidel Castro arrived in Managua within days and suggested publicly that if the Americans had offered his government aid, "Cuba would not have the problems it has today."[86] The new Sandinista regime, moreover, now announced that elections would not take place for at least five years. This was "appalling," Wright wrote Ortega. Cuba was a "dictatorship," and many Americans remained "apprehensive" about the direction

Nicaragua was taking. Republican conservatives, Wright warned, now had an excuse for their rigid policies.[87]

Fortunately for Wright—or unfortunately, from the broader perspective—the December 1979 Soviet invasion of Afghanistan overshadowed the disappointing developments in Nicaragua. The invasion, spawned by the growth of Islamic fundamentalism that threatened the Soviet border, shocked the West and led Carter to announce a boycott of the 1980 Summer Olympics in Moscow.[88] An angry Congress also refused to ratify the SALT II agreement, which had been signed but was still pending. His idealistic faith in diplomacy challenged, Wright fell back on his traditional support for the chief executive in time of crisis. Carter had proceeded in a "steady, firm and patient way," Wright recorded in his diary, and the situation might promote "a sense of unity."[89]

It was not to be. Not only did Afghanistan dominate the news, but the deteriorating situation in Iran soon undercut what support Carter still enjoyed. For Wright it was yet another challenge to his balance of idealism and pragmatism. The Iranian leader, Shah Mohammad Reza Pahlavi, was, once again, an American ally with an atrocious record of democratic rights, a record that fueled another fundamentalist Islamic movement led by the Ayatollah Ruhollah Khomeini. Given Iran's strategic location, Wright had long supported the shah. As late as 1977 he had even lobbied for the sale of military helicopters to the regime from his district.[90] In January 1979, however, with the shah out of the country, Khomeini seized power.

Wright immediately understood the complexity of the situation. Khomeini "may be insane," Wright told the press, but America's "influence has been vast." The United States had "failed to grasp fully the significance of change [within Iran]." Diplomats had shown "insensitivity" toward Iran's religious traditions. They "offended Moslems with their attire," and had appeared "too aloof from the people who have no shoes." Torn by anger on the one hand and his recognition of American culpability on the other, Wright feared the revolution's implications.[91]

With the new Iranian government demanding the return of the shah for trial, Carter, far from exhibiting the "firmness" Wright had attributed to him, wrestled with the international repercussions of every action. The shah, meanwhile, began a year of transiency, traveling from nation to nation seeking a permanent refuge. To make matters more complex, the shah was growing ill and needed medical treatment. Finally, in October 1979, Carter allowed the shah, then in Mexico, entrance into the United States, assuming his stay for diagnosis and treatment would be relatively simple and brief.

It proved anything but. The shah had terminal cancer, and, in November, so-called "students" in Tehran seized the American embassy, taking fifty-two hostages. Mexico then reneged on a promise to take the shah back. With the United States in a precarious position, Wright complained to the Mexican ambassador, noting America's "many small acts of friendship over many years." It was a "betrayal" at the "most inopportune moment." Wright's tone, the ambassador responded, was "unjustified."[92] Fortunately, Panama agreed to take the exiled leader. It was there that the shah died in July 1980, his supporters angry at Carter and the hostage crisis deepening.

The long, horrible ordeal drained what political support Carter had left. When Carter attempted a military rescue of the hostages in April 1980, Wright approved of the move, but the mission failed. If it had succeeded, Wright remarked, Carter "would have been a hero."[93] "Poor Jimmy Carter," Wright wrote in his diary as the presidential campaign was beginning. It was a sentiment he surely felt throughout 1980.[94] The hostage crisis ultimately lasted until the day Carter's successor, former California governor Ronald Reagan, took his inaugural oath. The release of the hostages on the same day that Reagan became president was one final Iranian slap at Jimmy Carter.

"The 1980 elections pose a great challenge to our party," the Democratic Congressional Campaign Committee wrote Wright in January 1979, in an obvious understatement.[95] Even before the foreign policy turmoil, powerful forces had aligned against the Democrats. Perhaps it was an inevitable reaction to long-entrenched Democratic power, part of a natural political cycle.[96] Perhaps, as Wright well knew, the Democratic embrace of civil rights had cost the party support in the South. Or, perhaps in a greater sense, the party's growing liberalism had alienated many Americans who feared cultural decay and a growing lack of respect for the nation around the world. Regardless, the economic woes exacerbated it all and helped to form what some were already calling the New Right.[97] Joining the likes of Barry Goldwater and others who were ideologically opposed to taxes and regulation was a reborn Religious Right that had been dormant since the 1950s and was becoming more and more frustrated with the growing libertine culture.[98]

Wright had long wrestled with the former but was learning quickly of the latter. The Moral Majority, formed by televangelist Jerry Falwell in 1979, attacked Wright for his tenuous balance on abortion.[99] Even as Republican Henry Hyde, a congressman from Illinois and a champion of prohibiting federal funding for abortions, acknowledged Wright as an ally, the Moral Majority lumped Wright together with the more liberal northern

Democrats as apostates.[100] Wright thought abortion was a matter best left to the states—his attempt at compromise—but declared himself "disturbed by the increasing incidence of abortion." He did not support a constitutional amendment outlawing it and accepted exceptions for rape or incest to any prohibitions. As Wright hoped to sidestep the emotional issue that was growing increasingly partisan by promoting adoption, the Religious Right demanded purity.[101] "Jim Wright has hurt this country," televangelist James Robison declared to a Dallas rally in August 1980.[102]

To activist Phyllis Schlafly, Wright's support for the Equal Rights Amendment (ERA) was a dagger at the heart of the nuclear family.[103] With only a few states needed for ratification but with the deadline approaching, Wright once again sought a compromise and fell short of the purity the Religious Right demanded. Wright agreed with the liberals who were proposing an extension for ratification, but he accepted the possibility of states reversing their earlier votes, pressed to do so by conservatives. Under attack from many in his own district—the ERA represented "a socialistic or totalitarian government," said one constituent—Wright moved to shore up his conservative bona fides. When Attorney General Griffin Bell ruled for the liberals on ratification, Wright called the decision "manifestly one-sided and unfair."[104]

The attacks were personal and frequently fallacious. Fliers distributed at churches, for example, proclaimed that Wright favored homosexuality. Wright had always tried to stay above the more Machiavellian, personal style of aggressive politics, but the no-compromise, more ideological, sectarian-driven movement he now encountered did not bode well for the collegiality he still espoused. Embodying all that Wright feared and loathed was a new PAC formed in 1975 to promote the GOP's union of social and fiscal conservatives, the National Conservative Political Action Committee.[105] Empowered by a 1976 Supreme Court ruling allowing PACs to make unlimited contributions to groups that did not coordinate with candidates, NCPAC raised considerable funds from anonymous donors and then identified, trained, and funded congressional challengers. The majority leader was an obvious target.[106]

As NCPAC mobilized, Wright's old suitor, the jilted wealthy oilman Eddie Chiles, attacked him with an equal vengeance, charging that Wright had become a flaming liberal. In fact, Wright was hardly the radical populist he had been at the outset of his career. Even as the election approached and Wright endorsed a holiday honoring Martin Luther King Jr., he supported cuts to achieve a balanced budget, the reinstitution of a national draft, and legislation "to prompt welfare recipients to work."[107] A liberal group, Americans for Democratic Action, rated him correct only 37 percent of the time. The AFL-CIO dropped its rating from 95 percent to 59 percent, while the Republican-leaning Chamber of Commerce improved it from 29 percent to 41 percent.[108]

The forty-eight-year-old Chiles hammered away nevertheless. In a series of commercials, Chiles said that he was "mad" that Wright had "shifted to the left." Soon bumper stickers appeared declaring "I'm mad too, Eddie." When reporters noted that Chiles's own oil interests benefited from less regulation, Chiles denied self-interest and kept his earlier flirtation with Wright under wraps. The government, he told reporters, just needed to "leave us the hell alone."[109] When conservative Texan Charlie Stenholm suggested that Wright's moderation might help "restrain" the real liberals, Chiles rebuked the new congressman directly. "If Jim Wright is the best the Democratic Party can hope for as Majority Leader," Chiles wrote, "then the Democratic Party is totally bankrupt." Soon Stenholm notified Wright that his office had received a flood of letters repeating exactly the same sentiments, the obvious product of a well-coordinated campaign.[110] When, in August 1979, Wright's supporters held a dinner to honor his quarter century in Congress, and the president of the Chamber of Commerce attended, Chiles publicly renounced his membership.[111]

As the *National Journal* reported that "Corporate PACS Come Through for the GOP," Chiles promised $300,000 to oust Wright, a total that eventually surpassed half a million, a sum unthinkable for a House challenger only a few years before.[112] Soon the media reflected the attacks. "Is Jim Wright Leaning Too Much to the Left?" asked *Texas Business*. The magazine was impartial in its answer, but the simple fact that the question was on the table did nothing to help Wright, given the broader drift in the Texas electorate.[113]

The beneficiary of all this energy and money, the champion of NCPAC and Chiles, was Fort Worth businessman Jim Bradshaw. As a Fort Worth councilman and later mayor pro tem, Bradshaw had dined with Wright and thanked him for helping the city. He had even attended Wright's anniversary dinner, the same celebration that so enraged Chiles. By December 1979, however, Chiles had hired a New York Republican polling firm to convince Bradshaw that Wright was vulnerable and promised all the support Bradshaw's candidacy would need.[114]

The battle joined, Bradshaw's campaign quickly came to reflect NCPAC's tactics. Anonymous fliers took Wright's votes out of context, proclaiming

Wright to be a "smooth talker" who favored "bureaucracies," a "liberal's liberal" who lied and was "against" Texas.[115] Although these charges were relatively boilerplate, they benefited from the additional money and coordination that Bradshaw enjoyed. Wright had never before faced such an onslaught. Bradshaw, Texas Republican governor Bill Clements stated, had "no ambition to assume leadership of some party you don't want to agree with."[116] The longtime chairman of Fort Worth's largest precinct suddenly announced that he was voting Republican, which caused the local Democratic Party to declare his position "automatically vacant." Two more Democratic precinct chairmen followed.[117] Reflective of the new Religious Right, Southern Baptist pastor Jimmy Draper told his congregation they should be "grateful for men like Jim Bradshaw."[118]

It was not only a matter of scale: the personal attacks were especially vehement. Proclaiming that Wright would surely attack Bradshaw "with personal innuendoes," Bradshaw's allies employed exactly that tactic. While Wright's employment of his tarnished aide, John Mack, escaped charges of nepotism, Republican operatives skewered Wright's past. His sudden wealth was proof of his dishonest character, they claimed.[119] "Wright Should See Handsome Profits from Wells," read one headline.[120] And once again, Wright was "aiding the forces of homosexuality." He held debt he never intended to repay. He cheated on his taxes and his wife. He had to be stopped.[121] One Fort Worth man, Wright's staff recalled, "got extremely mad and upset and started yelling and cursing" about Wright's perceived lying, even throwing a potted plant against the campaign office wall.[122] Wright had certainly never faced this before.

Wright responded that "lean pork" paid for itself in economic growth and reminded voters of all his accomplishments for Fort Worth. Shoring up his right flank, Wright welcomed the Washington for Jesus rally in April 1980 that brought thousands of conservative Christians to Washington. Though Wright had been invited to join the president on a campaign swing in Texas, Wright convinced Congressman Stenholm to attend in his place. "You are a true friend," Wright later wrote.[123] Asked about the Religious Right's attacks, Wright resisted the impulse to respond in kind and quoted the Bible's First Corinthians on the importance of love and suffering. It was the perfect passive aggressive response, and the quote left the impression that Wright was the true Christian.[124]

Wright Appreciation Committee fliers underscored Wright's conservatism.[125] When Cuban exiles held in Florida detention centers rioted, Wright took the opportunity to burnish his law-and-order credentials. The United

States would not tolerate those who "disobey its lawful authority," he proclaimed.[126] When in a televised debate Bradshaw claimed Wright was failing to pay his campaign workers' Social Security taxes, Wright laughed it off as "silliest nonsense." Federal law did not require it.[127]

Although Wright wanted to avoid personal attacks, he still could counterpunch. Bradshaw's city council record, Wright claimed, showed he "ignored senior citizens." A theme ran through Wright's attacks: Bradshaw was simply the tool of Chiles and big corporations.[128] In the end it was difficult to tell truth from fiction amid the charges and countercharges. The Bradshaw campaign complained that Wright supporters were spreading a rumor in African American neighborhoods that Bradshaw's family had owned slaves.[129] The Wright campaign complained that a Bradshaw aide had approached an aspiring county commissioner and offered a contribution for criticizing Wright. After the Wright campaign publicized an article in *D Magazine* that it had selectively edited, the publisher sued. The edited version, Wright replied, was the product of "well-intentioned but over-eager campaign volunteers."[130] Wright's connections infuriated Bradshaw. On the same day that the *Fort Worth Star-Telegram* included an advertising booklet that the Bradshaw campaign had purchased, the paper also included a full-page Wright advertisement. "Needless to say we've been suspicious of the coverage," Bradshaw responded, suggesting collusion. In the end, Accuracy in Media, a self-proclaimed "watchdog," concluded that both campaigns had tested the bounds of fairness.[131] While it was doubtful that Wright knew of every action taken on his behalf, there was enough mud to go around.

The Wright campaign was, after all, a large operation. Community leaders—led by Amon Carter Jr.—sent out letters calling Wright a "truly enormous asset." A number of congressmen, led by Wright acolyte Martin Frost and the conservative Stenholm, and including new member Phil Gramm of Texas, a man who would later cause Wright trouble, added their endorsements.[132] Having their representative as majority leader was valuable, the campaign reminded voters. Employing computerized lists, the campaign sent out regular pleas for money.[133] The resulting media blitz included not only short commercials but also one thirty-minute advertisement that his staff still thought ineffective. The campaign solicited the support of football stars and, especially, of Republicans.[134] It sponsored community events such as a Tarrant County "Energy Fair."[135] Things did not always run smoothly, however. There was infighting among the staff, with accusations of "unjustified outbursts" and resignations. "Clashes of personality are simply inevitable," Wright explained to a supporter.[136]

As the election approached, several polls suggested a close race. An exuberant Bradshaw exclaimed, "We're going to pull it off!"[137] Wright, meanwhile, admitted in his diary that it "rankled" him that the media was "salivating at the prospect of the defeat of leadership figures by right wing opponents."[138] The struggle for the Democratic nomination between Carter and liberal Massachusetts senator Ted Kennedy did not help. Wright, of course, was behind Carter, once again annoying many in his own party.[139] At the convention, Wright lambasted Republican "prophets of doom," but he could not avoid public discontent. "The good news is that we face the bad news frankly," Wright declared.[140]

Unfortunately for the Democrats, the Republican nominee, Ronald Reagan, was hardly easy to cast as an angry, pessimistic "prophet of doom." When Reagan confidently strode across the stage with a bright smile and an outstretched hand in his first debate with Carter, Wright thought, "Round one for Reagan." When Carter, perhaps reading the polls, went on the attack, Wright knew that it was his own candidate who appeared "angry and petty." Wright was no rookie. He recognized that the combination of Reagan's personality and his well-run, well-funded political machine did not bode well for the November elections.[141]

Throughout 1980 Wright did what he could. When Carter's campaign opened its Fort Worth headquarters, Wright gave an encouraging speech. Not only did he travel with Carter to Texas during the summer Washington for Jesus rally, but he welcomed First Lady Rosalynn Carter when she arrived in early October.[142] As for Wright's congressional colleagues, the Wright Majority Congress Committee reported that it had distributed over $184,000. Included among the recipients were the expected, such as Martin Frost, and new recipients, such as Phil Gramm.[143] Occupied with his own serious challenge, Wright was unable to campaign for others as much as he would have liked, but when he did he always drew a large crowd and tremendous thanks.[144] Reflecting the importance of Texas, Carter came to Fort Worth only days before the election. Wright chose the location of the rally in the city's old historic North Side because, he claimed, it was a working-class community. He did not add that it was near the redevelopment area that he had long championed. The crowd was impressive, but the cold, gray sky appeared as ominous as Carter's chances. Wright prepared himself for the worst, telephoning Speaker O'Neill and lamenting not only the effectiveness of the new hard-hitting campaigns but also what the future would hold under Republican dominance. It was not a pretty picture.[145]

Tuesday, November 4, proved a historic day, although bittersweet for Wright. With 61.4 percent of the vote, Wright crushed Bradshaw. The upstart, with his daughter wiping away her tears behind him, graciously conceded defeat, but added, "[Wright] may just have to face me again."[146] At the same time, however, Reagan's victory was even more impressive. Carrying all but five states and the District of Columbia, Reagan won every southern state but Georgia. The Republicans won a majority in the Senate, their strength clearly in the South and Midwest, with many blue-collar whites ceding their traditional allegiance to the party of Franklin Roosevelt. These conservative "Reagan Democrats" promised an even greater wave of Republican resurgence. Although the Democrats maintained control of the House, they lost an astounding thirty-four seats. Wright's own district had gone for Reagan even as it had returned him to office. It all appeared to be a tectonic shift in American politics.[147]

Wright could read the tea leaves. As his supporters celebrated, he stood in the corner of his rented ballroom and again phoned O'Neill. "I agonize for some of my friends," he told the press.[148] Across town at the Hilton, Chiles focused on the larger outcome. "[Bradshaw] didn't get elected," Chiles stated, "but he kept half a dozen others from getting elected." After receiving a phone call from Reagan, Bradshaw concluded the same. "I suspect [Reagan] wants to thank us for keeping Jim Wright home," he laughed.[149]

As he had done so often before, Wright set about taking stock of the political world that had shifted around him. The president that he admired so much, a man with whom he shared so much, had been crushed. No longer did Wright have an overwhelming majority. Entering the White House was not a man who shared Wright's assumptions about government, or even a Republican like Eisenhower or Nixon. Reagan was a new brand of Republican, an ideologue with a mandate. "Ultimately," Wright consoled himself in his diary, "I believe that the inevitable excesses of this right wing crowd will be their own undoing."[150] Such thoughts were undoubtedly comforting, even if, in the end, they were off the mark. The new decade, in fact, promised a Washington unlike one Wright had ever faced before.

PART IV

Victory and Defeat in the Age of Reagan

———

CHAPTER 15

A Challenge Like None Before

REAGAN (1980–1982)

"For the first time in more than fifty years the Congress is divided," Wright told the Dallas Democratic Forum just after the November 1980 elections. "A Democratic House and a Republican Senate must develop ways to work together." If they did not, a "national paralysis" might result. "I pledge to you," Wright concluded, "we shall not let that happen."[1] Several weeks later, citing his New Year's resolutions in his diary, Wright promised to "cultivate a more equitable disposition" and to remain "unruffled" in the face of "unreasonable demands." It was necessary, Wright wrote, if he were to reach consensus with those who opposed him.[2]

If Wright quietly hoped that the new political order was an aberration, or that "cooperation not confrontation" with the new, more stringent conservatives might still produce an outcome he could welcome, he soon learned otherwise. Initially, at least, it appeared the Democrats might unite in reaction to their collective rebuke. Wright's reelection as majority leader brought promises of fidelity from both liberals and conservatives.[3] When a group of southern conservatives led by Phil Gramm, emboldened by the national elections, pushed to "broaden the base of the Democratic Party," Wright worked to assure collegiality. The group, the media reported, was "careful not to appear threatening to the House leadership."[4] When Gramm, noting his concern for the debt, lobbied for an appointment to the powerful Budget Committee, Wright took up his cause. Gramm promised not to cause trouble and thanked Wright for his PAC's financial contributions. "I pledge to you that in return for your support for a seat on the Budget Committee," Gramm wrote Wright, "I will work diligently to assure that Democrats in the House are presented budget resolutions they can enthusiastically support."[5]

Wright also agreed to champion another Texas conservative, Kent Hance, for the Ways and Means Committee. If Wright would assist him, Hance promised, "I will be your most loyal member." Appointment to these two committees, which had such sway over taxes and spending, was competitive, and Wright knew that he had leverage. To ensure cooperation, he extracted a promise from both men to support the leadership's position when their committee bills reached the House floor. They could make their argument within the committee, but, whatever the outcome, they would subsequently follow the leadership.[6]

O'Neill and Wright worked to soothe all the ambitious members of their flock. When the powerful Wright ally Dan Rostenkowski requested the chairmanship of the Ways and Means Committee over the position of chief whip, Wright agreed to lend his support. The latter position, both Wright and Rostenkowski understood, was on the traditional ladder to the Speakership. With Wright one step ahead, however, the media surmised that Rostenkowski did "not want to wait that long." The former position, by contrast, offered immediate power—and, perhaps, an alternative path to the Speakership. In this respect, however, it posed a potential challenge to Wright.[7] Anxious to reward Rostenkowski for his efforts, and with the big Chicagoan also promising loyalty, Wright agreed to lend his support.[8] For chief whip, O'Neill selected Washington State's Tom Foley, while Wright selected Arkansas's Bill Alexander as deputy whip. Wright also ensured that his Texan acolyte Martin Frost emerged as one of the zone whips. They were all, Wright stressed, members of a team led by O'Neill.[9]

Wright clearly felt comfortable as the Speaker-in-waiting. He thanked voters when his portrait was hung in the Texas State Capitol, and he admitted that, given the efforts of NCPAC, Chiles, and Bradshaw the previous November, his margin of victory was particularly "gratifying." Given the political mud, he said, "I can't think of one that was sweeter."[10] The redistricting that followed the 1980 census, moreover, assured him of a "safe home base." Republicans in the Texas Legislature had hoped to use the influx of new suburban voters to redraw congressional districts, but Wright's allies made his security a priority. Legislators, one state representative acknowledged, "are aware of Wright's influence . . . and the additional power he would get if he becomes House Speaker."[11] Looking toward the future, Wright received words of encouragement from the departing Carter administration. Wright had a "significant legacy of accomplishment," wrote domestic adviser Stuart Eizenstat. The Carter administration, added national security adviser Zbigniew Brzezinski, "owes you a great debt."[12]

As Wright surveyed the postelection landscape for hope, Reagan's personality stood out. Wright had first met Reagan when he was California governor and genuinely thought him a friendly person. Several weeks after the election, Reagan met with O'Neill and Wright at the Capitol, entertaining the Democrats with humorous stories from his past. He did not seem a confrontational sort, and to Wright, he appeared somewhat ignorant of the issues and process. Reagan's inaugural speech did little to change this impression. His famous line, "Government is not the solution to our problem, government is the problem," struck Wright as simplistic, boilerplate campaign semantics. Nothing indicated an unwillingness to compromise.[13] Protocol required Wright to escort both the outgoing Carter and the incoming Reagan, and once again Reagan appeared good-natured. At the luncheon in Statuary Hall that followed the inauguration, Wright found the mother of the new First Lady to be delightful, and the light mood was enhanced by the news that the Iranians had at long last freed the American hostages. Just over two weeks later, Nancy Reagan invited leading Democrats to a surprise seventieth birthday party for the new president. With a cake too tall for her to light the candle, House Minority Leader Bob Michel and Wright each took a knee and offered her a boost. The symbolism of bipartisanship was hard to miss. Wright gave Reagan a tie clip of a gold boot with a spur, a gesture of goodwill.[14]

The first inkling Wright had of the magnitude of the trouble he now faced came in early February. Although Congress had regularly raised the national debt ceiling, Reagan stated that his request to do so was "made with deep regret," and was only to buy time for legislators to "change our basic economic policies."[15] Days later, Reagan submitted a "new comprehensive economic program" that included the controversial "Kemp-Roth tax cuts," named for the two Republican legislators who championed them, Congressman Jack Kemp and Senator William Roth.[16] In what *Newsweek* magazine later termed "Reaganomics," the new president drew heavily from "supply-side" economists. Fully implemented, the policy sought to tighten the money supply and cut tax rates, the tax cuts larger among the wealthy to unleash investment. Accompanying tremendous cuts to federal spending would be a wave of deregulation to encourage job creation.[17]

Democrats had their own word for it: "trickle-down economics." The spending cuts would hurt the poor, they claimed, while the tax cuts, combined with higher interest rates—raising the cost of borrowing, a point Wright had always made—would exacerbate inflation. The economy would weaken and deficits would swell. By the time Reagan later proposed massive increases in defense spending, arguing that the tax cuts would create enough new jobs—and thus enough new revenue despite the lower tax rates—to reduce the national debt, it was clear to Wright that Reagan was not like his predecessors.

Wright initially sought to cool tensions. While promising to "alter the tax package so it won't be so inflationary," Wright noted that there was much he could "enthusiastically embrace." Some of the new president's proposals were for "goals which I share."[18] With Wright advocating compromise, the Democratic leadership noted "grave doubts about the wisdom of the so-called Kemp Roth proposal," but also promised to "work closely with the Reagan Administration."[19] "I want the president to succeed," Wright remarked on the show *Meet the Press*, "because I want our country to succeed."[20]

Just as the White House sent the Democratic leadership a letter with "cordial regards," Wright was aghast to learn that another letter on Reagan's personal stationary had gone out to names on a National Republican Committee mailing list. Reagan's letter did not speak of compromise, only defeating the Democrats. When Wright contacted the White House, Reagan's aides apologized and claimed that the president had not authorized the letter. It would stop. Twice more the mailings appeared, however, and each time Wright protested. Each time the White House claimed a mistake. "The whole thing seems so flagrantly two-faced," Wright recorded in his diary, a bad omen.[21]

Reagan then followed with a bombshell, suggesting that Congress make Social Security voluntary. While the proposal was in one sense courageous, and demographics suggested that some reform was necessary, Democrats knew the program was politically sacrosanct. It was, in the words of one report, "a godsend for Democrats in their search for an issue on which the Reagan administration is vulnerable."[22] Predictably, Wright sought conciliation. Yes, Reagan had correctly identified a problem, Wright stated, but he proposed savings at the "expense of the elderly."[23]

With tensions building, a bipartisan group of congressional leaders met Reagan twice in March. The nonpartisan Congressional Budget Office had questioned the administration's economic projections, and Wright found that Reagan backed up what appeared to be ideological conclusions with simple anecdotes. "I don't think the President knows beans about the economy," Wright lamented in his diary.[24] In fact, at the time Reagan could honestly cite the theories of Arthur Laffer, in particular the so-called Laffer Curve hypothesizing that tax cuts increased, rather than decreased, revenues by promoting economic growth. It was not until more years of additional data were available that most economists rejected Laffer's central hypothesis. Tax cuts, properly timed and placed, could increase revenues enough to offset debt, but this could not be taken as a guiding, uniform assumption. Accurate or not, Wright understood that Reagan did not even acknowledge the debate, another bad omen.[25]

Working with the House Budget Committee throughout the spring to craft an alternative budget, Wright argued that the Democrats should offer "maximum cooperation" but stress that "no president has ever achieved enactment of his entire program." They should agree with Reagan's goal of economic growth and debt reduction, but argue that his plans would hamper both. To stress bipartisanship, Wright sent Reagan some jalapeño jelly beans.[26] Yes, Reagan was popular, Wright acknowledged, but Carter had been more popular at the same time during his presidency.[27] Worried that crafting a Democratic alternative would exacerbate party divisions, Wright accepted Deputy Whip Bill Alexander's idea for a "central coordinator" to vet specifics in private. Democrats needed to have short, one-minute speeches television-ready, Wright agreed.[28]

In early April, the Democrats released their "lean federal budget." It agreed to cut spending and taxes, but neither to the levels Reagan proposed. It also agreed to increase funding for the military, but again, to levels nowhere near what Reagan wanted. The draft kept a number of programs that Wright argued were stimulative and stressed the need for energy initiatives and efforts to combat inflation. In total, the Democrats claimed, the package reduced the debt by billions over the Republican plan.[29]

Reagan, however, refused to budge. Struggling to hold back his temper, Wright noted that even Republicans had publicly questioned the administration's projections. In fact, Reagan had not forgotten his pledge for bipartisanship; he was simply playing a strong political hand. Never before had Wright been in so weak a position. Not only had Republicans won a landslide, but Reagan had just survived an assassination attempt, and his popularity was soaring. "Honey, I forgot to duck," the press quoted him remarking to the

First Lady. It was an "incomprehensive thing," Wright mused on a flight back from Texas with Vice President George H. W. Bush. Bush, Wright observed, was admirably composed while Reagan's survival remained in doubt.[30]

Reagan had an additional motive not to compromise too readily. The conservative Democrat Phil Gramm, the man who had promised Wright fidelity, had met secretly with Reagan's budget adviser, David Stockman. If he could shape an alternative bill working with Stockman that was more agreeable to conservatives, Gramm now calculated, he would vote against the Democratic bill and lobby fellow southern conservative Democrats to do the same. As the White House understood, such a bill would allow Reagan to claim bipartisanship, muting Wright's charges. Learning of the plan and once again struggling to contain his temper, Wright reminded Gramm of their agreement. Gramm denied having broken his word and claimed that he had only promised to support whatever bill passed the "Committee of the Whole," the entire House. In other words, the promise was meaningless.

The Gramm-Latta bill, named for Gramm and Ohio Republican Delbert Latta, differed little from the earlier administration proposal. To make matters worse for Democrats, Reagan wrote in late April requesting the opportunity to address Congress to thank them for their support during his recent crisis.[31] The resulting speech focused almost entirely on the looming budget battle. Reagan ignored the Congressional Budget Office's conclusions and cast the Democratic bill in the worst possible light. Caught off guard, O'Neill requested from the networks time to reply. With O'Neill's request denied, Wright released a statement that lacked his earlier tone of collegiality. Reagan's remarks were "factually inaccurate" and "deliberately misleading," he stated. "The saddest thing personally" was that Reagan had broken his word for bipartisanship.[32]

With the stage set for a floor vote, Wright lobbied both the public and his congressional colleagues. To the former, he stressed debt reduction and the "striking similarities" between the competing bills, obviously aware of the popularity Reagan still wielded.[33] To the latter, Wright and his whips insisted that it was a gut-check time. For their part, the Republicans focused on the southern conservatives in what one such Democrat described as "the most well-orchestrated operation" he had ever encountered. Reagan called members individually, employing the grandeur of the Oval Office. Using computerized contributor lists, the Republicans contacted conservative business leaders in each district, using them for additional leverage.[34]

It was too much for Wright and his allies. Several dozen southern conservative Democrats split from their party and Reagan had the victory he sought. Complaints from some liberal Democrats that O'Neill and Wright had failed them were a "bum rap," according to Texan Charlie Wilson.[35] Still, however, the liberals grumbled. According to Californian George Miller, "repercussions are going to run deep." When O'Neill retired, Wright would have cause for concern. "Natural ascension [to the Speakership] may not necessarily be the order of the next Congress."[36]

Wright was not thinking in such terms, and not yet conceding defeat. Gramm-Latta was only a budget resolution, setting the parameters for spending. The task now was to flesh out the specifics in actual appropriations for individual programs and departments. The bottom line was set, but, for Wright and the other Democrats, the opportunity to mitigate the damage now lay in the so-called "reconciliation bill."

Still annoyed by the way in which the budget had unfolded, Wright approached Minority Leader Michel of Illinois—a "responsible Republican," according to Wright—and stressed the need for "true bipartisanship."[37] As Wright spoke, Reagan was holding a closed-door session with a group of southern Democrats, promising them that the Republican Party would not campaign against them if they backed the White House. The Budget Committee was considering a number of amendments, but Reagan also informed O'Neill that Stockman had just submitted a White House amendment. As Wright later claimed, O'Neill asked about the amendment's provisions, but Reagan said that he was not sure. The amendment, it turned out, was only a one-page summary of spending cuts that surpassed the original Gramm-Latta resolution. Recognizing, first, that one omnibus amendment was unusual, and, second, that delayed consideration allowed them time to mobilize opposition, O'Neill and Wright argued that it would be ridiculous to consider such broad cuts with only one vote.[38]

With the House set to vote on the rule under which it would consider reconciliation, the White House operation again kicked into high gear. The House, it argued, should consider the amendment, now dubbed Gramm-Latta II, in one vote. "Is there anything I can do for you?" Democrat Wilson recalled Reagan asking. Fellow Texan Ralph Hall agreed to support the single amendment when Reagan agreed to support the repeal of fuel-conversion requirements that the Texas utility companies opposed.[39] "We've got a president who's willing to go to the mat," Latta proudly declared. Gramm, for his part, complained that the Democratic leadership was using "storm trooper methods." When the vote came, Wright and his allies once again found themselves short. The amendment passed as one vote. "The President must have been up half the night making phone calls," O'Neill lamented.[40]

"Surely it was your right to vote as you did yesterday," Wright wrote the wayward southern conservatives. But, he continued, how could anyone "honestly say . . . what's in it?" Wright had a valid point. Just as the rule vote took place, the administration forwarded a more detailed amendment. The one-page memorandum was now almost a thousand pages. It was the "sloppiest piece of draftsmanship I ever saw," Wright later wrote, noting the incorrect page numbers, incomplete references, and corrections marked through with pen. The substitute was, obviously, rushed.[41]

The House considered the reconciliation bill throughout the summer of 1981. In the floor debate, Wright focused on provisions expanding the power of the White House's Office of Management and Budget, which, Wright argued, infringed upon congressional prerogative. Obviously struggling with his temper, Wright even got personal. Stockman, he stated, was "dangerous in his thirst for power."[42] The eleven provisions revising Social Security, Wright pled emotionally, hurt retirees and the poor. It was clearly more than a battle over data for Wright, who perceived a direct challenge to the core functions of good government, including the responsibility of a humane society to protect its most vulnerable. It offended his idealism.[43]

Paralleling the debate over spending during the summer was the related debate over taxes, the specifics of the Kemp-Roth proposals to meet the budget resolution. Seeking a conservative southern Democrat on the Ways and Means Committee, the White House courted Kent Hance, whom Wright had pressed onto the committee in the first place. When Reagan contacted him initially, Hance dutifully reported the solicitation to Wright. "He wants me to be his Phil Gramm on the tax bill," Hance stated, "but I'm going to tell him I can't do it."[44] Feeling confident, Wright privately speculated that Reagan's "sop to the right wing" was probably "doomed."[45]

Of course, it was not. Hance felt the pressure, both inside Congress and from his district's conservatives. Once again, Wright felt the sting of betrayal. Once again the liberal critics complained. Recognizing their weak hand, O'Neill and Wright met with Reagan, presenting a last-ditch compromise, a more modest 5 percent tax cut the first year. Reagan listened, but, not surprisingly, he again refused to yield.[46] Now more convinced than ever that Reagan was ideological and ill-informed, an angry Wright advised Democrats to stand firm. His idealism overcoming his pragmatism, Wright refused any additional compromises.

Rostenkowski thought otherwise, and, as the new chair of the committee deciding the issue, was not afraid of making his views known. The Democrats should continue to negotiate, he argued, until enough conservatives returned to the fold to block a worst-case scenario. It was, the *Wall Street Journal* declared, "divide and conquer tactics."[47] Rostenkowski told O'Neill that the public zeitgeist simply did not match Wright's perception of government. The Democrats were too vulnerable on the issue of debt. O'Neill reluctantly agreed, and Wright, for once, had to acquiesce.

The political world noticed. One Republican remarked that Rostenkowski had been "brilliant" and had bought the Democrats additional time. The media speculated about an internal Democratic power struggle, suggesting that Rostenkowski might emerge as the next Speaker after all. He had, biographer Richard Cohen concluded, "signaled that he would not readily surrender influence."[48] Behind the scenes things were less dramatic. Wright claimed that there had been no affront, while Rostenkowski told him "how much I personally appreciated your support."[49]

In the big picture—predictably—it mattered little. The Kemp-Roth bill, labeled the Economic Recovery Act of 1981, passed Congress along the same lines as the reconciliation vote. The new law made across-the-board reductions in income tax rates over three years of approximately 25 percent, Reagan having reduced his first-year rate cuts from 10 percent to 5 percent. Wright later tried to take credit for this small victory, citing his last-minute proposal, but in reality Reagan had grown concerned that the debt might initially explode before his program rebounded the economy. Congressional elections, Reagan understood, loomed.[50] The bill, he remarked at the signing, "represented a turnaround of almost a half a century of a course this country's been on." It was an apt description. With the Omnibus Budget Reconciliation Act of 1981 signed at the same time, Reaganomics had begun.[51]

Wright was left to find consolation where he could get it. Just as he had predicted, the reductions in Social Security that Reagan had forced through as part of the reconciliation bill soon proved unpopular.[52] Pressing this advantage, Wright stated that Reagan had been mean-spirited in attacking the "defenseless" recipients.[53] Sensing vulnerability, Reagan signed a temporary measure in December 1981 reinstituting the minimum payment and allowing additional borrowing to ensure solvency. For the long run, both sides agreed to create a bipartisan National Commission on Social Security Reform to investigate alternative solutions.[54] It was simply a kick down the road. For Wright, however, it was at least something.

It had been a rough year for Wright, but as it wound down he returned to the advice of his father. Swallowing his anger and pride, Wright congratulated Reagan for his "stunning victories."[55] In later years, writers would praise the relationship between Reagan and O'Neill, who were often projected as two old Irishmen battling during the day but sharing a drink at night. While there was some truth in this view, a reflection of Wright's idealized vision of Congress, Wright knew just how frustrated O'Neill was. Once after Reagan promised to "go the extra mile" in negotiations, O'Neill publicly implied that Reagan was lying. The president, O'Neill said sarcastically, "must go first." Like Wright, O'Neill was struggling to maintain the traditions he valued when precedents seemed to be falling every day. When an opportunity arose to turn the tables, the Democratic leadership was ready to attack.[56]

The opportunity was not long in coming. The economy continued to falter, and by the middle of 1982, unemployment in certain areas was approaching 12 percent. The "Reagan Revolution" had just begun, but citizens now spoke of the "Reagan Recession." It was an image that both Wright and O'Neill exploited. In reality, the recession had more to do with the Federal Reserve's hard money policies, the continuing energy shortages, and the new competition from Asian economies than with the administration's policies. Wright had predicted from the start of Fed Chairman Volcker's tenure that his monetarist policies would lead to a recession. What he had failed to see, however, was that the rising unemployment and stagnating wages were necessary to break the cycle of inflation. In the end, the energy cartel, OPEC, fell apart, energy prices fell, and the 1982 recession passed.[57]

At the time, many Democrats just wanted to stall. A bad economy meant an unpopular president. Wright wanted to attack, however, pressing for emergency appropriations to fund a massive jobs training program. As Democrat David Obey agreed, it would "start off the new year with a victory over the president."[58] "Once more Mr. Reagan resorts to role playing," Wright said, mocking the president's Hollywood background. "He is an actor of many disguises."[59] When the anniversary of Reagan's 1981 legislative victories arrived, Wright publicized the "sad but important milestone" with a litany of depressing economic statistics.[60] With Volcker refusing to lower rates, Wright remarked that Volcker was like a "benign Buddha who pats you on the head."[61] He should resign, and, in lieu of such, Congress should pass legislation guiding the central bank.[62]

If Wright ultimately overplayed Reagan's role in bringing about the 1982 recession, his predictions of greater debt proved prescient. While in one sense the national debt naturally grew during any recession, growing numbers of economists began to place the blame for the sudden skyrocketing deficits on Reagan's combination of tax cuts and increased military spending. When Reagan took office, the nation had an annual deficit of $56 billion. The following year the deficit ballooned to $111 billion. The Laffer Curve, it appeared, did not work well with Reagan's overhaul, at least in regard to the national debt. Throughout the remainder of Reagan's term Democrats had a legitimate political sword. From 1983 to 1986, deficits grew to approximately $200 billion per year. As the recession finally ebbed and the economy exploded later in the 1980s, Reagan loyalists focused on the impressive boom. His detractors, meanwhile—Wright included—suggested that the growth was all on the national credit card.[63]

The Democrats, Wright believed, had the upper hand going into the budget battles for fiscal year 1983. Reagan, however, was not about to surrender the ground he had so arduously gained the previous year. When discussions stalled, Reagan agreed to meet directly with a bipartisan group of congressional leaders. But it did not go well. Reagan seemed excessively concerned about the seating, which suggested a photo opportunity. At one point, Reagan, still testy, told Wright to put down his pen. "Stop thinking about what you are going to say and listen to what I am trying to tell you," Wright recalled Reagan saying in one rather harsh admonishment.[64]

The final solution came not from O'Neill or Wright, but from Rostenkowski, whom Stockman approached because he believed him to be less rigid. Leveraging his key position once again, Rostenkowski was able to negotiate at least some rescission of the Kemp-Roth mandates, but, as the administration insisted, not the rates themselves. Reagan refused to consider increases in the tax rate structure, and as a result, the Tax Equity and Fiscal Responsibility Act of 1982 only closed certain tax loopholes and added several excise taxes. Along with other relatively minor provisions, the legislation only modestly increased revenue and hardly fulfilled its rather grandiose name. While it amused Wright that Reagan claimed victory, Wright's hopes for more progressivism in the tax structure went unfulfilled. When the *Washington Post* suggested that the Democrats had "sold out for nothing," Wright protested, obviously sensitive.[65] Reagan, meanwhile, tried to argue in a bit of silly semantics that he had not raised taxes, only fees. To the extent there was a victor as the debt continued to grow, it was perhaps Rostenkowski, a reality not lost on many members of the Democratic caucus.[66]

When it came to the appropriations process of the new budget, Wright and his allies had more success. Shaving the White House's defense request,

Wright helped pass additional spending for education and the elderly. When Reagan claimed that the Democratic leadership had broken a promise not to increase spending, Wright denied the charge by citing the aggregate figures. Unable to claim victory, Reagan vetoed the measure only to have Congress override the veto. It was, Wright later wrote approvingly, the first time Reagan had lost on a major bill, a turning point of sorts. Wright had hardly reversed Reaganomics, but Reagan did agree at the end of 1982 to sign a bill to improve the nation's transportation infrastructure. The bill was deficit neutral, with a hike in the gasoline tax to help cover the cost, and Reagan feared another veto override. Once again claiming that he had avoided taxes, only allowing fees, Reagan signed the measure. For Jim Wright, at least, the 97th Congress ended a little better than it had begun.[67]

One might conclude from it all that Wright had shifted to his political left, and that his policies had evolved in part as a result of Reagan's challenge to his sense of good government. There had always been a degree of reactive dynamism in Wright's policies to match his idealism, of course. Nevertheless, it was as much the dynamism in the political culture of Reagan's Washington as the changes in Wright himself that made Wright's position appear to be more liberal than before.

Environmental policy, where Reagan attacked regulation and funding like no president before, was a case in point. Environmentalists had grown ambivalent about Wright as the energy crisis had unfolded, but now, when they were faced with their political antichrist, Wright had never looked so good—or so liberal. When Wright protested that Reagan was cutting synthetic fuels, or had neglected public lands or clean air, environmentalists applauded him more than ever.[68] In 1981, in what appears foresighted today, Wright warned of "the buildup of carbon dioxide in the atmosphere." The following year he called for action against "acid rain."[69] Suddenly, to environmentalists, Wright's continued support for reclamation projects such as the Tennessee Tombigbee Waterway, then under construction, did not seem so bad.[70]

Wright remained a centrist. When it came to a proposed balanced budget amendment, he joined with House Minority Whip Trent Lott of Mississippi, and, of all people, Phil Gramm, to back a form of the amendment. Working for compromise, Wright's version required the president to submit a balanced budget but allowed exceptions for war, or for when the president requested a deficit for a specific purpose that Congress had approved. All additional expenditures beyond those approved would require additional revenue sources or specific cuts. If it turned out as the year progressed that revenues had dropped below expectations, across-the-board cuts would match the same percentage as the shortfall.

Many liberals were aghast. The press, Wright noted in his diary, "speculates on why I would offer such a thing."[71] One old liberal foe, Richard Bolling, a Democrat from Missouri, was, in Wright's words, "not wholly enthused." Worse for Wright was O'Neill's opposition. "I do a lot of things on my own," Wright stated defensively.[72] The Republicans, however, refused to bend on any his qualifications, and Wright had had enough. He announced that he opposed any amendment going forward.[73] The Republican proposal was "careless mischief." When Reagan's plan passed, but without the supermajority required, Wright was in the headlines—standing before the cameras with the liberals, an apparent ally in opposition.[74]

Certainly, Wright's support for an extension of the Voting Rights Act in 1982 was neither a profile in liberal courage nor any break from his past. The renewal was overwhelmingly popular, helped by rumors that the KKK might protest it. The debate, therefore, was never over renewal, only over specific compromises proposed by southern conservatives, including Wright. When the renewal passed virtually devoid of any qualifications, both Wright and Reagan could read the tea leaves. Both men kept their reservations to themselves and voiced their support for the act.[75]

As the Voting Rights Act played out in the halls of Congress, a more dramatic confrontation played out in the nation's airports. When the air traffic controllers went on strike in August 1981, Reagan refused to negotiate and ordered the strikers back to work in accordance with the Taft-Hartley Act of 1947. With the airports operating with non-union replacements, it was a tenuous situation until full staffing resumed four years later. It was, in short, a perfect chance for Democrats to couch Reagan as indifferent to the concerns of everyday Americans. Wright, however, did not take the bait. While he thought the union's grievances were legitimate, he held his tongue. Quietly, he even agreed with Reagan that public employees "in these positions of great responsibility" had no right to strike.[76]

Of course, in foreign policy Wright had always harbored the idealistic view that in time of national strife the nation should come together under its elected leader. He had grown sensitive to slights on congressional prerogative, which begged conflict with the executive branch, but for the most part he had not found the balance of powers particularly challenging when it came to foreign affairs. After all, he had shared Carter's worldview, and had enjoyed the increased international role that his friendship with Carter had brought him. As Reagan assumed office, therefore, Wright hoped for more of the same, and he called for Americans to support their chosen leader in his efforts around the world. Wright refused to join the liberal chorus couching Reagan as a dangerous warmonger. Once again, Wright began the new presidency as the moderate, the conciliator, even if time would prove the careful balance between the branches of government, between the two parties, and between the powerful and competing egos impossible to maintain. Moderate or not, nothing was the same.

No one doubted where Ronald Reagan stood in foreign policy. Although he did not publicly repudiate the SALT II agreement, which was still pending ratification, he ignored it and approached arms negotiations with skepticism. The buildup of American power, Reagan assumed, was the only thing the communists understood. This cynicism of diplomacy concerned the idealistic Wright but appealed to the old Cold Warrior in him. While Wright resisted the military buildup that Reagan's budget proposed, Wright's compromises still increased spending. "We cannot afford to place ourselves at the mercy of those who would have no mercy," he stated.[77]

Breaking from many in his own party—and breaking from the provisions of SALT II that he still advocated—Wright supported Reagan's call for the development of a new intercontinental ballistic missile system, the MX. With new submarine-based and air-based missile systems, Reagan argued, the United States could conduct diplomacy from a "position of strength and unity."[78] Wright agreed, although at reduced appropriations.[79] Similarly, when Reagan pressed for continued development of the supersonic B-1 bomber, Wright agreed that the plane was "very important," without adding that he hoped for construction in Fort Worth.[80] When in 1981 Reagan proposed selling Saudi Arabia airborne warning and command systems, or AWACS, Wright acknowledged that he was "generally opposed." Unlike many Democrats, however, Wright suggested requiring American operation as a compromise.[81]

When Reagan did make diplomatic overtures, Wright offered praise. Reagan's 1981 proposal to reduce ICBMs with the Soviets was "bold, imaginative, sensible and reasonable," in Wright's view.[82] As many Democrats cited Reagan's simultaneous military buildup as hypocritical, Wright "wholeheartedly and enthusiastically" helped pass a bipartisan resolution of support.[83] Although the proposal went nowhere, the Soviets wary of the military increases, Wright welcomed the evidence that Reagan was no mad bomber. Enthused, Wright even proposed that both nations reduce arms spending by

10 percent for five years, suggesting that the billions of dollars saved could be used to establish a fund "to benefit the needy of the world."[84] Although the Letter-to-Ivan-like proposal also went nowhere, Wright and the new president appeared, at least initially, to be an odd pair on a similar path.

As such, the growing nuclear freeze movement posed a challenge to Wright. In June 1982, a nuclear freeze rally brought a million people to New York City, and over 2 million Americans signed a petition to the United Nations. Liberal Democrats, undoubtedly hoping to put the administration on the defensive, proposed a resolution endorsing the demands.[85] In his diary Wright worried that the resolution might "pull the rug out from under [Reagan]," making Soviet compromise less likely. "I have tried to respect the right of every president of whichever party to speak for us in the councils of the world," he noted. At the same time, however, Wright could not help but wonder about Reagan's true goals, given how budget talks had gone. Was the military buildup really to strengthen America's diplomatic hand? In the end Wright voted for the resolution, which failed by two votes and left Wright wondering if he might have lobbied harder.[86]

Many conservatives today credit Reagan as having ended the Cold War, citing how his military buildup depleted the Soviet Union's smaller economy, contributing to its domestic unrest and national implosion. Wright disagreed. If Reagan had intended such a plan, he would have rejected diplomacy out of hand, Wright later said. Reagan's early promises to seek an arms agreement appeared to be genuine, according to Wright, and in fact, when the new Soviet leader Mikhail Gorbachev rose to power during Reagan's second term, Reagan did ultimately conclude an accord. Moreover, if it were true that Reagan sought to deplete Soviet resources, conservatives would have to acknowledge the complicity of the nuclear buildup in producing America's own exploding national debt.[87]

Both Reagan and Wright supported foreign aid, although from different perspectives. Wright agreed that American economic support defended against communism, but believed that humanitarian needs were paramount. Although both men worried about debt, both also resisted cuts to foreign aid as a solution.[88] Wright supported Reagan's Caribbean Basin Initiative, which promised trade benefits to key Latin American countries, even as many of Wright's liberal colleagues, angry over the ongoing appropriation battles, saw a chance at retribution. Stifling his own spite, Wright worked the floor, an apparent Reagan ally, helping the legislation pass.[89]

Wright initially welcomed the Reagan administration's call for additional aid to El Salvador. Salvadorian elections loomed, and Reagan believed the

country's leader, José Napoleón Duarte, was its best defense against growing leftist violence and communism. Many American liberals disagreed,
however, viewing Duarte as an authoritarian who was resistant to democratic reforms. Wright denied that Reagan had asked him to lobby for the
new aid, but did remark that it was important for the president to "speak
with a clear voice," and that a humanitarian crisis loomed.[90] To make matters more complex for Wright, the leftist insurgency appeared to flow from
Cuba through El Salvador's neighbor Nicaragua. Wright still supported aid
to Daniel Ortega's Sandinista government as leverage for moderation.

In late March 1982 a right-leaning coalition won El Salvador's national
elections. Although Duarte would later return as president, it all boded poorly
for peace. Accordingly, in April, Wright led a bipartisan congressional delegation to meet with leaders from Costa Rica, Panama, and Jamaica as well as
Ortega, Duarte, and the leaders of the new ruling junta. A "government of
national unity," Wright stated in El Salvador, required reforms. If the new
junta wanted aid, it would have to comply.[91] In Nicaragua, Wright was disappointed to find a virtual "police state." It was necessary, Ortega insisted,
because right-leaning guerrillas from El Salvador, fueled by the American aid
to that country, were threatening his country. As one of Wright's colleagues
suggested that Ortega was "paranoid," Wright was left to demand liberalization from the Sandinistas and threatened the loss of American aid.[92]

Much to Wright's dismay, Reagan did not want to wait. Appearing unconcerned about abuses from the right wing in El Salvador, the president
viewed Nicaragua's Ortega as a communist who was fermenting revolution
in his neighbor. After successfully pressing Congress to cancel the Nicaraguan aid, Reagan informed the congressional leadership, as required by
law, that he had authorized $19 million for covert CIA action against the
leftist guerrillas in El Salvador. Wright was skeptical, wondering if the aid
was actually going to the so-called Contras, the opposition force against the
Sandinistas in Nicaragua, as Ortega claimed.

Wright had good reason for his skepticism. Although the CIA director,
William Casey, denied it, his agency had in fact trained anti-Sandinista
paramilitary brigades in Florida and California and funneled weapons to
those within Nicaragua. It had encouraged Argentina to train the followers
of the former Nicaraguan leader, Somoza, so they could return and fight for
Ortega's overthrow. By the end of 1982, with reports leaking to the media,
it was becoming hard for the Reagan administration to hide such covert
activities. Wright watched and waited, weighing his idealism and pragmatism with his growing skepticism and frustration.[93]

For much of the media, the momentous developments throughout the 97th Congress raised a key question. In the words of the *National Journal*, "Are Democrats really in control?" Do they, the *Congressional Quarterly* followed, "control the House?" It was, without a doubt, one columnist answered, an "unruly Congress." Even Wright could not ignore the question. Democrats, he acknowledged, "have been accused . . . of being in disarray."[94]

It was, of course, understandable. The defection of southern conservatives in the budget battles—in particular, of a group termed "Boll Weevils," after a beetle that fed on cotton plants—made pundits wonder if the 1980 election was just the beginning. Was the almost-three-decades-long Democratic dominance in the House coming to an end?[95] For O'Neill and Wright, the first step to answering such questions was determining the fate of the rebels. The dissidents still professed fidelity, but they had coalesced as the Conservative Democratic Forum. Their continued allegiance, they insisted, required the party to stop its liberal bent.

Gramm, sure of his political hand, was the most outspoken of them. "Congressman Gramm is a highly popular figure around here," observed the *Mexia Daily News* in Gramm's district. Many constituents seemed to enjoy the publicity that Gramm's dissonance won and celebrated with a "Phil Gramm Appreciation Dinner." These appeared to be "bleak and arid times for liberalism in Texas," observed one pundit.[96] The Republican Party let Gramm know that its door was open; meanwhile, Texas's Republican governor, Clements, leaked the news that he had met with the Boll Weevils, saying that "switches" might follow.[97] Gramm was blunt; he would join the GOP if the Democrats removed him from the Budget Committee.[98]

That decision fell to the Steering and Policy Committee and, indirectly, to O'Neill and Wright. Many angry liberals had no mercy. "Why doesn't he admit that he's a Republican anyway?" wondered Houston's Mickey Leland. Most Democrats did not want an ideological purge but thought punishment necessary. Connecticut's Toby Moffett remarked that he could "easily get 50" Democrats to support Gramm's dismissal from the committee.[99]

Once again Wright was in the middle. "I feel like the wife who was asked whether she considered divorce," Wright laughed. "She answered, 'Divorce, no, murder, yes.'"[100] When Charlie Wilson, who had helped Wright get Hance on the Ways and Means Committee, offered to resign from his own committee as punishment, the pressure on Wright increased.[101] At the same time, the Conservative Democratic Forum counted forty-four members in its ranks, and no majority leader could afford such a defection. When the media speculated that Wright favored punishment, Wright replied that no one "should be punished for voting his convictions."[102] Trying to calm his caucus, he noted that he had helped to promote Tom Foley and Bill Alexander, who were both considered conservatives.[103] Speaking to his flock in September 1981, Wright claimed that "defectors voting against the position of our party isn't anything new." What was new was the unity "on the other side of the aisle."[104]

The solution, O'Neill and Wright got the caucus to agree, was to forgive all past affronts. In the future, however, prized committee positions would represent rewards for loyalty. When the Steering and Policy Committee designated certain votes a "litmus test," members could "expect to have their votes scrutinized." The leadership might allow exemptions "on the basis of conscience," but would punish members for "conniving with the opposition." The media cut through the semantics, saying the Democrats had "granted amnesty to the Boll Weevils."[105] The compromise, for one thing, said little about committee assignments for the next Congress, and liberals promised not to forget the betrayal. Wright simply tried to dodge the issue. "It is not the leadership but the membership which elects members to committees," Wright stated when asked his position. "It is uncertain what the membership will do to Congressman Gramm."[106]

In the end the liberals were true to their word, denying Gramm his Budget Committee assignment. Gramm, equally true to his word, resigned his congressional seat, and a special election took place for his replacement. In this election Gramm ran as a Republican—and won. Wright later insisted that he had taken no position on Gramm's committee assignment; in any event, Gramm's partisan switch hardly proved unique. Hance switched parties two years later, with a number of the "Yellow Dog Democrats" following.[107]

The liberal Democrats were not the only ones with a long memory and a sense of vindictiveness. Having failed to oust Wright in the 1980 election, the National Conservative Political Action Committee began an extensive campaign of undermining his support. Announcing that it had half a million dollars to use against the majority leader, "Nickpack" played loose with the facts and, despite its denials, fabricated evidence. Wright, it stated, for example, did not support the B-1 bomber. It cited votes out of context and misquoted Wright.[108] To a degree such tactics had become normal political operations, but NCPAC was more Machiavellian. When NCPAC began to run commercials, several Democrats implied that the stations could face libel suits. NCPAC immediately filed a $10 million lawsuit against Wright personally, charging that he had stifled the organization's free speech rights by directly intimidating four specific stations. Wright quickly denied it. "[NCPAC] is very careless with the truth, and I do not wonder that many self-respecting broadcasters throughout the country have declined their material," Wright stated. After extensive media coverage, NCPAC could not prove its charges; the station managers denied ever having spoken to Wright.[109] NCPAC then filed a complaint with the Federal Communications Commission (FCC). The FCC, however, held that organizations, unlike official candidates, did not have an affirmative right to present paid messages on private media outlets.[110]

Relentless, NCPAC then filed a complaint against Wright for distributing "political pamphlets" at public expense. One of Wright's newsletters had claimed that NCPAC was "attacking my reputation" with untruths.[111] The bipartisan Committee on Congressional Mailing Standards ruled unanimously, however, that Wright had broken no rule. Indeed, Wright had obtained a legal ruling before his mailing and argued afterward that the attacks were coordinated to cast doubt regardless of specific vindications. It was, in the words of another Democrat, a "new wave of McCarthyism."[112]

Wright, angry once again, had no plans to take the attacks lying down. A group of Fort Worth loyalists organized a "task force" to answer the constant charges and produced bumper stickers proclaiming, "Hang In there, Jim."[113] Wright argued that the politics of demonization hurt national unity and that the money flowing into PACs like NCPAC threatened the nation's two-party system.[114] As the charges and countercharges flew, both sides sent each other terse letters.[115] In fact, even as Wright complained about the money, he still armed himself well. Even as he decried personal attacks, his own rhetoric coarsened. Whatever his ideals, he had to be pragmatic. Although Wright was not directly involved, a group of Democrats leveled dubious charges that NCPAC had violated election laws by coordinating with House Republicans.[116] In the words of the *Washington Post*, "Democrats Copy GOP Campaign Tactics—Almost."[117]

It all took a toll on Wright, whose schedule remained brutal. Up early, Wright read the paper on his way to work and often ate a quick bowl of Raisin Bran at the office. A new computerized "electronic mail" system arrived—a "new and innovative form of communications"—but Wright had little time to learn its operations. Meetings followed one after the other, often costing Wright lunch. In the evenings there remained speeches and dinners, often quite late. With little time for recreation, Wright wrestled with insomnia, the attacks replaying in his brain.[118] Betty had grown accustomed to Wright's work ethic, but his ability to control his temper now impressed her. In one instance, Wright accepted an invitation to dinner that included the televangelist James Robison. Although Wright had just supported a resolution denouncing the Texas atheist Madalyn Murray O'Hair's efforts to prohibit a congressional chaplain, Robison was blunt and accusatory.[119] "I kept my temper despite two or three verbal provocations," Wright recorded in his diary. "Only once, when the self-appointed judge of the motives of others interrupted something I was trying to say to accuse me of misrepresenting myself, did I answer sharply, insisting that a productive conversation could not proceed on the plane of personal accusations."[120] Had Robison known that Wright had stopped attending church regularly—a product of exhaustion and a source of guilt—he undoubtedly would have attacked again. The Religious Right, after all, appeared to Wright to have become as brutal as NCPAC.[121]

Perhaps it was his exhaustion, or perhaps it was his single-minded focus on Reagan, but Wright remained amazingly cavalier in his own dealings. Far from anticipating that the more forceful critics might delve into his financial past to use his actions against him, Wright continued to make their job easier. Not only did Wright continue to push to the boundaries of propriety in his investments, but his business relationship with his friend Mallick deepened. As their investment company, Mallightco, prospered, with Betty as vice-president, Wright saw no problem with borrowing $120,000 from the company, his personal and corporate finances becoming entwined to a troublesome degree. Mallick, moreover, let Betty drive his wife's Cadillac, technically a company car. When Betty ended up taking the car to Washington, it opened even more lines of possible attack.[122] In another instance, in 1982, a staffer wrote Wright's top assistant, Marshall Lynam, saying that their boss was coming close to the legal limit on honoraria. After an organization to which Wright had given a speech made a charitable donation in his name, the aide argued that the donation should be counted as earned income. "I just don't want the day to come on down the road when his tax report is scrutinized and found lacking," the aide noted. Wright, however, was not worried, and indeed nothing came of it. It was, however, indicative of Wright's blind spot—and, sadly for Wright in the end, somewhat prophetic.[123]

In 1982, at least, Wright's finances remained out of the spotlight— surprisingly, given the vehemence of the attacks he faced. As the midterm election approached, it might have had something to do with Wright's apparent invulnerability. NCPAC's attacks, it appeared, had barely dented Wright's district poll numbers. NCPAC had hoped to encourage a conservative to run against Wright in the Democratic primary, but it found no takers. Two years before, after all, the well-funded Bradshaw had come up short. With the conservative PACs unable to coalesce around a single candidate, the GOP ended up running Jim Ryan of Euless, Texas, a plain-spoken carpenter who seemed to enjoy espousing ultraconservative views that were unpopular in Wright's crafted district.[124] "My opposition in Fort Worth is not as formidable as before," Wright said, summarizing his situation to a supporter.[125]

NCPAC's attacks may have hurt Wright nationally, but his district's voters still knew what Wright had done for them. As Reagan proceeded with deregulation, Braniff Airlines went bankrupt, leaving thousands of Wright's constituents unemployed. The Airline Deregulation Act of 1978, Wright wrote the White House, required compensation, despite Reagan's "philosophical opposition."[126] At the same time, Wright lobbied for American Airlines at DFW Airport, saying it deserved new international flights.[127] When a massive flood struck Fort Worth late in 1981, Wright toured the area in a helicopter and promised to ensure that the administration declared a disaster area.[128] It was, perhaps, a tribute to Wright's enduring popularity that even during NCPAC's unprecedented assault, bumper stickers appeared in Fort Worth reading "Wright for President." Rumors had spread that Edward Kennedy was considering another run for the presidency in 1984 and that he considered Wright a possible opponent—or a running mate. Moreover, O'Neill had hinted at his own retirement. "Sure I have sad days," O'Neill stated in a sentiment Wright undoubtedly understood. "I've always thought that I would like to come back here as kind of an elder statesman."[129]

When it came to the 1982 congressional elections, Wright had reason for optimism, and not just about his own prospects. Despite reports that "money flows to the Right in the 1982 campaign," and despite the accusations that continued to fly, polls indicated that the Democrats had the advantage.[130] "November 2nd is probably the most critical election America has faced in many years," Wright stated hyperbolically. "Because of misguided Republican economies, friends and neighbors of yours and mine have lost their jobs."[131] Freed of any threat to his reelection, Wright went on the road for others, regaining some of the goodwill the budget battles had cost.

It was indeed a good day for Democrats when the election finally arrived. Wright walloped Ryan 69–32 percent while his party gained twenty-six House seats. Every candidate for whom Wright had campaigned had won, and Governor Clements, who had so ardently solicited the Boll Weevils, had lost. As Wright savored the prospect of welcoming the reinforcements, a more sober analysis might have urged caution. The Democrats had not picked up one Senate seat, and Reagan undoubtedly remained obstinate. Clements owed his loss more to a Southern Methodist University football booster scandal than to his policies. Taken as a whole, the election results were about the economy—but the economy could recover, and Reagan still had two years in office. It was easy to assume at the time that the Republicans' slow inroads in winning the South, and their once promising New Right coalition, had petered out. At least, like Wright, one could hope. In fact, the reality was a lot less clear.[132]

_____

CHAPTER 16

Rallying the Opposition

FRIENDS AND ENEMIES (1982–1986)

With the 1982 election an apparent salve for the Democrats' woes, the *New York Times* proclaimed that Wright was "riding high." He was, the *Fort Worth Star-Telegram* added, "returning to Washington with more clout."[1] Wright seemed to agree, proposing—"with no particular pride of authorship"—a massive stimulus program, grandly labeled "Program for National Economic Revival." To pay for the spending, Wright proposed to delay Reagan's tax cuts and reduce his military expenditures.[2] Former vice-president Walter Mondale agreed but cautioned that many Americans still shared Reagan's distrust of government. Democrats, he advised, "must show that we are squarely on the side of entrepreneurship."[3]

With Wright at the fore, the Democratic caucus promised to flesh out an "alternative budget."[4] O'Neill, meanwhile, reminded members of the previous year's agreement. On the designated critical votes, Democrats "were expected to vote with the party."[5] Across the aisle, Newt Gingrich sought the ear of his own caucus, suggesting that Republicans should "obstruct House proceedings" as a protest against partisan committee membership ratios.[6] When the Democrats made it harder to include unrelated amendments to budget bills—in the words of one Democrat, "the license of the little guy . . . to make waves"—the Republicans howled in unison.[7]

Watching it all, pundits predicted gridlock. When pressed on the program *Meet the Press* how he could think of such an expansive program "when you've done so little the last two years," Wright replied simply that the Democrats "are in a far better position."[8] He did not mention Reagan's reaction to his proposals. Apparently dismissing the election results, Reagan pressed for additional cuts in domestic programs and even more expansion of the military. "Tip [O'Neill] came unglued," Wright later wrote. "God damn it, Tip," Reagan answered. "We do care about [the poor]."[9] Working to calm tensions, Wright suggested a compromise, a limited jobs bill in lieu of a larger budget agreement. Reagan was "uncomfortable and anxious to adjourn," Wright recalled, but as they departed, Reagan's adviser Donald Regan, who was then secretary of the treasury, surprised O'Neill by whispering that "we're not that far apart on the jobs thing."[10] Reagan, it appeared after all, was on the defensive, and did not want to appear uncaring in the depth of the recession.

The result, an emergency supplemental appropriation, was perhaps the best evidence that Reagan recognized the new political dynamic and was willing to compromise—at least in some respects. The bill authorized a one-time spending increase for the ongoing fiscal year, with the money to be spread among domestic and military programs. The bill was a shadow of what he had originally proposed, but Wright praised the compromise nevertheless, ignoring the fact that Congress itself had received a salary increase.[11] When a few weeks later the report of the bipartisan National Commission on Social Security Reform, created in the previous Congress, suggested that the program's solvency demanded concessions on both sides, Wright again saw the opportunity for compromise. The report, he claimed, "contains a redeeming symmetry."[12]

As Congress debated Social Security, Wright argued that it was "an outrage" that the program blocked disability benefits to participants with mental illness.[13] Wright supported tax credits for older Americans who worked longer, thereby saving costs, but insisted that the Democrats would never "cut benefits." A better solution, he added, was to augment the revenue. "There are any number of sources . . . to make Social Security trust funds solvent forever."[14]

The commission's report did not promise to make Social Security solvent forever, but rather to increase its solvency for seventy-five years. It recommended keeping the program's "fundamental structure," neither privatizing it nor significantly altering its budgeting format, but implementing both cuts and new revenue. The former was what Wright had suggested the Democrats would reject.[15] Having accepted the report at the start, Wright accepted the bill that emerged at the end. The Social Security Amendments of 1983 clearly represented a compromise. They increased the age of retirement gradually and delayed cost-of-living adjustments. They also increased taxes on wealthier participants and added contributions from federal employees.[16] Wright did not get the disability benefits he sought—at least initially. Within a year Congress passed the Social Security Disability Benefits Reform Act of 1984, which codified the benefits available to the blind and mentally ill. Wright watched with some satisfaction as Reagan, who had once called for privatization, now spoke of the nation's "ironclad commitment to Social Security."[17]

If the emergency stimulus bill and Social Security reform suggested that Reagan recognized that the election had diminished his sway, he still drew the line in the larger, ongoing debate over the regular budget. This confounded Wright, who suggested that in regard to further domestic cuts, "we've already squeezed that lemon pretty tightly."[18] The key, Wright agreed with many Democrats, was to cap the tax cuts Reagan had passed for the wealthiest Americans.[19] The Democrats, he argued, should demonstrate that Reagan's program would have "a devastating impact" on the national debt.[20] They should stress that they proposed not cuts to the armed forces, but a lower rate of increase.[21] When Reagan responded by ridiculing the Democrats' ideas publicly, Wright described Reagan's comments as "an intemperate outburst," a "theatrical display aimed at image-building."[22]

By the spring of 1983, the larger Democratic majority had passed a budget resolution that Wright remarked proved that his party could "accept responsibility" and act realistically.[23] By June, both houses of Congress had reached a compromise on the resolution, not to the level Wright sought, but to levels significantly different from the existing appropriations. The resolution included a smaller increase in defense spending and caps on tax cuts for the wealthy, which Wright proclaimed "would reduce President Reagan's huge deficit."[24] The battle over specific appropriations then commenced, challenging Wright to keep his troops in line. Wright spoke of the "mandate" that the Democrats had agreed to the previous year and threatened individual sanctions for a lack of loyalty. When necessary, he notified the whips, in one instance suggesting that a dissenter "baffled" him. It was a "matter of personal honor," Wright stated, implying punishment for a sin he considered grave.[25] At the same time, however, in his typical style, Wright frequently tried to soothe ruffled feathers, to reach consensus without coercion. "I think I can understand some of the pressures you're under," Wright scribbled to one wayward Democrat. "Please help us if you can."[26]

Operating under continuing resolutions, Congress knew the importance of the budget impasse as the second session of the 98th Congress began in 1984. There was, in the words of one headline, a "climate of uncertainty." Wright tried to project optimism, but, like many other Democrats, he demonstrated his exasperation. "[Reagan's] lack of leadership does not bode well for serious deficit reduction," Wright stated bluntly.[27] A few weeks later a poll of members of Congress demonstrated that frustration ruled the day. "Even Congress Is Unhappy with Congress," *U.S. News and World Report* declared.[28]

As the budget talks resumed, Wright described the national debt in almost apocalyptic terms: "staggering," "overpowering," and "stupendous." Ignoring the impact of the recession and the multitude of factors involved, he laid the blame on Reagan. It was "bitter irony" that the White House blamed the Democrats, he said.[29] White House Chief of Staff James Baker let Wright know that his rhetoric was not appreciated. "We must communicate with each other directly rather than through the press," Baker wrote.[30] With negotiators regularly meeting—as an "ad hoc exploratory group," in Wright's words—Wright then backed off his more aggressive claims. "The public is very cynical about Congress' ability to do anything," Wright agreed. "Let's prove them wrong."[31] With Rostenkowski and Budget Committee chairman Jim Jones playing greater roles, Wright still hoped for what later generations would term a "grand bargain," a sweeping and impactful bill. Reagan's position appeared "fixed in stone," however, as one Democrat termed it. If the White House did not budge on the tax cuts enacted previously, only a small, temporary solution would result. The nation would suffer.[32]

In the end, it happened just as Wright feared. The Omnibus Reconciliation Act, signed on April 18, 1984, largely maintained the status quo, only reducing federal employee benefits. The Deficit Reduction Act, signed three months later, included approximately one hundred provisions that tweaked the tax code to increase revenue but did not adjust the tax rates that most economists thought necessary.[33] In short, without the significant reforms that Wright had hoped for, Reaganomics continued largely intact—for good or ill.

In time, both appeared to take place. As 1984 progressed, the nation's economy recovered rapidly, undoubtedly aided by the tax cuts and the disarray within OPEC as well as by a cut in interest rates. Wright seized upon the latter as evidence that he had been correct all along, even though the high rates had, by this point, helped break the Carter-era inflation. In an interesting aside, Wright also denounced the concept of the variable rate mortgage, allowed by Reagan's reforms. Unusually low rates might lure unsophisticated homebuyers into mortgages they could not afford, Wright warned, causing a bubble that could cost the nation. It was, of course, the very scenario that unfolded in 2008 at the beginning of the Great Recession.[34]

The tremendous economic growth buoyed Reagan's popularity. By the end of 1984, personal income had risen by its highest annual rate since World War II.[35] By 1989, the economy had produced 16 million new jobs and the nation's gross domestic product (GDP) had doubled. Reaganomics worked, Republicans happily exclaimed, beginning to elevate Reagan to the status of a political icon.[36] Wright and his fellow Democrats had lost a key argument—but some of their complaints were still legitimate. By the time Reagan left office, the nation owed approximately $2 trillion. The debt, it appeared, was not just the result of the 1982 recession, but something more systemic. Wright continued to claim that Reagan's tax cuts, combined with his military increases, were to blame, while Republicans countered that the cause was excessive domestic spending. The Democrats also found another issue that played to their advantage, the growing international trade deficit. In time they complained that the economy was growing unevenly. Disparity in wealth was increasing, and poverty rates remained high.[37]

The Democrats were not shy about pointing out these flaws, and at least in one respect Reagan made their job easier. Reagan's glitz lent an optimistic aura about the White House, and yet it contrasted nicely for his opponents with the dramatic increase in the number of homeless people on the streets. In the words of one political scientist, the homeless were one of Reagan's "enduring legacies."[38] Later termed "the decade of greed," the Reagan era proved a study in contrasts: it brought tremendous economic growth, which Republicans crowed about, but also the cracks in society that the Democrats emphasized.[39]

Collegiality and bipartisanship, meanwhile, continued to ebb. In one instance, Gingrich played to the C-SPAN cameras by attacking Massachusetts Democrat Edward Boland's patriotism. Aware that the camera was focused narrowly on him, Gingrich demanded that Boland respond. With his speech technically occurring after Congress had adjourned and with the chamber virtually empty and Boland absent, Gingrich left the impression that Boland had no response. Livid, O'Neill ordered the cameras to pan the chamber when congressmen spoke in the future. Because he did not notify the GOP beforehand, however, the next day Pennsylvania Republican Robert Walker looked "like a fool" talking to an empty chamber.[40] O'Neill's order was, in the words of Minority Leader Bob Michel, an "act of dictatorial retribution." A few days later, with Gingrich lambasting Democrats in personal terms and refusing to yield the floor for a response, O'Neill simply interrupted him. An angry O'Neill declared Gingrich's actions "the lowest thing I have ever seen," and Republicans complained that O'Neill's interruptions were out of order. After the parliamentarian agreed, Gingrich won a standing ovation from his party colleagues.[41]

The scuffle depressed Wright but he increasingly leveled his own coarse charges. Reagan, he once claimed, was "outrageous and irresponsible" and didn't "care about the future."[42] For Wright, at least, his sharper elbows had an alternative motive. After the New York Times quoted O'Neill as having remarked that he might stay in Congress one more term, a media frenzy speculated that he wanted to be appointed the ambassador to Ireland and that the Speakership would be open.[43] Many southerners still believed, as conservative Charlie Stenholm put it, that O'Neill was "the problem," and that the next Speaker should be one of their own.[44] Wright felt comfortable with his conservative credentials and recognized that his emphasis on the debt appealed to the fiscal hawks. As historian Karl Gerard Brandt put it, some southern conservatives had come to perceive their "principle of fiscal responsibility as having been sullied by Reaganomics."[45] At the same time, however, Wright recognized that the liberals were the most aggrieved at Reagan. Attacking Reagan would therefore endear himself to the liberals at the exact time they, too, needed new leadership. The old liberal thorn in Wright's side, Phillip Burton, had died suddenly of a ruptured artery, and his fellow challenger, Richard Bolling, appeared to have lost his drive for the top job. "I think Jim has done a good job," Bolling stated as Wright's words became more cutting.[46]

If Wright faced a real challenge, it came from his erstwhile ally Dan Rostenkowski. Rostenkowski was coy about his own ambitions, but when he reminded the press that Wright was known for his hot temper, he fueled speculation. Ignoring Wright's career-long effort to cultivate a network of supporters, Rostenkowski suggested that Wright would have trouble "walking onto the floor of the House, putting his arm around a guy and saying, 'You son of a gun, what else are we going to do tonight?'" Undoubtedly enjoying a potential fight, the press overlooked the two Democratic leaders' continuing cooperation. It was a "long-simmering feud" to columnists, a "family feud."[47]

It was in the midst of all the fierce politics that Wright, in an astounding lack of judgment, once again stumbled into a situation that would open him up to criticism. He would later claim that he was too busy with the budget impasse to realize that he was giving the appearance of impropriety—or approaching it. Wright's actions showed his growing willingness to push the edges of the legal envelope. It suggested hubris, but also the fact that Wright mistakenly assumed that his actions were too common to attract attention. Even as the nature of politics evolved, Wright handed his growing number of enemies the ammunition they needed.

As the 1984 election approached, one of Wright's friends, the former teamster Carlos Moore, approached him about publishing a book of photographs. When Wright replied that he wanted the book to say something, Moore suggested a compilation of Wright's writings, a project that would become *Reflections of a Public Man*. In addition to Moore, Fort Worth publisher Mark Williams bid to produce the book. Both proposed an unusual payment. Williams offered Wright a 50 percent royalty on the book's gross, while Moore offered 55 percent. With royalties for most authors substantially less, either was sure to raise eyebrows as a potential sweetheart deal. Wright later noted that if money had been his main concern, he could have charged more for the book. He wanted a cheap volume to attract college students and a volume to help his anticipated run for the Speakership. Indeed, Wright quickly distributed the book throughout his caucus.[48]

In selecting Moore's Madison Publishing, Wright made another mistake. A decade before, Moore had sought to help another politician by embezzling funds from a union account. To make matters even more unseemly, Moore had also contracted with Wright's campaign committee in the 1982 elections. With payments going to and from Moore, the deal had all the appearance of money laundering, an easy target for critics. Wright at least recognized that his profits might exceed congressional limits on outside income; accordingly, he received assurances from attorneys that book royalties were exempted.[49]

To work on the book, Wright let one staffer go to hire another, George Mair. Congressional rules prohibited public employees from working on private congressional projects, but Wright felt comfortable with the arrangement. Mair had other office duties and it was commonplace—even by critics such as Gingrich—to use staffers on personal publications. Moreover, unlike so many other congressmen whose employees had ghostwritten their books, Wright reasoned, Mair had only assisted with clerical and production work.[50]

Digging his hole still deeper, Wright agreed to give the Lyndon B. Johnson Lecture at Southwest Texas State University, where his sister taught. When Wright refused to accept the honoraria because he had reached the congressional limit for his speeches, the university's president suggested using the money to buy Wright's book for distribution to political science students. Wright agreed, as he had hoped the book would serve as an educational tool. "That set a pattern," Wright later wrote. Friends began to purchase multiple copies as "gifts."[51] One, George Payte, admitted that he had purchased a thousand copies "just trying to make a contribution to Jim's income." Another bulk buyer, Gene Wood, did so "to help Jim."[52] The teamsters purchased a thousand copies, as did the Democratic national chairman and Boston University president John Silber, who later became a candidate for governor of Massachusetts. It never hurt to have an ally in a rising Democratic star.[53]

Later, when it became apparent that 90 percent of the 20,000 copies sold were in purchases of a thousand or more, Wright argued that Madison Publishing, not he, sold the book. While that was technically true, it was also true that Wright's own staff had often suggested the purchase to organizations where Wright had spoken. No one ever described the purchase as a requirement for the appearance, but it clearly tread a fine line. To Wright, lobbyists paid honoraria all the time; many congressmen had for years at least skirted the intent of the law. Wright was correct that book royalties were exempted from limits on honoraria and that he had broken no law. Exploiting a loophole, however, was hardly the actions of a man who had so ardently championed ethics, and, if it ever became public, a man who surely would pay a cost.[54]

For the time being, Wright continued his careful political balancing act, cultivating allies across the spectrum for whatever lay ahead. In addition to supporting the creation of a national holiday honoring Martin Luther King Jr., Wright wrote Reagan urging him not to repeal affirmative action goals for federal contractors.[55] When the long-fought battle over the Equal Rights Amendment finally ended with the measure three states short of the required supermajority required for ratification, Wright chastised Reagan for his opposition and won the praise of leading feminists.[56] Wright ardently defended the Department of Education against White House efforts to abolish it, and he maintained his long-fought struggle for synthetic fuels, pleasing most environmentalists.[57]

At the same time, however, Wright agreed with Reagan on the need for school prayer, even winning a "beautiful certificate" of thanks from the Moral Majority, which had so criticized him earlier.[58] "Should I be fortunate enough to become Speaker," Wright replied, "I do not favor abortion."[59] When Reagan expressed the need to crack down on criminals, Wright suggested that there was no need for "partisan finger-pointing." There was a growing "get-tough consensus in the Congress," Wright stated, a "common goal."[60] The Comprehensive Crime Control Act of 1984, which resulted, established the federal death penalty, made bail more difficult, and created the United States Sentencing Commission to guide federal judges. Years later, critics claimed, the bill unnecessarily flooded the nation's prisons, straining their resources. If the bill indeed caused the increase in the prison population, both Wright and Reagan had a hand in that result.[61] In the end, Wright told University of Texas students in January 1984, partisans could still get along for the common good. Moderation was the key, and politics did not have to be "filthy and corrupted." Wright still professed that sentiment, ignoring, at least for the moment, any actions of his own that contributed to the very problems he had bemoaned.[62]

While Wright's moderation had left him open to Reagan's foreign policy, the ongoing budget battles began to strain any alliance that existed. Increasingly, in Wright's opinion, Reagan had no need for moderation—or, for that matter, for Congress. When Wright tried to argue that smaller increases in defense spending were necessary because of the debt, Reagan seemed to believe that anything short of the maximum left America horribly vulnerable. When in March 1983 Reagan proposed the Strategic Defense Initiative (SDI), asking for millions of dollars to develop a system of lasers capable of knocking nuclear missiles from the skies, Wright was skeptical. He had always supported new military technology, but scientists questioned the SDI's feasibility. After remaining quiet on the issue for two years, Wright finally, in 1985, settled on a compromise, a limited program that Reagan resisted.[63] Similarly, in the 97th Congress Wright had supported Reagan's development of the MX missile, albeit at levels that Reagan thought insufficient. Now, far from compromising, Reagan proposed additional funds for the missiles' deployment in new, more resistant silos dubbed "dense pack." Rather than seeing any need for moderation in light of the debt, Reagan saw only surrender if the United States did not pursue his defense initiatives.[64]

Wright initially supported Reagan in his deployment of American troops as part of a multinational peacekeeping force in war-torn Lebanon. Serving on a congressional Ad Hoc Committee on Lebanon, Wright agreed to support the mission if Reagan respected congressional prerogative, including compliance with the War Powers Act. The result of the mission, however, was tragic. In October 1983, taking advantage of insufficient security, a truck bomb killed 241 American soldiers as they slept. Reagan promised continued support for the mission, but Wright and his colleagues had grown wary, and withdrawal promptly followed in February 1984.[65] In his memoirs, Wright claimed that the Democrats did not "make political capital of the tragedy." They had earlier learned from a congressional visit by Pennsylvania's John Murtha that security was lax, but they did not "demand to know why Reagan's team had not heeded Murtha's advice."[66] In fact, Wright indirectly implied it was Reagan's fault by telling the press the troops were "clustered in a militarily indefensible position like so many fish in a barrel."[67] When Reagan responded that the "climate in Congress" had weakened respect for American power, Wright exploded. "Confronted by failures," Wright stated, "Mr. Reagan repeatedly engages in unfair and untrue attributions of blame."[68]

The blame game did not last long. The day following the bombing, Reagan called the congressional leadership to the White House for a "matter of highest national security." Believing that the new left-leaning government in Grenada was stockpiling Cuban weapons, presenting a threat to hemispheric stability—including a threat to several hundred American medical students on the island—Reagan announced that he planned to invade the following morning—"unless you gentlemen strongly object."[69]

Wright was skeptical, but agreed. He had no intelligence to counter Reagan's claim, and the president, once again, deserved unity as commander-in-chief. As Reagan left the meeting, however, he stated that it would be great to see the island's citizens waving little American flags on the sidewalks as the troops liberated them. O'Neill asked Wright where he thought the president had conjured up such an image, only to be told by another that it was a scene from the old Hollywood movie *A Bell for Adano*. It was not, Wright assumed, a tremendous omen. In any event, the invasion went as well as Reagan could have hoped, and the island was under control in a matter of days. The American public largely applauded the invasion, and a congressional panel assigned to review it found it to have been justified.[70]

While Wright did not complain, he still had his doubts about the president's truthfulness. The island's students had not felt there had been any danger to them, and he knew Reagan thought the island's airport was a threat to the Panama Canal. And then, Wright wondered, was the attack on Grenada planned to wipe Lebanon from the headlines? The bombing in Lebanon, after all, "was swept entirely off the front pages."[71] Moreover, when a Soviet fighter shot down a Korean Air Lines plane, Reagan quickly labeled the incident a deliberate act of "barbarism." But could it have been an accident? Just before it happened, an American military aircraft had ventured to the edge of Soviet airspace, and, according to the National Security Council, the Soviet air defense system was in "something like chaos." Reagan had cast the Soviet Union as an "evil empire," and the appearance of the Grenada problem just seemed so convenient.[72]

Reagan seemed not to care what any Democrat thought. With many Republicans seeking to cut aid to the International Monetary Fund (IMF), which Reagan believed was a useful anticommunist tool, the White House did seek Democratic support. Afterward, however, the Republican Party attacked the very same Democrats for dumping "money down foreign rat holes." Wright, no longer willing to give Reagan the benefit of the doubt, immediately assumed his complicity.[73] When Wright in the summer of 1983 led another bipartisan delegation abroad, this time to the Far East, his dissatisfaction with Reagan's militancy was not hard to discern. Writing from Malaysia, Wright declared that the United States should "accept with patience the limits of our invincibility," always respecting the "values and sensitivities of those unlike ourselves."[74]

Wright was hardly the only one questioning Reagan's veracity. Despite White House denials, reports continued to leak out of Central America that American military aid was, in fact, flowing not just to the Salvadorans, for their own defense, but also to the Nicaraguan Contras, in their attempt to topple the ruling Sandinistas. Accordingly, in its lame duck session, the 97th Congress attached the Boland Amendment to a defense appropriations bill. The amendment, advanced by the Massachusetts liberal whom Gingrich had assailed, did not prohibit military support for the right-leaning government of El Salvador, but did prohibit efforts to overthrow the Sandinista government next door. Wright recognized that if the aid continued, it presented a direct challenge to the congressional power of the purse. The

White House saw things differently, believing the amendment to be an affront to the executive's constitutional right to conduct foreign policy. Now unable to deny that the aid in fact continued, the White House replied that the administration's actions were technically legal, because whatever the Contras sought, the administration did not intend to overthrow the Sandinistas, but rather simply to harass them into negotiating an end to their own efforts in El Salvador.[75]

Confident in this premise, the administration unleashed a public relations blitz. With rhetoric Wright described as "more confrontational," Reagan stated that his opponents counseled "passivity, resignation, and defeatism."[76] It was to one observer a strategy "to go for broke, threaten Congress with blame, and watch legislators run for cover."[77] Upping the stakes, the White House reassigned the foremost State Department advocate of negotiations with the Sandinistas, closed all Nicaraguan consulates, and staged a joint military operation with Honduras, another Nicaraguan neighbor.[78]

These actions annoyed Wright, but he feared as well that his own liberal colleagues would react by cutting all support for El Salvador, which Wright still wanted as leverage.[79] "Please don't follow the McGovern line," Wright wrote Walter Mondale, after the former vice-president criticized El Salvador's human rights record. "At least they are an elected government."[80] Without continued aid, the Salvadorian "Marxists" would win. Wright recognized that advocating continued economic aid might make him appear to support the White House's efforts to fund the Contras. Indeed, conservative pundits spoke of his "courageous approval."[81]

When liberals began to press for cancellation of all Salvadorian funding, as he had feared they would, Wright suggested a compromise prohibiting money for intelligence gathering in Nicaragua but not directly against Contra funding. In the meantime, he suggested, the United States should call on the Organization of American States for mediation. Recognizing that its hopes hung on moderates, the White House sought to buy time by appointing a commission to make recommendations. This became the Kissinger Commission, named for its chairman Henry Kissinger, and it included Wright.[82] Kissinger, it turned out, had a surprisingly good sense of humor. Approached by armed guards in Central America, he called for Wright to stand near him. "If anyone's going to be shot, we all are going to be shot," Kissinger quipped. "That's what I call bipartisanship." In any event, Reagan had appointed its members, so it was no surprise that the Kissinger Commission largely supported the administration's position in its January 1984 report. And it hardly surprised Wright that Reagan "selectively ignored" its recommendations to seek a regional solution and continue economic aid, but stressed the recommendation to continue military pressure on the Sandinistas. It confirmed to Wright that Reagan was not trustworthy.[83]

As the Kissinger Commission conducted its investigation in late 1983 and the expiration of the Boland Amendment approached, evidence grew that the CIA was behind attacks on Nicaraguan ports—attacks that were beyond the capabilities of the Contras. After the White House encouraged members of the Senate Intelligence Committee to investigate, a delegation tried to land in Managua only to learn that an attack on the airport was prohibiting them from doing so. When it subsequently became evident through official documents that the attack had been an ill-advised CIA effort to convince the senators that the demise of the Sandinistas was inevitable, the White House was left to claim weakly that "free agents" among the Contras were at fault.[84]

By this point, the administration's military operations against Nicaragua had coalesced in the so-called Restricted Interagency Group (RIG), composed of selected members of the CIA, the National Security Council (NSC), and the State Department. Among the group was the NSC staffer Lieutenant Colonel Oliver North, who would soon emerge as a central player. At the time, however, the group was already arguably violating the constitutional separation of powers by deliberately misleading the congressional oversight committees. Wright and his colleagues had no knowledge of the interagency group. The administration "treated us like mushrooms," one congressman recalled. "They keep us in the dark and cover us with manure."[85]

When news broke that the CIA had mined Nicaraguan harbors, Congress even won some Republican support for a resolution condemning the action. Reagan dismissed the resolution even as the World Court agreed that the United States had violated international law. With the Boland Amendment expired, liberal efforts to cut off all aid to El Salvador—including economic aid—gained steam. Once again in an uncomfortable position, Wright supported a compromise that became known as the "Second Boland Amendment." It allocated roughly half the funds previously allocated and then only after February 1985. To receive the money, the administration would have to certify that it was necessary to combat Sandinista efforts in El Salvador. In other words, Congress prohibited funds for offensive CIA actions directly in Nicaragua. Wright did not know—nor did any other member of Congress—that the RIG had the White House's approval to explore other methods of funding, such as via contributions from Saudi Arabia or Israel.[86]

Whether feeling the pressure from Reagan or trying to take advantage of world opinion, Daniel Ortega announced early in 1984 that the Sandinista government would hold free elections later that year. Wright was ecstatic, hoping once again for a fledgling democracy. Alfonso Robelo, a Nicaraguan moderate whom Ortega had forced into exile, convinced Wright that an opposition victory was possible. Taking his advice, Wright and a group of Democrats wrote Ortega "to commend you . . . for taking steps to open up the political process." If free elections took place, bilateral relations would improve and peace would prevail.[87]

The White House was aghast. The letter may have been "naïve," Wright responded, but to ignore Ortega's promise was to "commit ourselves" to either a "hostile Marxist state" or a long war. It was "defeatism to settle for either."[88] Predictably, Newt Gingrich led a verbal assault on the House floor, even boasting that he had sent copies of the letter to the districts of all signatories. The letter, he wrote Wright, was an "example of Congressional interference in the effective execution of America's foreign policy."[89] It was nonsense to suggest that the letter represented direct independent bilateral negotiations, Wright replied; Congress had corresponded with foreign governments since the dawn of the republic. As this constitutional question festered, Ortega invited Wright and other congressmen to observe the elections, an invitation Wright declined, no doubt sensitive to the issue. According to Wright, Arturo Cruz, a moderate Nicaraguan banker, expressed an interest in running only to have the Reagan administration dissuade him. Moreover, when Secretary of State George Shultz proposed his own peace plan, Reagan rejected it by stating that the Sandinistas only respected force. When, ultimately, Ortega won the election with 60 percent of the vote, Reagan dismissed the conclusions of Western European observers that the voting was fair.[90]

Reagan did not feel the same way about the elections in El Salvador, appointing Wright to lead a delegation to ensure fairness, an obvious bow to Wright's efforts to ensure continued funding, and, perhaps, a peace offering of sorts. The vote appeared to be legitimate and in fact resulted in the return of José Napoleón Duarte, whom the Americans had earlier supported. Wright found it somewhat annoying that Reagan spoke of the Salvadorans' "determination to choose ballots over bullets" when he did not share the same sentiments for the beleaguered nation next door.[91] As the elections in the United States approached, Wright could be forgiven if through all his struggles on Central America and the economy, he felt a little beleaguered himself.

The Democratic sweepstakes for the opportunity to challenge Reagan in 1984 began early. At the outset, Wright appeared to support Ohio senator John Glenn, noting his "good work."[92] When Glenn began to fade, however, Wright endorsed Walter Mondale, the "mainstream of our party." In fact, although Mondale was the "establishment candidate," he was arguably more liberal than Wright. Wright might have endorsed Gary Hart, who refused PAC money, but the Colorado senator was somewhat of an unknown upstart. Liberal civil rights activist Jesse Jackson was never a consideration.[93] But Wright may have had other motivations in backing Mondale. Several Democrats had noted that Wright was the perfect running mate for Mondale and that Texas was a crucial state. Letters arrived at the Democratic National Committee (DNC) praising Wright's "distinguished stature." Wright, predictably, dismissed such speculation, but he continued advising Mondale as the primaries unfolded. "You know how much I value your counsel," Mondale replied.[94]

At the San Francisco convention in July, Wright played a key role, having agreed to serve as O'Neill's representative on the DNC's executive committee.[95] Requesting a limousine and rooms for a staff of twenty-five, Wright hosted a dinner for congressmen while asking that the calendar not include his social events. "When Jim Wright throws a party, they come to rub elbows," noted one report. Wright knew "who to put the strong arm on," observed another. Tony Coelho, the Democratic Campaign Congressional Committee chairman, was succinct: "Jim Wright is going to be the next speaker."[96] When Mondale selected New Yorker Geraldine Ferraro as his running mate, Wright stressed that the Democrats "opened the doors" to all people while the GOP remained just for the wealthy. "We must carry Texas to win," Wright said when rallying his own constituents after the convention.[97]

Wright sensed that the general campaign was not going well. Pollsters suggested that Reagan appeared to be gaining strength among southern conservatives, and many Democratic candidates reported heckling at their rallies.[98] The DNC warned of "intimidation of voters."[99] When Reagan remarked that the Democrats offered no solutions, Wright snapped back, uncharacteristically, "That is a lie." His exasperation showed before he regained his composure and tried to walk back the description.[100] Wright could focus on the national race because, as the *Fort Worth Star-Telegram* put it, he had "no rivals in sight."[101]

Unfortunately, for the Democrats, the election was worse than expected. Reagan won forty-nine states, including all of the South, in a historic landslide.

Mondale won only 25 percent of the white southern vote. In his first run for the Senate, Wright's nemesis, Gramm, torched Lloyd Doggett, for whom Wright had campaigned vigorously. The GOP gained fourteen House seats, including four in Texas. Republicans quickly claimed a mandate, although at closer inspection, the results actually ensured additional legislative obstructionism. The Democrats, after all, still controlled the House, leaving Wright to plead once again that a divided Congress required compromise and collegiality.[102]

Certainly the 99th Congress was significant for Jim Wright. After O'Neill confirmed in January 1985 what everyone had suspected—that he would retire at the end of the new Congress in 1986—Wright decided to preempt any challengers for the Speakership. Calling in his chits—reminding Democrats of his many favors—by February Wright had the endorsements of 184 Democrats, two-thirds of the caucus and more than enough to assure him the top job. His strong stance against Reagan had won him some liberal support, and many members of the younger generation had their own reasons for supporting him. The new caucus chairman, Richard Gephardt, had presidential ambitions, while the equally ambitious Coelho calculated that his best move was to run for Wright's vacated post, where he would await his turn on the leadership ladder. Most liberals would have welcomed one of their own but accepted Wright as inevitable. Although he might "say the right things," the cynical New Yorker Richard Ottinger predicted, "W-R-I-G-H-T will be a significant turn to the R-I-G-H-T."[103]

Of course, the actual caucus vote would be almost two years later, and the outcome was not assured. As one periodical put it, "How firm were those early commitments?" And then there was the matter of Dan Rostenkowski, who was conspicuously absent from the lists of endorsements. The Chicagoan had promised Wright that he would "get back to him," but then remained coy. Whether Rostenkowski still hoped to win the Speakership or simply enjoyed the leverage a potential candidacy afforded him, the race was clearly not devoid of the "rumors and intrigue" that Wright had hoped to dispel.[104]

Over the next two years Wright worked to make his promotion a fait accompli. It was not always easy. Reports persisted that both the Wright camp and the Rostenkowski camp were spreading rumors about the other's drinking, a charge that both men denied. Wright's temper, moreover, was never far below the surface, which Republicans exploited. In June 1985, several witnesses claimed that Wright had threatened to punch two House members who had refused to budge on a vote. Republicans added that he smelled of liquor. "Get your ass off the floor or you will never be speaker," O'Neill yelled, according to one witness.[105] In another instance, a reporter for USA Radio claimed that Wright "blew his top" and shoved him, which Wright denied. "The reporter was a plant," Wright's office claimed, who had been working closely with International Christian Media, a forceful Wright critic.[106]

As Wright drew close to his goal, he had even less time for his family. His firstborn, forty-one-year-old Jimmy, had returned from Vietnam, but was struggling to find direction; he had worked in a variety of jobs and was living with his wife in a converted trading post in Taos, New Mexico. Apparently rejecting the high-stakes, high-roller life of his father, he explained that he simply wanted "to choose my own lifestyle." Wright's eldest daughter, thirty-seven-year-old Ginger, was divorced with two sons and working for the House Banking Committee—a job that carried the risk of new charges of nepotism. Two years younger than Ginger, his other daughter, Kay, had divorced Wright's controversial aide, John Mack, and remarried a navy engineer. With her husband abroad, she had returned to her mother's Texas home. Wright's youngest, twenty-seven-year-old Alicia, was newly married but embroiled in her own mini-scandal. After pulling the newlyweds over for a broken taillight, police had found amphetamines and a pistol in Alicia's purse, not exactly the news an aspiring Speaker needed.[107]

The timing could not have been worse. One of the priorities for the 99th Congress was a "war on drugs." O'Neill, recognizing a "sure-fire campaign issue," in the words of one report, appointed Wright to coordinate a get-tough omnibus bill. When Wright strong-armed committee chairmen into packaging together a number of bills that had languished and getting them quickly through hearings, Republicans—also seeking advantage—applauded. "Let's hope this is the way that Jim Wright is going to run the house," remarked one.[108] The final result, the Anti–Drug Abuse Act of 1986, was indeed the type of significant legislation Congress had intended—but in the end was not as successful as Congress had hoped. Mandating minimum sentences flooded the judicial system and had little impact on drug abuse. Eventually Congress revised its policies, suggesting that Wright and his colleagues had overstepped while rushing to capitalize on public outrage.[109]

Another priority for Wright and the new Congress was the national debt, but, once again, the ultimate solution proved inadequate. The Gramm-Rudman-Hollings Balanced Budget Act of 1985 mandated across-the-board spending cuts if Congress failed to meet scheduled deficit targets.[110] Wright saw the new law as a "political straightjacket," an "act of desperation" that took away legislative prerogative.[111] Nevertheless, he again recognized public sentiment. A vote against the bill would appear to be a vote for the debt. Wright consoled himself; at least Congress had done something.[112]

The problems became apparent quickly. The law's tighter deadlines for budget resolutions proved difficult for negotiators to manage. Disgruntled legislators complained when they learned "their fair share of the appropriation shortfall."[113] More significantly, the Supreme Court ruled that the cuts Congress had mandated violated the separation of powers. Congress could pass laws, but not execute them.[114] While Congress subsequently passed an acceptable revision, the sad experience of Reagan's successor, Republican George H. W. Bush, ultimately showed that the law was ineffectual. Faced with a mandate for a balanced budget in 1991, Bush agreed to raise taxes as part of a compromise. Having therefore broken his 1988 pledge never to do so, violating a principle that was by then sacrosanct to the New Right, Bush lost his 1992 reelection bid.[115] For Republicans, it appeared, additional taxes were forever off the table. Congress eventually weakened the legislation's mandates, and deficits continued apace.[116]

The Immigration Reform and Control Act of 1986 fit the same pattern— it was another piece of legislation that seemed significant at the time, but it did not live up to its billing. Many conservatives complained of unauthorized immigration, while many liberals bemoaned the exploitation of migrants. Both, meanwhile, wanted to win the Hispanic vote.[117] When Congress passed a bill that outlawed employment of illegals outside of migrant agricultural workers, and increased border security, many conservatives still decried the bill for allowing some early migrants application for permanent residence—"amnesty." Not wanting the bill to die, Wright suggested a "two-tier system": a probationary period would ensure immigrant compliance with established criteria before application for permanent status was permitted. His "language and tone," however, upset the Hispanic caucus.[118] Pleading for all to compromise, Wright ultimately won passage only to find that it made no difference. The sanctions for illegal employment proved inadequate, and the budget cuts weakened border security just as economic conditions in Mexico were deteriorating. Illegal migration only grew.[119]

The most significant domestic legislation of Reagan's second term was hardly a success for Wright. To win enough Democratic support to simplify the tax code, Reagan agreed to close loopholes and raise the capital gains tax. The result, the Tax Reform Act of 1986, reduced the number of marginal tax rates, including a huge reduction in the top bracket, while combining lower brackets in a way that hurt many of the poor, arguably furthering the administration's supply-side efforts. Wright protested this and the fact that Reagan had assured Congress that the bill was revenue neutral. Referring to Congress, Wright warned, "[We must] come to our senses and recognize the stern reality of [the debt]."[120] Liberals, meanwhile, complained that Wright had caved after promising tax breaks for Texas's oil and savings-and-loan industries. Rostenkowski would "love to nail Jim Wright" as a protector of the oil industry, some speculated. Certainly, the chair of the Ways and Means Committee had cultivated his own group of loyalists with specific deals, and thus enhanced his own chances for the Speakership.[121]

Rostenkowski's obvious ambition was a concern, but the fact remained that months had passed and still no liberal had announced for the Speakership. With each passing day Wright appeared more certain despite any legislative frustrations. At the end of 1985, Wright hosted a Fort Worth "Cowtown Jamboree" to raise cash for Democrats in the coming 1986 election. With 5,000 guests paying $1,000 each, the total was impressive. In addition to the main event at the Tarrant County Convention Center, participants celebrated at the honkytonk Billy Bob's, the jewel of Fort Worth's Stockyard District. With lobbyists at every turn, Coelho was blunt: "There ain't no way to stop him now."[122]

As the 99th Congress progressed, Wright told all who would listen that the next Congress would finally reverse Reaganomics. He noted that he had led a Democratic Task Group on Trade that had taken testimony and that he planned legislation to correct the trade imbalance.[123] He also noted that he had fought for additional funding to combat domestic terrorism— "anti-U.S. activity"—but that Reagan's administration had rejected it as too expensive. He planned to resume the fight.[124] Wright promised additional transportation and water development as well as a more equitable revision of taxes that would actually reduce the debt. And then, of course, there was the issue of foreign policy, which for Wright had always provided both opportunities and frustration.

Congress and Reagan continued to jockey over foreign policy throughout the 99th Congress. Even when agreement existed, the road was never easy. At a state dinner for British prime minister Margaret Thatcher in February 1985, Reagan asked Wright to arrange a Democratic delegation to attend an arms control summit that the administration and new Soviet leader Mikhail Gorbachev had set for Geneva that November. Wright agreed that demonstrating unity was important, and allowed himself to hope that maybe, after it all, the administration's militarization was simply a means to a better end, as Reagan still insisted.[125] No sooner had Wright rounded up participants, however, than conservative pundits complained that he was trying to share Reagan's limelight. As Democrats began to withdraw, Wright saved the day by arranging for Reagan to state that he had invited them.[126]

As the summit approached, the State Department asked Wright and several other Texas congressmen to host a Soviet delegation on a trip to their state. Wright agreed, once again showcasing Billy Bob's. It all looked good until the White House began to court conservative Democrats in a renewed push for the MX missile. Wright had already agreed to accept the weapon, albeit not to the extent that Reagan advocated, but angry liberals quickly claimed that the summit was a ruse. Wright, still harboring his own reservations about Reagan's veracity, had to convince his colleagues that they had no choice. Geneva was too important, a "unique opportunity to wage peace."[127]

In the end, the Geneva summit accomplished little of substance but allowed Reagan and Gorbachev to develop a rapport. "Breaking the ice" was enough for Wright, who congratulated Reagan and even invited Gorbachev to Texas.[128] Wright's enthusiasm, unfortunately, did not last. In early 1986, as the talks continued, Reagan called for the deployment of new ICBMs. Congress had never ratified the Carter-era SALT II limits, and Reagan had avoided raising the issue, since the MX missile arguably was permitted under the agreement. The new proposal clearly was not, however, and, in Wright's view, it threatened to derail the ongoing talks. "Breaking the SALT II limits," Wright stated, was a "blow to the credibility of U.S. foreign policy" and "embarrassing" because the Soviets had complied.[129]

Just before Reagan and Gorbachev met in a second summit in Reykjavik, Iceland, in mid-October 1986, Reagan invited Wright to a White House breakfast. The two talked amicably and Wright stated his concerns. The United States might seek agreements on chemical weapons and antisatellite weaponry, Wright proposed, but put off a decision on nuclear testing and adherence to SALT II. The next day, Reagan thanked him for "taking time from your busy schedule," but reiterated that the Soviets would negotiate "only when they believe they will do better at the negotiating table than they do through a continued arms buildup." If Democrats rejected his request, the Soviets might delay "believing they could get a better deal from Congress later."[130]

After Reagan departed for Iceland, he called O'Neill and Wright long distance for one more appeal. In the interest of unity, both men agreed to press their caucus for the appropriation of several weapons programs that Reagan sought. Afterward, Wright watched with amazement as the

Reykjavik conference unfolded as a "high-stakes game of chicken" for world opinion. Gorbachev made far-reaching disarmament proposals, but in the end, what he demanded in return—including an end to Reagan's Strategic Defense Initiative—was too much, and the talks once again ended with only promises to continue in the future. The lack of anything concrete dismayed Wright, but like much of the rest of the world, he found the astounding proposals somewhat dizzying. It all promised so much for the future.[131]

"Trust but verify," Reagan famously said of his arms negotiations, paraphrasing an old Russian proverb. By the time of the Reykjavik talks—which took place only weeks before the 1986 congressional elections and the official birth of Wright's Speakership—Wright was still not sure that he could trust Reagan. Geneva and Reykjavik were good signs, but Central America still suggested otherwise. After the 1984 elections in both Nicaragua and El Salvador, Reagan at first dropped his request for military aid to the Contras. Congress, assured that the Second Boland Amendment prohibited any funds for offensive actions against the Sandinistas, agreed to provide El Salvador and the Contras with humanitarian aid. Soon, however, and much to Wright's chagrin, Reagan reversed himself and once again pressed for a new military allocation, suggesting that it was needed for defense only. After Reagan went on national television with his plea, O'Neill asked Wright to offer the Democratic rebuttal. Peace would only come when the United States treated Latin America with respect, Wright told the nation, his idealism on display. "The way to have a friend is to be a friend."[132]

The following morning, the Democratic caucus gave Wright a standing ovation, and within weeks the House rejected the money Reagan had requested. Wright had prevailed—or at least so he thought. Quietly, Reagan continued to encourage foreign nations to provide the Contra funding he wanted. The Second Boland Amendment prohibited only public funds, the White House rationalized. Whether Reagan had a valid argument or not, Saudi Arabia and several other nations agreed to provide the funding. Reagan knew that even as he had lost his battle in Congress, the Contras had not lost their battle to overthrow the Sandinistas.[133]

There was more that Congress did not know. As the 99th Congress passed, the CIA proposed an opening to Iran. If America sold military hardware through an Israeli intermediary, Iran might use its leverage to win the release of hostages that Islamic radicals held. Reagan believed that he was not negotiating with terrorists—he had publicly promised not to do so—but only making a strategic overture to moderates inside a geopolitical enemy. Again, whether this logic was valid or not, Reagan had the power to take such actions, provided that he notified Congress. On this, it turned out, there was no doubt. Congress received no word as the national security laws required. If this were not enough, matters became even more complex as the 1986 elections approached. Reagan's national security adviser, John Poindexter, gave Oliver North at the Restricted Interagency Group permission to divert money the Iranians had paid for the weapons to the Contras. Reagan had no knowledge of the diversion, but to North and the others involved it was simply combining two approved programs to advance the national interest.

In retrospect, although the hostages won their freedom, it was all bound to unravel. As Reagan departed for Reykjavik in early October 1986, intermediaries involved in the exchange threatened to go public. A day before the US elections on November 4, the Lebanese media reported the arms sale. The White House denied it, but it was clear that however the elections turned out, the new Congress, the nation's one hundredth, might have more on its plate than originally expected. Whether, after all the struggles over the economy, the debt, and foreign policy, Jim Wright believed Reagan or not, it was growing obvious that the presumptive Speaker would play a pivotal role at a critical time. It was just what Jim Wright had always sought, just what he had worked so hard to achieve throughout his long career.

———

CHAPTER 17

On the Mountaintop

SPEAKER OF THE HOUSE (1986–1989)

"I believe we make a bigger mistake when we think too small than when we think too big," Jim Wright told reporters as his swearing in as Speaker of the House approached.[1] It was an understandable sentiment. He had just swamped Republican Don McNeil in the 1986 elections, which had also rewarded the Democrats control of the Senate for the first time in six years. McNeil had run a lackluster campaign that Wright had largely ignored, confident that Fort Worth was excited about his pending Speakership. Wright's million-dollar campaign fund had plastered the district with 31,000 yard signs, and McNeil had complained that "my many calls [for debates] have gone unreturned." Moreover, Wright assumed that the explosive revelations just before the election about the Iranian hostage deal had put Reagan on the defensive. Preparing for his caucus's leadership vote, Wright had the wind at his back.[2]

Reagan did his best, going on television a week after the election to argue that the funds had not gone directly to Iran and did not constitute a quid pro quo. Reagan, however, still did not know the full extent of his troubles. As the congressional intelligence committees began closed-door investigations, Reagan soon learned of the Restricted Interagency Group's diversion of funds to the Contras. He quickly fired both John Poindexter and Oliver North and appointed his own investigatory commission led by John Tower. Within weeks, Reagan had testified before the Tower Commission appearing unsure whether he had authorized the arms sale. At the same time, the US Court of Appeals appointed Judge Lawrence Walsh as an independent counsel with unlimited prosecutorial power. Wright doubted Reagan's claim that he had no knowledge of the diversion, but he quietly harbored reservations about all the Democrats' glee. He did not want the scandal to complicate the big accomplishments he anticipated.[3]

When the Democrats finally caucused, Wright's vote went as expected and Washington's Thomas Foley won as majority leader. Northern liberals accepted the end of the old "Boston-Austin Axis" of leadership in part because Tony Coelho, a young liberal from California, had emerged as the new majority whip. Wright had championed Foley, confident of his loyalty, but accepted the overtly ambitious Californian because he promised fidelity and it strengthened party cohesion.[4] Wright took it as a good sign when Coelho hired Wright's former press secretary. Moreover, Wright felt confident in his own appointment of David Bonior of Michigan as deputy whip. Bonior was known as a young reformer, but he had supported Wright's position on Central America and served on the Rules Committee.[5]

Wright wanted complete control of that critical committee but found that all of its Democrats were returning. Although O'Neill's reforms had allowed the Speaker to make the appointments, Wright wanted to send a message without making enemies. Shrewdly, he made all incumbents formally ask for reappointment—previously return appointments had been considered automatic—thus quietly reiterating their subservience. The other critical committee Wright needed to control was the Steering and Policy Committee. O'Neill had let the various party factions select one of their own for the appointments allotted to him, but Wright wanted to take a different tack. When he appointed several members to the Steering and Policy Committee who also served on the Ways and Means Committee, it was obvious that Wright was challenging the chairman of the latter, Rostenkowski. Wright also rearranged the Capitol offices, sending messages through the assignment of choice real estate.[6]

For his swearing-in on January 6, 1987, Wright spared no expense—at least of taxpayer dollars. He received legal approval for donations to pay for an elaborate reception in the Cannon Caucus Room and had the ceremony televised to Fort Worth's Will Rogers Coliseum.[7] Addressing the caucus, Wright stated that he preferred "cooperation to controversy," and "bipartisan consensus." Nevertheless, he added, "we will not shrink from legislative action."[8] Letters poured in with congratulations. Even the Association of American Editorial Cartoonists congratulated Wright, obviously anticipating with pleasure his prominent eyebrows, a genetic gift from his maternal grandfather.[9] The popular political journal *Roll Call* declared that "the eyes of Texas are on Jim Wright." Meanwhile, Wright's aide Marshall Lynam quietly acknowledged "the uneasy feeling that our work is really just beginning."[10]

Instructing his committee chairs to devise specific packages, Wright arranged with the House parliamentarian to have the bills for his priorities numbered sequentially 1–5. First was clean water, then highway construction, both hardly surprising. The trade bill that had languished was third, followed by housing and education bills. Demanding that all chairs have the bills reported out of their committees according to established deadlines, Wright wanted to ensure there would be no more "autonomous field barons each pursuing a leisurely independent course."[11] Not forgetting the importance of public relations, Wright invited the homeless advocate Mitch Snyder, who had illegally set up a protest camp on the Capitol grounds, to his office. Rather than evict him, Wright agreed to tour a homeless shelter in exchange for Snyder's departure. The cameras followed, of course, allowing Wright to press publicly for the inclusion of homeless provisions in his housing bill, a nice contrast to Reagan. As for Reagan, Wright let the White House know that he planned to press Congress to postpone the scheduled tax cuts for the wealthy, a cornerstone of Reaganomics and an action that worried many conservatives in his caucus.

When Reagan gave the annual State of the Union Address on January 27, Wright agreed to share the Democratic response with the new Senate majority leader, Robert Byrd. In his address, Reagan had denounced the debt—which had led to sarcastic Democratic applause—and Wright fought back as well. Democrats, he declared, would work with Reagan, but with no "gimmicks" or the "selling off [of] assets." Two days later when the Democratic leadership met with Reagan, it was obvious that the president did not appreciate the comments. He reacted harshly when Wright proposed new revenue. Wright, perhaps a bit cocky, retorted that it was time to "confront reality." The Wright agenda promised to be a battle of political titans.[12]

Wright's clean water initiative, termed the Water Quality Act of 1987, provided $20 billion for waste treatment centers. It was the first through Congress for the session. As Wright expected, few congressmen wanted to appear anti-environment. When Reagan predictably vetoed the measure, Wright had the votes for an override. Congress had been in session only three weeks, and Wright had won the first skirmish.[13] The highway bill, which promised $88 billion for road repairs and mass transit, soon followed. Reagan complained about "special interest projects" that ballooned the debt, but Minority Leader Bob Michel warned him that he did not have the votes to sustain a veto.[14] Reagan, however, needed to show he was "in charge," in the words of Republican Bob Dole, and vetoed the bill anyway. Wright then simply designated the vote a matter of party loyalty and reminded his colleagues that committee assignments were on the line. Wright also mobilized the unions and let western Republicans know that if they sustained the veto, he would resist raising the speed limit as they wanted. It was "petulant," Wright suggested, for Reagan to veto a bill whose costs were covered by the Highway Trust Fund. Such tactics proved effective. In early April, Congress overrode the veto, and the Surface Transportation and Uniform Relocation Assistance Act of 1987 became law. Wright had won again.[15]

Wright's promise to the activist Snyder to pass legislation to help the homeless was more difficult to keep. When the Senate attached an amendment denying a congressional pay increase that had been scheduled by an independent commission, and that was set to take effect barring a vote otherwise, the legislation looked in doubt. To vote for the homeless bill was to deny themselves a raise; to vote against it would look terrible politically. Facing an uproar in his caucus, Wright found an out. He craftily manipulated the rules. With the raise set to take effect, Wright adjourned Congress, only taking up the Senate bill after the deadline had passed. Members could then vote for the Senate version, but the amendment denying the raise would be void. The Stewart B. McKinney Homeless Assistance Act of 1987 utilized $50 million that Congress had already allocated for emergencies.[16] When a reluctant Reagan, not anxious to face another veto override, signed the bill in late July, a relieved Wright sounded self-congratulatory. The law, he stated, "was one that I had vowed to myself I'd pass."[17]

The housing legislation that Wright championed was another example of his legislative acumen. With troublesome amendments in both chambers, Wright allowed a voice vote that did not require members to go on record. He then whittled down the funds, allowing Reagan to declare the bill "transformed from a budget-buster" and to sign it. The Housing and Community Development Act of 1987 still gave Wright most of what he sought, including funds to develop neighborhoods and to expand Federal Housing

Administration (FHA) insurance. Wright even had a defense against charges of profligate spending.[18]

Compromises saved the education bill as well. To offset Republican concerns about the costs, Wright allowed "English-only" bilingual programs and an amendment that banned pornographic telephone services. The Hawkins-Stafford Elementary and Secondary School Improvement Amendments of 1988 authorized over $8 billion in new funds, much of it for low-income students.[19] Reagan thought the bill excessive, but with the compromises, he had political cover. He signed the bill proclaiming that it gave parents "greater flexibility."[20]

Of all Wright's designated priorities, the trade proposal required the most effort. The administration favored free trade, but the issue was complex, in part because the strong dollar encouraged imports and discouraged exports, and many countries placed high tariffs on American products. The unions, moreover, had their own demands. With the encouragement of the Democratic Leadership Council, the new bloc of conservative Democrats, Wright organized a National Conference on Competitiveness with experts on all aspects of the problem. The Reagan administration, however, feared protectionism and lobbied Republicans not to participate.

Undaunted, Wright's conference produced a new bill that Wright claimed fully addressed the complex issues of globalization. Broader than simple protectionism, the bill provided new funds for math, science, engineering, foreign languages, and the semiconductor industry. It also provided almost $1 billion for displaced American workers. When new Democratic caucus chairman Richard Gephardt added an amendment that required negotiations with countries that enjoyed a large trade surplus resulting from unfair high tariffs, and promised immediate sanctions if the country refused reform, the reaction was predictable. Wright agreed, but Reagan denounced it as an attack on free trade. When the European Parliament also protested, Wright appeared not to care. "This is good; it shows that they got the message," he stated.[21]

Rostenkowski, however, had a different perspective. Seeking to exert his influence, he declared that Gephardt's amendment assured a successful veto. Once again, Wright had to navigate through the legislative weeds. He promised caucus skeptics that he would appoint moderates to any resulting conference committee, and have that committee drop the Gephardt amendment if it appeared the Senate could not override a veto. The promise worked, but it required a tough vote and engendered some resentment among his flock. In the promised conference committee, Wright helped negotiate away some of the harsher aspects of the Gephardt amendment, which now spoke of trade barriers, not actual trade figures. It also no longer mandated retaliation. The fight, however, persisted. When Wright then accepted a Senate provision requiring companies to provide sixty days' notice before massive layoffs, Reagan promised a veto. Once again Rostenkowski challenged Wright, predicting the veto's success.[22]

Wright ignored the warning, flexed his muscles again, and successfully guided the bill to passage. To add pressure on Reagan, Wright held his own signing ceremony, which reportedly was "carefully staged for maximum political impact." When Reagan still issued his veto and the Senate was unable to override it, Wright proved that he had one more card up his legislative sleeve. He agreed to remove the controversial notice provision and submit it as a separate bill. Under more pressure to acquiesce, Reagan signed the Omnibus Trade and Competitiveness Act of 1988, as Wright expected he would. Wright then held the remaining bill until closer to the election, when, as Wright knew, unions would apply greater pressure. Indeed, facing new demands from his fellow Republicans, Reagan let the notice bill become law without his signature. Wright had made additional enemies through it all, but, yet again, he had won.[23]

Wright wanted more. Complaining of the "slowness of the Senate," where the rules "are not as malleable as ours"—unintentionally demonstrating his own forceful hand—Wright did not rest with just his priorities.[24] The Computer Security Act of 1987, which provided for stronger protections of federal data, had wide bipartisan support and posed little problem.[25] The Civil Rights Restoration Act of 1987, however, took more time. After the Supreme Court ruled that Title IX of the Education Amendments of 1972 only prohibited gender discrimination in university programs that received direct financial assistance, Wright encouraged a bill to prohibit discrimination in all programs of any recipient.[26] Democrats quickly passed the bill, but Reagan vetoed it as an infringement upon religious liberty. Once again Wright found himself twisting arms for an override, declaring that Reagan wanted to "turn the clock back on civil rights."[27] It was a harsh assessment, but, in the end, an effective one.

No one in Washington could miss that the American farmer needed aid. Because of declining exports, many farms faced bankruptcy. A televised benefit concert by Willie Nelson, John Mellencamp, and other musicians, dubbed "Farm Aid," brought publicity, but the Farm Credit System remained weak as a result of poor loans. Congress had strengthened federal oversight in 1985, but it had not provided the federal assistance that many farmers thought necessary. With farmers writing that they had "given up on the administration," Wright demanded quick action. Farmers were plentiful in the South, he knew, and the 1988 election was approaching.[28] The result, the Agricultural Credit Act of 1987, again reorganized the troubled lending institution, but this time it also provided $4 billion in new funds.[29] Reagan did not like the bill's "unnecessary spending," but with the strong majorities Wright had helped assemble, he signed it, knowing that he did not have the votes for an override.[30]

Some bills moved quickly because the Democratic leadership and Reagan agreed. Although Reagan thought its outlays were too great, he still praised the Civil Liberties Act of 1988, which provided reparations to the victims of World War II–era Japanese-American internment camps.[31] During the debate over the Anti–Drug Abuse Act of 1988, which established the White House Office of National Drug Control Policy, Wright and Reagan fought for political credit. When Reagan's new attorney general, Richard Thornburgh, accused Wright of manipulating the debate for partisan advantage, Wright replied that the bill "deserves better."[32] The competition to appear tough on drugs was in spite of early but growing evidence that the emphasis on interdiction and criminalization was insufficient. Returning from a congressional fact-finding trip to Colombia, Wright wrote Reagan expressing "very serious concerns" about the government's get-tough strategy.[33] Wright wanted to consider additional options, but he also recognized that, given public sentiment, a shift in strategies was not possible unless the Democrats allowed Reagan to have the upper hand politically.

When it came to health care, it was Wright who protested that Reagan was manipulating the debate. Both men supported the Health Maintenance Organization Amendments of 1988, which gave employers more leeway in selecting HMO coverage, and the Medicare Catastrophic Coverage Act of 1988, which limited enrollees' copayments, expanded coverage to outpatient drugs, and capped hospital bills. Reagan's support, Wright complained, was only to deflect criticism of his proposed cuts to Social Security. The competitive rush to reform did little in the long run to enhance either party's reputation. By the time Wright left Congress, the press spoke of the "Catastrophic Care Debacle."[34] The legislation, it turned out, had done nothing for long-term nursing care, the greatest cost facing the elderly. It had also paid for the reforms with a surtax that many retirees could not afford.[35]

The White House claimed one unmitigated victory over Wright's Democrats. Republicans argued that the Federal Communications Commission's Fairness Doctrine, which required broadcasters to present both sides of political debates, was antiquated in the age of cable television, and a violation of free speech rights.[36] Wright tried to calm such concerns with legislation codifying the doctrine, but Reagan was able to sustain his subsequent veto. Then, in what Wright termed a "cavalier demolition" of broadcasters' social responsibility, Reagan's FCC voted to eliminate the doctrine completely.[37]

It did not take long for Wright to recognize the magnitude of his defeat. Political talk radio exploded, with conservatives dominating and Wright a principal focus of their wrath. From 82 all-talk stations at the beginning of Reagan's term to over 1,300 by the 1990s, it was not hard to find criticism of Wright.[38] Among the beneficiaries was Rush Limbaugh, whose show went national with his combination of sarcastic attacks and humor. Limbaugh played on conservative fears that the media did not adequately represent their views. Just prior to the FCC ruling, Democrats had rejected Reagan's Supreme Court nomination of Robert Bork, whom many conservatives believed had been unfairly cast as an extremist. In the words of journalist John Barry, Reagan nominated the controversial Bork to "regain the initiative," having lost the offense to Wright's legislative blitzkrieg. Republican outrage at the "borking" of a Supreme Court nomination played well on talk radio. Just as Wright feared, it all posed another blow to collegiality and bipartisanship. Wright did not have to turn on the radio to hear himself eviscerated. Wyoming Republican and future vice-president Dick Cheney, for one, called Wright "a heavy handed SOB." By 1988, Wright's initial agenda was in large part the law of the land—even if his problems clearly remained.[39]

The problems were not just with the White House. Despite Wright's obvious success, many Democrats resented his forceful hand. "The price of this headlong rush to pass legislation has been some trampled sensibilities," the New York Times explained. "Some say Mr. Wright shoots from the hip and is too quick to legislate to solve a problem, with one dubbing his effort to crank out legislation 'The Bill-of-the-Month Club.'"[40] Wright's deadlines annoyed members, as did his tightening of filibuster rules. The coordination that Wright demanded often challenged traditional committee jurisdictions, and, as some grumbled, he dictated more than he consulted. Liberals complained that Wright compromised too much to win the bipartisan label he cherished. Many members wanted longer weekends to fly to their districts, but Wright scheduled Friday and Monday sessions. Although he scheduled noncontroversial bills for Monday mornings, his urgency still annoyed many.[41] "Down the road," predicted one Democrat, "there's going to be a blowup."[42]

Of course, the greatest complaint Wright faced was his insistence on tax increases. The annual appropriations process was playing out at the same time that Wright was pushing his agenda, which demanded new revenues to avoid the debt that he denounced. Conventional wisdom suggested that Walter Mondale had lost the 1984 presidential race because he had openly advocated taxes, and ever since, the phrase "tax-and-spend liberal" had been a deadly epithet. Many of Wright's colleagues feared the label. O'Neill, accordingly, had highlighted the debt but avoided specifics, leaving it to Reagan to reconcile. The impatient Wright had no time for such political games.[43]

Republicans saw opportunity. Noting that Wright was "more involved," and anticipating that he would clash with Rostenkowski, Republicans on the Ways and Means Committee refused to produce their own minority budget, which was often presented as an alternative vision, thus drawing attention to Wright's taxes.[44] At first Wright struggled to respond, arguing only that legislators had a responsibility to be honest with their constituents. This approach hardly calmed fearful Democrats, so Budget Committee chairman William Gray proposed a "public markup session." There would be no new proposals, and both sides would simply vote on items from the previous year's budget. In this way Republicans would have to go on record cutting popular programs or adding specific taxes.[45]

Wright agreed, but when the markup began, the Republicans simply voted "present" on every item. Wright counseled Democrats to remain firm, but Rostenkowski publicly disagreed. Thankfully for Wright, polls began to show that the Republican tactic was unpopular, and thus Wright succeeded in getting the House to pass his budget resolution. Of the resolution's $36 billion in deficit reduction, half came from new taxes and half from spending cuts. Of the cuts, half were to domestic programs and half to defense. When Reagan complained, Wright ridiculed his claim that the Republican budget "was ignored by Congress."[46]

The next step was a conference committee, which soon deadlocked. Convinced that the Senate would not pass the House's version, and breaking precedent by interjecting himself into the committee's negotiations, Wright approved a conference committee bill more akin to the upper chamber's than his own. This bill, in turn, meant less money for domestic needs, angering House liberals. Breaking the impasse again required Wright's leg-islative skill. Arranging additional concessions and employing some account-ing gimmicks, Wright finally had a resolution. At least for the moment, the party had not irrevocably split.[47]

With a resolution in place and thirteen specific tax and appropriations bills before committees, Wright called Congress back early from its July 4 recess without any votes scheduled—the act of a dictator, some grumbled.[48] To put pressure on the White House, Wright wanted the thirteen bills pre-sented as one omnibus bill. Vetoing such a bill, Wright calculated, would shut the government down. Wright's patience was obviously wearing thin. When Reagan read off notecards, Wright appeared, to one participant, "to be looking around the room for a spittoon."[49] Aiding Wright was the approach of the Gramm-Rudman budget deadline, which highlighted the debt and added a sense of urgency.[50]

As the summer turned to fall in 1987, Wright's job grew even more com-plex. Worried by the potential fallout from the taxes the emerging reconcil-iation bill promised, conservative Democrats, led by Charlie Stenholm, submitted a bill calling for a balanced budget amendment to the Constitu-tion. Republicans applauded, sensing that it would shift the blame for the debt and help splinter the Democrats, undermining the reconciliation pro-cess. Wright had already angered members by permitting only 57 percent of floor votes under "open rules"—allowing for amendments at that stage—but now he felt that he had no choice but to be muscular with the rules again. Arguing that a constitutional amendment bill required a supermajor-ity that did not exist, Wright refused to bring Stenholm's bill to the floor. Frustrated by Wright's power play, Stenholm then pressed for a "discharge petition," a vote to override the leadership. Wright pressured Democrats not to sign the discharge, arguing that they could publicly support the amend-ment but quietly deny it a floor vote.[51]

Suddenly, and unexpectedly, "Black Monday" changed all calculations. On October 19, 1987, the stock market plummeted, with the Dow Jones Industrial Average suffering its greatest single-day loss ever. As panic set in, Wright couched the financial tsunami as a product of debt—"living off borrowed money"—and thus a reason to pass his reconciliation bill.[52] Repub-licans, however, saw an opportunity to reset the table and called for a bud-get summit, which Wright, having worked so hard to get to this point, was reluctant to agree to. Forcing a vote on reconciliation in light of the crash was "bad form," according to one Republican. No, Wright responded, a vote first on the reconciliation bill would "calm the markets."[53]

It proved a moot point. Public demand for immediate action forced negotiators to settle on a loose agreement to cut spending and raise taxes evenly.
Republicans then argued that the spending cuts and tax increases should
occur simultaneously, because the Democrats could not be trusted to hold
up their end of the bargain. This demand, Wright answered, infringed on
congressional prerogative. As the two sides argued over the accuracy of the
Office of Management and Budget (OMB) figures, Wright lost his temper.
Finally, Stenholm and the conservative Democrats agreed to support the
reconciliation bill provided that its welfare reforms were removed, a provision that Wright agreed to allow in a rules vote that preceded the final vote.
When liberals learned of this change, however, they noted that Wright had
promised them that the reforms would be included in the final bill. Apparently caught between his conflicting promises, Wright decided to let the
rules vote go forward with the reforms included.[54]

It did not go well for Wright. Stenholm, who was now the one angry, led
a successful opposition, and the vote failed. Reconciliation therefore rested
on a second vote with welfare reform removed. As Wright pled with the
liberals to concede, arguing that Reagan wanted to start the whole process
anew, the Republicans stalled. Wright wanted the new vote immediately,
but congressional rules prohibited a second rules vote on the same day.
Wright had always prided himself on equity in congressional debates and
esteem for his colleagues—his idealism, once again. Now, however, success
demanded that he violate the spirit of the rules. In a victory for pragmatism,
Wright ordered Congress adjourned and immediately reconvened, a techni-
cality that he argued allowed for a new vote.

As Republicans howled, the vote proceeded, and it was agonizingly close.
When the time for balloting elapsed with Wright's bill one vote short, Wright
kept the clock running, claiming that another member was on his way to
the chamber. In reality, Wright's aide John Mack was in the cloakroom
lobbying Texan Jim Chapman, whom Wright had helped win his seat. With
Republicans growing angrier with each passing minute, Chapman burst in
and announced that he was switching his vote.[55]

Wright had won—but at considerable cost. "Bush league," Republicans
cried, a mockery of the bipartisanship Wright supposedly supported. The
outrage of the Bork nomination, one journal concluded, was "patty-cake"
compared to "Wright's parliamentary handling of the reconciliation bill."[56]
It was not just Republicans. Liberals resented Wright's pressure, and even
the conservatives now wondered if they could ever trust Wright again.
Wright understood the cost and had trouble sleeping. After all, it was just a

House vote; the Senate and Reagan still had their say. The thought of more negotiations on an imperfect bill that had already cost him so much kept Wright turning in the night.[57]

The delay in producing a budget weighed on the markets, but it also added pressure as negotiators from both congressional chambers and the White House met for a final resolution—in essence, the summit that had been proposed. The urgency of the late hour drove all sides to agreement but in doing so also assured an ever smaller deficit reduction. In the end it was almost anticlimactic. Reagan agreed to new taxes and cuts in defense, things he had promised never to allow—and thus it was a victory for Wright's Democrats—even as he claimed savings from asset sales and referred to taxes as "user fees." Wright's spending priorities were a shadow of their original incarnation and his taxes equally small.[58]

Wright had his "victory," but, in reality, as Reagan signed the Omnibus Budget Reconciliation Act of 1987 three days before Christmas, few were happy. "We let the opportunity slip by," wrote one budget hawk, ignoring all the time and costs Wright had invested. Reagan certainly did not like making the concessions Wright had forced upon him, and took an indirect swipe at the majority leader as he affixed his signature. Passing "thousand-page bills on the eve of Christmas" was "not the way to do business," Reagan remarked. When Reagan denounced the bill's small deficit reductions, Wright struggled to hold his tongue. Wright, too, had wanted so much more. The long-fought battle had cost Wright. It had helped change the nature of Congress, but represented only a dent in the national debt. To this extent, Wright had swung for the fences and hit a single.[59]

If the Iran-Contra affair and the hearings that began as Wright took office did not assure Wright a significant role in foreign affairs during the 100th Congress, other events soon did. With arms talks scheduled to resume in Moscow, Soviet Leader Gorbachev invited Wright and a bipartisan delegation to the Soviet capital. Although many assumed that the Soviets hoped to use the delegation to widen a gap between the executive and legislative branches, Reagan approved of the mission as an encouragement of *perestroika* and *glasnost*, Gorbachev's new economic and social liberalization plans.[60] Aware that Wright's group would represent the highest-ranking congressional delegation ever to visit the communist country, Secretary of State George Shultz anticipated help with arms negotiations. Shultz, Wright recorded, "expressed an interest in learning what impressions [were] gained from our visit."[61]

Preparations for the eleven-day April 1987 trip, which also included stops in Madrid, Kiev, and West Berlin, began immediately. Ignoring that his cochair was his harsh Wyoming critic Cheney, Wright studied a briefing book provided by the Congressional Research Service and agreed to meet with fellow congressmen and private lobbies who had their own agendas.[62] The "Divided Spouses Coalition," one Wright aide reported, "is bugging us with phone calls." One congressman asked Wright to bring a "peace quilt" his constituents had sewn. Fort Worth even asked Wright to promote its Van Cliburn piano competition.[63] Wright agreed to discuss African food shortages and, more controversially, human rights, for which the Commission on Security and Cooperation in Europe prepared its own briefing book.[64]

After departing Andrews Air Force Base on April 10, the delegation arrived first in Madrid, where Wright addressed the European Parliament at the International Hall of the Spanish Congress. Two days later, it was off to Kiev, where Wright met members of the Ukrainian Supreme Soviet and visited historical sites and a cattle breeding farm. More notably, the Soviets allowed the delegation to visit Chernobyl, the site of a nuclear disaster one year before.[65] When Ukrainian leader Valentina Schevchenka told Wright that he had visited Fort Worth, Wright said that he already knew. "Your picture is hanging in Billy Bob's."[66]

Arriving in Moscow on April 15, the delegation stayed at the ornate Sovietskaya Hotel. In addition to a trip to the Bolshoi Theatre and a wreath-laying ceremony at the Memorial to the Unknown Soldier, there were meetings with top Soviet leaders, which went well. When Wright spoke of human rights, the Soviets noted the imprisoned Native American activist Leonard Peltier. When Foreign Minister Eduard Shevardnadze remarked that "Congress looks at things in a realistic way," Wright did not take the bait. "Partisanship," Wright responded, "stops at the water's edge."[67] For the most part, however, Wright found the leaders to be sincere. His discussions with Gorbachev were "a very free exchange laced with humorous banter."[68] As per diplomatic protocol, Wright hosted the Soviets at the American embassy. While Wright thought security seemed lax, the Texas-themed reception added to a sense of goodwill. "We couldn't feed our Russian friends four-alarm chili," one delegate laughed. "They'd think we were doing something to them."[69]

In anticipation of his meeting with Gorbachev, Wright sent to the Soviet embassy a copy of his twenty-eight-year-old "Letter to Ivan," the fictional letter to a hypothetical Soviet citizen that he had penned for his Christmas 1958 newsletter. It professed a hope for peace and proposed mutual arms reductions with the profits going to domestic needs. As his meeting with Gorbachev ended, Wright handed the Soviet leader another copy. "Twenty-eight years ago?" Gorbachev asked. "Have you calculated how many billions of dollars and rubles—well, perhaps trillions—we both might have saved?"[70] When Wright returned to his hotel, the American embassy called and told him that Gorbachev had invited him to address the Soviet public on the prime-time television news program *Vremya* (Time). Assured that the Soviets would not edit his remarks, Wright immediately began to compose his fifteen-minute speech. As the Soviets expected, Wright reflected the same sentiments he had expressed in his old letter. Americans and Soviets were citizens of the world. Wright got the Soviets to display his name and Capitol address on the screen and told his audience that if they wrote him, he would forward a small lapel pin of Soviet and American flags, the same pin the State Department had given him.[71]

The response was overwhelming. Thousands of letters poured in from people of all ages, from children to retirees, and were translated, when necessary, by the Congressional Research Service. Almost all the letter-writers applauded Wright's televised speech. "I wish you great success," wrote one Soviet man. A Muscovite woman worried that "someone crazy will give an order to start a war."[72] Only a few were skeptics. The speech was "only your opinion," wrote one Belarusian, noting Reagan's arms buildup.[73] Americans wrote as well, and the only negative comments were from conservatives who were unaware of Reagan's approval of the mission. The conservative *Manchester Union Leader* in Britain described the speech as "appeasement politics" and suggested, incorrectly, that Wright had abused his franking privileges in sending the pins.[74]

The outpouring required private corporate funding. With help from the World Freedom Foundation, over 5,000 pins were sent to embassies in Moscow, Prague, Budapest, and Warsaw.[75] Wright had good reason for pride. For the first time ever, an American politician had spoken directly to Soviet citizens. The speech helped break Soviet distrust, and Gorbachev obviously assumed that it advanced his perestroika and glasnost programs. A group of Americans began a "pen pal" relationship with their counterparts that one Louisianan termed "vital to obtaining mutual trust."[76]

Undoubtedly basking in the praise, Wright's delegation stopped in West Berlin on its way home. In his speech at the Kongresshalle, Wright reported with obvious pride on his Moscow visit.[77] In addition to touring the Reichstag and the Brandenburg Gate, Wright visited the Berlin Wall. There, in remarks that received far less publicity, he implied the very sentiments that

Reagan would famously exclaim at the same spot two months later. "I'd like to see this wall come down," Wright stated.[78] Back in Washington, Wright wrote congressmen to make sure they knew of his success and followed up with a letter of thanks to Gorbachev, adding that in "all due candor," more remained to be done. Gorbachev did not seem to mind, sending Wright a beautiful lacquer box.[79] Even some Republicans detoured from the growing partisan rancor. Wright was "a world-class statesman," acknowledged one. He did not carry himself as "a partisan Democrat," observed another.[80]

After his return, Wright remained amazingly active in foreign affairs, given the unfolding domestic agenda. South Korea's president, for one, thanked Wright for his "sustained efforts" at cooperation.[81] By the end of the 100th Congress, Wright had led delegations around the globe, including ones to India, Turkey, and Britain, and several to the Middle East. In Australia, he visited his old World War II airfield.[82] For the most part, Reagan had no problems with Wright's sojourns; he even invited Wright to the meetings of the World Bank and the International Monetary Fund.[83] When the American cruiser USS *Vincennes* mistakenly shot down an Iranian airliner, Wright defended the White House and denied reports that he had recommended reparations.[84]

Central America, however, was a different story. Wright certainly did not want to appear a partisan demagogue regarding the Iran-Contra affair. When his old nemesis the National Conservative Political Action Committee complained that Democrats were ignoring the "funding of leftists in El Salvador," Wright took the advice of his aides "not to be involved" and ignored the charge.[85] When the Tower Commission issued its report one month after Congress convened, Wright avoided the harsh criticism of some of his liberal colleagues. The report criticized Reagan for weak control of the National Security Council and for failing to notify Congress of his actions, but largely absolved him of knowingly violating the law.[86] Wright issued only a brief statement, saying that a "full rebirth of public confidence" required the White House to keep Congress informed. At the same time, however, Wright had no intention of letting the matter lie, or of not pressing the advantage it offered him. After all, Wright knew that Special Counsel Walsh and congressional investigators were still at work. That work, Wright suggested, should be resolved "expeditiously."[87]

The scandal aside, the matter of continued funding for the Contras and El Salvador remained. Congress had made public funding for the offensive actions of the Contras against the Nicaraguan Sandinistas illegal, but not other funding. Moreover, in late 1986 Congress had even weakened some of the military restrictions, and by early 1987 additional military aid had resumed, albeit for defensive purposes only. The administration immediately began to lobby for the restoration of all funding. To deny it, Secretary Shultz wrote Wright, was to "abandon in midstream the resistance."[88] Wright responded passive aggressively at first, noting that the United States was "a defender of democracy and an upholder of law."[89] Wright, after all, still did not agree with liberals who sought to deny all funding. Aid constituted leverage. Reagan, however, declared that the public had lost interest in the televised congressional hearings, and Wright exploded like the most liberal hardliner. The president, he hissed, had shown "arrogance, lawlessness, and greed."[90]

Aware of Wright's relative moderation, Reagan sent an emissary to calm the waters. Tom Loeffler, a former Texas congressman whom Wright respected, stated that the White House wanted to work together on a bipartisan peace plan for Nicaragua and El Salvador. Liberals immediately smelled a rat. By floating a peace plan that the Nicaraguan leader, Ortega, would reject, they argued, Reagan hoped to increase the odds that Congress would renew all funding. Wright, on one hand, still doubted Reagan's veracity and did not want to be a patsy, but, on the other, he did not want to dismiss even the slightest chance for a diplomatic solution. If Reagan had indeed shifted his policy, he deserved a chance, as commander-in-chief. Assured by his White House contacts that the scandal had muted Reagan's most militant advisers, Wright agreed. He also knew that the region's leaders planned to meet in Esquipulas, Guatemala. If nothing else, the hopes for a change in American policy might energize those talks. Wright contacted Costa Rica's Óscar Arias, who agreed, adding that he thought Ortega was in trouble politically. Arias promised to keep Wright informed from Esquipulas.[91]

In Washington, Wright realized that many Republican hardliners would not welcome a peace plan, believing it to be a surrender. To ensure adequate bipartisanship, he invited a number of congressional leaders, including Minority Leader Michel, to meet with Nicaraguan ambassador Carlos Tunnermann in Wright's "hideaway" office just off the Capitol rotunda. Tunnermann's comment that he had never met with anyone from the White House astounded Wright, but his assertion that his country would abide by any new peace plan was reassuring.[92]

The plan, Wright immediately proposed, should include several major provisions: the suspension of all Contra military aid; a simultaneous end to all Soviet and Cuban Sandinista aid; the restoration of civil liberties; a commission to prepare for free elections; and, once scheduled, an international group for monitoring. Shultz recommended some minor changes and the bipartisan leadership agreed. On August 5, 1987, an obviously proud Wright appeared with Reagan at the White House to announce the initiative. The press conference went well until Reagan handed Wright a piece of paper as they departed. The paper seemed to assume that the peace plan would fail, promising a resumption of Contra military aid if the Sandinistas did not comply with a list of strict deadlines.[93]

Wright, too preoccupied with making the agreement successful to worry about failure, paraphrased John Lennon's famous song "Give Peace a Chance" in a radio address.[94] Ortega's insistence that the United States deal directly with his government—which Reagan still refused to do—appeared to Wright to be an obstacle that negotiators could overcome. The important thing was that Ortega had agreed to negotiations. Meanwhile, the Contras had sent word that Wright's plan was "not perfect," but "good."[95] At the same time, many conservatives, aware of the strict deadlines, appeared confident of failure and reveled in the defiance of Oliver North before the Iran-Contra congressional committees.[96]

Then came word from Esquipulas. Richard Peña, a former staffer whom Wright had dispatched to Guatemala, reported that the Central American leaders had reached their own accord. Wright was ecstatic, claiming that his plan had "served as the catalyst" and that the agreement included many of the American provisions.[97] Signed by five nations, the "framework for peace" rejected the interference of any group in the government of a neighbor and created a reconciliation committee to oversee the peace process. Assured that the Contras and Sandinistas would comply, Wright predicted that the United States would welcome the new agreement. "We never had the impression that we possessed the almighty wisdom to dictate precise terms," Wright stated. Reagan's response was lukewarm, if not a bit foreboding. The United States welcomed efforts that were "consistent with our interests and the interests of the Nicaraguan resistance."[98]

Initially, at least, all seemed to go well. Ortega issued a blanket amnesty and flew to Cuba to negotiate the withdrawal of all Cuban forces. El Salvador's Duarte offered his own amnesty. Meeting a group of Contra leaders at the DFW Airport, Wright learned that they planned their own concession, the placement of all American military aid into escrow until the peace process was complete. After Costa Rica's Arias won the Nobel Peace Prize for his efforts in Esquipulas, Wright proposed to invite him to address a joint session of Congress. Wright's motivation was obvious. Contra appropriations were set to expire just days after the scheduled address, and Wright feared that any push from angry Republicans for renewed military aid would rattle the tenuous peace process. "We do not talk about military aid," Wright told the press.[99] Predictably, Reagan objected. Wright then agreed to cancel Arias's formal address, but Reagan even balked at an informal one. In the end, Arias addressed Congress despite Reagan's disapproval. Not surprisingly, he remarked, like Wright, that the peace process needed a chance to play out.[100]

Many Democrats who earlier had argued that Wright's joint plan with Reagan was foolish now applauded Wright. The process, it appeared, had advanced so far that Reagan could not stop it. Wright had initially acknowledged that he "might be getting rolled." Now, however, he relished the praise from the ardent liberals. In the words of one report, "Democrats are downright boastful of their Speaker—who, finally, has given them something to be for instead of against."[101]

Such assumptions did not last long. As intermittent fighting broke out, Reagan, in mid-September, renewed his calls for additional military aid. The unfolding peace process did not allow adequate compliance safeguards, he now suggested. Could it be that the liberals were right after all, Wright once again found himself asking, and that it was the budget fiasco again? Wright fought back, even implying harshly that Reagan really did not want peace. "I've had a very difficult time getting any cooperation," Wright told the press.[102] Appearing to be the champion of peace gave Wright the upper hand, and with Democrats controlling Congress, Reagan soon realized that his hopes for new military aid stood little chance at passage. When Reagan retreated, agreeing to request military aid only after the peace process had concluded—and, obviously, in his view, failed—Wright was able to win enough liberals to pass new humanitarian aid for the Contras—a "stinker" bill, Reagan noted in his diary.[103]

Despite the periodic fights, Wright reiterated, all sides remained committed to the process. The biggest hurdles were the Sandinistas' refusal to negotiate directly with the Contras and the White House's refusal to do the same with the Sandinistas. Implying again that the White House really did not want peace, Wright won at least a small change in the administration's position. The White House, it announced, might consider direct negotiations with the Sandinistas if they first met the Contras.[104] Some liberals saw another Trojan horse, but most pundits recognized that Wright was gaining the upper hand. Polls supported the peace process, and the scandal had weakened Reagan. It was the "new Contra politics," one report claimed, with Wright the "dominant force."[105] The release of the congressional report on the Iran-Contra scandal in mid-November helped. The report still did not conclude that Reagan knew of the diversion of Iranian funds, but its indictment was much harsher than the Tower Commission's, speaking of Reagan's "persuasive dishonesty and inordinate secrecy."[106]

Not about to miss his new momentum, Wright pressed for an intermediary to overcome the impasse of direct negotiations. Contacting both the Contras and the Sandinistas—including Ortega, whom the administration still refused to deal with—Wright recommended Cardinal Miguel Obando y Bravo, the Catholic archbishop of Managua. After both sides agreed, Wright arranged to meet with the cardinal at Washington's papal embassy. Wright then learned, however, that Ortega would also be present—a delicate situation. In Wright's recollection, Shultz stopped by his office on another matter and remarked that the meeting "would be fine" as long as Wright did not negotiate directly with Ortega.[107] In his later account of the exchange, journalist John Barry disagreed. Shultz did not protest strenuously but concluded, "I would decline if I were you." Writing still later, Wright almost appeared to respond to Barry. If Shultz did not want him to proceed, Wright wrote, "I'm afraid I missed the point."[108]

In the end, it mattered little. Wright was already clearly involved in the negotiations, which appealed to him on many levels. Not only were the political winds at his back, but the negotiations spoke to his idealism and his lifelong interest in Latin America. They appealed to his ambition and his desire for a signature accomplishment. Wright believed that he knew the key players better than anyone and that the White House had invited him into the negotiations in the first place. The White House had changed directions, not him. The real issue was not whether Wright was negotiating, but the underlying constitutional balance of powers. Wright still claimed that the executive branch deserved deference, as the president was commander-in-chief, but his years in Congress had made him sensitive to congressional prerogative. Wright was correct when he argued that Congress had long been involved in diplomacy. But the constitutional dilemma had never been as prominent as it was in Wright's planned meeting, which was bold by any account. Previously, after all, Wright's efforts had always been in concurrence with, if not with the express approval of, the executive branch. This time, however, it was different. In some respects, the United States did not have a unified foreign policy, an obviously explosive situation.

When Wright arrived for the meeting on November 13, Obando wasted little time in getting at the heart of the matter. Was he just a messenger, or a true arbiter? Ortega pushed the former, clearly hoping to have the negotiations continue in Washington with Wright as a connection to the administration. Wright, undoubtedly sensitive to his own position and having faith in Obando, took a stern stance otherwise. Obando should have real power and continue the negotiations in Central America. Ortega reluctantly agreed, and the group departed with the press waiting anxiously for a report.[109]

Wright had little idea of the storm his meeting would ignite. The press focused as much on his role as the chance for peace. "I don't need the administration's permission," Wright, obviously annoyed, answered journalist Tom Brokaw.[110] Soon an array of Republicans rushed to harshly condemn Wright in personal terms. The meeting was an "exercise in guerilla theater," stated one unnamed administration figure, whom Wright assumed was Assistant Secretary of State Elliott Abrams. It was a "media event" that would "screw up the real process," stated another. Even Minority Leader Michel, who valued his relationship with the Speaker, complained vigorously. Ortega was a "liar," Reagan exclaimed, obviously wishing to link Wright with the Nicaraguan leader, who was still unpopular in America. The "Wright-Reagan plan" had become the "Wright-Ortega plan."[111] Wright struggled to reply, defending the role of Congress and adding that the administration knew of the meeting. Clearly, however, the criticism was taking its toll. Wright was "doing what the president should do," the friendly *Fort Worth Star-Telegram* editorialized, but it was still a "risky gamble." Labeling Wright the "Speaker of State," the *New York Times* concluded, "It would be better all-around if the Speaker, who is not shy about claiming co-equal authority in foreign affairs, could leave Latin American policy to the executive branch." Other news outlets were less charitable. "Wright was wrong," concluded one editorial bluntly, an egomaniac who thought that he was president. He was a "national embarrassment" added one Texas columnist.[112]

Wright was "skirting close" to violating the Constitution, claimed political scientist Norman Ornstein. He may not have violated the "letter of the Constitution," but "you do have a question of the spirit." Some noted that the Supreme Court had spoken in 1936 of the "exclusive power of the President" in international relations. Others noted that Wright's old hero Sam Rayburn had written that he was "loath to make any moves" because foreign affairs were "so definitely an executive function." Carter's former defense secretary, Harold Brown, perhaps put it best. "It's always a matter of degree," he said.[113] The situation was complex, and Wright had clearly pushed the law to its limits once again.

Tempers ran high. "If you people have something to say to me," Wright told White House Chief of Staff Howard Baker, "please say it to my face."[114] Reagan agreed to meet with Wright, but after calling Ortega a liar again, simply walked out, claiming another commitment. Wright then complained to Shultz about the personal attacks that he assumed Shultz's assistant Abrams had made. "If a member of my staff ever leaked a story like that about you, Mr. Secretary, I'd fire his ass," Wright complained.

Wright was in a fighting mood but agreed to a joint press conference with Shultz, mediated by Dallas power broker Robert Strauss. Wright and Shultz were "burying the hatchet," concluded one report. They were "ending a war over peace," concluded another. While the two indeed agreed to work for peace together, nothing really had changed. "Wright made it very clear that he's not going to discontinue doing anything," one congressional aide remarked.[115] In fact, as the political sniping continued, Wright spoke of his "hope to visit several Central American nations" to "build momentum for the Arias peace plan."[116] Addressing the Costa Rican Legislative Assembly on one trip, Wright noted that he spoke "on behalf of a great many fellow countrymen," and that he came as a representative of Congress. "In our country," he told Costa Rican press, "we have an equality of the branches of the government."[117] More to the point, when word reached him that Obando's talks had "hit a snag," Wright wrote Ambassador Tunnermann and explained that he had just made recommendations to Arias. "I would appreciate very much your discussing this matter with President Ortega," Wright added.[118] Soon, conservatives began to complain that Wright was violating the Logan Act, which prohibited private citizens from conducting diplomacy. Wright, of course, was not acting as a private citizen, and left it to his allies to make the distinction. "I suspect that those members who have of late hurled the Logan Act as a parliamentary rotten tomato are themselves chronic offenders of the same law," Colorado Democrat Patricia Schroeder stated.[119]

Twice more, as 1987 turned to 1988, Reagan pushed to renew Contra military funding, but both times Wright helped block the bill. When Ortega called Wright to suggest some mechanism to verify that military aid had in fact stopped, Wright suggested that he discuss the matter with his liaison, Peña. Aware of the political implications, Wright then asked Peña to record his recollections and share the transcript "with someone in the Administration."[120] Defeating military aid did not mean that Wright had an easy time pushing humanitarian aid to the Contras. In what Wright ascribed to a new low in partisanship, angry conservatives united with liberals in an odd coalition against Wright's bill. Wright finally succeeded in passing an alternative humanitarian package, but it still seemed that some conservatives were more interested in defeating Wright than in passing aid to the Contras they supported.[121]

It all came to a head in the spring of 1988. As Wright encouraged the Obando talks—"the negotiations have reached a critical stage," he wrote—the Sandinistas launched an incursion into Honduras.[122] Ortega argued that the assault was defensive, to disrupt the Contra attacks from that country, but it convinced Reagan to dispatch the 82nd Airborne. Reagan just wanted an excuse to give military aid to the Contras, Wright's aide Lynam replied. "The White House had squandered its credibility."[123] On the House floor, Wright reminded his colleagues that the Iran-Contra report had documented the administration's "intelligence misrepresentations for policy purposes."[124]

In the midst of this, developments in Nicaragua once again overtook the Washington debate. On March 23 at the tiny town of Sapoa, the Sandinistas and the Contras formally—and finally—signed the cease-fire promised at Esquipulas. While the new agreement still allowed continuing negotiations, it was broader than the earlier accord and included key specifics, such as the exchange of prisoners and a process for compliance verification. It was just what Wright needed. "Wright's High-Risk Strategy on Central America Pays Off," declared the *Washington Post*. "Peace Try by Wright Bears Fruit," added the *Fort Worth Star-Telegram*. Despite the presence of American forces in Honduras, moreover, the peace appeared firm.[125]

As Wright declared victory in his political war with Reagan, the White House, in a bit of déjà vu, still refused to yield. Claiming that Ortega would certainly break the new accord, Reagan called once again for Contra military funding. Wright, in disbelief as much as in anger, responded in a way that exacerbated tensions even more, pushing the proverbial envelope to its extremes once again. Wright told the press that the CIA had worked clandestinely to provoke the Sandinistas into an overreaction that would help Congress renew military aid. As Reagan blasted Wright for disclosing classified materials from the House Intelligence Committee, Wright argued that he had said nothing more than what was already public. "The Speaker really came to a gut conclusion," a spokesman from the committee agreed.[126] Asked to provide proof of his charge, Reagan artfully dodged the question. To answer, Reagan replied, would be to commit "the same violation."[127]

SPEAKER OF THE HOUSE   371

With the presidential elections only months away, Republicans pressed for the House Ethics Committee to investigate Wright's remarks. Democrats shot back that a State Department political appointee, Dan Wattenberg, had orchestrated the episode to embarrass Wright. Wattenberg had encouraged Contra leaders to reveal private conversations in which Wright had mentioned the well-documented CIA activities earlier in the 1980s. Wattenberg assumed, correctly as it turned out, that the media would ask Wright about the conversations and provoke an answer that the Republicans could use against him.[128] Defending himself, Wright noted that Congress had "clear testimony" on CIA activities. He meant the evidence uncovered in the Iran-Contra affair, but the Republicans fanned the flames of suspicion, demanding that the Intelligence Committee release all relevant testimony. When Democrats on the committee balked, Republicans then charged in a press conference that Wright was hiding from investigation. Wright replied that he had asked to testify but to no avail. In the end, the committee released the requested materials, but there was no smoking gun. Nothing came of it all except a political culture rubbed raw.[129]

The death threats began to accumulate. In Chicago, a talk radio caller suggested that "somebody should blow [Wright] away." Describing Wright as a "filthy treasonous bastard," one letter writer noted ominously that other traitors had been assassinated.[130] In Washington, a group calling itself the Council for Inter-American Security fanned the anger by labeling Wright "treasonous" and "pro-Communist." After the group claimed to have prominent Republicans on its board, Wright requested that three of those listed—retired admiral E. R. Zumwalt, former Republican National Committee chairman Paul Laxalt, and the antitax congressman Jack Kemp—denounce the organization. In what proved to be a rare act of collegiality, all three agreed.[131] It was, of course, still an election year, and Wright's old nemesis NCPAC was salivating at the opportunity to make another run at Wright. Wright had violated the Constitution, it claimed as it released a series of "demands."[132]

Wright did his best to remain optimistic. The sudden heart attack and death of his old aide Craig Raupe did not help, but Wright clearly looked forward to the battles still on the horizon. The new computers, Wright believed, were "astonishing electronic marvels" that would help for years to come, but he still preferred the manual typewriters. Wright expanded his Virginia home to host large dinner parties and remodeled his offices, including painting part of it the University of Texas burnt orange. When 10,000 people showed up at the Will Rogers Coliseum to show their support,

Wright denounced the "phony charges" that had been leveled against him and promised great things to come. "Together," Wright exclaimed, "we'll make it come true!"[133]

Two weeks before the 1988 elections, the *Washington Post* declared that he was ending the term "as he began it two years ago: at the center of a controversy of his own making." Recounting Wright's impressive accomplishments, the paper noted that it had all come with a cost. Republicans were furious, and Democrats, in the words of one of Wright's colleagues, acknowledged "some concerns."[134] Wright's style of taking risks, his demands and discipline, had not always pleased his fractious flock. Politics had grown more partisan and personal, and Wright had enemies. For many, he was an excellent target.

The *Post* had a point. As the 1988 election approached, the future looked uncertain. Wright, wrestling with his ambition, balancing his idealism with pragmatism, and always working to keep his party united, was hardly an innocent bystander in the devolution of political civility. He had pushed the edges of the envelope many times, in the process leaving his flanks open. His tremendous successes were historic, but, in the dynamic context of Washington politics, it all ensured payback. Wright still promised great accomplishments to come, but he still had no idea of how deep his problems ran. The end of Jim Wright's long and impressive career was nigh, whether he recognized it or not.

CHAPTER 18

In the Valley

RESIGNATION AND ITS AFTERMATH (1987–2015)

The end for Jim Wright began quietly, the proverbial cancer that grows slowly but ultimately proves fatal. It metastasized from the keen mind of Newt Gingrich, in fact, who, by the 100th Congress, was in his fifth term and enjoyed a reputation as an intelligent but Machiavellian grand strategist. As Wright consolidated power and notched his initial victories, Gingrich saw the potential for a "great Speaker," a "very, very formidable" opponent who needed to be neutralized before more damage was done. Recognizing the new media culture and the prominence of ethics, Gingrich saw the means to his end. The Democrats, Gingrich began to argue, had grown accustomed to power and had arrogantly abused it. Moreover, the flawed Jim Wright, properly cast, could easily appear to be the exemplar of corruption, the perfect foil.[1]

To lay the groundwork, Gingrich helped organize a group of young Republicans as the Conservative Opportunity Society. The group quickly produced a pamphlet titled *The House of Ill Repute*. The title itself spoke volumes. After reading old articles on Wright's debt and use of campaign funds, Gingrich dispatched an aide, Karen Van Brocklin, to study Wright's past for other possible negative stories. Planning a coordinated media strategy, Gingrich soon had a formidable arsenal of rumors and fact.[2]

The assault began in the summer of 1987. Letters mailed to legislators and journalists described Wright's aide John Mack as a "violent criminal" without adding anything about his punishment or rehabilitation. Old newspaper articles were attached. Although the letters claimed to be from a Virginia policeman, the media noted that they carried Washington postmarks and included information not universally known. "This is somebody who works, or had worked, in this Capitol," noted a visibly upset Mack.[3] As Wright defended Mack, conservative pundits picked up on the reports. Fortunately for Wright, the major news outlets, sensing a smear campaign, did not.[4] Undeterred, Gingrich then told attendees at a US Chamber of Commerce brunch "several facts about Jim Wright." Not only had he "converted $100,000 from his campaign funds to his personal use," but he had handed Egyptian president Muhammad Anwar el-Sadat a personal letter lobbying for oil concessions on behalf of a business partner. He had pressed the Carter administration to lower the price of national forest oil leases to another business partner. Finally, he had "forced the Appropriations Committee" to give "an unmatched, unrequested grant" to Fort Worth for a project that benefited his friends.[5]

If Gingrich's "facts" were twisted, conveniently avoiding the context of Wright's actions or his explanations, Wright had nevertheless made himself vulnerable. Indeed, Wright had left himself open to a newly emerging charge that seemed to give credence to the old. The high interest rates of the late 1970s had helped undermine the savings and loan industry, and deregulation had allowed risky investments. In Texas, these "thrifts" had invested heavily in real estate, which, unfortunately, collapsed around the same time that Wright set his eyes on the Speakership.[6] When key Texas thrifts complained that the Federal Savings and Loan Insurance Corporation (FSLIC) was unfairly pressuring them when they simply needed more time to recoup their losses, Wright got the FSLIC to back off by delaying a bill recapitalizing it. The failure of the thrifts would have cost the Texas economy millions, Wright believed, and, like the Egyptian deal, he was simply carrying the torch for his constituents. It was prudent and ethical. When one of the beneficiaries contributed more money to Wright's PAC than the law allowed, Wright returned the contribution, noting that he felt "strongly about the integrity of the political process."[7]

Soon, however, Wright found himself flooded with complaints about the FSLIC from numerous other thrifts. Wright asked his business partner

George Mallick to investigate, which proved an ill-advised move, as Mallick was not up to the task. Mallick's report supported the charges of partisan prosecutions without noting that many of the thrifts had engaged in unethical behavior. Broadening his intervention, Wright pressured the Federal Home Loan Bank Board chairman, Edwin Gray, who oversaw the FSLIC, to rein in his agency. Preoccupied with Reagan and the broader agenda, however, Wright failed to do his due diligence. When Wright criticized one regulator who was homosexual, critics claimed that he was using the regulator's sexuality to pressure him to drop his investigation, a charge Wright vehemently denied. Worse still, Wright took up the defense of Texan Don Dixon, unaware that he had milked his Vernon Savings and Loan for millions of dollars.[8]

As reports emerged that Wright had flown on Dixon's jet, an annoyed Gray remarked that Wright's lobbying "did violence to regulatory procedures." In another ill-advised move, Wright let his anger get the best of him and he insulted one of the regulators, Bill Black. Seeking revenge, Black contacted Van Brocklin. "It was my birthday and I wanted to go home," the Gingrich aide recalled. "[Black] just started unloading these stories on me."[9]

Any ignorance Wright had of the savings and loan fraud did not last long. Federal authorities indicted one of Wright's thrift acquaintances, Thomas Gaubert.[10] Wright argued in vain that he had ultimately supported the FSLIC recapitalization bill that the regulators wanted, but Gingrich—who had actually voted against the bill—had all the ammunition he needed.[11] Wright pled that his office "interceded with one or another agency of the bureaucracy on behalf of private citizens many times each month," and, indeed, no one had accused Wright of breaking the law.[12] It little mattered, however. Gingrich's portrait was taking shape. With each new report, Wright replied quickly. "Your recent article," Wright wrote *Bankers Monthly* early in the 100th Congress, "does your publication and your readers a disservice."[13] "Your story contains unintentional inaccuracies," Wright added to the *Washington Post*.[14]

In the midst of the savings and loan accusations, the story on Wright's book deal emerged, cast as a conflict of interest, if not a violation of law. Seeking to cut off the speculation, Wright announced that he was putting all his assets into a blind trust. He owed the public an "assurance" that his actions were not "colored by considerations of financial well-being."[15] When the chorus of accusations continued, Wright's allies urged him to sever ties with Mallick. Wright, however, could not abandon a friend. Reporters even pressed Wright when he added a fireplace to the Speaker's office. "In no way whatever is it any personal property," Wright exclaimed, reminding them that the Capitol had more than one hundred fireplaces.[16]

Having laid the groundwork, Gingrich was ready by the end of 1987 to unleash the next wave of his campaign of destruction. Without noting his own complicity, Gingrich cited the large number of "respected publications" that had written on Wright. Congress, he claimed, had an "obligation to examine these articles and their allegations." The attorney general should launch a formal inquiry, and Congress should consider a special ad hoc ethics committee. If Congress chose to let the standing House Ethics Committee handle the matter, the committee should "suspend all other investigations." If members had questions, Gingrich concluded, they should contact "me or Karen Van Brocklin."[17]

Some Republicans, such as Minority Leader Michel, had reservations. "Newt has his own way of operating," Michel stated. "I have from time to time problems with his methodology."[18] Gingrich could have cared less. As he began calling Wright a "dangerous man," Gingrich worked to tie Wright to Democrat Gary Hart, who had left the presidential race facing charges of an extramarital affair only to reenter. The Wright allegations merited an investigation, Gingrich stated. They were "clearly as important as Gary Hart's sex life." As Gingrich spoke, Fort Worth Democrats reported fake Wright phone calls endorsing Hart, who was unpopular in the district. "This is an urgent message from Jim Wright," the recordings stated. "Our friend Gary Hart got himself back into the race and we want to welcome him back."[19]

"What is good for the goose is good for the gander," Democrats responded, beginning their own opposition research. Seeking to separate Gingrich from other Republicans, one Democratic congressional aide noted that he had "a history of cheap shots against Reagan." Many Republicans were uneasy with his slash-and-burn tactics, the aide stated, and Democrats should cast Gingrich as "juvenile and rabble rousing," always "eager to get his name in the paper."[20] As the first session of the 100th Congress concluded, Wright's policy successes stood out—and his reputation for corruption was beginning to as well.

In terms of political scandal, the new session of the 100th Congress in January 1988 began where the previous one had ended. Jim Wright could not get a break. Anxious to refute the inaccurate stories, Wright's press aide, George Mair, protested to media outlets with letters that seemed unprofessional and threatening.[21] Angry reporters quickly noted that the letters contained misspellings and inaccuracies. The misspellings, Mair responded, were intentional to ferret out the origin of leaks from Wright's staff. Now, in short, it appeared that Wright's staff was as vindictive as their boss was corrupt.[22] Moving to quash the story, Wright invited reporters to lunch and apologized, quipping, when the waiters brought the entrée, "Is this crow?"[23]

Gingrich had great plans for the new session. He hoped to force Wright to resign as the chair of the upcoming Democratic National Convention. If the Ethics Committee launched a formal inquiry of Wright, Gingrich told his fellow Republicans, Wright would have to step down, adding credence to the charges facing him, or, alternatively, remain as chair, thereby casting the shadow of scandal over the entire party. "I think the Democrats are boxed," laughed Karl Rove, a young Republican political operative.[24] Gingrich was optimistic that the Ethics Committee would act. The press had broken the story of Wright's book royalties and appeared to be digging deeper into his company with Mallick, Mallightco.

Michel, however, still had reservations about Gingrich's tactics. Two Republican congressmen, both lawyers, had reviewed Van Brocklin's dossier on Wright and concluded that the charges lacked substance.[25] While Gingrich promised to mobilize "three or four thousand of my friends" to protest Wright's ethics at the Democratic convention, the press reported that a staged "mock trial" of Wright "didn't draw enough spectators to form a jury pool."[26] Michel did not want the new Congress deadlocked with partisanship, but the Democrats had responded to all the accusations by calling for the Ethics Committee to investigate Gingrich.[27] The media began to report that Gingrich conducted questionable fundraising, had accepted payment to write a book that had never materialized, and had used congressional staff on personal projects.[28] When the press reported that Van Brocklin had contacted former Wright acquaintances seeking new allegations, Gingrich was caught off guard. "If anybody has reasonable suspicion that the man third in line to the presidency is corrupt," Gingrich snapped, "how could they justify not using their staff to investigate it?"[29] The argument, one report concluded, constituted a "double standard." Gingrich was confident that the Ethics Committee would act, but Wright was increasingly confident otherwise. The tide had begun to shift against that "Georgia jerk," Wright wrote colleagues. "The storm . . . seems to have abated."[30]

Wright was wrong. The respected good-government lobby group Common Cause announced that it supported a Wright investigation. Gingrich had pressed the nonprofit's president, Fred Wertheimer, for months, and on May 18, Wertheimer wrote Ethics Committee chairman Julian Dixon.

Stressing that his call did not imply Wright's guilt, Wertheimer suggested that the Ethics Committee retain outside counsel to "ensure that the results of the inquiry are credible."[31] Caught off guard himself, Wright noted that Common Cause had never contacted his office and had only corresponded with Gingrich. Wright did not believe Common Cause had conspired with Gingrich, as some Democrats claimed, but he did view the nonprofit as "the handmaiden of a partisan political initiative."[32]

Wright understood that the winds had now shifted against him. Confident of his exoneration, he also began pressing for the Ethics Committee to act—but openly and quickly. It was best, Wright now calculated, to appear cooperative and get past the matter as soon as possible. On June 9—just as Wright won on the trade bill—the Ethics Committee complied after meeting for over six hours. Denying Wright's pleas to address the committee immediately, Dixon stated that a preliminary investigation would focus on the issues raised in a formal complaint that Gingrich had filed in late May. Wright noted that Gingrich's complaint held the signatures of his most ardent opponents on Central America, but no moderates. Michel was not on the list; nor were the two Republicans who had reviewed Van Brocklin's dossier. The complaint included the charge that Wright had lobbied for companies in which he had invested, an accusation that Wright's royalties on his book were improper, and claims that the book was nothing more than a vehicle to convert campaign funds to personal use. Common Cause had also requested an investigation of Wright's role in the thrift crisis.[33]

In later years, Wright recalled that his allies warned him that politics, not facts, would prove determinative. He should do as other Speakers facing scandal had done, and indeed, as Reagan had done—appoint his own investigative committee. Wright, however, rejected the idea. He believed in his innocence and wanted full exoneration. The Ethics Committee was the only path forward.[34] Of course, Wright claimed publicly that the charges were timed to cloud the Democratic convention. "If that isn't politics," Wright stated, "I don't know what is."[35] He also claimed publicly that he welcomed an independent counsel, but privately he lobbied against it. A special counsel, he feared, might not understand House rules, and bring additional publicity. Worse still was the possibility of a politically motived partisan investigator. To answer whatever came, Wright hired the former Federal Election Commission (FEC) counsel William Oldaker. Oldaker, Wright knew, understood both the law and politics.[36]

Only a month before the Democrats met in Atlanta, the politics were obvious. Republican National Committee chairman Frank Fahrenkopf called on the clear Democratic nominee, Michael Dukakis, to state whether he supported the investigation of Wright. Wright was the new poster boy for Republican fliers, which always cited Common Cause. Feeling the pressure, the liberal magazine *New Republic* described Wright as an "albatross."[37] Most Democrats, however, rallied around Wright and downplayed the investigation. Wright, one column declared, "takes it all in stride." With the northern liberal Dukakis as the party's candidate, Wright remained key to Democratic unity. Only once did Wright blunder. Appearing on *Face the Nation*, he stated that he had the written apologies of three Republicans. When asked who they were—surely an expected question—Wright stated that he wanted to spare them embarrassment. True or not, the response smacked of Senator Joe McCarthy's anonymous letters alleging communism four decades before.[38]

At the convention, Wright's speech praising the accomplishments of the 100th Congress won a standing ovation from the crowd, many wearing "I love Jim Wright" buttons. The investigation would be over within two months, Wright predicted to the press.[39] After the convention, he introduced Dukakis at a "general campaign kick-off rally" in Houston, predicting a Democratic victory in Texas. It was a stiff order; Dukakis's opponent was Texas's own George Bush. Wright liked Bush, although he questioned his knowledge of the Iran-Contra scandal in his years as Reagan's vice-president. At least Bush appeared to be less ideological than Reagan.[40]

One week after the convention—and after Reagan called for a special prosecutor—the Ethics Committee appointed a past president of the Chicago Bar Association, Richard J. Phelan, as special counsel to investigate Wright. When Wright asked Chairman Dixon why the committee did not select someone knowledgeable of House rules, mentioning moderate Republican John Anderson, Dixon replied that the Republicans were insistent. Wright later claimed that Indiana Republican John Myers had pressed for Phelan, who had lobbied for the job.[41] If in fact Phelan had Republican backing, Gingrich was not among them. Gingrich declared himself "outraged" because Phelan had contributed to Democratic senator Paul Simon of Illinois. Phelan, Van Brocklin added, was a "Democratic activist." The charges put Phelan on the defensive, which, Wright later concluded, was exactly Gingrich's plan.[42]

The official investigation then proceeded quietly, with the only development of public note being the testimony of Wright in mid-September. Wright told the press that he had waited for "some ninety days" to tell his side of the story and that he had refuted all the "erroneous, incomplete and misleading charges."[43] For the remainder of the 100th Congress, the presidential campaign overshadowed Wright's woes. Rumors, some far-fetched and others less so, kept arising nevertheless. Wright was a wife-beater and had padded his resume. He was behind the death of an old Texas political opponent, a claim now four decades old. He had hired a half-brother, Stephen Byrd, an illegitimate child from Wright's father. It was, of course, left to Wright to question the relationship. Upon learning of the possible connection, Wright responded, he had quickly ended Byrd's employment.[44] More critically, reports continued to trickle out about Wright's finances—the openings that Wright's own actions had created. Wright had to acknowledge that his office had paid for an aide's expenses working on his book. He had to revise his 1987 financial disclosure forms when researchers uncovered "minor discrepancies." New accusations against Betty particularly angered Wright. "Mrs. Wright has not abandoned the right to pursue constructive career goals of her own," Wright reminded the press."[45]

As friends advised him that the scandal was a "media game," Wright was aghast to learn that Dixon had allowed Phelan to expand his investigation beyond the original complaints. Two of Wright's former opponents reported that Phelan was simply fishing, asking for "anything illegal or unethical that you know or suspect."[46] As Republicans began to defend Phelan, claiming that it was "not unusual for someone to follow up on various leads," Wright's supporters mocked him, charging that Phelan was looking "into the whole history of Texas politics since World War II." Fearing that Phelan had his own political aspirations and wanted to make a name for himself, Wright began to complain that Phelan socialized with some of Wright's harshest critics and had taken Ethics Committee members to dinner. "Can you imagine a district attorney fraternizing with members of a jury?" Wright later wrote incredulously. In fact, Wright also socialized with several committee members, attending a fundraiser for Californian Vic Fazio. "How can you have a judge co-host a fund-raiser with a person who's on trial?" Gingrich asked the press, equally incredulously.[47] By all accounts, the politics were hard to miss.

The 1988 presidential campaign revealed more about the state of politics than the actual election results did. It was a brutal campaign, marked by Bush's campaign manager, Lee Atwater, arguably pandering to fear and racism in his aggressive attacks highlighting the Dukakis-paroled convict Willie Horton. Charges and countercharges flew, including false accusations that Bush had engaged in an affair. From such a harsh climate came somewhat surprising results. Bush won in a landslide, but Democrats gained two seats in the House and one in the Senate. The results promised more of the same—perhaps encouraging for Wright in terms of policy, but not for his own reputation.[48]

Although a group called Citizens for Reagan distributed "Foley for Speaker" buttons and put up "Wanted" posters for Wright, there remained no serious challenge to Wright's reelection as Speaker. No Democrat wanted to appear to be in cahoots with the opposition. In an unprecedented move, Michel announced that the Republicans would back any Democrat who ran. "I'm tired of this horseshit," Wright muttered.[49] At least, in a symbolic gesture, the president-elect promised to come to Capitol Hill to discuss cooperation. Bush told Wright he would do nothing that "impinges on your honor and integrity."[50]

If anything, policy was almost a respite for Wright. In the coming weeks, the new secretary of state, James Baker, helped broker a compromise on Central America. The new administration agreed to support the ongoing peace process, ending military efforts, and to support any leader who won a fair election in Nicaragua, scheduled for 1990.[51] Confident that Bush and the Sandinistas would uphold the agreement, Wright finally had all he had hoped for in his long struggle with Reagan. Meanwhile, he delved into the annual budget negotiations and a debate over increasing the minimum wage, in both instances finding Bush a formidable opponent. While Bush vetoed a Democratic minimum-wage bill, he was no ideologue, and ultimately the two sides compromised on both issues.[52]

Much to Wright's dismay, however, one policy issue leaked into the clouds of scandal that seemed to follow him everywhere. With Congress facing another scheduled pay raise, barring a vote otherwise, Wright wanted to avoid another public outcry like the one that had taken place two years before. The raise once again was popular among legislators but not with the public. Wright hoped to stall until the deadline had passed. Sensing political opportunity, however, the Republican leadership demanded a vote, anticipating that Democrats would force Wright to block the measure. He would appear to be sneaking a stealth pay raise past the public. Looking to extricate himself, Wright proposed a vote on a smaller raise combined with a ban on honoraria—not coincidentally, one of the issues that interested Phelan. Hoping to poll his members, Wright found that few complied, suggesting that his ambitious whip, Tony Coelho, was already anticipating a post-Wright Congress. Still struggling, Wright then proposed to let the raise take effect. Only at that point would Congress vote to reduce the raise and ban honoraria. Leaked to the press, the new plan pleased no one. The raise was still too high for the public, and Wright and his party appeared to be both scheming and greedy. Talk radio exploded. Forced into a corner, Wright ended up calling a vote before the deadline, and the Democrats, seeking to shield themselves, voted overwhelmingly against the raise—and, as Wright knew, against their true feelings. They had lost the raise, and yet they still suffered public wrath—and they blamed Wright. Wright had shaken the support that he would need the most in the coming weeks.[53]

In the midst of this ill-timed "gaffe," as one journal termed it, the Senate Democrats rejected Bush's nomination of Wright's old nemesis John Tower for secretary of defense. Tower had been chairman of both the Senate Armed Services Committee and the president's commission investigating the Iran-Contra affair. Ignoring his obvious credentials, the Democrats focused on allegations of drinking and womanizing. It was, the Republicans believed, the worst sort of character assassination. As Tower bemoaned the "new and rather ugly phase in American politics"—sentiments Wright knew well—Wright remained relatively quiet. Although he did not repudiate the attacks, he did in one instance toast Tower at a Texas Independence Day celebration.[54]

"You need to know, Mr. Speaker, that the John Tower rejection has hardened the ranks in my party against you," one Republican warned Wright after the vote. "They want to go Hammurabi one better." So, Wright responded, "an eye for an eye and a tooth for a tooth?" It was more than that, came the answer. It was a "Texan for a Texan." The national press agreed. "The big loser of the Tower debacle is Jim Wright," one anonymous congressional aide told the media. "He's got to be cringing because he's next."[55]

The storm clouds appeared increasingly ominous. The appointment of Atwater as the new National Republican Committee chairman promised more hardball politics. Soon Wright received word that Atwater supported Gingrich's assault.[56] Leaks from Phelan's investigation indicated that the Teamsters had refused to comply with a subpoena to testify about their mass-purchase of Wright's book. Moreover, it appeared that Mallick had failed in his own testimony to reveal Betty's use of their company car. As the press began to speculate that his future lay with Phelan's report, Wright for the first time appeared genuinely worried, offering to resign his Speakership if his Democratic support eroded. "I don't have to be Speaker," Wright stated defensively, unintentionally implying that the end was near.[57]

Phelan officially submitted his report in late February 1989. At almost five hundred pages, it was detailed and damning, the charges manifold. The book royalties were meant to surpass the limits on honoraria, it claimed. Supporters had purchased large quantities for Wright's benefit. Wright and Mallick's company, Mallightco, was a "sham" intended to facilitate gifts. Betty did no real work, and Mallick had direct interest in legislation before Congress, the key ingredient for a rule violation. Wright, moreover, had exerted undue pressure on behalf of key savings and loans. He had used his office to advance his own investments.[58]

Addressing the committee after Phelan, Wright's attorney, Oldaker, argued that the report failed to consider context and had left out exculpatory evidence. It appeared to interpret terms such as "gifts" or "direct interest" in ways that served Phelan's biased purposes. Such distinctions were critical, Oldaker understood, because Wright had parsed the rules so carefully in his actions. He had so often gone to the edge of propriety that it was easy for Phelan to blur the differences.[59] It was, of course, a difficult defense to make politically to the reporters who waited anxiously outside.

What followed was perhaps predictable. When Democrats blocked Republican efforts to release the report before the committee voted on whether to level formal charges, the leaks began to appear. The Republicans began to argue that the standard to proceed was low, only a "reason to believe." Final determination of guilt or innocence, after all, was for later in the process. Democrats countered that there was no need to go further given that the report had failed to meet the standard for conviction, "clear and convincing." As the Republicans argued that failing to vote for formal charges would add to the perception of Congress as corrupt, committee Democrats received hundreds of letters and phone calls orchestrated by talk radio and Republican lobbies.[60]

The committee finally voted in early April. Dismissing the oil investments and thrift accusations, among others, it ruled against Wright on several key issues. Mallick, the committee voted, had a direct interest in legislation. Betty's employment and compensation, including the car and condo, constituted gifts. Betty did no real work. Wright's large book royalty was not a violation—Wright having exploited a loophole—but the bulk purchases constituted an effort to surpass honoraria limits. If these matters were not enough, the committee packaged them into sixty-nine specific violations of House rules, which one Republican member later acknowledged was an attempt to prejudice Wright. The car alone brought twenty-two charges.[61]

Although Wright held an emotional press conference to plead for fairness, many Democrats began to distance themselves, undoubtedly recalling the new pay raise debacle, if not Wright's heavy-handed leadership. Older conservative Democrats tended to rally to Wright's side more than the younger liberals. Nothing seemed to go Wright's way. Coelho, now suddenly under a similar cloud of suspicion for questionable junk bond purchases, appeared unwilling to rally the caucus. Sensing that Oldaker was too focused on the legal minutiae and had too much faith in the committee chair, Dixon, Wright hired Houston litigator Stephen Susman to better manage the politics. Susman's harsh personal attacks on Phelan, however, backfired. In a bit of irony not lost on Wright, Phelan emerged as the victim of a smear campaign. In fact, Phelan, confident that he had a committee majority, refused to turn over all the evidence as the rules required, offering only partial evidence and summaries. When Wright asked to testify again, noting that Gingrich's initial charges had all been dismissed, and that he had not had the opportunity to address the new accusations, the committee delayed. The media, meanwhile, appeared to welcome it all as good copy. When one of Wright's bulk book buyers, Gene Payte, offered an affidavit to support his claim that Phelan had misrepresented his testimony, the press largely ignored it. By the end of April, pundits were no longer speculating on whether Wright would resign, but when.[62]

The stories were relentless. On May 4, the *Washington Post* ran an exposé on John Mack's violent past, the same story it had earlier rejected. The next day, the *New York Times* reported that Wright had not recorded the income from an investment in a nursing home company. Wright argued that he had lost money, but the preferential treatment the story implied remained. Finally, on May 19, the *Los Angeles Times* reported that the IRS planned a criminal investigation of Wright. Oldaker protested, and the IRS denied the story, but the denial carried little weight and barely made the news.[63] The momentum against Wright was simply too great.

Struggling to sleep, his blood pressure elevated, Wright found reporters camped outside his home in a proverbial death watch. Wright could not walk the halls of Congress without heads turning. His colleagues stiffened and looked awkwardly away. They understood the reality; in the minds of many Americans, Wright was guilty—of something. There was too much smoke. Wright had become the embodiment of the public's distrust of Congress, the exemplar of all the suspicions and frustrations the public harbored toward politicians. For Wright, the important matters—the policies, the institution to which he had devoted his life—appeared almost to be an afterthought for his colleagues. What good was his position if he had no power and his agenda was stalled, and perhaps even hurt by his presence? His reputation, which had always been important to him, was in tatters, and the collegial relationships he had long cultivated seemed suddenly inconsequential. It was not fun anymore; the politics were now too brutal.[64]

Wright's instincts told him to fight, but the reality was now too hard to miss. Yet another group of new advisers, the venerable strategist Clark Clifford and his partner Robert Altman, appeared to be at odds with Oldaker and Susman. Even if he could get the gift and direct-interest charges related to Mallick dropped, the book charge appeared certain to lead to a reprimand and a floor vote that no one wanted. Rostenkowski, while surprisingly supportive, let Wright know that a majority of Democrats thought him an albatross. In the very least, his days as Speaker were numbered.[65] Wright assumed that the assault would never stop. Minority Leader Foley faced rumors of questionable stock dealings and connections to homosexual prostitution. Whip William Gray faced accusations of campaign irregularities. Coelho, watching it all, decided to bow out quickly and save what reputation he had left, a decision that Wright noticed won praise as a selfless sacrifice.

Quietly, behind the scenes, negotiations began. When Phelan offered to drop the charges against Betty in exchange for Wright's immediate resignation and the appointment of a Speaker pro tem, the offer struck Wright as arrogant and insulting to his high elected office. Phelan, Wright noticed, did not seem to understand that if he had agreed, the Speaker pro tem would have had no authority.[66] Phelan countered, offering to have the direct-interest charges dropped but adding a threat. If Wright still refused, he would have the committee look into oil investments Wright held near Sabine Lake along the Texas-Louisiana border. Wright saw no problem with the investments but realized it little mattered. As the media, citing leaks, began to report that Wright was plea-bargaining, Wright was as furious as he was powerless. Under no circumstances would he ever negotiate the future of such an important position on such petty matters. If he were to resign, he would do so on his own terms and with the House left in good order.[67]

Stealthily slipping away to a friend's house in the Shenandoah Valley on the Memorial Day weekend, Wright found his family was up for the fight. Ginger said she would quit her job to help. Polls still suggested that most constituents felt the same, and supportive letters arrived daily. "Don't throw in the towel!" read one. "Let's give Newt Gingrich the fight of his life!" read another. It all lifted Wright's spirits but did little to change the reality. Continuing the fight would cost thousands of dollars he could ill afford and could drag on throughout the entire 101st Congress. Resignation was not fair, but it was, perhaps, best for everything in which he believed.[68]

Wright finally, reluctantly, made his peace. He would not resign immediately as demanded—he was not, he still insisted, negotiating—but would announce his resignation publicly on the floor of the institution he loved, pending the vote on his successor. He would use his resignation speech, and all of his renowned rhetorical skills, to draw what good he could from such a bleak situation. Politics had to change. He would, in short, leave with a shred of dignity, and, who knows, something positive might come of his political demise after all.[69]

Suddenly it was over. As his colleagues offered an awkward combination of congratulations for his speech and condolences for his fate, their expressions honest or otherwise, Wright found himself surprised. He had every reason to sulk in self-pity or lash out in bitter anger, but his overriding emotion was simply relief. The cameras largely vanished. The press no longer stalked him, and suddenly, he slept better. A great burden had been lifted, and it was now more obvious than ever just how much a personal toll his long agony had taken.

After writing his many supporters letters of thanks, something that he had meant to do but had rarely had the time to carry out, Wright attended a meeting of the Democratic caucus a few days after his speech. Rising to a standing ovation, Wright formally nominated Foley as the new Speaker and then sat down—again to a standing ovation.[70] In the days that followed, he kept the veneer of normalcy, the routine but nonsubstantive responsibilities of his office. These included his last official act, calling the complete House to order for the election of his successor. As the media now hovered around Foley, one wayward reporter asked Wright about his future. Was he planning to run for governor of Texas? Wright could not help but laugh.[71]

Wright had arranged for his extensive collection of personal papers and memorabilia to go to Texas Christian University. TCU had assumed that Wright, as a former University of Texas student, would opt for his alma mater. In fact, UT had contacted him. After a series of discussions with TCU chancellor William Tucker, however, Wright had decided on the university in his hometown. It was, perhaps, one more service for his district. TCU provost Larry Adams came to Washington as Wright's staff cleaned out their offices. There Adams helped Wright identify materials for transfer. Wright, Adams recalled, was "in very good spirits." TCU agreed to pay for the transfer and planned to store the materials until the university could build in its library an appropriate facility for their permanent collection.[72]

The construction at the Mary Couts Burnett Library began not long after the trucks arrived with the papers, which were contained in over 4,000 cubic feet of boxes. The archives' primary storage area was on the library's lowest level, complete with appropriate temperature, humidity, and lighting controls. The second floor housed the archivists' offices and a reading room. Outside the offices were nine display cases exhibiting the highlights of Wright's career, including such items as the "Letter to Ivan" and glowing letters from presidents. Nowhere, however, was there mention of Wright's painful downfall. After TCU hired Glenda Stevens as lead archivist, Stevens began the arduous task of cataloging the massive volumes.[73]

Wright, meanwhile, was busy boxing up all his possessions in his McLean home. He had decided with Betty to purchase a home in Mira Vista, a nice development in southwest Fort Worth, not far from where he planned to have an office downtown. "There's no room for that," Betty admonished Wright as they packed. "We've talked and talked about that." Wright, once able to ram legislation through Congress but now apparently unable to sway even his wife, gave her a sheepish smile. "I know we did, but I thought I had prevailed." Gone was the basement bar, Wright's man cave that he called his "Tex-Mex Room." In exchange, Wright won a broadsword that a Cambodian leader had given him. And so it went.[74]

To welcome him back to Fort Worth, over 3,000 supporters jammed the Round Up Hotel Convention Center and cheered his arrival. An obviously moved Wright alluded to his scandal and even implied his own role, thanking them for tolerating "my problems, my eccentricities and my mistakes."[75] The 3,500-square-foot, two-story antebellum residence at the end of Wright's 1,400-mile journey was quite a consolation. It was perfect for visits from Wright's children and his now four grandsons. The Wrights kept two dogs, a terrier named Maggie McTavish and a bichon frise named Gigi. The home had a pool out back and the development's practice golf range out front, and Betty told the local media that Wright now truly had time to relax. "That is," she added skeptically, "if I can keep him from being a workaholic."[76]

Of course, she could not. With his federal benefits and pension, Wright maintained a 2,100-square-foot office on the ninth floor of the Fritz Lanham Federal Building. An assistant who had worked for him for eighteen years, Norma Ritchson, handled the many requests that still arrived daily. Without a dogged prosecutor following him, Wright invested wisely—with,

Wright noted sarcastically, Betty's help. Turning down lobbying jobs, Wright signed on as a "management consultant" with the American Income Life Insurance Company, led by his lifelong friend Bernard Rapoport. Much of his time, however, was spent traveling. "For the first five years," Wright recalled, "I was on the speaking circuit." He also served as a consultant for Arch Petroleum Company, which required the occasional visit to Mexico. Returning to Latin America was never a problem for Wright.[77]

As the years passed, Wright agreed to teach a course at TCU, "Congress and the Presidents." As much personal reflections as a set curriculum, the course was clearly an outlet for his still-considerable oratory skills. In the words of one reporter who attended the first class, "It would have been difficult for even the laziest student to nod off." When one student asked Wright which presidents he had "served under," Wright gave a grandfatherly smile and replied that he had "served with" eight.[78] Only once did his past cast a shadow. Not long after his arrival, the Federal Election Commission ruled that his PACs had not correctly reported plane trips afforded him.[79]

Not surprisingly, Wright also wrote. In addition to serving as a semi-regular columnist for the *Fort Worth Star-Telegram*, he produced three significant books. First came the 322-page *Worth It All*, his recounting of his long struggle for peace in Central America. Cast in historical context and written in Wright's well-crafted style, the story implies that his downfall resulted from his success. In the end, he argues, events proved him correct. He had made mistakes, but it was "worth it all."[80] The next volume, *Balance of Power: Presidents and Congress from the Era of McCarthy to the Age of Gingrich*, constituted Wright's major memoirs. As its title implies, the book proceeds chronologically and does not shy away from his fatal scandal. The new politics of attack are cast as the clear villain. With the obvious exception of Gingrich, and, to a lesser extent, Reagan, Wright is relatively generous to those whom he fought. Having lauded collegiality, after all, Wright knew better than to stock his memoirs full of derogatory allegations. Finally, at the age of eighty-three, Wright published *The Flying Circus: Pacific War—1943—as Seen Through a Bombsight*. The product of a conversation with his grandson, who had inquired of his war service, the book once again told of hard work and sacrifice for great accomplishments.

Life went on. "An old man has certain things in common with a car," Wright wrote. "Body parts begin to wear out and need fixing."[81] Wright's first challenge came in 1991. Just a few days before his sixty-ninth birthday, Wright felt a bump in his mouth. The doctors at Houston's M. D. Anderson Cancer Center diagnosed cancer and removed a portion of Wright's tongue, leaving the orator extraordinaire with a slight speech impediment. "It was like being an artist without a brush or a carpenter without a saw," Wright later laughed. Characteristically, Wright approached the treatment optimistically. Earlier in his life, he remarked, he had been "consumed by being speaker." He would have "ignored that BB-sized lump."[82] With such a positive attitude and speech therapy, Wright was able to continue his teaching, and even participated in an experimental trial of a cancer drug, cis-retinoic acid.

Through it all, Wright continued to insist that he was not bitter. "To bear a grudge, or harbor anger and hate, doesn't hurt the object of the anger," Wright remarked. "It hurts you."[83] The winter of his life brought him many joys. The awards came—from the American Civil Liberties Union, the Anti-Defamation League, the University of Texas, and many others. In 1996, Weatherford proclaimed August 5 "Jim Wright Day" and opened an extensive exhibit on his life. Wright also agreed to contribute to a short booklet, *Weatherford Days: A Time of Learnin'*, produced for the exhibit and recounting his boyhood.[84] Matching the recognition from his lifelong friends was the formal unveiling of his portrait in Congress's Statuary Hall. Better still, old colleagues from both sides of the aisle were on hand for the event. Michel even toasted his former colleague. "I can't think of another man who deserves our respect and honor more," stated Texan Jack Brooks.[85]

For the most part, Wright was successful in demonstrating that he had put his troubles behind him. When Gingrich called Wright a crook in 1995, Wright did not take the bait, responding only passive aggressively. "Mr. Gingrich lacks dignity," Wright stated. "It would be demeaning for me to respond in kind."[86] When Republicans successfully proposed slashing the retirement benefits of former Speakers—all those still living were Democrats—reporters noted that it was a slap at Wright. Wright, however, remained silent.[87] When Congress received testimony that the CIA under Reagan had clandestinely monitored his discussions with Central American leaders, Wright did not join the public outcry but stated simply that he was "not surprised."[88]

To the extent that he remained active in politics, Wright for the most part let his newspaper columns speak for him. He attended the 1992 Democratic National Convention, but, unlike four years before, sat quietly among the 5,000 convention delegates. "I'm enjoying not having too many responsibilities," he told a reporter. When Dallas billionaire Ross Perot launched his independent presidential bid that year, Wright advised Democratic candidate Bill Clinton to avoid attacking the wealthy Texan. "It's quite obvious that Perot and President Bush detest one another," Wright stated, adding that they would most likely attack each other. Slinging political mud was never a good option.[89] The death of Tip O'Neill in early 1994 hit Wright hard, reminding him not only that life had to be lived in the moment but also of the collegiality of days past. O'Neill was a "relic of a better age," Wright remarked solemnly. He set out to "exalt rather than degrade."[90]

As the new millennium approached, with his eightieth birthday not far behind, Wright moved from his palatial downtown offices to an office at TCU next to his archives. Congress's recent reduction in the pay allotted to retired Speakers had precipitated the move, but Wright understood as well that he could no longer maintain his schedule. He and Betty sold their Mira Vista home and downsized to one in Overton Park, closer to his new office. "It will be different, but he's the engine that runs this thing," Ritchson stated.[91] His appearances slowed, but his writing did not. "It was a delight to hear from you and to learn that you are doing so well," wrote Senator Ted Kennedy. Visitors came and went, with the public still occasionally stopping the old man to say hello.[92] "A guy gets to be my age, and people think of him as history," Wright laughed. "The memories are so full, so many, and I wouldn't trade them for anything."[93]

Just as Wright adjusted, however, old age took its toll again; the cancer returned, this time in his jaw. In a thirteen-hour operation back at M. D. Anderson, the surgeons transplanted a portion of Wright's femur to his jaw and some skin from his thigh to his tongue. The operation left him with a speech impediment that no speech therapy could erase, but once again, Wright refused to wallow in self-pity. He laughed when an old friend joked that he had been trying for forty years to keep his foot out of his mouth but now had his whole leg in it. Despite the assumptions of friends, Wright insisted on still teaching. The students, he assured them, could still understand him. "The good news is that they got all of the cancer and I have a new jaw and it seems to be working," Wright told the press. In fact, Wright's graft produced unexpected complications, requiring additional reconstructive surgery. The letters of concerned friends poured in, ranging from President Clinton to his old high school chums. "These days I've been nursed, wheeled around, fed, medicined, chauffeured, pampered, and made to feel virtually helpless," Wright wrote, lauding humility and patience. Life had taught him yet another lesson, and he was a better man for it.[94]

Every morning, Wright still woke looking forward to the day, even as old friends and acquaintances fell increasingly to Father Time. "I don't want to be idle," he explained. "I want to get up every morning and look forward to having something to do."[95] This, at least, was a life lesson that Wright had learned early. Wright continued to teach almost a decade into the new millennium. In time, his eyes failing and with an annoying case of ischemia making him occasionally dizzy, he had to give this up as well. Still, however, the keen mind and the writing remained, as did the attitude. His thick eyebrows had thinned, and his stature had shrunk, but Wright still found reason to joke. The radiation treatments had left one side of his face unable to grow whiskers, he noted. "Maybe if I live long enough, I can save enough money on razors to pay for my surgery."[96]

Still Wright followed the news. In November 2013, he made it to the voting booth only to discover that he did not have the proper identification. Texas Republicans had passed legislation requiring a photo ID, a requirement that Democrats decried as a way to decrease voter participation among the poor and elderly. It was no coincidence, perhaps, that the media learned of the situation and it made national news.[97] Wright, in his ninety-first year, still appeared to be a political operative. Jim Wright, it was obvious to everyone, still cared.

The Politics of Scandal and the Judgment of History

Reflecting on his role in history, Wright claimed that his departing plea for collegiality and cooperation, his emotional call for an end to the politics of personal destruction, was "the biggest damn miscalculation of my life."[1] Far from changing, Congress did not return to the political culture of days past that Wright so idealized. As one report read just after Wright's resignation, "There are few signs that partisan warfare is about to end." No sooner had Wright returned to the Lone Star State than Gingrich declared that he had a "list" of Democrats to investigate. Of course by then Gingrich was as much prey as predator, as the Ethics Committee was investigating his own book deals and campaign financing. In a bit of irony that Wright surely appreciated, the committee's Democratic chairman who had distanced himself from Wright, Julian Dixon, had to reveal his own wife's questionable investments.[2] Moreover, in 1992, the media reported that many congressmen were regularly and without penalty overdrawing their House bank accounts. The scandal ended with dozens of official reprimands and several criminal convictions. Yet again, the institution that Wright cherished found itself in the political muck.[3]

Together with a poll-tested Republican agenda termed the "Contract with America," the House bank scandal contributed to a massive Republican sweep in the 1994 congressional elections. A significant number of the seventy-three freshmen had no legislative experience and were ideologically antigovernment. They had nothing in common with the old guard.[4] As Wright watched the nightmare that he had tried to prevent for decades unfold, his old acquaintance Bob Michel retired, paving the way for the new, younger Republicans to reward the man they believed to be responsible for their good fortune. Newt Gingrich, to the shock of many, was the new Speaker of the House. Wright might have made an emotional appeal to end the "mindless cannibalism," but the success of Gingrich's aggressive, accusatory style of politics spoke much louder. Indeed, Gingrich quickly orchestrated a government shutdown to pressure his opposition on the budget. Wright had some consolation when Richard Phelan unsuccessfully sought public office—proving Wright's claim that his former tormentor had political aspirations—but Congress's continued fall into disrepute was more than dismaying to the old man in Fort Worth.[5]

After a wave of successful initial proposals, Gingrich and his allies overplayed their hand, both rhetorically and legislatively. Their harsh hyperbole—including, for example, equating the Environmental Protection Agency with the Gestapo—and their proposals to eliminate a number of popular programs began to erode their support. Gingrich now personified Congress—and Congress remained an institution that was hardly held in esteem. Gingrich, Wright noted, "has sown the seeds of hate whose weeds now threaten his own garden." The media soon reported that Gingrich had called First Lady Hillary Clinton a "bitch," and the Ethics Committee fined him $300,000 for fundraising transgressions and forced him to return a $4.5 million book advance. The Democrats made sure the public recognized the irony.[6]

Given the tide, Bill Clinton won reelection in 1996, but, with little change in the makeup of Congress in the same year, Gingrich saw no need for a tactical adjustment. A booming economy and a nation at peace provided ample time for the media to sensationalize scandal, which came to dominate Clinton's second term. Dogged throughout his presidency by accusations of illegal investments and illicit affairs, Clinton provided his opposition, which was now armed with its new subpoena power, with considerable ammunition. The result was a special prosecutor, Kenneth Starr, who appeared to be as determined to bring down Clinton as Phelan had been to oust Wright. By 1998, new accusations that Clinton had carried on an affair with an intern, Monica Lewinsky, had led Starr in a new direction. Denying the affair under oath—a denial that he later acknowledged to be untruthful—Clinton gave Republicans the opportunity they had long sought. In a wave of partisanship, the Republican House impeached Clinton. Although he was officially acquitted by the Senate, Clinton remained the first president tainted by impeachment since Andrew Johnson 131 years before. It was a scandal bar none.[7]

There appeared to be no end to the attacks. Democrats increasingly found Gingrich to be the perfect foil in the same way that Wright had been to the GOP, and the public concluded that the impeachment was partisan overreach, punishing Republicans at the polls. Facing a party revolt, Gingrich resigned as Speaker and, in a parallel to Wright that few missed, left Congress, becoming the second Speaker to resign under a cloud.[8] Wright, at least, quietly savored the irony and harsh justice. Unsatisfied, however, the Democrats charged that the new Speaker-designate, Louisiana's Robert Livingston, had called for Clinton's resignation only to have the press uncover his own simultaneous affair. As Democrats angrily shouted from the House floor, "Resign! Resign!," Livingston agreed, stating that he could not do the job he wanted to do "under the present circumstances."[9] Wright, sadly, knew what he meant.

Campaign spending—which Wright, having failed to curb, had ironically embraced—exploded. Partisanship and scandal, driven in part by more efficient gerrymandering and the proliferation of new media, now defined government in a way that had not been seen since the days of McCarthyism, the days when the young Jim Wright first envisioned a career in government. The consensus politics that had welcomed Wright during the Eisenhower years, and the moderate Republicans who had led his opposition during the decades that had followed, were now as much an anachronism as Wright himself. The club-like collegiality was gone, and with it much of congressional efficiency. The presidencies that followed, as George W. Bush and Barack Obama entered the Oval Office in turn, each struggled to overcome such a climate, each facing an unrelenting assault of hostility. The rise of the activist Tea Party, the new American populists, led to a renewed government shutdown and even faint calls for another presidential impeachment. The political template was set in stone.[10]

Wright had been unable to turn the biggest stain on his legacy to the larger good, and the traditional Democratic coalition for which he had fought so long was no longer dominant. In 1994, the year of Gingrich's greatest triumph, the Republicans won the majority of the southern vote and, for the first time since Reconstruction, held more House seats throughout the entire South than the Democrats did. "The party of northern aggression has become the party of southern dominance," boasted GOP strategist Karl Rove, who by then had become an adviser to George W. Bush. Wright's old southern conservative Democrats began to fade away. In 1994 alone, almost half a dozen such "Blue Dog Democrats" switched parties in the House, following a path that Phil Gramm had blazed over a decade before.[11] The Texas delegation now included eleven Republicans. The South, once solidly Democratic, was now growing almost as solidly Republican, a process that continued with each passing year. In 1998, Republicans swept all of Texas's statewide offices. Having won a majority in the Texas Senate in 2000, the year of a census, the Republicans crafted new congressional boundaries assuring future victories in Congress. In 2004, Texas Republicans won their first congressional majority since Reconstruction. By this point, Wright's own seat had fallen to the GOP. In the end Wright may have bridged the gap between the liberals and conservatives within his caucus for an impressive period of time, but his resignation signaled the end of the "Austin-Boston axis" of Democratic leadership that had lasted almost half a century. The alliance was now just another remnant of the past, a Congress that no longer existed.[12]

Of course, Wright's legacy was more than just politics. All the years of trying to fulfill his burning ambition, calculating when and how to act as Congress evolved, struggling to balance his idealism with pragmatism, his sense of the balance of powers, was hardly in vain. His long fight for Central American diplomacy—which he continued to insist contributed to his downfall—was to Wright perhaps his greatest accomplishment. As Wright had predicted, and as he confirmed as an official observer, the long-anticipated 1990 Nicaraguan elections went smoothly—and with a surprise outcome. Daniel Ortega lost, and the Sandinistas relinquished power voluntarily. Two subsequent elections, in 1996 and 2001, confirmed democracy's nascent rise. Ortega returned to power in 2006 and won again in 2011, but by this point it was clear that though the Nicaraguan democracy remained tenuous, the days of brutal dictatorship had ended. Wright savored the vindication.[13]

Wright, understandably, thought highly of his foreign policy record, including his historic address to the Soviets and his role in the Camp David Accords. Less prominent in Wright's recollections was his continued support for the Vietnam War, a position that challenged Wright just as it did many of his colleagues. Wright's experiences demonstrated not only the passions that conflict elicited but the Cold War assumptions that underscored the entire debacle. Wright took pride in his civil rights and environmental records, and, indeed, he had helped to bring about several milestones in both realms. At the same time, however, his policies had evolved as society—and his own political position—changed. It was a struggle many in Congress knew well. Like many of his generation, Wright never understood the cultural revolution that was transforming the nation's young people. On many social issues, such as drugs and crime, Wright's manifold accomplishments reflected the tensions that tore at America.

As Wright liked to remind anyone who was willing to listen, the 100th Congress was one of the nation's most productive, the volume of legislation impressive. Wright's skillful use of the Public Works Committee—yet another reflection of Congress—benefited Fort Worth in more ways than one. Wright never lost touch with his constituents, a lesson for every politician. As one Fort Worth citizen noted, "Fort Worth grew and prospered at a steady pace, and it was clearly obvious who had the clout in Washington."[14] Significantly, Wright played a pivotal role in the development of the Dallas–Fort Worth International Airport, the major engine of economic growth for one of the nation's leading metropolitan areas. Although in one sense Wright was the prototypical "pork-barrel" politician, a congressional stereotype, in another sense his efforts helped advance needed infrastructure around the nation, most notably in highway funding and in water reclamation and treatment. His long advocacy of debt reduction proved futile, and perhaps, to opponents, seemed hypocritical. In the very least, Wright symbolized the larger economic debate over what exactly constituted stimulus and waste, the Keynesian policies that underscored so much postwar legislation. From energy to education to taxes, Wright left his fingerprints on virtually every major policy issue in the second half of the twentieth century. He interacted with towering figures in modern American history, and, indeed, stood among them—whatever he or anyone else might conclude of his relative success. Wright made a lot of headlines, and, as the writer Silas Bent penned, "harmony rarely makes headlines."[15]

A child of the Depression, Wright witnessed firsthand the challenges that so many Americans endured. He was not alone in gaining from the ordeal a concern for the common man and an abiding faith in the good that government could accomplish. Wright knew as well the hardships of one of the world's most destructive wars, sharing the sacrifices and heroism of so many in his generation. It instilled in him and many others a patriotism that ran deep. Wright's life exemplified the postwar boom, as his prosperity was hardly unique. He was in so many ways an exemplar of a generation that defined America in its heyday, his long record of leadership aside. Simply put, the legacy Wright left was wide and deep, as complex as the man himself.

"You really took me by surprise when you asked how I would like to be remembered," Wright wrote one journalist late in his career. He wanted to be remembered as a successful legislator with an influential record of benefiting others, Wright replied, but that was not the most important thing. It was most critical that people remembered him as "a man of my word."[16] In this regard, perhaps, Wright fell a little short. The scandal that precipitated his historic resignation left a cloud on his good name. For many Americans, Wright will live on only in infamy. In truth, Wright's long life was so much more. To understand Jim Wright in all his complexity, with all his flaws and mistakes, all his strengths and triumphs, is to understand much of the American past and the politicians who guided it. The story of Jim Wright, whether a tragedy or triumph, is a story of America.

The inevitable end of James Claude Wright Jr.'s story came quietly, far removed from the majesty of the Capitol Dome and the Halls of Congress where he had spent so much of his life. In the early morning hours of Wednesday, May 6, 2015, Jim Wright passed in his sleep in a Fort Worth nursing home. His life had spanned the globe but ended only miles from where it had begun. Six days later, hundreds turned out to mourn their city's famous son. The streets surrounding the First United Methodist Church in downtown Fort Worth were closed for the funeral, the mourners encouraged to park offsite where buses were waiting. Fort Worth police officers lined up on horseback across the street from the church's main entrance while a fire truck hoisted a giant American flag at an intersection nearby. Inside, a soloist sang "Let There Be Peace on Earth," an appropriate tribute to the many family, friends, admirers—and, of course, politicians—in attendance. From Washington came statements of condolences, including from President Barack Obama and former president George H. W. Bush. Afterward, the funeral procession headed west on Interstate 30 toward Weatherford, a journey Wright knew well. There, in the family plot inside the historic Greenwood Cemetery, Jim Wright was laid to rest.

Former Texas representative Martin Frost, the onetime Wright acolyte who knew more than most the importance of Wright's legacy, summarized the thoughts of many who heard the news. The accomplishments, the failures, and the controversies aside, Wright, the student of history, had earned his place in history. "We will never," Frost declared, "see his like again."[17]

Acknowledgments

"Writing is utter solitude," Franz Kafka reportedly remarked, "the descent into the cold abyss of oneself." Kafka, of course, never wrote a historical biography. At each stage of writing this book, from the initial research to the final product, I had to rely not on the cold abyss of myself but the warm embrace of others. For this I owe tremendous thanks. The archivists and librarians at Texas Christian University's Mary Couts Burnett Library Special Collections, which houses the Jim Wright Papers, were unbelievably helpful and patient as I kept asking questions and requesting photocopies. I particularly wish to thank Lisa Pena and Jensen Branscombe. TCU also granted copyright permission for the photographs, which I appreciate. The archivists at the Gerald R. Ford Presidential Library in Ann Arbor, Michigan, and the Jimmy Carter Presidential Library in Atlanta, Georgia, were always professional and efficient. I wish to thank the congressmen, journalists, family members, and activists who agreed to oral histories, and, of course, Speaker Wright himself, who granted dozens of hours for taped interviews and even allowed me access to his personal diaries that would not otherwise have been available. I could always count on the Speaker's longtime secretary, Norma Ritchson, for squeezing me into the schedule.

At my own university, librarian Dennis Miles was tremendously helpful, just as he was for my earlier books. When it comes to the hard work of publication, I can attest to why the University of Texas Press is so well regarded. My editor Robert Devens was terrific, and the staff there outstanding. I would like to thank, in particular, Sarah McGavick, Lindsay Starr, Lynne Chapman, Colleen Ellis Devine, Nancy Lavender Bryan, and the absolutely amazing freelance copyeditor Katherine Streckfus. Finally, I can hardly forget the support and patience of my wife, Celeste, whose comments tremendously improved the final product. With such support on all fronts, I was always fortunate and, unlike, apparently, Kafka, never in solitude.

Notes

JWP   Jim Wright Papers, Texas Christian University Special Collections
LAT   Los Angeles Times
NAII   National Archives II
NYT   New York Times
OPL   Office of Public Liaison Files
PSQ   Presidential Studies Quarterly
RC   Roll Call
TM   Texas Monthly
WDH   Weatherford Daily Herald
UCSB   University of California–Santa Barbara
USIA   US Information Agency
WD   Weatherford Democrat
WHCMF   White House Congressional Mail File
WHSF   White House Staff Files
WSW   The Wright Slant on Washington
WT   Washington Times

INTRODUCTION

1. Quoted in *Milwaukee Journal*, February 21, 1983, Part 1, 6.

2. Interview, Tom Downey, July 31, 2014.

3. Committee on Standards of Official Conduct, *Statement of the Committee on Standards of Official Conduct in the Matter of Representative James C. Wright, Jr.* (Washington, DC: US Government Printing Office, 1989); Committee on Standards of Official Conduct, *Report of the Special Outside Counsel in the Matter of Speaker James C. Wright, Jr.* (Washington, DC: US Government Printing Office, 1989); letter, Julian Dixon and John Myers to colleague, August 4, 1988, Folder "Wright Ethics," Box 968, Series 2, JWP.

4. Jim Wright, *Reflections of a Public Man* (Fort Worth: Madison, 1984).

5. "The Facts About the Phelan Report," undated, Folder "Ethics Materials," Box 1060, Series 2, JWP.

6. Jim Wright, *Balance of Power: Presidents and Congress from the Era of Eisenhower to the Age of Gingrich* (Atlanta: Turner, 1996), 481–487.

7. Janet Hook, "Wright Inquiry Turns Spotlight on Bastion of Anonymity," *CQWR* (February 25, 1989): 363–368; see Jacob Straus, *CRS Report for Congress: House Committee on Ethics: A Brief History of Its Evolution and Jurisdiction* (Washington, DC: Bibliogov, 2013).

8. Hays Gorey, "The Games Congress Plays," *Time* (February 13, 1989): 38.

9. Janet Hook, "Passion, Defiance, Tears: Jim Wright Bows Out," *CQWR* (June 3, 1989): 1289–1294; Robert Strong, "Character and Consequences: The John Tower Confirmation Battle," in Michael Nelson and Barbara A. Perry, eds., *41: Inside the Presidency of George H. W. Bush* (Ithaca, NY: Cornell, 2014), 122–139; see John Tower, *Consequences: A Personal and Political Memoir* (New York: Little, Brown, 1991).

10. *NYT*, May 5, 1989, 1; *LAT*, May 18, 1989, 1.

11. Letter, Wright to Hugh Raupe, February 28, 1989, Folder "Correspondence, January–March, 1989," Box 673, Series 2, JWP.

12. Tom Morganthau and Eleanor Clift, "Looking for an Exit: Ensnarled in Ethics Questions, Jim Wright Prepares His Last Hurrah," *Newsweek* (June 5, 1989): 18–20.

13. Interview, Jim Wright, July 22, 2012; John Barry, *Ambition and Power: A True Story of Washington* (New York: Penguin, 1990), 748–749.

14. *NYT*, May 18, 1989, 1; interview, Jim Wright, July 22, 2012.

15. Barry, *Ambition*, 742, 745.

16. Interview, Jim Wright, July 22, 2012.

17. *NYT*, May 27, 1981, 1.

18. Quoted in Hook, "Passion, Defiance, Tears," 1293.

19. Douglas Franz and David McKean, *Friends in High Places: The Rise and Fall of Clark Clifford* (New York: Little, Brown, 1995), 348–349.

20. Catherine Collins and Jeanne Clark, "Jim Wright's Resignation Speech: De-Legitimization or Redemption," *Southern Communication Journal* 58, no. 1 (1992): 67–75.

21. *CR*, 101st Cong., 1st sess., vol. 135, no. 69 (May 31, 1989): H2238–2247; Video, Resignation Speech, Speaker Jim Wright, C-SPAN, www.c-span.org/video/?7822–1 /resignation-speech-speaker-wright, accessed July 9, 2014; *LAT*, June 1, 1989, 1.

22. *CR*, 101st Cong., 1st sess., vol. 135, no. 69 (May 31, 1989): H2238–2247; Resignation Speech, Speaker Jim Wright, C-SPAN, www.c-span.org/video/?7822–1 /resignation-speech-speaker-wright; *LAT*, June 1, 1989, 1; James Riddlesperger Jr., Anthony Champagne, and Dan Williams, eds., *The Wright Stuff: Reflections on People and Politics by Former Speaker Jim Wright* (Fort Worth: Texas Christian University Press, 2013), 261–281.

23. Interview, Mike Andrews, July 14, 2014.

24. Robert Remini, *Henry Clay: Statesman for the Union* (New York: Norton, 1991), 193–209, 345–364; Neil Rolde, *Continental Liar from the State of Maine: James G. Blaine* (Gardiner, ME: Tilbury, 2000), 133–162; Doris Kearns Goodwin, *Bully Pulpit: Theodore Roosevelt, William Howard Taft, and the Golden Age of Journalism* (New York: Simon and Schuster, 2013), 628–629; Anthony Champagne, Douglas Harris, James Riddlesperger, and Garrison Nelson, *The Austin-Boston Connection: Five Decades of House Leadership, 1937–1989* (College Station: Texas A&M University Press, 2009), 188.

25. Quoted in Janet Hook, "Speakers Have Faced Trouble, But None Have Been Toppled," *CQWR* (March 11, 1989): 505–506.

26. Interview, James Riddlesperger, May 23, 2012.

27. Interview, Betty Lee Wright, February 1, 2013.

28. Quoted in *Chicago Tribune*, June 1, 1989, 1.

29. Letter, Edolphus Towns to Wright, March 16, 1989, Folder "Speaker's Mail," Box 939, Series 2, JWP; letter, Richard Ray to Wright, Folder "Speaker's Mail," Box 939, Series 2, JWP.

30. Letter, Jane Thomson to Wright, May 30, 1989, Folder "Correspondence—Resignation from Congress," Box 1179, Series 2, JWP; letter, Ervin Daye to Wright, June 5, 1989, Folder "Correspondence—Resignation from Congress," Box 1179, Series

2, JWP; letter, C. R. Brewer to Wright, May 30, 1989, Folder "Correspondence—Resignation from Congress," Box 1179, Series 2, JWP; letter, J. T. Vaughn Jr. to Wright, Folder "Correspondence, 1989," Box 936, Series 2, JWP.

31. Interview, Mike Andrews, July 14, 2014; quoted in Barry, *Ambition*, 756.

32. Interview, William Whitehurst, December 29, 2012.

33. Quoted in *LAT*, June 1, 1989, 1.

34. Quoted in Janet Hook, "Confusion, Tension, Despair: Wright Case Takes Its Toll," *CQWR* (May 20, 1989): 1165–1166; Margaret Carlson, "How Many Will Fall?" *Time* (June 5, 1989): 34–35.

35. Interview, Mike Andrews, July 14, 2014.

36. Tom Brokaw, *The Greatest Generation* (New York: Random House, 1998).

37. Karl Brandt, *Ronald Reagan and the House Democrats: Gridlock, Partisanship, and the Fiscal Crisis* (Columbia: University of Missouri Press, 2009), 3.

38. Diary, Jim Wright, June 6, 1979, Restricted Access, TCU Special Collections (hereafter Wright diary).

39. Katie Sherrod, "Power Who Runs Fort Worth?" *D Magazine*, November 1995, www.dmagazine.com/publications/d-magazine/1995/november/power-who-runs-fort-worth, accessed July 14, 2014.

40. See Champagne et al., *Austin-Boston*.

41. Interview, Mike Andrews, July 14, 2014.

CHAPTER I

1. Randolph Campbell, *Gone to Texas: A History of the Lone Star State* (New York: Oxford University Press, 2003), ix; Robert Pace and Donald Frazier, *Frontier Texas: History of a Borderland to 1880* (Abilene, TX: State House Press, 2004), 82–89.

2. Letter, W. B. Lamb to James Pylant, undated, Folder "Biographical Materials, Genealogy," Box 1201, Series 3, JWP; Lyster Family Tree, Folder "Wright Family History," Box 993, Series 2, JWP.

3. Wright Genealogy, Folder "Biographical Materials, Genealogy," Box 1201, Series 3, JWP; interview, Jim Wright, May 18, 2012; photocopy, uncited article, Edward Blum, "Jim Wright: Majority Leader," September 1984, Folder "Biographical Materials, Clippings 2 of 3, Box 1201, Series 3, JWP.

4. Wright Family History, undated manuscript, Folder "Wright Family History," Box 993, Series 2, JWP.

5. Wright speech, "A Mother's Day Meditation," May 9, 1993, Folder "Speeches—General, 1993," Box 1290, Series 3, JWP.

6. Quoted in Barbara Newberry and David Aiken, *Images of Weatherford, Texas* (Charleston, SC: Arcadia, 1999), 7–8; Henry Smythe, *Historical Sketch of Parker County and Weatherford, Texas* (Memphis, TN: General Books, 2012), 113.

7. *FWST*, May 13, 2001, 4F.

8. Judith McArthur and Harold Smith, *Texas Through Women's Eyes: The Twentieth-Century Experience* (Austin: University of Texas Press, 2010), 9–11, 25; see Joan Burstyn, *Victorian Education and the Ideal of Womanhood* (New York: Rowman and Littlefield, 1980); interview, Jim Wright, May 18, 2012.

9. Quoted in Jim Wright, *Weatherford Days: A Time for Learnin'* (Fort Worth: Madison, 1996), 68.

10. Quoted in *FWST*, August 20, 2001, 6F.

11. Wright speech, "Mother's Day Meditation," Folder "Speeches—General, 1993," Box 1290, Series 3, JWP; *FWST*, December 9, 1986, Special Section, 2.

12. Interview, Betty Lee Wright, February 1, 2013; Jim Wright, *FWST*, June 20, 1999, 3E.

13. Interview, Betty Lee Wright, February 1, 2013; Jim Wright, *FWST*, June 20, 1999, 3E.

14. Jim Wright, *Balance of Power: Presidents and Congress from the Era of McCarthy to the Age of Gingrich* (Atlanta: Turner, 1996), 23.

15. John Storey, "Pagodas amid Steeples," in John Storey and Mary Kelly, eds., *Twentieth-Century Texas: A Social and Cultural History* (Denton: University of North Texas Press, 2008), 135–136.

16. Wright speech, "Mother's Day Meditation," Folder "Speeches—General, 1993," Box 1290, Series 3, JWP.

17. Quoted in John Barry, "Man of the House," *NYT Magazine* (November 23, 1986): Section VI, 61; interview, Jim Wright, May 18, 2012.

18. Quoted in *FWST*, June 19, 1994, Folder "Post Congressional News Clips, January 6, 1994–June 19, 1994," Box 1206, Series 3, JWP.

19. T. R. Fehrenbach, *Lone Star: A History of Texas and the Texans* (New York: Tess, 1968), 689; Anthony Quiroz, "The Quest for Identity and Citizenship: Mexican-Americans in Twentieth-Century Texas," in Storey and Kelly, eds., *Twentieth-Century Texas*, 43; Cary Wintz, "The Struggle for Dignity: African-Americans in Twentieth-Century Texas," in Storey and Kelly, eds., *Twentieth-Century Texas*, 83–84; Alwyn Barr, *Black Texans: A History of African-Americans in Texas, 1528–1995*, 2nd ed. (Norman: University of Oklahoma Press, 1996), 139; Walter Buenger, "Memory and the 1920s Ku Klux Klan in Texas," in Gregg Cantrell and Elizabeth Turner, eds., *Lone Star Pasts: Memory and History in Texas* (College Station: Texas A&M University Press, 2007), 119–142; see Kenneth Jackson, *The Ku Klux Klan in the City, 1915–1930* (New York: Oxford University Press, 1967); interview, Jim Wright, May 18, 2012.

20. Interview, Betty Lee Wright, February 1, 2013; quoted in Wright speech, "Mother's Day Meditation," Folder "Speeches—General, 1993," Box 1290, Series 3, JWP; interview, Jim Wright, May 18, 2012.

21. *FWST*, February 17, 1985, C1; December 9, 1986, Special Section, 2.

22. US Department of Commerce, Bureau of the Census, *Fourteenth Census of the United States, 1920*, vol. 2 (Washington, DC: US Government Printing Office, 1922), 133; Mary Kelley, "Private Wealth, Public Good," in Storey and Kelly, eds., *Twentieth-Century Texas*, 331; see Robert Fairbanks, *For the City as a Whole: Planning, Politics, and the Public Interest in Dallas, Texas, 1900–1965* (Columbus: Ohio State University Press, 1998).

23. See Lucy Moore, *Anything Goes: A Biography of the Roaring Twenties* (New York: Penguin, 2011).

24. *FWST*, June 20, 1999, 3E; David Kennedy, *Freedom from Fear: The American People in Depression and War* (New York: Oxford University Press, 1999), 43–69.

25. *FWST*, May 13, 2001, 4F.

26. Jim Wright, *Reflections of a Public Man* (Fort Worth: Madison, 1984), 5–6; interview, Jim Wright, May 18, 2012.

27. *DMN*, December 7, 1986, E1; quoted in *FWST*, May 13, 2001, 4F; interview, Jim Wright, May 18, 2012.

28. Interview, Jim Wright, May 18, 2012; Wright speech, "Mother's Day Meditation," Folder "Speeches—General, 1993," Box 1290, Series 3, JWP; Wright speech, March 15, 2012, Folder "Biographical Sketches, 1 of 3," Box 1201, Series 3, JWP.

29. Interview, Betty Lee Wright, February 1, 2013; *FWNT*, January 2, 1987, B1; interview, Jim Wright, May 18, 2013.

30. *FWST*, December 9, 1986, Special Section, 2.

31. Wright, *Reflections*, 11–12.

32. Quoted in interview, Jim Wright, May 18, 2013; *HP*, December 7, 1986, 26.

33. Quoted in *FWST*, February 17, 1985, C1.

34. Nat Fleischer, *Jack Dempsey: The Idol of Fistiana* (New Rochelle, NY: O'Brien, 1929); Wright speech, Folder "Biographical Sketches, 1 of 3," Box 1201, Series 3, JWP.

35. Quoted in Barry, "Man of the House," 61.

36. Quoted in *HP*, December 7, 1986, 26.

37. Quoted in ibid.

38. Quoted in *Athens (TX) Daily Review*, December 26, 1986, 4.

39. Quoted in Barry, "Man of the House," 61; Wright Column, "My Father's Act Is a Tough One to Follow," undated, Folder "Post Congressional News Clips, January 1, 1994–June 19, 1994," Box 1206, Series 3, JWP.

40. Interview, Betty Lee Wright, February 1, 2013; quoted in Barry, "Man of the House," 61.

41. Wright speech, "Mother's Day Meditation," Folder "Speeches—General, 1993," Box 1290, Series 3, JWP.

42. Quoted in *FWST*, February 17, 1985, C5.

43. Interview, Betty Lee Wright, February 1, 2013; quoted in interview, Jim Wright, May 18, 2012.

44. Quoted in *FWST*, February 17, 1985, C4.

45. History of Duncan, Oklahoma, Historical Society, www.digital.library.okstate.edu/encylopedia/entries/D/DU0, accessed January 18, 2013.

46. Wright, *Weatherford Days*, 93.

47. Interview, Betty Lee Wright, February 1, 2013; *FWST*, May 13, 2001, F4.

48. Wright, *Balance*, 22–23; interview, Jim Wright, May 18, 2012; *FWST*, December 9, 1986, Special Section, 2.

49. Wright speech, "Mother's Day Meditation," Folder "Speeches—General, 1993," Box 1290, Series 3, JWP.

50. Interview, Betty Lee Wright, February 1, 2013; Wright Sketchbook, Folder "Scrapbook, 1936, Research Copy," Box 1240, Series 3, JWP; interview, Jim Wright, May 18, 2012.

51. Edgar Rice Burroughs, *Tarzan of the Apes* (Chicago: McClurg, 1914); Harry Hansen, ed., *The Complete Works of O'Henry* (New York: Doubleday, 1903).

52. Quoted in Wright, "My Father's Act Is a Tough One to Follow," undated, Folder

"Post Congressional News Clips, January 1, 1994–June 19, 1994," Box 1206, Series 3, JWP.

53. Interview, Jim Wright, May 18, 2012.

54. James Riddlesperger Jr., Anthony Champagne, and Dan Williams, eds., *The Wright Stuff: Reflections on People and Politics by Former Speaker Jim Wright* (Fort Worth: Texas Christian University Press, 2013), 49; Wright speech, "Mother's Day Meditation," Folder "Speeches—General, 1993," Box 1290, Series 3, JWP.

55. Wright speech, "Mother's Day Meditation."

56. Quoted in *FWST*, June 20, 1999, 3E.

57. Interview, Jim Wright, May 25, 2012.

58. Ibid.

59. Quoted in *DMN*, December 7, 1986, E2.

60. Quoted in *FWST*, February 17, 1985, C1.

61. Interview, Betty Lee Wright, February 1, 2013; quoted in *FWST*, December 9, 1986, Special Section, 2.

62. Interview, Jim Wright, May 18, 2012.

63. Quoted in Wright Scrapbook, Folder "Scrapbook, 1936, Research Copy," Box 1240, Series 3, JWP; History of Seminole, Oklahoma, Historical Society, http://digital .library.okstate.edu/encyclopedia/entries/S/SE014.html, accessed January 21, 2013.

64. Reprinted article, "Newspapers Like This Trade Day Plan," *Texas Press Messenger*, Folder "Campaign (1953?), 1954," Box 1203, Series 3, JWP.

65. Reprinted article, "Small Towns Fight Back," *West Texas Today*, January 1941, Folder "Campaign (1953?), 1954," Box 1203, Series 3, JWP.

66. Interview, Betty Lee Wright, February 1, 2013; interview, Jim Wright, May 18, 2012.

67. Reprinted article, "Small Towns Fight Back," *West Texas Today*, January 1941, Folder "Campaign (1953?), 1954," Box 1203, Series 3, JWP.

68. Ibid.; Barry, "Man of the House," 61; *DMN*, December 7, 1986, E2; transcript, interview, Jeanne Grisham with Wright, October 1, 1992, Folder "Jim Wright Interview," Box 1213, Series 3, JWP.

69. Bill O'Neal, *The Texas League, 1888–1987: A Century of Baseball* (Austin: Eakin, 1987); interview, Jim Wright, May 18, 2012; see Roy Stewart, *Born Grown: An Oklahoma City History* (Oklahoma City: Fidelity Bank, 1974).

70. *FWST*, December 9, 1986, Special Section, 2.

71. Wright, *Balance*, 25; interview, Jim Wright, May 18, 2012.

72. Interview, Jim Wright, May 18, 2012.

73. Ibid.; interview, Betty Lee Wright, February 1, 2013.

74. Interview, Betty Lee Wright, February 1, 2013; 1939 Adamson Yearbook, Special Collections, TCU; *FWST*, February 17, 1985, C1.

75. Jim Wright, unpublished manuscript, "To Make a Difference: The Self-Told Story of House Speaker Jim Wright," Folder "Biographical Sketches, 1 of 3," Box 1201, Series 3, JWP; reprinted article, "Newspapers Like This Trade Day Plan," *Texas Press Messenger*, Folder "Campaign (1953?), 1954," Box 1203, Series 3, JWP.

76. Interview, Betty Lee Wright, February 1, 2013; interview, Jim Wright, May 18, 2012.

77. Quoted in Jim Wright, *Worth It All* (Washington, DC: Brassey's, 1993), 8.

78. Ibid., 8–13.

79. Interview, Jim Wright, May 18, 2012; Wright speech, "Mother's Day Meditation," Folder "Speeches—General, 1993," Box 1290, Series 3, JWP.

80. Interview, Jim Wright, May 18, 2012; quoted in *FWST*, February 17, 1985, C4.

81. Quoted in Jim Wright, *The Flying Circus: Pacific War as Seen Through a Bombsight* (Guilford, CT: Lyons, 2005), 83.

82. Quoted in Barry, "Man of the House," 61.

83. Wright, *Balance*, 25.

84. Quoted in ibid.

85. Wright, "To Make a Difference," Folder "Biographical Sketches, 1 of 3," Box 1201, Series 3, JWP; interview, Jim Wright, May 18, 2012.

86. Quoted in *DMN*, December 7, 1986, E6.

87. Jeffrey Prince, "The Speaker in Winter," *Fort Worth Weekly*, vol. 12, no. 15 (July 4, 2007): 18; quoted in *FWST*, February 17, 1985, C4.

88. Interview, Betty Lee Wright, February 1, 2013.

89. Quoted in *FWST*, February 17, 1985, C4; Adamson Yearbook, Special Collections, TCU.

90. Quoted in *Athens (TX) Daily Review*, December 26, 1986, 1.

91. Quoted in *DTH*, July 21, 1985, III, 1.

92. Quoted in Wright Column, "My Father's Act," June 19, 1994, Folder "Post Congressional News Clips, January 6, 1994–June 19, 1994," Box 1206, Series 3, JWP.

93. Wright speech, March 15, 2012; Folder "Biographical Sketches, 1 of 3," Box 1201, Series 3, JWP; Adamson Yearbook, Special Collections, TCU.

94. Adamson Yearbook, Special Collections, TCU; interview, Jim Wright, May 18, 2012.

95. Dale Carnegie, *How to Win Friends and Influence People* (New York: Simon and Schuster, 1936); interview, Jim Wright, May 25, 2012.

96. See James Clark, *Three Stars for the Colonel: A Biography of Ernest O. Thompson* (New York: Random House, 1954); quoted in *DTH*, July 21, 1985, III, 1.

97. Quoted in *DMN*, December 7, 1986, E1.

98. Remarks to Graduation Class, June 1939, Folder "Wright Background," Box 993, Series 2, JWP.

99. Quoted in Wright Column, "My Father's Act," June 19, 1994, Folder "Post Congressional News Clips," January 6, 1994–June 19, 1994," Box 1206, Series 3, JWP.

100. Eileen McNamara, "The Man Who Would Be Speaker," *Boston Globe Magazine* (April 21, 1985): 12.

101. Jim Wright, "The Message in the Watch," *This Week* (April 8, 1956): 2; quoted in Wright, *Reflections*, 13.

CHAPTER 2

1. Interview, Betty Lee Wright, February 1, 2013.

2. Wright diary, April 30, 1972.

3. Quoted in *DMN*, December 7, 1986, E2, E6.

4. Ibid.

5. Jim Wright, *The Flying Circus: Pacific War as Seen Through a Bombsight* (Guilford, CT: Lyons, 2005), 191; Jim Wright, *Weatherford Days: A Time for Learnin'* (Fort Worth: Madison, 1996), 97.

6. Frederick Rudolph, *The American College and University: A History* (New York: Vintage, 1962), 355–372; Wright, *Weatherford Days*, 97.

7. Interview, Betty Lee Wright, February 1, 2013; Wright, *Weatherford Days*, 96–97; interview, Jim Wright, June 18, 2012.

8. Jim Wright, *Balance of Power: Presidents and Congress from the Era of McCarthy to the Age of Gingrich* (Atlanta: Turner, 1996), 26.

9. Barbara Newberry and David Aiken, *Images of Weatherford, Texas* (Charleston, SC: Arcadia, 1999), 76; Wright, *Weatherford Days*, 99.

10. Quoted in Wright, *Weatherford Days*, 104.

11. Interview, William Whitehurst, December 29, 2012.

12. Wright, *Weatherford Days*, 108–109.

13. *FWST*, February 17, 1985, 5.

14. Interview, Betty Lee Wright, February 1, 2013; interview, Jim Wright, June 18, 2012.

15. Interview, Jim Wright, June 18, 2012; Wright, *Weatherford Days*, 109.

16. Interview, Jim Wright, June 18, 2012.

17. Wright, *Weatherford Days*, 100–101.

18. Ibid.

19. Ibid., 101–102.

20. Ibid., 102; interview, Jim Wright, June 18, 2012; James MacGregor Burns, *Roosevelt: Soldier of Freedom* (New York: Harcourt, Brace, Jovanovich, 1970), 120, 142, 264, 271.

21. Wright, *Weatherford Days*, 102; interview, Jim Wright, June 18, 2012; see Betty DeBerg, *Ungodly Women: Gender and the First Wave of American Fundamentalists* (Macon, GA: Mercer University Press, 2000), and Ralph Giordano, *Satan in the Dance Hall: Rev. John Roach Straton, Social Dancing, and Morality in 1920s New York City* (New York: Scarecrow, 2008).

22. *FWST*, December 9, 1986, Special Section, 2; Wright, *Weatherford Days*, 110–111.

23. Quoted in *FWST*, February 17, 1985, 4.

24. Wright, *Weatherford Days*, 104–105, 107; see William Pelfrey, *Billy, Alfred, and General Motors: The Story of Two Unique Men, a Legendary Company, and a Remarkable Time in American History* (New York: Amacon, 2006).

25. Wright, *Weatherford Days*, 105.

26. Interview, Jim Wright, June 18, 2012.

27. Ibid.; Wright, *Weatherford Days*, 107; Carol Roark, ed., *Fort Worth and Tarrant County* (Fort Worth: TCU, 2003), 12.

28. Quoted in Robert Caro, *The Years of Lyndon Johnson: The Path to Power* (New York: Alfred Knopf, 1982), 676.

29. Ibid., 677, 690–691; Wright, "To Make a Difference," Folder "Biographical Sketches, 1 of 3," Box 1201, Series 3, JWP; interview, Jim Wright, May 18, 2012; see John Keegan, *The Second World War* (New York: Viking, 1989), 54–87, 173–208.

30. Quoted in Caro, *The Years of Lyndon Johnson: The Path to Power*, 689.

31. Quoted in Wright, "To Make a Difference," Folder "Biographical Sketches, 1 of 3," Box 1201, Series 3, JWP; interview, Jim Wright, June 18, 2012.

32. Ralph Wooster, "Over Here: Texans on the Home Front," in John Storey and Mary Kelly, eds., *Twentieth-Century Texas: A Social and Cultural History* (Denton: University of North Texas Press, 2008), 182; see also T. R. Fehrenbach, *Lone Star: A History of Texas and the Texans* (New York: Tess, 1968), 639; interview, Jim Wright, June 18, 2012.

33. Wright, *Flying Circus*, 32.

34. Wright, "To Make a Difference," Folder "Biographical Sketches, 1 of 3," Box 1201, Series 3, JWP; interview, Jim Wright, June 18, 2012; Burns, *Roosevelt, Soldier of Freedom*, 25–29, 43–49, 130–131.

35. Wright, *Flying Circus*, 7.

36. Tom Brokaw, *The Greatest Generation* (New York: Random House, 1998); Wright, *Weatherford Days*, 105.

37. Jim Wright, *Of Swords and Plowshares* (Fort Worth: Stafford-Lowdon, 1967), 54.

38. Wright, *Flying Circus*, 11–12; see Tom Skeyhill, *Sergeant York and the Great War* (San Antonio, TX: Vision Forum, 1998).

39. Wright, *Flying Circus*, 11–12; interview, Jim Wright, June 18, 2012.

40. *FWST*, February 17, 1985, 4.

41. Laura Hillenbrand, *Unbroken: A World War II Story of Survival, Resilience, and Redemption* (New York: Random House, 2010), 52.

42. Quoted in *Life*, vol. 121 (February 1989): 106–109; Wright, *Flying Circus*, 15.

43. Interview, Jim Wright, June 18, 2012.

44. *FWNT*, January 2, 1987, 10B; *FWST*, August 9, 1985, 16; February 17, 1985, 4; *DMN*, December 7, 1986, E2.

45. 41 Stat 787 (1920); Harold McNiece and John Thorton, "Military Law from Pearl Harbor to Korea," *Fordham Law Review* 22, no. 2 (1953): 156.

46. Wright, *Flying Circus*, 23; *FWST*, August 9, 1985, 16.

47. Interview, Jim Wright, June 18, 2012; Wright, *Flying Circus*, 24.

48. Hillenbrand, *Unbroken*, 61; Wright, *Flying Circus*, 28, 36.

49. Letter, undated, 1942, Folder "Personal Notes and Writings, 1942–1964," Box 995, Series 2, JWP.

50. Quoted in *FWST*, December 9, 1986, Special Section, 2; Wright, *Flying Circus*, 31–37.

51. Wright, *Flying Circus*, 36–37; interview, Jim Wright, June 18, 2012.

52. Quoted in *FWST*, December 9, 1986, Special Section, 2; February 17, 1985; Erin O'Donnell, *FWNT*, January 2, 1987, 10B.

53. Interview, Jim Wright, June 18, 2012.

54. Hillenbrand, *Unbroken*, 59–61, quoted on 61.

55. Wright, *Flying Circus*, 42, 45–47, 50, 53–55; interview, Jim Wright, June 18, 2012.

56. Interview, Jim Wright, June 20, 2012.

57. Wright, *Flying Circus*, 60–63.

58. Richard Selcer, *Fort Worth* (Austin: Texas State Historical Society, 2004), 53; interview, Jim Wright, June 20, 2012; Paul S. Boyer, Clifford E. Clark Jr., Sandra McNair Hawley, Joseph F. Kett, Andrew Rieser, Neal Salisbury, Harvard Sitkoff, and

Nancy Woloch, *Enduring Vision: A History of the American People*, 6th ed. (Boston: Houghton Mifflin, 2009), 809–812; see Morton Blum, *V Was for Victory: Politics and American Culture During World War II* (New York: Mariner, 1977).

59. Hillenbrand, *Unbroken*, 79; Wright, *Flying Circus*, 88; interview, Jim Wright, June 20, 2012.

60. Hillenbrand, *Unbroken*, 53. Wright, *Flying Circus*, 71.

61. Hillenbrand, *Unbroken*, 813, Wright, *Flying Circus*, 95–96; Richard Frank, *Guadalcanal* (New York: Random House, 1992), 259–260; Rex Alan Smith and Gerald Meehl, *Pacific War Stories: In the Words of Those Who Survived* (New York: Abbeville, 2004), 171–172.

62. Wright, *Flying Circus*, 91, 95.

63. David Kennedy, *Freedom from Fear: The American People in Depression and War* (New York: Oxford University Press, 1999), 562.

64. Interview, Jim Wright, June 20, 2012.

65. Kennedy, *Freedom from Fear*, 811–812; John Dower, *War Without Mercy: Race and Power in the Pacific War* (New York: Pantheon, 1986), 221; interview, Jim Wright, June 20, 2012.

66. Kennedy, *Freedom from Fear*, 589; see Ian Toll, *Pacific Crucible: War at Sea in the Pacific* (New York: Norton, 2011).

67. Wright, *Flying Circus*, 106, 109.

68. Ibid., 109, 111, 152–153, 155.

69. Memo, Wright to Flying Personnel, October 7, 1943, Folder "Wright Personal Papers, Academic and Military, 1938–1952," Box 995, Series 2, JWP; memo, Wright to Enlisted Personnel, October 7, 1943, Folder "Wright Personal Papers, Academic and Military, 1938–1952," Box 995, Series 2, JWP.

70. Memo, Wright to Flying Personnel, October 7, 1943, Folder "Wright Personal Papers, Academic and Military, 1938–1952," Box 995, Series 2, JWP; memo, Wright to Enlisted Personnel, October 7, 1943, Folder "Wright Personal Papers, Academic and Military, 1938–1952," Box 995, Series 2, JWP.

71. Quoted in John Barry, "Man of the House," *NYT Magazine* (November 23, 1986): Section VI, 62.

72. Wright article, "Appointment with War," Folder "Wright Personal Papers—Academy and Military, 1938–1952," Box 995, Series 2, JWP.

73. Letter, Wright to Joseph Ball, March 17, 1943, Folder "Pre-Congressional Correspondence, March 17, 1943—December 11, 1943," Box 1204, Series 3, JWP; letter, Joseph Ball to Wright, April 10, 1943, Folder "Correspondence, 1943," Box 1203, Series 3, JWP; see Stephen Schlesinger, *Act of Creation: The Founding of the United Nations* (New York: Basic Books, 2004).

74. Wright, *Flying Circus*, 183–184.

75. Memo, Wright to Commanding Officer, April 8, 1943, Folder "Wright Personal Papers—Academic and Military, 1938–1952," Box 995, Series 2, JWP; memo, F. W. Miller to Wright, April 16, 1943, Folder "Wright Personal Papers—Academic and Military, 1938–1952," Box 995, Series 2, JWP.

76. Quoted in *FWST*, August 12, 2001, E5; Smith and Meehl, *Pacific War Stories*, 254.

77. Smith and Meehl, *Pacific War Stories*, 254; *NYT*, August 17, 1943, 4; interview, Jim Wright, June 20, 2012.

78. Photocopy, uncited article, Folder "Jim Wright in World War II," Box 1202, Series 3, JWP.

79. Kennedy, *Freedom from Fear*, 564; Boyer et al., *Enduring Vision*, 806.

80. Wright, *Flying Circus*, 115, 127; *FWST*, August 12, 2001, E5.

81. Dallas Isom, *Midway Inquest* (Bloomington: Indiana University Press, 2007), 1–2, 279–282: Frank, *Guadalcanal*, vii–x.

82. *NYT*, December 20, 1943, 12; Kennedy, *Freedom from Fear*, 563, 654.

83. Interview, Jim Wright, June 20, 2012; Wright, *Flying Circus*, 130, 141, 144–146, 160, 177–178.

84. Interview, Jim Wright, August 20, 2012, Wright, *Flying Circus*, 178–181, 185.

85. Interview, Jim Wright, June 20, 2012; Wright, *Flying Circus*, 189–190.

86. Biography, Folder "Speech Files, Biography—Biography of Majority Leader," Box 1280, Series 3, JWP; interview, Jim Wright, June 20, 2012; Institute of Heraldry, Secretary of the Army, www.tioh.hqdha.pentagon/Awards, accessed February 19, 2013; see Peter Elphick, *Liberty: The Ships That Won the War* (Annapolis, MD: US Naval Institute, 2006).

CHAPTER 3

1. Quoted in *Brownwood Bulletin*, June 30, 1985, 1.

2. Jim Wright, *The Flying Circus: Pacific War as Seen Through a Bombsight* (Guilford, CT: Lyons, 2005), 190–191; Wright, "To Make a Difference," Folder "Biographical Sketches, 1 of 3," Box 1201, Series 3, JWP.

3. History of Lincoln Air Base, Strategic Air Command, www.strategic-air-command.com/bases/Lincoln_AFB, accessed February 22, 2013; History of Lincoln AFB, Lincoln AF Base Museum, www.lincolnafb.org/history.php, accessed February 21, 2013.

4. Quoted in *DTH*, July 21, 1985, III, 16.

5. Untitled article, December 2, 1944, Folder "Speech Files: Defense—Newspaper Articles Written by JW While on Active Duty," Box 1284, Series 3, JWP; untitled article, November 30, 1944, Folder "Speech Files: Defense—Newspaper Articles Written by JW While on Active Duty," Box 1284, Series 3, JWP; untitled article, December 1, 1944, Folder "Speech Files: Defense—Newspaper Articles Written by JW While on Active Duty," Box 1284, Series 3, JWP.

6. Letter, Wright to Manager, October 12, 1944, Folder "Correspondence, Oct., 1944," Box 1203, Series 3, JWP; Wright, *Flying Circus*, 196–197.

7. Letter, Wright to Gentlemen, October 23, 1944, Folder "Wright Personal Papers—Academic and Military, 1938–1952," Box 995, Series 2, JWP.

8. Letter, Wright to Dublin Development Corporation, October 12, 1944, Folder "Correspondence, October 12, 1944–November 4, 1944," Box 1203, Series 3, JWP.

9. Letter, W. P. Hallmark to Wright, October 17, 1944, Folder "Correspondence, Oct., 1944," Box 1203, Series 3, JWP.

10. Quoted in *FWST*, December 9, 1986, Special Section, 2; quoted in Jim Wright, *Balance of Power: Presidents and Congress from the Era of McCarthy to the Age of Gingrich* (Atlanta: Turner, 1996), 27–28.

11. Quoted in *FWST*, February 17, 1985, 5.

12. Quoted in *FWST*, December 9, 1986, Special Section, 4–5.

13. Wright, "To Make a Difference," Folder "Biographical Sketches, 1 of 3," Box 1201, Series 3, JWP; interview, Jim Wright, June 26, 2012.

14. Interview, Jim Wright, June 26, 2012; Wright, *Flying Circus*, 193.

15. *FWST*, December 9, 1986, Special Section, 2; interview, Jim Wright, June 26, 2012; Wright, *Flying Circus*, 194.

16. Wright, "To Make a Difference," Folder "Biographical Sketches, 1 of 3," Box 1201, Series 3, JWP.

17. See Kenneth Jackson, *Crabgrass Frontier: The Suburbanization of the United States* (New York: Oxford University Press, 1985).

18. Letter, H. Y. Price to Wright, December 11, 1945, Folder "Pre-Congressional Correspondence, March 17, 1943–December 11, 1945," Box 1204, Series 3, JWP; letter, Edwin Elliot to Wright, December 3, 1945, Folder "Pre-Congressional Correspondence, March 17, 1943–December 11, 1945," Box 1204, Series 3, JWP; letter, Hila Weathers to Wright, October 22, 1945, Folder "Pre-Congressional Correspondence, March 17, 1943–December 11, 1945," Box 1204, Series 3, JWP.

19. Interview, Jim Wright, June 26, 2012.

20. Quoted in Edward Blum, "Jim Wright: Majority Leader," article, September 1984, Folder "Latin America," Box 709, Series 2, JWP.

21. Robert Dallek, *Lone Star Rising: Lyndon Johnson and His Times, 1908–1960* (New York: Oxford University Press, 1991), 260–264, quoted on 261; T. R. Fehrenbach, *Lone Star: A History of Texas and the Texans* (New York: Tess, 1968), 657–659; Paul S. Boyer, Clifford E. Clark Jr., Sandra McNair Hawley, Joseph F. Kett, Andrew Rieser, Neal Salisbury, Harvard Sitkoff, and Nancy Woloch, *Enduring Vision: A History of the American People*, 6th ed. (Boston: Houghton Mifflin, 2009), 727.

22. Interview, Jim Wright, June 26, 2012; Wright, *Balance*, 28; Wright, "To Make a Difference," Folder "Biographical Sketches, 1 of 3," Box 1201, Series 3, JWP.

23. Interview, Jim Wright, June 26, 2012.

24. Quoted in *HC*, December 7, 1986, 8; *DMN*, December 7, 1986, 6E; *FWST*, February 17, 1985, 4.

25. Wright speech, TX Democrats, undated, Folder "Speech Files: Democratic Party, 1946 Executive Committee," Box 1285, Series 3, JWP.

26. Quoted in *FWNT*, January 2, 1987, 10B.

27. Wright speech, Legislative Pay, undated, Folder "Miscellaneous," Box 995, Series 2, JWP; letter, Wright to John Granbury, May 19, 1946, Folder "Pre-Congressional Correspondence, January 9, 1946–July 22, 1946," Box 1204, Series 3, JWP.

28. Letter, Wright to Sidney Gregory, September 2, 1946, Folder "Pre-Congressional Correspondence, September 2, 1946–December 31, 1946," Box 1204, Series 3, JWP.

29. Letter, Drew Nichols to Wright, April 20, 1946, Folder "Pre-Congressional Correspondence, January 9, 1946–July 22, 1946," Box 1204, Series 3, JWP.

30. Letter, Garth Hester to Wright, October 20, 1946, Folder "Pre-Congressional Correspondence, September 2, 1946–December 31, 1946," Box 1204, Series 3, JWP.

31. Letter, Wright to Jim, May 28, 1947, Folder "Pre-Congressional Correspondence, March 20, 1947–June 12, 1951," Box 1204, Series 3, JWP.

32. Wright speech, Marshall Plan, undated, Folder "Speech Files, Foreign Affairs—Marshall Plan, 1947," Box 1287, Series 3, JWP.

33. Letter, Fred Schmidt to Wright, April 13, 1946, Folder "Pre-Congressional Correspondence, January 9, 1946–July 22, 1946," Box 1204, Series 3, JWP; letter, Wright to Mr. Schmidt, April 17, 1946, Folder "Pre-Congressional Correspondence, January 9, 1946–July 22, 1946," Box 1204, Series 3, JWP; letter, Fred Schmidt to Wright, April 20, 1946, Folder "Pre-Congressional Correspondence, January 9, 1946–July 22, 1946," Box 1204, Series 3, JWP; letter, Wright to Mr. Schmidt, April 24, 1946, Folder "Pre-Congressional Correspondence, January 9, 1946–July 22, 1946," Box 1204, Series 3, JWP.

34. Quoted in photocopy, uncited article, Edward Blum, "Jim Wright: Majority Leader," September 1984, Folder "Biographical Materials, Clippings, 2 of 3," Box 1201, Series 3, JWP.

35. Interview, Jim Wright, June 26, 2012; Wright, *Balance*, 28.

36. See Elisabeth Clemons, *The People's Lobby: Organizational Innovation and the Rise of Interest Group Politics* (Chicago: University of Chicago Press, 1997).

37. Jim Wright, *Of Swords and Plowshares* (Fort Worth: Stafford-Lowdon, 1967), 17–18, 20.

38. Photocopy, uncited article, Edward Blum, "Jim Wright, Majority Leader," Folder "Biographical Materials, Clippings, 2 of 3," Box 1201, Series 3, JWP.

39. Quoted in ibid.; Wright speech, Teachers Association, undated, Folder "Speech Files: Education—Classroom Teachers Association of Fort Worth, 1949," Box 1287, Series 3, JWP.

40. Summary, Teacher Pay Bill, Folder "Correspondence (Misc.)," Box 1203, Series 3, JWP.

41. Letter, Wright to John Granbury, May 19, 1946, Folder "Pre-Congressional Correspondence, January 9, 1946–July 22, 1946," Box 1204, Series 3, JWP.

42. Wright broadcast, February 16, 1947, Folder "Personal Notes and Writings, 1942–1964," Box 995, Series 2, JWP; letter, Wright to Board of Education, January 9, 1946, Folder "Pre-Congressional Correspondence, January 9, 1946–July 22, 1946," Box 1204, Series 3, JWP.

43. Wright speech, Teachers Association, undated, Folder "Speech Files: Education—Classroom Teachers Association of Fort Worth, 1949," Box 1287, Series 3, JWP.

44. Letter, Wright to Frank White, April 18, 1946, Folder "Pre-Congressional Correspondence, January 9, 1946–July 22, 1946," Box 1204, Series 3, JWP; letter, Wright to John Granbury, May 19, 1946, Folder "Pre-Congressional Correspondence, January 9, 1946–July 22, 1946," Box 1204, Series 3, JWP; interview, Jim Wright, June 26, 2012; David Kennedy, *Freedom from Fear: The American People in Depression and War* (New York: Oxford University Press, 1999), 252, 783.

45. Quoted in *DMN*, December 7, 1986, E6.

46. See Lawrence Goodwyn, *The Populist Moment: A Short History of the Agrarian Revolt in America* (New York: Oxford University Press, 1978), and Lauren Sklaroff, *Black Culture and the New Deal: The Quest for Civil Rights in the Roosevelt Era* (Chapel Hill: University of North Carolina Press, 2009).

47. *FWST*, December 9, 1986, Special Section, 4.

48. Ibid.; Oral History Interview, Henry B. Sirgo with Jim Wright, April 10, 1998, 3, Folder "Oral History: Henry Sirgo," Box 1213, Series 3, JWP.

49. Interview, Jim Wright, June 26, 2012; Randolph Campbell, *Gone to Texas: A History of the Lone Star State* (New York: Oxford University Press, 2003), 337–338, 421–422.

50. Letter, Wright to John Granbury, May 19, 1946, Folder "Pre-Congressional Correspondence, January 9, 1946–July 22, 1946," Box 1204, Series 3, JWP.

51. Letter, J. Socre to Wright, April 14, 1946, Folder "Pre-Congressional Correspondence, January 9, 1946–July 22, 1946," Box 1204, Series 3, JWP; letter, Wright to J. R. Reese, April 12, 1946, Folder "Pre-Congressional Correspondence, January 9, 1946–July 22, 1946," Box 1204, Series 3, JWP.

52. Letter, Wright to Margaret Carter, undated, Folder "Pre-Congressional Correspondence, September 2, 1946–December 31, 1946," Box 1204, Series 3, JWP; letter, Don Sorelle to Wright, undated, Folder "Pre-Congressional Correspondence, January 9, 1946–July 22, 1946," Box 1204, Series 3, JWP.

53. Quoted in *DMN*, December 7, 1986, E6.

54. Wright diary, January 1, 1981.

55. *FWST*, February 17, 1985, 4.

56. Ibid.; Paul West, "The Curious History of the Next Speaker of the House," *New Republic* 193 (October 14, 1985): 22.

57. See John Gladchuk, *Hollywood and Anti-Communism: The Evolution of the Red Menace* (New York: Routledge, 2006).

58. Letter, James Spencer to Mr. Speaker, undated, Folder "Pre-Congressional Correspondence, March 20, 1947–June 12, 1951," Box 1204, Series 3, JWP.

59. Interview, Jim Wright, June 26, 2012.

60. Oral History, Sirgo with Wright, April 10, 1998, 3, Folder "Oral History: Henry Sirgo," Box 1213, Series 3, JWP.

61. Interview, Jim Wright, June 26, 2012.

62. Ibid.

63. *FWST*, February 17, 1985, 1.

64. *FWST*, December 9, 1986, Special Section, 4; interview, Jim Wright, June 26, 2012.

65. *HP*, December 7, 1986, 26; quoted in *DTH*, July 21, 1985, III, 16.

66. *FWST*, February 17, 1985, 1.

67. *DMN*, December 7, 1986, E6.

68. *WP*, June 14, 1987, G8.

69. *FWST*, December 9, 1986, Special Section, 4.

70. Interview, Jim Wright, June 26, 2012.

71. Quoted in West, "Curious History," 23.

72. Wright, *Balance*, 29; interview, Jim Wright, June 26, 2012.

73. Quoted in photocopy, uncited article, Edward Blum, "Jim Wright, Majority Leader," September 1984, Folder "Biographical Materials, Clippings, 2 of 3," Box 1201, Series 3, JWP.

74. Quoted in *FWST*, December 9, 1986, Special Section, 3; interview, Jim Wright, June 26, 2012.

75. Jim Wright, "Legislation and the Will of God," in John Anderson, ed., *Congress and Conscience* (Philadelphia: Lippincott, 1970), 27; interview, Jim Wright, June 26, 2012.

76. Quoted in *DTH*, July 21, 1985, III, 16.

CHAPTER 4

1. Quoted in *DTH*, July 21, 1985, III, 16; *DMN*, December 7, 1986, E6.

2. US Department of Commerce, Bureau of the Census, Series P-60, no. 15 (April 27, 1954), www.census.gov/prod2/popscan/p60-015.pdf, accessed February 28, 2013.

3. Interview, Jim Wright, July 28, 2012.

4. Ibid.

5. Quoted in transcript, interview, Jeanne Grisham with Wright, October 1, 1992, Folder "Jim Wright Interview," Box 1213, Series 3, JWP.

6. *Kansas City Times*, July 28, 1965, 13; quoted in *HP*, December 7, 1986, 26; quoted in *DMN*, December 7, 1986, E6.

7. Quoted in *St Louis Post-Dispatch*, April 5, 1987, B10.

8. Photocopy, uncited article, Edward Blum, "Jim Wright, Majority Leader," September 1984, Folder "Biographical Materials, Clippings, 2 of 3," Box 1201, Series 3, JWP.

9. Advertisement, Conrad Russell, undated, Folder "Scrapbook, 1950–1951, Research Copy," Box 1241, Series 3, JWP; advertisement, Veterans Committee for Wright, January 4, 1950, Folder "Scrapbook, 1950–1951, Research Copy," Box 1241, Series 3, JWP; *FWST*, February 17, 1985, 4; interview, Jim Wright, July 28, 2012.

10. Advertisement, E. B. Buffington, undated, Folder "Scrapbook, 1950–1951, Research Copy," Box 1241, Series 3, JWP; advertisement, E. B. Buffington, undated, Folder "Scrapbook, 1950–1951, Research Copy," Box 1241, Series 3, JWP.

11. Wright, handwritten comments on *WDH*, January 3, 1950, Folder "Scrapbook, 1950–1951, Research Copy," Box 1241, Series 3, JWP.

12. *WDH*, January 18, 1950, 4; quoted in January 19, 1950, 1; interview, Jim Wright, June 28, 2012.

13. *FWP*, January 19, 1950, 8; copy, editorial, *WDH*, January 26, 1950, Folder "Scrapbook, 1950–1951, Research Copy," Box 1241, Series 3, JWP.

14. *WDH*, February 9, 1950, 1; interview, Jim Wright, June 28, 2012.

15. *WDH*, February 9, 1950, 1; interview, Jim Wright, June 28, 2012; *WD*, January 26, 1950, 1; *WDH*, January 20, 1950, 1.

16. John Kenneth Galbraith, *The Affluent Society*, 2nd ed. (New York: Houghton Mifflin, 1969); see Adam Rome, *The Bulldozer in the Countryside* (New York: Cambridge University Press, 2001).

17. *WDH*, February 9, 1950, 1.

18. *WD*, February 9, 1950, 1; interview, Jim Wright, June 28, 2012.

19. *WDH*, February 2, 1950, 1; February 16, 1950, 1.

20. *WD*, March 9, 1950, 1; September 14, 1950, 4.

21. Quoted in *WDH*, February 2, 1950, 6.

22. Quoted in ibid. and February 16, 1950, 1.

23. *WD*, January 26, 1950, 1; June 29, 1950, 1.

24. *WD*, March 16, 1950, 1; March 23, 1950, 1; April 27, 1950, 1; *WDH*, April 13, 1950, 2.

25. *WDH*, March 20, 1950, 3; *WD*, March 9, 1950, 2; September 14, 1950, 1.

26. Quoted in *Corsicana Daily Sun*, June 12, 1950, photocopy, Folder "Scrapbook, 1950–1951, Research Copy," Box 1241, Series 3, JWP.

27. Wright, statement on Emergency Plan, July 6, 1950, Folder "Correspondence, Disasters," Box 1204, Series 3, JWP; *WD*, July 6, 1950, 1.

28. Quoted in *WD*, April 13, 1950, 1; June 8, 1950, 1; October 19, 1950, 1.

29. *WDH*, June 22, 1950, 1; quoted in *WD*, June 22, 1950, 1.

30. *WD*, June 22, 1950, 1; *WD*, June 22, 1950, 5.

31. *WD*, June 15, 1950, 1.

32. *WDH*, May 25, 1950, 2.

33. *WD*, March 3, 1951, 1.

34. Unmarked articles and photographs, Folder "Scrapbook, 1950–1951," Box 1241, Series 3, JWP.

35. Oral History, Grisham with Wright, October 1, 1992, 3, Folder "Jim Wright Interview," Box 1213, Series 3, JWP.

36. Wright, Application to Dubuque, December 26, 1950, Folder "Pre-Congressional Correspondence, March 20, 1947–June 12, 1951," Box 1204, Series 3, JWP.

37. Letter, Harry Turner to Wright, December 22, 1950, Folder "Pre-Congressional Correspondence, March 20, 1947–June 12, 1951," Box 1204, Series 3, JWP.

38. *FWST*, January 31, 1951, 7; *WD*, October 19, 1950, 1; November 22, 1950, 1; *WDH*, December 9, 1950, 2; Jim Wright, *Weatherford Days: A Time for Learnin'* (Fort Worth: Madison, 1996), 118–119.

39. Quoted in *FWST*, February 6, 1951, II, 2; *WD*, January 11, 1951, 1.

40. Interview, Jim Wright, June 28, 2012; *WDH*, January 13, 1951, 2.

41. *WDH*, November 2, 1950, 1; July 26, 1951, 2; Wright, *Weatherford Days*, 119.

42. Wright, handwritten comments, undated, Folder "Scrapbook, 1950–1951, Research Copy," Box 1241, Series 3, JWP.

43. *WD*, July 19, 1951, 1; *WDH*, October 25, 1951, 3; interview, Jim Wright, June 28, 2012.

44. Quoted in Oral History, Sirgo with Wright, April 10, 1998, 11, Folder "Oral History, Henry B. Sirgo," Box 1213, Series 3, JWP.

45. *FWST*, October 19, 1951, 10; *WD*, October 18, 1951, 1.

46. *WDH*, December 1, 1951, 3; December 6, 1951, 1; December 13, 1951, 1; *WD*, January 10, 1952, 1; January 31, 1952, 1; *FWST*, January 31, 1952, II, 3; February 7, 1952, 1; February 14, 1952, 1; Wright, *Weatherford Days*, 117; interview, Jim Wright, June 28, 2012.

47. Flier, Weatherford Chamber of Commerce, Folder "Scrapbook, 1952, Research Copy," Box 1241, Series 3, JWP.

48. Quoted in *WD*, February 14, 1952, 1.

49. Interview, Jim Wright, June 28, 2012; Wright, *Weatherford Days*, 118.

50. Quoted in *FWST*, February 17, 1985, C4; *Kansas City Times*, July 28, 1954, 13; interview, Jim Wright, July 6, 2012; Wright, *Weatherford Days*, 121.

51. Quoted in *DMN*, December 7, 1986, E8, and in photocopy, uncited article, Edward Blum, "Jim Wright, Majority Leader," September 1984, Folder "Biographical Materials, Clippings, 2 of 3," Box 1201, Series 3, JWP; *FWNT*, January 2, 1987, B6.

52. Oral History, Grisham with Wright, October 1, 1992, 3, Folder "Jim Wright Interview," Box 1213, Series 3, JWP; Jim Wright, *Balance of Power: Presidents and Congress from the Era of McCarthy to the Age of Gingrich* (Atlanta: Turner, 1996), 30; Wright, *Weatherford Days*, 120; interview, Jim Wright, June 28, 2012; *DMN*, December 7, 1986, E6.

53. Quoted in Paul West, "The Curious History of the Next Speaker of the House," *New Republic* 193 (October 14, 1985): 23.

54. Quoted in *FWST*, June 20, 1999, 3E.

55. Transcript, broadcast, 1952, Folder "Speech Files—Economics: Debate with Teague and Elkins," Box 1286, Series 3, JWP.

56. Memo, Information Office, Federal Civil Defense Administration (FCDA), March 1952, Folder "Pre-Congressional Correspondence, March, 1953," Box 1204, Series 3, JWP; letter, William McGill to James Wright, March 7, 1953, "Pre-Congressional Correspondence, March, 1953," Box 1204, Series 3, JWP; quoted in Jim Wright, *Of Swords and Plowshares* (Fort Worth: Stafford-Lowdon, 1967), 22–23.

57. *WD*, March 12, 1953, 1; January 31, 1953, 1; January 1, 1952, 1; *WDH*, January 1, 1952, 2.

58. Oral History, Grisham with Wright, October 1, 1992, 13–14, Folder "Jim Wright Interview," Box 1213, Series 3, JWP; interview, Jim Wright, July 1, 2012.

59. Oral History, Grisham with Wright, October 1, 1992, 17, Folder "Jim Wright Interview," Box 1213, Series 3, JWP.

60. Maeva Marcus, *Truman and the Steel Seizure Case: The Limits of Presidential Power* (New York: Columbia University Press, 1977), 26; Philip Wood, *Southern Capitalism: The Political Economy of North Carolina, 1880–1980* (Durham, NC: Duke University Press, 1976), 151; see *Vital Speeches of the Day* vol. 15, no. 20 (August 1, 1949): 629.

61. Oral History Interview, Jeanne Grisham with Willard Barr, September 30, 1992, 8–9, Folder "Bert Willard Interview," Box 1213, Series 3, JWP.

62. Transcript, Jim Greer Interview, October 16, 1992, 4, Folder "Jim Greer Interview," Box 1213, Series 3, JWP.

63. Oral History, Grisham with Barr, September 30, 1992, 3–4, Folder "Bert Willard Interview," Box 1213, Series 3, JWP; Oral History, Grisham with Wright, October 1, 1992, 4, Folder "Jim Wright Interview," Box 1213, Series 3, JWP; interview, Jim Wright, July 1, 2012.

64. Oral History, Grisham with Wright, October 1, 1992, 4, Folder "Jim Wright Interview," Box 1213, Series 3, JWP.

65. Ibid., 5.

66. Ibid., 15.

67. Transcript, Greer Interview, October 16, 1992, 6–13, Folder "Jim Greer Interview," Box 1213, Series 3, JWP.

68. Ibid., 16; Recollections of Carlos Hartnett, undated, Folder "News Clippings, 1999," Box 1207, Series 3, JWP; Oral History, Grisham with Wright, October 1, 1992, 7–12, Folder "Jim Wright Interview," Box 1213, Series 3, JWP; interview, Jim Wright, July 1, 2012.

69. Interview, Jim Wright, July 1, 2012; Oral History, Grisham with Wright, October 1, 1992, 11, Folder "Jim Wright Interview," Box 1213, Series 3, JWP.

70. Wright, *Balance*, 31; transcript, Greer Interview, October 16, 1992, 6–13, Folder "Jim Greer Interview," Box 1213, Series 3, JWP.

71. Script, TV advertisement, Folder "Speeches: General," Box 1290, Series 3, JWP; interview, Jim Wright, July 1, 2012; Wright, *Balance*, 31; see Roger Morris, *Richard Milhous Nixon: The Rise of an American Politician* (New York: Henry Holt, 1990), 825–835.

72. Interview, Jim Wright, July 1, 2012; transcript, Greer Interview, October 16, 1992, 6–7, Folder "Jim Greer Interview," Box 1213, Series 3, JWP.

73. Recollections of Carlos Hartnett, undated, Folder "News Clippings, 1999," Box 1207, Series 3, JWP; interview, Jim Wright, July 1, 2012.

74. Wright speech, December 5, 1953, Folder "Speech: Correspondence," Box 1290, Series 3, JWP.

75. Untitled speech, Folder "Speeches: General—(n.d.)," Box 1290, Series 3, JWP; "Peace Is Possible," 1953, Folder "Speech Files, Foreign Affairs—Peace Is Possible," Box 1287, Series 3, JWP; "The State on Which Our Future Depends," 1954, Folder "Speech Files, Communism—The State on Which Our Future Depends," Box 1282, Series 3, JWP.

76. Answers to Media Inquiries, 1954, Folder "Speeches: General," Box 1290, Series 3, JWP.

77. *DMN*, December 7, 1986, E6.

78. *FWST*, December 9, 1986, Special Section, 4; see Ted Morgan, *Reds: McCarthyism in Twentieth-Century America* (New York: Random House, 2004), and Thomas Reeves, *McCarthyism* (Malabar, FL: Krieger, 1978).

79. Quoted in *FWST*, February 17, 1985, 5.

80. Oral History, Grisham with Wright, October 1, 1992, 9, Folder "Jim Wright Interview," Box 1213, Series 3, JWP.

81. Quoted in transcript, Greer Interview, October 16, 1992, 6, Folder "Jim Greer Interview," Box 1213, Series 3, JWP; Recollections of Carlos Hartnett, undated, Folder "News Clippings, 1999," Box 1207, Series 3, JWP.

82. *DTH*, July 21, 1985, 16; interview, Jim Wright, July 1, 2012.

83. Wright address, 1954, Folder "Campaign (1953?), 1954," Box 1203, Series 3, JWP.

84. Transcript, Greer Interview, October 16, 1992, 15, Folder "Jim Greer Interview," Box 1213, Series 3, JWP.

85. Letter, Duncan Gault to Wright, July 5, 1954, Folder "Correspondence," Box 699, Series 2, JWP; letter, G. Shields to *Fort Worth Press*, July 7, 1954, Folder "Correspondence," Box 699, Series 2, JWP.

86. Quoted in interview, Jim Wright, July 1, 2012.

87. Oral History, Grisham with Wright, October 1, 1992, 18, Folder "Jim Wright Interview," Box 1213, Series 3, JWP.

88. Quoted in ibid., 21–22.

89. *FWST*, July 22, 1954, 1; interview, Jim Wright, July 1, 2012.

90. *FWST*, July 24, 2004, 17.

91. *FWST*, July 23, 1954, 8; transcript, Greer Interview, October 16, 1992, 9, Folder "Jim Greer Interview," Box 1213, Series 3, JWP; transcript, Oral History, Grisham with Wright, October 1, 1992, 14, Folder "Jim Wright Interview," Box 1213, Series 3, JWP; interview, Jim Wright, July 1, 2012.

92. Interview, Jim Wright, July 1, 2012.

93. Quoted in *FWST*, July 24, 2004, 17.

94. Oral History, Grisham with Wright, October 1, 1992, 14, Folder "Jim Wright Interview," Box 1213, Series 3, JWP.

95. Marshall Lynam, *Stories I Never Told the Speaker: The Chaotic Adventures of a Capitol Hill Aide* (Dallas: Three Forks, 1998), 15–16; quoted in *FWST*, July 24, 2004, 17.

96. Marshall Lynam, *Stories I Never Told the Speaker: The Chaotic Adventures of a Capitol Hill Aide* (Dallas: Three Forks, 1998), 15–16; quoted in *FWST*, July 24, 2004, 17; Oral History, Grisham with Wright, October 1, 1992, 14, Folder "Jim Wright Interview," Box 1213, Series 3, JWP; interview, Jim Wright, July 1, 2012; Kathy Kiely, *HP*, December 7, 1986, 26; flier, Folder "Scrapbook, 1950–1951," Box 1242, Series 3, JWP.

97. Interview, Betty Lee Wright, February 1, 2013; interview, Jim Wright, July 1, 2012.

98. Letter, Joe Crumble to Wright, August 4, 1954, Folder "Correspondence," Box 699, Series 2, JWP; letter, Mrs. R. M. Clay to Wright, August 1, 1954, Folder "Correspondence," Box 699, Series 2, JWP.

99. Telegram to Jim Wright, December 16, 1954, Folder "Correspondence, 1954," Box 1203, Series 3, JWP; letter, F. C. Zeigler to Jim Wright Sr., August 3, 1954, Folder "Correspondence," Box 699, Series 2, JWP.

100. Quoted in *FWST*, July 24, 2004, 17.

101. Ibid.; *DMN*, December 7, 1986, E6.

CHAPTER 5

1. Erwin Knoll, "The Truth About Desegregation in the Washington, DC Public Schools," *Journal of Negro Education* 28, no. 2 (Spring 1959): 92–97; *WDH*, December 29, 1954, 4; Jim Wright, *Balance of Power: Presidents and Congress from the Era of McCarthy to the Age of Gingrich* (Atlanta: Turner, 1996), 34–35.

2. Quoted in Oral History, Sirgo with Wright, April 10, 1998, Folder "Oral History: Henry B. Sirgo," Box 1213, Series 3, JWP.

3. Telegram, Sam Rayburn to Wright, November 5, 1954, Folder "Scrapbook," Box 1242, Series 3, JWP; Paul West, "The Curious History of the Next Speaker of the House," *New Republic* 193 (October 14, 1985): 23.

4. Quoted in Stephen Ambrose, *Eisenhower: The President* (New York: Simon and Schuster, 1984), 219.

5. Quoted in Chester J. Pach Jr. and Elmo Richardson, *The Presidency of Dwight D. Eisenhower* (Lawrence: University of Kansas Press, 1991), 52.

6. Fred Greenstein, *The Hidden-Hand Presidency: Eisenhower as Leader* (Baltimore: Johns Hopkins University Press, 1982), 42.

7. Wright, *Balance*, 37; interview, Jim Wright, July 1, 2012.

8. Quoted in *NYT*, March 22, 2013, 16; see Norman Ornstein, *The Broken Branch: How Congress Is Failing America and How to Get It Back on Track* (New York: Oxford, 2008).

9. Quoted in Mickey Edwards, *The Parties Versus the People* (New Haven, CT: Yale University Press, 2012), 172.

10. Interview, Jim Wright, July 1, 2012; *FWST*, January 5, 1955, 3.

11. See Robert Stein, *Perpetuating the Pork Barrel: Policy Subsystems and American Democracy* (New York: Cambridge University Press, 1997); Wright, *Balance*, 42.

12. Quoted in West, "Curious History," 23; interview, Jim Wright, July 1, 2012.

13. *WDH*, December 29, 1954, 1; *FWST*, January 5, 1955, 3.

14. Interview, Jim Wright, July 1, 2012; quoted in *DTH*, July 21, 1985, III, 17.

15. Interview, Jim Wright, July 1, 2012.

16. Ibid.; *FWP*, January 28, 1955, 1; *FWST*, January 5, 1955, 3.

17. *FWST*, January 12, 1955, 3; April 29, 1955, 2; *WD*, January 19, 1955, 1; *FWP*, January 12, 1955, 4; *Glenrose Reporter*, April 29, 1955, 1.

18. Photocopy, uncited article, "Wright Seeks Funds to Soundproof School," January 8, 1955, Folder, "Scrapbook," Box 1242, Series 3, JWP; *Arlington Citizen*, January 13, 1955, 1.

19. *CR*, 84th Cong., 1st sess., vol. 101, pt. 1 (January 24, 1955): H634–H635; *FWP*, January 7, 1955, 2; photocopy, uncited article, "Jim Wright Makes Plea to Save Soil Program," January 24, 1955, Folder, "Scrapbook," Box 1242, Series 3, JWP.

20. *FWP*, March 8, 1955, 3; photocopy, uncited article, Folder "Scrapbook," Box 1242, Series 3, JWP; *WD*, July 28, 1955, 1.

21. Letter, Wright to Jack Langdon, February 1, 1955, Folder "84th Congress, 1st Leg., Public Works Committee, 1/17–2/26/55," Box 1326, Series 1, JWP; Wright statement, May 11, 1955, Folder "Trinity River Project," Box 1122, Series 2, JWP; *FWST*, May 12, 1955, 4; March 8, 1955, 2; March 28, 1955, 1.

22. Quoted in Elmo Richardson, *Dams, Parks, and Politics: Resource Development and Preservation in the Truman-Eisenhower Era* (Lexington: University of Kentucky Press, 1973), 114.

23. Ibid., 115–116.

24. *Mansfield News*, February 17, 1955, 3; "Wright Tells Position on Foreign Trade," uncited article, Folder "Scrapbook," Box 1242, Series 3, JWP; Ambrose, *Eisenhower*, 155–156; see Richard Cupitt, *Reluctant Champions: U.S. Presidential Policy and Strategic Export Controls, Truman, Eisenhower, Bush and Clinton* (New York: Routledge, 2000).

25. Interview, Jim Wright, July 1, 2012.

26. "Mailing Bill for Churches Introduced by Jim Wright," uncited article, Folder "Scrapbook," Box 1242, Series 3, JWP; *FWST*, March 9, 1955, 5.

27. David Halberstam, *The Fifties* (New York: Fawcett Columbine, 1993), 53; quoted in *FWST*, January 25, 1955, 1; Wright speech, "The Sinews of Freedom," Folder "Speech Files: Defense—The Sinews of Freedom," Box 1284, Series 3, JWP.

28. Greenstein, *Hidden-Hand*, 20–25; Ambrose, *Eisenhower*, 231–235.

29. Wright statement, March 16, 1955, Folder "Communism—The Propaganda War," Box 1282, Series 3, JWP.

30. Wright speech, March 26, 1955, Folder "Speech Files—Defense—National Security Speech," Box 1284, Series 3, JWP.

31. Joseph Petulla, *American Environmental History* (San Francisco: Boyd and Frazier, 1977), 375; Victor Scheffer, *The Shaping of Environmentalism in America* (Seattle: University of Washington Press, 1991), 152; Samuel Hays, *Beauty, Health and Permanence: Environmental Politics in the United States, 1955–1985* (New York: Cambridge University Press, 1987), 152.

32. Paul Milazzo, *Unlikely Environmentalists: Congress and Clean Water, 1945–1972* (Lawrence: University of Kansas Press, 2006), 7.

33. Ibid., 5–7, quoted on 7.

34. Letter, Wright to Helen Sullivan, March 1, 1955, Folder "84th Congress, 1st Leg., Public Works Committee, 1/17–2/26/55," Box 26, Series 1, JWP; Telegram, Wright to Henry Holle, June 11, 1956, Folder "84th Congress, 1st Leg., General," Box 26, Series 1, JWP.

35. Water Pollution Control Act, P.L. 80–845; quoted in *WD*, June 21, 1956, 2.

36. *CR*, 84th Cong., 2nd sess., vol. 102, pt. 8 (June 13, 1956): H10237, H10247; *FWP*, June 15, 1956, 5.

37. P.L. 84–660; Robert Durant, *When Government Regulates Itself* (Knoxville: University of Tennessee Press, 1985), 20; Clarence Davies, *The Politics of Pollution* (New York: Pegasus, 1970), 40.

38. Letter, Horace Albright to Wright, April 8, 1955, Folder "84th Congress, 1st Leg., Public Works Committee, April–May, 1955," Box 26, Series 1, JWP; letter, Milton Weilermann to Wright, July 5, 1955, Folder "84th Congress, 1st Leg., Public Works Committee, June–July, 1955," Box 26, Series 1, JWP; Wallace Stenger, *This Is Dinosaur: Echo Park Country and Its Magic Rivers* (New York: Knopf, 1955).

39. *Arlington Citizen*, March 8, 1956, 4.

40. Richardson, *Dams, Parks, and Politics*, 142–147; see Mark Harvey, *A Symbol of Wilderness: Echo Park and the American Conservation Movement* (Seattle: University of Washington Press, 2000).

41. Kenneth Jackson, *Crabgrass Frontier: The Suburbanization of the United States* (New York: Oxford University Press, 1985), 248–249; see Tom Lewis, *Divided Highways: Building the Interstate Highways, Transforming American Life* (New York: Penguin, 1999).

42. Letter, Ottis Lock to Wright, January 31, 1955, Folder "84th Congress and Public Works, October, 1954–April, 1955," Box 27, Series 1, JWP; letter, Harry Gibson to Wright, July 16, 1955, Folder "84th Congress, 1st Leg., Pro Highway," Box 26, Series 1, JWP.

43. Letter, Wright to H. R. Mundhenke, February 3, 1955, Folder "84th Congress and Public Works—General, October, 1954–April, 1955," Box 27, Series 1, JWP.

44. *FWST*, July 6, 1955, 1; *WD*, July 11, 1955, 1; Wright, *Balance*, 48.

45. Quoted in *FWP*, February 10, 1956, 6; *FWST*, February 10, 1956, 3.

46. Quoted in *Washington Daily News*, April 9, 1956, 15; *Labor News*, April 12, 1956, 2.

47. *Washington Post and Times Herald*, March 19, 1956, 10; see US House Committee on Public Works, *Federal Highway Act of 1956: Hearings Before the U.S. House Committee on Public Works, Subcommittee on Roads* (Ann Arbor: University of Michigan Press, 1956).

48. Quoted in Wright, *Balance*, 48.

49. Quoted in ibid., 49.

50. Quoted in Ambrose, *Eisenhower*, 301.

51. P.L. 84–627; Piers Brendon, *Ike: His Life and Times* (New York: Harper and Row, 1986), 12.

52. Letter, Wright to V. Y. Cain, May 31, 1956, Folder "84th Congress, 1st Leg., Public Works Committee, May–June, 1956," Box 26, Series 1, JWP; Ambrose, *Eisenhower*, 528.

53. Letter, Paul Vickers to Wright, May 28, 1956, Folder "84th Congress, 1st Leg., Public Works Committee, June–May, 1956," Box 26, Series 1, JWP; memo, William Miller to Wright, undated, Folder "84th Congress, 1st Leg., General, June, 1956," Box 26, Series 1, JWP.

54. Wright statement, June 16, 1956, Folder "Speech File: Congressional Reform: Let's Remove the Patronage Tumor," Box 1282, Series 3, JWP; *FWST*, January 17, 1956, 2.

55. Quoted in Ambrose, *Eisenhower*, 151.

56. Quoted in photocopy, uncited article, March 10, 1955, Folder "Scrapbook," Box 1242, Series 3, JWP.

57. Quoted in *Arlington Journal*, October 30, 1955, 1.

58. Quoted in *FWST*, January 3, 1956, 4.

59. Interview, Jim Wright, July 1, 2012; *FWST*, October 2, 1956, 6.

60. Quoted in *FWP*, June 6, 1956, 2; *FWST*, June 11, 1956, 13.

61. Quoted in *Mansfield News*, May 12, 1955, 1.

62. *RC*, February 23, 1956, 3.

63. Quoted in *WD*, January 12, 1956, 1; *FWP*, January 18, 1956, 1.

64. Quoted in photocopy, uncited article, August 9, 1955, Folder "Scrapbook," Box 1242, Series 3, JWP.

65. Quoted in *FWP*, September 7, 1955, 3.

66. Quoted in *FWST*, June 28, 1955, 1.

67. Interview, Jim Wright, July 1, 2012; *Arlington Journal*, December 1, 1955, 4.

68. Letter, Wright to Friends and Neighbors, July 6, 1956, Folder "Scrapbook," Box 1243, Series 3, JWP.

69. *FWST*, February 26, 1956, 1.

70. *Washington Post and Times Herald*, March 20, 1956, 4; *FWST*, March 20, 1956, 2.

71. *FWST*, October 22, 1956, 9; *WD*, March 22, 1956, 5; March 26, 1956, 4.

72. Quoted in *FWST*, July 23, 1955, 8.

73. Quoted in *Cleburne Times-Review*, December 15, 1956, 1.

74. *The Brookeville, Pennsylvania, American*, May 29, 1955, 7; *FWST*, May 28, 1955, 6.

75. Quoted in *FWP*, December 20, 1955, 3; *WD*, February 6, 1956, 1; April 23, 1956, 1.

76. Photocopy, uncited article, "Ground Broken for Boat Factory for Weatherford," Folder "Scrapbook," Box 1243, Series 3, JWP; *FWST*, February 1, 1956, 2; February 15, 1956, 6; *Hood County News Tablet*, December 20, 1956, 1; *FWST*, April 4, 1956, 1; *FWP*, February 15, 1956, 1.

77. *FWST*, January 26, 1956, 1; July 20, 1956, 1; *FWP*, December 7, 1956, 3.

78. Letter, Charles Cotton to Wright, January 4, 1956, Folder "84th Congress, Public Works Committee, Willis Bridge, 1956," Box 30, Series 1, JWP; letter, Wright to Charles Cotton, January 19, 1956, Folder "84th Congress, Public Works Committee, Willis Bridge, 1956," Box 30, Series 1, JWP; Telegraph, Wright to Charles Cotton, June 27, 1956, Folder "84th Congress, Public Works Committee, Willis Bridge, 1956," Box 30, Series 1, JWP.

79. Letter, L. S. Mosley to Robert Stuart, August 7, 1962, Folder "Jim Wright," Box 36, CLF, USIA, Record Group 306, NAII, College Park, Maryland; memo, Jean Wolberg to Mr. Johnston, September 20, 1955, Folder "Jim Wright," Box 36, CLF, USIA, Record Group 306, NAII.

80. *WD*, March 24, 1955, 1.

81. *Alavardo Bulletin*, January 13, 1956, 1; *Hood County News Tablet*, January 26, 1956, 2.

82. Quoted in *WD*, May 17, 1956, 1; *Alvarado Bulletin*, May 18, 1956, 3; *Grapevine Sun*, May 24, 1956, 6; *Venus Express*, May 24, 1956, 4.

83. Interview, Jim Wright, July 1, 2012; quoted in *FWP*, July 24, 1956, 7; July 30, 1956, 2.

84. Quoted in uncited article, "New Voter Just 21 Years Too Young," July 28, 1956, Folder "Scrapbook," Box 1243, Series 3, JWP.

85. Interview, Jim Wright, July 1, 2012; quoted in *FWP*, August 9, 1956, 1.

86. Jim Wright, "Shaping the Democratic Nomination," May 28, 1956, Folder "Speech Files: Democratic Party, Shaping the Democratic Nomination," Box 1285, Series 3, JWP.

87. Quoted in Jim Wright, *You and Your Congressman* (New York: G. P. Putnam's Sons, 1965), 109; Robert Dallek, *Lone Star Rising: Lyndon Johnson and His Times, 1908–1960* (New York: Oxford University Press, 1991), 500.

88. Dallek, *Lone Star Rising*, 505; *FWST*, March 8, 1956.

89. Quoted in Dallek, *Lone Star Rising*, 500; Halberstam, *Fifties*, 429–441.

90. Quoted in interview, Jim Wright, July 1, 2012.

91. *Lufkin Daily News*, October 19, 1956, 1; Pach and Richardson, *The Presidency of Dwight D. Eisenhower*, 125; Ambrose, *Eisenhower*, 346; *Edinburg (TX) Daily Review*, October 31, 1956, 1; *Tyler Morning Telegraph*, November 2, 1956, 1; *(McAllen, TX) Valley Evening Monitor*, October 31, 1956, 1.

92. Quoted in *Abilene Reporter News*, October 28, 1956, 12.

93. Photocopy, uncited article, "Wright Says GOPs 'Repeal' Demo Plans," Folder "Scrapbook," Box 1243, Series 3, JWP; *WD*, October 11, 1956, 1; photocopy, uncited article, "What They Are Saying," Folder "Scrapbook," Box 1243, Series 3, JWP.

94. *FWP*, May 8, 1956, 2; *Cleburne Times News*, May 8, 1956, 1.

95. See David Nichols, *Eisenhower, 1956: The President's Year of Crisis—Suez and the Brink of War* (New York: Simon and Schuster, 2011); Brendon, *Ike*, 333.

96. Brendon, *Ike*, 332–334; Ambrose, *Eisenhower*, 370; *FWP*, December 30, 1956, 8.

CHAPTER 6

1. Quoted in Sherman Adams, *Firsthand Report* (New York: Harper, 1961), 365.

2. *Esquire* 50, no. 3 (September 1958): 29; *FWST*, August 7, 1958, 11; *DMN*, September 21, 1958, IV, 4; *FWP*, August 27, 1958, 13.

3. *FWP*, September 15, 1958, 7; editorial, *HC*, September 20, 1958, C6.

4. Photocopy, uncited article, *Midland Reporter Telegram*, Folder "Scrapbook," Box 1245, Series 3, JWP.

5. Photocopy, uncited article, "Unity Needed, Wright Says," Folder "Scrapbook," Box 1245, Series 3, JWP.

6. *Arlington Citizen*, January 17, 1957; 4; *Hood County News Tablet*, January 31, 1957, 5.

7. *Rocky Mountain News*, January 18, 1957, 5; quoted in *FWP*, January 17, 1957, 2.

8. Photocopy, uncited article, "Wright's Plan to Ease Water Problem Gets Enthusiastic Response," Folder "Scrapbook," Box 1244, Series 3, JWP; *FWP*, February 15, 1957, 10.

9. Ezra Benson, *Farmers at the Crossroads* (New York: Devin-Adair, 1956), 4.

10. Stephen Ambrose, *Eisenhower: The President* (New York: Simon and Schuster, 1984), 460–461.

11. John Opie, *Nature's Nation: An Environmental History of the United States* (Orlando, FL: Harcourt, Brace, 1998), 328–329; see Stephen Sturgeon, *The Politics of Western Water: The Congressional Career of Wayne Aspinall* (Tucson: University of Arizona Press, 2002).

12. Quoted in *FWST*, May 26, 1957, 1; *WD*, May 27, 1957, 1.

13. *DMN*, May 31, 1957, 12.

14. Photocopy, uncited article, "Jim Wright Writes from Washington," June 27, 1957, Folder "Scrapbook," Box 1244, Series 3, JWP.

15. Quoted in *FWP*, September 26, 1957, 10.

16. See Herbert Hoover et al., *The Hoover Commission Report on Organization of the Executive Branch of the Government* (New York: McGraw-Hill, 1949); photocopy, uncited column, "The Home Towner," Folder "Scrapbook," Box 1244, Series 3, JWP.

17. Photocopy, uncited article, "Postal Unit Move Here Confirmed," January 10, 1957, Folder "Scrapbook," Box 1244, Series 3, JWP; photocopy, uncited article, "Postal Workers to Hold Rally," February 10, 1957, Folder "Scrapbook," Box 1244, Series 3, JWP; quoted in photocopy, uncited article, "Post Office Abandons Unit Move," February 28, 1957, Folder "Scrapbook," Box 1244, Series 3, JWP.

18. *FWP*, September 26, 1957, 10; *Arlington Journal*, September 26, 1957, 1.

19. *WD*, January 21, 1957, 1; *Burleson News*, February 1, 1957, 1; photocopy, uncited article, "Texas Co-Op Power," January 1957, Folder "Scrapbook," Box 1244, Series 3, JWP.

20. Quoted in *FWST*, March 22, 1957, 12.

21. Richard Selcer, *Fort Worth* (Austin: Texas State Historical Society, 2004), 99–101; *FWST*, March 27, 1957, 1; quoted in March 28, 1957, 1.

22. Quoted in *FWP*, October 6, 1957, 11.

23. See Joseph Stone, *Prime Time and Misdemeanors: Investigating the 1950s T.V. Quiz Scandal* (New Brunswick, NJ: Rutgers University Press, 1994); *FWST*, August 16, 1957, 15.

24. Hermann Remmers, *The American Teenager* (Indianapolis: Bobbs-Merrill, 1957); quoted in *Hood County News Tablet*, February 21, 1957, 3; *Longview Daily News*, February 18, 1957, 4; see James Gilbert, *A Cycle of Outrage: America's Reaction to Juvenile Delinquency in the 1950s* (New York: Oxford University Press, 1988).

25. Alton Lee, *Dwight D. Eisenhower: Soldier and Statesman* (Chicago: Nelson Hall, 1981), 269; quoted in *Cleburne Times Review*, 6.

26. Quoted in Fred Greenstein, *The Hidden-Hand Presidency: Eisenhower as Leader* (Baltimore: Johns Hopkins University Press, 1982), 121.

27. Chester J. Pach Jr. and Elmo Richardson, *The Presidency of Dwight D. Eisenhower* (Lawrence: University of Kansas Press, 1991), 168–169; quoted in *FWP*, February 24, 1957, 21.

28. Jim Wright, *Of Swords and Plowshares* (Fort Worth: Stafford-Lowdon, 1967), 99–100; Ambrose, *Eisenhower*, 388–391; quoted in photocopy, uncited article, "Hoover Group Lauds Congressman Wright," June 20, 1957, Folder "Scrapbook," Box 1244, Series 3, JWP.

29. Letter, J. C. Liddell to Wright, January 31, 1958, Folder "85th Cong., 2nd Leg., Armed Services, June 22, 1957–August 13, 1958," Box 77, Series 1, JWP; letter, Wright to J. C. Liddell, February 6, 1958, Folder "85th Cong., 2nd Leg., Armed Services, June 22, 1957–August 13, 1958," Box 77, Series 1, JWP.

30. Melvin Baker, "Productivity Management in the Defense Supply Agency," *Public Administration Review* 32, no. 6 (November–December 1972): 771–776; Wright, *Swords and Plowshares*, 97–99; *Detroit Times*, February 9, 1957, 22; *FWST*, March 15, 1957, 18; *Arlington Journal*, March 14, 1957, 8.

31. Pach and Richardson, *Eisenhower*, 54; photocopy, uncited article, "Hard Money Problem Failure, Wright Says," Folder "Scrapbook," Box 1244, Series 3, JWP.

32. *Arlington Citizen*, February 18, 1957, 9.

33. Michael Beschloss, *Eisenhower: A Centennial Life* (New York: Harper Collins, 1990), 160; Ambrose, *Eisenhower*, 460; Lee, *Dwight D. Eisenhower*, 269.

34. Interview, Jim Wright, July 1, 2012.

35. Wright speech, September 26, 1957, Folder "Speech Files: Civil Rights—Women in Civic Affairs," Box 1282, Series 3, JWP.

36. Quoted in Jim Wright, *Balance of Power: Presidents and Congress from the Era of McCarthy to the Age of Gingrich* (Atlanta: Turner, 1996), 52–53.

37. "The Southern Manifesto," March 12, 1956, in Waldo Martin, ed., Brown v. Board of Education: A Brief History with Documents (New York: Bedford/Saint Martin's, 1998), 220–223; interview, Jim Wright, July 1, 2012.

38. John Barry, Ambition and Power: A True Story of Washington (New York: Penguin, 1990), 52; quoted in FWST, March 24, 1956, 2.

39. John Gilmour, "The Powell Amendment Voting Cycle: An Obituary," Legislative Studies Quarterly 26, no. 2 (May 2001): 249–262; interview, Jim Wright, July 1, 2012.

40. FWST, July 25, 1957, 1.

41. See Karen Anderson, Little Rock: Race and Resistance at Central High School (Princeton, NJ: Princeton University Press, 2009); interview, Jim Wright, July 1, 2012.

42. Time 69, no. 7 (February 18, 1957): 12; Robert Dallek, Lone Star Rising: Lyndon Johnson and His Times, 1908–1960 (New York: Oxford University Press, 1991), 523–526.

43. Bruce Dierenfield, The Civil Rights Movement (Harlow, UK: Pearson, 2004), 50; Arlington Journal, May 2, 1957, 12; photocopy, uncited column, "Jim Wright Writes from Washington," June 27, 1957, Folder "Scrapbook," Box 1244, Series 3, JWP.

44. Quoted in Wright, Balance, 54.

45. Ibid.; P.L. 85–315.

46. John Hope Franklin and Alfred Moss, From Slavery to Freedom: A History of African-Americans, 7th ed. (New York: McGraw-Hill, 1994), 494; Gary May, Bending Toward Justice: The Voting Rights Act and the Transformation of American Democracy (New York: Basic Books, 2013), 49, 96–97.

47. FWP, March 5, 1957, 21; FWST, April 2, 1957, 3; May 30, 1957, 18; WD, July 8, 1957, 8.

48. Interview, Jim Wright, June 26, 2012.

49. Interview, Jim Wright, July 1, 2012; WSW, August 3, 1959, Folder "Newsletter Master File," Box 1003, Series 2, JWP; quoted in FWST, December 8, 1986, Special Section, 4.

50. FWP, June 12, 1957, 17; photocopy, article, June 23, 1957, Folder "Scrapbook," Box 1244, Series 3, JWP.

51. Quoted in Arlington Journal, October 31, 1957, 4; Mansfield News, November 9, 1957, 9.

52. Interview, Jim Wright, July 1, 2012; photocopy, Wright Letter Home III, "Turkish Terrain Very Much Like West Texas, Congressman Finds," undated, Folder "Scrapbook," Box 1244, Series 3, JWP; photocopy, Wright letter, November 12, 1957, Folder "Scrapbook," Box 1244, Series 3, JWP; photocopy, Wright letter, November 13, 1957, Folder "Scrapbook," Box 1244, Series 3, JWP.

53. Interview, Betty Lee Wright, February 1, 2013; Wright, "To Make a Difference," Folder "Biographical Sketches, 1 of 3," Box 1201, Series 3, JWP; photocopy, uncited article, "Jim Wright's Son, Who Posed Happily for Yule Card, Dies," Folder "Scrapbook," Box 1244, Series 3, JWP.

54. Ralph Levering, The Cold War, 1945–1987 (Arlington Heights, IL: Harlan Davidson, 1988), 78; NYT, October 10, 1957, 32; Washington Star News, January 6, 1958, 12.

55. Wright, Balance, 47; quoted in photocopy, uncited article, "Wright Praised for Club Idea," January 21, 1958, Folder "Scrapbook," Box 1245, Series 3, JWP.

56. Letter, Joel Bacon to Wright, March 14, 1958, Folder "85th Cong., 2nd Leg., Education and Labor," Box 77, Series 1, JWP; letter, Wright to Joel Bacon, March 18, 1958, Folder "85th Cong., 2nd Leg., Education and Labor," Box 77, Series 1, JWP.

57. *DMN*, January 19, 1958, 15; quoted in photocopy, uncited article, "Wright Bill for Science Approved," July 3, 1958, Folder "Scrapbook," Box 1245, Series 3, JWP.

58. *Washington Daily News*, August 26, 1958, 12; quoted in *FWP*, August 28, 1958, 8.

59. P.L. 85–864; Wright, *Balance*, 47.

60. Matthew 10; Newsletter, *WSW*, April 25, 1958, Folder "Newsletter Master File," Box 1003, Series 2, JWP.

61. *WSW*, June 27, 1958, Folder "Newsletter Master File," Box 1003, Series 2, JWP; quoted in *FWP*, July 20, 1958, 13.

62. *WSW*, July 10, 1958, Folder "Newsletter Master File," Box 1003, Series 2, JWP.

63. Wright, *Swords and Plowshares*, 21.

64. See Saki Dockrill, *Eisenhower's New-Look National Security Policy, 1953–1961* (New York: Palgrave, 1996); interview, Jim Wright, July 7, 2012; Robert Burk, *Dwight D. Eisenhower: Hero and Politician* (Boston: Twayne, 1986), 129–130; George Moss, *Moving On: The American People Since 1945*, 3rd ed. (Upper Saddle River, NJ: Prentice Hall, 2005), 115.

65. Jim Wright, *You and Your Congressman* (New York: G. P. Putnam's Sons, 1965), 253–254.

66. "A Highway to Unite the American Nations," *Highway Highlights* (December 1958): 6–7.

67. *CR*, 85th Cong., 2nd sess., vol. 104, pt. 4 (March 13, 1958): H4338.

68. Quoted in *FWP*, November 6, 1958, 12.

69. Quoted in *Midland Reporter-Telegram*, November 13, 1958, 4.

70. Eisenhower, Letter to Congress, Inter-American Highway, April 1, 1955, Public Papers of the Presidents, Dwight Eisenhower, APP, UCSB, accessed April 28, 2013, www.presidency.ucsb.edu/ws/?pid=10443; quoted in "A Highway to Unite the American Nations," *Highway Highlights* (December 1958): 7; Kelly Lytle Hernandez, "The Crimes and Consequences of Illegal Immigration: A Cross-Border Examination of Operation Wetback," *Western Historical Quarterly* 37, no. 4 (Winter 2006): 421–444.

71. Ambrose, *Eisenhower*, 157–158; Wright, *Balance*, 62–63; see Terrence Cole, *Fighting for the Forty-Ninth Star: C. W. Snedden and the Crusade for Alaska Statehood* (Fairbanks: University of Alaska Press, 2010).

72. *WSW*, June 2, 1958, Folder "Newsletter Master File," Box 1003, Series 2, JWP; *CR*, 85th Cong., 2nd sess., vol. 104, pt. 7 (May 26, 1958): H9507; *FWST*, May 29, 1958, 2.

73. Quoted in uncited article, "Congressman Wright Has Silvery Tongue," Folder "Clippings, 1957–1961," Box 1205, Series 3, JWP.

74. Letter, Harold Foster to Wright, May 30, 1958, Folder "85th Cong., 2nd Leg., Armed Services, January 29, 1958–July 10, 1958," Box 77, Series 1, JWP.

75. P.L. 85–508 and P.L. 86–3; Dallek, *Lone Star Rising*, 554–555; interview, Jim Wright, July 7, 2012; Wright, *Balance*, 562–563.

76. *WSW*, July 29, 1958, Folder "Newsletter Master File," Box 1003, Series 2, JWP; interview, Jim Wright, July 7, 2012.

77. *WSW*, December 22, 1958, Folder "Russian Letter, Trip File, Wright's Notes on Russia (December 22, 1958)," Box 1328, Series 3, JWP; interview, Jim Wright, July 7, 2012.

78. Letter to Ivan, in James Riddlesperger Jr., Anthony Champagne, and Dan Williams, eds., *The Wright Stuff: Reflections on People and Politics by Former Speaker Jim Wright* (Fort Worth: Texas Christian University Press, 2013), 197–202.

79. *Washington Star*, December 21, 1958, 16; *FWST*, December 21, 1958, 17; photocopy, uncited article, "Texas Rep. Jim Wright Asks Ivan to Help Peace Move," Folder "Clippings, 1957–1961," Box 1205, Series 3, JWP; photocopy, uncited article "It's a Strange Christmas," Folder "Clippings, 1957–1961," Box 1205, Series 3, JWP; Wright, *Balance*, 65; interview, Jim Wright, July 7, 2012.

80. Adams, *Firsthand Report*, 372–373; Wright, *Balance*, 58.

81. *WSW*, February 24, 1958, Folder "86th Cong., 1st Leg., Public Works Committee, February 23–March 1, 1958," Box 115, Series 1, JWP; *FWST*, March 19, 1958, 10; *FWP*, March 11, 1958, 15; interview, Jim Wright, July 7, 2012.

82. *FWP*, April 17, 1958, 2.

83. Dwight Eisenhower, *White House Years: Waging Peace, 1953–1961* (New York: Doubleday, 1965), 306.

84. *Calhoun County Times*, April 14, 1958, 1; quoted in *Amarillo Daily News*, April 16, 1958, 9; photocopy, uncited article, "Wright Hits Liaison Gap," April 12, 1958, Folder "Scrapbook," Box 1245, Series 3, JWP.

85. Quoted in *NYT*, April 17, 1958, 20.

86. *Des Moines Register*, April 17, 1958, 5; *El Paso Herald Post*, April 17, 1958, 2.

87. William Link and Arthur Link, *American Epoch*, vol. 2, 7th ed. (New York: McGraw-Hill, 1993), 546; Jeff Alexander, *Pandora's Locks: The Opening of the Great Lakes–St. Lawrence Seaway* (East Lansing: Michigan State University Press, 2011), xvi–xvii.

88. Wright, *You and Your Congressman*, 62.

89. *WSW*, February 24, 1958, Folder "86th Cong., 1st Leg., Public Works Committee, February 23–March 1, 1958," Box 115, Series 1, JWP; quoted in uncited article, "Mrs.-merized," April 6, 1958, Folder "Scrapbook," Box 1245, Series 3, JWP; *HP*, February 18, 1958, 16; quoted in photocopy, uncited article, "Wright to Push Project for Retarded Case Funds," March 30, 1958, Folder "Scrapbook," Box 1245, Series 3, JWP; photocopy, uncited article, "Wright Urges Oil Controls," June 11, 1958, Folder "Scrapbook," Box 1245, Series 3, JWP.

90. *FWST*, June 6, 1958, 1; quoted in June 5, 1958, 5.

91. Adams, *Firsthand Report*, 448–450; quoted in *FWP*, June 19, 1958, 11.

92. Quoted in photocopy, uncited article, "Fighting Texan Backs Rayburn on East Front," July 10, 1958, Folder "Scrapbook," Box 1245, Series 3, JWP.

93. Interview, Jim Wright, July 10, 2012; *FWST*, November 6, 1958, 1; photocopy, uncited article, "Wright Hits Trail for Candidates," October 14, 1958, Folder "Scrapbook," Box 1245, Series 3, JWP.

94. Piers Brendon, *Ike: His Life and Times* (New York: Harper and Row, 1986), 365–366; *WSW*, January 5, 1959, Folder "Newsletter Master File," Box 1003, Series 2, JWP.

95. Quoted in Ambrose, *Eisenhower*, 496.

96. *CR*, 86th Cong., 1st sess., vol. 105, pt. 2 (February 9, 1959): H2171–H2172; *WSW*, February 16, 1959, Folder "Newsletter Master File," Box 1003, Series 2, JWP; interview, Jim Wright, July 7, 2012.

97. Wright statement, February 25, 1959, Folder "Speech Files: Economics— Retire National Debt Speech," Box 1286, Series 3, JWP.

98. *Washington Star*, February 12, 1959, 14; editorial, "Slow But Not Sure," *DMN*, February 18, 1959, 12; *FWP*, February 26, 1959, 15; *FWST*, March 8, 1959, 4.

99. Quoted in uncited article, "Wright Debt Cut Plan Backed, But Where'll Cash Come From?" June 18, 1959, Folder "Scrapbook," Box 1246, Series 3, JWP.

100. Quoted in *DTH*, June 12, 1959, 2.

101. Wright, "To Make a Difference," Folder "Biographical Sketches, 1 of 3," Box 1201, Series 3, JWP; *FWP*, April 13, 1959, 5.

102. Letter, Wright to B. L. Powell, May 6, 1959, Folder "86th Cong., 1st Leg., Public Works Committee, April 1–April 17, 1959," Box 115, Series 1, JWP; "Jim Wright's Record," Folder "86th Cong., 2nd Leg., Jim Wright's Voting, 2 of 2," Box 123, Series 1, JWP.

103. *WSW*, February 8, 1960, Folder "Committee on Public Works," Box 928, Series 2, JWP; *WSW*, May 9, 1960, Folder "Committee on Public Works," Box 928, Series 2, JWP.

104. Letter, Wright to Rob Griffin, September 14, 1959, Folder "86th Cong., 1st Leg., Public Works Committee, August 5–August 9, 1959," Box 116, Series 1, JWP.

105. Letter, Wright to Charles Stewart, April 13, 1959, Folder "86th Cong., 1st Leg., Public Works Committee, April 1–April 17, 1959," Box 115, Series 1, JWP.

106. Letter, Wright to Roy Robertson, April 17, 1959, Folder "86th Cong., 1st Leg., Public Works Committee, April 1–April 17, 1959," Box 115, Series 1, JWP; letter, Wright to Burton Ford, August 31, 1959, Folder "86th Cong., 1st Leg., Public Works Committee, August 5–August 9, 1959," Box 116, Series 1, JWP; Ambrose, *Eisenhower*, 527–528; O. H. Brownlee and Walter Heller, "Highway Development and Financing," *American Economic Review* 46, no. 2 (May 1956): 232–250.

107. Letter, Wright to Bryson Rash, August 29, 1959, Folder "86th Cong., 1st Leg., Public Works Committee, August 5–August 9, 1959," Box 116, Series 1, JWP.

108. *WSW*, September 9, 1959, Folder "Public Works Committee," Box 928, Series 2, JWP.

109. *FWST*, February 24, 1959, 2; *WSW*, March 7, 1960, Folder "Newsletter Master File," Box 1003, Series 2, JWP.

110. Letter, Charles Callison to Wright, June 17, 1959, Folder "86th Cong., 1st Leg., Public Works Committee, June 1–June 14, 1959," Box 116, Series 1, JWP.

111. Pach and Richardson, *Eisenhower*, 212; Michael Hunt, *The World Transformed: 1945 to the Present* (Boston: Bedford/St Martin's, 2004), 95–99.

112. *WSW*, March 22, 1960, Folder "Committee on Public Works," Box 928, Series 2, JWP.

113. Dallek, *Lone Star Rising*, 556–557; Wright, *Swords and Plowshares*, 57; *WSW*, August 10, 1959, Folder "Newsletter Master File," Box 1003, Series 2, JWP.

114. *WSW*, August 10, 1959, Folder "Newsletter Master File," Box 1003, Series 2, JWP; Pach and Richardson, *Eisenhower*, 212–213; letter, Wright to Otis Gardner, December 30, 1960, Folder "RC Box 150," Box 396, Series 1, JWP; uncited article, "Wright Urges Passage of Labor Reform Bill," Box 1246, Series 3, JWP.

115. P.L. 86–449; letter, Wright to Webb Joiner, February 9, 1959, Folder "86th Cong., 1st Leg., General, February 6–May 13, 1959," Box 115, Series 1, JWP; Franklin and Moss, *From Slavery to Freedom*, 497–498; Link and Link, *American Epoch*, 549; Dallek, *Lone Star Rising*, 562–564; Pach and Richardson, *Eisenhower*, 156; List, Civil Rights Measures Supported by Jim Wright, Folder "Majority Leader 100, 1976–1978," Box 993, Series 2, JWP; interview, Jim Wright, July 7, 2012.

116. *WSW*, May 11, 1959, Folder "Newsletter Master File," Box 1003, Series 2, JWP; interview, Jim Wright, June 18, 2012.

117. *WSW*, May 23, 1960, Folder "Newsletter Master File," Box 1003, Series 2, JWP; Levering, *Cold War*, 81–82; Link and Link, *American Epoch*, 497–498; interview, Jim Wright, July 7, 2012.

118. Tom Weiner, *Legacy of Ashes: The History of the CIA* (Norwell, MA: Anchor, 2008), 92–104, 106–119; Moss, *Moving On*, 115–116; *WSW*, May 23, 1960, Folder "Newsletter Master File," Box 1003, Series 2, JWP.

119. Brendon, *Ike*, 384–385; see Marifeli Perez-Stable, *The Cuban Revolution: Origins, Course, and Legacy* (New York: Oxford, 2011).

120. *CR*, 86th Cong., 2nd sess., vol. 106, pt. 5 (March 21, 1960): H6153–H6155; Jim Wright, *Worth It All* (Washington, DC: Brassey's, 1993), 23–24; Wright, *Swords and Plowshares*, 20–22; Wright, *You and Your Congressman*, 167.

121. Jim Wright, "The Challenge of the Sixties," June 10, 1960, Folder "Speeches: General, 1959–1961," Box 1290, Series 3, JWP; Norman Graebner, "Eisenhower's Popular Leadership," in Dean Albertson, ed., *Eisenhower as President* (New York: Hill and Wang, 1963), 141–142.

CHAPTER 7

1. *FWST*, February 26, 1959, 8.

2. Interview, Jim Wright, July 8, 2012.

3. Doris Kearns, *Lyndon Johnson and the American Dream* (New York: Harper and Row, 1976), 160–161.

4. Interview, Jim Wright, July 8, 2012.

5. Ibid.; Jim Wright, *Balance of Power: Presidents and Congress from the Era of McCarthy to the Age of Gingrich* (Atlanta: Turner, 1996), 67–68.

6. Quoted in interview, Jim Wright, July 8, 2012.

7. Quoted in ibid.

8. Wright, *Balance*, 68–69.

9. Wright speech, June 14, 1960, Folder "Speech Files: Democratic Party, Keynote Speech," Box 1285, Series 3, JWP.

10. Herbert Parmet, *JFK: The Presidency of John F. Kennedy* (New York: Penguin, 1984), 23.

11. Letter, Wright to Hyott, August 21, 1960, Folder "Correspondence, 1960–1964," Box 1127, Series 2, JWP.

12. Richard Reeves, *President Kennedy: Profile of Power* (New York: Simon and Schuster, 1993), 17.

13. Interview, Jim Wright, July 8, 2012.

14. Theodore Sorenson, *Kennedy* (New York: Harper and Row, 1965), 126–127, 138–139.

15. *CR*, 86th Cong., 2nd sess., vol. 106, pt. 14 (August 31, 1960): H18882–H18885.

16. Jonathan Aitken, *Nixon: A Life* (Washington, DC: Regnery, 1993), 280; interview, Jim Wright, July 8, 2012; letter, Wright to Hyott, August 21, 1960, Folder "Correspondence, 1960–1964," Box 1127, Series 2, JWP.

17. William Martin, *With God on Our Side: The Rise of the Religious Right in America* (New York: Broadway, 1996), 53–54; Garry Wills, *Head and Heart: American Christianities* (New York: Penguin, 2007), 458.

18. Interview, Jim Wright, July 8, 2012.

19. Ibid.; Wright, *Balance*, 70–71.

20. *DMN*, December 7, 1986, E2; see Gary Donaldson, *The First Modern Campaign: Kennedy, Nixon, and the Election of 1960* (New York: Rowman and Littlefield, 2007).

21. Interview, Jim Wright, July 8, 2012; Wright, *Balance*, 73.

22. Senate Announcement, November 18, 1960, Folder "Senate Candidacy Announcement," Box 994, Series 2, JWP.

23. Randolph Campbell, *Gone to Texas: A History of the Lone Star State* (New York: Oxford University Press, 2003), 432–433.

24. Flier, "Meet Jim Wright," Folder "Jim Wright for U.S. Senator," Box 397, Series 1, JWP.

25. Letter, George Boller to Wright, March 8, 1961, Folder "RC Box 150, 1329-74-143, #17," Box 396, Series 1, JWP; *FWST*, December 9, 1960, 2; *WD*, November 20, 1960, 10.

26. Letter, Larry Blackmon to Truett Smith, March 20, 1961, Folder "Lists," Box 396, Series 1, JWP; Project Motorcade, undated, Folder "Campaign," Box 397, Series 1, JWP; Block Captains, Folder "Harris County," Box 396, Series 1, JWP; Negro Ministers, Folder "Harris County," Box 396, Series 1, JWP.

27. Letter, Wright to Richard Gemmer, February 29, 1961, Folder "Harris County," Box 396, Series 1, JWP; Newspaper Endorsements, undated, Folder "Senate Campaign, Newspapers," Box 397, Series 1, JWP.

28. Report, President's Advisory Committee on Natural Resources, January 1, 1961, Folder "Speeches, General, 1959–1961," Box 1290, Series 3, JWP; photocopy, uncited article, January 1, 1961, Folder "Senate Campaign Reprints," Box 397, Series 1, JWP.

29. Press release, undated, Folder "Senate Campaign, General," Box 397, Series 1, JWP; interview, Jim Wright, July 8, 2012.

30. Interview, Jim Wright, July 8, 2012.

31. Map, Democratic Vote, April 1961, Folder "Distribution of Democratic Vote, Election, April 4, 1961," Box 1178, Series 2, JWP.

32. Letter, Wright to Don Hammill, May 5, 1961, Folder "Travis," Box 396, Series 1, JWP; 1961 Special Election for U.S. Senate, Texas State Almanac, Texas State Historical Society, accessed May 22, 2013, www.texasalmanac.com/topics/elections /senatorial-elections-and-primaries-1906%E2%80%932008–0.

33. Letter, Wright to W. M. Mallory, June 15, 1961, Folder "Harris County," Box 396, Series 1, JWP; letter, Wright to Emmett Lack, April 10, 1961, Folder "Hardin," Box 396, Series 1, JWP; letter, Wright to Margaret Carter, May 18, 1961, Folder "Tarrant," Box 396, Series 1, JWP.

34. Paul Burka, "The Wright House," *TM* 14 (December 1986): 242.

35. Campbell, *Gone to Texas*, 433–435; Mark Brewer and Jeffrey Stonecash, "Class, Race Issues, and Declining White Support for the Democratic Party in the South," *Political Behavior* 23, no. 2 (June 2001): 131–155; quoted in *FWST*, July 5, 1961, 1; interview, Jim Wright, July 8, 2012.

36. Letter, Wright to Roland Childress, May 11, 1961, Folder "Travis," Box 396, Series 1, JWP; letter, Wright to James Redford, September 16, 1965, Folder "89th Leg., General, 1965," Box 274, Series 1, JWP.

37. Letter, Si Grant to Gilbert Adams, June 24, 1961, Folder "Re: Governor," Box 397, Series 1, JWP.

38. Letter, Wright to Julian Read, May 9, 1961, Folder "Tarrant," Box 396, Series 1, JWP; letter, John Crooker to Wright, May 5, 1961, Folder "1961 Senate Campaign Expenses," Box 397, Series 1, JWP; letter, Wright to John Crooker, May 7, 1961, Folder "1961 Senate Campaign Expenses," Box 397, Series 1, JWP; letter, Wright to Lynn Darden, June 3, 1961, Folder "Wichita," Box 396, JWP.

39. Letter, Wright to Walter Humphrey, May 10, 1961, Folder "Senate Campaign Newspaper, 1961," Box 397, Series 1, JWP; letter, Wright to Donna White, May 10, 1961, Folder "Senate Campaign, General," Box 397, Series 1, JWP.

40. Letter, Wright to Sam Keith, May 18, 1961, Folder "Senate Campaign, General," Box 397, Series 1, JWP.

41. Quoted in *DMN*, December 7, 1986, E2.

42. Wright, *Balance*, 75; interview, Jim Wright, July 8, 2012.

43. Quoted in *FWST*, December 9, 1986, Special Section, 7.

44. Interview, Betty Lee Wright, February 1, 2013; quoted in *FWST*, December 9, 1986, Special Section, 5.

45. *FWST*, July 29, 1961, 13.

46. Interview, Jim Wright, July 8, 2012; Wright, *Balance*, 100.

47. Interview, Jim Wright, July 8, 2012; Wright, *Balance*, 100.

48. Quoted in *DMN*, December 7, 1986, E8.

49. *Mansfield News-Mirror*, June 8, 1961, 9; *FWST*, July 6, 1961, 6.

50. Quoted in Burka, "Wright House," *TM* 14 (December 1986): 242.

51. Letter, Silas Grant to W. A. Byrum, August 5, 1961, Folder "Tarrant (?) Young," Box 397, Series 1, JWP.

52. Letter, Reagan Legg to Wright, April 6, 1961, Folder "Senate Campaign, General," Box 397, Series 1, JWP.

53. Photocopy, uncited article, "Wright in Waiting, Views His Chances," Folder "JW Press Clippings, 1961," Box 397, JWP.

54. *HC*, November 26, 1961, 7; quoted in *FWST*, June 18, 1961, 8; photocopy, newspaper article, Folder "JW Press Clippings, 1961 (4)," Box 397, Series 1, JWP.

55. Letter, Wright to Fritz Keller, March 9, 1961, Folder "Letter of Thanks for Contributors," Box 396, Series 1, JWP.

56. Letter, Wright to J. W. Walker, May 10, 1961, Folder "Hale," Box 396, Series 1, JWP; letter, Wright to Ed Boling, July 31, 1961, Folder "Hardeman," Box 396, Series 1, JWP; letter, Wright to Silas Grant, May 31, 1961, Folder "Letters over Doctor Grant's Signature," Box 397, Series 1, JWP.

57. Letter, Wright to J. W. Walker, May 10, 1961, Folder "Hale," Box 396, Series 1, JWP; letter, Wright to Ed Boling, July 31, 1961, Folder "Hardeman," Box 396, Series 1, JWP; letter, Wright to Silas Grant, May 31, 1961, Folder "Letters over Doctor Grant's Signature," Box 397, Series 1, JWP; letter, Wright to John Crawford, June 26, 1961, Folder "Travis," Box 396, Series 1, JWP; letter, D. D. Williams to Wright, April 25, 1961, Folder "Tarrant (?) Young," Box 397, Series 1, JWP; letter, Wright to Martin Wiginton, June 3, 1961, Folder "Wharton," Box 396, Series 1, JWP; photocopy, uncited article, "Wright Acts as if Governor Job Alluring," September 29, 1961, Folder "JW Press Clippings, 1961 (4)," Box 397, Series 1, JWP; uncited article, "Rep. Jim Wright's Backers Looking to Governor's Race," June 6, 1961, Folder "JW Press Clippings, 1961 (4)," Box 397, Series 1, JWP.

58. *FWST*, June 25, 1961, 2.

59. Press release, September 16, 1961, Folder "Personal + ?," Box 1203, Series 3, JWP.

60. Quoted in photocopy, uncited article, December 12, 1961, Folder "JW Press Clippings, 1961 (4)," Box 397, Series 1, JWP; open letter, Margaret Carter, undated, Folder "Tarrant," Box 396, Series 1, JWP.

61. Photocopy, uncited article, "Wright to Tell Political Plans in Few Days," December 12, 1961, Folder "JW Press Clippings, 1961 (4)," Box 397, JWP.

62. Letter, Wright to Joe Swanner, December 28, 1961, Folder "Out of State," Box 395, Series 1, JWP; *WDH*, December 16, 1961, 1.

63. Richard Reeves, *President Kennedy: Profile of Power* (New York: Simon and Schuster, 1993), 55–56; Sorensen, *Kennedy*, 339–342.

64. *WSW*, January 1, 1963, Folder "Newsletter Master File," Box 1003, Series 2, JWP.

65. Wright, *Balance*, 76.

66. Letter, Frank Garvey to Wright, March 21, 1961, Folder "87th Cong., 1st Leg., Education and Labor (Minimum Wage), 21 Mar., 1961," Box 157, Series 1, JWP; letter, Lynn Boyd to Wright, April 17, 1961, Folder "87th Cong., 1st Leg., Education and Labor (Minimum Wage), 17 Apr., 1961," Box 157, Series 1, JWP.

67. Parmet, *JFK*, 92, 97; letter, Watt Kemble to Wright, undated, Folder "87th Cong., 1st Leg., Education and Labor (Minimum Wage), 17 Apr., 1961," Box 157, Series 1, JWP; letter, Wright to Watt Kemble, May 11, 1961, Folder "87th Cong., 1st Leg., Education and Labor (Minimum Wage), 17 Apr., 1961," Box 157, Series 1, JWP.

68. Letter, Wright to Herbert Petry, November 11, 1963, Folder "Correspondence,

1963," Box 1204, Series 3, JWP; *WSW*, November 3, 1963, Folder "Newsletter Master File," Box 1003, Series 2, JWP; P.L. 87–415.

69. *WSW*, April 16, 1962, Folder "Newsletter Master File," Box 1003, Series 2, JWP.

70. Letter, Wright to Harold Blackshear, October 10, 1963, Folder "88th Cong., 1st Leg., Armed Forces (National Guard), October 24, 1963–November 3, 1963," Box 22, Series 1, JWP; letter, Edwin Fifielski to Wright, Folder "Correspondence, 1960–1963," Box 1204, Series 3, JWP; letter, Lee Matthews to Wright, January 21, 1961, Folder "RC Box 150 (329-74-143, #17)," Box 396, Series 1, JWP.

71. *WSW*, May 14, 1962, Folder "Newsletter Master File," Box 1003, Series 2, JWP; Richard Godden and Richard Maidment, "Anger, Language, and Politics: John F. Kennedy and the Steel Crisis," *PSQ* 10, no. 3 (Summer 1980): 317–331.

72. Letter, Wright to Ray Greene, April 8, 1963, Folder "88th Cong., 1st Leg., Appropriation Committee, January 23, 1963–June 26, 1963," Box 219, Series 1, JWP; *WSW*, May 26, 1961, Folder "Committee–Public Works," Box 928, Series 2, JWP.

73. *WSW*, June 16, 1963, Folder "Newsletter Master File," Box 1003, Series 2, JWP; interview, Jim Wright, July 8, 2012.

74. P.L. 88–206; Linda Lear, "Rachel Carson's 'Silent Spring,'" *Environmental History Review* 17, no. 2 (Summer 1993): 23–48.

75. Wright, *Balance*, 92.

76. Interview, Jim Wright, July 8, 2012.

77. Letter, Floyd Deacon to Wright, February 9, 1961, Folder "87th Cong., 1st Leg., Agriculture, 31 January 1961–30 January 1961," Box 156, Series 1, JWP; letter, Stewart Chism to Wright, May 28, 1963, Folder "88th Cong., 1st Leg., District of Columbia, April 3, 1963–July 17, 1963," Box 220, Series 1, JWP.

78. Sorensen, *Kennedy*, 481; *WSW*, November 10, 1963, Folder "Wright Voting Record," Box 993, Series 2, JWP; interview, Jim Wright, July 8, 2012.

79. Jonathan Oberlander, *The Political Life of Medicare* (Chicago: University of Chicago Press, 2003), 17–35; letter, B. I. Brant to Wright, February 23, 1961, Folder "87th Cong., 1st Leg., Education and Labor (Federal Aid to Education), 6 January 1961–27 January 1961," Box 156, Series 1, JWP; letter, Jack McCullough to Wright, September 19, 1961, Folder "87th Cong., 1st Leg., Education and Labor (Federal Aid to Education), 6 January 1961–27 January 1961," Box 156, Series 1, JWP; letter, Wright to Jack McCulloch, November 16, 1961, Folder "87th Cong., 1st Leg., Education and Labor (Federal Aid to Education), 6 January 1961–27 January 1961," Box 156, Series 1, JWP.

80. Reeves, *President Kennedy*, 430; William Link and Arthur Link, *American Epoch*, vol. 2, 7th ed. (New York: McGraw-Hill, 1993), 592.

81. P.L. 87–794; letter, Wright to Frank Rand, July 2, 1962, Folder "87th Cong., 2nd Leg., Ways and Means—Trade and Tariff, 1962," Box 176, Series 1, JWP; *WSW*, February 5, 1962, Folder "Newsletter Master File," Box 1003, Series 2, JWP; letter, Webb Joiner to Wright, July 7, 1962, Folder "87th Cong., 2nd Leg., Ways and Means—Trade and Tariff, July–August 1962," Box 176, Series 1, JWP; *CR*, 87th Cong., 2nd sess., vol. 108, pt. 9 (June 28, 1962): H12056.

82. Press release, undated, 1962, Folder "Personal + ??," Box 1203, Series 3, JWP; Wright speech, October 13, 1961, Folder "Speech Files: Defense—Our National

Security System," Box 1284, Series 3, JWP; press release, September 21, 1961, Folder "Speech Files: Defense—Disarmament Agency," Box 1284, JWP.

83. *WSW*, July 26, 1963, Folder "Newsletter Master File," Box 1003, Series 2, JWP; Wright, *Balance*, 95; *WSW*, January 26, 1962, Folder "Newsletter Master File," Box 1003, Series 2, JWP; letter, Wright to Tim Paulsel, April 4, 1962, Folder "87th Cong., 2nd Leg., Ways and Means, Withholding, Tax Bill, April–May 1962," Box 176, Series 1, JWP; letter, Wright to D. T. Harbison, March 31, 1962, Folder "87th Cong., 2nd Leg., Ways and Means, Withholding, Tax Bill, April-May 1962," Box 176, Series 1, JWP; Allen Matusow, "John F. Kennedy and the Intellectuals," *Wilson Quarterly* 7, no. 4 (Autumn 1983): 140–153.

84. Interview, Jim Wright, July 8, 2012; Wright, *Balance*, 78.

85. Interview, Jim Wright, July 8, 2012; Wright, *Balance*, 78.

86. *WSW*, May 5, 1963, Folder "Newsletter Master File," Box 1003, Series 2, JWP; interview, Jim Wright, July 8, 2012.

87. Parmet, *JFK*, 218; interview, Jim Wright, July 8, 2012.

88. History DFW, homepage, DFW International Airport, http://bus-tst-vip .dfwairport.com/visitor/history.php, accessed May 29, 2013; interview, Jim Wright, July 8, 2012.

89. *FWST*, November 28, 1961, 1; *WSW*, August 6, 1962, Folder "Newsletter Master File," Box 1003, Series 2, JWP.

90. *WSW*, October 11, 1963, Folder "Newsletter Master File," Box 1003, Series 2, JWP; Wright, *Balance*, 96; interview, Jim Wright, July 8, 2012.

91. 370 U.S. 421 (1962); J. Brooks Flippen, *Jimmy Carter, the Politics of Family, and the Rise of the Religious Right* (Athens: University of Georgia Press, 2010), 74–75; Matthew Moen, "School Prayer and the Politics of Lifestyle Concern," *Social Sciences Quarterly* 65, no. 4 (1984): 1065–1071; James Hottois and Neil Milner, *The Sex Education Controversy: A Study of Politics, Education and Morality* (Lexington, MA: Heath, 1975), 14–15; quoted in Martin, *With God*, 78.

92. Shane Mountjoy, Engel v. Vitale: *School Prayer and the Establishment Clause* (New York: Chelsea, 2007), 96.

93. *WSW*, July 2, 1962, Folder "Newsletter Master File," Box 1003, Series 2, JWP.

94. John Hope Franklin and Alfred Moss, *From Slavery to Freedom: A History of African-Americans*, 7th ed. (New York: McGraw-Hill, 1994), 499–500; quoted in Link and Link, *American Epoch*, 597; Taylor Branch, *Parting the Waters: America in the King Years, 1954–1963* (New York: Simon and Schuster, 1988), 515–516, 693, 796–798, 823–824.

95. Letter, E. F. Burke to Wright, undated, Folder "88th Cong., 1st Leg., April 3, 1963–July 17, 1963," Box 220, Series 1, JWP; letter, Hugh Deaton to Wright, December 23, 1963, Folder "Correspondence, 1960–1963," Box 1204, Series 3, JWP; letter, Jeannette Christian to Wright, November 6, 1963, Folder "Correspondence, 1963," Box 1204, Series 3, JWP; letter, S. G. Swenson to Wright, November 8, 1963, Folder "Correspondence, 1963," Box 1204, Series 3, JWP; letter, T. W. Jolly to Wright, November 16, 1963, Folder "Correspondence, 1963," Box 1204, JWP; letter, Larry Tate to Wright, November 7, 1963, Folder "Correspondence, 1963," Box 1204, JWP; letter, C. W. Stewart to Wright, November 6, 1963, Folder "Correspondence, 1963," Box 1204, Series 3, JWP.

96. *CR*, 88th Cong., 1st sess., vol. 109, pt. 14 (October 17, 1963): H19802–H19803; Kearns, *Lyndon Johnson and the American Dream*, 190–191.

97. *WSW*, June 24, 1963, Folder "Newsletter Master File," Box 1003, Series 2, JWP; interview, Jim Wright, July 8, 2012.

98. Wright remarks, September 21, 1962, Folder "Speech Files: Defense—Peace Is Our Profession," Box 1284, Series 3, JWP.

99. *WSW*, April 7, 1963, Folder "Newsletter Master File," Box 1003, Series 2, JWP; Wright, *Balance*, 76; Piero Gleijeses, "Ships in the Night: The CIA, the White House, and the Bay of Pigs," *Journal of Latin American Studies* 27, no. 1 (February 1995): 1–42; Joshua Sandman, "Analyzing Foreign Policy Crisis Situations: The Bay of Pigs," *PSQ* 16, no. 2 (Spring 1986): 310–316.

100. Serge Ricard, "The Roosevelt Corollary," *PSQ* 36, no. 1 (March 2006): 17–26; Kris James Mitchener and Marc Weidenmier, "Empire, Public Goods, and the Roosevelt Corollary," *Journal of Economic History* 65, no. 3 (September 2005): 658–692.

101. Wright, *Balance*, 96–97; interview, Jim Wright, July 8, 2012; Timothy McKeown, "The Cuban Missile Crisis and Politics as Usual," *Journal of Politics* 62, no. 1 (February 2000): 70–87; see Robert Kennedy, *Thirteen Days: A Memoir of the Cuban Missile Crisis* (New York: Norton, 1999).

102. *CR*, 87th Cong., 2nd sess., vol. 108, pt. 12 (August 13, 1962): H16285; *Brownwood, Texas, Bulletin*, July 5, 1961, 2; *DMN*, September 29, 1961, 1; *WSW*, July 17, 1961, Folder "Newsletter Master File," Box 1003, Series 2, JWP.

103. Wright remarks, October 11, 1962, Folder "Speech Files: Foreign Affairs— Tarrant County Women's Club, October 11, 1962," Box 1283, JWP; quoted in Wright, *Balance*, 76, 85; Elizabeth Hoffman, *All You Need Is Love: The Peace Corps and the Spirit of the 1960s* (Cambridge, MA: Harvard University Press, 2000), 11–72.

104. Jeffrey Taffet, *Foreign Aid as Foreign Policy: The Alliance for Progress in Latin America* (New York: Routledge, 2007), 11–46; *WSW*, May 19, 1963, Folder "Newsletter Master File," Box 1003, Series 2, JWP.

105. Wright, *Balance*, 86.

106. *CR*, 87th Cong., 2nd sess., vol. 108, pt. 14 (September 14, 1962): H19459–H19460.

107. P.L. 87–195; *CR*, 87th Cong., 2nd sess., vol. 108, pt. 10 (July 11, 1962): H13131–H13133; Jim Wright, *Worth It All* (Washington, DC: Brassey's, 1993), 30; *WSW*, July 16, 1962, Folder "Newsletter Master File," Box 1003, Series 2, JWP; photocopy, uncited article, "Wright Effects Basic Change in Foreign Aid," August 22, 1962, Folder "Speech Files: Foreign Affairs—Let's Make Ourselves Clear on Cuba," Box 1287, Series 3, JWP; *HP*, September 1, 1961, 14.

108. Letter, Dean Rusk to Wright, September 28, 1962, Folder "Special Letter," Box 1125, Series 2, JWP; see Dean Rusk, *As I Saw It* (New York: Penguin, 1991).

109. Interview, Jim Wright, July 8, 2012.

110. Wright remarks, March 20, 1962, Folder "Sam Rayburn," Box 1047, Series 2, JWP; *WSW*, March 22, 1962, Folder "Newsletter Master File," Box 1003, Series 2, JWP.

111. Interview, Jim Wright, July 8, 2012; *RC* 8, no. 40 (April 10, 1963): 1.

112. Letter, B. E. Godfrey to Wright, August 17, 1961, Folder "Correspondence— Campaign '61 (6), Tarrant," Box 398, Series 1, JWP; letter, Wright to B. E. Godfrey,

August 26, 1961, Folder "Correspondence—Campaign '61 (6), Tarrant," Box 398, Series 1, JWP; letter, Joe Shosid to Wright, August 23, 1961, Folder "Correspondence—Campaign '61 (6), Tarrant," Box 398, Series 1, JWP.

113. Photocopy, uncited article, "Conservatives Talk of Wright Opponent," December 29, 1961, Folder "JW Press Clippings, 1961 (5)," Box 397, Series 1, JWP; photocopy, uncited article, "Area Republicans Eye Wright Spot," Folder "JW Press Clippings, 1961 (5)," Box 397, Series 1, JWP.

114. Letter, Wright to Jane Guerry, Folder "1962 Campaign," Box 397, Series 1, JWP; photocopy, uncited article, "Wright Johnson Pawn GOP Barron Charges," Folder "JW Press Clippings, 1961 (5)," Box 397, Series 1, JWP; letter, Wright to Thomas Abel, September 1, 1962, Folder "1962 Campaign," Box 397, Series 1, JWP.

115. Interview, Jim Wright, July 8, 2012; Wright, *Balance*, 102.

116. Quoted in Wright, *Balance*, 88.

117. Ibid., Wright, *Worth It*, 31; interview, Jim Wright, July 8, 2012.

118. *RC* 8, no. 40 (April 10, 1963): 1.

119. *RC* 8, no. 44 (May 22, 1963): 1; *WSW*, March 14, 1962, Folder "Newsletter Master File," Box 1003, Series 2, JWP; *WSW*, June 12, 1961, Folder "Newsletter Master File," Box 1003, Series 2, JWP.

120. Jim Wright, *You and Your Congressman* (New York: G. P. Putnam's Sons, 1965), 13.

121. Sorensen, *Kennedy*, 749.

122. Wright, *Balance*, 103–104.

123. Quoted in *FWST*, November 22, 1998, F8.

124. Quoted in ibid.; Parmet, *JFK*, 342–343; James Riddlesperger Jr., Anthony Champagne, and Dan Williams, eds., *The Wright Stuff: Reflections on People and Politics by Former Speaker Jim Wright* (Fort Worth: Texas Christian University Press, 2013), 285–295.

125. *DMN*, November 22, 1963, 14; interview, Jim Wright, July 8, 2012.

126. Documentary, PBS, *JFK: One P.M. Central Standard Time*, Colonial Pictures, Alastair Layzell director, aired November 13, 2013.

127. Interview, Jim Wright, July 8, 2012.

128. *WSW*, November 29, 1963, Folder "Newsletter Master File," Box 1003, Series 2, JWP; Wright, *Balance*, 108–109.

CHAPTER 8

1. Jim Wright, *Balance of Power: Presidents and Congress from the Era of McCarthy to the Age of Gingrich* (Atlanta: Turner, 1996), 111, 114.

2. Quoted in Michael Beschloss, *Taking Charge: The Johnson White House Tapes, 1963–1964* (New York: Simon and Schuster, 1997), 125.

3. Quoted in William Chafe, Harvard Sitkoff, and Beth Bailey, eds., *A History of Our Time* (New York: Oxford University Press, 2003), 104–106; Doris Kearns, *Lyndon Johnson and the American Dream* (New York: Harper and Row, 1976), 173; Robert Dallek, *Lyndon B. Johnson: Portrait of a President* (New York: Oxford, 2004), 163, 171–192.

4. Wright, *Balance*, 119.

5. Michael Harrington, *The Other America: Poverty in the United States* (New York: Macmillan, 1962); Maurice Isserman, *The Other American: The Untold Story of Michael Harrington* (New York: Public Affairs, 2000), 209–218; Jonathan Bell and Timothy Stanley, *Making Sense of American Liberalism* (Champaign: University of Illinois Press, 2012), 62–68; 233; interview, Jim Wright, July 12, 2012.

6. *WSW*, August 22, 1966, Folder "Newsletter Master File," Box 1003, Series 2, JWP.

7. Ibid.; Marshall Lynam, *Stories I Never Told the Speaker: The Chaotic Adventures of a Capitol Hill Aide* (Dallas: Three Forks, 1998), 55–58; Walter Raymond, *Dictionary of Politics*, 7th ed. (Lawrenceville, VA: Brunswick, 1992), 213; Paul S. Boyer, Clifford E. Clark Jr., Sandra McNair Hawley, Joseph F. Kett, Andrew Rieser, Neal Salisbury, Harvard Sitkoff, and Nancy Woloch, *Enduring Vision: A History of the American People*, 6th ed. (Boston: Houghton Mifflin, 2009), 903.

8. Quoted in Beschloss, *Taking Charge*, 216–218.

9. Quoted in interview, Jim Wright, July 12, 2012; Wright, *Balance*, 109.

10. Letter, Lee Rankin to Wright, March 24, 1964, Folder "Warren Commission," Box 1120, Series 2, JWP.

11. Address Before Congress, November 27, 1963, Public Papers of the Presidents, Lyndon Johnson, APP, UCSB, www.presidency.ucsb.edu/ws/index.php?pid=25988&st=Kennedy&st1, accessed June 12, 2013.

12. Letter, J. L. Haight to Wright, November 28, 1963, Folder "Correspondence, 1963," Box 1204, Series 3, JWP; letter, C. J. Bozeman to Wright, December 13, 1963, Folder "Correspondence, 1963," Box 1204, Series 3, JWP.

13. *CR*, 88th Cong., 2nd sess., vol. 110, pt. 2 (February 4, 1964): H1927.

14. Quoted in *FWP*, April 20, 1964, 10; interview, Jim Wright, July 8, 2012.

15. *WSW*, January 16, 1964, Folder "Newsletter Master File," Box 1003, Series 2, JWP; George Moss, *Moving On: The American People Since 1945*, 3rd ed. (Upper Saddle River, NJ: Prentice Hall, 2005), 157.

16. *WSW*, February 3, 1964, Folder "Newsletter Master File," Box 1003, Series 2, JWP; *WSW*, May 30, 1966, Folder "Newsletter Master File," Box 1003, Series 2, JWP; interview, Jim Wright, July 12, 2012.

17. P.L. 88–452; William Link and Arthur Link, *American Epoch*, vol. 2, 7th ed. (New York: McGraw-Hill, 1993), 606; interview, Jim Wright, July 12, 2012.

18. *WSW*, July 27, 1964, Folder "Newsletter Master File," Box 1003, Series 2, JWP.

19. Letter, Wright to Joe Stovall, August 24, 1965, Folder "89th Leg., General, 1965," Box 274, Series 1, JWP; letter, Wright to Tom Vandergriff, January 17, 1966, Folder "Tarrant, 65–66," Box 396, Series 1, JWP.

20. The National Food Stamp Act, P.L. 88–525; *WSW*, April 12, 1964, Folder "Newsletter Master File," Box 1003, Series 2, JWP.

21. P.L. 88–579; Mark Bauerlein and Ellen Grantham, eds., *National Endowment for the Arts: A History, 1965–2008* (Washington, DC: NEA, 2009), 15; interview, Jim Wright, July 12, 2012.

22. P.L. 88–577; interview, Jim Wright, July 12, 2012.

23. Federal Highway Act, P.L. 88–423, and Urban Mass Transportation Act, P.L. 88–365; Policy Positions, Folder "JW Voting Record, 1964," Box 1120, Series 2, JWP.

24. See, for example, Marilyn Young, *Vietnam Wars, 1945–1990* (New York: Harper-Collins, 1991), 33–46, and George Herring, *America's Longest War: The United States and Vietnam, 1950–1975* (New York: McGraw-Hill, 1985).

25. Mark Lawrence, *The Vietnam War: A Concise International History* (New York: Oxford University Press, 2008), 75–79; List of Newsletters, Folder "Voting Records, 1955–1979," Box 1003, Series 2, JWP.

26. See Stanley Karnow, *Vietnam: A History* (New York: Penguin, 1983), 15–27; Fredrik Logevall, *Embers of War: The Fall of an Empire and the Making of America's Vietnam* (New York: Random House, 2012), xv–xxii.

27. Interview, Jim Wright, July 14, 2012.

28. Ibid.; *WSW*, March 4, 1966, Folder "Newsletter Master File," Box 1003, Series 2, JWP; Daniel Yergin, *Shattered Peace: The Origins of the Cold War and the National Security State* (Boston: Houghton Mifflin, 1977), 401–403.

29. Message on US Policy in Southeast Asia, August 5, 1964, Public Papers of the Presidents, Lyndon Johnson, APP, UCSB, www.presidency.ucsb.edu/ws/index.php ?pid=26422&st=Vietnam&st1, accessed June 18, 2013.

30. Ibid.; P.L. 88–408.

31. *WSW*, August 8, 1964, Folder "Newsletter Master File," Box 1003, Series 2, JWP.

32. See Ezra Siff, *Why the Senate Slept: The Gulf of Tonkin Resolution and the Beginning of America's Vietnam War* (Westport, CT: Praeger, 1999); Donald Wester-feld, *War Powers: The President, the Congress, and the Question of War* (Westport, CT: Praeger, 1996), 3; Mariah Zeisberg, *The Politics of Constitutional Authority* (Princeton, NJ: Princeton University Press, 2013), 153–155, 164–166, 172–173; Karnow, *Vietnam*, 344–345, 360–363, 374–376; Kearns, *Lyndon Johnson and the American Dream*, 198–199.

33. Interview, Jim Wright, July 14, 2012.

34. Interview, Jim Wright, July 12, 2012; Wright, *Balance*, 124.

35. Karnow, *Vietnam*, 377, 396–397.

36. *FWP*, February 3, 1964, 3; interview, Jim Wright, July 12, 2012.

37. Letter, Harlan Friend to John Ramsfield, July 29, 1964, Folder "Out of State," Box 396, Series 1, JWP; John Ramsfield to Harlan Friend, August 3, 1964, Folder "Out of State," Box 396, Series 1, JWP; letter, John Ramsfield to Wright, August 3, 1964, Folder "Out of State," Box 396, Series 1, JWP.

38. *WP*, July 23, 1964, 16.

39. Dear Friend Letter, Amon Carter, undated, Folder "JW Literature," Box 1151, Series 2, JWP; photocopy, uncited photograph, "Bullish Situation," Folder "Correspon-dence, 1963–1964," Box 1120, Series 2, JWP.

40. Campaign flier, Folder "JW Literature," Box 1151, Series 2, JWP.

41. *FWP*, April 24, 1964, 16; *FWST*, April 12, 1964, IV, 4.

42. Interview, Jim Wright, July 12, 2012.

43. Press release, October 30, 1964, Folder "Speech Files: Democratic Party—Remarks of Congressman Jim Wright, 10/30/64," Box 1285, Series 3, JWP.

44. Goldwater Acceptance Speech, 28th Republican National Convention, July 16, 1964, *WP*, Historical Archives, www.washingtonpost.com/wp-srv/politics/daily/may

98/goldwaterspeech.htm, accessed June 20, 2013; Rick Perlstein, *Before the Storm: Barry Goldwater and the Unmaking of the American Consensus* (New York: Hill and Wang, 2001), 420–515.

45. Drew Weston, *The Political Brain: The Role of Emotion in Deciding the Fate of the Nation* (New York: Public Affairs, 2008), 55–57; interview, Jim Wright, July 12, 2012.

46. Robert Johnson, *All the Way with LBJ: The 1964 Presidential Election* (New York: Cambridge University Press, 2009), 292–299; Wright, *Balance*, 125.

47. Letter, Otho Crawford to Wright, November 21, 1964, Folder "JW Personal, Circa 1964," Box 1120, Series 2, JWP; letter, "Bill" to Wright, November 10, 1964, Folder "JW Personal, 1963–1964," Box 1120, Series 2, JWP.

48. Wright, *Balance*, 125.

49. *WSW*, January 11, 1965, Folder "Newsletter Master File," Box 1003, Series 2, JWP; *WSW*, August 9, 1965, Folder "Newsletter Master File," Box 1003, Series 2, JWP.

50. Interview, Jim Wright, July 12, 2012.

51. Quoted in Lewis Gould, *Lady Bird Johnson and the Environment* (Lawrence: University of Kansas Press, 1988), 162.

52. Quoted in photocopy, uncited article, "Wright Credited in Pushing Bill," Folder "Misc. Press Clippings, 1963–1966," Box 1150, JWP.

53. *Appalachia: A Report by the President's Appalachian Regional Development Commission, 1964*, homepage, Appalachian Regional Commission, www.arc.gov/about /ARCAppalachiaAReportbythePresidentsAppalachianRegionalCommission1964.asp, accessed June 23, 2013.

54. P.L. 89–4; *WSW*, March 10, 1965, Folder "Newsletter Master File," Box 1003, Series 2, JWP.

55. P.L. 89–10 and P.L. 89–329, respectively; Patrick McGuinn, *No Child Left Behind and the Transformation of Federal Education Policy* (Lawrence: University of Kansas Press, 2006), 21–48.

56. Wright remarks, May 2, 1968, Folder "Speech Files: Education—New Tools for Education," Box 1287, Series 3, JWP; Wright remarks, March 17, 1967, Folder "Speech Files: Education and Democracy," Box 1287, Series 3, JWP; letter, Wright to John Pessler, May 17, 1967, Folder "90th Cong., Education and Labor, 1967 (4 of 13)," Box 316, Series 1, JWP.

57. Letter, Wright to D. E. Wiggins, March 5, 1965, Folder "89th Leg., General," Box 274, Series 1, JWP; letter, Wright to Harold Johnson, March 9, 1965, Folder "89th Leg., General," Box 274, Series 1, JWP.

58. Memo, Bill Philips to DSG, February 23, 1965, Folder "Medicine," Box 1119, Series 2, JWP.

59. Letter, Wright to W. L. Leavy, June 1, 1965, Folder "89th Leg., General," Box 274, Series 1, JWP.

60. Letter, Wright to W. C. Boone, March 3, 1965, Folder "Ways and Means," Box 336, Series 1, JWP.

61. Letter, John McCormack et al. to colleagues, April 5, 1965, Folder "Medical Care," Box 1125, Series 2, JWP; Moss, *Moving On*, 158.

62. *WSW*, "Wright Voting Record," Box 993, Series 2, JWP; interview, Jim Wright, July 12, 2012.

63. *Whom Shall Welcome: Report of the President's Commission on Immigration and Naturalization* (Washington, DC: US Government Printing Office, 1953); Roger Daniels, *Guarding the Golden Door: America's Immigration Policy and Immigrants Since 1882* (New York: Hill and Wang, 2004), 132–139.

64. Letter, Wright to Lois Hardy, March 1, 1965, Folder "89th Leg., General," Box 274, Series 1, JWP; letter, Wright to Vernon Smith, July 9, 1965, Folder "89th Leg., General, 1965," Box 274, JWP; P.L. 89–236.

65. Letter, Wright to Don Hirst, November 13, 1967, Folder "90th Cong., District of Columbia, 1967," Box 316, Series 1, JWP; see Harry Jaffe and Tom Sherwood, *Dream City: Race, Power, and the Decline of Washington, D.C.* (New York: Simon and Schuster, 1994).

66. Letter, Wright to Bob Robinson, September 1, 1965, Folder "89th Cong., 1st Session, District of Columbia," Box 275, Series 1, JWP; letter, Wright to Fred Thornton, December 28, 1964, Folder "89th Cong., Leg., General," Box 274, Series 1, JWP.

67. P.L. 89–117 and P.L. 89–174; Gareth Davies, *From Opportunities to Entitlement: The Transformation and Decline of Great Society Liberalism* (Lawrence: University of Kansas Press, 1996), 77, 92; Sidney Milkis and Jerome Mileur, eds., *The Great Society and the High Tide of Liberalism* (Amherst: University of Massachusetts Press, 2005), xiv, 8, 239.

68. P.L. 234; List of Newsletters, Folder "Voting Records, 1955–1979," Box 1003, Series 2, JWP; *WSW*, January 29, 1963, Folder "Wright Voting Record," Box 993, Series 2, JWP; interview, Jim Wright, June 18, 2012.

69. Jim Wright, *The Coming Water Famine* (New York: Coward-McCann, 1966); photocopy, book review, *Chicago Tribune*, June 12, 1966, Folder "Scrapbook," Box 1248, Series 3, JWP; Wright, *Balance*, 130.

70. Wright remarks, October 30, 1967, Folder "Population and the Environment, (2)," Box 803, Series 2, JWP.

71. Letter, Wright to Henry Black, April 19, 1967, Folder "Legislation—90th Cong., House Administration, 1967," Box 317, Series 1, JWP.

72. *DMN*, May 13, 1966, D1; photocopy, uncited article, "Wright Backs Water Plan of Texas Solon," Folder "Scrapbook," Box 1248, Series 3, JWP.

73. See Gary May, *The Voting Rights Act and the Transformation of American Democracy* (New York: Perseus, 2013).

74. Letter, Wright to Jack Smoke, April 13, 1965, Folder "89th Leg., General," Box 274, Series 1, JWP.

75. *CR*, 89th Cong., 1st sess., vol. 111, pt. 12 (July 9, 1965): H16248–H16249.

76. Letter, Wright to H. R. Pipkin, August 11, 1965, Folder "89th Leg., General, 1965," Box 274, Series 1, JWP; letter, Wright to J. R. Foust, July 13, 1965, Folder "89th Leg., General, 1965," Box 274, Series 1, JWP.

77. P.L. 89–110; *WSW*, July 26, 1965, Folder "Newsletter Master File," Box 1003, Series 2, JWP; Alexander Keyssar, *The Right to Vote: The Contested History of Democracy in the United States* (New York: Basic, 2000), 211–244.

78. See Paul Krugman, *Conscience of a Liberal* (New York: Norton, 2009), 99.

79. Quoted in Beschloss, *Taking Charge*, 470.

80. *WSW*, May 5, 1965, Folder "Newsletter Master File," Box 1003, Series 2, JWP; Wright, *Balance*, 132.

81. Interview, Jim Wright, July 12, 2012.

82. "Let's Talk Trinity and Shipping on It: An Interview with Jim Wright," *Texas Metro* (December 1965): 19–23; quoted in Wright, *Balance*, 133.

83. Wright, *Balance*, 134; interview, Jim Wright, July 12, 2012.

84. Quoted in Jack Cleland, "Trinity Bill Handed to Johnson," *FWST*, 2.

85. Interview, Jim Wright, July 12, 2012.

86. Letter, Wright to Robert Pigg, October 5, 1965, Folder "89th Leg., General, 1965," Box 274, Series 1, JWP; letter, Wright to Harry Nolan, October 13, 1965, Folder "89th Leg., General, 1965," Box 274, Series 1, JWP.

87. Letter, Wright to Jack Moseley, October 14, 1965, Folder "Tarrant, 65–66," Box 396, Series 1, JWP.

88. Letter, Wright to W. M. Dressler, January 17, 1964, Folder "Tarrant, 65–66," Box 396, Series 1, JWP.

89. Letter, Wright to C. J. Bradley, February 8, 1965, Folder "Tarrant, 65–66," Box 396, Series 1, JWP.

90. Letter, Wright to Clyde Johnson, July 22, 1965, Folder "Travis II," Box 396, Series 1, JWP.

91. Letter, Wright to Marshall Lynam's List, September 16, 1965, Folder "Lists," Box 396, Series 1, JWP.

92. Letter, Wright to Jack Moseley, October 5, 1965, Folder "Tarrant, 65–66," Box 396, Series 1, JWP; letter, Wright to Herb Evans, March 2, 1965, unmarked folder, Box 396, Series 1, JWP.

93. Letter, Henry Kerry to Joe Tonahill, September 4, 1965, Folder "Tarrant, 65–66," Box 396, Series 1, JWP.

94. Letter, Don Ellinger to Wright, July 14, 1965, Folder "Out of State," Box 396, Series 1, JWP; letter, Wright to Don Ellinger, July 20, 1965, Folder "Out of State," Box 396, Series 1, JWP.

95. *FWST*, December 19, 1965, 12; interview, Jim Wright, July 12, 2012; photocopy, advertisement, December 16, 1965, Folder "Scrapbook," Box 1248, Series 3, JWP; photocopy, uncited article, "Wright Faces Tough Competition—TV Movie," Folder "Misc. Press Clippings, 1963–1966," Box 1150, Series 2, JWP.

96. Press release, January 8, 1966, Folder "Statement on Senate Race," Box 994, Series 2, JWP; *FWST*, January 9, 1965, 1.

97. Photocopy, uncited article, "Reasons for Wright Decision Puzzle Many," December 19, 1965, Folder "Misc. Press Clippings, 1963–1966," Box 1150, Series 2, JWP; letter, Wright to Clifford Williams, January 14, 1966, Folder "Tarrant, 65–66," Box 396, Series 1, JWP.

98. *FWST*, January 11, 1966, 10.

99. Photocopy, uncited article, "Wright as Speaker Termed Unlikely," December 2, 1965, Folder "Misc. Press Clippings, 1963–1966," Box 1150, Series 2, JWP.

CHAPTER 9

1. Child Nutrition Act, P.L. 89–642; National School Lunch Act, P.L. 90–302; Public Broadcasting Act, P.L. 90–129; Motor Vehicle Safety Act, P.L. 89–563; Social Security Act Amendments, P.L. 89–97; Housing and Urban Development Act, P.L. 89–117; Public Works and Economic Development Act, P.L. 89–136; Demonstration Cities and Metropolitan Development Act, P.L. 89–754.

2. Letter, Wright to William Morris, January 19, 1966, Folder "89th Cong., Leg., General," Box 274, Series 1, JWP.

3. *WSW*, June 1, 1964, Folder "Newsletter Master File," Box 1003, Series 2, JWP; *WSW*, January 8, 1966, Folder "Newsletter Master File," Box 1003, Series 2, JWP.

4. David Halberstam, *The Best and the Brightest* (New York: Ballantine, 1992), 159, 409, 476, 633; see John Prados and Margaret Porter, eds., *Inside the Pentagon Papers* (Lawrence: University of Kansas Press, 2004); interview, Jim Wright, July 12, 2012.

5. Letter, Wright to Michael Gately, April 1, 1966, Folder "World Affairs," Box 1017, Series 2, JWP.

6. Letter, Wright to Charles Loving, March 21, 1966, Folder "Vietnam," Box 1125, Series 2, JWP.

7. *CR*, 89th Cong., 2nd sess., vol. 112, pt. 4 (March 1, 1966): H4432–H4433.

8. *WSW*, January 8, 1966, Folder "Newsletter Master File," Box 1003, Series 2, JWP; Jim Wright, *Balance of Power: Presidents and Congress from the Era of McCarthy to the Age of Gingrich* (Atlanta: Turner, 1996), 136.

9. P.L. 89–358; *WSW*, February 21, 1966, Folder "Newsletter Master File," Box 1003, Series 2, JWP.

10. *WSW*, February 21, 1966, Folder "Newsletter Master File," Box 1003, Series 2, JWP; letter, Wright to W. A. Campbell, May 24, 1966, Folder "World Affairs," Box 1125, Series 2, JWP; *WSW*, March 4, 1966, Folder "Newsletter Master File," Box 1003, Series 2, JWP.

11. Wright remarks, April 20, 1965, Folder "Vietnam (3)," Box 1024, Series 2, JWP.

12. Letter, Wright to Lyndon Johnson, February 1, 1966, Folder "Vietnam, 1954–1966," Box 1125, Series 2, JWP.

13. Letter, Wright to J. W. Fulbright, February 9, 1966, Folder "World Affairs," Box 1125, Series 2, JWP.

14. Letter, J. W. Fulbright to Wright, February 12, 1966, Folder "World Affairs," Box 1125, Series 2, JWP.

15. Letter, Arthur Goldberg to Wright, February 25, 1966, Folder "World Affairs," Box 1125, Series 2, JWP.

16. Letter, Douglas MacArthur to Wright, February 25, 1966, Folder "World Affairs," Box 1125, Series 2, JWP.

17. Quoted in Wright, *Balance*, 138.

18. Doris Kearns, *Lyndon Johnson and the American Dream* (New York: Harper and Row, 1976), 295–296.

19. *WSW*, March 3, 1967, Folder "Newsletter Master File," Box 1003, Series 2, JWP.

20. Wright remarks, August 3, 1966, Folder "Speech Files: Economy—Hard

Money Hits Home," Box 1286, Series 3, JWP; *WSW*, April 4, 1966, Folder "Newsletter Master File," Box 1003, Series 2, JWP.

21. Wright, *Balance*, 145.

22. Photocopy, uncited article, April 15, 1966, Folder "Scrapbook," Box 1248, Series 3, JWP.

23. Letter, Wright to Earl Harrison, February 20, 1967, Folder "90th Cong., Interstate + (?), 1967 (4 of 4)," Box 317, Series 1, JWP; letter, Wright to Paul DeCleva, March 1, 1967, Folder "90th Cong., Interstate + (?), 1967 (4 of 4)," Box 317, Series 1, JWP.

24. Letter, Wright to Paul Mason, May 20, 1968, Folder "Ways and Means Committee," Box 336, Series 1, JWP.

25. P.L. 90–364; Irving Bernstein, *Guns or Butter: The Presidency of Lyndon Johnson* (New York: Oxford University Press, 1996), 372–377; Mark Updegrove, *Indomitable Will: LBJ in the Presidency* (New York: Random House, 2012), 214–215.

26. Letter, Wright to Radford Allen, September 28, 1967, Folder "90th Congress, Interior and Internal Affairs," Box 317, Series 1, JWP; letter, Wright to W. E. Hartmann, January 31, 1968, Folder "Ways and Means Committee," Box 336, Series 1, JWP; letter, Wright to L. B. Holmes, January 11, 1968, Folder "Ways and Means (Medical, Social Security, Excise Tax)," Box 336, Series 1, JWP.

27. Letter, Wright to Joe Hayslip, December 14, 1967, Folder "90th Cong., Education and Labor, 1967 (6 of 13)," Box 316, Series 1, JWP.

28. Wright, *Balance*, 142; interview, Jim Wright, July 12, 2012.

29. *WSW*, April 28, 1967, Folder "Newsletter Master File," Box 1003, Series 2, JWP; interview, Jim Wright, July 12, 2012.

30. Letter, Frank Andrews to Wright, November 17, 1967, Folder "90th Cong., Education and Labor, 1967 (6 of 13)," Box 316, Series 1, JWP.

31. Photocopy, uncited article, November 14, 1967, Folder "Scrapbook," Box 1248, Series 3, JWP.

32. Lewis Gould, *Lady Bird Johnson and the Environment* (Lawrence: University of Kansas Press, 1988), 179–180; Wright, *Balance*, 141.

33. Quoted in Kearns, *Lyndon Johnson and the American Dream*, 289–290.

34. Letter, Wright to Jack Phillips, June 26, 1969, Folder "91st Cong., 1st Leg., Judiciary, February 13, 1969—July 10, 1969," Box 362, Series 1, JWP; Charles Hamilton, *Adam Clayton Powell, Jr.: The Political Biography of an American Dilemma* (New York: Cooper Square, 1991), 429–478; Lee A. Daniels, "The Political Career of Adam Clayton Powell," *Journal of Black Studies* 4, no. 2 (December 1973): 115–138; photocopy, uncited article, "Wright Says House Acted Too Quick in Powell Ouster," January 18, 1967, Folder "Scrapbook," Box 1248, Series 3, JWP.

35. Jim Wright, "Clean Money for Congress," *Harper's Magazine* 235 (April 1967): 98–102, 105–106; letter, Wright to Ruth Briggs, April 24, 1967, Folder "Legislation, 90th Cong., House Administration, 1967," Box 317, Series 1, JWP.

36. Wright address, November 15, 1966, Folder "Speech Files: Defense—Responsibility of Elected Officials," Box 1285, Series 3, JWP.

37. *WSW*, January 27, 1967, Folder "Newsletter Master File," Box 1003, Series 2, JWP.

38. Photocopy, uncited article, "Wright Cites Cost of Holding Office," Folder "Scrapbook," Box 1248, Series 3, JWP.

39. Letter, Ed Gollett to Wright, August 22, 1967, Folder "Legislation, 90th Cong., House Administration, 1967," Box 317, Series 1, JWP; letter, Wright to Ed Gollett, September 7, 1967, Folder "Legislation, 90th Cong., House Administration, 1967," Box 317, Series 1, JWP; letter, Wright to Charles Ferguson, April 6, 1967, Folder "Legislation, 90th Cong., House Administration, 1967," Box 317, Series 1, JWP.

40. Jim Wright, "How Dirty Is Politics?" *Baptist Student* (May 1968): 19–22.

41. Letter, Wright to James Coffee, July 18, 1967, Folder "Legislative—90th Cong., House Administration, 1967," Box 317, Series 1, JWP; photocopy, uncited article, "Wright Tells Congress' Role in Movie," June 19, 1967, Folder "Scrapbook," Box 1248, Series 3, JWP.

42. Letter, Wright to Claudia Brummet, December 1, 1967, Folder "Governor's Race—1968 (Jim Wright)," Box 789, Series 2, JWP; letter, Wright to J. R. Brown, December 3, 1967, Folder "Governor's Race—1968 (Jim Wright)," Box 789, Series 2, JWP.

43. Letter, Doke to Wright, August 6, 1965, Folder "Correspondence, 1965–1986, 1 of 3," Box 1122, Series 2, JWP.

44. *FWST*, September 11, 1966, B1.

45. Wright, "To Make a Difference," Folder "Biographical Sketches, 1 of 3," Box 1201, Series 3, JWP; interview, Jim Wright, May 18, 2012; quoted in *FWST*, December 9, 1986, Special Section, 6.

46. Memo, Omar Burleson to Members, April 11, 1967, Folder "Legislation—90th Cong., House Administration, 1967," Box 317, Series 1, JWP; memo, Joe Shosid to Wright, August 5, 1965, Folder "Correspondence, 1965–1986, 1 of 3," Box 1122, Series 2, JWP.

47. Betty Friedan, *The Feminine Mystique* (New York: Norton, 1963); interview, Jim Wright, June 22, 2012; see William O'Neill, *The New Left: A History* (Arlington Heights, IL: Harlan Davidson, 2001).

48. Letter, Wright to George Madden, August 9, 1967, Folder "Legislative, Internal Security," Box 317, Series 1, JWP.

49. Wright remarks, November 18, 1967, Folder "Speech Files: Democratic Party—Remarks of JW, RCWC, November 18, 1967," Box 1285, JWP.

50. Letter, Wright to Lawrence Connor, March 31, 1965, Folder "89th Legislature, General," Box 274, Series 1, JWP.

51. Letter, Wright to W. R. Lambert, May 16, 1967, Folder "90th Cong., Education and Labor, 1967 (10 of 13)," Box 316, Series 1, JWP.

52. *FWP*, August 26, 1965, 12; letter, M. A. Hutchinson to Wright, April 3, 1967, Folder "90th Cong., Education and Labor, 1967 (1 of 13)," Box 316, Series 1, JWP.

53. Wright, *Balance*, 154.

54. Quoted in ibid., 170–172.

55. Letter, Wright to Pamela Brady, January 2, 1968, Folder "Vietnam (1)," Box 1024, Series 2, JWP.

56. *CR*, 90th Cong., 2nd sess., vol. 114, pt. 7 (April 3, 1968): H8919.

57. Letter, Wright to Robert Fenley, March 24, 1967, Folder "90th Cong., Armed Services, 2 of 2," Box 316, Series 1, JWP.

58. Interview, Jim Wright, July 12, 2012.

59. Ibid.; Wright, *Balance*, 144.

60. Interview, Jim Wright, July 12, 2012.

61. Wright remarks, October 27, 1967, Folder "Speech Files: Crime—On Protests and Patriotism," Box 1282, Series 3, JWP.

62. *WSW*, May 7, 1968, Folder "The Politics of Disruption," Box 994, Series 2, JWP.

63. Letter, Wright to R. M. Smith, July 20, 1967, Folder "90th Cong., Judiciary—General, 1967 (8 of 8)," Box 317, Series 1, JWP; letter, Wright to John Harley, August 22, 1967, Folder "90th Cong., Judiciary—General, 1967 (8 of 8)," Box 317, Series 1, JWP.

64. Letter, Wright to Charles Brewer, May 8, 1967, Folder "90th Cong., Judiciary—General, 1967 (8 of 8)," Box 317, Series 1, JWP; letter, Wright to Dub Rogers, June 5, 1967, Folder "90th Cong., Judiciary—General, 1967 (8 of 8)," Box 317, Series 1, JWP.

65. Press release, August 16, 1967, Folder "Speech Files: Crime—Protecting Police and Firemen," Box 1282, Series 3, JWP; photocopy, uncited article, "Wright Asks US Protection for Officials Fighting Riots," August 16, 1967, Folder "Speech Files: Civil Rights—Wright Asks US Protection of Officials," Box 1282, Series 3, JWP; letter, Crawford Martin to Wright, August 14, 1967, Folder "90th Cong., Judiciary—General, 1967 (7 of 8)," Box 317, Series 1, JWP.

66. P.L. 90–284; Wright statement, April 10, 1968, Folder "Wright Voting Record," Box 993, Series 2, JWP.

67. P.L. 90–351; Fact Sheet, Crime Act, Folder "Wright Voting Record," Box 993, Series 2, JWP; letter, Wright to Albert Ross, April 5, 1967, Folder "90th Cong., Judiciary, General, 1967 (1 of 8)," Box 317, Series 1, JWP; Wright remarks, July 9, 1968, Folder "Speech Files: Crime—Control of Violent Crime," Box 1282, Series 3, JWP.

68. Jim Wright, *Worth It All* (Washington, DC: Brassey's, 1993), 37.

69. *WSW*, July 5, 1965, Folder "Newsletter Master File," Box 1003, Series 2, JWP.

70. Wright, *Worth It*, 35–36; letter, Wright to Irwin Fruchtman, August 15, 1966, Folder "Dominican Republic Project," Box 717, Series 2, JWP; letter, Wright to Irwin Fruchtman, March 16, 1967, Folder "Dominican Republic Project," Box 717, Series 2, JWP; William Link and Arthur Link, *American Epoch*, vol. 2, 7th ed. (New York: McGraw-Hill, 1993), 627–628; interview, Jim Wright, July 12, 2012.

71. Wright remarks, July 17, 1965, Folder "Speech Files: Defense—Remarks to WWI Veterans," Box 1284, Series 3, JWP.

72. *WSW*, March 30, 1964, Folder "Newsletter Master File," Box 1003, Series 2, JWP; letter, Larry Blackmon to Wright, November 4, 1965, Folder "Larry Blackmon," Box 803, Series 2, JWP; letter, Larry Blackmon to Bill Rodgers, January 9, 1965, Folder "Larry Blackmon," Box 803, Series 2, JWP.

73. Letter, Wright to Parks Campbell, August 28, 1967, Folder "Leg., 90th Cong., Foreign Affairs, 1967," Box 317, Series 1, JWP; *WSW*, March 3, 1967, Folder "Newsletter Master File," Box 1003, Series 2, JWP; letter, Miguel Mendez to Wright, May 9, 1967, Folder "90th Cong., Internal and Insular Affairs," Box 317, Series 1, JWP.

74. Wright remarks, April 13, 1968, Folder "Latin America," Box 709, Series 2, JWP.

75. *WSW*, March 15, 1964, Folder "Newsletter Master File," Box 1003, Series 2, JWP; interview, Jim Wright, July 12, 2012.

76. *WSW*, September 27, 1967, Folder "Speech Files: Defense—British Mines," Box 1284, Series 3, JWP; *WSW*, March 1, 1964, Folder "Newsletter Master File," Box 1003, Series 2, JWP; interview, Jim Wright, July 12, 2012; George Moss, *Moving On: The American People Since 1945*, 3rd ed. (Upper Saddle River, NJ: Prentice Hall, 2005), 163.

77. *WSW*, April 10, 1966, Folder "Newsletter Master File," Box 1003, Series 2, JWP.

78. Quoted in Ralph Levering, *The Cold War, 1945–1987* (Arlington Heights, IL: Harlan Davidson, 1988), 111.

79. Quoted in photocopy, uncited article, "Wright Says Firmness, Unity Needed in Crisis," January 26, 1968, Folder "Scrapbook," Box 1248, Series 3, JWP; interview, Jim Wright, July 12, 2012; Mitchell Lerner, *The Pueblo Incident: A Spy Ship and the Failure of American Policy* (Lawrence: University of Kansas Press, 2002), 122–146.

80. *WSW*, June 16, 1967, Folder "Wright Voting Record," Box 993, Series 2, JWP.

81. Seth Kantor, "Ex-Kid Fighter, Jim Wright, Meets Hero, Dempsey, Again," *FWP*, January 6, 1965, 8.

82. History of Texas Redistricting, Texas Legislative Council, www.tlc.state.tx.us /redist/history/overview_congress.html, accessed July 11, 2013; photocopy, uncited article, June 7, 1965, Folder "Scrapbook," Box 1248, Series 3, JWP; letter, Wright to Frank Laverty, July 17, 1967, Folder "90th Cong., Judiciary, General, 1967 (8 of 8)," Box 317, Series 1, JWP.

83. Letter, Wright to Cecil Burney, March 14, 1968, Folder "Cecil Burney Reports," Box 789, Series 2, JWP; interview, Jim Wright, July 12, 2012; Dominic Sandbrook, *Eugene McCarthy: The Rise and Fall of Postwar American Liberalism* (New York: Anchor, 2004), 163–217.

84. Louis Gould, *1968: The Election That Changed America* (Chicago: Ivan Dee, 2010), 129–155; interview, Jim Wright, July 12, 2012.

85. Letter, Wright to Patricia Fletcher, April 2, 1968, Folder "Campaign, 1968 (National)," Box 789, Series 2, JWP; interview, Jim Wright, July 12, 2012.

86. *FWP*, May 24, 1968, 5; interview, Jim Wright, July 12, 2012; photocopy, uncited article, April 4, 1968, Folder "Scrapbook," Box 1248, Series 3, JWP.

87. *FWST*, May 24, 1968, 1; letter, J. M. Moudy to Wright, June 5, 1968, Folder "Wright Congressional Club," Box 1125, Series 2, JWP.

88. Memo, Fred Harris to Hubert Humphrey, May 6, 1968, Folder "Humphrey Campaign," Box 789, Series 2, JWP; Wright, *Balance*, 148.

89. Letter, Wright to J. H. Jackson, May 9, 1968, Folder "Humphrey Campaign," Box 789, Series 2, JWP; letter, Wright to E. J. Glaser, August 7, 1968, Folder "Campaign, 1968 (National)," Box 789, Series 2, JWP.

90. Wright remarks, undated, Folder "Remarks to Delegation (1968–1969)," Box 789, Series 2, JWP.

91. Jim Wright, "An Open Letter to Senator Eugene McCarthy," undated, Folder "Open Letter to Senator Eugene McCarthy (1968)," Box 789, Series 2, JWP.

92. Letter, Wright to Geoffrey Cowan, October 2, 1969, Folder "Campaign, 1968 (National)," Box 789, Series 2, JWP.

93. Wright, *Balance*, 149.

94. Gould, *1968: The Election That Changed America*, 104–128; see Frank Kusch, *Battleground Chicago: The Police and the 1968 Democratic National Convention* (Westport, CT: Greenwood, 2004).

95. Letter, Wright to Rosel H. Hyde, March 7, 1969, Folder "Letter to FCC Following DN Convention," Box 789, Series 2, JWP; letter, Rosel Hyde to Wright, April 11, 1969, Folder "Letter to FCC Following DN Convention," Box 789, Series 2, JWP.

96. Statement Regarding Jim Wright, Hubert Humphrey, August 30, 1968, Folder "Speech Files: Democratic Party Statement Regarding Congressman Jim Wright of Texas," Box 1285, Series 3, JWP.

97. Oral History, Sirgo with Wright, April 10, 1998, 5, Folder "Oral History Interview: Henry B. Sirgo," Box 1213, Series 3, JWP.

98. "The Texas Campaign," undated, Folder "Speech Files: Democratic Party—The Texas Campaign," Box 1285, Series 3, JWP; letter, Wright to Bureau Chief, Associated Press, October 5, 1968, Folder "Campaign, 1968 (National)," Box 789, Series 2, JWP; letter, Wright to W. R. Poage, December 2, 1968, Folder "Humphrey Campaign," Box 789, Series 2, JWP.

99. Interview, Jim Wright, July 12, 2012; quoted in Wright, *Balance*, 150.

100. Earl Black and Merle Black, *The Rise of the Southern Republicans* (Cambridge, MA: Harvard University Press, 2002), 25, 120, 210–211, 222, 225; Michael Schaller and George Rising, *The Republican Ascendancy: American Politics, 1968–2001* (Wheeling, IL: Harlan Davidson, 2002), 35–41, 46; Frank Brown, "Nixon's Southern Strategy and Forces Against Brown," *Journal of Negro Education* 73, no. 1 (Summer 2004): 191–208.

101. Letter, Larry O'Brien to Wright, November 27, 1968, Folder "Humphrey Campaign," Box 789, Series 2, JWP; letter, Hubert Humphrey to Wright, September 23, 1968, Folder "Humphrey Campaign," Box 789, Series 2, JWP.

102. Wright statement, November 6, 1968, Folder "Speech Files: Democratic Party—Statement Following the Election," Box 1285, Series 3, JWP.

CHAPTER 10

1. 1969 Inaugural Address, Public Papers of the Presidents, Richard Nixon, APP, UCSB, www.presidency.ucsb.edu/ws/?pid=1941, accessed July 18, 2013.

2. Tom Wicker, *One of Us: Richard Nixon and the American Dream* (New York: Random House, 1991), 539–541; Joan Hoff, *Nixon Reconsidered* (New York: Basic Books, 1994), 19–20; Conrad Black, *Richard Nixon: A Life in Full* (New York: Public Affairs, 2007), 474–485, 600–625, 643–655, 737–745; Jim Wright, *Balance of Power: Presidents and Congress from the Era of McCarthy to the Age of Gingrich* (Atlanta: Turner, 1996), 152.

3. Jeffrey Kimball, *Nixon's Vietnam War* (Lawrence: University of Kansas Press, 1998), 103–146; quoted in *FWST*, November 4, 1969, 1.

4. Wright, *Balance*, 157.

5. Photocopy, uncited article, October 15, 1969, Folder "Vietnam (1)," Box 1024, Series 2, JWP; interview, Jim Wright, July 13, 2012.

6. "President Nixon Receives Overwhelming Support of Vietnam Policy," *Commanders Digest* 7, no. 10 (December 6, 1969): 1; quoted in Wright, *Balance*, 158, and Stephen Ambrose, *Nixon: The Triumph of a Politician* (New York: Simon and Schuster, 1989), 311; letter, W. P. Mack to Wright, December 12, 1969, Folder "Vietnam Resolution," Box 984, Series 2, JWP.

7. Wright remarks, November 4, 1969, Folder "Vietnam Resolution," Box 984, Series 2, JWP; Wright remarks, November 15, 1969, Folder "Speech Files: Democratic Party—Remarks at State Young Democratic Convention," Box 1285, Series 3, JWP.

8. Questions, House Resolution 613, Folder "Vietnam Resolution," Box 984, Series 2, JWP; letter, Wright to Brock Adams, November 20, 1969, Folder "Vietnam Resolution (2)," Box 984, Series 2, JWP.

9. Bill Lee, "Wright Gives Nixon List of 300 House Backers," *FWST*, November 13, 1969, 1; Wright, *Balance*, 160–161; photocopy, uncited article, "Wright Blasts Mitchell View," November 12, 1969, Folder "Scrapbook," Box 1248, Series 3, JWP.

10. Interview, Jim Wright, July 13, 2012; Wright, *Balance*, 161.

11. *FWST*, December 2, 1969, 2; letter, Wright to Patsy Mink, November 20, 1969, Folder "Vietnam Resolution (2)," Box 989, Series 2, JWP; *FWST*, November 20, 1969, 2; Fact Sheet, Folder "Vietnam Resolution," Box 984, Series 2, JWP; Wright statement, undated, Folder "Vietnam Resolution," Box 984, Series 2, JWP.

12. Wright comments, Resolution 613, Folder "Vietnam (3)," Box 1024, Series 2, JWP.

13. "House Approves Resolution, 333–55," *WP*, 1; photocopy, editorial, *Washington Daily News*, December 4, 1969, Folder "JW Resolution, News Clippings (3), 1969–1970," Box 1151, Series 2, JWP.

14. *FWST*, November 11, 1969, 13; photocopy, uncited editorial, "The House Speaks," December 3, 1969; Folder "JW News Clippings (3), 1969–1970," Box 1151, Series 2, JWP; photocopy, uncited editorial, "A Whole Lot of Nothing," December 4, 1969, Folder "JW News Clippings (3), 1969–1970," Box 1151, Series 2, JWP; letter, Jack Butler to Wright, January 12, 1970, Folder "Wright Personal," Box 370, Series 1, JWP.

15. Letter, Richard Nixon to Wright, November 6, 1969, Folder "Vietnam Resolution (2)," Box 984, Series 2, JWP; letter, Bryce Harlow to Wright, December 26, 1969, Folder "Wright Personal," Box 370, Series 1, JWP; interview, Jim Wright, July 13, 2012.

16. Ambrose, *Nixon: Triumph*, 296.

17. *Sierra Club Bulletin* 54, no. 3 (March 1969): 9; Ross MacDonald and Robert Easton, "Santa Barbarans Cite an Eleventh Commandment," in Amos Hawley, ed., *Man and the Environment* (New York: New York Times Company, 1975), 130–145; J. Brooks Flippen, *Nixon and the Environment* (Albuquerque: University of New Mexico Press, 2000), 50–53; interview, Jim Wright, July 13, 2012.

18. Endangered Species and Conservation Act, P.L. 91–135; Resource Recovery Act, P.L. 91–512; Water Quality Improvement Act, P.L. 91–224; Family Planning and Population Research Act, P.L. 91–572; Clean Air Act Amendments, P.L. 91–604; Flippen, *Nixon and the Environment*, 48, 76, 109–110.

19. Letter, Wright to John McCormack, March 11, 1970, Folder "Wright Personal," Box 370, Series 1, JWP.

20. Wright remarks, April 22, 1970, Folder "Earth Day," Box 957, Series 2, JWP.

21. Letter, Wright to Butch, January 26, 1970, Folder "Wright, Personal, NF," Box 370, Series 1, JWP.

22. Letter, Wright to Bernard Rapoport, March 20, 1970, Folder "Wright Personal," Box 370, Series 1, JWP; Wright remarks, TCU Environmental Seminar, Folder "TCU Seminar on the Environment," Box 957, Series 2, JWP; letter, Charles Hogarth to Wright, May 11, 1970, Folder "Wright Personal," Box 370, Series 1, JWP; Wright remarks, May 8, 1970, Folder "Man's Environment, Man's Choice," Box 957, Series 2, JWP; Wright remarks, American Paper Institute, Folder "Pure Water," Box 957, Series 2, JWP.

23. Burton Abrams, "How Richard Nixon Pressured Arthur Burns: Evidence from the Nixon Tapes," *Journal of Economic Perspectives* 20, no. 4 (Fall 2006): 177–188; letter, Wright to colleague, September 19, 1969, Folder "Interest Rates," Box 1017, Series 2, JWP; letter, Wright to Wright Patman, September 3, 1969, Folder "Interest Rates," Box 797, Series 2, JWP.

24. Wright remarks, June 11, 1969, Folder "Speech Files: Economics—Interest Rates Must Be Rolled Back," Box 1286, Series 3, JWP; letter, Wright to colleague, February 25, 1970, Folder "Interest Rates," Box 1017, Series 3, JWP; letter, Wright to H. C. Alexander, January 12, 1971, Folder "92nd Cong., Appropriations—Banking and Currency, January 1971–July 1971, 1 of 2," Box 377, Series 1, JWP.

25. P.L. 91–172; letter, Wright to C. R. Kelley, September 24, 1969, Folder "Legislative, General," Box 361, Series 1, JWP; letter, Wright to Henry Sonner, November 21, 1969, Folder "Legislative, General," Box 361, Series 1, JWP; letter, Wright to Donna Leito, April 22, 1969, Folder "Legislative, General," Box 361, Series 1, JWP; Wicker, *One of Us*, 566; Jerry Tempalski, "Revenue Effect of Major Tax Bills," US Department of the Treasury, September 2006, www.treasury.gov/resource-center/tax-policy/tax-analysis/Documents/ota81.pdf, accessed July 21, 2013.

26. Ambrose, *Nixon: Triumph*, 288; letter, Wright to Laurence Kirk, February 19, 1969, Folder "Armed Services," Box 361, Series 1, JWP; Raymond Garthoff, "SALT I: An Evaluation," *World Politics* 31, no. 1 (October 1978): 1–25.

27. See Philip Caputo, *13 Seconds: A Look Back at the Kent State Shootings* (New York: Penguin, 2005); quoted in Ambrose, *Nixon: Triumph*, 348; interview, Jim Wright, July 13, 2012.

28. Letter, Wright to Ralph Estes, May 20, 1970, Folder "Wright Personal NF," Box 370, Series 1, JWP; letter, Wright to A. B. Clark, May 25, 1970, Folder "Vietnam (1)," Box 1024, Series 2, JWP.

29. Walter Trattner, *From Poor Law to Welfare State* (New York: Simon and Schuster, 1994), 337–341; George Rejda, "The Family Assistance Plan as a Solution to the Welfare Crisis," *Journal of Risk and Insurance* 38, no. 2 (June 1971): 169–179; Ambrose, *Nixon: Triumph*, 291; letter, Wright to J. E. Stockstill, May 17, 1971, Folder "92nd Cong., Appropriations—General (1971), 2 of 2," Box 377, Series 1, JWP.

30. *Stanley v. Georgia*, 394 U.S. 557 (1969); *WSW*, June 23, 1969, Folder "Speech Files: Crime—Wright Calls for Action on Halting High Jacking," Box 1282, Series 3,

JWP; Ambrose, *Nixon: Triumph*, 393; photocopy, uncited article, June 2, 1969, Folder "Speech Files: Crime—J. W. Seeks Bill to Stop Smut Mailings," Box 1282, JWP.

31. Wright remarks, June 20, 1970, Folder "Speech Files: Economics—Remarks to Nebraska Democratic Convention," Box 1286, Series 3, JWP.

32. Letter, Wright to James Ballard, May 18, 1970, Folder "Wright Personal (3rd Folder)," Box 370, Series 1, JWP.

33. Joe McGinnis, *The Selling of the President, 1968* (New York: Trident, 1969); letter, Wright to Leonard Sanders, March 9, 1970, Folder "Wright Personal," Box 370, Series 1, JWP.

34. Letter, Wright to Jim Quinn, November 6, 1969, Folder "Vietnam Resolution (2)," Box 984, Series 2, JWP.

35. Quoted in Wright, *Balance*, 165; interview, Jim Wright, July 13, 2012.

36. Photocopy, uncited article, March 16, 1969, Folder "Campaign, 1968 (National)," Box 789, Series 2, JWP; letter, Hubert Humphrey to Wright, March 31, 1969, Folder "Campaign, 1968 (National)," Box 789, Series 2, JWP.

37. Letter, George McGovern to Democrats, December 18, 1969, Folder "Party Structure and Delegate Selection," Box 797, Series 2, JWP; letter, Wright to George McGovern, October 8, 1969, Folder "Party Structure and Delegate Selection," Box 797, Series 2, JWP.

38. Interview, Jim Wright, July 13, 2012; Wright, *Balance*, 184; see Carl Albert and Danney Goble, *Little Giant: The Life and Times of Carl Albert* (Norman: University of Oklahoma Press, 1990).

39. Letter, Wright to Larry O'Brien, November 19, 1968, Folder "Speech Files: Democratic Party—JW's Proposal to Larry O'Brien," Box 1285, Series 3, JWP.

40. Letter, Wright to J. R. Saylor, January 19, 1970, Folder "Wright Personal," Box 370, Series 1, JWP; letter, Adlai Stevenson to Wright, March 13, 1970, Folder "Wright Personal," Box 370, Series 1, JWP.

41. Letter, Martin McKneally to colleague, January 26, 1970, Folder "Wright Personal," Box 370, Series 1, JWP; letter, Wright to Martin McKneally, January 27, 1970, Folder "Wright Personal," Box 370, Series 1, JWP.

42. "Wright Wants to Spar with Ellis or Frazier," *FWST*, January 28, 1970, C3; letter, Don Woodward to Wright, January 28, 1970, Folder "Wright Personal," Box 370, Series 1, JWP; letter, Ralph Yarborough to Martin McKneally, January 30, 1970, Folder "Wright Personal NF," Box 370, Series 1, JWP; letter, Keith Kahle to Wright, January 30, 1970, Folder "Wright Personal NF," Box 370, Series 1, JWP.

43. Interview, Jim Wright, July 13, 2012; Wright, *Balance*, 188–189; see Barbara Jordan and Shelby Hearon, *Barbara Jordan: A Self-Portrait* (New York: Doubleday, 1979).

44. Press release, August 5, 1970, Folder "Speech Files: Foreign Affairs—Articles for Australian Trip, August, 1970," Box 1287, Series 3, JWP; *FWST*, August 22, 1970, H8.

45. *WSW*, February 13, 1969, Folder "91st Cong., 1st Leg., Judiciary, February 17, 1969–March 5, 1969," Box 362, Series 1, JWP; photocopy, uncited article, February 11, 1969, Folder "Scrapbook," Box 1248, Series 3, JWP; letter, Wright to A. H. Rowan, February 24, 1969, Folder "91st Cong., 1st Leg., Judiciary, February 17, 1969–March 5, 1969," Box 362, Series 1, JWP.

46. Letter, Wright to Bill Lamb, October 6, 1971, Folder "Wright Personal (1st Folder)," Box 379, Series 1, JWP; interview, Jim Wright, July 13, 2012.

47. Letter, Wright to Hattie Hasie, November 22, 1971, Folder "Wright Personal (1st Folder)," Box 379, Series 1, JWP.

48. Letter, Wright to Ginger Brown, April 28, 1970, Folder "Wright Personal NF," Box 370, Series 1, JWP; letter, Wright to J. T. Rutherford, May 15, 1970, Folder "New Folder NF," Box 370, Series 1, JWP.

49. Letter, Wright to Hattie Hasie, May 11, 1970, Folder "Wright Personal NF," Box 370, JWP; letter, Wright to David Mann, May 11, 1970, Folder "Wright Personal NF," Box 370, JWP; letter, Wright to Butch, April 15, 1970, Folder "Wright Personal NF," Box 370, JWP.

50. Letter, Wright to Ginger Brown, March 20, 1970, Folder "Wright Personal," Box 370, Series 1, JWP; letter, Wright to Al Bourland, April 29, 1971, Folder "Wright Personal (1)," Box 392, Series 1, JWP; letter, Wright to Butch, March 9, 1970, Folder "Wright Personal," Box 370, Series 1, JWP.

51. Letter, Wright to Maurice Laufman, July 2, 1970, Folder "Wright Personal (3)," Box 370, Series 1, JWP; letter, Wright to Lisa Wright, July 17, 1970, Folder "Wright Personal (3)," Box 370, Series 1, JWP.

52. Interview, Betty Lee Wright, February 1, 2013; *DMN*, December 7, 1986, E8; *FWST*, December 9, 1985, Special Section, 7.

53. Quoted in *WP*, June 14, 1987, G8; interview, Jim Wright, July 13, 2012.

54. Quoted in interview, Jim Wright, July 13, 2012.

55. Quoted in *WP*, June 14, 1987, G7.

56. Quoted in *FWST*, October 3, 1973, B1.

57. Quoted in photocopy, uncited article, "Jim and Betty Wright: Independent Politics," November 1984, Folder "Betty Wright," Box 741, Series 2, JWP; *WP*, June 14, 1987, G1.

58. Quoted in *WP*, June 14, 1987, G7.

59. *WP*, June 14, 1987, G8; interview, Jim Wright, July 13, 2012.

60. Letter, Wright to Cermen Sasmore, September 29, 1972, Folder "Wright Personal (2)," Box 392, Series 1, JWP; letter, Wright to Vancil Trammel, August 15, 1972, Folder "Wright Personal (2)," Box 392, Series 1, JWP; quoted in *FWST*, October 3, 1973, B1; interview, Jim Wright, July 13, 2012.

61. Ambrose, *Nixon: Triumph*, 396, 413, 432; Flippen, *Nixon and the Environment*, 132–136; 1971 State of the Union, Public Papers of the Presidents, Richard Nixon, APP, UCSB, www.presidency.ucsb.edu/ws/?pid=3110, accessed July 26, 2013.

62. P.L. 92–512; David Billings, "Revenue Sharing: Impact and Renewal," *State and Local Government Review* 8, no. 1 (January 1976): 14–18; William Link and Arthur Link, *American Epoch*, vol. 2, 7th ed. (New York: McGraw-Hill, 1993), 669–670; interview, Jim Wright, July 13, 2012; Will. Myers, "A Legislative History of Revenue Sharing," *Annals of American Academy of Political and Social Science* 419 (May 1975): 1–11.

63. Ambrose, *Nixon: Triumph*, 158–159, 328; Flippen, *Nixon and the Environment*, 84–86.

64. P.L. 91–375; see John Potter, *The United States Postal Service: An American History, 1775–2002* (Washington, DC: USPS, 2003).

65. Letter, Charles Wilson to colleague, May 28, 1971, Folder "Wright Personal (1)," Box 392, Series 1, JWP; letter, Charles Wilson to Wright, June 1, 1971, Folder "Wright Personal (1)," Box 392, Series 1, JWP; letter, Wright to Charles Wilson, June 7, 1971, Folder "Wright Personal (1)," Box 392, Series 1, JWP; see Winton Blount, *Doing It My Way* (Old Lyme, CT: Greenwich, 1996).

66. Veto of Economic Opportunity Act Amendments, Public Papers of the Presidents, Richard Nixon, APP, UCSB, www.presidency.ucsb.edu/ws/?pid=3251, accessed July 29, 2013; Ambrose, *Nixon: Triumph*, 470.

67. Letter, James Sammons to Wright, September 13, 1971, Folder "92 Cong., Appropriations—Education and Labor (1 of 4)," Box 377, Series 1, JWP; letter, Wright to Robert Mayer, December 8, 1971, Folder "92 Cong., Appropriations—Education and Labor (1 of 4)," Box 377, Series 1, JWP; letter, Wright to James Sammons, December 16, 1971, Folder "92 Cong., Appropriations—Education and Labor (1 of 4)," Box 377, Series 1, JWP.

68. Letter, J. J. Pickle to Wright, May 17, 1971, Folder "Wright Personal (1)," Box 392, Series 1, JWP.

69. P.L. 92–55; Congressional Research Service, *A Legislative History of the Water Pollution Control Act Amendments of 1972* (Washington, DC: US Government Printing Office, 1973), 281–339; Harvey Lieber, *Federalism and Clean Water: The 1972 Water Pollution Control Act* (Lexington, MA: Lexington Books, 1975), 80–82; *BioScience* 22, no. 12 (December 1972): 728; interview, Jim Wright, July 13, 2012.

70. P.L. 93–344; Bruce Hopkins, "Congress Curtails Presidential Impoundment," *American Bar Association Journal* 60, no. 9 (September 1974): 1053–1057; James Pfiffner, *The President, the Budget, and Congress: Impoundment and the 1974 Budget Act* (Boulder: Westview Press, 1979).

71. Letter, Wright to Reagan Legg, July 7, 1971, Folder "Wright Personal (1st Folder)," Box 392, Series 1, JWP; letter, Wright to George Canada, July 22, 1971, Folder "Wright Personal (1)," Box 392, Series 1, JWP.

72. Ambrose, *Nixon: Triumph*, 391.

73. Letter, Wright to Morris Udall, April 26, 1971, Folder "Wright Personal (2)," Box 392, Series 1, JWP.

74. Letter, Wright to Frank Evans, March 22, 1971, Folder "Wright Personal (1)," Box 392, Series 1, JWP; letter, Wright to D. A. Taebel, November 3, 1971, Folder "92nd Cong., Interior and Internal Affairs, 1971, 1 of 3," Box 378, Series 1, JWP; photocopy, uncited article, April 28, 1971, Folder "Scrapbook," Box 1250, Series 3, JWP.

75. P.L. 92–225; John Bibby and Cornelius Cotter, "Presidential Campaigning, Federalism, and the Federal Election Campaign Act," *Publius* 10, no. 1 (Winter 1980): 119–134.

76. Quoted in Miles Hawthorne, "James C. Wright, Jr., Democratic Representative from Texas," *Ralph Nader Congress Project: Citizens Look at Congress* (New York: Grossman, 1972), 15; letter, Patrick Caffery to Wright, June 16, 1971, Folder "Wright Personal (1st Folder)," Box 392, Series 1, JWP; letter, John Blatnik to Wright, January 17, 1972, Folder "Wright Personal (2)," Box 392, Series 1, JWP; letter, Burton Miller to Wright, July 23, 1971, Folder "Wright Personal (1)," Box 392, Series 1, JWP; photocopy, uncited article, June 21, 1971, Folder "Scrapbook," Box 1248, Series 3, JWP.

77. Quoted in photocopy, uncited article, October 5, 1971, Folder "Scrapbook," Box 1248, Series 3, JWP.

78. Federal Environmental Pesticide Control Act, P.L. 92–516; Marine Protection, Research and Sanctuaries Act, P.L. 92–532; Marine Mammal Protection Act, P.L. 92–522; Flippen, *Nixon and the Environment*, 158–188.

79. Letter, Wright to Michael Frome, April 22, 1972, Folder "Wright Personal (2)," Box 392, Series 1, JWP; letter, Michael Frome to Wright, April 12, 1972, Folder "Wright Personal (2)," Box 392, Series 1, JWP.

80. Letter, Wright to Mark Warren, February 17, 1971, Folder "92nd Cong., Appropriations—Supersonic Transport (Feb., '71—Apr., '71)," Box 377, Series 1, JWP; letter, Wright to Kenneth Creaves, March 22, 1971, Folder "92nd Cong., Appropriations—General (1971), 1 of 2," Box 377, Series 1, JWP; letter, Wright to Knut Johansen, March 19, 1971, Folder "92nd Cong., Appropriations—General (1971), 1 of 2," Box 377, Series 1, JWP.

81. Quoted in photocopy, uncited article, "Wright Explains Environmental Act," Folder "Scrapbook," Box 1248, Series 3, JWP; letter, Wright to Edward Fritz, July 26, 1971, Folder "Wright Personal (1st Folder)," Box 392, Series 1, JWP; letter, Edward Fritz to Wright, July 22, 1971, Folder "Wright Personal (1st Folder)," Box 392, Series 1, JWP.

82. Hawthorne, "James C. Wright," 12; quoted in photocopy, uncited article, "Wright Attacks Douglas over Article," Folder "Scrapbook," Box 1248, Series 3, JWP; quoted in *FWST*, March 18, 1972, 3; see Jeffrey Stine, *Mixing the Waters: Environment, Politics, and the Building of the Tennessee-Tombigbee Waterway* (Akron, OH: University of Akron Press, 1993), and Flippen, *Nixon and the Environment*, 58–62.

83. Interview, Jim Wright, July 13, 2013; letter, Wright to Rhonda Lindley, October 2, 1972, Folder "Wright Personal (2)," Box 392, Series 1, JWP.

84. Letter, Wright to Jim Wright, May 5, 1971, Folder "Wright Personal (1)," Box 392, Series 1, JWP; letter, Wright to Jim Wright, May 11, 1971, Folder "Wright Personal (1)," Box 392, Series 1, JWP; *FWST*, April 30, 1971, 10.

85. Quoted in photocopy, uncited article, "Rep. Jim Wright Seeks Bill to Stop 'Smut' Mailings," Folder "Scrapbook," Box 1248, Series 3, JWP.

86. Quoted in photocopy, uncited article, January 27, 1972, Folder "Scrapbook," Box 1248, Series 3, JWP.

87. Photocopy, uncited article, June 19, 1971, Folder "Scrapbook," Box 1248, Series 3, JWP; letter, Wright to Jack Butler, March 9, 1971, Folder "Wright Personal (1st Folder)," Box 379, Series 1, JWP.

88. P.L. 92–218; letter, Wright to Ben Bird, May 5, 1971, Folder "92nd Cong., Judiciary, General, Jan. '71—May '71," Box 378, Series 1, JWP; letter, Wright to Carley Moore, May 3, 1971, Folder "92nd Cong., Judiciary, General, Jan. '71—May '71," Box 378, Series 1, JWP; Jonathan Aitken, *Nixon: A Life* (Washington, DC: Regnery, 1993), 395.

89. Letter, Wright to Frank Thompson, June 25, 1971, Folder "Foreign Affairs, Feb., '71–June, '71," Box 377, Series 1, JWP.

90. Paul McCracken, "Economic Policy in the Nixon Years," *PSQ* 26, no. 4 (Winter 1996): 165–177; Burton Abrams, "How Richard Nixon Pressured Arthur Burns: Evidence

from the Nixon Tapes," *Journal of Economic Perspectives* 20, no. 4 (Fall 2006): 177–188; interview, Jim Wright, July 13, 2012; Wright, *Balance*, 178.

91. *Swann v. Charlotte-Mecklenburg Board of Education*, 402 U.S. 1 (1970); Michael Schaller and George Rising, *Republican Ascendancy: American Politics, 1968–2001* (Wheeling, IL: Harlan Davidson, 2002), 37–38; letter, Gene Cain to Wright, July 15, 1971, Folder "92nd Cong., School Busing (1971) (3 of 10)," Box 379, Series 1, JWP; letter, Don Roach to Wright, July 21, 1971, Folder "92nd Cong., Appropriations—Departments (Supreme Court), Busing, July 21–July 22, 1971," Box 377, Series 1, JWP; letter, Roy Wood to Wright, November 4, 1971, Folder "92nd Cong., School Busing (1971) (9 of 10)," Box 379, Series 1, JWP.

92. Interview, Jim Wright, July 13, 2012; Wright quoted in photocopy, undated article, Folder "Scrapbook," Box 1248, Series 3, JWP.

93. Letter, Wright to D. R. Gaither, September 22, 1971, Folder "92nd Cong., School Busing (1971) (3 of 10)," Box 379, Series 1, JWP; letter, Wright to Edmond Gonzales, November 22, 1971, Folder "92nd Cong., School Busing (1971) (6 of 10)," Box 379, Series 1, JWP; Gareth Davies, "Richard Nixon and the Desegregation of Southern Schools," *Journal of Policy History* 19, no. 4 (October 2007): 367–394; Lawrence McAndrews, "The Politics of Principle: Richard Nixon and School Desegregation," *Journal of Negro History* 83, no. 3 (Summer 1998): 187–200.

94. Form Letter Template, Folder "92nd Cong., School Busing (1971) (1 of 10)," Box 379, Series 1, JWP; letter, Wright to Pat Gunn, July 27, 1971, Folder "92nd Cong., School Busing (1971) (1 of 10)," Box 379, Series 1, JWP.

95. *Engel v. Vitale*, 300 U.S. 412 (1962); *Lemon v. Kurtzman*, 403 U.S. 602 (1971).

96. Kevin McMahon, *Nixon's Court: His Challenge to Judicial Liberalism and Its Political Consequences* (Chicago: University of Chicago Press, 2011), 3; letter, James Dunn to Wright, November 1, 1971, Folder "92nd Cong., Judiciary, Anti-School Prayer (1971)," Box 379, Series 1, JWP.

97. *CR*, 92nd Cong., 1st sess., vol. 117, pt. 30 (November 8, 1971): H39888; letter, D. K. Sullivan to Wright, November 1, 1971, Folder "92nd Cong., Judiciary, Anti-School Prayer (1971)," Box 379, Series 1, JWP; letter, Harold Dahlike to Wright, November 2, 1971, Folder "92nd Cong., Judiciary, Anti-School Prayer (1971)," Box 379, Series 1, JWP; Richard Nixon, *In the Arena: A Memoir of Victory, Defeat, and Renewal* (New York: Simon and Schuster, 1990), 99–100.

98. Quoted in Wright, *Balance*, 181–183; see Chris Tudda, *Cold War Turning Point: Nixon and China, 1969–1972* (Baton Rouge: Louisiana State University Press, 2012).

99. Wright statement, April 21, 1972, Folder "Vietnam (1)," Box 1024, Series 2, JWP; *FWP*, April 22, 1972, 3.

100. Letter, Wright to Olin Teague, April 20, 1972, Folder "Wright Personal (2)," Box 392, Series 1, JWP; letter, Spiro Agnew to Wright, May 4, 1972, Folder "Wright Personal (2)," Box 392, Series 1, JWP; letter, Henry Kissinger to Wright, May 5, 1972, Folder "Wright Personal (2)," Box 392, Series 1, JWP; letter, Richard Nixon to Wright, April 24, 1972, Folder "Wright Personal (2)," Box 392, Series 1, JWP.

101. Letter, Wright to R. B. Bost, March 19, 1971, Folder "92nd Cong., General, Jan.–Dec., 1971," Box 377, Series 1, JWP; letter, Wright to Stan Wilson, July 14, 1971, Folder "Wright Personal (2)," Box 392, Series 1, JWP; letter, Wright to Wade Brower, July 22, 1971, Folder "Wright Personal (2)," Box 392, Series 1, JWP.

102. Wright, *Balance*, 187–188; Colorado River Basin Salinity Control Act, P.L. 93–320; Colorado River Basin Salinity Control Program, Natural Resources Conservation Service, www.nrcs.usda.gov/wps/portal/nrcs/detailfull/national/programs/alphabetical/?cid=stelprdb1044198, accessed August 4, 2013.

103. Jim Wright, *Worth It All* (Washington, DC: Brassey's, 1993), 37–38; see Tanya Harmer, *Allende's Chile and the Inter-American Cold War* (Chapel Hill: University of North Carolina Press, 2011).

104. Letter, Richard Nixon to Wright, August 6, 1971, Folder "Wright Personal (1st Folder)," Box 379, Series 1, JWP; interview, Jim Wright, July 13, 2012.

CHAPTER 11

1. *Haltom City (TX) News-Tribune*, March 31, 1972, 1.

2. Letter, Edmund Muskie to Wright, June 22, 1971, Folder "Wright Personal (1)," Box 392, Series 1, JWP.

3. Letter, Hubert Humphrey to Wright, November 24, 1971, Folder "Wright Personal (1st Folder)," Box 379, Series 1, JWP.

4. *FWST*, January 19, 1971, 1.

5. Letter, Lyndon Johnson to Wright, June 4, 1971, Folder "Wright Personal (1st Folder)," Box 392, Series 1, JWP.

6. Letter, Fred Rooney to Wright, October 17, 1971, Folder "Wright Personal (1st Folder)," Box 379, Series 1, JWP.

7. Letter, Wright to Edmund Muskie, February 2, 1972, Folder "Speech Files: Democratic Party—Remarking on Behalf of Ed Muskie," Box 1285, Series 3, JWP.

8. Wright remarks, Nucleus Club of Arizona, undated, Folder "Speech Files: Democratic Party—Remarking on Behalf of Ed Muskie," Box 1285, Series 3, JWP.

9. Letter, Edmund Muskie to Wright, June 7, 1972, Folder "Wright Personal (2)," Box 392, Series 1, JWP; quoted in uncited article, May 3, 1972, Folder "Scrapbook," Box 1250, Series 3, JWP; Carl Bernstein and Bob Woodward, *All the President's Men* (New York: Simon and Schuster, 1974), 127–129, 136–142.

10. Wright statement, May 2, 1972, Folder "1972 Democratic Election," Box 1150, Series 2, JWP.

11. Wright remarks, May 13, 1972, Folder "Speech Files: Democratic Party—JW's Remarks to TX Senatorial District," Box 1285, Series 3, JWP.

12. Letter, Wright to Glen Lauderdale, May 22, 1972, Folder "Wright Personal (2)," Box 392, Series 1, JWP.

13. Stephen Leshner, *George Wallace: American Populist* (Boston: Da Capo, 1995), 458–486; see Keith Olson, *Watergate: The Presidential Scandal That Shook America* (Lawrence: University of Kansas Press, 2003).

14. See Hunter Thompson, *Fear and Loathing on the Campaign Trail '72* (New York: Warner, 1973), 269–324.

15. Letter, Hubert Humphrey to Wright, July 26, 1972, Folder "Wright Personal (2)," Box 392, Series 1, JWP; letter, Wright to Jimmy Wright, June 8, 1972, Folder "Wright Personal (2)," Box 392, Series 1, JWP.

16. Letter, Wright to Jack Geddie, July 24, 1972, Folder "Wright Personal (2)," Box 392, Series 1, JWP.

17. See George McGovern, *Grassroots: The Autobiography of George McGovern* (New York: Random House, 1977), 214–215; Jim Wright, *Balance of Power: Presidents and Congress from the Era of McCarthy to the Age of Gingrich* (Atlanta: Turner, 1996), 197; Joshua Glasser, *The Eighteen-Day Running Mate: McGovern, Eagleton, and a Campaign in Crisis* (New Haven, CT: Yale University Press, 2012), 165–214.

18. Letter, Sargent Shriver to Wright, September 29, 1972, Folder "Wright Personal (2)," Box 392, Series 1, JWP.

19. Walter Isaacson, *Kissinger: A Biography* (New York: Touchstone, 1992), 459–469; Randolph Campbell, *Gone to Texas: A History of the Lone Star State* (New York: Oxford University Press, 2003), 443.

20. *FWP*, April 1, 1971, 4.

21. Photocopy, uncited article, January 24, 1972, Folder "Scrapbook," Box 1250, Series 3, JWP; Campbell, *Gone to Texas*, 443.

22. Interview, Jim Wright, July 13, 2012; see Bruce Eggler, *The Life and Career of Hale Boggs* (New Orleans: States-Item, 1973).

23. Anthony Champagne, Douglas Harris, James Riddlesperger, Garrison Harris *The Austin-Boston Connection: Five Decades of House Leadership, 1937–1989* (College Station: Texas A&M University Press, 2009), 204, 208–218.

24. Ibid., 182.

25. Quoted in Champagne et al., *Austin-Boston Connection*, 186.

26. Interview, Jim Wright, July 13, 2012.

27. Letter, Tip O'Neill to Wright, October 16, 1972, Folder "Whip (2), 1974," Box 797, Series 2, JWP.

28. Quoted in photocopy, uncited article, May 30, 1972, Folder "Scrapbook," Box 1250, Series 3, JWP.

29. Jim Jones, "Exhibit of Jim Wright's Paintings Set in Azle," *FWST*, February 3, 1973, B8.

30. Notes on Russia, December 28, 1972, Folder "Russia Letters Trip File, Wright's Notes on Russia (December 28, 1972)," Box 1328, Series 3, JWP; Wright, *Balance*, 192–195.

31. Quoted in photocopy, uncited article, "Europe Transit Impresses Wright," Folder "Scrapbook," Box 1250, Series 3, JWP; photocopy, uncited article, Folder "Scrapbook," Box 1250, JWP.

32. *FWP*, May 8, 1973, 14; letter, Wright to Alice Deming, May 31, 1973, Folder "House Administration," Box 441, Series 1, JWP.

33. *WP*, June 14, 1987, G8.

34. Quoted in uncited article, November 12, 1973, Folder "News Clippings, 1972–74," Box 1150, JWP.

35. Stanley Karnow, *Vietnam: A History* (New York: Penguin, 1983), 649–654; Stephen Ambrose, *Nixon: Ruin and Recovery, 1973–1990* (New York: Simon and Schuster, 1991), 38–58.

36. Letter, Richard Nixon to Wright, January 24, 1973, Folder "Peace in Vietnam," Box 1150, Series 2, JWP.

37. Letter, Wright to Shirley Parker, July 25, 1974, Folder "Armed Services," Box 411, Series 1, JWP.

38. Letter, Wright to MTST, February 23, 1973, Folder "Vietnam (1)," Box 1024, Series 2, JWP; *FWP*, February 16, 1975, 2.

39. Wright, *Balance*, 251.

40. Interview, Jim Wright, July 13, 2012.

41. P.L. 93–148; Mariah Zeisberg, *War Powers: The Politics of Constitutional Authority* (Princeton, NJ: Princeton University Press, 2013), 5–7, 168; Louis Fisher, "Foreign Policy Powers of the President and Congress," *Annals of the Academy of Political and Social Science* 488 (September 1985): 148–159.

42. 410 U.S. 113 (1973); Hal Miller, *Abandoned Middle: The Ethics and Politics of Abortion in America* (Salem, MA: Penumbra, 1988), 11–18.

43. J. Brooks Flippen, *Jimmy Carter, the Politics of Family, and the Rise of the Religious Right* (Athens: University of Georgia Press, 2010), 29–60.

44. Rickie Solinger, *Beggars and Choosers: How the Politics of Choice Shapes Adoption, Abortion, and Welfare in the United States* (New York: Hill and Wang, 2001), 11–12; Barbara Hinkson Craig and David O'Brien, *Abortion and American Politics* (Chatham, NJ: Chatham House, 1993), 158; Eric Uslaner and Ronald Weber, "Public Support for Pro-Choice Abortion Policies in the Nation and States: Changes and Stability After the *Roe* and *Doe* Decisions," in Carl Schneider and Maris Vinovskis, eds., *The Law and Politics of Abortion* (Lexington, MA: Heath, 1980), 215–218; Elizabeth Adell Cook, Ted Jelen, and Clyde Wilcox, *Between Two Absolutes: Public Opinion and the Politics of Abortion* (Boulder: Westview Press, 1992), 167.

45. Eva Rubin, *Abortion, Politics, and the Courts:* Roe v. Wade *and Its Aftermath* (Westport CT: Greenwood, 1987), 93–94; Cook et al., *Between Two Absolutes*, 114–117.

46. *CQWR* (May 6, 1972): 674; Craig and O'Brien, *Abortion and American Politics*, 159; Flippen, *Carter*, 64–65.

47. Rubin, *Abortion, Politics, and the Courts*, 155–157; see US Commission on Civil Rights, *Report on the Constitutional Aspects of the Right to Limit Childbearing* (Washington, DC: US Government Printing Office, 1975).

48. Legislative Fact Sheet, March 1977, Folder "Women and Abortion, March, 1977–September, 1977," Box 10, Margaret Costanza Files, OPL, WHSF, JCL; Cynthia Gorney, *Articles of Faith: A Frontline History of the Abortion Wars* (New York: Simon and Schuster, 1998), 348; Flippen, *Carter*, 66.

49. Letter, Wright to Anita Snow, October 24, 1974, unidentified folder, Box 411, Series 1, JWP; Wright Votes, undated, Folder "Abortion," Box 1006, Series 2, JWP; interview, Jim Wright, July 13, 2012.

50. Quoted in *FWST*, April 23, 1973, 10; photocopy, uncited article, "Highways Essential, Wright Tells Officials," Folder "Scrapbook," Box 1251, Series 3, JWP; *FWST*, May 9, 1973, 16.

51. *HC*, May 7, 1973, 9; photocopy, uncited article, "Wright Retains Highway Aid Bill," Folder "Scrapbook," Box 1251, Series 3, JWP; *FWP*, October 5, 1973, 3.

52. P.L. 93–87; quoted in photocopy, uncited article, "Roads Act Author Boosts Proposals as Innovations," Folder "Scrapbook," Box 1251, Series 3, JWP; *DMN*, August 12, 1973, 22.

53. Daniel Yergin, *The Prize: The Epic Quest for Oil, Power and Money* (New York: Simon and Schuster, 1991), 571–574.

54. Ibid.; Rogers Morton, "The Nixon Administration Energy Policy," *Annals of the Academy of Political and Social Sciences* 410 (November 1974): 65–74; photocopy, uncited article, "Wright Cites Lack of Leadership," Folder "Scrapbook," Box 1252, Series 3, JWP.

55. "A National Energy Plan of Action," November 30, 1973, no folder, Box 520, Series 1, JWP; *FWP*, November 30, 1973, 3; photocopy, uncited article, "Energy Trust Fund Proposed," Box 1252, Series 3, JWP.

56. Quoted in *FWST*, December 1, 1973, 1–2; letter, Wright to Hal Risner, July 18, 1973, Folder "Energy," Box 441, Series 1, JWP.

57. *FWP*, September 22, 1974, 3.

58. Quoted in *FWST*, August 28, 1974, 5.

59. Ruth Knowles, *America's Energy Famine* (Norman: University of Oklahoma Press, 1980), 60.

60. P.L. 93–159 and P.L. 93–319; Stanley Kutler, *Wars of Watergate* (New York: Knopf, 1990), 436–437; John Whitaker, *Striking a Balance: Environment and Natural Resources Policy in the Nixon-Ford Years* (Washington, DC: American Enterprise Institute, 1976), 110.

61. Letter, Wright to H. B. Fuqua, April 26, 1974, Folder "General," Box 411, Series 1, JWP; letter, H. B. Fuqua to Wright, April 11, 1974, Folder "General," Box 411, Series 1, JWP.

62. Letter, Wright to Hamilton Rogers, June 1, 1973, Folder "Interior and Insular Affairs," Box 441, Series 1, JWP; letter, Wright to James Byars, February 20, 1974, Folder "Energy," Box 411, Series 1, JWP; letter, Wright to Oliver Pettit, March 12, 1974, Folder "General," Box 411, Series 1, JWP.

63. Quoted in *FWP*, February 13, 1974, 5; and *Mid-Cities Daily News*, February 26, 1974, 7.

64. *FWP*, September 18, 1974, 11.

65. *CR*, 93rd Cong., 2nd sess., vol. 120, pt. 73 (May 23, 1974): H14342; *FWP*, June 1, 1973, 6; *FWST*, June 5, 1973, 4.

66. *DTH*, March 23, 1973, 15.

67. Letter, Wright to Penn Kimble, June 27, 1973, Folder "Coalition for a Democratic Majority," Box 984, Series 2, JWP; Folder "Coalition for a Democratic Majority," Box 984, Series 2, TCU; By-Laws, Folder "United Democrats of Congress," Box 984, Series 2, JWP.

68. Letter, Edmund Muskie to Wright, October 6, 1973, Folder "Speech File: Biography," Box 1280, Series 3, JWP; quoted in *FWP*, October 7, 1973, 27; interview, Jim Wright, July 13, 2012.

69. Transcript, Nixon White House Tapes, March 21, 1973, Presidential Recordings Program, Miller Center, University of Virginia, http://whitehousetapes.net/tran script/nixon/cancer-presidency, accessed October 3, 2013; quoted in *FWST*, August 14, 1974, 7; Wright, *Balance*, 206.

70. Anthony Lukas, *Nightmare: The Underside of the Nixon Years* (New York: Penguin, 1988), 369–396; Wright, *Balance*, 206.

71. Wright, *Balance*, 209; interview, Jim Wright, July 13, 2012.

72. Ambrose, *Nixon: Ruin*, 267–268; Olson, *Watergate*, 154.

73. Quoted in Wright, *Balance*, 221–222.

74. Letter, Wright to Peter Rodino, November 9, 1973, Folder "JW Letter to Judiciary Committee, Re: G. Ford for VP," Box 987, Series 2, JWP.

75. Letter, Wright to Gerald Ford, November 9, 1973, Folder "JW Letter to Judiciary Committee, Re: G. Ford for VP," Box 987, Series 2, JWP; letter, Gerald Ford to Wright, November 12, 1973, Folder "JW Letter to Judiciary Committee, Re: G. Ford for VP," Box 987, Series 2, JWP; letter, Wright to Jack Butler, November 14, 1973, Folder "JW Letter to Judiciary Committee, Re: G. Ford for VP," Box 987, Series 2, JWP.

76. Wright, *Balance*, 213.

77. Ibid., 213–214.

78. Letter, Wright to James Simmons, March 11, 1974, Folder "JW Campaign, General (2)," Box 783, Series 2, JWP; letter, James Simmons to Wright, March 1, 1974, Folder "JW Campaign, General (2)," Box 783, Series 2, JWP.

79. Letter, Charles Stokely to Wright, October 22, 1973, Folder "Impeachment Letters," Box 1195, Series 2, JWP; letter, E. M. Arnold to Wright, October 30, 1973, Folder "Judiciary (2), 1973," Box 1195, Series 2, JWP; letter, Ben Bird to Wright, October 31, 1973, Folder "Judiciary (3), 1973," Box 1195, Series 2, JWP; Questionnaire on Impeachment, undated, Folder "Impeachment," Box 1017, Series 2, JWP.

80. P.L. 93–344; Allen Schick, "The Battle of the Budget," *Proceedings of the American Academy of Political Science* 32, no. 1 (1975): 51–70; Tom Wicker, *One of Us: Richard Nixon and the American Dream* (New York: Random House, 1991), 512; Outline, Budget Committee, Folder "Budget Committee," Box 1151, Series 2, JWP.

81. Letter, Wright to Carl Albert, January 19, 1973, Folder "Whip (2), 1974," Box 797, Series 2, JWP; letter, Wright to Tip O'Neill, January 19, 1973, Folder "Whip (2), 1974," Box 797, Series 2, JWP.

82. Letter, Carl Albert to Editor, *FWP*, September 17, 1974, Folder "Budget Committee," Box 1151, Series 2, JWP.

83. Interview, Jim Wright, July 13, 2012; *DMN*, August 8, 1974, 14.

84. *DMN*, August 8, 1974, 14.

85. Quoted in *FWP*, July 21, 1974, 29.

86. Letter, Wright to Danny McCoy, April 28, 1974, Folder "General," Box 411, Series 1, JWP.

87. Wright, *Balance*, 218; interview, Jim Wright, July 13, 2012.

88. *United States v. Richard M. Nixon*, 418 U.S. 683 (1974); Wright statement, undated, Folder "General," Box 411, Series 1, JWP.

89. Wright statement, August 8, 1974, Folder "General," Box 411, Series 1, JWP.

90. Interview, Jim Wright, July 13, 2012; Wright, *Balance*, 215, 203.

CHAPTER 12

1. Press release, Garvey for Congress, October 7, 1974, Folder "General Election, 1974," Box 783, Series 2, JWP.

2. Garvey statement, September 18, 1974, Folder "Campaign Contributor Prospects," Box 1151, Series 2, JWP.

3. Letter, Wright to Kathi Miller, October 14, 1974, Folder "General Election, 1974," Box 783, Series 2, JWP.

4. Press release, JWAC, October 19, 1974, Folder "General Election, 1974," Box 783, Series 2, JWP.

5. Letter, Wright to friend, September 16, 1974, Folder "General Election, 1974," Box 783, Series 2, JWP; letter, Marshall Lynam to Fred Korth, October 10, 1974, Folder "General Election, 1974," Box 783, Series 2, JWP.

6. Press release, JWAC, November 3, 1974, Folder "General Election, 1974," Box 783, Series 2, JWP; advertisement, Wright Campaign, Folder "General Election, 1974," Box 783, Series 2, JWP.

7. Press release, JWAC, October 1, 1974, Folder "General Election, 1974," Box 783, Series 2, JWP; Wright statement, October 26, 1974, Folder "General Election, 1974," Box 783, Series 2, JWP.

8. Quoted in Jim Wright, *Balance of Power: Presidents and Congress from the Era of McCarthy to the Age of Gingrich* (Atlanta: Turner, 1996), 227–228; interview, Jim Wright, July 13, 2012.

9. Wright statement, October 4, 1974, Folder "General Election, 1974," Box 783, Series 2, JWP.

10. Statement by Robert Schur et al., October 25, 1974, Folder "General Election, 1974," Box 783, Series 2, JWP.

11. Memo, Marshall Lynam to Joe Shosid, July 18, 1974, Folder "Confidential, Garvey," Box 783, Series 2, JWP.

12. Wright statement, October 26, 1974, Folder "General Election, 1974," Box 783, Series 2, JWP.

13. 1974 Election Results, homepage, Office of the Clerk, House of Representatives, http://clerk.house.gov/member_info/electioninfo/1974election.pdf, accessed November 17, 2013; Wright, *Balance*, 230.

14. Jack McLeod, Jane Brown, and Lee Becker, "Watergate and the 1974 Congressional Elections," *Public Opinion Quarterly* 41, no. 2 (Summer 1977): 181–195; Schaller and Rising, *Republican Ascendancy: American Politics, 1968–2001* (Wheeling, IL: Harlan Davidson, 2002), 56–57; Wright, *Balance*, 241; interview, Jim Wright, July 13, 2012.

15. Letter, Wright to Julia Butler Hansen, May 17, 1974, Folder "House Administration," Box 412, Series 1, JWP.

16. Letter, Wright to Kenneth McClure, April 30, 1974, Folder "House Administration," Box 412, Series 1, JWP.

17. Interview, Jim Wright, July 13, 2012.

18. Ibid., Richard Cohen, *Rostenkowski: The Pursuit of Power and the End of the Old Politics* (Chicago: Ivan Dee, 1999), 89.

19. Wright, *Balance*, 240.

20. Letter, Wright to Russell Mauldin, June 7, 1974, Folder "House Administration," Box 412, Series 1, JWP.

21. P.L. 93–443; Election Law History, Federal Election Commission, www.fec.gov/info/appfour.htm, accessed January 20, 2014.

22. Joel Fleishman, "The 1974 Federal Election Campaign Act Amendments,"

Duke Law Journal 1975, no. 4 (September 1975): 851–899; interview, Jim Wright, July 13, 2012.

23. Interview, Jim Wright, July 13, 2012; "Congress Trying to Put Lid on Outside Income Heads for Sharp Debate," *Wall Street Journal*, February 22, 1977, 1; see William Leventrosser, "Financing Presidential Campaigns: The Impact of Reform Campaign Finance Laws on the Democratic Presidential Nomination of 1976," *PSQ* 11, no. 2 (Spring 1981): 280–288; Wright, *Balance*, 278.

24. Elizabeth Ray, *The Washington Fringe Benefit* (New York: Dell, 1976).

25. Letter, Wright to C. H. Linton, January 9, 1976, Folder "94th Congress, General (1976) (7 of 11)," Box 456, Series 1, JWP; letter, Wright to Wynona Thompson, June 7, 1976, Folder "94th Congress, General (1976) (7 of 11)," Box 456, Series 1, JWP; Wright radio broadcast, March 25, 1975, Folder "94th Congress, General (1976) (7 of 11)," Box 456, Series 1, JWP.

26. Wright diary, January 3, 1976.

27. P.L. 93–579; James Beverage, "The Privacy Act Amendments of 1974: An Overview," *Duke Law Journal* 1976, no. 2 (May 1976): 301–329; letter, Wright to Linda Blackburn, December 16, 1974, Folder "Government Operations," Box 412, Series 1, JWP.

28. Letter, Wright to E. L. Lancaster, June 26, 1974, Folder "House Administration," Box 412, Series 1, JWP.

29. Letter, William Timmons to Wright, November 7, 1974, Folder "Outgoing Correspondence by Name—Wright, Jim," Box 72, WHCMF, GRFL; letter, William Timmons to Wright, November 21, 1974, Folder "Outgoing Correspondence by Name—Wright, Jim," Box 72, WHCMF, GRFL; letter, William Timmons to Wright, September 12, 1974, Folder "Outgoing Correspondence by Name—Wright, Jim," Box 72, WHCMF, GRFL.

30. Mark Rozell, "President Ford's Pardon of Richard Nixon: Constitutional and Political Considerations," *PSQ* 24, no. 1 (Winter 1991): 121–137; see Barry Werth, *31 Days: Gerald Ford, The Nixon Pardon, and a Government in Crisis* (New York: Doubleday, 2006); *FWP*, September 9, 1974, 3; letter, Wright to Newell Baugh, October 8, 1974, Folder "Appropriations," Box 411, Series 1, JWP; letter, Nancy Lenihan to Earl Huckabee, October 22, 1974, Folder "Appropriations," Box 411, JWP.

31. Letter, Wright to Elmer Drier, October 8, 1974, Folder "General," Box 411, Series 1, JWP.

32. Yanek Mieczkowski, *Gerald Ford and the Challenges of the 1970s* (Lexington: University of Kentucky Press, 2005), 99–108, 113–114, 133–137.

33. Letter, Wright to colleague, January 30, 1975, Folder "Energy Conservation," Box 797, Series 2, JWP.

34. Wright speech, "To Revive the Economy," January 1975, Folder "Speech Files: Economics—To Revive the Economy Speech, January 13, 1975," Box 1286, Series 3, JWP.

35. Letter, Wright to Gerald Ford, October 1, 1974, Folder "General Election, 1974," Box 783, Series 2, JWP; Wright statement, February 4, 1975, Folder "Speech Files: Economics—Remarks to Subcommittee on Domestic Monetary Policy," Box 1286, Series 3, JWP.

36. Letter, Wright to Lewis Happer, January 12, 1976, Folder "94th Congress Budget (1976)," Box 457, Series 1, JWP.

37. Quoted in "Fair Energy Plan Sought," *DMN*, February 23, 1975, 14; *Wichita-Falls Times*, March 11, 1975, 9.

38. *FWST*, April 17, 1975, 7.

39. *FWST*, May 29, 1975, 12.

40. P.L. 94–163; Bruce Beaubouef, *The Strategic Petroleum Reserve: U.S. Energy Security and Oil Politics, 1975–2005* (College Station: Texas A&M University Press, 2007), 1, 7, 37; Robert Rogers, "The Effects of the Energy Policy and Conservation Act Regulation on Petroleum Product Prices, 1976–1981," *Energy Journal* 24, no. 2 (2003): 63–93.

41. Quoted in photocopy, uncited article, "Pollution Control Bill Left to Die in Congress," October 11, 1976, Folder "1976 News Clippings," Box 1151, Series 2, JWP.

42. George Moss, *Moving On: The American People Since 1945*, 3rd ed. (Upper Saddle River, NJ: Prentice Hall, 2005), 244.

43. Wright remarks, September 27, 1976, Folder "Sign It, Mr. President," Box 960, Series 2, JWP; Wright broadcast, April 20, 1976, Folder "Speech for Agriculture—Great Farm Pond Caper," Box 1280, Series 3, JWP.

44. Wright broadcast, April 13, 1976, Folder "Speech Files: Budget—Jobs, the Key to a Balanced Budget," Box 1282, Series 3, JWP.

45. Wright statement, March 23, 1976, Folder "Budget: Apparent Factual Misstatements in President's Budget," Box 1281, Series 3, JWP.

46. *WSW*, August 10, 1975, Folder "Foreign Affairs—Limits of Partnership," Box 1287, Series 3, JWP.

47. Wright broadcast, May 9, 1975, Folder "Vietnam (1)," Box 1024, Series 2, JWP.

48. Wright statement, May 13, 1975, Folder "Vietnam (1)," Box 2, JWP, TCU; see Rowan Roy, *Four Days of Mayaquez* (New York: Norton, 1975).

49. See Vassili Fouskas, "Uncomfortable Questions: Cyprus, October, 1973–August, 1974," *Contemporary European History* 14, no. 1 (February 2005): 45–63; Brendan O'Malley, *The Cyprus Conspiracy: America, Espionage and the Turkish Invasion* (New York: Tauris, 1990), 207–208, 214, 226–227; Wright, *Balance*, 258.

50. Wright statement, "The President's Pork Barrel—for Export Only," undated, Folder "Speech Files: Foreign Affairs—President's Pork Barrel—for Export Only, June, 1976," Box 1287, Series 3, JWP.

51. Wright speech, December 1975, Folder "Speech Files: Defense—Role of Congress in Formation of National Security," Box 1284, Series 3, JWP; interview, Jim Wright, July 13, 2012.

52. P.L. 95–223; Wright, *Balance*, 255–256; interview, Jim Wright, July 13, 2012.

53. *Sherman Democrat*, August 1, 1975, 3.

54. "Koreagate on Capitol Hill?" *Time* 108, no. 24 (December 13, 1976): 18; see Robert Boettcher, *Gifts of Deceit: Sun Myung Moon, Tongsun Park, and the Korean Scandal* (New York: Holt, Rinehart and Winston, 1980); Anthony Champagne, Douglas Harris, James Riddlesperger, and Garrison Nelson, *The Austin-Boston Connection: Five Decades of House Leadership, 1937–1989* (College Station: Texas A&M University Press, 2009), 186–187.

55. Seymour Lachman and Robert Polner, *The Man Who Saved New York: Hugh Carey and the Fiscal Crisis of 1975* (Albany: State University of New York Press, 2011), 109–112, 151–160.

56. Quoted in Wright, *Balance*, 248.

57. Quoted in ibid., 249.

58. Letter, Wright to R. R. Cheatham, November 14, 1975, Folder "General Banking and Currency, Aid to NYC (1 of 2)," Box 442, Series 1, JWP.

59. Letter template, November 6, 1975, Folder "General Banking and Currency, Aid to NYC (1 of 2)," Box 442, Series 1, JWP.

60. Letter, Wright to James Williams, November 21, 1975, Folder "General Banking and Currency, Aid to NYC (1 of 2)," Box 442, Series 1, JWP.

61. Wright address, June 8, 1978, Folder "NYC, Fiscal Assistance," Box 1019, Series 2, JWP.

62. Letter, Wright to R. C. Hollemon, August 31, 1976, Folder "94th Congress, Appropriation (3 of 3)," Box 456, Series 1, JWP; Abortion Votes, undated, Folder "Abortion," Box 1006, Series 2, JWP; letter, Wright to Hugh Rogers, May 14, 1976, Folder "94th Congress, General (1976) (11 of 11)," Box 456, Series 1, JWP; *DMN*, September 24, 1975, C6; *WSW*, September 26, 1975, Folder "Wright Voting Record," Box 993, Series 2, JWP.

63. Quoted in photocopy, uncited article, "Airline Chief Says Wright Worked Miracle," Folder "News Clippings, 1972–1980," Box 1054, Series 2, JWP; *FWST*, April 4, 1976, B1.

64. Wright broadcast, March 16, 1976, Folder "Speech Files: Aviation—Let's Keep America's Airlines Healthy," Box 1280, Series 3, JWP; Wright speech, April 12, 1976, Folder "Speech Files: Aviation—A Fresh Look at the Challenges of Aviation," Box 1280, Series 3, JWP.

65. "The Legislative Scene: A Fresh Approach," *Flight Local and Air Transport Yearbook* (June 1976): 36–37; *FWST*, April 4, 1976, B1.

66. J'Nell Pate, *North of the River: A Brief History of North Fort Worth* (Fort Worth: Texas Christian University Press, 1994), 153–157; History, Fort Worth Stockyards Historic District, www.fortworthstockyards.org, accessed January 8, 2014; interview, Jim Wright, July 13, 2012.

67. Photocopy, uncited article, Folder "News Clippings, 1972–1980," Box 1054, Series 2, JWP.

68. Photocopy, uncited article, Folder "Scrapbook, 1976," Box 1253, Series 3, JWP; *FWST*, June 3, 1975, C4.

69. Quoted in *WP*, June 14, 1987, G7.

70. Quoted in photocopy, uncited article, Folder "Biographical Materials, Clippings, 2 of 3," Box 1201, Series 3, JWP.

71. Quoted in Champagne et al., *Austin-Boston Connection*, 225.

72. Quoted in photocopy, uncited article, "New House Leader? Missouri's Richard Bolling, Bread and Butter Liberal, Looks Like a Winner," November 1976, Folder "Majority Leader, 1976–1977," Box 993, Series 2, JWP.

73. Quoted in *FWST*, March 10, 1974, C6.

74. Quoted in *DMN*, July 20, 1976, 4.

75. Marshall Lynam, *Stories I Never Told the Speaker: The Chaotic Adventures of a Capitol Hill Aide* (Dallas: Three Forks, 1998), 150–171; John Barry, *Ambition and Power: A True Story of Washington* (New York: Penguin, 1990), 15.

76. Quoted in "Is Jim the Wright Man?" *RC* 21, no. 42 (May 27, 1976): 1.

77. *HP*, June 15, 1976, 4; photocopy, uncited article, June 11, 1976, Folder "1976 Scrapbook," Box 1253, Series 3, JWP.

78. Barry, *Ambition*, 21–22.

79. Quoted in Cohen, *Rostenkowski*, 97.

80. Quoted in Champagne et al., *Austin-Boston Connection*, 231.

81. Quoted in Barry, *Ambition*, 57.

82. Quoted in *Washington Star*, December 12, 1976, 8.

83. Letter template, JWAC, June 2, 1976, Folder "Wright Appreciation Committee, 1976 Reception," Box 519, Series 1, JWP.

84. Bruce Oppenheimer and Robert Peabody, "How the Race for Majority Leader Was Won," *Washington Monthly* 9 (November 1977): 46–56.

85. Letter, Wright to Joe Shosid, August 27, 1976, Folder "Pollution," Box 1150, Series 2, JWP; Wright remarks, September 17, 1976, Folder "Speech Files: Democratic Party—Remarks at State Convention," Box 1285, Series 3, JWP.

86. Letter, Wright to friend, October 25, 1976, Folder "Pollution," Box 1150, Series 2, JWP; Wright, *Balance*, 265.

87. Letter, Wright to Jeff Isbell, November 1, 1976, Folder "94th Congress, General (1976) (1 of 11)," Box 456, Series 1, JWP.

88. Myron Struck, "Wright Entry Heats Up Majority Leader's Race," *RC* 22, no. 3 (August 5, 1976): 1; quoted in Champagne et al., *Austin-Boston Connection*, 234.

89. Quoted in Barry, *Ambition*, 23–24.

90. Ibid., 24; letter, Wright to Arthur Temple, August 23, 1986, Folder "MCC Contributors, 1976, Pre-MCC (?)," Box 519, Series 1, JWP.

91. *FWST*, August 1, 1976, G8; Champagne et al., *Austin-Boston Connection*, 235; interview, Jim Wright, July 13, 2012.

92. *WP*, November 22, 1976, 8.

93. Barry, *Ambition*, 25–26.

94. Letter, Dan Rostenkowski to colleagues, November 17, 1976, Folder "Majority Leader, 1976–1977," Box 993, Series 2, JWP.

95. Quoted in Barry, *Ambition*, 26; Champagne et al., *Austin-Boston Connection*, 238–239.

96. Betty Glad, *Jimmy Carter: In Search of the Great White House* (New York: Norton, 1980), 400–405; interview, Jim Wright, July 13, 2012.

97. Oppenheimer and Peabody, "How the Race for Majority Leader Was Won," 54; Champagne et al., *Austin-Boston Connection*, 235; Barry, *Ambition*, 27.

98. *Wall Street Journal*, November 19, 1976, 4; Wright, *Balance*, 265–266; Champagne et al., *Austin-Boston Connection*, 241–242; Barry, *Ambition*, 28–29; interview, Jim Wright, July 13, 2012.

99. "After the Walkover, a Squeaker," *Time* 108, no. 25 (December 20, 1976): 20–21; quoted in Oppenheimer and Peabody, "How the Race for Majority Leader Was Won," 55.

100. Oppenheimer and Peabody, "How the Race for Majority Leader Was Won," 56; Cohen, *Rostenkowski*, 98.

101. *WP*, December 7, 1976, 1; Wright, *Balance*, 266; quoted in Barry, *Ambition*, 29.

CHAPTER 13

1. Photocopy, column, Rowland Evans and Robert Novak, "The Wright Consequences," December 1976, Folder "Majority Leader, 1976–77," Box 993, Series 2, JWP.

2. *WP*, December 10, 1976, 28; *FWST*, December 8, 1976, 7.

3. *DMN*, December 8, 1976, 11; letter, Harry Hopkins to Wright, December 13, 1976, no folder, Box 486, Series 1, JWP; letter, J. B. Witherspoon to Wright, December 8, 1976, no folder, Box 486, Series 1, JWP.

4. *WP*, December 14, 1976, 2.

5. *DMN*, January 27, 1977, B10; *Washington Star*, January 30, 1977, C12; photocopy, uncited article, Folder "Ethics Investigation," Box 743, Series 2, JWP; photocopy, uncited article, July 18, 1977, Folder "October, 1977," Box 703, Series 2, JWP.

6. *WP*, December 14, 1976, 2.

7. Press release, February 21, 1977, Folder "Betty Wright—Retirement from House Public Works," Box 960, Series 2, JWP; Betty Wright speech, August 9, 1977, Folder "Betty Wright Speeches," Box 707, Series 2, JWP.

8. Quoted in *FWST*, January 27, 1977, B1.

9. Telegram, Wright to Philip Lacovara, July 19, 1977, Folder "Korea Probe," Box 812, Series 2, JWP; Telegram, Philip Lacovara to Wright, July 20, 1977, Folder "Telegram Exonerating Wright in Investigation," Box 998, Series 2, JWP; *Washington Star*, July 22, 1977, 6.

10. Wright statement, July 18, 1977, Folder "Korea Probe," Box 812, Series 2, JWP; *DMN*, July 18, 1977, 1; *HP*, July 24, 1977, 4; *Abilene Reporter News*, July 19, 1977, 2; Jim Wright, *Balance of Power: Presidents and Congress from the Era of McCarthy to the Age of Gingrich* (Atlanta: Turner, 1996), 277.

11. Interview, Jim Wright, July 14, 2012; photocopy, uncited article, July 19, 1977, Folder "October, 1977," Box 703, Series 2, JWP; photocopy, uncited article, July 21, 1977, Folder "October, 1977," Box 703, Series 3, JWP; *San Angelo Standard*, July 22, 1977, 1.

12. "The Protégé and the Victim: A Brutal Tale Resurfaces and Shakes the Capitol," *Newsweek* (May 15, 1989): 38; "Wright's Aide: Too Little, Too Late," *Newsweek* (May 22, 1989): 41; *DMN*, August 2, 1987, 10.

13. US Department of Commerce, Bureau of the Census, Current Population Reports, Series P-60, no. 109, January 1978, http://www2.census.gov/prod2/popscan/p60–109.pdf, accessed February 3, 2013; John Barry, *Ambition and Power: A True Story of Washington* (New York: Penguin, 1990), 230.

14. Barry, *Ambition*, 225–229.

15. Interview, Jim Wright, July 14, 2012.

16. Kenneth Morris, *Jimmy Carter, American Moralist* (Athens: University of Georgia Press, 1996), 7; Jimmy Carter, *Keeping Faith: The Memoirs of a President* (New York: Bantam, 1982), 68.

17. James Patterson, "Jimmy Carter and Welfare Reform," in Gary Fink and Hugh Graham, eds., *The Carter Presidency: Policy Choices in the Post–New Deal Era* (Lawrence: University of Kansas Press, 1998), 123; Betty Glad, *Jimmy Carter: In Search of the Great White House* (New York: Norton, 1980), 417–418; quoted in Morris, *Carter*, 243–244.

18. Wright, *Balance*, 267.

19. Ibid., 268–269; interview, Jim Wright, July 14, 2012.

20. Interview, Jim Wright, July 14, 2012.

21. Glad, *Carter: In Search*, 417; quoted in Anthony Champagne, Douglas Harris, James Riddlesperger, and Garrison Nelson, *The Austin-Boston Connection: Five Decades of House Leadership, 1937–1989* (College Station: Texas A&M University Press, 2009), 248.

22. Wright speech, "The Responsibilities of the Majority Leader as I View Them," Folder "JW Majority Leader and FW Congressman," Box 993, Series 2, JWP.

23. Quoted in *FWST*, December 9, 1986, Special Section, 7.

24. Quoted in *DMN*, December 7, 1986, E8.

25. *Wall Street Journal*, July 27, 1981, 1; quoted in Barry, *Ambition*, 31.

26. Quoted in *Wichita-Falls Record News*, December 8, 1976, 1.

27. John Jacobs, *A Rage for Justice: The Passion and Politics of Phillip Burton* (Berkeley: University of California Press, 1995), 323–324.

28. Press release, December 10, 1976, Folder "Majority Leader, 1976–77," Box 993, Series 2, JWP; Richard Cohen, *Rostenkowski: The Pursuit of Power and the End of the Old Politics* (Chicago: Ivan Dee, 1999), 98.

29. Wright speech, January 27, 1977, Folder "National Prayer Breakfast Speech, January 27, 1977," Box 707, Series 2, JWP; quoted in Wright, *Balance*, 271.

30. Interview, Jim Wright, July 14, 2012; Wright, *Balance*, 272.

31. Wright, *Balance*, 279.

32. Wright remarks, January 14, 1977, Folder "Congress, General," Box 708, Series 2, JWP.

33. Whip Advisory Number 18, February 17, 1977, Folder "Ethics," Box 719, Series 2, JWP; Whip Advisory Number 23, February 22, 1977, Folder "Ethics," Box 719, Series 2, JWP; Wright remarks, March 2, 1977, Folder "Ethics," Box 719, Series 2, JWP.

34. Letter, Richard Preyer to colleagues, July 29, 1977, Folder "Ethics Committee," Box 693, Series 2, JWP; letter, Wright to Stephen Crockett, April 20, 1977, Folder "Ethics," Box 473, Series 1, JWP; photocopy, uncited article, September 22, 1977, Folder "Congressional Reforms," Box 943, Series 2, JWP; letter, Walter Mondale to Wright, March 17, 1977, Folder "Letter for the President," Box 726, Series 2, JWP; Wright, *Balance*, 277–278; Cohen, *Rostenkowski*, 101–102; interview, Jim Wright, July 14, 2012.

35. Letter, Wright to High Spitzer, March 14, 1978, Folder "House Administration," Box 524, Series 1, JWP.

36. Wright statement, March 21, 1977, Folder "Campaign Financing," Box 708, Series 2, JWP.

37. P.L. 95–521.

38. Memorandum for the Record, April 12, 1977, Folder "Jim Wright, TX," Box 273, James Free Files, CLF, SOF, JCL.

39. Letter, Wright to James Schlesinger, April 12, 1977, Folder "White House General," Box 1045, Series 2, JWP; letter, Wright to Jimmy Carter, March 28, 1977, Folder "Letters to the President," Box 1045, Series 2, JWP.

40. Letter, Wright to Jimmy Carter, March 29, 1977, James Free Files, CLF, SOF, JCL; letter, Jimmy Carter to Wright, March 30, 1977, James Free Files, CLF, SOF, JCL.

41. Letter, Wright to Jimmy Carter, April 18, 1977, Folder "Letters to the President," Box 1045, Series 2, JWP.

42. National Energy Plan Address, April 20, 1977, Public Papers of the Presidents, Jimmy Carter, APP, UCSB, www.presidency.ucsb.edu/ws/index.php?pid=7372&st=energy&st1, accessed February 27, 2014; John Barrow, "The Age of Limits: Jimmy Carter and the Quest for a National Energy Policy," in Fink and Graham, eds., *Carter Presidency*, 162–166.

43. Wright Actions, Independent Petroleum, 1977–1978, Folder "Energy," Box 693, Series 2, JWP; letter, Wright to John Palmer, June 23, 1977, Folder "Energy (1st Folder)," Box 491, Series 1, JWP.

44. Quoted in Minutes, DSPC, July 26, 1977, Folder "Democratic Steering and Policy Committee," Box 718, Series 2, JWP; Wright remarks, March 16, 1977, Folder "Energy," Box 709, Series 2, JWP.

45. Wright statement, August 8, 1977, Folder "Energy, 1977 (2)," Box 1012, Series 2, JWP; Barrow, "Age of Limits," 166–167; letter, Tip O'Neill and Wright to colleagues, October 13, 1978, Folder "Dear Colleague Letters, 1977–1978," Box 715, Series 2, JWP.

46. *WSW*, July 7, 1978, Folder "Wright Voting Record," Box 993, Series 2, JWP; Wright, *Balance*, 317.

47. Quoted in photocopy, uncited article, "Energy Bill Efforts Praised by FW Oilmen," October 20, 1978, Folder "Energy, 1977 (2)," Box 1012, Series 2, JWP; letter, Preston Geren to Wright, January 23, 1978, no folder, Box 486, Series 1, JWP; letter, Burford King to Wright, November 10, 1978, no folder, Box 486, Series 1, JWP.

48. Wright statement, "Texas Congressmen Make Improvements in the Energy Bill," undated, Folder "Energy, 1977 (2)," Box 1012, Series 2, JWP.

49. Memo, Frank Moore to Jimmy Carter, June 24, 1977, Folder "6/24/77 (1)," Box 27, SSF, PF, JCL.

50. Notes, Democratic Leadership, February 8, 1977, Folder "White House Briefings," Box 1045, Series 2, JWP; Carter, *Keeping Faith*, 69–71; letter, Jimmy Carter to Wright, November 8, 1977, Folder "Letters for President Carter," Box 1045, Series 2, JWP; interview, Jim Wright, July 14, 2012.

51. P.L. 95–91; David Bardin, "The Role of the New Department of Energy," *National Resources Lawyer* 10, no. 4 (1978): 633–638.

52. Interview, Jim Wright, July 14, 2012.

53. Letter, Wright to Jesse Brown, June 23, 1977, Folder "Budget," Box 473, Series 1, JWP.

54. Bruce Schulman, "Slouching Toward the Supply Side," in Fink and Graham, eds., *Carter Presidency*, 54–55; letter, Wright to colleagues, September 14, 1977, Folder "Dear Colleague Letters, 1977–78," Box 715, Series 2, JWP.

55. Quoted in William Leuchtenburg, "Jimmy Carter and the Post–New Deal Presidency," in Fink and Graham, eds., *Carter Presidency*, 13.

56. Letter, Wright to George Thompson, June 20, 1978, no folder, Box 530, Series 1, JWP; letter, Ross Wilson to Wright, March 17, 1978, Folder "Agriculture," Box 718, Series 2, JWP; letter, Dolph Briscoe to Wright, April 10, 1978, Folder "Agriculture," Box 524, Series 1, JWP.

57. Letter, Wright to Melvin Price, June 6, 1977, Folder "Defense," Box 718, Series 2, JWP; letter, Wright to colleagues, September 26, 1977, Folder "Dear Colleague Letters, 1977–78," Box 715, Series 2, JWP; Wright remarks, July 6, 1977, Folder "Speech Files: Defense—A Time for Tough Decisions," Box 1284, Series 3, JWP; Wright statement, June 30, 1977, Folder "Speech Files: Defense—Comments on B-1," Box 1284, Series 3, JWP.

58. Wright statement, March 28, 1977, Folder "Water Projects," Box 722, Series 2, JWP.

59. Memo, Frank Moore to Jimmy Carter, September 21, 1978, James Free Files, CLF, SOF, JCL.

60. Wright remarks, October 5, 1978, Folder "Vetoes," Box 1024, Series 2, JWP.

61. *Washington Star*, April 1, 1977, 11.

62. Photocopy, *Boston Globe* editorial, September 9, 1978, Folder "Appropriations," Box 524, Series 1, JWP; photocopy, *WP* editorial, October 2, 1978, Folder "Appropriations," Box 524, Series 1, JWP; photocopy, *Idaho Statesman* editorial, September 10, 1978, Folder "Appropriations," Box 524, Series 1, JWP; letter, Wright to colleagues, October 4, 1978, Folder "Appropriations," Box 524, Series 1, JWP.

63. Letter, Wright to Jimmy Carter, June 14, 1978, Folder "Letters to President Carter," Box 1045, Series 2, JWP; letter, Jimmy Carter to Wright, June 14, 1978, Folder "Letters from President Carter," Box 1045, Series 2, JWP.

64. Carter, *Keeping Faith*, 156; Noel Maurer and Carlos Yu, *The Big Ditch: How America Took, Built, Ran, and Ultimately Gave Away the Panama Canal* (Princeton, NJ: Princeton University Press, 2010), 264–312; see Douglas Brinkley, *The Unfinished Presidency: Jimmy Carter's Quest for Global Peace* (New York: Penguin, 1998).

65. Ted Smith and Michael Hoegh, "Public Opinion and the Panama Canal Treaties," *Public Opinion Quarterly* 51, no. 1 (Spring 1987): 5–30; R. M. Koster, *In the Time of Tyrants: Panama, 1968–1990* (New York: Norton, 1990), 118–235; Charles Bartlett, "Panama and Selfish Lapses," *Washington Star*, August 1, 1978, 14.

66. Koster, *Time of Tyrants*, 70–71.

67. *HC*, November 17, 1977, 5; Carter, *Keeping Faith*, 159; letter, W. B. Hallmark to Wright, July 27, 1977, Folder "General," Box 524, Series 1, JWP.

68. Interview, Jim Wright, July 14, 2012.

69. Letter, Jimmy Carter to Wright, September 19, 1977, Folder "Letters from President Carter," Box 1045, Series 2, JWP.

70. Telegram, Wright to Jimmy Carter, August 8, 1977, Folder "Letters to the President," Box 1045, Series 2, JWP; Memorandum for the Record, July 1, 1977, Folder "Panama Canal," Box 720, JWP.

71. Letter, Wright to colleagues, August 17, 1977, Folder "International Relations," Box 518, Series 1, JWP.

72. Photocopy, *WP* column, John Wayne, October 25, 1977, Folder "Panama Canal (2)," Box 1019, Series 2, JWP.

73. Letter, Wright to Jimmy Lakas, April 28, 1978, Folder "Panama Canal," Box 720, Series 2, JWP; Carter, *Keeping Faith*, 178–179.

74. Letter, Omar Torrijos to Wright, May 31, 1978, Folder "Panama Canal," Box 720, Series 2, JWP.

75. Letter, Carl Levin to Wright, September 28, 1979, Folder "Senator Correspondence," Box 724, Series 2, JWP.

76. Letter, Zbigniew Brzezinski to Wright, September 27, 1979, Folder "Panama Canal," Box 720, Series 2, JWP.

77. David Skidmore, "Foreign Policy Interest Groups and Presidential Power: Jimmy Carter and the Battle over Ratification of the Panama Canal Treaties," *PSQ* 23, no. 3 (Summer 1993): 477–497; letter, David Jones to Wright, September 27, 1979, Folder "Panama Canal," Box 720, Series 2, JWP.

78. Adam Clymer, *Drawing a Line at the Big Ditch: The Panama Canal Treaties and the Rise of the Right* (Lawrence: University of Kansas Press, 2008), 40–52; letter, E. B. Morgan to Wright, March 16, 1979, Folder "General," Box 526, Series 1, JWP.

79. Koster, *Time of Tyrants*, 145–149, 189–190, 232, 235–239.

80. Mohamed Kamel, *The Camp David Accords* (New York: Routledge, 1986), 8–61; letter, Sabah Kabbani to Wright, June 17, 1977, Folder "World Affairs," Box 523, Series 1, JWP; letter, Wright to Sabah Kabbani, July 12, 1977, Folder "World Affairs," Box 523, Series 1, JWP.

81. Interview, Jim Wright, July 14, 2012; Wright, *Balance*, 298.

82. Interview, Jim Wright, July 14, 2012.

83. Ibid.; quoted in Wright speech, November 16, 1977, Folder "Speech Files: Foreign Affairs—Anwar Sadat Before Congressional Panel," Box 1287, Series 3, JWP.

84. Wright speech, November 19, 1977, Folder "Speech Files: Foreign Affairs—Remarks on the Problems of the Border," Box 1287, Series 3, JWP.

85. Ibid.; quoted in Jim Wright, "Dispatch from Jerusalem," November 22, 1977, Folder "Speech Files: Foreign Affairs—Remarks on the Problems of the Border," Box 1287, Series 3, JWP.

86. Interview, Jim Wright, July 14, 2012; Wright remarks, June 20, 1978, Folder "Speech Files: Foreign Affairs—Remarks for Egyptian Delegation," Box 1287, Series 3, JWP.

87. White House Briefing, March 26, 1978, Folder "White House Briefing," Box 1045, Series 2, JWP; "The Lion and the Lamb," *Newsweek* 91, no. 8 (February 20, 1978): 35.

88. Letter, Louis Lechenger to Wright, February 20, 1978, Folder "World Affairs," Box 523, Series 1, JWP.

89. Press release, May 7, 1978, Folder "Speech Files: Democratic Party—Democrats Blast Saudi Arms Sale," Box 1285, Series 3, JWP; press release, May 8, 1978, Folder "Speech Files: Democratic Party—Democrats Blast Saudi Arms Sale," Box 1285, Series 3, JWP.

90. Wright statement, August 8, 1978, Folder "Letters to President Carter," Box 1042, Series 2, JWP.

91. Press release, August 31, 1978, Folder "Speech Files: Foreign Affairs—The Chance for Peace in the Middle East," Box 1288, Series 3, JWP.

92. Quoted in transcript, *Face the Nation*, September 10, 1978, Folder "Energy," Box 709, Series 2, JWP; William Quandt, "Camp David and Peacemaking in the Middle East," *PSQ* 101, no. 3 (1986): 357–377.

93. White House Briefing, March 4, 1979, Folder "White House Briefings," Box 1045, Series 2, JWP; interview, Jim Wright, July 14, 2012.

94. Letter, Wright to colleagues, May 23, 1977, Folder "Dear Colleague Letters, 1977–78," Box 715, Series 2, JWP; letter, Wright to colleagues, October 31, 1977, Folder "Dear Colleague Letters, 1977–78," Box 715, Series 2, JWP; letter, Tip O'Neill to Wright, October 26, 1978, Folder "O'Neill, Thomas," Box 1118, Series 2, JWP.

95. Wright remarks, 1977, Folder "Wright Congressional Record Remarks, 1977," Box 715, Series 2, JWP; Wright remarks, 1978, Folder "Wright Congressional Record Remarks, 1978," Box 715, Series 2, JWP.

96. Memo, Walter Mondale to Jimmy Carter, June 7, 1977, Folder "6/24/77 (1)," Box 27, SSF, PF, JCL.

97. Letter, Jimmy Carter to Joseph Biden, June 24, 1977, Folder "6/24/77 (1)," Box 27, SSF, PF, JCL.

98. P.L. 95–511; Wright statement, June 28, 1977, Folder "Intelligence," Box 719, Series 2, JWP; letter, Griffin Bell to Wright, September 21, 1978, Folder "Intelligence," Box 719, Series 2, JWP.

99. Julia Angwin, *Dragnet Nation: A Quest for Privacy, Security, and Freedom in a World of Relentless Surveillance* (New York: Henry Holt, 2014), 25–26, 34, 115.

100. Memo, Jimmy Carter to Stuart Eizenstat, June 24, 1977, Folder "6/24/77 (1)," Box 27, SSF, PF, JCL.

101. P.L. 95–87; Minutes, DSPC, April 26, 1977, Folder "Democratic Steering and Policy Committee," Box 718, Series 2, JWP; letter, Cecil Andrus to Wright, October 9, 1979, Folder "Internal and Interior Affairs," Box 526, Series 1, JWP; Samuel Hays, *Beauty, Health and Permanence: Environmental Politics in the United States, 1955–1985* (New York: Cambridge University Press, 1987), 145–146.

102. Letter, Wright to Doug Costle, October 26, 1978, Folder "Environment (General)," Box 719, Series 2, JWP; letter, T. L. Austin to Wright, September 26, 1978, Folder "Thank You," Box 523, Series 1, JWP; letter, Wright to colleagues, October 3, 1978, Folder "Water Projects," Box 722, Series 2, JWP.

103. P.L. 95–217; letter, Wright to colleagues, June 2, 1977, Folder "Wetlands," Box 1015, Series 2, JWP; letter, Wright and James Cleveland to Jimmy Carter, February 23, 1978, Folder "Letters for the President," Box 726, Series 2, JWP; photocopy, uncited article, September 9, 1979, Folder "Environment (General)," Box 719, Series 2, JWP; letter, Wright to Jimmy Carter, September 13, 1979, Folder "Environment (General)," Box 719, Series 2, JWP.

104. Letter, Wright to Edward Fritz, June 7, 1977, Folder "Wetlands," Box 1015, Series 2, JWP; letter, Robert Edgar and James Jeffords to Wright, February 12, 1979, Folder "Environment (General)," Box 719, Series 2, JWP.

105. Melvyn Dubofsky, "Jimmy Carter and the End of the Politics of Productivity," in Fink and Graham, eds., *Carter Presidency*, 96.

106. Dubofsky, "Jimmy Carter and the End of the Politics of Productivity," 105–107; letter, William Solomon to Wright, October 28, 1977, Folder "Education and Labor," Box 524, Series 1, JWP; letter, Delbert Ward to Wright, February 8, 1978, Folder "Education and Labor," Box 524, Series 1, JWP; letter, Wright to Delbert Ward, February 8, 1978, Folder "Education and Labor," Box 524, Series 1, JWP.

107. Letter, Wright to colleagues, June 6, 1978, Folder "Dear Colleague Letters, 1977–78," Box 715, Series 2, JWP; letter, Lewis Rudin to Wright, July 26, 1978, Folder "Bank, Finance, and Urban Affairs," Box 524, Series 1, JWP; letter, Walter Young to Wright, June 10, 1978, Folder "General," Box 524, Series 1, JWP; Ernest Wohlenberg, "The 'Geography of Civility' Revisited: New York Blackout Looting, 1977," *Economic Geography* 58, no. 1 (January 1982): 29–44.

108. Wright statement, September 21, 1978, Folder "DFW/Love Fidel," Box 1011, Series 2, JWP.

109. Theodore Farris and Stephen Swartz, "The Wright Amendment: Time for Repeal," *Transportation Journal* 45, no. 1 (Winter 2006): 52–60.

110. Memo, Lloyd Rivard to Wright, July 31, 1978, Folder "Public Works and Transportation," Box 526, Series 1, JWP; letter, Wright to Donald Pacheco, August 3, 1978, Folder "Minorities," Box 720, Series 2, JWP.

111. Photocopy, article, "Even When Jim's Vote Rankles, Texas Gains," Folder "JW Majority Leader and FW Congressman," Box 993, Series 2, JWP; *FWST*, July 3, 1977, 21; *Mid-Cities Daily News*, March 22, 1978, 5; *Springtown Epigraph*, March 22, 1978, 1; *DMN*, January 5, 1978, D1.

112. Letter, Wright to Jimmy Carter, June 8, 1977, Folder "6/30/77," Box 28, SSF, PF, JCL.

113. Letter, Wright to Ray Marshall, April 22, 1977, Folder "White House, General," Box 1045, Series 2, JWP; letter, Wright to Bert Lance, April 22, 1977, Folder "White House, General," Box 1045, Series 2, JWP; *FWST*, June 23, 1978, 1; June 24, 1978, 1.

114. Letter, John Dalton to Wright, June 27, 1978, Folder "Thank You," Box 523, Series 1, JWP.

115. *DMN*, June 11, 1978, B9; quoted in *FWST*, June 24, 1978, J5.

116. P.L. 95–523; Murray Weidenbaum, "The Case Against the Humphrey Hawkins Bill," *Challenge* 19, no. 4 (September/October 1976): 21.

117. Quoted in *DMN*, March 18, 1978, 4.

118. Photocopy, uncited article, January 8, 1978, Folder "Scrapbook, 1978," Box 1255, Series 3, JWP.

CHAPTER 14

1. Richard Cohen, "The Return of Phil Burton?" *National Journal* (February 4, 1978): 196; quoted in *NYT*, February 23, 1978, 43.

2. "They Won't Take Jim Wright for Granted This Time," *National Journal* (May 6, 1978): 712–714.

3. *DMN*, January 2, 1978, 8.

4. *HP*, January 8, 1978, 13; letter, Wright to Basil Condos, January 4, 1978, Folder "MCC-1978, General," Box 519, Series 1, JWP.

5. Photocopy, uncited article, "The Wright Time for the Wright Crowd," Folder "1978 Scrapbook," Box 1255, Series 3, JWP; photocopy, uncited article, "Wright Becoming Fund-Raising Dean," Folder "1978 Scrapbook," Box 1255, Series 3, JWP.

6. *FWST*, February 1, 1978, D2; *WP*, February 2, 1978, 14; letter, Wright to Leslie Israel, February 14, 1978, Folder "MCC-1978, General," Box 519, Series 1, JWP.

7. Letter, Wright to colleague, September 27, 1978, Folder "Dear Colleague Letters, 1977–78," Box 715, Series 2, JWP; remarks of Louis Harris, September 27, 1977, Folder "Dear Colleague Letters," Box 715, Series 2, JWP; letter, Wright to Ralph Nader, February 18, 1978, Folder "Education and Labor," Box 524, Series 1, JWP.

8. Letter, Wright to Frank Annunzio, March 1, 1978, Folder "Dear Colleague Letters," Box 715, Series 2, JWP; memo, Jim Corman and Wright to Democrats, October 3, 1977, Folder "Dear Colleague Letters, 1977–78," Box 715, Series 2, JWP; Wright article, "How to Make Low-Cost, Hard-Hitting Campaign Radio Spots Using Testimonials from Constituents," May 5, 1978, Folder "Speech Files: Elections—How to Make Low Cost Hard Hitting Campaign Radio Spots, May, 1978," Box 1287, Series 3, JWP.

9. Interview, Jim Wright, July 14, 2012; *FWST*, February 7, 1978, C7.

10. Interview, Jim Wright, July 14, 2012; quoted in *FWST*, April 30, 1978, I4.

11. Letter, George Troutman to friend, undated, Folder "JW Appreciation Committee—1978, Mags and Copies of Letters," Box 519, Series 1, JWP.

12. Letter, Wright to John Berry, April 13, 1978, Folder "Majority Cong. Cmte, 1978, Trips on Behalf of Others," Box 519, Series 1, JWP; letter, Wright to Gary Hindes, September 11, 1978, Folder "Majority Cong. Cmte, 1978, Trips on Behalf of Others," Box 519, Series 1, JWP; Trips Made on Behalf of Colleagues, 1978, Folder "MCC-General, 1978," Box 519, Series 1, JWP.

13. Letter, Wright to Sheldon Labovitz, June 29, 1978, Folder "Fort Worth Club, 7/7/78—Martin Frost," Box 519, Series 1, JWP; letter, Martin Frost to Wright, May 30, 1978, Folder "Fort Worth Club, 7/7/78—Martin Frost," Box 519, Series 1, JWP.

14. *DTH*, May 8, 1978, 12; Jim Wright, *Balance of Power: Presidents and Congress from the Era of McCarthy to the Age of Gingrich* (Atlanta: Turner, 1996), 310.

15. *DMN*, January 19, 1978, 26; handwritten notes on letter, Jesse Helms to Wright, June 8, 1978, Folder "Senator Correspondence," Box 724, Series 2, JWP.

16. Letter, Jimmy Carter to Democratic Leaders, October 17, 1978, Folder "Letters from President Carter," Box 1045, Series 2, JWP.

17. Sandy Maisel, "Congressional Elections in 1978: The Road to Nomination, the Road to Election," *American Politics Research* 9, no. 1 (January 1981): 23–47; Michael Schaller and George Rising, *Republican Ascendancy: American Politics, 1968–2001* (Wheeling, IL: Harlan Davidson, 2002), 74–77.

18. Thomas Edsall, "Congress Turns Rightward," *Dissent* 25, no. 1 (Winter 1978): 12–18.

19. History, Texas Republican Party, www.texasgop.org/about-the-party/overview-and history, accessed March 3, 2014; Schaller and Rising, *Republican Ascendancy*, 76–77.

20. Letter, Burt Hall to Ben Carroll, November 17, 1978, Folder "Budget," Box 526, Series 1, JWP.

21. *DTH*, November 8, 1978, 13; December 5, 1978, 1.

22. *San Angelo Standard-Times*, November 26, 1978, 7; *Bonham Daily Favorite*, December 14, 1978, 1.

23. Wright remarks, December 4, 1978, Folder "Congress, General," Box 708, Series 2, JWP; *El Paso Herald-Post*, December 13, 1978, 1.

24. Photocopy, uncited article, November 26, 1978, Folder "1978 Scrapbook," Box 1256, Series 3, JWP.

25. Quoted in *FWST*, November 7, 1978, 3.

26. Ibid.; photocopy, uncited column, George Will, "A Convict in the House Is Decadent," Folder "House Administration," Box 526, Series 1, JWP.

27. Wright diary, March 1, 1979; letter, Albert Battaglini to Wright, January 29, 1979, Folder "House Administration," Box 526, Series 1, JWP.

28. Letter, Jay Montague to Wright, March 1, 1979, Folder "Standards of Official Conduct," Box 518, Series 1, JWP.

29. History, C-SPAN homepage, www.c-span.org/about/history, accessed March 17, 2014; letter, Charles Peete to Wright, February 28, 1979, Folder "Standards of Official Conduct," Box 518, Series 1, JWP.

30. Wright diary, March 1, 1979.

31. John Barry, *Ambition and Power: A True Story of Washington* (New York: Penguin, 1990), 366–367; quoted in Wright, *Balance*, 318.

32. Clarence Lusane, "Unity and Struggle: The Political Behavior of African-American Members of Congress," *Black Scholar* 24, no. 4 (Fall 1994): 16–29; see Carolyn Dubose, *The Untold Story of Charles Diggs: The Public Figure, The Private Man* (Brandon, SD: Barton, 1999).

33. Wright diary, June 27, 1979.

34. Quoted in Andrew Radoff, "Rep. Wright Issues Warning on Press-Congress Relations," *Editor and Publisher* (November 24, 1979): 12; handwritten note, Jimmy Carter to Wright, undated, Folder "Letters from the President," Box 1042, Series 2, JWP; letter, Frank Moore to Wright, December 19, 1979, Folder "Letters from the President," Box 1042, Series 2, JWP.

35. Letter, Wright to colleague, October 22, 1979, Folder "Dear Colleague Letters, 1979–80," Box 715, Series 2, JWP.

36. See Robert Greene, *The Sting Man: Inside Abscam* (New York: Penguin, 2013); "House Votes to Conduct 'Full and Complete Inquiry' in 'Abscam' Bribery Probe," *CQWR* (April 5, 1980): 913.

37. Wright statement, November 21, 1978, Folder "Guyana Massacre," Box 997, Series 2, JWP; Rebecca Moore, *Understanding Jonestown and the People's Temple* (Westport, CT; Praeger, 2009), 87–94, 103–105, 109–111, 127–128.

38. *DMN*, November 23, 1978, 17.

39. Interview, Jim Wright, June 18, 2012; photocopy, uncited article, "In Jim's Future: TV or Not TV?" Folder "News Clippings, 74–78 (2)," Box 1152, Series 2, JWP.

40. Interview, Jim Wright, July 14, 2012; photocopy, uncited article, "In Jim's Future: TV or Not TV?" Folder "News Clippings, 74–78 (2)," Box 1152, Series 2, JWP; *DTH*, July 21, 1985, 17; Barry, *Ambition*, 230–231.

41. Interview, Jim Wright, July 14, 2012; Barry, *Ambition*, 231.

42. Paul West, "The Curious History of the Next Speaker of the House," *New Republic* (October 14, 1985): 22–25.

43. Letter, Wright to Cyrus Vance, March 19, 1979, Folder "Letter to Cyrus Vance," Box 1047, Series 2, JWP.

44. Letter, Wright to Muhammad Anwar el-Sadat, March 27, 1979, Folder "Things to Save," Box 678, Series 2, JWP.

45. West, "Curious History," 22–25; *DTH*, July 21, 1985, 17.

46. Quoted in Cort Kirkwood, "Jim Wright Makes It the Old-Fashioned Way," *National Review* 39 (October 23, 1979): 42; letter, Jim Wright et al. to Cecil Andrus, September 29, 1979, Folder "Campaign Material (4)," Box 696, Series 2, JWP; interview, Jim Wright, July 14, 2012.

47. Interview, Jim Wright, June 18, 2012.

48. Quoted in *Atlanta Constitution*, November 15, 1979, 1.

49. Wright diary, February 12, 1979.

50. John Barrow, "The Age of Limits: Jimmy Carter and the Quest for a National Energy Policy," in Gary Fink and Hugh Graham, eds., *The Carter Presidency: Policy Choices in the Post–New Deal Era* (Lawrence: University of Kansas Press, 1998), 168.

51. Quoted in *FWST*, March 10, 1979, 6.

52. Letter, Wright to Jimmy Carter, March 6, 1979, Folder "Letter to President Carter," Box 1045, Series 2, JWP.

53. Energy address, April 5, 1979, Public Papers of the Presidents, Jimmy Carter, APP, UCSB, www.presidency.ucsb.edu/ws/index.php?pid=32159&st=&st1=, accessed May 9, 2014; *FWST*, June 7, 1979, 13.

54. Address on Energy and National Goals, July 15, 1979, Public Papers of the Presidents, Jimmy Carter, APP, UCSB, www.presidency.ucsb.edu/ws/index.php ?pid=32596&st=&st1=, accessed May 9, 2014; letter, Wright to colleague, June 29, 1979, Folder "Dear Colleague Letters, 1979–80," Box 715, Series 2, JWP; Seth Kantor, "Energy Plans Frustrating," *Kansas City Times*, November 15, 1979, 21; Barrow, "Age of Limits," 172; press release, October 31, 1979, Folder "Energy (1)," Box 1012, Series 2, JWP.

55. Wright diary, June 15, 1979.

56. Letter, Jimmy Carter to Wright, November 21, 1979, Folder "Letters from President Carter," Box 1045, Series 2, JWP.

57. Letter, Barry Goldwater to Wright, August 1, 1979, Folder "Republican Correspondence," Box 726, Series 2, JWP.

58. See Joseph Treaster, *Paul Volcker: The Making of a Financial Legend* (New York: John Wiley, 2004); quoted in *FWST*, October 17, 1979, 52; *Dalhart Texan*, October 24, 1979, 6; letter, Wright to Jimmy Carter, March 31, 1980, Folder "Letters to President Carter," Box 1045, Series 2, JWP; press release, February 29, 1980, Folder "Speech Files: Economics—An Anti-Inflation Strategy," Box 1286, Series 3, JWP.

59. William Silber, *Volcker: The Triumph of Persistence* (New York: Bloomsbury, 2012), 165–215; Carl Biven, *Jimmy Carter's Economy: Policy in an Age of Limits* (Chapel Hill: University of North Carolina Press, 2002), 237–246; Herbert Stein, *Presidential Economics: The Making of Economic Policy from Roosevelt to Clinton* (Washington, DC: American Enterprise Institute, 1994), 229–230, 390–392; Bruce Schulman, "Slouching

Toward the Supply Side," in Fink and Graham, eds., *Carter Presidency*, 60–67; Bradford DeLong, "America's Peacetime Inflation: The 1970s," in Christina Romer and David Romer, eds., *Reducing Inflation: Motivation and Strategy* (Chicago: University of Chicago Press, 1997); see John Woolley, *Monetary Politics: The Federal Reserve and the Politics of Monetary Policy* (New York: Cambridge University Press, 1984).

60. Quoted in *FWST*, October 17, 1979, B5.

61. Wright statement, October 26, 1979, Folder "Wright Voting Record," Box 993, Series 2, JWP; Wright diary, October 28, 1979.

62. Robert Reich and John Donahue, "Lessons from the Chrysler Bailout," *California Management Review* 27, no. 4 (Summer 1985): 157–183; see Charles Hyde, *Riding the Roller Coaster: A History of the Chrysler Corporation* (Detroit: Wayne State University Press, 2003).

63. Alfred Sumberg to Wright, June 18, 1979, Folder "Government Operations," Box 526, Series 1, JWP; letter, Gregory Humphrey to Wright, June 8, 1979, Folder "Government Operations," Box 526, Series 1, JWP; letter, Cadar Parr to Wright, October 4, 1978, Folder "Government Operations," Box 526, Series 1, JWP.

64. Letter, Eugene Hardy to Wright, June 1, 1979, Folder "Government Operations," Box 526, Series 1, JWP; letter, William Clements to Wright, May 29, 1979, Folder "Government Operations," Box 526, Series 1, JWP.

65. Wright diary, October 2, 1979.

66. Ibid., December 22, 1979.

67. Quoted in *FWST*, February 16, 1979, 3; February 20, 1979, 3; interview, Jim Wright, July 14, 2012.

68. Wright broadcast, September 24, 1979, Folder "Speech Files: Foreign Affairs—Alliance with Mexico—Shift from Old to New," Box 1288, Series 3, JWP.

69. Quoted in *Greenville Herald-Banner*, 6.

70. "Wright on Tour of Europe Plants," *FWST*, June 29, 1979, 2; *FWST*, July 5, 1979, B6.

71. Interview, Jim Wright, July 14, 2012; letter, Jimmy Carter to Wright, June 18, 1979, Folder "Arms Control," Box 718, Series 2, JWP; Wright, *Balance*, 320; Jean Garrison, "Explaining Change in the Carter Administration's China Policy," *Asian Affairs* 29, no. 2 (Summer 2002): 83–98; Robert Strong, *Working in the World: Jimmy Carter and the Making of American Foreign Policy* (Baton Rouge: Louisiana State University Press, 2000), 73, 173, 191, 222, 261, 274. See Dan Caldwell, *The Dynamics of Domestic Politics and Arms Control: The SALT II Treaty Ratification Debate* (Columbia: University of South Carolina Press, 1991).

72. Wright diary, July 25, 1979.

73. Press release, January 5, 1980, Folder "Speech Files: Foreign Affairs—Majority Leader Trip to South Africa, Nigeria, Etc.," Box 1288, Series 3, JWP.

74. *FWST*, January 10, 1980, D6; letter, Wright to Jimmy Carter, June 10, 1980, Folder "Letters to President Carter," Box 1045, Series 2, JWP; trip report, January 10, 1980, Folder "Speech Files: Foreign Affairs—Sasolburg, South Africa (1980)," Box 1288, Series 3, JWP.

75. Memorandum for the Record, Bill Newbold, February 21, 1980, Folder "Foreign Dignitary Correspondence," Box 693, Series 2, JWP.

76. Cyrus Vance statement, March 6, 1980, Folder "Speech Files: Biography—Wright Foreign Travel," Box 1280, Series 3, JWP.

77. Shirley Christian, "Nicaragua and the United States," *World Affairs* 149, no. 4 (Spring 1987): 177–182; Richard Fagan, "Dateline Nicaragua: The End of the Affair," *Foreign Affairs* 37 (Autumn 1979): 178–191; see Anthony Lake, *Somoza Falling: A Case Study of Washington at Work* (Amherst: University of Massachusetts Press, 1990); letter, Byron Galle to Wright, September 25, 1978, Folder "World Affairs," Box 523, Series 1, JWP; letter, Charles Singletary to Wright, Folder "World Affairs," Box 523, Series 1, JWP.

78. Marx Lewis, "Zorinski and Wright Support Sandinistas," *Washington Weekly* (June 17, 1980): 9; Jim Wright, *Worth It All* (Washington, DC: Brassey's, 1993), 43.

79. Letter, Wright to Jimmy Carter, June 10, 1980, Folder "Letters to President Carter," Box 1045, Series 2, JWP.

80. Wright, *Worth It*, 44.

81. Ibid.

82. Press release, June 6, 1980, Folder "Latin America," Box 709, Series 2, JWP; interview, Jim Wright, June 18, 2012.

83. Wright diary, June 8, 1980; *WSW*, June 30, 1980, Folder "Latin America," Box 709, Series 2, JWP.

84. Interview, Jim Wright, June 18, 2012; Wright, *Worth It*, 46.

85. Wright diary, June 8, 1980; letter, Wright to colleague, June 12, 1980, Folder "Latin America," Box 709, Series 2, JWP.

86. Quoted in Wright, *Worth It*, 47.

87. Letter, Wright et al. to Daniel Ortega, September 4, 1980, Folder "Nicaragua," Box 702, Series 2, JWP; Richard Fly, "Wright, Colleagues Express Concern at Delaying of Nicaraguan Elections," *DTH*, September 25, 1980, 26.

88. See Nicholas Sarantakes, *Dropping the Torch: Jimmy Carter, the Olympic Boycott, and the Cold War* (New York: Cambridge University Press, 2010).

89. Wright diary, December 16, 1979.

90. James Buchan, *Days of God: The Revolution in Iran and Its Consequences* (New York: Simon and Schuster, 2012), 1–26, 79–98, 177–242; press release, March 15, 1977, Folder "Speech Files: Iranian Government Order—March 15, 1977," Box 1287, Series 3, JWP.

91. Wright statement, December 2, 1979, Folder "Middle East," Box 770, Series 2, JWP; quoted in photocopy, uncited article, "Insensitivity Triggered Hostility, Wright Says," Folder "Scrapbook, 1979," Box 1258, Series 3, JWP; quoted in *FWST*, April 11, 1979, B6.

92. Letter, Wright to Hugo Margain, December 4, 1979, Folder "Foreign Dignitary Correspondence," Box 693, Series 2, JWP; Letter, Hugo Margain to Wright, December 14, 1979, Folder "Shah of Iran," Box 696, Series 2, JWP.

93. Buchan, *Days of God*, 271–272; see Paul Ryan, *The Iranian Rescue Mission: Why It Failed* (Annapolis, MD: Naval Institute Press, 1985); Wright statement, April 17, 1980, Folder "Middle East," Box 770, Series 2, JWP; quoted in *WP*, April 27, 1980, 10; *DTH*, April 26, 1980, B3.

94. Wright diary, July 21, 1979.

95. Letter, James Corman to Wright, January 23, 1979, Folder "Democratic Congressional Committee Campaign (Prior to 1981)," Box 723, Series 2, JWP.

96. See Arthur Schlesinger Jr., *The Cycles of American History* (New York: Houghton Mifflin, 1986).

97. Laura Kalman, *Right Star Rising: A New Politics, 1974–1980* (New York: Norton, 2000), 21–37.

98. William Martin, *With God on Our Side: The Rise of the Religious Right in America* (New York: Broadway, 1996), 148–161. See Michael Lienesch, *Redeeming America; Piety and Politics in the New Christian Right* (Chapel Hill: University of North Carolina Press, 1993).

99. Interview, Jerry Falwell, July 24, 2003; J. Brooks Flippen, "A Tale of Two Baptists: Jimmy Carter and Jerry Falwell," *Baptist History and Heritage* 48, no. 3 (Fall 2013): 33–56.

100. Letter, Henry Hyde to Wright, June 18, 1979, Folder "Republican Correspondence," Box 726, Series 2, JWP; interview, Jim Wright, July 14, 2012.

101. Wright statement, September 1979, Folder "Abortion," Box 910, Series 2, JWP.

102. J. Brooks Flippen, *Jimmy Carter, the Politics of Family, and the Rise of the Religious Right* (Athens: University of Georgia Press, 2010), 284–285; *FWST*, July 9, 1980, 3; interview, Jim Wright, July 18, 2012.

103. Interview, Phyllis Schlafly, December 4, 2009.

104. Donald Mathews and Jane Sherron De Hart, *Sex, Gender, and the Politics of ERA: A State and the Nation* (New York: Oxford University Press, 1990), 56, 80, 86, 97, 222; letter, Joe Stovall to Jimmy Carter, June 12, 1978, no folder, Box 530, Series 1, JWP; Wright statement, April 3, 1978, Folder "Thorton's ERA Remark About Wright," Box 1039, Series 2, JWP.

105. James Kitchens, "An Analysis of the National Conservative Political Action Committee and Its Involvement in the 12th Congressional District of Texas, 1980," undated, Folder "An Analysis of NCPAC in 12th District," Box 1178, Series 2, JWP; Clyde Wilcox, "Political Action Committees of the New Christian Right: A Longitudinal Analysis," *Journal for the Scientific Study of Religion* 27, no. 1 (March 1985): 60–71; Keith Poole and Thomas Romer, "Patterns of Political Action Committee Contributions to the 1980 Campaigns for the United States House of Representatives," *Public Choice* 47, no. 1 (1985): 63–111.

106. 424 U.S. 1 (1976); *Wall Street Journal*, October 22, 1980, 1; *WP*, October 24, 1980, 2; interview, Jim Wright, July 14, 2012.

107. Wright remarks, November 13, 1979, no folder, Box 530, Series 1, JWP; press release, March 19, 1980, Folder "Speech Files: Budget—$21 Billion to Budget Reduction," Box 1281, Series 3, JWP; *DMN*, April 10, 1980, 24; *FWST*, April 13, 1979, 8; April 13, 1979, 12; *DTH*, March 13, 1979, 1; interview, Jim Wright, July 18, 2012; letter, Wright to Joseph Califano, February 17, 1977, Folder "Welfare," Box 722, Series 2, JWP; *WSW*, June 30, 1978, Folder "Welfare," Box 722, Series 2, JWP.

108. Summary of Organization Ratings, Folder "Voting Studies," Box 722, Series 2, JWP.

109. Quoted in *DMN*, April 22, 1979, 32; February 11, 1979, D1.

110. Quoted in *DMN*, April 22, 1979, 32; February 11, 1979, D1; letter, H. E. Chiles to Charles Stenholm, November 14, 1979, Folder "Colleagues," Box 516, Series 1, JWP; letter, Charles Stenholm to H. E. Chiles, November 27, 1979, Folder "Colleagues," Box 516, Series 1, JWP; letter, Charlie Stenholm to Craig Raupe, undated, Folder "Colleagues," Box 516, Series 1, JWP.

111. *FWST*, August 25, 1979, 1; interview, Jim Wright, July 18, 2012; Wright, *Balance*, 330–331.

112. Maxwell Glen, "At the Wire, Corporate PACS Come Through for the GOP," *National Journal* (February 3, 1979): 174–177; *DTH*, November 3, 1980, 1.

113. Scott Bennett, "Is Jim Wright Leaning Too Much to the Left?" *Texas Business* (February 1980): 28–30.

114. Wright, *Balance*, 331.

115. Flier, Bradshaw for Congress, undated, Folder "Campaign Materials (2)," Box 696, Series 2, JWP; *FWST*, January 30, 1980, B1; photocopy, uncited article, "Bradshaw Claims Wright Has Become 'Liberal's Liberal,'" Folder "Scrapbook, 1980 Campaign," Box 1265, JWP; photocopy, uncited article, "Bradshaw Charges Wright 'Against' Texas," Folder "Scrapbook, 1980 Campaign," Box 1265, JWP.

116. Quoted in *FWST*, August 26, 1980, B1.

117. *DTH*, April 24, 1980, 6; *DMN*, September 25, 1980, 37.

118. Quoted in *FWST*, September 1, 1980, 20.

119. Interview, Jim Wright, July 18, 2012; *FWST*, May 4, 1980, 40; March 5, 1980, B1; August 21, 1980, G2.

120. *DTH*, September 29, 1980, C3; August 1, 1980, 8; Wright statement, September 12, 1980, Folder "Revelation of the Bradshaw Accusation in the 1980 Campaign," Box 960, Series 2, JWP; Marshall Lynam statement, July 29, 1980, Folder "Speech Files: Biography—Explanation of JW's Interest in Neptune Oil and Gas," Box 1280, Series 3, JWP.

121. Photocopy, uncited article, "Berman Says House Leader 'Confused,'" Folder "Eddie Chiles, 1979," Box 990, Series 2, JWP.

122. *FWST*, August 26, 1980, B4.

123. Photocopy, uncited article, "Wright Fights for Political Life," November 2, 1980, Folder "Scrapbook, November–December, 1980," Box 1262, Series 3, JWP; letter, Wright to Charlie Stenholm, April 29, 1980, Folder "Stenholm, Charlie," Box 735, Series 2, JWP.

124. Transcript, March 18, 1980, Folder "Speech Files: National Affairs—Transcript of Deena Clark Show," Box 1289, Series 3, JWP.

125. "The Wright Approach," Special Edition, April 10, 1980, Folder "Campaign Material (1)," Box 696, Series 2, JWP.

126. Letter, Wright to Zbigniew Brzezinski, June 2, 1980, Folder "Cuba Refugees," Box 706, Series 2, JWP.

127. Quoted in *DTH*, October 14, 1980, C3.

128. Quoted in photocopy, uncited article, November 3, 1980, Folder "Scrapbook, November–December, 1980," Box 1262, Series 3, JWP; campaign flier, Folder "Campaign Materials (1)," Box 696, Series 2, JWP; *FWST*, October 28, 1980, 14.

129. *DMN*, October 21, 1980, D5.

130. *FWST*, November 1, 1980, C1; *Austin American-Statesman*, November 1, 1980, 11.

131. Quoted in *FWST*, October 17, 1980, 8; *DTH*, November 1, 1980, 14.

132. Letter, Amon Carter Jr. et al. to Fellow Citizens, August 7, 1980, Folder "Campaign Material (4)," Box 696, Series 2, JWP; letter, Martin Frost et al. to People of Tarrant County, undated, Folder "Campaign Material (4)," Box 696, Series 2, JWP.

133. Campaign flier, October 10, 1980, Folder "Campaign Material (1)," Box 696, Series 2, JWP.

134. Memo, Joe Shosid to Wright, August 4, 1980, Folder "Campaign Material (2)," Box 696, Series 2, JWP; memo, unsigned, May 5, 1980, Folder "Campaign Material (4)," Box 696, Series 2, JWP.

135. *DTH*, July 24, 1980, B4; *DMN*, August 9, 1980, F1.

136. Letter, Judy Welch to Wright, May 8, 1980, Folder "Office, Fort Worth," Box 699, Series 2, JWP; letter, Wright to Judy Welch, May 12, 1980, Folder "Office, Fort Worth," Box 699, Series 2, JWP.

137. Interview, Jim Wright, July 18, 2012; quoted in *DTH*, November 3, 1980, 7; photocopy, uncited article, November 4, 1980, Folder "Scrapbook, November–December, 1980," Box 1262, Series 3, JWP.

138. Wright diary, December 21, 1980.

139. Timothy Stanley, *Kennedy vs. Carter: The 1980 Battle for the Democratic Party's Soul* (Lawrence: University of Kansas Press, 2010), 92–169.

140. Quoted in *DTH*, October 9, 1980, 12.

141. Schaller and Rising, *Republican Ascendancy*, 81; interview, Jim Wright, July 18, 2012; Wright, *Balance*, 337.

142. *Fort Worth East Side News*, September 25, 1980, 3; *FWNT*, September 26, 1980, 5.

143. *FWST*, October 30, 1980, 11.

144. Letter, Morris Udall to Wright, September 28, 1980, Folder "Udall, Morris," Box 735, Series 2, JWP.

145. *Odessa American*, October 12, 1980, 1; interview, Jim Wright, July 18, 2012; Wright, *Balance*, 337–338.

146. *DMN*, November 5, 1980, 1; quoted in *FWST*, November 5, 1980, 14.

147. Andrew Busch, *Reagan's Victory: The Presidential Election of 1980 and the Rise of the Right* (Lawrence: University of Kansas Press, 2005), 163–190; *Odessa American*, November 5, 1980, 1.

148. Quoted in *DTH*, November 5, 1980, 12; interview, Jim Wright, July 18, 2012.

149. Quoted in *FWST*, November 5, 1980, 14.

150. Wright diary, December 7, 1980.

CHAPTER 15

1. Wright remarks, December 18, 1980, Folder "Speech Files: Democratic Party—Remarks at Dallas Democratic Forum," Box 1285, Series 3, JWP.

2. Wright diary, January 1, 1981.

3. Letter, Jamie Whitten to Wright, November 13, 1980, Folder "Whitten, Jamie," Box 735, Series 2, JWP.

4. Quoted *DTH*, November 16, 1980, 11.

5. Letter, Phil Gramm to Wright, September 22, 1980, Folder "Gramm, Phil (Texas)," Box 818, Series 2, JWP; letter, Phil Gramm to Wright, December 30, 1980, Folder "Gramm, Phil (Texas)," Box 818, Series 2, JWP.

6. Interview, Jim Wright, July 21, 2012; quoted in Jim Wright, *Balance of Power: Presidents and Congress from the Era of McCarthy to the Age of Gingrich* (Atlanta: Turner, 1996), 351.

7. Richard Cohen, *Rostenkowski: The Pursuit of Power and the End of the Old Politics* (Chicago: Ivan Dee, 1999), 116–120; "New Role for Rostenkowski Gets Him into the Thick of House Power-Playing," *CQWR* (May 16, 1981): 863–866.

8. Interview, Tom Downey, July 31, 2014; interview, Mike Andrews, July 14, 2014; *FWST*, November 16, 1980, 31; press release, Dan Rostenkowski, December 5, 1980, Folder "Rostenkowski, Dan," Box 734, Series 2, JWP.

9. Quoted in *FWNT*, December 19, 1980, C1.

10. Quoted in photocopy, uncited article, November 5, 1980, Folder "Scrapbook, 1980 Campaign," Box 1265, Series 3, JWP.

11. Quoted in *DMN*, November 30, 1980, C1; *FWST*, April 28, 1981, 16; "Major Victory for GOP in Texas Redistricting," *CQWR* (August 15, 1981): 1517; *FWNT*, May 18, 1981, 1.

12. Letter, Stuart Eizenstat to Wright, January 14, 1981, Folder "Letters for the President—Bush," Box 726, Series 2, JWP; letter, Zbigniew Brzezinski to Wright, January 14, 1981, Folder "Letters for the President—Bush," Box 726, Series 2, JWP.

13. Wright diary, January 20, 1981.

14. Schedule, January 20, 1981, Folder "Inauguration," Box 696, Series 2, JWP; *DMN*, February 7, 1981, 1; interview, Jim Wright, July 21, 2012; Wright, *Balance*, 343–344.

15. Letter, Ronald Reagan to Wright, February 4, 1981, Folder "Letters for the President—Reagan," Box 726, Series 2, JWP.

16. Wright diary, February 8, 1981; Craig Jenkins and Craig Eckert, "The Right Turn in Economic Policy: Business Elites and the New Conservative Economics," *Sociological Forum* 15, no. 2 (June 2000): 307–338; Kim Phillips Fein, *Invisible Hands: The Businessman's Crusade Against the New Deal* (New York: Norton, 2009), 183, 203, 229–230, 244.

17. Milton Friedman, "Reaganomics and the Interest Rate," *Newsweek* (September 21, 1981): 39; Steven Hayward, *The Age of Reagan: The Fall of the Old Liberal Order, 1964–1980* (New York: Three Rivers, 2001), 690.

18. Wright statement, February 19, 1981, Folder "Speech File: Budget—Budget Remedies of JW," Box 1281, Series 3, JWP; Wright statement, February 18, 1981, Folder "Speech Files: Defense—President's Proposals, National Defense," Box 1284, Series 3, JWP.

19. Letter, Wright to Democrats, February 18, 1981, Folder "Dear Colleague Letters, 1980–81," Box 715, Series 2, JWP.

20. Transcript, *Meet the Press*, Folder "Speech Files: National Affairs—Meet the Press," Box 1289, Series 3, JWP.

21. Wright diary, February 3, 1981; *Washington Star*, February 8, 1981, 4; letter, Max Friedersdorf to Wright, March 12, 1981, Folder "Letters for the President—Bush," Box 726, Series 2, JWP; letter, Ronald Reagan to Craig Raupe, undated, Folder "GOP Campaign Letters," Box 725, Series 2, JWP; letter, Wright to Max Friedersdorf, March 17, 1981, Folder "GOP Campaign Letters," Box 725, Series 2, JWP; letter, Wright to Rodger Summers, December 4, 1981, Folder "Letters to the President," Box 726, Series 2, JWP.

22. See Edward Berkowitz, *Robert Ball and the Politics of Social Security* (Madison: University of Wisconsin Press, 2005); "Social Security Cutback Faces Review," *CQWR* (August 15, 1981): 1467.

23. Wright remarks, May 13, 1981, Folder "Social Security (2)," Box 721, Series 2, JWP.

24. Wright diary, February 8, 1981.

25. Uriel Spiegel and Joseph Templeman, "A Nonsingular Peaked Laffer Curve: Debunking the Traditional Laffer Curve," *American Economist* 48, no. 2 (Fall 2004): 61–66; Aasim Husain, "Domestic Taxes and External Debt Laffer Curve," *Economica* 64, no. 25 (August 1997): 519–525; see Arthur Laffer and Stephen More, *Return to Prosperity: How America Can Regain Its Economic Superpower Status* (New York: Threshold Editions, 2010); interview, Jim Wright, July 21, 2012; Wright, *Balance*, 346–347.

26. Interview, Tom Downey, July 31, 2014; letter, Wright to Ronald Reagan, February 24, 1981, Folder "Letters to the President," Box 1045, Series 2, JWP; letter, Wright to Democrats, March 5, 1981, Folder "Dear Colleague Letters, 1980–81," Box 715, Series 2, JWP.

27. Letter, Wright to Democrats, March 2, 1981, Folder "Dear Colleague Letters, 1980–81," Box 715, Series 2, JWP.

28. Economic Initiatives, February 2, 1981, Folder "Alexander, Bill," Box 730, Series 2, JWP; memo, Bill Alexander to Tip O'Neill and Wright, March 4, 1981, Folder "Alexander, Bill," Box 730, Series 2, JWP.

29. Press release, April 8, 1981, Folder "Democratic Caucus," Box 723, Series 2, JWP.

30. Wright diary, March 30, 1981; quoted in Edmund Morris, *Dutch: A Memoir of Ronald Reagan* (New York: Random House, 1999), 431; interview, Jim Wright, July 21, 2012.

31. Address on Economic Recovery Program, April 28, 1981, Public Papers of the Presidents, Ronald Reagan, APP, UCSB, accessed June 3, 2014, www.presidency.ucsb .edu/ws/index.php?pid=43756&st=&st1=.

32. Interview, Mike Andrews, July 14, 2014; Jim Wright, Comments on President Reagan's Address to Congress, April 28, 1981, Folder "Speech Files: National Affairs—Comments on President Reagan's Address to Congress," Box 1289, Series 3, JWP.

33. Wright remarks, May 4, 1981, Folder "Speech Files: National Affairs—Critical Choices for the Future," Box 1289, Series 3, JWP.

34. Quoted in *WP*, May 10, 1981, 3.

35. Interview, Jim Wright, July 21, 2012; quoted in *DTH*, May 20, 1981, 14.

36. Quoted in *FWST*, July 31, 1981, 6.

37. Transcript, *Face the Nation*, Folder "Speech Files: National Affairs—Transcript, *Face the Nation*, May 24, 1981," Box 1289, Series 3, JWP.

38. Interview, Jim Wright, July 21, 2012; Wright, *Balance*, 358; letter, Tip O'Neill to Democrats, June 24, 1981, Folder "Dear Colleague Letters, 1980–1981," Box 715, Series 2, JWP.

39. Interview, Tom Downey, July 31, 2014; quoted in *FWST*, June 26, 1981, 2.

40. Quoted in *FWST*, June 26, 1981, 1.

41. Letter, Wright to Democrats, June 26, 1981, Folder "Stenholm, Charlie," Box 735, Series 2, JWP; interview, Jim Wright, July 21, 2012; Wright, *Balance*, 360.

42. Quoted in *FWST*, July 19, 1981, 1.

43. Letter, Ronald Reagan to Wright, May 21, 1981, Folder "Social Security," Box 721, Series 2, JWP; letter, Ronald Reagan to Tip O'Neill, July 18, 1981, Folder "Reagan Correspondence with O'Neill," Box 726, Series 2, JWP; Wright statement, July 19, 1981, Folder "Social Security (2)," Box 721, Series 2, JWP; letter, Wright to colleagues, July 20, 1981, Folder "Dear Colleague Letters, 1980–81," Box 715, Series 2, JWP.

44. Quoted in Wright, *Balance*, 363.

45. Wright diary, February 16, 1981.

46. Wright, *Balance*, 364; interview, Jim Wright, July 21, 2012.

47. *Wall Street Journal*, June 24, 1981, B1.

48. Cohen, *Rostenkowski*, 146.

49. Interview, Mike Andrews, July 14, 2014; letter, Dan Rostenkowski to Wright, July 31, 1981, Folder "Rostenkowski, Dan," Box 734, Series 2, JWP.

50. Edward Delaney, "The Economic Recovery Tax Act of 1981," *American Bar Association Journal* 67, no. 10 (October 1981): 1266–1269; Steve Pressman, "A Tale of Two Taxpayers: The Effects of the Economic Recovery and Tax Act of 1981," *Journal of Post-Keynesian Economics* 9, no. 2 (Winter 1986): 226–236; Economic Recovery Tax Act of 1981, P.L. 97–34; Morris, *Dutch*, 446; Wright, *Balance*, 364.

51. Omnibus Budget Reconciliation Act, P.L. 97–35; Remarks on Economic Recovery Tax Act, August 13, 1981, Public Papers of the Presidents, Ronald Reagan, APP, UCSB, www.presidency.ucsb.edu/ws/index.php?pid=44161&st=&st1, accessed May 25, 2014.

52. Harris Poll, "Americans Reluctant to Accept Cuts in Social Security to Balance Federal Budget," October 8, 1981, Folder "Public Opinion," Box 720, JWP.

53. *WP*, September 18, 1981, 7; *DMN*, September 19, 1981, 13.

54. Letter, Wright to colleagues, November 5, 1981, Folder "Dear Colleague Letters, 1980–81," Box 715, Series 2, JWP; letter, Wright to Jack Tinsley, November 13, 1981, Folder "Taxation," Box 721, Series 2, JWP; P.L. 97–123; *WP*, September 26, 1981, 10.

55. Letter, Wright to Ronald Reagan, August 4, 1981, Folder "Letters to the President—Reagan," Box 726, Series 2, JWP.

56. Interview, Jim Wright, July 21, 2012; see Chris Matthews, *Tip and the Gipper: When Politics Worked* (New York: Simon and Schuster, 2013); see Daniel Marans, "The

Reagan-O'Neill Myth of Bipartisan Social Security Reform," *Huffington Post*, November 20, 2012, www.huffingtonpost.com/daniel-marans/the-reaganoneill-myth-of-_b_2162028.html, accessed May 25, 2014; *WP*, April 22, 1982, 6.

57. Michael Schaller and George Rising, *Republican Ascendancy: American Politics, 1968–2001* (Wheeling, IL: Harlan Davidson, 2001), 91; William Link and Arthur Link, *American Epoch*, vol. 2, 7th ed. (New York: McGraw-Hill, 1993), 745; George Moss, *Moving On: The American People Since 1945*, 3rd ed. (Upper Saddle River, NJ: Prentice Hall, 2005), 250, 287.

58. Wright remarks, January 28, 1982, Folder "Unemployment," Box 722, Series 2, JWP; *FWST*, June 9, 1982, 17; memo, David Obey to Tip O'Neill, January 26, 1982, Folder "Unemployment," Box 722, Series 2, JWP.

59. Letter, Wright to colleagues, May 11, 1982, Folder "Dear Colleague Letters, 1981–82," Box 715, Series 2, JWP; letter, Wright to colleagues, May 21, 1982, Folder "Dear Colleague Letters, 1981–82," Box 715, Series 2, JWP; letter, Wright to colleagues, June 16, 1982, Folder "Dear Colleague Letters, 1981–82," Box 715, Series 2, JWP; Wright, *Balance*, 376–377; Wright address, July 19, 1982, Folder "Budget," Box 707, Series 2, JWP.

60. Wright remarks, September 29, 1982, Folder "Speech Files: Economics—Address, A New Dimension," Box 1286, Series 3, JWP; letter, Wright to colleagues, July 28, 1982, Folder "Dear Colleague Letters, 1981–1982," Box 715, Series 2, JWP.

61. Quoted in *WP*, June 9, 1982, D11.

62. Wright testimony, March 30, 1982, Folder "Interest Rates—Testimony, Banking, March 30, 1982," Box 719, Series 2, JWP; letter, Wright et al. to Ronald Reagan, August 17, 1982, Folder "Inflation," Box 1017, Series 2, JWP; letter, Wright to colleagues, August 10, 1982, Folder "Inflation," Box 1017, Series 2, JWP; Wright statement, August 12, 1982, Folder "Inflation," Box 1017, Series 2, JWP.

63. See Michael Boskin, *Reagan and the Economy: The Successes, Failures, and Unfinished Agenda* (Ithaca, NY: Cornell University Press, 1988), and Bruce Bartlett, *The New American Economy: The Failure of Reaganomics and a New Way Forward* (New York: Macmillan, 2009); Link and Link, *American Epoch*, 745.

64. Interview, Jim Wright, July 21, 2012; quoted in Wright, *Balance*, 378.

65. P.L. 97–248; letter, Wright to Thomas Edsall, Folder "Press Letters—Correspondence," Box 702, JWP.

66. Letter, Dan Rostenkowski to Wright, November 12, 1982, Folder "Social Security," Box 721, Series 2, JWP.

67. Interview, Jim Wright, July 21, 2012; Wright, *Balance*, 381; Surface Transportation Assistance Act, P.L. 97–424.

68. Interview, William Reilly, June 26, 1998; interview, Russell Train, July 8, 1998; interview, Philip Berry, June 19, 1998; Samuel Hays, *Beauty, Health and Permanence: Environmental Politics in the United States, 1955–1985* (New York: Cambridge University Press, 1987), 491–526; letter, Wright to Ronald Reagan, July 16, 1981, Folder "Letters to the President—Reagan," Box 726, Series 2, JWP.

69. Wright statement, September 21, 1981, Folder "Energy, 1981," Box 709, Series 2, JWP; Wright statement, November 18, 1982, Folder "Response to Wright's Position on Acid Rain," Box 957, Series 2, JWP.

70. Letter, Jim Wright et al. to colleagues, July 20, 1981, Folder "Dear Colleague Letters, 1980–81," Box 715, Series 2, JWP; Jeffrey Stein, *Mixing the Waters: Environment, Politics, and the Building of the Tennessee-Tombigbee Waterway* (Akron, OH: University of Akron Press, 1993), 28–32.

71. Wright diary, March 22, 1981; photocopy, uncited article, March 22, 1981, Folder "1981 Scrapbook," Box 1266, Series 3, JWP.

72. Quoted in *FWST*, March 20, 1981, 1; quoted in *HC*, March 21, 1981, 7.

73. Interview, Jim Wright, July 21, 2012; letter, Wright to colleagues, August 12, 1982, Folder "Dear Colleague Letters, 1981–82," Box 715, Series 2, JWP; letter, Wright to colleagues, August 13, 1982, Folder "Dear Colleague Letters, 1981–82," Box 715, Series 2, JWP.

74. Quoted in *WP*, October 1, 1982, 1, 8; *WP*, October 2, 1982, 1.

75. P.L. 97–205; Thomas Boyd and Stephen Markman, "The 1982 Amendments to the Voting Rights Act: A Legislative History," *Washington and Lee University Law Review* 40, no. 4 (September 1, 1983): 1342–1428; Gary May, *Bending Towards Justice: The Voting Rights Act and the Transformation of American Democracy* (New York: Basic Books, 2013), 214–232; Wright speech, "Trust the People," October 5, 1982, Folder "Speech Files: Elections—In Support of Voting Rights Act," Box 1287, Series 3, JWP.

76. Interview, Jim Wright, July 21, 2012; see Joseph McCartin, *Collision Course: Ronald Reagan, the Air Traffic Controllers, and the Strike That Changed America* (New York: Oxford University Press, 2011).

77. Wright address, December 8, 1982, Folder "Speech Files: Defense—Price of Defense," Box 1284, Series 3, JWP.

78. Letter, Ronald Reagan to Wright, July 15, 1982, Folder "Letters for the President—Reagan," Box 726, Series 2, JWP.

79. *WP*, October 3, 1981, 12; Wright statement, December 7, 1982, Folder "MX," Box 1019, Series 2, JWP; letter, Ronald Reagan to Wright, December 6, 1982, Folder "Letters for the President—Reagan," Box 726, Series 2, JWP.

80. *CR*, 97th Cong., 1st sess., vol. 127, pt. 21 (November 18, 1981): H28039.

81. Wright statement, undated, Folder "Speech Files: Foreign Affairs—Remarks of JW on AWACs Sale," Box 1288, Series 3, JWP; Link and Link, *American Epoch*, 754–755.

82. Quoted in *DTH*, November 20, 1981, 4.

83. *CR*, 97th Cong., 1st sess., vol. 127, pt. 21 (November 19, 1981): H28154–H28155.

84. "Wright: Ten Percent Arms Reduction Would Make Possible Vast Improvements Worldwide," *Capital Baptist* 28, no. 15 (September 23, 1982): 1.

85. Lawrence Wittner, "The Nuclear Freeze and Its Impact," *Arms Control Today* 40, no. 10 (December 2010): 53.

86. Wright diary, August 5, 1982.

87. Interview, Jim Wright, July 21, 2012; see James Mann, *The Rebellion of Ronald Reagan: A History of the End of the Cold War* (New York: Penguin, 2009), and James Wilson, *The Triumph of Improvisation: Gorbachev's Adaptability, Reagan's Engagement, and the End of the Cold War* (Ithaca, NY: Cornell University Press, 2014).

88. Letter, Ronald Reagan to Wright, December 8, 1981, Folder "Letters for the

President—Reagan," Box 726, Series 2, JWP; letter, Wright to colleagues, December 9, 1981, Folder "Dear Colleague Letters, 1981–82," Box 715, Series 2, JWP.

89. History of Caribbean Basin Initiative, Office of the US Trade Representative, www.ustr.gov/trade-topics/trade-development/preference-programs/caribbean -basin-initiative-cbi, accessed May 30, 2014; letter, Ronald Reagan to Wright, December 16, 1982, Folder "Letters for the President—Reagan," Box 726, Series 2, JWP; P.L. 98–67; interview, Jim Wright, July 21, 2012.

90. Quoted in *DMN*, March 13, 1981, 14.

91. *HP*, March 13, 1981, 5; *Laredo News*, April 9, 1982, 1; *Plano Star-Courier*, April 13, 1982, 2; *Amarillo Globe Times*, April 12, 1982, 1; quoted in *Port Arthur News*, April 12, 1982, 3.

92. Quoted in *Terrell Tribune*, April 18, 1982, 1.

93. Thomas Walker, *Reagan Versus the Sandinistas: The Undeclared War on Nicaragua* (Boulder: Westview Press, 1987), 6; Barry Rubin, "Reagan Administration Policymaking and Central America," in Robert Leiken, ed., *Central America: Anatomy of a Conflict* (New York: Pergamon, 1984), 309; Christian Smith, *Resisting Reagan: The U.S. Central American Peace Movement* (Chicago: University of Chicago Press, 1996), 24–25.

94. Richard Cohen, "They're Still a Majority, but Are Democrats Really in Control?" *National Journal* (January 31, 1981): 189–191; "Do Democrats Control the House?" *CQWR* (April 25, 1981): 739; *Birmingham News*, December 23, 1982, 13; December 13, 1982; Wright remarks, September 16, 1981, Folder "Democratic Caucus," Box 723, Series 2, JWP.

95. *WP*, April 4, 1982, 6; "The Boll Weevils: Who, What, Why," *U.S. News and World Report* (August 17, 1981): 36.

96. *DTH*, August 17, 1981, 2; quoted in "How a Maverick Lawmaker Goes Over Back Home," *U.S. News and World Report* (August 17, 1981): 37; *DTH*, August 17, 1981, 14.

97. Quoted in *FWST*, June 2, 1981, 9.

98. *DMN*, August 7, 1981, 3.

99. Quoted in *DMN*, July 12, 1981, 32; quoted in *DMN*, June 17, 1981, 15.

100. Quoted in photocopy, uncited article, June 11, 1981, Folder, "Gramm, Phil (TX)," Box 818, Series 2, JWP.

101. *DTH*, July 7, 1981, 5.

102. Membership List, Folder "Conservative Democratic Forum," Box 718, Series 2, JWP; letter, Wright to James Wright, September 22, 1981, Folder, "Speech Files: Democratic Party—Response to DMN Editorial," Box 1285, Series 3, JWP.

103. Vernon Louviere, "Conservative Democrats: New Power in the House," *Nation's Business* (January 1981): 29–32.

104. Wright remarks, September 16, 1981, Folder "Colleagues," Box 708, Series 2, JWP.

105. *WP*, September 17, 1981, 1.

106. Letter, Wright to Greg Curtis, September 13, 1982, Folder "Letters to the Media," Box 678, Series 2, JWP; letter, Wright to Sydney Reagan, December 7, 1982, Folder "Gramm, Phil (TX)," Box 818, Series 2, JWP.

107. Ross Baker, "Party and Institutional Sanctions in the U.S. House: The Case of Congressman Gramm," *Legislative Studies Quarterly* 10, no. 3 (August 1985): 315–337; interview, Jim Wright, July 21, 2012.

108. NCPAC flier, Folder "NCPAC," Box 725, Series 2, JWP; "The War of the Wolf PAC's," *Newsweek* (June 1, 1981): 39–41; "Wright, Two Others Still on Hit List," *DMN*, June 12, 1981, 8; Tom Wicker, "U.S. Agency Should Look at Dolan's Outfit," *FWST*, May 14, 1981, 24.

109. *DMN*, December 8, 1981, 18; December 16, 1981, 14.

110. *NYT*, April 2, 1982, 14.

111. Letter, Wright to friends, undated, Folder "NCPAC," Box 725, Series 2, JWP.

112. NCPAC Action Report, undated, Folder "NCPAC," Box 725, Series 2, JWP; *FWST*, October 2, 1981, B4; October 22, 1981, 1; *DMN*, October 22, 1981, 5; Complaint, *John Dolan v. Jim Wright*, undated, Folder "Frank Case, 1981," Box 673, Series 2, JWP; letter, Stanley Brand to Wright, September 25, 1981, Folder "NCPAC," Box 1019, Series 2, JWP; photocopy, uncited article, "Texas Educator Predicts New Wave of McCarthyism," undated, Folder "NCPAC," Box 725, Series 2, JWP.

113. Wright Task Force, undated, Folder "NCPAC," Box 725, Series 2, JWP.

114. Letter, Wright to friends, March 12, 1981, undated, Folder "Democratic Congressional Committee Campaign," Box 723, Series 2, JWP.

115. Letter, Terry Dolan to Wright, June 17, 1981, Folder "NCPAC," Box 725, Series 2, JWP; letter, Wright to John Dolan, July 9, 1981, Folder "NCPAC," Box 725, Series 2, JWP.

116. Photocopy, uncited article, September 28, 1981, Folder "NCPAC," Box 725, Series 2, JWP.

117. *DMN*, June 20, 1981, 32; *WP*, July 13, 1981, 10.

118. Letter, Wright to colleagues, July 1, 1980, Folder "Dear Colleague Letters, 1979–1980," Box 715, Series 2, JWP; interview, Jim Wright, July 21, 2012.

119. Letter, Wright to colleagues, March 25, 1982, Folder "Dear Colleague Letters, 1981–82," Box 715, Series 2, JWP; photocopy, article, "Wright Receives Christian Statesman Award," Folder "1981 Scrapbook," Box 1266, Series 3, JWP; Wright diary, January 14, 1981.

120. Quoted in Wright diary, January 14, 1981.

121. Ibid., December 21, 1981.

122. John Barry, *Ambition and Power: A True Story of Washington* (New York: Penguin, 1990), 231.

123. Memo, Kim to Marshall Lynam, undated, Folder "Approaching Legal Limit Honoraria (1982)," Box 993, Series 2, JWP.

124. *DMN*, January 30, 1982, 32; *FWST*, February 2, 1982, 2.

125. Letter, Wright to Leo Melamed, October 20, 1982, Folder "Wright Appreciation Cmte. (1981–88) (6 of 6)," Box 670, Series 2, JWP.

126. Letter, Wright to Ronald Reagan, May 18, 1982, Folder "Letters to the President—Reagan," Box 726, Series 2, JWP.

127. Letter, Wright to Dan Rostenkowski, May 20, 1981, Folder "Letter to Dan Rostenkowski," Box 994, Series 2, JWP; letter, R. L. Crandall to Wright, September 3, 1982, no folder, Box 562, Series 1, JWP.

128. Wright flier, undated, Folder "1982 Election," Box 688, Series 2, JWP; *FWST*, October 17, 1981, 6.

129. *FWNT*, July 23, 1982, 14; *Wall Street Journal*, June 18, 1982, 1.

130. "Money Flows to the Right in 1982 Campaign," *CQWR* (February 27, 1982): 482; Harris Poll, May 20, 1982, Folder "Public Opinion," Box 720, Series 2, JWP.

131. Wright address, October 22, 1982, Folder "Speech Files: Democratic Party— Vote Democratic on November 2 Radio Address," Box 1285, Series 3, JWP.

132. Gary Jacobson and Samuel Kernel, "Strategy and Choice in the 1982 Congressional Elections," *PS* 15, no. 3 (Summer 1982): 423–430; Alan Abramowitz, "National Issues, Strategic Politicians, and Voting Behavior in the 1980 and 1982 Congressional Elections," *American Journal of Political Science* 28, no. 4 (November 1984): 710–721; John McAdams and John Johannes, "The Voter in the 1982 House Elections," *American Journal of Political Science* 28, no. 4 (November 1984): 778–781; interview, Jim Wright, July 21, 2012; Wright, *Balance*, 381.

CHAPTER 16

1. "The Winners: New Faces of '82," *Newsweek* (November 15, 1982): 36–37; Martin Tolchin, "The Majority Leader Is Riding High," *NYT*, August 1, 1983, 32; Dave Montgomery, "Voters Give Wright Some Team Players," *FWST*, November 4, 1982, 1, 13.

2. Letter, Wright to Bill Alexander, January 24, 1983, Folder "Dear Colleague Letters, 1982–83," Box 715, Series 2, JWP; Program for Economic Revival, undated, Folder "Dear Colleague Letters, 1982–83," Box 715, Series 2, JWP.

3. Letter, Walter Mondale to Wright, February 28, 1983, Folder "Correspondence with Presidential Hopefuls," Box 713, Series 2, JWP.

4. Letter, Thomas O'Neill et al. to Democrats, March 2, 1983, Folder "Dear Colleague Letters," Box 715, Series 2, JWP.

5. Thomas O'Neill et al. to Democrats, March 22, 1983, Folder "Dear Colleague Letters, 1982–83," Box 715, Series 2, JWP.

6. Letter, Newt Gingrich et al. to Republicans, November 17, 1983, Folder "Republican Correspondence," Box 726, Series 2, JWP.

7. Quoted in *NYT*, January 4, 1983, 1.

8. Quoted in transcript, *Meet the Press*, November 7, 1982, Folder "Media Transcripts," Box 722, Series 2, JWP.

9. Jim Wright, *Balance of Power: Presidents and Congress from the Era of McCarthy to the Age of Gingrich* (Atlanta: Turner, 1996), 389.

10. Ibid., quoted on 390.

11. P.L. 98–63; interview, Jim Wright, July 21, 2012.

12. Wright testimony, February 2, 1983, Folder "Dear Colleague Letters, 1982–83," Box 715, Series 2, JWP.

13. Quoted in *FWST*, April 14, 1983, 6.

14. Quoted in *FWST*, November 8, 1982, 1.

15. Chapter 2, Report, National Commission on Social Security Reform, January 1983, Social Security Administration homepage, Reports and Studies, www.ssa.gov /history/reports/gspan5.html, accessed June 12, 2014.

16. P.L. 98–21; Daniel Beland and Alex Waddan, *The Politics of Policy Change: Welfare, Medicare and Social Security Reform in the United States* (Washington, DC: Georgetown University Press, 2012), 125, 131–132, 134–135.

17. Remarks on Social Security Act Amendments, Public Papers of the Presidents, Ronald Reagan, APP, UCSB, www.presidency.ucsb.edu/ws/index.php?pid=41211&st=&st1=, accessed June 13, 2014.

18. Wright Reports From Washington, August 1983, Folder "Newsletter, August, 1983," Box 688, Series 2, JWP.

19. Letter, Wright to colleague, June 3, 1983, Folder "Dear Colleague Letters, 1982–83," Box 715, Series 2, JWP.

20. Letter, Wright to colleague, February 22, 1983, Folder "Dear Colleague Letters, 1982–83," Box 715, Series 2, JWP.

21. Letter, Wright to friends, April 15, 1983, Folder "Dear Colleague Letters, 1982–83," Box 715, Series 2, JWP.

22. Letter, Wright to Democrats, March 22, 1983, Folder "Dear Colleague Letters, 1982–83," Box 715, Series 2, JWP; letter, Wright to colleague, May 24, 1983, Folder "Dear Colleague Letters, 1982–83," Box 715, Series 2, JWP.

23. Letter, Wright to colleague, March 25, 1983, Folder "Dear Colleague Letters, 1982–83," Box 715, Series 2, JWP.

24. Wright Response to Reagan Address, June 25, 1983, Folder "Speech Files: Budget—Jim Wright Response," Box 1281, Series 3, JWP.

25. Letter, Wright to Bill Alexander, October 31, 1983, Folder "Alexander, Bill," Box 730, Series 2, JWP.

26. Letter, Wright to Tom Bevill, November 3, 1983, Folder "Bevill, Tom," Box 730, Series 2, JWP.

27. Quoted in *WP*, February 8, 1984, 3.

28. "Even Congress Is Unhappy with Congress," *U.S. News and World Report* (April 23, 1984): 37–39.

29. Wright statement, April 16, 1983, Folder "Speech Files: Economics—The Deficit Problem and Hard Choices," Box 1286, Series 3, JWP; Wright Response to Reagan Address, October 1, 1983, Folder "Speech Files: National Affairs—Response to President, October 1, 1983," Box 1289, Series 3, JWP.

30. Letter, James Baker to Wright and Dan Rostenkowski, February 8, 1984, Folder "James A. Baker," Box 741, Series 2, JWP.

31. Letter, Wright to James Baker, February 16, 1984, Folder "Deficits," Box 718, Series 2, JWP.

32. *Wall Street Journal*, June 23, 1984, 1; letter, Wright to James Baker, February 9, 1984, Folder "Budget—WH Conf. '84—Wright Proposals," Box 924, Series 2, JWP; letter, Wright to James Baker, February 28, 1984, Folder "Correspondence, 1983–89," Box 922, Series 2, JWP; letter, Bill Goodling to Wright, February 16, 1984, Folder "Deficits," Box 718, Series 2, JWP.

33. P.L. 98–270 and P.L. 98–369.

34. Wright statement, May 15, 1984, Folder "Speech Files: Economics—Anti-Variable Rate Mortgage," Box 1286, Series 3, JWP; Neil Fligstein and Adam Goldstein,

"The Roots of the Great Recession," in David Grusky, Bruce Western, and Christopher Wimer, eds., *The Great Recession* (New York: Russell Sage, 2011), 31–57.

35. William Link and Arthur Link, *American Epoch*, vol. 2, 7th ed. (New York: McGraw-Hill, 1993), 761; George Moss, *Moving On: The American People Since 1945*, 3rd ed. (Upper Saddle River, NJ: Prentice Hall, 2005), 290.

36. Michael Schaller, *Ronald Reagan* (New York: Oxford University Press, 2011), 45; see Robert Metzger, *Reagan: American Icon* (Philadelphia: University of Pennsylvania Press, 1989), and Will Bunch, *Tear Down This Myth: How the Reagan Legacy Has Distorted Our Politics and Haunts Our Future* (New York: Free Press, 2009).

37. Marissa Chappel, *The War on Welfare* (Philadelphia: University of Pennsylvania Press, 2011), 199–241; Michael Schaller and George Rising, *Republican Ascendancy: American Politics, 1968–2001* (Wheeling, IL: Harlan Davidson, 2001), 91–93; Moss, *Moving On*, 290; Schaller, *Ronald Reagan*, 46.

38. Peter Dreier, "Reagan's Legacy: Homeless in America," Shelterforce Online, National Housing Institute, June 2004, www.nhi.org/online/issues/135/reagan.html, accessed June 14, 2014.

39. Quoted in Steve Fraser, *Everyman a Speculator: A History of Wall Street in American Life* (New York: HarperCollins, 2005), 538; Graham Thompson, *American Culture in the 1980s* (Edinburgh, UK: Edinburgh University Press, 2007), 10–15.

40. Tip O'Neill and William Novak, *Man of the House: The Life and Political Memories of Speaker Tip O'Neill* (New York: Random House, 1987), 354.

41. Quoted in Karl Brandt, *Ronald Reagan and the House Democrats: Gridlock, Partisanship, and the Fiscal Crisis* (Columbia: University of Missouri Press, 2009), 128; *WP*, May 16, 1984, 1.

42. Letter, Wright to colleague, May 23, 1983, Folder "Dear Colleague Letters, 1982–83," Box 715, Series 2, JWP; quoted in transcript, CNN, *Evans and Novak*, January 30, 1983, Folder "Evans and Novak," Box 1289, Series 3.

43. Brandt, *Reagan*, 173–174; Martin Tolchin, *NYT*, March 1, 1984, 1.

44. Quoted in *USA Today*, December 4, 1984, 1.

45. Brandt, *Reagan*, 91.

46. "Last of the Red Hot Liberals," *Newsweek* (April 25, 1983): 27; quoted in transcript, PBS, *The Lawmakers*, March 3, 1983, Folder "Media Transcripts," Box 722, Series 2, JWP.

47. Quoted in "A Family Feud Among House Democrats," *Newsweek* (March 7, 1983): 36; *DTH*, April 9, 1984, 12.

48. Interview, Jim Wright, July 21, 2012; John Barry, *Ambition and Power: A True Story of Washington* (New York: Penguin, 1990), 391–392.

49. Robert Williams, *Political Scandals in the USA* (Edinburgh, UK: Keele University Press, 1998), 109; Barry, *Ambition*, 392.

50. Interview, Jim Wright, July 21, 2012; Barry, *Ambition*, 625.

51. Wright, *Balance*, 486.

52. Interview, Betty Lee Wright, February 1, 2013; interview, Jim Wright, July 21, 2012; quoted in Barry, *Ambition*, 632.

53. Barry, *Ambition*, 585.

54. Ibid., 696–697; interview, Jim Wright, July 21, 2012.

55. Letter, Wright to colleague, August 1, 1983, Folder "Dear Colleague Letters, 1982–83," Box 715, Series 2, JWP; Wright remarks, August 27, 1983, Folder "Civil Rights," Box 708, Series 2, JWP; Wright speech, October 5, 1984, Folder "Speech Files; Civil Rights—75 Years of Progress," Box 1282, Series 3, JWP; letter, Wright et al. to Ronald Reagan, September 6, 1985, Folder "Affirmative Action," Box 1058, Series 2, JWP.

56. Letter, Geraldine Ferraro to Wright, November 16, 1983, Folder "Ferraro, Geraldine," Box 818, Series 2, JWP.

57. Letter, Wright to colleague, November 15, 1983, Folder "Dear Colleague Letters, 1982–83," Box 715, Series 2, JWP; Wright flier, November 3, 1983, Folder "Speech Files: Education—President Reagan's Current Education Policy," Box 1287, Series 3, JWP; Wright speech, July 10, 1983, Folder "Speech Files: Education—Education and Our Future," Box 1287, Series 3, JWP; letter, Wright to colleague, March 22, 1983, Folder "Dear Colleague Letters, 1982–83," Box 715, Series 2, JWP.

58. Letter, Roy Jones to Wright, September 25, 1984, Folder "Moral Majority," Box 1019, Series 2, JWP.

59. Letter, Wright to Jerry Falwell, August 25, 1985, Folder "Falwell Letter," Box 833, Series 2, JWP.

60. Wright statement, June 25, 1984, Folder "Speech Files: Crime—JW Urges Passage of Justice Assistance," Box 1284, Series 3, JWP.

61. P.L. 98–473; Stephen Trott, "Implementing Criminal Justice Reform," *Public Administration Review* 45 (November 1985): 795–800.

62. Wright address, January 30, 1984, Folder "Speech Files: Democratic Party—The Lifeblood of Democracy," Box 1285, Series 3, JWP.

63. Interview, Jim Wright, July 21, 2012; Frances FitzGerald, *Way Out There in the Blue: Reagan, Star Wars, and the End of the Cold War* (New York: Touchstone, 2000), 265–313.

64. Wright statement, July 16, 1983, Folder "Speech Files: Defense—JW No Commitment Regarding Role of MX," Box 1284, Series 3, JWP; Edmund Morris, *Dutch: A Memoir of Ronald Reagan* (New York: Random House, 1999), 467–468; Wright statement, July 20, 1983, Folder "Speech Files: Defense—Statement on MX Missile and Bennett Amendment," Box 1284, Series 3, JWP.

65. Norman Graebner, Richard Burns, and Joseph Sircause, eds., *Reagan, Bush, Gorbachev: Revisiting the End of the Cold War* (Westport, CT: Praeger, 2008), 40–44; letter, Tip O'Neill to Wright, April 5, 1984, Folder "O'Neill, Thomas," Box 1118, Series 2, JWP; letter, Ronald Reagan to Tip O'Neill, December 14, 1983, Folder "Reagan Correspondence with O'Neill," Box 726, Series 2, JWP.

66. Wright, *Balance*, 394.

67. Wright statement, October 24, 1983, Folder "Speech Files: Foreign Affairs—Statement by Majority Leader Jim Wright, 10/24/83," Box 1288, Series 3, JWP.

68. Wright statement, September 28, 1984, Folder "Wright Voting Record," Box 993, Series 2, JWP.

69. Interview, Jim Wright, July 21, 2012; quoted in Wright, *Balance*, 394–395.

70. Interview, Jim Wright, July 21, 2012; quoted in Wright, *Balance*, 394–395;

letter, Ronald Reagan to Tip O'Neill, October 25, 1983, Folder "Reagan Correspondence with O'Neill," Box 726, Series 2, JWP.

71. Colin Dueck, *Hard Line: The Republican Party and U.S. Foreign Policy Since World War II* (Princeton, NJ: Princeton University Press, 2010), 215–216, 218, 220; interview, Jim Wright, July 21, 2012; Wright *Balance*, 395.

72. Farooq Hassan, "The Shooting Down of Korean Airlines 007 by the Soviets and the Future of Air Safety for Passengers," *International and Comparative Law Quarterly* 33, no. 3 (July 1984): 7612–7725; interview, Jim Wright, July 21, 2012; quoted in Peter Grier, "The Flight of Korean Airlines Flight 007," *American Air Force Magazine Online*, America Air Force Association, January 2013, www.airforcemag.com/magazinearchive /pages/2013/january%202013/0113korean.aspx, accessed May 18, 2014.

73. Letter, Ronald Reagan to Wright, July 13, 1983, Folder "Letters for the President— Reagan," Box 726, Series 2, JWP; interview, Jim Wright, July 21, 2012; quoted in Wright, *Balance*, 392.

74. Letter, Tip O'Neill to George Shultz, July 28, 1983, Folder "Far East Trip, Friday, August 5–Thursday, August 13, 1983," Box 684, Series 2, JWP; *DMN*, August 13, 1983, 31; Wright Reflections on Asia, undated, Folder "Far East Trip, Friday, August 5– Thursday, August 13, 1983," Box 684, Series 2, JWP.

75. *WP*, May 3, 1983, 12: Jim Wright, *Worth It All* (Washington, DC: Brassey's, 1993), 56.

76. Wright, *Balance*, 412; Address on Central America, April 27, 1983, Public Papers of the Presidents, Ronald Reagan, APP, UCSB, www.presidency.ucsb.edu/ws/index.php ?pid=41245&st=&st1.

77. I. M. Destler, "The Elusive Consensus: Congress and Central America," in Robert Leiken, ed., *Central America: Anatomy of a Conflict* (New York: Pergamon, 1984), 330.

78. Christian Smith, *Resisting Reagan: The U.S. Central American Peace Movement* (Chicago: University of Chicago Press, 1996), 31.

79. *CR*, 98th Cong., 2nd sess., vol. 130, pt. 9 (May 10, 1984): H11871–H11872.

80. Letter, Wright to Walter Mondale, June 21, 1983, Folder "Correspondence with Presidential Hopefuls," Box 713, Series 2, JWP.

81. *WP*, May 6, 1983, 17.

82. Letter, Ronald Reagan to Wright, May 9, 1984, Folder "Letters for the President— Reagan," Box 726, Series 2, JWP; interview, Jim Wright, July 21, 2012.

83. *Report of the National Bipartisan Commission on Central America* (Washington, DC: US Government Printing Office, 1984); List of Appearances, August 31– November 2, 1983, Folder "Bipartisan Commission on Central America," Box 718, Series 2, JWP; List of Individuals Consulted, October 9–16, 1993, Folder "Bipartisan Commission on Central America," Box 718, Series 2, JWP; Wright, *Worth It*, 64–65; Smith, *Resisting Reagan*, 31; quoted in Wright, *Balance*, 392; letter, Henry Kissinger to Ronald Reagan, January 10, 1984, Folder "Bipartisan Commission on Central America," Box 718, Series 2, JWP; Wright statement, January 11, 1984, Folder "Speech Files: Foreign Affairs—Statement on Report of Kissinger Commission," Box 1288, Series 3, JWP.

84. Quoted in Wright, *Balance*, 423.

85. Wright, *Worth It*, 61, quoted on 63–64.

86. Bob Woodward, *Veil: the Secret Wars of the CIA, 1981–1987* (New York: Simon and Schuster, 2005), 349–350, 396–398; Wright, *Worth It*, 73–74.

87. Letter, Wright et al. to Daniel Ortega, March 20, 1984, Folder "Nicaragua," Box 688, Series 2, JWP; letter, Wright to George Melloan, April 24, 1984, Folder "Nicaragua," Box 688, Series 2, JWP; interview, Jim Wright, July 21, 2012; Wright, *Worth It*, 65–66.

88. Letter, Wright to Jack Germond, April 23, 1984, Folder "Daniel Ortega," Box 1045, Series 2, JWP.

89. Letter, Newt Gingrich to Wright, April 23, 1984, Folder "Congressional Correspondence," Box 726, Series 2, JWP.

90. Letter, Manuel Cordero to Wright, August 17, 1984, Folder "Foreign Dignitary Correspondence," Box 693, Series 2, JWP; Woodward, *Veil*, 391–392; Wright, *Worth It*, 74.

91. Letter, Ronald Reagan to Wright, April 18, 1984, Folder "Letters for the President—Reagan," Box 726, Series 2, JWP.

92. Letter, Alan Cranston to Wright, January 24, 1983, Folder "Correspondence with Presidential Hopefuls," Box 713, Series 2, JWP; letter, John Glenn to Wright, May 26, 1983, Folder "Correspondence with Presidential Hopefuls," Box 713, Series 2, JWP; letter, Wright to John Glenn, June 2, 1983, Folder "Correspondence with Presidential Hopefuls," Box 713, Series 2, JWP.

93. Wright statement, March 6, 1984, Folder "Speech Files: Democratic Party—Why I Support Mondale," Box 1285, Series 3, JWP.

94. Letter, Walter Mondale to Wright, April 9, 1984, Folder "Correspondence with Presidential Hopefuls," Box 713, Series 2, JWP; *Wall Street Journal*, February 28, 1984, 17; letter, Charles Manatt to Eli Corak, February 23, 1983, Folder "Democratic National Committee," Box 724, Series 2, JWP.

95. Letter, Tip O'Neill to Dorothy Bush, January 2, 1985, Folder "Democratic National Committee," Box 724, Series 2, JWP; letter, Wright to Tip O'Neill, February 4, 1985, Folder "Democratic National Committee," Box 724, Series 2, JWP.

96. Memo, Marshall Lynam to Rosalind Wyman, March 19, 1984, Folder "1984 Democratic National Convention—San Francisco—July," Box 684, Series 2, JWP; *DTH*, July 18, 1984, 7.

97. Wright statement, July 19, 1984, Folder "Speech Files: Democratic Party—Opening Door Speech," Box 1285, Series 3, JWP; letter, Wright to Timothy Goggans, August 9, 1984, Folder "84 Campaign," Box 993, Series 2, JWP.

98. "Southern Strategy?" *Barron Report* 171 (February 28, 1983): 1–2; letter, Wright to J. J. Pickle, September 27, 1984, Folder "Dear Colleague Letters, 1983–84," Box 715, Series 2, JWP.

99. Letter, Charles Manatt to Wright, October 29, 1984, Folder "Democratic National Committee," Box 724, Series 2, JWP.

100. *NYT*, March 16, 1984, 21; *San Antonio Light*, March 19, 1984, 1.

101. *FWST*, May 6, 1984, 33.

102. Walter Mondale, *The Good Fight* (New York: Scribner, 2010), 292–307; Eric Woodrum, "Moral Conservatism and the 1984 Presidential Election," *Journal of the Scientific Study of Religion* 27, no. 2 (June 1988): 192–210; Stephen Johnson and

Joseph Tamney, "The Christian Right and the 1984 Presidential Election," *Review of Religious Research* 27, no. 2 (December 1985): 124–133; David Kinder, Paul Gronke, and Gordon Adams, "Economics and Politics in the 1984 Presidential Election," *American Journal of Political Science* 33, no. 2 (May 1989): 491–515; Stephen Rosenstone, "Explaining the 1984 Presidential Election," *Brookings Review* 2, no. 2 (Winter 1985): 25–32; Schaller and Rising, *Republican Ascendancy*, 102.

103. Interview, Jim Wright, July 21, 2012; "Jim Wright: On the Road to Being Speaker," *CQWR* (April 7, 1984): 775–778, quoted on 777; *FWST*, February 6, 1985, 1.

104. Wright statement, February 7, 1985, Folder "Latin America," Box 709, Series 2, JWP; *DMN*, February 7, 1985, 1; *WP*, February 8, 1985; Richard Cohen, "Despite Rumblings in Democratic Ranks, Jim Wright Favored to Be Next Speaker," *National Journal* (March 1, 1986): 499–503.

105. Quoted in John Sansing, "Things Get Nasty on the Floor as Speaker Battle Intensifies," *Washingtonian* (August 1985): 9.

106. Quoted in *FWST*, September 15, 1985, 2; memo, Don to Marshall Lynam, September 13, 1985, Folder "Hyatt Regency Demonstration, September 13, 1985," Box 675, Series 2, JWP.

107. Quoted in *FWST*, December 9, Special Section, 7.

108. Quoted in *DTH*, September 14, 1986; *FWST*, September 12, 1986, 1; May 21, 1986, 18; Wright address, August 26, 1986, Folder "Drugs," Box 686, Series 2, JWP; Wright statement, May 20, 1986, Folder "Drugs," Box 686, Series 2, JWP.

109. P.L. 99–570; see Dan Baum, *Smoke and Mirrors: The War on Drugs and the Politics of Failure* (New York: Little, Brown, 1996), 196–198, 205, 233–234.

110. Balanced Budget and Emergency Deficit Control Act, P.L. 99–177.

111. *CR*, 99th Cong., 1st sess., vol. 131, pt. 22 (November 1, 1985): H31192–H30193; letter, Connie Mack to Wright, December 11, 1985, Folder "Congressional Correspondence," Box 726, Series 2, JWP.

112. Wright remarks, November 13, 1985, Folder "Speech Files: Economics—Liquidity Crisis," Box 1286, Series 3, JWP; interview, Jim Wright, July 21, 2012.

113. Statement of Frank Annunzio, January 29, 1986, Folder "Democratic Caucus," Box 924, Series 2, JWP; letter, James Miller to Wright, November 4, 1986, Folder "Executive Office of the President—Office of Management and Budget," Box 726, Series 2, JWP; letter, William Gray to Wright, January 24, 1986, Folder "Budget," Box 924, Series 2, JWP.

114. *Bowsher v. Synar*, 478 U.S. 714 (1986).

115. Balanced Budget and Emergency Deficit Control Reaffirmation Act, P.L. 100–119; Schaller and Rising, *Republican Ascendancy*, 106–109; David Farber, *The Rise and Fall of Modern American Conservatism* (Princeton, NJ: Princeton University Press, 2010), 224, 238.

116. Budget Enforcement Act, P.L. 101–508; Robert Kelly, *The National Debt of the United States, 1941–2008* (Jefferson, NC: McFarland, 2008), 289–336.

117. P.L. 99–603; Roger Daniels, *Coming to America: A History of Immigration and Ethnicity in American Life*, 2nd ed. (New York: HarperCollins, 2002), 391–397.

118. Letter, Wright to colleague, June 12, 1984, Folder "Dear Colleague Letters," 1983–84," Box 715, Series 2, JWP; Wright remarks, April 1984, Folder "Speech Files:

Foreign Affairs—J. Wright Amendment, April, 1984," Box 1288, Series 3, JWP; Fact Sheet, undated, Folder "Jim Wright Sponsored Amendment to Immigration Bill, Simpson-Mazzoli, 1984," Box 717, Series 2, JWP; Robert Garcia to colleague, undated, Folder "Jim Wright Sponsored Amendment to Immigration Bill, Simpson-Mazzoli, 1984," Box 717, Series 2, JWP; *NYT*, January 20, 1984, 22.

119. Brad Plumer, "Congress Tried to Fix Immigration Back in 1986. Why Did It Fail?" Wonkblog, *WP*, January 30, 2013, www.washingtonpost.com/blogs/wonkblog/wp/2013/01/30/in-1986-congress-tried-to-solve-immigration-why-didnt-it-work, accessed June 24, 2014; Roger Daniels, *Guarding the Open Door: American Immigration Policy and Immigrants Since 1882* (New York: Hill and Wang, 2004), 219–260.

120. P.L. 99–514; Wright statement, December 17, 1985, Folder "Wright Voting Record," Box 993, Series 2, JWP; see Joel Slimrod, *Do Taxes Matter? The Impact of the Tax Reform Act of 1986* (Cambridge, MA: MIT Press, 1990).

121. Quoted in *WP*, April 1, 1985, 1; Richard Cohen, *Rostenkowski: The Pursuit of Power and the End of the Old Politics* (Chicago: Ivan Dee, 1999), 148.

122. Quoted in *FWST*, November 15, 1985, 19; November 17, 1985, 33.

123. Chronology of Trade Bill, Folder "Press Releases," Box 678, Series 2, JWP; letter, Wright to Dan Rostenkowski, September 10, 1985, Folder "Rostenkowski, Dan," Box 734, Series 2, JWP.

124. Letter, Wright to friends, July 31, 1985, Folder "Speech Files: Crime—Dear Friend (1985)," Box 1284, Series 3, JWP; quoted in *FWST*, July 11, 1985, 3.

125. Press release, Folder "Defense—Wright Heads Delegates to Arms Control Talks," Box 1284, Series 3, JWP; interview, Jim Wright, July 21, 2012.

126. Interview, Jim Wright, July 21, 2012; Wright, *Balance*, 400–401.

127. Wright statement, March 26, 1985, Folder "Speech Files: Foreign Affairs—Bipartisan Group in Geneva," Box 1288, Series 3, JWP; Wright column, "Ronald Reagan's Unique Opportunity to Wage Peace," Folder "RR's Unique Opportunity to Wage Peace," Box 1284, Series 3, JWP; Wright, *Balance*, 406; interview, Jim Wright, July 21, 2012.

128. Letter, Wright et al. to Ronald Reagan, November 22, 1985, Folder "Letters to the President—Reagan," Box 726, Series 2, JWP; letter, Anatoly Dobrynin to Wright, January 27, 1986, Folder "Correspondence, January–April, 1986," Box 670, Series 2, JWP.

129. *CR*, 99th Cong., 2nd sess., vol. 132, pt. 9 (June 3, 1986): H12102; Wright statement on SALT II, undated, Folder "1986 Press Releases," Box 675, Series 2, JWP.

130. Letter, Ronald Reagan to Wright, October 8, 1986, Folder "Letters for the President—Reagan," Box 726, Series 2, JWP.

131. Ken Adelman, *Reagan at Reykjavik: Forty-Eight Hours That Ended the Cold War* (New York: Broadside, 2014), 38–40, 84–85, 304–322; Vivek Viswanatham, "Fallout from Reykjavik: Reagan's Stand and the Fate of Arms Control," *New York History* 87, no. 1 (Winter 2006): 135–143; Wright, *Balance*, 408.

132. Wright, *Balance*, 430–435, quoted on 435.

133. Interview, Jim Wright, July 21, 2012; see Lawrence Walsh, *Firewall: The Iran Contra Conspiracy and Cover-up* (New York: Norton, 1997).

CHAPTER 17

1. Quoted in "A Modern Speaker for Modern Times," *CQWR* (March 22, 1986): 691.

2. Flier, Don McNeil for Congress, Folder "1986 Campaign," Box 699, Series 2, JWP; letter, Don McNeil to Wright, August 14, 1986, Folder "1986 Campaign," Box 699, Series 2, JWP; *DTH*, October 22, 1986, 1, 15.

3. Malcolm Byrne, *Iran-Contra: Reagan's Scandal and the Unchecked Abuse of Presidential Power* (Lawrence: University of Kansas Press, 2014), 262–295, 307–329; Edmund Morris, *Dutch: A Memoir of Ronald Reagan* (New York: Random House, 1999), 616.

4. Lynne Brown and Robert Peabody, "Patterns of Succession in House Democratic Leadership: The Choices of Wright, Foley, Coelho, 1986," paper presented at the American Political Science Association Annual Meeting, Chicago, September 3–6, 1987.

5. Ibid.; press release, January 4, 1989, Folder "1989 Press Releases," Box 678, Series 2, JWP; letter, David Bonior to Wright, February 10, 1989, Folder "Democratic Response, 1989," Box 724, Series 2, JWP; *NYT*, December 9, 1989, 1, 12; John Barry, *Ambition and Power: A True Story of Washington* (New York: Penguin, 1990), 78–81.

6. Interview, Paul Driscoll, July 17, 2014; Alan Ehrenhalt, "Speaker's Job Transformed Under O'Neill," *CQWR* (June 22, 1985): 1247; Barry, *Ambition*, 69–70, 81–83.

7. Memo, William Oldaker to Marshall Lynam, December 4, 1986, Folder "Swearing-In, January 6, 1986," Box 671, Series 2, JWP; letter, George White to Wright, December 1, 1986, Folder "P.I. RC Box 1114B—Swearing In (Ceremony Folder)," Box 671, Series 2, JWP.

8. Wright remarks, December 8, 1986, Folder "1986 Press Releases," Box 675, Series 2, JWP.

9. Letter, Etta Hulme to Wright, February 1, 1987, Folder "Political Cartoons," Box 1145, Series 2, JWP.

10. Tim Richardson, "The Eyes of Texas Are on Jim Wright," *RC* 32, no. 22 (December 11, 1986): 1, 20; letter, Marshall Lynam to Joseph Eley, December 26, 1986, Folder "Correspondence, September–December, 1986 (3 of 3)," Box 670, Series 2, JWP.

11. Janet Hook, "Speaker Jim Wright Takes Charge in the House," *CQWR* (July 11, 1987): 1483; interview, Jim Wright, July 22, 2012; Jim Wright, *Balance of Power: Presidents and Congress from the Era of McCarthy to the Age of Gingrich* (Atlanta: Turner, 1996), 446.

12. Democratic Response, Folder "Speech Files: National Affairs—Jim Wright Response to President's State of the Union," Box 1289, Series 3, JWP.

13. P.L. 100–4; quoted in *WP*, February 3, 1987, 1.

14. Letter, Ronald Reagan to Wright, March 19, 1987, Folder "Letters for the President—Reagan," Box 726, Series 2, JWP.

15. P.L. 100–17; Wright statement, March 23, 1987, Folder "1987 Press Releases," Box 686, Series 2, JWP; Barry, *Ambition*, 180–182, 189–192, 198–199, quoted on 180.

16. P.L. 100–77; interview, Paul Driscoll, July 15, 2014; History, McKinney-Vento Act, National Coalition for the Homeless Fact Sheet #18, June 2006, www.national homeless.org/publications/facts/McKinney.pdf, accessed July 19, 2014.

17. Transcript, Jim Wright Recollections, February 12, 1987, Folder "Wright Transcripts and Speech Interview," Box 943, Series 2, JWP.

18. P.L. 100–242; interview, Paul Driscoll, July 15, 2014; letter, Wright to Fellow Americans, June 30, 1988, Folder "1988 Press Releases," Box 678, Series 2, JWP; Remarks on Signing of Housing and Community Development Act, Public Papers of the Presidents, Ronald Reagan, APP, UCSB, www.presidency.ucsb.edu/ws/index.php?pid=35099&st=&st1=, accessed July 19, 2014.

19. P.L. 100–297; Janet Hook, "100th Congress Wraps Up Surprisingly Busy Year," *CQWR* (October 29, 1988): 3118.

20. Remarks on Signing of Hawkins-Stafford Amendments, Public Papers of the Presidents, Ronald Reagan, APP, UCSB, www.presidency.ucsb.edu/ws/index.php?pid=35745&st=&st1=, accessed July 24, 2014.

21. Interview, Paul Driscoll, July 15, 2014; interview, Mike Andrews, July 14, 2014; Kent Hughes, "American Trade Politics: From the Omnibus Act of 1988 to the Trade Act of 2002," paper presented at Global Economy Seminar on Congress and Trade Policy, November 17, 2003, Woodrow Wilson International Center for Scholars.

22. Interview, Paul Driscoll, July 15, 2014; Barry, *Ambition*, 177–179, 267–278, 614–615.

23. Barry, *Ambition*, 620–621, 627–628, 640; Chronology of Trade Bill, August 9, 1988, Folder "Press Releases," Box 678, Series 2, JWP; P.L. 100–418; *FWST*, July 19, 1988, 9; Ronald Reagan, *Reagan Diaries* (New York: Harper, 2009), 606.

24. Transcript, Wright Recollections, undated, Folder "Wright Interview and Speech Transcripts," Box 943, Series 2, JWP.

25. P.L. 100–235; interview, Jim Wright, July 22, 2012.

26. 465 U.S. 555 (1984); Michael Villalobos, "The Civil Rights Restoration Act of 1987: Revitalization of Title IX," *Marquette Sports Law Review* 149 (1990), http://scholarship.law.marquette.edu/cgi/viewcontent.cgi?article=1005&context=sportslaw, accessed July 23, 2014.

27. Message Returning Without Approval Civil Rights Restoration Act of 1987, Public Papers of the Presidents, Ronald Reagan, APP, UCSB, www.presidency.ucsb.edu/ws/index.php?pid=35559&st=&st1=, accessed July 23, 2014; Wright statement, March 16, 1988, Folder "Speech Files: Civil Rights—Statement of JW on Civil Rights Restoration Act," Box 1282, Series 3, JWP; P.L. 100–259.

28. Kenneth Meier, J. L. Polinard, and Robert Wrinkle, "Politics, Bureaucracy, and Farm Credit," *Public Administration Review* 59, no. 4 (July 1999), 293–302; memo, Bill Alexander to Wright, March 17, 1987, Folder "Alexander, Bill," Box 734, Series 2, JWP; letter, Wright to Fellow Americans, June 30, 1988, Folder "1988 Press Releases," Box 678, Series 2, JWP.

29. P.L. 100–233; David Freshwater, "Competition and Consolidation in the Farm Credit System," *Review of Agricultural Economics* 19, no. 1 (Spring-Summer 1997): 219–227; History, Farm Credit Administration, www.fca.gov/about/history/historyFCA_FCS.html, accessed July 24, 2014.

30. Remarks on Signing of Agricultural Credit Act, Public Papers of the Presidents, Ronald Reagan, APP, UCSB, www.presidency.ucsb.edu/ws/index.php?pid=36256&st =&st1=, accessed July 25, 2014.

31. P.L. 100–383; see Leslie Hatamiya, *Righting a Wrong: Japanese-Americans and the Passage of the Civil Liberties Act of 1988* (Palo Alto, CA: Stanford University Press, 1994).

32. P.L. 100–690; letter, Wright to friend, October 21, 1987, Folder "Speech Files: Crime—Congressional Letter on Drugs," Box 1284, Series 3, JWP; telegram, Wright to Richard Thornburgh, November 4, 1988, Folder "1988 Press Releases," Box 678, Series 2, JWP.

33. Letter, Wright to Ronald Reagan, March 20, 1987, Folder "Letters to the President—Reagan," Box 726, Series 2, JWP.

34. P.L. 100–517 and P.L. 100–360, respectively; letter, Wright to Robert Anderson, April 24, 1987, Folder "112280–112326," Box 640, Series 1, JWP; *NYT*, October 9, 1989, 1.

35. Richard Himmelfarb, *Catastrophic Politics: The Rise and Fall of the Medicare Catastrophic Coverage Act of 1988* (State College: Pennsylvania State University Press, 1995), 29–30, 53–54; Christine Day, "Older Americans' Attitudes Toward the Medicare Catastrophic Coverage Act of 1988," *Journal of Politics* 55, no. 1 (February 1993): 167–177; letter, Bill Young to Wright, November 20, 1987, unmarked folder, Box 729, Series 2, JWP.

36. Craig Smith, "The Campaign to Repeal the Fairness Doctrine," *Rhetoric and Public Affairs* 2, no. 3 (Fall 1999): 481–505; see Steven Simmons, *The Fairness Doctrine and the Media* (Berkeley: University of California Press, 1978).

37. Letter, Wright to colleague, December 2, 1987, Folder "Dear Colleague Letters That the Speaker Signed Onto," Box 702, Series 2, JWP.

38. David Brock, *The Republican Noise Machine* (New York: Crown, 2004), 296–298.

39. William Coleman and Donald Bliss, *Counsel for the Situation: Reshaping the Law to Realize America's Promise* (Washington, DC: Brookings Institution, 2010), 323–334; interview, Paul Driscoll, July 15, 2014; interview, Jim Wright, July 22, 2012; Barry, *Ambition*, 304; quoted in Richard Cohen, "Full Steam Ahead," *National Journal* (January 1, 1988): 238.

40. *NYT*, April 7, 1987, 34.

41. Interview, Paul Driscoll, July 15, 2014; interview, Mike Andrews, July 14, 2014; interview, Jim Wright, July 22, 2012.

42. Quoted in *WD*, March 1, 1987, 7.

43. Interview, Jim Wright, July 22, 2014; Barry, *Ambition*, 143.

44. Quoted in Richard Cohen, *Rostenkowski: The Pursuit of Power and the End of the Old Politics* (Chicago: Ivan Dee, 1999), 159.

45. Interview, Paul Driscoll, July 15, 2014; Barry, *Ambition*, 168–169.

46. Barry, *Ambition*, 172–173, 178–179, 204–208; Wright statement, June 16, 1987, Folder "Speech Files: Budget—Jim Wright's Response to Reagan," Box 1282, Series 3, JWP.

47. Interview, Paul Driscoll, July 15, 2014; Barry, *Ambition*, 283–285, 288–296, 300.

48. Barry, *Ambition*, 300; interview, Mike Andrews, July 14, 2014.

49. Quoted in Morris, *Dutch*, 579.

50. Statement on Signing of Federal Debt Ceiling Bill, Public Papers of the Presidents, Ronald Reagan, APP, UCSB, www.presidency.ucsb.edu/ws/index.php?pid=33467&st=&st1=, accessed July 23, 2014; Barry, *Ambition*, 383–386, 400.

51. Karl Brandt, *Ronald Reagan and the House Democrats: Gridlock, Partisanship, and the Fiscal Crisis* (Columbia: University of Missouri Press, 2009), 196; interview, Jim Wright, July 22, 2012; Barry, *Ambition*, 408–409.

52. Didier Sornette, *Why Stock Markets Crash* (Princeton, NJ: Princeton University Press, 2003), 228–230; see Tim Metz, *Black Monday: The Stock Market Catastrophe of October 19, 1987* (Frederick, MD: Beard, 2003); Wright statement, October 27, 1987, Folder "1987 Press Releases," Box 686, Series 2, JWP.

53. Letter, Robert Michel to Wright, October 21, 1987, Folder "Republican Leader Correspondence," Box 726, Series 2, JWP; quoted in *FWST*, October 29, 1987, 1, 22.

54. Interview, Paul Driscoll, July 15, 2014; Barry, *Ambition*, 419–447.

55. Barry, *Ambition*, 448–473.

56. Brandt, *Reagan*, 193–194; James Barnes, "Political Focus: Partisanship," *National Journal* (November 7, 1987): 282.

57. Interview, Jim Wright, July 22, 2012; interview, Mike Andrews, July 14, 2014; Barry, *Ambition*, 474–482.

58. Summit Agreement, November 20, 1987, Folder "Fairness Doctrine," Box 1054, Series 2, JWP; interview, Paul Driscoll, July 15, 2014; letter, Ronald Reagan to Wright, December 1, 1987, Folder "Letters for the President," Box 726, Series 2, JWP; Brandt, *Reagan*, 194–195; Barry, *Ambition*, 483–493, 496–497, 515–522.

59. P.L. 100–203; letter, Bill Goodling to Wright, January 19, 1988, Folder "Republican Correspondence #2," Box 726, Series 2, JWP; Remarks on the Signing of Omnibus Budget Reconciliation Act, Public Papers of the Presidents, Ronald Reagan, APP, UCSB, www.presidency.ucsb.edu/ws/index.php?pid=33852&st=&st1=, accessed July 23, 2014.

60. Mikhail Gorbachev and George Shriver, *On My Country and the World* (New York: Columbia University Press, 1999), 2, 30, 57–66, 204–205, 276, 277; press release, March 11, 1987, Folder "JW—Soviet Trip, 1987," Box 833, Series 2, JWP; *WP*, January 11, 1987, C1; *FWST*, April 5, 1987, 29.

61. Letter, Wright to James Howard, April 28, 1987, Folder "Soviet Union Trip, 1987," Box 671, Series 2, JWP.

62. Letter, Joseph Ross to Wright, April 2, 1987, Folder "Russian Letters Trip File, Briefing Book for Congressional Members," Box 1328, Series 3, JWP; letter, Wright to Thomas Foley, March 30, 1987, Folder "Russia Trip, Soviet Trip Project, Immigrants, March 25, 1987–March 31, 1987," Box 1329, Series 2, JWP.

63. Letter, Mickey Leland to Wright, April 9, 1987, Folder "Russian Letters Trip Files, Briefing Book for Congressional Members," Box 1328, Series 3, JWP; letter, Clay Shaw to Wright, March 31, 1987, Folder "Russia Trip, Soviet Trip Project, Immigrants, March 25, 1987–March 31, 1987," Box 1329, Series 2, JWP; letter, Les AuCoin to Wright, April 2, 1987, Folder "Russia Trip, Soviet Trip Project, Immigrants, March 25, 1987–March 31, 1987," Box 1329, Series 2, JWP; letter, Barney Frank to Wright, April 9, 1987,

Folder "Russian Trip, 17/60, Soviet Trip Project, Immigration, April 2, 1987–July 21, 1987," Box 1329, Series 2, JWP; memo, Don to Marshall Lynam, March 29, 1987, Folder "Trip to Soviet Union, 1987, 17/60, Trip, USSR—3, Human Rights in Soviet Union," Box 1328, Series 3, JWP; letter, Nancy Bass to Wright, March 25, 1987, Folder "Trip to Soviet Union, 1987, 17/60, Trip, USSR—3, Human Rights in Soviet Union," Box 1328, Series 3, JWP.

64. Letter, Wright to Ralph Regula, April 1, 1987, Folder "Soviet Union Trip, April, 1987 (Second Folder)," Box 671, Series 2, JWP; letter, Steny Hoyer to Wright, March 16, 1987, Folder "Soviet Union Trip, April, 1987 (Second Folder)," Box 671, Series 2, JWP; letter, Steny Hoyer to Wright, April 6, 1987, Folder "Trip to Soviet Union, 1987, 17/60, Trip, USSR—3, Human Rights in Soviet Union," Box 1328, Series 3, JWP.

65. Trip schedule, Folder "Soviet Union Trip, April, 1987," Box 671, Series 2, JWP; *DTH*, April 15, 1987, 6.

66. Quoted in *DMN*, April 15, 1987, 4.

67. Letter, Steny Hoyer to Wright, May 4, 1987, Folder "Soviet Union Trip, April, 1987," Box 677, Series 2, JWP; quoted in *DMN*, April 20, 1987, 1.

68. *FWST*, April 30, 1987, 20; quoted in *FWST*, April 16, 1987, 14.

69. *FWST*, April 10, 1987, 10; quoted in *DMN*, April 18, 1987, 22.

70. Quoted in James Riddlesperger Jr., Anthony Champagne, and Dan Williams, eds., *The Wright Stuff: Reflections on People and Politics by Former Speaker Jim Wright* (Fort Worth: Texas Christian University Press, 2013), 197–202; *FWST*, April 12, 1987, 1, 12; quoted in Wright, *Balance*, 454.

71. Quoted in Riddlesperger et al., *Wright Stuff*, 202–204.

72. Letter, Marshall Lynam to Joseph Ross, May 1, 1987, Folder "Soviet Union Trip, April 10–21, Thank You," Box 671, Series 2, JWP; letter, Alexandrov Samuilovich to Wright, April 26, 1987, Folder "Russian Letters, Ala–Ale," Box 1291, Series 3, JWP; letter, Tatyana Agalakova to Wright, April 24, 1987, Folder "Russian Letters, Ala–Ale," Box 1291, Series 3, JWP.

73. Letter, Alexeyev Alexnadrovich to Wright, April 20, 1987, Folder "Russian Letters, Ala–Ale," Box 1291, Series 3, JWP.

74. Letter, Sue Abrahamson to Wright, May 20, 1987, Folder "Russian Letter, Trip File, Correspondence, General," Box 1329, Series 2, JWP; letter, Walter Hornsby to Wright, April 28, 1987, Folder "Russian Letters, Trip File, Correspondence, General," Box 1329, Series 2, JWP; photocopy, *Manchester Union Leader* editorial, undated, Folder "Sack the Quarterback," Box 675, Series 2, JWP.

75. Letter, Armand Hammer to Wright, May 14, 1987, Folder "Russian Letters, Trip File—Correspondence, General," Box 1329, Series 2, JWP; letter, Peter Palecek to Wright, April 23, 1987, Folder "Russian Letters, Trip File—Correspondence, General," Box 1329, Series 2, JWP.

76. Interview, Jim Wright, July 22, 2012; Pen Pal List, undated, Folder "Russia Trip File, 17/60, Soviet Pen Pal Project, 1 of 2," Box 1329, Series 2, JWP; letter, Paul Graff to Wright, May 19, 1987, Folder "Russia Trip, 17/60, Soviet Pen Pal Project, 1 of 2," Box 1329, Series 2, JWP.

77. Wright remarks, April 20, 1987, Folder "Speech Files: Foreign Affairs—When the Wall Comes Down," Box 1288, Series 3, JWP.

78. Quoted in *FWST*, April 21, 1987, 9; letter, Wright to Kurt Mattick, June 16, 1987, Folder "Soviet Union Trip, April 10–21, Thank You," Box 677, Series 2, JWP.

79. Letter, Wright to colleague, May 21, 1987, Folder "Russia Letter, Trip File—Correspondence, General," Box 1329, Series 2, JWP; letter, Wright to Anatoly Dobrynin, May 11, 1987, Folder "Soviet Union Trip, April 10–21, Thank You," Box 671, Series 2, JWP; letter, Wright to Mikhail Gorbachev, May 11, 1987, Folder "Soviet Union Trip, April, 1987," Box 671, Series 2, JWP; letter, Wright to Mikhail Gorbachev, June 1, 1987, Folder "Soviet Union Trip, April, 1987," Box 671, Series 2, JWP; letter, Wright to Mikhail Gorbachev, January 13, 1988, Folder "JW—Soviet Trip, 1987," Box 833, Series 2, JWP.

80. Quoted in *FWST*, April 19, 1987, 29.

81. Letter, Wright to Abdel Raouf El Reedy, June 27, 1988, Folder "Correspondence, April–June, 1988," Box 673, Series 2, JWP; letter, Wright to C. P. Chang, September 23, 1987, Folder "Correspondence, July–September, 1987," Box 671, Series 2, JWP; letter, Chiang Ching-kuo to Wright, October 21, 1987, Folder "Correspondence, October–December, 1987," Box 671, Series 2, JWP.

82. Letter, Don Camp to Marshall Lynam, August 14, 1987, Folder "India Trip," Box 672, Series 2, JWP; letter, Seyfi to Marshall Lynam, July 18, 1987, Folder "Turkey," Box 672, Series 2, JWP; letter, Marshall Lynam to Halis Komili, November 30, 1987, Folder "Turkey," Box 672, Series 2, JWP; trip schedule, Folder "Speaker Trip to UK, July 1–July 6, 1988," Folder 672, Series 2, JWP; letter, Wright to Bernard Weatherhill, November 24, 1987; Folder "Trip to United Kingdom, 1988," Box 697, Series 2, JWP; trip schedule, Folder "Australia Trip, August 19–September 2, 1988," Box 672, Series 2, JWP; trip schedule, Folder "Israel Trip, 1987," Box 672, Series 2, JWP; letter, Yosef Lamdan to Wright, January 21, 1988, Folder "Israel Trip, 1987," Box 672, Series 2, JWP; *FWST*, January 14, 1988, D6.

83. Letter, James Baker to Wright, August 26, 1987, Folder "Secretary of the Treasury," Box 726, Series 2, JWP.

84. Press release, July 7, 1988, Folder "Speech Files: Foreign Affairs—Downed Iranian Airliner Reparations," Box 1288, Series 3, JWP.

85. Memo, Dorothy to Marshall Lynam, undated, Folder "NCPAC," Box 1019, Series 2, JWP.

86. Byrne, *Iran-Contra*, 284–286, 291; United States, President's Special Review Board, *The Tower Commission Report: The Full Text of the President's Special Review Board* (New York: Bantam, 1987).

87. Wright statement, undated, Folder "1987 Press Releases," Box 686, Series 2, JWP.

88. Letter, George Shultz to Wright, March 10, 1987, Folder "Secretary of State," Box 726, Series 2, JWP.

89. Statement of Principles for Alternative Policy, Folder "Contra Aid," Box 1011, Series 2, JWP; Wright statement, March 10, 1987, Folder "Contra Aid," Box 1011, Series 2, JWP.

90. Memo, Matthew to Wright, June 18, 1987, Folder "DCCC—Philadelphia, June 19, 1987," Box 1145, Series 2, JWP; Wright statement, July 28, 1987, Folder "Contras, July 28, 1987," Box 1145, Series 2, JWP.

91. Interview, Jim Wright, July 22, 2012; Jim Wright, *Worth It All* (Washington, DC: Brassey's, 1993), 94–106.

92. Wright, *Worth It.*

93. Plan for Peace, undated, Folder "Nicaragua Peace Plan, 1987," Box 1019, Series 2, JWP; *DMN*, August 7, 1987, 13; Wright, *Worth It*, 198; interview, Jim Wright, July 22, 2012; Remarks on Central American Peace Initiative, Public Papers of the Presidents, Ronald Reagan, APP, UCSB, www.presidency.ucsb.edu/ws/index.php?pid=34648&st=&st1=, accessed May 13, 2014.

94. Wright address, August 8, 1987, Folder "Nicaraguan Peace Plan," Box 1019, Series 2, JWP.

95. Quoted in *FWST*, August 6, 1987, 1; August 7, 1987, 1.

96. William LeoGrande, *Our Own Backyard: The United States and Central America, 1977–1992* (Chapel Hill: University of North Carolina Press, 2000), 481–483, 493–503, 510; Christian Smith, *Resisting Reagan: The U.S. Central American Peace Movement* (Chicago: University of Chicago Press, 1996), 351; letter, Ike Skelton to Ronald Reagan, August 7, 1987, Folder "Correspondence, 1983–1989," Box 922, Series 2, JWP.

97. Wright speech, undated, Folder "Nicaragua," Box 702, Series 2, JWP.

98. Democratic Study Group, September 9, 1987, Folder "Nicaragua," Box 702, Series 2, JWP; *DTH*, August 10, 1987, 1.

99. *DMN*, August 27, 1987, 12; August 28, 1987, 7; interview, Jim Wright, July 22, 2012.

100. Quoted in *FWST*, August 26, 1987, 10.

101. "Surprise! It's the Wright Stuff," *U.S. News and World Report* 103 (September 7, 1987): 8.

102. Quoted in *WP*, September 16, 1987, 28.

103. Reagan, *Reagan Diaries*, 581–589; *FWST*, October 29, 1987, 12; September 24, 1987, 7.

104. *DMN*, November 10, 1987, 1.

105. Interview, Mike Andrews, July 14, 2014; John Felton, "New Contra Politics: Wright the Dominant Force," *CQWR* (October 31, 1987): 266.

106. US Congress, House Select Committee to Investigate Covert Arms Transactions with Iran and Senate Select Committee on Secret Military Assistance to Iran and the Nicaraguan Opposition, *Report of the Congressional Committees Investigating the Iran-Contra Affair: With Supplemental, Minority, and Additional Views* (Washington, DC: US Government Printing Office, 1987), 13; interview, Jim Wright, July 22, 2012.

107. Interview, Jim Wright, July 22, 2012; Wright, *Balance*, 468.

108. Barry, *Ambition*, 500–501; Wright, *Worth It*, 140.

109. Interview, Jim Wright, July 22, 2012; Wright, *Worth It*, 144–146; Barry, *Ambition*, 504–505.

110. Quoted in Barry, *Ambition*, 509.

111. Quoted in *WP*, November 15, 1987, 1, 36.

112. *FWST*, November 17, 1987, 17; November 22, 1987, III, 1; *NYT*, November 17, 1987, 21; *DMN*, November 14, 1987, 30; November 18, 1987, 23.

113. Quoted in *FWST*, November 18, 1987, 1, 2; *United States v. Curtis-Wright Export Corporation*, 209 U.S. 304 (1936).

114. Quoted in Wright, *Worth It*, 150–151; *FWST*, November 17, 1987, 1; interview, Jim Wright, July 22, 2012.

115. *DTH*, November 18, 1987, 1; *FWST*, November 18, 1987, 1; interview, Jim Wright, July 22, 2012.

116. Letter, Wright to Roberto Ordonez, December 2, 1987, Folder "Correspondence, October–December, 1987," Box 671, Series 2, JWP.

117. *FWST*, November 10, 1987, 2; December 1, 1987, 1; quoted in December 2, 1987, 2; Wright remarks, December 1, 1987, Folder "Latin America," Box 709, Series 2, JWP; Wright Remarks for Ceremony, December 1, 1987, Folder "Latin America," Box 709, Series 2, JWP.

118. Letter, Wright to Carlos Tunnermann, December 8, 1987, Folder "Nicaragua," Box 1019, Series 2, JWP.

119. Letter, Patricia Schroeder to colleague, December 19, 1987, Folder "Negative Press," Box 943, Series 2, JWP.

120. Letter, Ronald Reagan to Wright, February 3, 1988, Folder "Letters for the President—Reagan," Box 726, Series 2, JWP; transcript, telephone conversations, February 3, 1988, Folder "Nicaragua," Box 702, Series 2, JWP; letter, Ronald Reagan to Wright, February 11, 1988, Folder "Letters for the President—Reagan," Box 726, Series 2, JWP.

121. Letter, George Miller et al. to friends, February 26, 1988, Folder "Nicaragua," Box 702, Series 2, JWP; letter, Wright to Robert Michel, March 30, 1988, Folder "Republican Leader Correspondence," Box 726, Series 2, JWP; letter, Wright to Ronald Reagan, March 30, 1988, Folder "Letters to the President—Reagan," Box 726, Series 2, JWP; Wright, *Worth It*, 168–169.

122. Telegram, Wright to Directors of Nicaraguan Resistance, Folder "Nicaragua," Box 702, Series 2, JWP.

123. Robert Kagan, *A Twilight Struggle: America and Nicaragua, 1977–1990* (New York: Free Press, 1996), 587–590; letter, Marshall Lynam to W. E. Turner, March 18, 1988, Folder "Correspondence, January–March, 1988," Box 673, Series 2, JWP.

124. Quoted in Kagan, *Twilight Struggle*, 591.

125. *WP*, April 4, 1988, 1; *FWST*, March 25, 1988, 1.

126. *NYT*, October 11, 1988, 26; quoted in September 22, 1988, 15.

127. Wright statement, September 23, 1988, Folder "1988 Press Releases," Box 678, Series 2, JWP; quoted in *WT*, September 22, 1988, 1.

128. Interview, Mike Andrews, July 14, 2014; Reagan, *Reagan Diaries*, 617; *USA Today*, September 22, 1988, 1; *Newsday*, September 23, 1988, 6; Wright, *Worth It*, 208–209.

129. Transcript, press conference, undated, Folder "Nicaragua," Box 760, Series 2, JWP; *WT*, September 25, 1988, 3; *NYT*, September 25, 1988, 1; *WP*, September 29, 1988, 8; October 5, 1988, 5; letter, Wright to Julian Dixon, October 5, 1988, Folder "Press Releases," Box 678, Series 2, JWP.

130. Quoted in Report on WLS and Wade Matter, Folder "Dirty Tricks," Box 691, Series 2, JWP; letter, Wright to Robert Finley, July 7, 1988, Folder "Correspondence, July–September, 1988," Box 673, Series 2, JWP; letter, Paul Resnick to Wright, May 1, 1988, Folder "New Republic," Box 692, Series 2, JWP; letter, A. R. Caggiano

to Squad C-4, FBI, September 22, 1988, Folder "New Republic," Box 692, Series 2, JWP.

131. Flier, Council for Inter-American Security, undated, Folder "Memo, 1988, (2)," Box 1018, Series 2, JWP; letter, Wright to Jack Kemp, March 23, 1988, Folder "Council for Inter-American Security," Box 675, Series 2, JWP; letter, Paul Laxalt to Francis Bouchey, February 11, 1988, Folder "Dirty Tricks," Box 691, Series 2, JWP; letter, E. R. Zumwalt to Wright, March 29, 1988, Folder "Nicaragua," Box 1019, Series 2, JWP; letter, E. R. Zumwalt to Francis Bouchey, March 29, 1988, Folder "Nicaragua," Box 1919, Series 2, JWP.

132. Letter, Maiselle Shortly to Wright, March 16, 1988, Folder "Republican Mailings," Box 692, Series 2, JWP.

133. Marshall Lynam, *Stories I Never Told the Speaker: The Chaotic Adventures of a Capitol Hill Aide* (Dallas: Three Forks, 1998), 208; *Hood County News*, October 15, 1988, 1; Wright statement, October 14, 1988, Folder "1988 Press Releases," Box 678, Series 2, JWP; letter, Wright to Donald Anderson, August 4, 1988, no folder, Box 759, Series 2, JWP; Barry, *Ambition*, 143, 380; *DMN*, October 12, 1988, 23; Wright remarks, October 11, 1988, Folder "1988 Press Releases," Box 678, Series 2, JWP.

134. Quoted in *WP*, October 23, 1988, H1.

CHAPTER 18

1. Sean Theriault, *The Gingrich Senators: The Roots of Partisan Warfare in Congress* (New York: Oxford University Press, 2013), 24–25; Steven Gillon, *The Pact: Bill Clinton, Newt Gingrich, and the Rivalry That Shaped a Generation* (New York: Oxford University Press, 2008), 61, 69; David Mariness and Michael Weiskoff, *Tell Newt to Shut Up: Prize Winning Washington Post Journalists Reveal How Reality Gagged the Gingrich Revolution* (New York: Touchstone, 1996), 6; quoted in John Barry, *Ambition and Power: A True Story of Washington* (New York: Penguin, 1990), 161–162.

2. Robert Remini, *The House: A History of the House of Representatives* (New York: HarperCollins, 2006), 472–475; Barry, *Ambition*, 214; Dan Renburg, ed., *House of Ill Repute* (Princeton, NJ: Princeton University Press, 1987).

3. Quoted in AP Wire Report, "Aide Target of Letter Writing Campaign," August 1, 1987, Folder "John Mack," Box 1018, Series 2, JWP.

4. Letter, Diane Stadler to Wright, August 7, 1987, Folder "John Mack," Box 1018, Series 2, JWP; photocopy, uncited article, "Letter Writer Dogs Wright Aide over Conviction for 1973 Assault," Folder "John Mack," Box 1018, Series 2, JWP; interview, Jim Wright, July 22, 2012.

5. Gingrich remarks, Chamber of Commerce, July 6, 1987, Folder "Correspondence, July–September, 1987," Box 671, Series 2, JWP.

6. See Martin Mayer, *The Greatest Bank Robbery Ever: The Collapse of the Savings and Loan Industry* (New York: Scribner, 1990), and Stephen Pizzo, Mary Fricker, and Paul Muolo, *Inside Job: The Looting of America's Savings and Loans* (New York: McGraw-Hill, 1989).

7. Letter, Wright to William Harvey, October 14, 1986, Folder "Wright Appreciation Committee (1981–1988) (1 of 6)," Box 670, Series 2, JWP; Barry, *Ambition*, 216–219.

8. Letter, Wright to Edwin Gray, October 10, 1987, Folder "Correspondence (2)," Box 729, Series 2, JWP; interview, Jim Wright, July 22, 2012; Barry, *Ambition*, 223.

9. *DMN*, June 30, 1987, 1, 8; quoted in *Austin American-Statesman*, March 5, 1988, 7; quoted in Barry, *Ambition*, 240.

10. *WP*, March 16, 1988, F1; *DMN*, March 16, 1988, 1.

11. *DTH*, January 12, 1988, 1.

12. Wright Statement on FSLIC, undated, "Wright Ethics," Box 968, Series 2, JWP.

13. Letter, Wright to Robert Slater, March 24, 1988, Folder "Bankers' Monthly," Box 675, Series 2, JWP; Response to Allegations, Bankers' Monthly, Folder "S+L's," Box 675, Series 2, JWP.

14. Interview, Mike Andrews, July 14, 2014; letter, Wright to Kathleen Day, February 16, 1988, Folder "S+L's," Box 675, Series 2, JWP.

15. Wright statement, October 16, 1987, Folder "Blind Trust," Box 675, Series 2, JWP; *WP*, October 17, 1987, 4.

16. Interview, Mike Andrews, July 14, 2014; interview, Jim Wright, July 22, 2012; Wright statement, September 22, 1987, Folder "1987 Press Releases," Box 686, Series 2, JWP.

17. Letter, Newt Gingrich to colleague, December 15, 1987, Folder "Newt Gingrich," Box 1002, Series 2, JWP.

18. Quoted in *FWST*, December 20, 1987, 14.

19. Quoted in *DTH*, December 16, 1987, 3; quoted in *DTH*, December 31, 1987, 4.

20. Memo, Beryl Anthony to Wright, December 7, 1987, Folder "Democratic Congressional Campaign Committee—Anthony," Box 724, Series 2, JWP; press release, DCCC, Folder "Democratic Congressional Campaign Committee—Anthony," Box 724, Series 2, JWP; letter, James Traficant to colleague, December 18, 1987, Folder "Negative Press," Box 943, Series 2, JWP; memo, Dan Buck to Dave Worley, November 12, 1987, Folder "Ethics Investigations," Box 743, Series 2, JWP.

21. Letter, George Mair to Richard Smith, December 15, 1987, Folder "Letters to the Media," Box 678, Series 2, JWP; letter, George Mair to Robert Bartley, December 15, 1987, Folder "Letters to the Media," Box 678, Series 2, JWP; letter, George Mair to Larry Jinks, December 15, 1987, Folder "Letters to the Media," Box 678, Series 2, JWP.

22. *Arizona Republic*, January 20, 1988, 14; *DMN*, January 25, 1988, 11; *FWST*, January 18, 1988, 1.

23. Interview, Jim Wright, July 22, 2012; quoted in *FWST*, January 22, 1988, 6; January 19, 1988, 1.

24. Interview, Mike Andrews, July 14, 2014; *NYT*, June 23, 1988, B7; *DTH*, June 21, 1988, 1, 14; quoted in *FWST*, June 14, 1988, 8.

25. Barry, *Ambition*, 602–604.

26. *WP*, July 20, 1988, 21.

27. Letter, Beryl Anthony to colleagues, January 26, 1988, Folder "Democratic Party," Box 1011, Series 2, JWP; *WP*, February 13, 1988, 13.

28. Press release, DCCC, May 26, 1988, Folder "Ethics Investigations," Box 743,

Series 2, JWP; *FWST*, June 8, 1988, 1; *DMN*, June 8, 1988, H2; *WP*, February 21, 1988, 6; *HC*, June 11, 1988, 16.

29. Letter, George Green to Wright, February 12, 1988, Folder "Sack the Quarterback," Box 675, Series 2, JWP; quoted in photocopy, uncited article, "Gingrich Has Aide Probing Wright Case," Folder "Ethics Investigations (2)," Box 743, Series 2, JWP.

30. Red Gest, "Capitol Crimes and Double Standards," *U.S. News and World Report* (June 13, 1988): 20–21; letter, Wright to Bill Alexander, October 21, 1988, Folder "Correspondence, October–December, 1988," Box 673, Series 2, JWP; letter, Wright to Sue Byrnes, March 16, 1988, Folder "Correspondence, January–March, 1988," Box 673, Series 2, JWP.

31. Letter, Fred Wertheimer to Julian Dixon, May 18, 1988, Folder "Ethics Investigation," Box 743, Series 2, JWP.

32. Press release, May 18, 1988, Folder "1988 Press Releases," Box 678, Series 2, JWP.

33. Complaint, Committee on Standards of Official Conduct, May 26, 1988, Folder "Ethics Investigations," Box 743, Series 2, JWP; press release, CSOC, June 9, 1988, Folder "Ethics Investigations," Box 743, Series 2, JWP; Resolution, CSOC, June 9, 1988, Folder "Ethics Investigations," Box 743, Series 2, JWP.

34. Interview, Jim Wright, July 22, 2012.

35. Wright statement, June 10, 1988, Folder "Wright Interview and Speech Transcripts (Brown Folder)," Box 943, Series 2, JWP; letter, Wright to Julian Dixon, May 24, 1988, Folder "General Correspondence (2)," Box 729, Series 2, JWP; letter, Wright to Julian Dixon and John Myers, June 10, 1988, Folder "Ethics Investigation," Box 743, Series 2, JWP; quoted in *DMN*, June 13, 1988, 3.

36. *DMN*, June 17, 1988, 6; Terence Moran, "Representative Wright Retains Counsel," *Legal Times* (May 30, 1988): 1.

37. Quoted in *DMN*, May 20, 1988, 4; letter, Mark Siljandar to friend, June 29, 1988, Folder "Public Advocate," Box 675, Series 2, JWP; "Albatross," *New Republic* (June 20, 1988): 5.

38. *WP*, August 7, 1988, 14; *DTH*, June 13, 1988, 5.

39. Transcript, Wright speech, Democratic National Convention, undated, Folder "Speech Files: Democratic Party—Democratic Congressional Accomplishments, Speech, Democratic National Convention, Atlanta, July 17, 1988," Box 1285, Series 3, JWP; *DTH*, June 18, 1988, 1.

40. Letter, Lloyd Bentsen to Wright, August 23, 1988, Folder "Democratic Presidential Campaign, 1988," Box 724, Series 2, JWP.

41. Quoted in Wright, "To Make a Difference," Folder "Biographical Sketches, 1 of 3," Box 1201, Series 3, JWP.

42. Quoted in *WP*, July 26, 1989, 12.

43. Wright statement, September 14, 1988, Folder "1988 Press Releases," Box 678, Series 2, JWP.

44. *WP*, April 29, 1988, E5; *WT*, March 7, 1988, 15; September 12, 1988, 8; *DMN*, June 9, 1988, 29.

45. Wright statement, September 7, 1988, Folder "Penthouse, 1988," Box 759, Series 2, JWP; *WT*, June 9, 1988, 1, 8; *DMN*, June 7, 1988, 3.

46. Letter, Steve Skardon to Wright, June 29, 1988, Folder "Wright Ethics," Box 968, Series 2, JWP; quoted in Wright, "To Make a Difference," Folder "Biographical Sketches, 1 of 3," Box 1201, Series 3, JWP.

47. Quoted in Terence Moran, "A Texas-Style Inquiry," *Legal Times* 11, no. 22 (October 31, 1988): 1; Wright, "To Make a Difference," Folder "Biographical Sketches, 1 of 3," Box 1201, Series 3, JWP; quoted in *FWST*, June 25, 1988, 11.

48. David Gopoian, "Images and Issues in the 1988 Presidential Election," *Journal of Politics* 55, no. 1 (February 1993): 151–166; Alan Abramowitz, "Beyond Willie Horton and the Pledge of Allegiance: National Issues in the 1988 Elections," *Legislative Studies Quarterly* 15, no. 4 (November 1990): 565–580; Timothy Naftali, *George H. W. Bush* (New York: Henry Holt, 2007), 61–62; see John Brady, *Bad Boy: The Life and Politics of Lee Atwater* (Cambridge, MA: Da Capo, 1996).

49. Barry, *Ambition*, 644, 667–668, quoted on 668.

50. Jim Wright, *Balance of Power: Presidents and Congress from the Era of McCarthy to the Age of Gingrich* (Atlanta: Turner, 1996), 479; quoted in Barry, *Ambition*, 662.

51. Letter, James Baker to Wright, April 28, 1989, Folder "Nicaragua," Box 702, Series 2, JWP; Christian Smith, *Resisting Reagan: The U.S. Central American Peace Movement* (Chicago: University of Chicago Press, 1996), 356–357; press release, White House, March 24, 1989, Folder "Nicaragua," Box 702, Series 2, JWP; Naftali, *Bush*, 70–71; Wright, *Balance*, 480.

52. Larry Bartels, *Unequal Democracy: The Political Economy of the New Gilded Age* (Princeton, NJ: Princeton University Press, 2008), 234–235; Naftali, *Bush*, 66–68; Michael Schaller and George Rising, *Republican Ascendancy: American Politics, 1968–2001* (Wheeling, IL: Harlan Davidson, 2001), 108.

53. Interview, Mike Andrews, July 14, 2014; Barry, *Ambition*, 669–675.

54. Larry Martz, "Profiles in Courage," *Newsweek* (February 13, 1989): 14–16; interview, Mike Andrews, July 14, 2014; Robert Strong, "Character and Consequence: The John Tower Confirmation Battle," in Michael Nelson and Barbara A. Perry, eds., *41: Inside the Presidency of George H. W. Bush* (Ithaca, NY: Cornell University Press, 2014), 122–140; *FWST*, December 9, 1989, 7; *NYT*, March 10, 1989, 1; quoted in Barry, *Ambition*, 676; Wright, *Balance*, 484; see John Tower, *Consequences: A Personal and Political Memoir* (New York: Little, Brown, 1991).

55. Wright, *Balance*, 484–485; *DMN*, March 20, 1989, 27; quoted in Eloise Salhoez, "Ready for Wright: A GOP Grudge Match," *Newsweek* (March 20, 1989): 28.

56. Memo, Phil Duncan to Wright, March 9, 1989, Folder "1990 Election," Box 678, Series 2, JWP.

57. *FWST*, March 20, 1989, F2; Barry, *Ambition*, 665; interview, Mike Andrews, July 14, 2014; quoted in *LAT*, February 22, 1989, 1, 16.

58. Committee on Standards of Official Conduct, *Report of the Special Outside Counsel in the Matter of Speaker James C. Wright, Jr.* (Washington, DC: US Government Printing Office, 1989), 3–24.

59. Interview, Mike Andrews, July 14, 2014; Barry, *Ambition*, 683–703.

60. Barry, *Ambition*, 704, 708, 710; Wright, *Balance*, 484.

61. Barry, *Ambition*, 715.

62. Ibid., 725–726, 729–730, 732, 737, 742; letter, Wright to Julian Dixon, April 16,

1989, Folder "1989 Press Releases," Box 678, Series 2, JWP; Janet Hook, "Speaker Draws Battle Lines in Fight for Political Life," *CQWR* (April 15, 1989): 789–792; interview, Mike Andrews, July 14, 2014.

63. Barry, *Ambition*, 734; Wright, *Balance*, 489; Michael Oreskes, "Wright Aide's Past Shocks Capitol," *NYT*, May 5, 1989, 1; *NYT*, May 5, 1989, 1; interview, Jim Wright, July 22, 2012.

64. Interview, Mike Andrews, July 14, 2014; interview, Betty Lee Wright, February 1, 2013; interview, Jim Wright, July 22, 2012.

65. Terence Moran, "Speaker Wright's Final Days: Outmaneuvered Defense Contends with Chaos," *Legal Times* 12, no. 1 (May 29, 1989): 1, 17–18; Barry, *Ambition*, 731–732, 741.

66. Margaret Carlson, "How Many Will Fall?" *Time* (June 5, 1989): 34–35; interview, Mike Andrews, July 14, 2014; Barry, *Ambition*, 746–752.

67. Interview, Jim Wright, July 22, 2012; Barry, *Ambition*, 749.

68. Letter, John Jones to Wright, May 25, 1989, Folder "Correspondence, 1989," Box 936, Series 2, JWP; letter, Mrs. Willie Harper to Wright, May 30, 1989, Folder "Correspondence, Resignation from Congress," Box 1179, Series 2, JWP; interview, Betty Lee Wright, February 1, 2013.

69. Interview, Jim Wright, July 22, 2012; Barry, *Ambition*, 751–752.

70. Barry, *Ambition*, 757.

71. Quoted in *FWST*, June 7, 1989, 13.

72. Oral History, Larry Adams, April 4, 1994, Folder "Oral History, Larry Adams," Box 1213, Series 3, JWP.

73. Stephanie Radway, "Where the Gavel Came to Rest," *TCU Image* (October 1991): 10–12.

74. Quoted in *FWST*, December 1, 1989, 1–2.

75. Quoted in *NYT*, July 1, 1989, 13; September 13, 1989, 11.

76. Quoted in *FWST*, November 10, 1990, D1.

77. Interview, Jim Wright, July 22, 2012; AP, *NYT*, September 7, 1989, 14; *FWST*, August 22, 1998, B8.

78. Quoted in Joe Nick Patoski, "Class Speaker: Jim Wright Is Passing Out Copies of His Book Again—and This Time It's Required Reading," *Texas Monthly* 19, no. 10 (October 1991): 98, 112–114; *TCU Daily Skiff*, August 28, 1991, 1.

79. Interview, Jim Wright, July 22, 2012; *FWST*, December 8, 1990, 9.

80. Jim Wright, *Worth It All* (Washington, DC: Brassey's, 1993), 258–259.

81. Jim Wright column, "Ordinary Miracles," April 4, 1998, Folder "1998," Box 1207, Series 3, JWP.

82. Quoted in *FWST*, August 26, 2001, G1.

83. Quoted in *FWST*, April 3, 1996, 1.

84. *FWST*, June 6, 1998, B6; August 6, 1996, B4; interview, Jim Wright, July 22, 2012; interview, Betty Lee Wright, February 1, 2013.

85. Quoted in *DMN*, May 8, 1991, 7.

86. Quoted in *FWST*, January 21, 1995, 8.

87. *FWST*, March 28, 1993, 8.

88. Quoted in *FWST*, September 21, 1991, 2.

89. Quoted in *FWST*, July 14, 1992, 7.

90. Quoted in *FWST*, January 6, 1994, 7.

91. Interview, Jim Wright, July 22, 2012; *TCU Daily Skiff*, September 3, 1998, 1; quoted in *FWST*, August 22, 1998, G1.

92. Letter, Ted Kennedy to Wright, January 25, 1999, Folder "News Clippings, 1999," Box 1207, Series 3, JWP; interview, Jim Wright, July 22, 2012.

93. *Fort Worth Metro*, November 14, 1999, B8.

94. Quoted in *FWST*, April 3, 1999, B3; Jim Wright column, "Keys to Healing," April 25, 1999, Folder "1999," Box 1207, Series 3, JWP.

95. Jeff Prince, "The Speaker in Winter: True to His Golden Glove Past, Jim Wright Answers the Bell for Another Round," *Fort Worth Weekly* 12, no. 15 (July 4, 2007): 12–18, quoted on 12.

96. Quoted in ibid., 18.

97. *NYT*, November 5, 2013, 14.

EPILOGUE

1. Interview, Jim Wright, July 22, 2012.

2. *FWST*, June 7, 1989, 14; John Barry, *Ambition and Power: A True Story of Washington* (New York: Penguin, 1990), 758–759.

3. Michael Dimock and Gary Jacobson, "Checks and Choices: The House Bank Scandal's Impact on Voters in 1992," *Journal of Politics* 57, no. 4 (November 1995): 1143–1159; David Niven, "A Fair Test of Media Bias: Party, Race, and Gender in Coverage of the 1992 House Bank Scandal," *Polity* 36, no. 4 (July 2004): 637–649; Charles Stewart, "Let's Go Fly a Kite: Correlates of Involvement in the House Bank Scandal," *Legislative Studies Quarterly* 19, no. 4 (November 1994): 521–535.

4. David Brady et al., "The Perils of Presidential Support: How the Republicans Took the House in the 1994 Midterm Elections," *Political Behavior* 18, no. 4 (December 1996): 345–367; Everett Ladd, "The 1994 Congressional Elections: The Post-Industrial Realignment Continues," *Political Science Quarterly* 110, no. 1 (Spring 1995): 1–23; Michael Schaller and George Rising, *Republican Ascendancy: American Politics, 1968–2001* (Wheeling, IL: Harlan Davidson, 2002, 128–131.

5. Bob Woodward, *The Choice: How Clinton Won* (New York: Simon and Schuster, 1996), 318–324, 326–328, 341–342.

6. *NYT*, September 19, 1995, 1; February 5, 1995, 7; November 30, 1995, 1; quoted in *FWST*, January 20, 1995, 1.

7. Stephen Gillon, *The Pact: Bill Clinton, Newt Gingrich, and the Rivalry That Defined a Generation* (New York: Oxford University Press, 2008), 223–248, 254–255; Bill Clinton, *My Life* (New York: Knopf, 2004), 773–776, 800–803, 824, 826, 834–836; interview, Jim Wright, July 22, 2012.

8. Diane Heath, "The Polls, Polling for a Defense: The White House Public Opinion Apparatus and the Clinton Impeachment," *PSQ* 30, no. 4 (December 2000): 783–790; Carol Silva, "Why Did Clinton Survive the Impeachment Crisis? A Test of Three Explanations," *PSQ* 37, no. 3 (September 2007): 468–485; William Connelly and

John Pitney, "The House GOP's Civil War: A Political Science Perspective," *Political Science and Politics* 30, no. 4 (December 1997): 699–702; Gillon, *Pact*, 247–248, 257–258, 273–283.

9. Quoted in *WP*, December 20, 1998, 1.

10. Opinion poll, Partisan Polarization Surges, Pew Research Center for the People and the Press, www.people-press.org/2012/06/04/partisan-polarization-surges-in-bush-obama-years, accessed October 1, 2014; Kevin Arceneaux, "Who Wants to Have a Tea Party? The Who, What, and Why of the Tea Party Movement," *Political Science and Politics* 45, no. 4 (October 2012): 700–710; Michael Takiff, *A Complicated Man: The Life of Bill Clinton as Told by Those Who Know Him* (New Haven, CT: Yale University Press, 2011), 258–263.

11. Schaller and Rising, *Republican Ascendancy*, 129–131, quoted on 131; see David Lublin, *The Republican South: Democratization and Partisan Change* (Princeton, NJ: Princeton University Press, 2004).

12. Kathryn Pearson, "Demographic Change and the Future of Congress," *Political Science and Politics* 43, no. 2 (April 2010): 235–238.

13. See Leslie Anderson and Lawrence Dodd, *Learning Democracy: Citizen Engagement and Electoral Choice in Nicaragua, 1990–2001* (Chicago: University of Chicago Press, 2005); *FWST*, August 14, 1994, 4.

14. Photocopy, uncited letter, Clarence Davis to editor, Folder "Post Congressional News Clippings," Box 1205, Series 3, JWP.

15. Silas Bent, *Strange Bedfellows: A Review of Politics, Personalities, and the Press* (New York: Horace Liveright, 1928), 81.

16. Letter, Wright to Dave Montgomery, August 25, 1985, Folder "JW Majority Leader and FW Congressman," Box 993, Series 2, JWP; interview, Jim Wright, July 22, 2012.

17. *DMN*, May 7, 2015, 1; quoted in *DMN*, May 12, 2015, B5.

Index

Capital letters indicate pages in the unnumbered photo section.